DISCARDED

Pass
Corpus Christi
Laredo
Mac Allen
Brownsville
Reynosa · Matamoros
Ciudad Victoria
Carboneras
Tampico
Ciudad Valles
Tuxpam
Poza Rica
Pachuca

GULF OF ME

Puerto Progreso
Celestún
Mérida
Chichén Itzá
Uxmal
Campeche

Río Lagartos

CARIBBEAN COAST ★

★ **EL TAJÍN**
★ **TEOTIHUACÁN**
Puebla
Veracruz
XICO CITY
POPOCATÉPETL
PICO DE ORIZABA
5 452 M

MAYAN SITES IN YUCATÁN

Felipe Carillo Puerto

Chetumal

GOLFO DE CAMPECHE

Escárcega

BELIZE
Belize City

Coatzacoalcos · Villahermosa
PALENQUE
RESERVA DE LA BIÓSFERA MAYA

Belmopan

ISTMO DE TEHUANTEPEC
Tuxtla Gutiérrez
Yaxchilán
Bonampak

San Pedro Sula

Chilpancingo
OAXACA
ADRE DEL SUR
Juchitán de Zaragoza
SAN CRISTÓBAL DE LAS CASAS
GUATEMALA
HONDURAS

Puerto Escondido · Puerto Ángel
Tapachula
Guatemala

EL SALVADOR

is hidden by forest and tropical mist.

OAXACA
The elegant jewel of the South, the capital of the Zapotec and Mixtec cultures and a magnet for artists, captivated by the harmony of its

colonial architecture and its entrancing baroque chapel.

PÁTZCUARO
A mountain city, the heart of Purépecha country, overlooking a lake where fishing boats work engulfed in mist.

ZACATECAS
In a dreamlike setting, an elegant town made of chiseled pink stone, situated at the edge of the desert.

GUANAJUATO
The silver mines gave rise to the colonial

splendor of this city of hills and alleyways.

SIERRA TARAHUMARA
This part of the Sierra Madre, with pine-clad heights and tropical vegetation in the canyons, is the land of the Tarahumara Indians.

Mexico

KNOPF GUIDES

● Encyclopedia section

NATURE The natural heritage: species and habitats characteristic to Mexico, annotated and illustrated by naturalist authors and artists.

HISTORY The impact of international events on local history, from the arrival of the first inhabitants to modern times, with key dates appearing in a timeline above the text.

ARTS AND TRADITIONS Customs and traditions and their continuing role in contemporary life.

ARCHITECTURE The architectural heritage, focusing on style and topology; a look at rural and urban buildings, and major civil, religious and military monuments.

AS SEEN BY PAINTERS A selection of paintings by different artists and schools from around the world, arranged chronologically or thematically.

AS SEEN BY WRITERS An anthology of texts, taken from works of writers from several periods and nationalities, arranged thematically.

◆ Mexico City: The historic center

▲ Itineraries

Each itinerary begins with a map of the area to be explored.

★ **NOT TO BE MISSED** These sites should be seen at all cost. They are highlighted in gray in the margins.

INSETS On richly illustrated double pages, insets turn the spotlight on subjects deserving more in-depth treatment.

◆ Practical information

All the travel information you will need before you go and when you get there.

USEFUL ADDRESSES A selection of hotels, restaurants, cafés, and so forth.

PLACES TO VISIT A handy table of addresses and opening times.

APPENDICES Bibliography, list of illustrations and index.

MAP SECTION Maps of areas covered by the guide; these are marked out with letters and figures, making it easy for the reader to pinpoint a town, region or site.

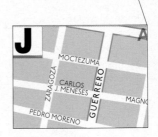

Each map in the map section is designated by a letter. In the itineraries, all the sites of interest are given a grid reference (for example: ◆ **F** C1).

The mini-map pinpoints the itinerary within the wider area covered by the guide.

The itinerary map shows the main sites as well as those not to be missed.

● ■ ▲ ◆
The above symbols within the text provide cross-references to a place or a theme discussed elsewhere in the guide.

▲ Chiapas

The southern border of colonial Mexico (New Spain) was formed by the Isthmus of Tehuantepec. Until Independence in 1821, Chiapas was the gateway to a less important border province, the Captaincy General of Guatemala (or Kingdom of Guatemala), which corresponded to modern Central America and whose capital was Antigua. The Sierra Madre, whose highest point – the Tacaná volcano 13,450 feet (4,100 m) – marks the beginning of the long volcanic chain running along the Pacific coast, is a fragment of the American continental shield. The coast of Chiapas is a karstic ridge – the niguinula (Tacuala), with their highest point at the Cerro Tzontehuitz (9,840 feet/3,000 m), extend into the Sierra de los Cuchumatanes whose foothills are formed by the great arc of middle-range mountains in the north and east (Cretaceous). The Lacandón Forest marks the start of the tropical forest of Petén (Guatemala) and Belize.

San Cristóbal de las Casas ◆ E D4

San Cristóbal lies at an altitude of 6,955 feet (2,120 m), in a deep depression bounded by three extinct volcanoes. It was founded during the early days of colonial rule, and is one of the oldest Spanish towns in South America. The idea of building a town was first conceived in 1524 by Bernal Díaz del Castillo during his long battle against the rulers of Chamula, who occupied the territory at the time. The idea was turned into a reality in 1528 by Captain Diego de Mazariegos, who only lived there for a few months. Torn between the fear of Indian uprisings and the need to come to terms with its Indian inhabitants (who today account for almost half the population), the town developed within the human shield of its barrio of loyal Indians. The inhabitants were slowly 'de-Hispanicized' and the new Creole population severed ties with Spain in 1821, initially hesitating between the statute of a free and sovereign country and allegiance to Mexico. They finally voted to join Mexico in 1824, but had to fight frequent battles to maintain their federal status. In fact, Chiapas has fought constantly to retain its identity within the

SAN CRISTÓBAL DE LAS CASAS ★ San Cristóbal has a good hotel infrastructure, with accommodation to suit every purse. It makes an ideal base for exploring Chiapas.

FROM 'CHÍA' TO CHIAPAS Chía is a sort of sage whose seeds are used to make a refreshing drink (chía fría) and to produce the oil used to make lacquer ▲ 281.

Mexican Constitution. Under the leadership of Joaquín Miguel Gutiérrez until 1838, and then Angel Albino Corzo, it struggled to resist the centralism advocated by the Conservatives and then Maximilian I. Later, under Miguel Utrilla, it pressed for free elections. Armed struggle was involved in each case. The choice of San Cristóbal by Zapata's National Liberation Army as the seat of the uprising of January 1, 1994, ● 29 was partly due to this tradition of insurgence. The town's stockbreeders and landowners – who had blocked the 1910 Revolution – perpetuated the marginalization of San Cristóbal, with the majority of the population reaping no benefit from the wealth generated by the region's agriculture, hydroelectric dams, oil, coffee or tourism. The anarchists built new towns to the north and south, in the shadow of the historic town. Between 1980 and 1990, the population of San Cristóbal de las Casas doubled and today stands at more than 100,000.

Central Plaza ◆ P B2

THE CATHEDRAL. The Mudejar bell tower, whose height has been reduced by several earthquakes, was once a separate structure. The WEST FAÇADE was completed in 1696. The restoration (in 1993) of its original colors (using natural colorings) has re-created the effect of an architectural huipil – yellow ocher from the soil of Chamula ▲ 260 and red ocher from Cuxtitali, colors once used for the

THE FIRST CHAMPION OF INDIAN RIGHTS Fray Bartolomé de las Casas, the son of one of Columbus's caravel pilots, became Bishop of Chiapas in 1543. He had already denounced the encomiendas – a system that subjugated the Indians to the Spanish – in Hispaniola (present-day Cuba) and Venezuela. He sent a report in the form of an indictment to Charles V – the Brevísima relación de la destrucción de las Indias – and was an instigator of the new laws that made cruelty illegal and prepared for the abolition of slavery. He failed to get the laws adopted in Chiapas and returned to Spain, bequeathing his name to the town.

'CARACOLES ZAPATISTAS' The five autonomous Indian capitals of Chiapas – whose name derives from caracol, the 'snail' or spiral shell that is an omnipresent motif in Mayan glyphs – are constantly visited by militants from Mexico and other countries In recent years, the EZLN ● 29 has undertaken the construction of an alternative society in these cities.

252

253

In the margins, the symbol 🅽 indicates walks recommended by the authors.

◆ B A6-B6 F C1
This reference pinpoints the place's location on one of the maps at the back of the book.

★ This symbol indicates a place not to be missed.

● Encyclopedia section

▲ Itineraries in Mexico

◆ Practical information

Mexico City and around

The Gulf coast

Yucatán peninsula

Chiapas

Puebla–Oaxaca–
Pacific coast

Occidente

The colonial cities of
northern Mexico

The missions of the Sierra
Madre Oriental

The North and Baja
California

MEXICO CITY ▲ 127
AND AROUND (THE CENTRAL PLATEAU) ▲ 159
From the colonial center, with its Aztec nucleus still visible, to the Chapultepec Wood, via the Paseo de la Reforma and the modern neighborhoods of Roma and Condesa. Not to mention the old villages of Coyoacán and San Ángel and the picturesque canals of Xochimilco. In the area around Mexico City, a dazzling tour of the central plateau: Teotihuacán, the 'City of the Gods'; Tepotzotlán, apogee of Jesuit baroque; Taxco, the silver city; and lastly Acapulco.

THE GULF COAST ▲ 183
Veracruz, the first city founded by Cortés, is also the center of a hot, humid region with a Caribbean soul, where the first great pre-Hispanic civilization, the Olmecs, took root (see the museums in Xalapa and Villahermosa). To the north, in El Tajín, the Totonacs built a strange and unique tiered pyramid.

YUCATÁN PENINSULA ▲ 199
These chalky lowlands were the setting for numerous Mayan cities, most notably Uxmal and Chichén Itzá, with their delightful range of architectural styles. Follow the Río Bec Route to the Puuc Route through Tulum, a fortified site overlooking the sea. Along the Caribbean coast lie idyllic beaches, while, between the colonial treasures of Campeche and Mérida, the North is dotted with *haciendas*, monasteries and mangrove swamps full of birds.

CHIAPAS ▲ 251
Just like the tropical mists, the Indian spirit thrives in the highlands of Chiapas. In San Cristóbal de las Casas, colonial architecture stands side by side with indigenous markets; in the forests, the sites of Palenque, Yaxchilán and Bonampak are still replete with Mayan treasures. As for the natural scenery, the lagoons of Montebello stretch to the national border, while, in the west of the state, the Sumidero Canyon opens up a dizzying breach.

PUEBLA–OAXACA–PACIFIC COAST ▲ 283
Descent from the central plateau to the Pacific. Take the back roads to catch the colonial and baroque splendors between Puebla and Oaxaca, as many churches are tucked away along the winding paths through the red, cactus-studded Tehuacán Valley. Around Oaxaca, discover the world of the Zapotecs and Mixtecs and the craftwork of the South, before reaching the Pacific Coast.

OCCIDENTE ▲ 309
This western region may be unassuming but it is a remarkable repository of tradition. In the State of Michoacán, the Purépecha (or Tarasc) identity is palpable in Pátzcuaro, around its lake shrouded in mist and at the foot of the young volcano Paricutín. As for Jalisco, it is proud of its capital, Guadalajara, the country's second city, and its status as the birthplace of three of the symbols of Mexico: the *charro*, the mariachi and tequila. The Huichol Indians live nearby, and there are still some untouched beaches behind the Sierra Madre.

THE COLONIAL CITIES OF NORTHERN MEXICO ▲ 333
In the north of Mexico, the mild climate and subsoil rich with silver gave rise to a series of sumptuous towns in the colonial era, with civil and religious architecture rivaling each other for glory. From Querétaro to San Luis Potosí, Guanajuato, San Miguel de Allende, right up to Zacatecas and Real de Catorce, on the fringes of the desert, there lies a parade of color and baroque exuberance.

THE MISSIONS OF THE SIERRA MADRE ORIENTAL ▲ 357
An unusual and moving itinerary revealing forgotten Franciscan and Jesuit monasteries, from the depths of the Sierra Gorda to the edges of Huasteca.

THE NORTH ▲ 367 AND BAJA CALIFORNIA ▲ 383
Two places stand out in the vast expanses of the northern desert: from Chihuahua to the Pacific, the Sierra Madre Oriental, the land of the Tarahumara Indians, which can be crossed by train; and, to the east, Monterrey, an American-style city fast growing into a fascinating megalopolis. Between the Pacific and the Mar de Cortés, Baja California stretches for 930 miles (1,500 km), its arid lands home to forests of cactuses and seas that lap unspoilt beaches and provide a breeding ground for gray whales.

MANY ACADEMICS AND MEXICAN EXPERTS HAVE COLLABORATED ON THIS GUIDE. ALL THE INFORMATION CONTAINED HEREIN WAS SUBMITTED FOR THEIR APPROVAL.

MICHEL ANTOCHIW
A French anthropologist resident in Mexico for forty-five years. Author of numerous books on Mexican history, cartography and ethno-history. Currently involved in the creation of the Historical Documentation Center of the State of Campeche. Pages 200–50 (itinerary), 206–7

ANDRÉ AUBRY
Frenchman living in Chiapas since 1973, founder of an institute of applied anthropology, currently director of the Historical Archives of San Cristóbal. Pages 252–82 (itinerary)

CLARA BARGELLINI
Researcher and professor of art history at the National Autonomous University of Mexico City (UNAM). Author of numerous books and articles on the art of New Spain. Pages 168–9

CLAUDE-FRANÇOIS BAUDEZ
Archeologist, honorary director of research at the CNRS. Specialist in Mayan iconology. Pages 24, 30–1, 72–5, 200–50 (archeology); 196–7, 214–17, 252–82 (archeology), 264–5, 272–3

JOSÉ LUIS BERMEO VEGA
Philosopher and theologian, winner of the Fray Bernadino de Sahagún Prize. Professor at the Iberoamerican University. Pages 334–56 and 358–66 (itineraries)

MICHEL BOCCARA
Sociologist and moviemaker specializing in the Mayans. Research supervisor at the CNRS, research director at the Doctoral School of Research in Psychoanalysis (Université de Paris-VII). Pages 232–3

ALAIN BRETON
Ethnologist and ethno-historian, specialist in the Mayans, research director at the CNRS. Pages 40–1, 46–55, 252–82 (itinerary), 328–9

NORA L. BRINGAS RÁBAGO
Lecturer and researcher in city planning and the environment in the Colegio de la Frontera Norte (Tijuana). Pages 392–400 (itinerary)

THOMAS CALVO
Professor at the University of Paris X-Nanterre. Specialist in the history of Mexico, particularly Guadalajara and its region. Former director of the CEMCA (French Center of Mexican and Central American Studies) in Mexico City. Pages 34–5, 76–9, 310–32 (itinerary)

GUÉNOLA CAPRON
Geographer and city planner, researcher at the CNRS in Toulouse and Mexico City, specialist in major Latin American cities (Buenos Aires, Mexico City, Rio). Pages 378–82

ISHTAR CARDONA
Sociologist and cultural organizer. Doctoral student at the Université de Paris-III. Pages 56–7

JULIETA CONTRERAS GARFIAS
Socio-anthropologist. Professor at the Iberoamerican University. Specialist in social development issues. Pages 334–56 and 358–66 (itineraries)

MARIE-LAURE COUBÈS
Researcher and lecturer in demography at the Colegio de la Frontera Norte (Tijuana). Pages 384–91 (itinerary)

JEAN-PIERRE COURAU
Photographer and author. Extensive experience in Mexico since 1965, when he was sent there as photographer and topographer for the French Architectural and Ethnological Mission. Pages 324–5

LEONOR CUAHONTE
Art historian and exhibition curator, specialist in 20th-century Mexican art and architecture. Pages 86–90

MARTINE DAUZIER
Lecturer in literature at the Université de Paris XII-Val-de-Marne. Lived for ten years in Mexico City, where she ran the CEMCA. Page 44

NOËLLE DEMYK
Professor of geography at the Université de Paris-VII-Diderot, specialist in developing countries and Latin America, member of the SEDET Laboratory. Pages 16–22

FABIENNE FAVRE
Lived for 25 years in Mexico, working as a translator. Pages 160–82 (itinerary), 178–9, 184–93, 198, 284–308 (itinerary)

MARTHA FERNÁNDEZ
Art historian specializing in Mexican colonial art. Professor at the UNAM and researcher at the Institute of Esthetic Studies in the same university. Pages 80–83

CHRISTINE FRÉROT
Specialist in the history of modern and contemporary Latin American art. Researcher at the EHESS, course supervisor at the Université de Paris-III. Art critic. Author of *Art contemporain d'Amérique latine, chroniques françaises 1990–2005* (L'Harmattan, 2005). Pages 38–9, 92–8, 100–4, 140–1, 346–7

JACQUES GALINIER
Ethnologist, research director at the CNRS, author of *La Moitié du monde. Le corps et le cosmos dans le rituel des Indiens Otomi*. Pages 40–1, 46–55, 328–9

MIGUEL GLEASON
Journalist and photographer for several magazines, including *México desconocido*. Moviemaker responsible for an award-winning film on a Mexican expedition in the Himalayas. Co-author of the CD-ROM *Mexico in France* and the DVD *Mexico in the UK*. Pages 368–75

SALOMÓN GONZÁLEZ ARELLANO
Architect-city planner, doctor in national and regional development, specialist in the mutations of Mexican cities. Pages 378–82

SCIENTIFIC CONSULTANT: MARÍA EUGENIA COSIO-ZAVALA
Professor of demography at the University of Paris-X-Nanterre, director of the CREDAL
(Center of Research and Documentation on Latin America,
CNRS-Université de Paris-III-Sorbonne nouvelle)

THE AUTHORS OF THIS GUIDE

JOANI HOCQUENGHEM
Writer, translator and journalist, living in Mexico City since 1975, author of *Le Stade aztèque* (Payot-Voyageurs, 1994). Writer of articles in the magazine Chimères and co-author of *La Fragile Armada* (Métailié, 2001). Responsible, with the moviemaker Jacques Kebadian, for the films *Calle San Luis Potosí 181* (1991) and *La Fragile Armada* (2004). Pages 32–3, 128–58 (itinerary), 134–5

JEAN-NOËL LABAT
Botanist, professor at the National Museum of Natural History (MNHN) in Paris. Research into Mexican vegetation spanning a period of ten years. Pages 240–1, 278–9, 388–9

YVON LE BOT
Sociologist at the CNRS, author of several works on Latin America. Curator of the

exhibition 'Indians: Chiapas–Mexico City–California' in the Parc de la Vilette (2002). Pages 42–3

PASCAL MONGNE
Archeologist and art historian, specializing in the Americas. Responsible for the course 'Arts of the Americas' in the École du Louvre. Participant in numerous expeditions to Mexico. Pages 300–1

BERNARD OUDIN
Historian, author of *Vila, Zapata et le Mexique en feu* (Découvertes Gallimard). Pages 26–9, 36–7

DANIELLE PECH-CAVALERI
Ethno-historian. Director of Ethnic A, an association mainly responsible for accompanying programs evaluating craftwork in Mexico. Editor of *Textiles mayas. La trame d'un peuple* (published by UNESCO). Pages 62–5, 258–9

MARTINE PÉDRON
Ethnologist, photographer and visiting lecturer on Indian civilizations. Pages 66–70, 194–5, 376–7

EMILIO QUESADA ALDANA
Historian. Founder and director for over thirty years of the program of guided tours at the National Institute of Anthropology and History (INAH). Professor of Mexican art history at the University and author of numerous works on the subject. Pages 334–56, 358–66 (itineraries)

ESTHER SAINT-DIZIER
Founding member (1989) and director of 'Rencontres cinémas d'Amérique latine' in Toulouse. Member of the editorial board of the (trilingual) magazine *Cinémas d'Amérique latine*. Pages 60–1

FRÉDÉRIC SAUMADE
Anthropologist specializing in the

study of European and Mexican bullfighting cultures. Pages 58–9

MARÍA TERESA URIARTE
Doctor of history, director of the Institute of Esthetic Studies in the UNAM. Author of numerous books and articles published in Mexico and abroad, including one devoted to the cave paintings of Lower California. Pages 394–5

KARLA AURORA VEGA MANJARREZ
Journalist for the press and media. Jointly responsible for the gastronomy sections in the magazine *Donde ir* in Mexico City and the supplement to *Sky* magazine. Co-author of pages 415–30

The **PRACTICAL INFORMATION** was compiled by Martin Angel, Hervé Basset, France Bourboulon and Karla Vega.

This is a Borzoi Book published by Alfred A. Knopf

Copyright © 2006 Alfred A. Knopf, New York. All rights reserved under International and Pan-American Copyright Conventions. Published in the United States by Alfred A. Knopf, a division of Random House, Inc., New York, and simultaneously in Canada by Random House of Canada Limited, Toronto. Distributed by Random House, Inc., New York.

Originally published in France by Nouveaux Loisirs, a subsidiary of Editions Gallimard, Paris, 2006. Copyright © 2006 by Editions Nouveaux-Loisirs.

Knopf, Borzoi Books, and the colophon are registered trademarks of Random House, Inc
www.aaknopf.com

First American Edition
ISBN 0 375 71125 2

Series editors
Clémence Jacquinet and Shelley Wanger
Translated by
Wendy Allatson and Matthew Clarke
Mexico as seen by writers compiled by
Lucinda Gane

Edited by
Grapevine Publishing Services Ltd, London
Typeset by
Adrian McLaughlin
Printed and bound in Italy by
Editoriale Lloyd

ORIGINAL FRENCH EDITION
Edited by
France Bourboulon, with Clarisse Deniau
Picture research by
Natalie Saint-Martin
Typesetting by
Laure Massin
Cartography by
Édigraphie
With thanks to:
Claude-François Baudez, Alain Breton, Patrick John Buffe, Thomas Calvo, Jean-Pierre Courau, Ferrante Ferranti, Christine Frérot, Jacques Galinier, Danielle Pech-Cavaleri, Martine Pédron, Sylvie Tailland, Alfonso Alfaro, Pauline Delomez, Claire Du Parc, Cándida Fernández de Calderón, Gaelle Le Calvez, Caroline Levent, Carlos Monroy Valentino, Margarita de Orellana, Cristina Prum, Alberto Ruy Sánchez

Encyclopedia section

An actor takes a break among the agaves during the filming of *La Escondida* (Juan Rulfo, 1955)

The church of Parangaricutiro stands defiant against the imminent threat from the Paricutín volc

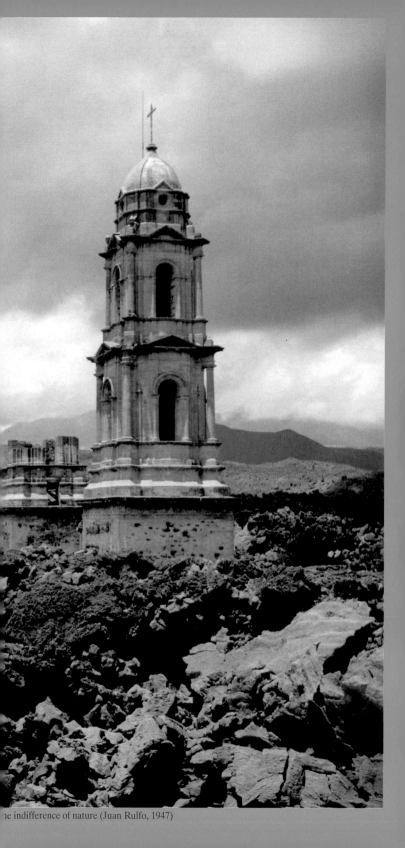

The indifference of nature (Juan Rulfo, 1947)

Women ring a hilltop church bell (Juan Rulfo, 1940)

Three dancers in traditional masks and costumes (Juan Rulfo, 1956)

Nature

● Geomorphology

HIGH BASINS
In the center-west of the neo-volcanic axis, Lake Pátzcuaro
(*right*) ▲ *316*, dotted with islands, spreads across a flat-
bottomed basin surrounded by small old volcanoes, at an
altitude of 6,692 ft (2,040 m). The landscape is a mosaic of
cultivated fields and clumps of pine trees.

Mexico is a country with a dramatic relief: 80% of its surface area reaches over 3,250 ft (1,000 m) above sea level, while 40% surpasses 6,500 ft (2,000 m). Three morpho-structural units can be distinguished. In the north, two large mountain ranges facing N–NW/S–SE extend for over 620 miles (1,000 km), flanking the high, rugged plateaus of the altiplano, which ranges in height from 3,250 to 4,000 ft (1,000 to 1,200 m) to the north to over 6,500 ft around the basins of the central region. The cordilleras, made of volcanic and metamorphic rocks to the west (Sierra Madre Occidental) and folded rocks – particularly limestone – to the east (Sierra Madre Oriental), dominate the coastal plains, which are wider on the shores of the Gulf of Mexico. The sedimentary plains of the Gulf prolong the plain of Texas and share its oil deposits.

GEOLOGY
The geological complexity of the mountainous masses bears witness to the importance of volcanic activity, old and new, as well as the major tectonic accidents and powerful fault systems that structure the central neo-volcanic region. These are the cause of the steep cliffs plunging down to the Pacific, and the collapsed basins such as the Río Balsas depression.

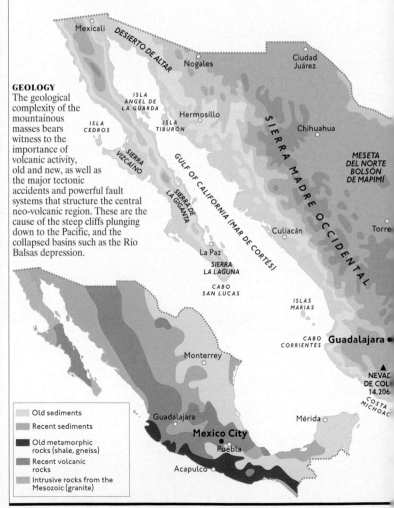

Old sediments
Recent sediments
Old metamorphic rocks (shale, gneiss)
Recent volcanic rocks
Intrusive rocks from the Mesozoic (granite)

THE SIERRAS

The Barranca del Cobre (*right*) ▲ 372 is about 3,250 ft (1,000 m) deep and is bisected by the River Urique for over 30 miles (50 km). It forms part of a group of canyons that cut through the mountains of the Sierra Madre Occidental (8,200–9,750 ft/2,500–3,000 m).

THE NEO-VOLCANIC AXIS

The neo-volcanic axis runs between the latitudinal lines of 19° and 20° north, slicing the southern meridians of northern Mexico. This axis is a structural accident that modified an older platform, leading to the formation of a more recent mountain complex. This is punctuated by volcanoes that are often still active; some soar to heights of over 16,400 ft (5,000 m), and many loom over the altiplano (at over 6,500 ft/2,000 m) and the land to the south (over 9,750 ft/3,000 m). The various basins (Mexico, Morelia, Puebla, Guadalajara, El Bajío) serve as the country's main population centers.

THE SOUTH

The Sierra Madre del Sur forms a steep mountainous front in Oaxaca that interrupts the isthmus of Tehuantepec, a mere 125 miles (200 km) wide. Beyond this, the mountains of Chiapas herald the reliefs of Central America.

THE YUCATÁN PENINSULA

This original ensemble of low plateaus is made up of tertiary limestone sediments.

Map labels:

SIERRA PIRRO

Monterrey

LAGUNA MADRE

ORIENTAL

San Luis Potosí

Mexico City
Toluca
IXTACCÍHUATL 17,343 ft
LA MALINCHE 14,636 ft
GOLFO DE CAMPECHE
Veracruz
NEVADO E TOLUCA 14,954 ft
POPOCATÉPETL 17,887 ft
Puebla
PICO DE ORIZABA 18,406 ft
LAGUNA DE TÉRMINOS

Mérida •

Cancún

YUCATÁN PENINSULA

CARIBBEAN SEA

capulco

SIERRA MADRE DEL SUR

ISTMO DE TEHUANTEPEC

SIERRA MADRE DE CHIAPAS

GOLFO DE TEHUANTEPEC

	6560–16,400 ft
	3280–6560 ft
	1690–3280 ft
	655–1690 ft
	0–655 ft
▲	Volcanoes

● Biogeography

Opposite: the altiplano
near Durango

The vegetal landscapes reflect the great diversity of the natural conditions in Mexico. In a humid, tropical setting, evergreen forest extends to 20° latitude in the area facing the Gulf of Mexico. Savannah has often replaced cleared forests on the southern plains. If the dry season lasts for more than four months, the thick equatorial forest turns into a tropical forest with deciduous trees. The driest regions are marked by discontinuous vegetal formations, such as the *pastizal*, or grassy steppe, and the *matorral*, or bush with thorny shrubs and cacti. Higher ground is usually distinguished between the *monte bajo*, covered with low prickly shrubs, and the *monte alto*, endowed with more substantial bushes or forest with taller deciduous trees.

THE MISTY FOREST
On the extremely humid western slopes of the Sierra Mazateca, in the State of Veracruz, the forest (*below*) has adapted to the permanent presence of fog and wind at around 6,500 ft (2,000 m). The trees are swathed in epiphytes and clumps of moss, and the ground is carpeted with large ferns.

Mexicali

Nogales

Ciudad Juárez

Hermosillo

Chihuahua

Torreón

Culiacán

La Paz

Guadalajara

TYPES OF VEGETATION
The map shows the extent of aridity in Mexico – embracing over half its surface area – as well as the variety of forest formations, which are determined by the configuration of the mountains. The temperate forest of oaks and pines takes over from the semi-perennial tropical forest in high, cold areas.

Evergreen forest

Perennial and semi-perennial forest

Temperate mountain forest (conifers and deciduous trees)

Herbaceous steppes with prickly shrubs and cacti ('pastizal')

Bush with prickly shrubs ('matorral')

Aquatic and subaquatic vegetation (marsh, mangroves)

Although the northeast of Mexico manages to stay free of total aridity, parts of the northwest, isolated by the Sierra Madre Occidental, experience conditions typical of a desert. An uncultivable semi-desert occupies most of Baja California and southeast Sinaloa, while western Sonora and central Baja California, around the Mar de Cortés, are fully fledged desert with bare rocks and constantly shifting dunes. This landscape abruptly changes to scrubland toward the far northwest of the peninsula, and high temperate forests to the west.

THE ALTIPLANO

The altiplano is characterized in northern Mexico by vast flat expanses stretching into the distance, occasionally interrupted by reliefs, often in the form of a table with steep sides. The bare earth is sparsely vegetated with clumps of thorny bushes and the odd lone cactus.

THE HIGH FORESTS

The high plateaus of the Sierra Tarahumara (the northern part of Sierra Madre Occidental), gouged by canyons with vertical walls, are covered with forests of pines, cypresses and oaks at altitudes between 6,900 and 8,850 ft (2,100 and 2,700 m). The slopes and the bottoms of the canyons are home to tropical species requiring varying degrees of water, creating even more contrasts in the landscape.

Lake Cusárare, near Creel, in the Sierra Tarahumara

YUCATÁN

These limestone plateaus are divided into a more humid northern region, occupied by thick forest, and a drier northern region with sparser forest and *matorral*.

THE GULF COAST

Tabasco and Campeche are bordered by large lakes and marshes, while the lower coastline has been taken over by mangrove swamps ▲ *240*.

19

● An unstable terrain

At a height of 7,218 ft (2,200 m), the immense mass of Mexico City sprawls between the feet of two protective volcanoes, Ixtaccihuatl and Popocatépetl.

Mexico's territory is intersected by the American Pacific cordilleras, an area of great seismic and volcanic activity running along major breaks in the earth's crust. It has registered 160 earthquakes of a magnitude greater than or equal to 6.5 on the Richter scale since 1910; the strongest were those of Jalisco (magnitude of 8.2, June 3, 1932) and Michoacán (8.1, September 19, 1985). The latter's most destructive effects were felt in Mexico City, over 375 miles (600 km) from the epicenter.

SUBDUCTION EARTHQUAKES

Most earthquakes take place at a depth of less than 25 miles (40 km) in the subduction area of the Pacific coast. Superficial tremors occurring within tectonic plates are less common but they can cause severe damage in heavily populated areas, in just the same way as earthquakes caused by subduction movements in the depths of the oceanic plates under the continent.

THE 1985 EARTHQUAKE

Mexico has experienced numerous earthquakes over the course of its history. The shock waves of September 19–20, 1985, responsible for over 25,000 deaths, were transmitted and amplified by resonance in the poorly consolidated lacustrine clay that makes up the soil. The most badly hit buildings were government buildings, hospitals, schools and public housing units.

EPICENTERS OF THE EARTHQUAKES OCCURRING IN THE LAST 100 YEARS

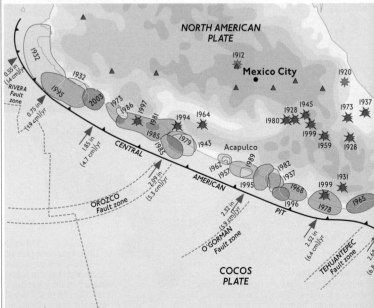

FAULTS AND EARTHQUAKES IN LOWER CALIFORNIA

In northern Mexico and the United States, subduction leads to sliding and thrusting between the Pacific and North American plates. The Pacific plate moves northwestward along an old oceanic distension ridge associated with fault zones defined as 'transforming'.

The Cierro Prieto and Imperial faults in northern Lower California are prolongations of the San Andreas Fault in California. Numerous earthquakes have been created at low depths by plates rubbing together; some of these have exceeded a magnitude of 6.5 (1915 and 1934).

SUBDUCTION OF THE COCOS PLATE UNDER THE NORTH AMERICAN PLATE

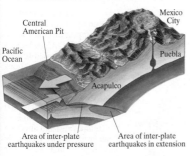

Area of inter-plate earthquakes under pressure   Area of inter-plate earthquakes in extension

The destruction in Mexico City after the 1985 earthquake (*below right*) was on a massive scale. Buildings of 6 to 15 floors were particularly badly hit, even if they conformed to the anti-earthquake construction regulations.

SUBDUCTION

The phenomenon known as subduction results from the meeting of two tectonic plates: one passes below the other under the effect of the impetus and differences in density. This occurs with the Rivera and Cocos oceanic plates, which are under the North American continental plate. The subduction zone extends from Puerto Vallarta to Chiapas and then continues into Central America; this corresponds to the Mesoamerican Undersea Pit, also known as the Acapulco Pit. Deformations in the earth's crust under the sea can trigger tsunamis, as in 1985 and 1995 in the seas off Colima-Jalisco, or in the Indian Ocean in 2004.

● Climate

Mexico, situated between the latitudes of 14° and 32° north, displays a variety of climates, from semiaridity in the north (or almost half the country) to tropical humidity. Its large mountain ranges are an essential factor in this diversity of patterns of temperature and rainfall. Their meridian arrangement, coupled with the dual shoreline, creates a significant division between, on the one hand, the Mexico of the high plateaus and the mountain basins and, on the other, the tropical Mexico of the coastal regions. Furthermore, strong climatic contrasts can also be found at a local level.

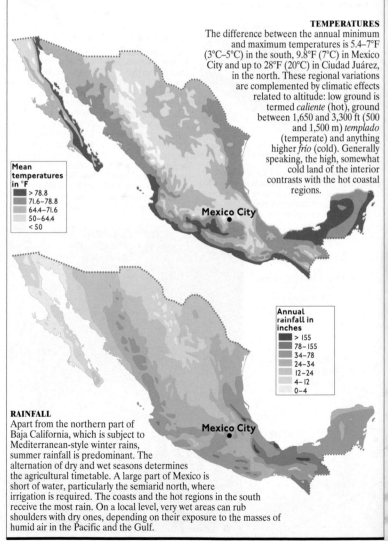

TEMPERATURES
The difference between the annual minimum and maximum temperatures is 5.4–7°F (3°C–5°C) in the south, 9.8°F (7°C) in Mexico City and up to 28°F (20°C) in Ciudad Juárez, in the north. These regional variations are complemented by climatic effects related to altitude: low ground is termed *caliente* (hot), ground between 1,650 and 3,300 ft (500 and 1,500 m) *templado* (temperate) and anything higher *frío* (cold). Generally speaking, the high, somewhat cold land of the interior contrasts with the hot coastal regions.

Mean temperatures in °F
- \> 78.8
- 71.6–78.8
- 64.4–71.6
- 50–64.4
- \< 50

Mexico City

Annual rainfall in inches
- \> 155
- 78–155
- 34–78
- 24–34
- 12–24
- 4–12
- 0–4

Mexico City

RAINFALL
Apart from the northern part of Baja California, which is subject to Mediterranean-style winter rains, summer rainfall is predominant. The alternation of dry and wet seasons determines the agricultural timetable. A large part of Mexico is short of water, particularly the semiarid north, where irrigation is required. The coasts and the hot regions in the south receive the most rain. On a local level, very wet areas can rub shoulders with dry ones, depending on their exposure to the masses of humid air in the Pacific and the Gulf.

History

Apogee of La Venta (Olmec)	−600/−100 Cuicuilco (Mexico basin)	250/500 Apogee of Teotihuacán	
−7000	−2500	−1000	−500	0	500

| −7000/−5000 Attempts at horticulture and growing cereals | −2500/−1500 Settling process, start of agriculture and pottery | −600 Start of monumental architecture in Nakbé (Mayan) | −32 Stele C in Tres Zapotes (Gulf Coast) | 292 Stele 29 in Tikal (Mayan) | 500–9 Monte Albán (Zapo |

The Origins

SEMINOMADS

Men first arrived on the American continent at least 20,000 years ago, taking advantage of the access provided by a glaciation over the Bering Strait, which made it possible to travel on foot from Siberia to Alaska. Nomadic hunter-gatherers first appeared in Mesoamerica around 11,000 years ago. The seminomads of the archaic period (7000–2500 BC) migrated on a seasonal basis, in accordance with the behavior patterns of the animals they hunted and the ripening of edible plant species. When local resources became sufficiently abundant to permit a settled lifestyle, the first hamlets came into being. Attempts at horticulture led to the domestication of some plants.

The Preclassical era (2500 BC–AD 300)

THE OLMEC STYLE

In the ANCIENT PRE-CLASSICAL ERA (2500–900 BC), human groups created hamlets and villages, produced their own food, then conserved it and cooked it in pottery vessels. Complex cultures developed after the emergence and diffusion of the Olmec style, shared to varying degrees by the cultures of the Gulf coast (San Lorenzo), Puebla-Tlaxcala (Chalcatzingo), the Mexico basin (Tlatilco) and Oaxaca. In the MIDDLE PRE-CLASSICAL ERA (900–300 BC), the Olmec style ▲ 196 and its underlying political and religious concepts reached their apogee in La Venta, a settlement meticulously laid out by means of large-scale public works (*below*, head no. 9). The oldest traces of writing were discovered at the archeological site of San José Mogote (Oaxaca). In the Mayan lowlands, the large site of Nakbé features stone platforms and temples, some of them 58 ft (18 m) high. In this period, the Olmecs passed on many cultural characteristics to the Mayans, undoubtedly through direct contact. In the RECENT PRE-CLASSICAL ERA (300 BC–AD 300), the basic elements of the classical Mayan civilization were put into place. Dates and inscriptions become more common on monuments (such as Stele C in Tres Zapotes, Stele 2 in Chiapa de Corzo). In the highlands of Guatemala, the major settlement of Kaminaljuyu was proof of the burgeoning skill in these fields and acted as a center for the transmission of Olmec culture; in the following period, it served as a link between the Mayans and Teotihuacán. In Oaxaca, Monte Albán became an important site, and its king commemorated his military conquests with stone sculptures of the mutilated corpses of his enemies.

INTENSIVE FARMING

Techniques associated with intensive farming (terraces, raised fields, irrigation) became widespread in several regions. Specialization in craftwork, made with sharp stone tools, encouraged the development of long-distance trading.

The Classical era (AD 300–900)

APOGEE OF TEOTIHUACÁN

The ANCIENT CLASSICAL ERA (300–600) was dominated by the size and outreach of Teotihuacán (Mexico basin), which reached its apogee during this period. It was spread over 5 sq. miles (13 sq. km) and its population is thought to have been about 125,000. The city was crisscrossed by a network of orthogonal roads and was divided into neighborhoods, sometimes revolving around a specific trade. Teotihuacán developed an original style, which was particularly apparent in mural painting, stone sculpture and pottery. This metropolis left in its wake other great Mesoamerican cultures, such as those of El Tajín, Monte Albán and Matacapan (on the Gulf coast).

| 600 | 800–50 Decline of the Mayan central lowlands | 900 | 950 The Toltecs in Tula | 1000 | 1300 | 1345 Foundation of Tenochtitlán | 1500 | 1519–21 Hernán Cortés conquers the Aztecs and founds Mexico City | 1700 |

| 600–800 Apogee of the Mayan classical civilization | 909 Last Mayan classical stele in Toniná | 1220–1400 Fall of Chichén Itzá and hegemony of Mayapán in Yucatán | 1492 Columbus discovers America, then with a total population of approx. 100 million | 1697 The Spanish capture Tayasal, the last Mayan stronghold |

THE MAYAN KINGDOMS

The Mayan kingdoms multiplied and declared their power by means of writing and the calendar ▲ *214*. Calakmul and Tikal vied for a position of hegemony. The political landscape changed constantly, reflecting new alliances and conflicts. Architecture developed with the help of the Mayan vault and the embellishment of façades with stone sculptures. The official rituals of power took concrete form, such as the pitches for Mayan ball games. (*Above*, Sayil.)

THE RECENT CLASSICAL ERA (AD 600–900)

This flourishing of the Mayan civilization was brought to an abrupt end by the abandonment of the cities of the central lowlands in the 9th century. At this time, the cities of Yucatán, such as Uxmal, were at the height of their glory. The Mayan collapse was mainly caused by the imbalance between population growth (70,000 inhabitants in Tikal, Guatemala) and agricultural resources. In the Puebla-Tlaxcala region, the fall of Teotihuacán led to the development of original cultures (Xochicalco, Cantona, Cacaxtla).

The Postclassical era (AD 900–1520)

THE TOLTECS

In THE ANCIENT POST-CLASSICAL ERA (900–1200), the Toltecs, with their capital in Tula (apogee c. 950 with 37,000 inhabitants), occupied what had been Teotihuacán. Chichén Itzá was then the biggest Mayan city in Yucatán, its culture heavily marked by elements taken from Tula and El Tajín. Tula was abandoned in the late 12th century, Chichén Itzá around 1250, and new centers such as Mitla and Yagul came to the fore in the Oaxaca area between 700 and 1000. The Tarasc (or Purépacha) civilization of Michoacán spanned 15,500 sq. miles (40,000 sq. km) by 1000, and its capital, Tzintzuntzan, had 35,000 inhabitants. In THE RECENT POST-CLASSICAL ERA (1200–1520), the major Mayan centers were Mayapán and Tulum, both protected by city walls. In Oaxaca, the Mixtecs succeeded the Zapotecs in Mitla, Zaachila and Monte Albán.

THE AZTECS

The first mention of the Aztecs, or Mexicas, dates from 1300, when they were mercenaries of Culhuacán Their success led them to found their capital, Tenochtitlán, between 1345 and 1370 ▲ *134*. Its 200,000–300,000 inhabitants, its network of canals, its ceremonial area (complete with 70 buildings) and its huge pyramids astonished the *conquistadores*, who seized it in 1521. The Aztecs received tributes from vast territories, which they controlled with the help of *pochteca*, a powerful class of traveling merchant-spies.

The Conquest

The Spanish conquest of the Americas began with the colonization of Cuba and Hispaniola (now Haiti and the Dominican Republic), and continued with expeditions launched from these islands. In 1517, Hernández de Córdoba set off in search of slaves and new territory. He discovered the Isla Mujeres, near Cozumel, then sailed along the Yucatán peninsula to Champotón, where he suffered heavy casualties at the hands of the Mayans. The next expedition, commanded by Juan de Grijalva, rounded the peninsula in five months and went up the River Panuco. Finally, Hernán Cortés (*right*) set off with eleven ships on February 18, 1519. He sailed along the peninsula into the Gulf of Mexico and landed in Veracruz, where he burnt his vessels and went on to conquer the Aztecs in the space of two years ● *32*.

'Cry of Dolores' and
start of the revolt

1821 Independence
of Mexico

1520	1550	1650	1810	1815	1820

1522 Cortés
governor of
New Spain

1535 Installation
of first viceroy

1683 Pillage of
Veracruz by
Dutch pirates

Defeat of the
Insurgents

1823 Iturbide, the
'Emperor' of Mexico,
is overthrown

'New Spain' (1521–1821)

The colonial period lasted for three hundred years, from the capture of Tenochtitlán in 1521 until the Treaty of Independence in 1821 ● 32. In 1535, the Spanish king, Carlos V, established the territory as a vice-royalty, and over the years some 200,000 Spaniards settled there. New Spain enjoyed relative prosperity, its borders unthreatened, apart from the occasional coastal raid by English and Dutch pirates. The colonizers built numerous towns in accordance with the Spanish model, developed agriculture and bred livestock on their *haciendas* ● 84, mined minerals, particularly silver ▲ 178, and traded with Europe, via Veracruz, and with the Far East, via Acapulco. The Catholic Church soon left its mark on the territory. Mexico became an archbishopric in 1546, the Inquisition was set up there in 1571 and the Jesuits arrived the following year. Whereas the Indians to the north of Mexico were spurned, here they formed part of colonial society (once baptized), although they usually occupied the lowest rung on the ladder. Despite their semi-serfdom, they often mingled with the whites and a mestizo (mixed-race) stratum emerged as an incipient middle class. Dissent began to appear among the top Spanish ranks in the late 18th century, as the rich Creole smallholders, born in Mexico, grew to resent the dominant position of the Gachupines, immigrants from the metropolis who monopolized the top administrative and religious posts.

THE WAR OF INDEPENDENCE (1810–21)

The example of the United States inspired the Mexican Creoles, whose desire for independence was shared by the Indians and mestizos. The shake-up in Spain, where Napoleon had placed his brother Joseph on the throne, gave the Mexicans an unexpected opportunity. In 1810, a plot was hatched in Querétaro, under the auspices of an officer, Ignacio de Allende, and Miguel Hidalgo ▲ 356, the priest from Dolores, the neighboring village. On September 10, the latter issued the signal for the uprising. The 'Cry of Dolores' met with an enthusiastic public response. Hidalgo (*left*) proved to be a leader, but not a strategist. His men captured Guanajuato, where the Spanish were massacred, and marched on Mexico City. The viceroy regrouped his forces, however, while some Creoles were appalled by the excessive brutality of the Indians. The Insurgents were defeated, Allende was killed and Hidalgo captured and shot in 1811. Another village priest, the mestizo José María Morelos, took up the torch by seizing Acapulco, where he proclaimed independence and the equality of races; he held out against the Spanish for four years, before being captured and shot in 1815. Although the military defeats and the return of the Bourbons in Madrid dampened hope, the movement found new impetus in the political arena. General Iturbide, responsible for overcoming Morelos, rallied to the cause of the autonomists and finally imposed the Treaty of Córdoba, the seal of the country's independence, on the viceroy in 1821.

The time of the 'Caudillos' (1821–55)

Independent Mexico got off to a bad start. A Constitution inspired by that of the United States was adopted, but nobody respected it, least of all Iturbide, who assumed absolute power, along with the title of Emperor Agustín I. He was overthrown in 1823, ushering in an extraordinary succession of *pronunciamientos* and generals-presidents, most notably Antonio López de Santa Anna (1795–1876), who took and lost power no less than five times. Covetous eyes were cast on this debilitated Mexico, and in 1829 the Spanish attempted a reconquest, only to be overcome in Tampico by Santa Anna. He was less successful, however, against the revolt of the Mexican colonialists in Texas. He massacred the garrison of Fort Alamo in 1836, but was defeated shortly after by Sam Houston in San Jacinto and had to recognize the independence of Texas. Worse was to follow in the war of 1846, when Mexico found itself the target of the expansionist American president James Polk. Santa Anna held back General Taylor in California, but General Scott attacked from the rear, landing in Veracruz and seizing Mexico City, despite the heroism of the cadets of Chapultepec (Niños Heroes). The Treaty of Guadalupe Hidalgo (1848) was disastrous for Mexico,

| 1830 | **1836** Defeat of Santa Anna in Texas | 1840 | 1850 | 1860 | **1867** Execution of Maximilian | 1870 | **1876** First election of Porfirio Díaz | 1880 |

1833 First dictatorship of Santa Anna   **1846–7** War against the United States   **1858** Benito Juárez president   **1862** Maximilian emperor of Mexico   **1872** Death of Juárez

as it relinquished a third of its territory. For the sum of $15 million, the United

States purchased California and New Mexico (territory encompassing today

not only these two states but also Arizona and southern Utah and Nevada).

The Río Grande became the frontier between the two countries.

Juárez and the French intervention

This dismembered Mexico was both impoverished and lacking in direction. In 1854, the liberals launched the Ayutla Plan, designed to reestablish respect for the Constitution. This is the period of the 'Reforma'. Power was given back to civilian governments, under Ignacio Comomfort (1855) and Benito Juárez (1858). The Catholic Church had lost its status of state religion, so it excommunicated civil servants who swore to abide by it. Juárez then confiscated the clergy's assets. There followed a civil war (1858–61) from which Juárez emerged victorious, but not without difficulty. The new order had barely been restored when a new calamity hit: the

country's coffers were empty. Jecker, a Swiss banker who had lent the government 15 million pesos, succeeded in making France responsible for the debt, after paying a commission to the Duke of Morny. Napoleon III, meanwhile, was dreaming of a Latin empire. The United States was distracted by the Civil War, and it was tempting for France to take advantage of the situation. French troops landed in 1862, took Mexico City after a fierce battle, and installed a Hapsburg as Emperor Maximilian. Juárez continued the fight from the north. In 1866, a weary Napoleon withdrew his troops. Maximilian was captured and shot

in 1867 (*above*: *The Execution of Emperor Maximilian*, by Édouard Manet, 1868). Once he was re-elected president,

Juárez tried to implement his reformist program – with uneven results at the time of his sudden death in 1872.

JUÁREZ
Benito Juárez (1806–72) embodied the 19th-century ideals of laicism. An Indian of very humble origins, he rose up through hard work, becoming a lawyer, then the governor of his home province of Oaxaca and, finally, the president of Mexico in 1848. He was a serious man, who always dressed in black, yet he aroused fervor in the populace. This hero of independence in the face of foreign intervention remained in power until his death.

1900   **1910**   **1915**   **1920**

1913 Madero assassinated by Huerta

1920 Assassination of Carranza

Start of the revolution

1911 Fall of Porfirio Díaz

1914 Fall of Huerta

1919 Death of Zapata in an ambush

The longest dictatorship: the Porfiriat (1876–1911)

The interlude of the civilian governments proved to be brief, as another general, Porfirio Díaz, snatched power in 1876. Unlike his military predecessors, he clung to office for 35 years, with the help of sham elections. The record sheet of the Porfiriat is not entirely negative. Competent ministers – known as the *científicos* – attracted foreign capital and managed to boost the economy by creating a railroad network, developing mining and introducing industrialization. Mexico City became one of the most attractive cities in Latin America ● *86*. This veneer of modernity concealed a backward society, however, with corruption and cronyism at the top and extreme social deprivation at the bottom. The rural masses were maintained in a state of near-serfdom by the *hacendados* (wealthy landowners). Díaz finally succumbed to the two-pronged opposition of the democrats – led by Francisco Madero

(*above*), a middle-class liberal – and the oppressed peasants. The elections of 1910 were fixed (true to form), but nevertheless they provided the opportunity for Madero to launch an uprising. This was thwarted at first, forcing Madero to flee to the United States, but he soon found support from two other rebels, both with a gift for leadership: Pancho Villa in the north and Emiliano Zapata in the south. The capture of Ciudad Juárez by Villa and Madero in the spring of 1911 marked the end for Díaz, who who was then forced into exile.

The troubled times of the Revolution (1911–24)

'TIERRA Y LIBERTAD!'

Once president, Madero set about introducing reforms, but in phases. Zapata, however, advocated the immediate redistribution of land, and took up arms once again to the cry of '*Tierra y Libertad!*' ('Land and freedom') ● *36*. To win this new battle, Madero had to throw his hand in with a military oligarchy that hated him. February of 1913 saw the start of the 'Tragic Decade' in Mexico City. General Huerta, a brutal drunk, suddenly turned against Madero, arresting him and killing him. However, Huerta's dictatorship proved short-lived. Pancho Villa, who had remained faithful to Madero and fled to the United States, returned on March 16, 1913 with eight companions. Before long, thousands had rallied to his cause. Zapata, in the south, and Carranza, a provincial governor in the north, rebelled in their turn. Huerta was defeated on all fronts and took the road to exile in July 1914. In December, Zapata and Villa entered Mexico City in triumph, but in the following years the two leaders argued ceaselessly; neither ever possessed the status of a true statesman. The third rebel, Carranza, took advantage of the situation to impose his authority, but only at the cost of further bloody battles. He succeeded in overcoming Villa and Zapata with the backing of General Obregón – who promptly turned against him. The three rebels all met with a tragic end: Zapata was ambushed and killed in 1919, Carranza was then overthrown and assassinated in 1920, and Pancho Villa was murdered in 1923.

1926–29
Rebellion of
the Cristeros

1994
Uprising in
Chiapas

1925   1930   1990   2000   2005

1923 Assassination
of Pancho Villa

1934 Cárdenas
president

2000 Vicente Fox
elected president

A LULL

With Alvaro Obregón and his successor, Plutarco Calles, the Revolution entered a period of greater calm, despite a final attempt at a coup d'état in 1924. The government made reforms, reduced the illiteracy rate and developed technical education. These years were also fruitful in economic terms, as Mexico became responsible for a quarter of the world's oil production.

REVOLT OF THE 'CRISTEROS'

Yet again, the country was brutally put to the test from 1926 to 1929: the staunchly anticlerical policies of the government incited a revolt among the Catholic peasants, who were known as the 'Cristeros'. Fanaticism reigned on both sides, however, and consequently the repression was unpitying. Obregón was assassinated by a Catholic student in 1923 ● 37.

The institutionalization of the Revolution (1934–90)

Lázaro Cárdenas, who became president in 1934, introduced calm and emerged as the true founder of modern Mexico. He gradually restored religious freedom and brought in progressive economic policies, coupled with agrarian reform and nationalization of the oilfields. Breaking with the autocracy of Plutarco Calles, who had proclaimed himself *Jefe máximo*, Cárdenas renounced the single-party system, while his own party took on the highly symbolic name of the Institutional Revolutionary Party (PRI). The convulsions of the past gave way to a stability rarely found in Latin America. Pluralism and freedom of expression are still respected and political violence has been eradicated (apart from the bloody suppression of student protests in 1968). The preeminence of the PRI totally distorted the workings of democracy, however: right to the end of the century, every single president came from the ranks of the PRI.

The contemporary era

By opting for more liberal economic policies, Mexico has moved closer to the United States, and in 1994 it joined NAFTA (the North American Free Trade Agreement). The country's economic development has continued apace, as the world oil crisis enabled it to take fuller advantage of its own resources. Enormous problems remain to be solved, however: poverty, corruption, foreign debt and major demographic imbalances. While the capital has grown into a megalopolis, some regions have declined. In 1994, this reality of a two-speed Mexico sparked the Indian rebellion in Chiapas, in the far south of the country. Over a decade later, the situation seems to have reached a stalemate. The federal troops in the area have not been able to eradicate the rebel movement, but the latter, despite its government-authorized 'march on Mexico City' in 2001, has not succeeded in expanding and taking on board the mass of the Mexican people. Finally, on the political level, the key event of the early years of this century was the end of the all-powerful reign of the PRI. The election of a center-left mayor in Mexico City (Cuauhtémoc Cárdenas, the son of the former president) in 1997 and, above all, that of Vicente Fox Quesada to the presidency of Mexico in 2000 demonstrate that power can still be peacefully handed over among the highest ranks of the state.

EL 'SUBCOMANDANTE'

Subcomandante Marcos, the head of the EZLN (Ejército Zapatista de Liberación Nacional), now an idol of activists all over the world, has managed to maintain both his legend and his anonymity. He is particularly fond of using the Internet as his means of communication. In 1995 the authorities identified him as Rafael Guillén, a former philosophy teacher born in 1957. Marcos denied this and has always refused to unmask himself, even in Mexico City. Does this reflect political symbolism, as he himself claims, or, as his detractors suspect, a need to hide a face overly white for an Indian leader? Or merely the desire to preserve an image that has stuck in people's minds?

● Mesoamerica

Aztec breastplate, a mosaic of turquoise, shell and mother-of-pearl on wood

Mesoamerican Area

At the time of the Conquest, Mesoamerica was an area settled by crop growers who lived in central and southern Mexico, Guatemala, Belize, El Salvador and parts of Honduras, Nicaragua and Costa Rica.

Its northern frontier gave way to an arid zone (less than 24 inches [600 mm] of rain per year) roamed by groups of nomadic hunter-gatherers. To the south, the small chiefdoms of Central America were less developed cultures than the civilizations of Mesoamerica.

ECONOMY

The subsistence economy was based on the cultivation of corn, beans and squashes, complemented by a wide variety of plants, such as tomato, amaranth and chili. In the warmer regions, fruit trees and avocados were grown, along with cacao (used as money ▲ 178), cotton and tobacco. Extensive farming was supplemented by intensive farming, made possible by irrigation. The most profitable technique, the *chinampa*, involved the creation of artificial islets in shallow freshwater lakes ▲ 135.

SOCIAL HIERARCHY

Mesoamerican societies were strictly hierarchic. An extremely centralized hereditary elite maintained control of politics and religion. The strata between this elite and the masses were made up of military orders, guilds of specialized craftsmen and merchants. The latter traded over long distances with utilitarian goods such as obsidian and luxury items – jade, cacao, turquoise and the highly coveted bronze-green feathers of the quetzal ▲ 278.

Right: Mixtec representation of Tlaloc, the god of rain

WRITING

Of all the writing techniques in use in Mesoamerica, that of the Mayans was the most efficient. It was a mixed system that used both logograms (words and morphemes) and phonograms (sounds, syllables) ▲ *214*. It was closely linked to language and was capable of transcribing any utterance in a visual form. The Zapotec, Aztec and Mixtec writing systems rarely featured phonetic signs, preferring instead ideograms and the rebus system.

CALCULATIONS

These were based on a system that used multiples of 20. Two complementary calendars were consulted to calculate time: one ritual and divinatory, with 13 groups of 20 days (260 days); the other solar, with 18 months of 20 days each, with 5 extra days added. The two calendars started on the same day every 52 years. The Mayans were the only people to go past this 52-year 'century', writing out their history in a cycle of over 5,125 years.

CITIES

The cities were centers of political, religious and economic power that controlled regions of varying size, along with a group of satellite communities. Tiered pyramids crowned with temples dominated the urban space. The community buildings were made up of a stone palace, which was covered with painted stucco, pitches for the ball games, and the houses, which were arranged around courtyards.
● *72–5*.

THE CODEX

All these peoples possessed manuscripts (made of cork paper or leather covered with a thin layer of stucco) folded like an accordion, containing historical records, genealogies, almanacs, and instructions for rituals, myths and prophecies (*right*, temple of Tenochtitlán, *Ixtlilxochil Codex*).

RELIGION

An underlying animism – whereby every animate or inanimate element in the universe possesses a soul or a sacred nature (mountains, rivers, animals, plants, stars, periods of the calendar, and so forth) – later gave rise to individualized, generally anthropo-morphic divinities, which can be identified by their costume and attributes, as well as by specific symbols. Some gods and goddesses, such as the god of rain, the god of the wind and the goddess of corn, were common to various civilizations. The earth, with its four directions, was the subject of a major cult that varied in form from one place to another. Human sacrifice and self-immolation (in the form of painful, self-inflicted draining of blood) constituted the most important rituals; they were accompanied by processions, dancing and singing, burning of incense and a variety of offerings.

The Spanish Conquest

Feathered headdress presented by Moctezuma to Cortés, who, in July 1519, sent it to Carlos V, who passed it on to his nephew

On February 18, 1519, Hernan Cortés set sail from Cuba – where the Spanish had been established ever since the voyages of Columbus – with 500 soldiers, 16 horses and 10 cannons on a journey to the limits of the known world, out of reach of all jurisdiction. Cuba's governor, Diego Velázquez, fearing insubordination, issued orders to arrest Cortés at the last moment and never ceased trying to track him down.

FIRST CONTACT

After landing on the continent, Cortés came across Jerónimo de Aguilar. Aguilar, who had been washed on to the shores of Yucatán in 1519, became Cortés' Mayan interpreter. Cortés then followed the coastline to Tabasco, where a cacique offered him 20 slaves, including Malinche, a woman snatched from the Aztecs. She spoke Nahuatl and became Cortés' concubine. Aguilar and Malinche gave him the advantage of language when he received Moctezuma's envoys.

MALINCHE

Malinche opened the doors to the Aztec world for Cortés, but in doing so she earned the contempt of her own people. She played a key role in the 'discovery' of Mexico, and because of this her name is now synonymous with treachery: a 'malinchista' is somebody who denies his or her Indian roots out of admiration for foreign values.

VERACRUZ, THE FIRST CITY

Cortés created a city, Veracruz, and sent his booty of gold and a report on the expedition in his own name directly to Carlos V, over the head of Velázquez. On August 16, after scuttling his remaining ships to prevent any thought of retreat, Cortés, as captain of the new municipality, penetrated inland and set about climbing the sierra.

THE MEETING WITH MOCTEZUMA

Beyond the mountains, Moctezuma, the lord of Tenochtitlán, was stricken by anxiety. The omens announced the fulfillment of an ancient prophecy: was the god Quetzalcóatl coming to reclaim possession of his earthly kingdom? Moctezuma spied on the newcomer, set him traps and sent him gifts (unwittingly whetting his appetite for gold), all the while begging him to leave. Moctezuma's enemies from Tlaxcala were swelling the foreign forces, which were also being helped by his Totanac vassals. The nearby town of Cholula followed suit, so he resignedly went to meet Cortés. With great pomp and ceremony, on the huge embankment that linked the central island with the south bank, he offered the Spaniard his palaces and treasures, as if returning them to their rightful owner.

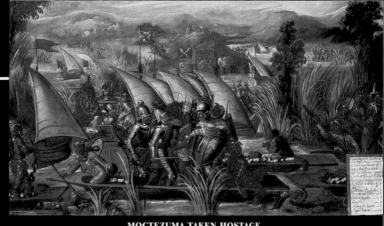

MOCTEZUMA TAKEN HOSTAGE

For safety's sake, the Spanish clapped Moctezuma in irons. The atmosphere was tense; and in early 1520, Pánfilo de Narváez, sent by Velázquez to detain Cortés, landed with a strong military force. When Cortés rushed to meet him, Pedro de Alvarado, his second-in-command, almost immediately massacred the Aztecs who had assembled for the festival of Toxcatl. The city rose up and attacked the palace. Cortés flaunted gold to convince Narváez's troops to rally to his cause, and then recaptured Tenochtitlán. He persuaded Moctezuma to go out on to the palace roof to calm his subjects. He was stoned to death by his people or, according to another version, executed by his jailers.

Below and right: the meeting of two worlds

aztatlan

THE 'SAD NIGHT'

The Spanish were encircled. They hastily melted down Moctezuma's carved gold headdresses into ingots and fled in confusion. Weighed down by the gold, many of them sank into the lake. On that night of June 30, known as the *noche triste* (sad night), Cortés lost all his treasure and half his men.

THE FINAL ASSAULT

A year later, Cortés returned from Tlaxcala with 80,000 soldiers, carrying 13 brigs (two-masted ships) which he had ordered them to build; he captured the coastal towns and besieged Tenochtitlán. On August 13, 1521, the Spanish captured Cuauhtémoc, the last Aztec king. The city was razed to the ground, its pyramids destroyed, its streets piled with corpses and wreckage. The new capital was built on these flattened ruins, and Mesoamerica became New Spain. The effects of the invasion were aggravated by epidemics: the population of around 10 million in 1519 had declined to a mere 1 million in 1605.

33

New Spain

A. Palacio Re.
B. Cathedral.
C. Cafa de Cabildo.
D. Cafa Arp.
F. Univerfidad.
G. Alameda.

From 1519 to 1821, the future Mexico was conquered, exploited and evangelized by the Spanish monarchy. As the jewel in the latter's crown, it had to be a replica of the motherland, so Cortés christened it New Spain – although at that time it took almost a year and a half for an order to leave Madrid and a reply to arrive back. This was no virgin territory – the Spanish found a densely populated world with rich cultures. Later on, other ethnic groups (Africans) were added to the mix, while the Spanish residents became acclimatized. A new Creole society was born, thereby consolidating the language, religion and power of the Spanish state throughout the colonial era.

THE FUTURE OF THE INDIAN POPULATION

History has known few cataclysms of the dimensions of the decline of the Indian population from 10 million to 1 million between 1519 and 1619. The causes are manifold – among them massacres, exploitation and thoughtless squandering of manpower. The decimated population was regrouped, assimilated or protected by the Crown from the encroachment of the landowners. The native population gradually recovered its strength and integrated into the colonial structure (not without the odd revolt), but always in the context of their own communities (*altepelt*, now known as *pueblos*).

EVANGELIZATION

This is the key word, the supreme justification for the Conquest. It was initially undertaken by mendicant orders (particularly the Franciscans) driven by evangelical zeal. They advocated a 'separate development' of two republics, one Indian and one Spanish. However, the failure of the Indian Church (due to lack of indigenous priests) led the ecclesiastical authorities to take on the burden of evangelization from about 1570, when the episcopal structures were put in place. Except in the marginal areas (which were left to missionaries), the Church held sway, spreading the cults of the Counter-Reformation – from the Virgin to images of saints – through spectacular displays of devotion, while the whole country, particularly the towns, was peppered with baroque churches.

A MIXED URBAN SOCIETY

In 1519, Tenochtitlán could stand comparison with European capitals. By 1800, Mexico City had grown into the continent's foremost city. Spain invested heavily in its development, spurred by the desire to manifest the national ideals of civilization as an example to the downtrodden. So, in a display of strength, the city center gathered together all the key elements of power on its Plaza Mayor (*zócalo*). The colonial city was not a mere copy of the metropolis, however: it had a Roman-style grid system ● 76, and its population provided the demographic blueprint for a multiracial Mexico. Blacks, mulattos and mestizos formed a substantial part of the teeming urban population.

AN EXPORTING COLONIAL COLONY

The colonial relationship required the colony to deliver its raw materials – silver, dyestuffs – to the metropolis in exchange for certain necessary manufactured goods. In the case of Mexico, this system revolved around the production of silver ▲ 178. By 1800, the country was producing two-thirds of the world's silver, with the main seams situated in the north. Mexico was also being populated, however, and the colonizers wanted the same diet that was to be found in Europe. Large cereal and livestock farms emerged very quickly, encroaching on Indian territory and taking over the unoccupied lands of the north. Labor came from various sources, including Indians dislocated from their communities. The hot lands (today's Morelos) proved ripe for a plantation economy based on the cultivation of sugar cane by slaves.

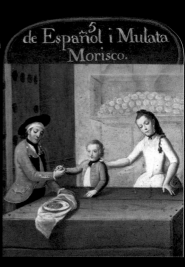

de Español i Mulata
Morisco.

TOWARD INDEPENDENCE

The 'second Conquest' started in 1760. This time, the administrative, a expression of the despotism of the Enlightenment embodied by taxation and bureaucrats sent from Spain. The Creole elite became increasingly frustrated and the distribution of wealth increasingly inequitable. Add to this the examples of the American fight for independence and the French Revolution, and the events of 1910 are easier to understand even if they took a long time coming.

Below: Pancho Villa. His flamboyant personality attracted American journalists, who peddled tales of his ferocity and love of women.

If the events that shook the country between 1910 and 1929 had not been quite so bloody – the death count is reckoned to be 1 million – it would be tempting to focus on the picturesque aspects: the sun-drenched Latin setting with all the atmosphere of a Hollywood Western, the colorful characters, the soldiers with cartridges and sombreros galloping through the desert to attack armored trains in a struggle packed with incident…. The truer story, however, is replete with battles fought without quarter, coups d'état and treason, all of which were marked by a mixture of personal conflicts and clashes of ideology. This dark period bled the country dry, but it nevertheless created the foundations for modern Mexico.

THE 'CONSTITUTIONALISTS'

Although the party of this name did not appear until 1913, the term had been used to designate advocates of a 'bourgeois revolution', bent on political rather than social reforms. Their guiding light was Francisco Madero, an intellectual from a rich family who launched the revolt against Porfirio Díaz in 1910 but who was assassinated in 1913. Others, such as Venustiano Carranza, in power from 1915 to 1920, and his successors Obregón and Calles, gave the revolution a more 'presentable' face, eliciting support from the United States that would never have been forthcoming for Villa or Zapata.

EMILIANO ZAPATA: 'LAND AND FREEDOM'

A small landowner from the State of Morelos in the south, Zapata (*right*) was no outsider, but he rose up against the exactions of the *hacendados* (big landowners). He embodied the most uncompromising wing of the peasant revolt, demanding radical agrarian reform, and it is no accident that today's rebels (EZLN ● *29*) invoke his name. For nine years, the 'Attila of the South' fought with the same fervor against the dictators (Díaz and Huerta) and 'constitutionalists' (Madero and Carranza) in power in Mexico City, before he was lured into an ambush and killed in 1919.

A RAILROAD WAR

Trains played a key role. The leaders set up their HQs on them, while the troops piled on board with their *soldaderas*, wives or girlfriends, who organized supplies and provided healthcare, as well as occasionally lending a hand in the fighting. Battles often took place along the main railroad lines; the most famous such episode was the capture of Ciudad Juárez in 1913, featuring a modern version of the Trojan Horse. Villa sent a telegram to the garrison with news of the arrival of reinforcements, boarded a train with his men and took the city by surprise.

PANCHO VILLA AND HIS LEGEND

His name symbolizes the Mexican Revolution. The 'Centaur of the North' (he was originally from Chihuahua) was not an ideologue, but a rebel, endowed with inexhaustible energy. He showed his enemies no mercy and was a born leader of men, as well as a brilliant tactician on the battlefield. He was finally defeated by the better equipped army of Obregón and retired in 1920, before being murdered in 1923.

Above right: Pancho Villa's men charging the federal troops. Right: the historic meeting of Villa and Zapata in Mexico City (1914). Below: Emiliano Zapata.

AN ANTICLERICAL REVOLUTION

The privileges inherited from the colonial era by the Church – still mired in the 19th century – rebounded against it. Although Zapata's peasants displayed images of the Virgin of Guadalupe, the revolutionaries in the big cities fostered a virulent anticlericalism. Some extremists held parties in churches and forced priests to marry, under pain of death. In his novel *The Power and the Glory* (1940) ● *119,* Graham Greene described these harassments – part tragic, part ludicrous – which would lead in 1926 to the violent revolt of the Cristeros, the last upheaval of the revolutionary period (*below,* a group of Cristeros).

Mexico, land of inspiration

In 1935, an exhibition in New York gathered together photos by Cartier-Bresson, the Mexican Manuel Álvarez Bravo and the American Walker Evans.

Right from its emergence in Mexico City in 1922, the Muralist Movement – which gave both cultural and political support to the national ideal – had internationalist aspirations. Spurred by the historical need to redefine the mission of painting and attracted by the prevailing freedom of expression (both iconographic and ideological), muralists, artists and intellectuals (particularly from Europe and the United States) came to live and work in the new country. Meanwhile, Mexican artists abroad played an extremely important role in establishing the path of international modern art in the 1930s.

Left: *Woman on strike* (1928), Tina Modotti

1920–30: THE MURALIST MOVEMENT'S POWER OF ATTRACTION

One of the first foreign artists to tread Mexican soil was the French painter and engraver Jean Charlot (1898–1979), who arrived in the early 1920s. In the following decade, there was a steady influx. The American Paul (Pablo) O'Higgins (1904–83) developed his entire artistic career in Mexico; the Catalan graphic artist Josep Renau (1907–82) worked with David Alfaro Siqueiros on the mural for the electricians' union in 1939; and the Japanese-American Isamu Noguchi (1904–88) was invited by Diego Rivera to create a high-relief mural in the Abelardo Rodríguez market in Mexico City (1936).

Below: Breton, Rivera and Trotsky in 1938, in the company of Jacqueline Lamba

THE 1940s

According to the Russian painter Vlady Serge (1920–2005), 'Mexico is a country where everything is possible.' It welcomed the following artists, mostly refugees from European Fascism: the Spaniards Remedios Varo (1908–66) and Vicente Rojo (b. 1932), the Austrian Wolfgang Paalen (1905–59), the English Surrealists Leonora Carrington (b. 1917) and Gordon Onslow Ford (1912–2003) and the German sculptor Mathias Goeritz (1915–90). Also from Germany came the art critic Paul Westheim (1886–1963), while the ex-director of the Bauhaus, the Swiss Hannes Meyer, taught in the City Planning Institute in Mexico City (1939–49) and the Frenchman Vladimir Kaspé built the French Institute of Latin America (1945) and the French Lycée (1950). These people contributed immeasurably to the renewal of Mexico's artistic life.

UNDER THE AEGIS OF ANDRÉ BRETON

Mexico, 'the Surrealist land par excellence', was chosen by the French poet in 1940 as the site of an international organization bringing together Mexican artists and a cohort of European Surrealists. Although the show aroused protests and criticism, it also marked a turning point in the artistic life of the Mexican nation.

PHOTOGRAPHY

During the 1920s and 1930s, several foreign photographers produced striking images of Mexican culture and society, in the process helping photography gain recognition as an art form as well as creating an invaluable record of life at the time. The American Edward Weston (1886–1958) and the Italian Tina Modotti (1896–1942) ▲ *152* worked together from 1923 to 1926, capturing aspects of popular life: Henri Cartier-Bresson (1908–2004) took numerous photos between 1934 and 1964, which are collected in his *Carnets mexicains*, while Gisèle Freund visited Mexico in 1948. The Hungarian Kati Horna (1912–2000) devoted forty years of her life to depicting Mexican society.

MOVIES
Sergei Eisenstein left an unfinished film *¡Qué viva México!* (1931, *above*), along with many outtakes. Luis Buñuel arrived in 1946 and created some masterpieces: *Los Olvidados*, 1950; *Subida al cielo*, 1951; *La Vida criminal de Archibaldo de la Cruz*, 1955. John Huston shot *The Night of the Iguana* in 1964, with local director of photography Gabriel Figueroa.

México (1934), Henri Cartier-Bresson

THE AURA OF THE MEXICAN PAINTERS
During the 1930s, the great muralists enjoyed an international reputation, particularly in the United States, where they were sought out by the future luminaries of modern art. Louise Nevelson (1899–1988) and the painter Ben Shahn (1898–1969) collaborated with Diego Rivera ● *100* in 1930 in the New Workers School (New York). In 1936, David Alfaro Siqueiros ● *101* settled in New York and founded the Siqueiros Experimental Workshop. His research into materials, techniques and tools attracted painters such as Jackson Pollock (1912–56), who first experimented with dripping paint under his auspices, while Philip Guston (1913–80) was his assistant in Los Angeles in 1932.

● The Indian presence today

Contrary to popular belief, Mexican Indians are not on the verge of extinction. Far from it, in fact: they are more numerous today than they have ever been, despite epidemics, colonization, deportation and wars, not to mention mixing with other cultures. Their exact numbers are extremely difficult to calculate (although there are over 10 million native speakers of Indian languages), but no demographic data can do justice to the vast differences in the evolution of the various groups.

SOCIAL EXCLUSION
Today's Indians have inherited a colonial situation that continues to establish marked social divisions – hence the temptation to escape this discrimination by ceasing to speak in Indian languages, a stigma of the most wretched poverty.

THE INDIGENOUS ORGANIZATIONS
Although this situation has hardly changed overall since colonization, Indians are asserting their presence in mainstream society. This is because there is an increased awareness of identity and a mushrooming of indigenous associations that defend local languages and cultures, which have been encouraged by the media coverage of recent rebellions, such as that of the EZLN (Ejército Zapatista de Liberación Nacional) in Chiapas ● 29. The situation has also improved because of the influx of foreign tourists and their appreciation of Indian craftwork and culture.

THE LANGUAGES
Although some fifty indigenous languages – inevitably divided into a considerable number of dialects – are now spoken in Mexico, others have completely disappeared throughout recent decades (for example, Pai Pai and Kiliwa in Lower California), or are very close to total extinction (such as Tlahuica and Azinca in the State of Mexico). Others, however, such as Mayan and Nahuatl (which is spoken by the descendants of the Aztecs) are thriving, with more than a million and a half speakers for each language (although monolinguism is becoming increasingly uncommon in the 21st century).

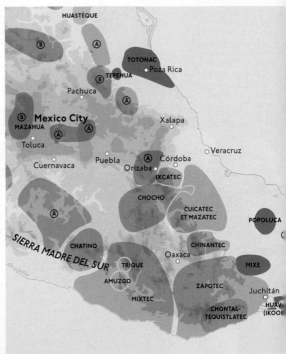

Map labels:
Tijuana, CUCAPA, KUMIAI, PAPAGO, UNITED STATES, KILIWA, COCHIMI, PAIPAI, SERI, PIMA, YAQUI, TARAHUMARA, MAYO, Monterrey, CORA, HUICHOL, PAME, HUASTEC, Guadalajara, OTOMÍ, Mérida, PURÉPACHA (TARASC), Mexico City, MAYAN, NAHUATL, TLAPANEC, BELIZE, Acapulco, GUATEMALA, MAZAHUA, HONDURAS

THE 'MARÍAS'

The Indian populations of Mexico City, known as 'marías', are concentrated in the old historic center and, above all, in the city's crowded suburbs, but they are also found in more upmarket residential areas, where there is a heavy demand for domestic staff.

LINGUISTIC FAMILIES

- Macro-Nahuatl or Uto-Uahuatl group
- Ⓐ NAHUATL
- Macro-Mixtec or Otomi group
- Ⓑ OTOMI
- Macro-Yuman or Hokano group
- Macro-Mayan group

THE CURRENT REDISTRIBUTION OF INDIGENOUS GROUPS

The most spectacular changes in the last few years have occurred as a result of the redistribution of indigenous groups over the map of Mexico. The capital has a magnetizing effect on populations in search of a better life and has become a veritable ethnic kaleidoscope, untainted by any temptation to create linguistic ghettos. Meanwhile, the emigration to the United States that is bleeding indigenous communities ● *42* has given rise to heavy indigenous concentrations on the American border, in Tijuana, Mexicali and Ciudad Juárez, where the new Indian speakers are now Mixtecs and Zapotecs from the State of Oaxaca, or Mayans.

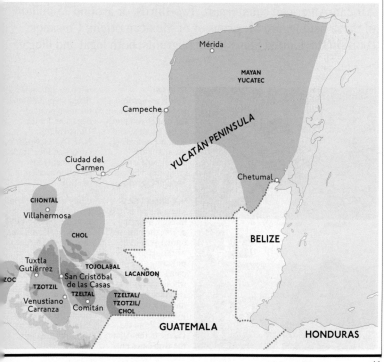

Map labels:
Mérida, MAYAN YUCATEC, Campeche, YUCATÁN PENINSULA, Ciudad del Carmen, Chetumal, CHONTAL, Villahermosa, CHOL, BELIZE, Tuxtla Gutiérrez, TOJOLABAL, LACANDON, ZOC, San Cristóbal de las Casas, TZOTZIL, TZELTAL, Venustiano Carranza, Comitán, TZELTAL/ TZOTZIL/ CHOL, GUATEMALA, HONDURAS

'Del Otro Lado':
Mexican migrants in the United States

In the United States, the conquest of the West also involved the annexation of a third of Mexico, from Texas to California ● 27, in the mid-19th century. Ever since then, Mexicans have headed north, in successive and increasingly large waves. In the last two decades, migration has exploded, amid talk of the silent reconquest of the lost territories. The Hispanic population is now more numerous to the north of the Río Grande than its African-American counterpart. Two-thirds, or around 25 million of these people, are Mexicans or of Mexican origin: Chicanos (born in the United States), and migrants, both legal and illegal.

LEAVING
This is an uprooting and an adventure. In the center and north of the country, and also increasingly in the south, the countryside is emptying. These days, Mexico City can often be little more than a stepping-stone, the main point of departure for the United States. NAFTA (the North American Free Trade Agreement) has served to accelerate the flow.

'LA FRONTERA'
Many migrants pass through Tijuana ▲ 386, the busiest border post in the world, set in a pulsating area of contact and transit whose darker side is reflected by the multiple murders of women in Ciudad Juárez. From the Pacific to the Atlantic, the twin cities on either side of the line, the subcontracted factories (known as *maquiladoras* ▲ 379), the migrant smugglers and the drug traffickers all forge strong links between the two countries, despite the miles of wall, the deserts, the rivers, the Border Patrol and the strict anti-immigrant militia.

'DEL OTRO LADO' (FROM THE OTHER SIDE)

Los Angeles, where almost half the population is Hispanic, is the biggest Mexican city after the country's capital, and in 2005 it elected a mayor with a background in this migratory flow. The southwest of the United States is gradually becoming Mexican-American and the influx is also penetrating the rest of the country. Partisans of the Anglo-Saxon model of identity warn of the threat of a 'Mexican invasion', but without this imported manpower whole swathes of the American economy (agriculture, restaurants, cleaning services and gardening) would collapse.

THE CIRCLE OF MIGRATION

Migrants also allow Mexico itself to move ahead. The *remesas*, or sums of money sent to relatives and home communities, constitute Mexico's main source of legal revenue apart from oil and tourism. Migrants also introduce new values, lifestyles and consumer trends. Although they may come back to get married, to pay for the most splendid fireworks at the village fiesta, or to build homes in which to enjoy their final years, most usually return to the US, in pursuit of the Mexican-American dream.

Below: San Ysidro frontier post, between Tijuana and San Diego

THE MOVIES

Mexican cinema ● *60* has a history of presenting the Mexican-American dream as a nightmare, and migrants as deserters or victims. At the same time, Hollywood has exalted many Mexican stars, from Dolores del Río to Salma Hayek, while still presenting a negative image of their compatriots as violent, alcoholic machos, or as femmes fatales or prostitutes. Some independent movies – American, Chicano and European – have conjured up a more complex vision: *The Salt of the Earth* (Herbert Biberman, 1954), *Touch of Evil* (Orson Welles, 1958), *Zoot Suit* (Luis Valdez, 1981), *The Border* (Tony Richardson, 1982) and *Bread and Roses* (Ken Loach, 2000).

● Languages

Mexican Spanish

This variant of Spanish is slower and gentler on the ear, with none of the terse authority of Castilian speech. It also lacks, to the horror of Spaniards, the dental pronunciation of the *z* and *c* and the distinction between *b* and *v*. Another feature is the plethora of diminutives that serve to stretch out time (beware the *momentito* and the *ratito*, as these can last for ever!). It is more ceremonious, with its *usted* and *ustedes* ('Your Grace', from the glory days of the Colony) replacing *tú* and *vosotros*, thus sparing travelers the need to learn two more forms of conjugation. Regional speech is often dotted with archaisms, particularly in the south, while dozens of words have different meanings than in Spain. A *tortilla* here is a corn pancake and only recovers the sense of omelet when qualified as *española*. Even the most luxurious bus is called a *camión* (a truck in Spain), while towns revolve around a *zócalo* (apparently derived from the socle of a royal statue), rather than a Plaza de Armas or Plaza Mayor.

THE FIGURES
Mexico is the world's biggest Spanish-speaking country, with 104 million inhabitants, as against 41 million Spaniards and 43 million Colombians. Pedants will argue that some 2 or 3 million Indian women and children still do not speak Spanish; but, to make up for this, there are even more Mexicans living in Chicago or California who do speak it.

The Indian heritage

In Mexico, the largest Indian country in the Americas, between 10 and 15 million peasants or migrants speak one of the 60 languages spoken before the Conquest ● 40. The Indians sitting on the sidewalks of Mexico City greet each other in Otomí or Triqui, the traders of Oaxaca use Zapotec as their primary means of expression, just as the women of the southeast use Tzotzil, Tzeltal or Yucatán Mayan. Mestizos are familiar, above all, with Nahuatl, the language of the central plateaus, of Tenochtitlán-Mexico City, of the Aztec world and its commercial networks. The letter *x* conveys a sound relatively close to the *jota*, as in *México*. Nahuatl gave the *conquistadores* and the Spanish tongue the words *chocolate*, *cacao*, *tomate*, *aguacate* (avocado) and *nopal* (cactus), among others. And today's traveler still admires embroidered *huipils* (blouses) or buys leather *huaraches* (sandals), as well as eating tamales (cornmeal pasta) in the *tianguis*, open-air markets in villages and cities alike, or opting for *tlacoyos*, blue corn pancakes, or grilled *elotes* (corncobs). A child (*escuintle*) will ask for a *popote* (straw) to drink a soda, before running behind a *papalote* (kite). So, despite the conquest of souls in the 16th century and the Revolution of 1910, which both tended to rename the world according to the conquerors' saints and heroes, the volcanoes of Popocatépetl and Ixtaccihuatl, the beaches of Huatulco, the mines of Taxco, the markets of Oaxaca and the neighborhoods of Mexico City all stake out a firmly Indian toponymy and space.

Spanglish

Cultural convergence continues apace, since the American language is absorbing Spanish heedless of protests against the encroachment of 'Spanglish'. Similarly, Anglicisms like *fútbol* and *bistec* have not only been long integrated into Mexican speech, they have also acquired a Hispanic spelling. The contact is particularly fruitful in the northern states, where pickups are *trocas* (from *trucks*), but throughout Mexico office workers classify *folders* before eating a sandwich in a *lonchería*.

Arts and traditions

One of Mexico's most striking paradoxes is that Catholicism plays a preponderant role – the diocese of Mexico City has the biggest Catholic allegiance in the world – but at the same time pre-Hispanic lore still has a palpable presence in everyday life, although it often remains hidden, or at least buried in the unconscious, until it bursts into the open in times of tension, suffering or anguish. This alliance of the two poles of Mexican religion can barely be summed up by the word 'syncretism', however. Christian and pagan elements are sometimes consciously dissociated by the Indians themselves, but it is not unusual for ritual practices of an autochthonous origin to be considered locally as 'Spanish', and vice versa. Indian beliefs and practices cannot be found in their 'pure' form anywhere in Mexico.

THE NEO-INDIANS

Urban Mexico is today witnessing the emergence of new assertions of identity, the most spectacular being the 'neo-Indians', city dwellers who, by means of supposedly Aztec dances (see the Zócalo of Mexico City ▲ 130), advocate the return to an 'authentic' religion that is unsullied by any Spanish influence, and in which the pre-Hispanic deities are to some extent humanized, in perpetual harmony with the cosmos. Every year, at the time of the spring equinox, the 'neo-Indians' take over the most prestigious archeological sites to capture cosmic vibrations in a New-Age atmosphere. These ceremonies attract Mexicans of all political and religious persuasions, as well as numerous foreigners combining tourism with mysticism (in Teotihuacán, more than a million people throng to the Pyramid of the Sun and its annexes ▲ 163 on this day).

The religious kaleidoscope of contemporary Mexico has been considerably diversified by the development of ██████ *istas* (Protestant sects) in both Indian communities and the ci██ along with the upsurge in Salvationist religions (the mushrooming of temples, in even the most remote regions, bears witness to the outreach of this grass-roots movement). This volatility reflects the emergence of new religious experiments in these times of globalized beliefs, reflecting a search for an alternative to monolithic religion, typified by triumphant Catholicism.

EASTER WEEK

The celebration of Corpus Christi and Holy Week varies markedly from region to region. Among the Tarahumara ▲ *376* and Cora populations to the north of the country, they are major events in the devotional cycle, but incorporate many elements from the religion that predate contact with the Spanish. Ostentatious Christian displays (processions of penitents closely resembling those found in Spain) should not be allowed to obscure the persistence of strong beliefs about nature, animal doubles and the beings inhabiting the cosmos and the underworld. In many places, the invocation of Christ, the Virgin and the saints is superimposed on that of a whole series of pre-Hispanic deities whose characteristics have barely changed since the Conquest. Powerful symbols such as the Cross are components of a twin tradition, both Native American and European.

THE DEVIL

The devil occupies a significant place among the primordial entities of the cosmos. This ambivalent figure – who shares many characteristics with Tezcatlipoca (meaning 'smoking mirror'), a prominent member of the old Aztec pantheon – has served as a mask disguising a large number of pre-Hispanic deities who are in some way connected with death and sacrifice, as well as agricultural fertility, thus affording them the opportunity to escape the iconoclastic zeal of the evangelizers. Even today, the devil still remains an essential reference in Indian religions: he forges the intermediary link between two world views, one of American Indian origin, the other European.

● The cult of the dead

Candies for the
Día de los Muertos
(Day of the Dead)

For outsiders, the cult of the dead undoubtedly constitutes the most spectacular and most disconcerting – or even distressing – aspect of Mexican spirituality, on account of the omnipresence of the theme of death and its corresponding iconography, both in urban settings and in the most far-flung Indian communities, as well as the celebratory atmosphere surrounding the rituals for the Day of the Dead. This establishes an intense communion between the living, the deceased and the great ancestors, made manifest in ostentatious gifts and magnificent oblations, in the form of both flowers and food. This tradition, rooted in the local mind-set since pre-Hispanic times, has survived absolutely unaltered by evangelization, although it has merged with Christian practices.

THE CONCEPT OF DEATH

Life is in death, death is in life: the essence of indigenous thought is expressed in this chiasmus (which Western reason finds great difficulty in endorsing). Hence the apparent levity accompanying tragic events and the burlesque approach to depictions of death. In western Mexico, the Xantolo festival – a local variant of the ceremonies for the Day of the Dead (All Souls' Day in the West) – is nothing short of untrammeled revelry, distinguished by performances by masked dancers with a strong erotic content. Similarly, the Carnival – the key event in the ritual cycle throughout central and southern Mexico – reenacts a 'primordial scene' of the birth of humanity, thereby ushering the ancestors back into the community of the living to guarantee its perpetuity and to make its women fertile.

THE DAY OF THE DEAD
The celebration of the dead, or 'Todos Santos', on November 2, is often the most important festival in the annual cycle, especially in the mestizo and Indian areas of central and western Mexico. Mixquic, a southern suburb of Mexico City, has even become a tourist attraction, renowned for the nighttime devotions held in its candlelit cemetery.

ON THE ZÓCALO OF MEXICO CITY
The Zócalo is transformed into a giant cemetery, with its bakery, its stages, its wrestling matches and its shrines, each striving to outdo the other in refinement, imagination and humor, not to mention forthright political protest. (*Above*: a tram car heading for Mictlan, the world of the dead in ancient Mexican belief.)

COMMUNING VIA FOOD
The period of Todos Santos (All Saints) is the most powerful manifestation of the fascinating beauty of Mexico's indigenous and mestizo cultures, whether in the large cities, the colonial towns or the most remote outpost of Indian community. It is also the time of the year when food is at its most abundant and sophisticated, ranging from the anthropomorphic *pan de muertos* (bread of the dead) to delicious drinks such as *atole* (which is made from corn dough) and regional specialties ● 67. Streets are invaded with stands crammed with candies in the form of skulls and skeletons (favorites with children), as well as T-shirts and disguises portraying the figure of death.

SHRINES
The end of October is marked by the appearance of shrines, found everywhere from humble huts to the department stores in big cities. Their creators let their imaginations run wild, often uniting time-honored subjects with modern references. The dead return to the living every year, in various guises, reflecting the type of death (natural or violent). They are supposed to be honored in high style and given sophisticated food. This obligation is respected everywhere, as any negligence entails severe punishment. Visits to the cemetery are an intrinsic part of the reunion with the dead. The tombs are bedecked for the occasion with French marigolds (*cempoalxochtil*), the autumnal flower symbolizing the dead, whose orange color enhances the beauty of these ritual compositions.

49

● Festivals

Below left: carnival in Tenejapa
Below right: Independence Day in Mexico City

There is hardly a single day in the Mexican calendar that is
not devoted to a festival. Villages provide the financial backing
for events from the Christian celebratory cycle (with the day of
the locality's eponymous saint given pride of place) as well as
those of pre-Hispanic inspiration. Among the Indians, festivals
are an indispensable source of the *respeto* (prestige) that is an
essential prerequisite of social success. Music is ever-present,
and the volume is as high as possible, not just for the instruments
but also for the successive crescendos of fireworks, in which even
the most impoverished village will not hesitate to invest a small
fortune. No community – Indian, mestizo, peasant or urban – is
immune to this festive spirit, which is indicative of an
immoderation that escapes all control.

THE FESTIVALS OF THE LIFE CYCLE

Throughout Indian, mestizo and urban Mexico, the main phases of the life cycle – birth, marriage, death – are marked by festivities.
In addition, urban areas hold rites of passage, such as adolescent girls' attainment of adulthood at the age of fifteen (the *quinceañeras*, *left*): this family celebration represents a new variant of the christening ceremony (*padrinazgos*), a veritable institution that brings together generations and cultures. The *padrinazgos* begins with the christening of a child, but above all it creates lifelong links of mutual assistance between the parents and godparents (converted into *compadres*). The accumulation of these links of symbolic parentage enhances the indispensable *respeto*, the social prestige that ensures a person's status as a citizen of the local community, particularly in Indian country. Inviting a mestizo (particularly a trader) to be your child's godfather generates a beneficial commercial relationship that overrides the religious implications of the ceremony.

THE 'PIÑATA'

This is a vital part of every festival. Blindfolded children burst open these objects (often in the shape of a star or bell) decorated with strips of paper and loaded with candies.

'FIESTAS PATRIAS' (PATRIOTIC FESTIVALS)

These commemorate the major events of Mexico's postcolonial history: February 5, the Day of the Constitution; March 21, birthday of Benito Juárez; May 1, Labor Day; May 5, the anniversary of the defeat of the French expedition in Puebla, marked every year by a reconstruction of the battle; September 16, Independence Day; and, finally, November 20, the Day of the Revolution. These all exalt a strong nationalistic sentiment and assert a composite Mexican identity, free from the influence of colonial powers and the interference of foreign governments in the country's public affairs.

'EL DÍA DE INDEPENDENCIA'

Every year, on the eve of Independence Day (September 16), the 'Cry of Dolores' ('*el grito de Dolores*') that was issued in that town by Father Hidalgo, the hero of the Independence ▲ *356*, is taken up by the president of the republic from the top of the Government Palace, and echoed by all the country's administrative authorities.

Below: festive atmosphere in San Cristóbal de las Casas, Chiapas

THE LITURGICAL AND PATRONAL FESTIVALS

Ritual activity permeates these festivals throughout the country. The feast day of the eponymous saint of a village, the major high points in the Christian calendar (such as All Souls ● 48, Christmas and Easter week ● 47) and Carnival are always honored with specific devotions, innumerable processions, offerings of food, sumptuous floral compositions and colourful firework displays. The organization and funding for these extravagant festivals depend on a system of collective participation in the form of posts (*cargos*) of varying degrees of responsibility and position. These posts are sometimes arranged in a hierarchical fashion, and they invariably plunge their incumbent into debt. This constraining factor guarantees the functioning of a profligate economy centered on religion. Christmas is above all an urban and mestizo festival. The evening of December 16 marks the start of the Christmas *novena*, punctuated by *posadas* (stops for the Virgin). Mary and Joseph, borne in procession, pass through the streets in search of a lodging. It is considered an honor to welcome the couple, who are regaled along their route with chanting and recitations of the rosary. This scene is repeated every night until December 24, when the Holy Family arrives in Bethlehem (the church, where the manger has been prepared).

● Traditional music and dance

Dancing is associated with festivals and was a highly codified means of expression in the pre-Hispanic era. The Spanish very quickly understood the benefits to be reaped from this form of ritual representation in their quest to colonize the Indian imagination, and it is for this reason that many dances with an indigenous content have survived to this day. Music and singing also play an important part in ceremonies and celebrations. Archaic structures can be found intermingled with old Spanish folk tunes, while Christian hymns have not entirely displaced Indian threnodies, such as the chants for the dead that are performed by the Chol in Chiapas, or the shamanic incantations of the H'men of Yucatán.

THE DANCES OF THE CONQUEST
In the years just after the Conquest, Spanish dances illustrating the recent victories of Christians over Arabs were adapted to the new reality. The *baile de Cortés*, for example, pitted the conqueror of Mexico against the Aztec emperor Moctezuma. The dance of the Matachines (*above*), which is connected to the cycle of the 'Moros y Cristianos', is still widely performed by the Indians of the northwest, where it honors the Virgin of Guadalupe and celebrates the end of the harvest.

COMMEMORATIVE DANCES AND RITUAL HUMOR
Although most dances have a mythical or historical basis and contribute to the commemoration of saints and ancestors, several others serve to parody the immoral customs of animals ('prehuman' creatures) or to pour scorn on the Ladinos (mestizos), using a type of ritual humor greatly appreciated by indigenous audiences.

'EL PALO VOLADOR'
The symbolism of this Toltec ritual ▲ *193 (right)*, still very much alive in eastern Mexico, has been substantially modified over time, mixing Christian faith with pre-Hispanic dance rituals.

TRADITIONAL MASKS
Masks, often carved from soft wood and painted in bright colors, represent mythical creatures – animals, devils *(right)*, ancestors – and historical figures. Like all effigies, they are treated as living beings: vigils are kept over them, as if they were saints, and they are fed, just as if they were alive. The words uttered by their voice are sacred.

FLUTE AND CYLINDRICAL DRUM
This is the most common combination in indigenous musical groups. The flute and the big cylindrical drum *(right)* with a membrane made of animal skin accompany all the journeys made by performers in ritual processions. They are played outside churches and punctuate speeches made at the gates of the sanctuaries of brotherhoods.

INSTRUMENTS PAST AND PRESENT

The Mayan wind instruments – 'whistling vases', pipes, and so forth – have largely been replaced by all kinds of flutes of European origin, not to mention the highly popular brass bands (*bandas*). Percussion instruments have persisted longer, whether as vibrating strips of wood (*teponaztli*) or vertical drums (*huehuetl*). Conches (or whelks), traditionally used for calling or raising the alarm, have nowadays metamorphosed into tortoise shells, struck with corncobs, used in the Bachajón carnival to accompany the performers and to represent the 'savage' powers of the forest. They have also attracted the attention of the Neo-Indians ● *46*, who use them for their 'cosmic dance'. Violins, harps and guitars are distinguished from their Spanish models by their rusticity; the community of Chamula (Chiapas) is a major production center for these instruments. Although violins and guitars are very widespread, the harp, particularly prized by the Tzotzils, has become the symbol of *jarocha* music (State of Veracruz).

● Shamanism

Right and opposite, far right:
Pre-Columbian medicinal plants,
facsimile of the *Codex Bodiano*

The term 'shamanism',
used with reference to
both Asia and the Americas, is applied to a wide range of
different cultural realities, but these all have in common the
existence of religious specialists who communicate with spirits to
fight against misfortune and disease. In Mexico, the shaman plays
an important role in Indian communities as the keeper of
knowledge about the world, its origins and its future. His
capacities set him apart not only from herbal healers, whose
abilities are confined to the field of the profane, but also from the
'priors', masters of the recitation of biblical texts. Nevertheless, a
shaman's work incorporates symbolic objects and references
pertaining to Christianity, but absorbed, consciously or otherwise,
into a worldview drawing on the animistic traditions and other
beliefs that preceded it.

THE PERSON

According to
traditional beliefs, the
human body is
vulnerable to
aggression because it
possesses unstable
elements outside the
body proper, such as
the *tona*, the animal
double. The life cycle
of this being runs
parallel to that of all
other beings, and the
dividing line between
animal, vegetable and
human entities is
extremely thin. There
is a possibility at all
times of reversible
metamorphoses of
human beings into
wild animals, or
nahuales, and, if
deemed necessary,
the shaman can
effect these changes
at will.

Below: Huichol
shaman

DISEASE AND THERAPY

Shamanic rituals
involve the struggle
against misfortune
through divination
and ceremonies to
request good harvests
or rain, as well as
through acts of
sorcery. All bodily
ailments, along with
conditions of the
mind or spirit, such as
jealousy, terror or
the loss of the soul,
lead to accusations
of sorcery, as the
idea of disease from
natural causes is alien
to the Indian way of
thinking.

Above: purification ritual (*limpia*) in the Tuxtlas
Left: ritual objects
Bottom: *temazcal* (steam bath ▲ *195*)

SHAMANS AND MEDICINE

These days, biomedicine plays an important role in the day-to-day life of Indian communities, and shamans do not hesitate to send their patients to a mainstream clinic or hospital; however, if this recourse fails, the patient may well return to the indigenous expert. Similarly, the therapeutic methods of the shamans themselves borrow elements from both Western medicine and traditional practices. Catholicism – and also, to an increasing extent, Protestantism – will decisively determine the suitability of different treatments.

'ÍDOLOS'

Throughout the Mesoamerican region, therapeutic practices involve an infinite variety of supplications and offerings to the rulers of the natural world: the masters of animals, cultivated plants, deities of the underworld and heavenly images, the cohort of saints and Virgins, who are often merged with various solar and lunar divinities. The shamanic pantheons thus embrace significant figures from Christian tradition. These beliefs continue to reflect the overriding influence of a concept of the body inherited from the pre-Hispanic era, which revolves around the practice of manipulatng energy to restore good health. The Indians of western Mexico (Nahua, Tepehua, Otomi) still represent the entities of the other world in the form of figurines made with bark paper, called *ídolos*, which the shamans cut up in a healing ceremony or to which they appeal for a good harvest.

● Mexican music today

Prickly subjects associated with the border (such as drug smuggling and illegal migration) characterize the lyrics of *norteño* songs.

From the tiniest village to the big city, the notes of a *cumbia*, a *ranchera* or a pop song emanate from the houses, enshroud the clients of the minibuses used for public transport and echo through the market stalls. The sound systems are turned up to full volume in the doors of stores to lure in customers, and the regional bus drivers who generously share their musical tastes with their passengers ensure that it is impossible to travel anywhere in Mexico without a continuous sound track: this is a manifestation not only of the pleasure found by Mexicans in musical expression but also of their fear of emptiness and silence.

Below: Vicente Fernández

Sigo siendo EL REY
JOSÉ ALFREDO JIMÉNEZ

THE MIXING OF GENRES

After the Revolution and the great rural exodus to the cities, several cultural forms took on a new life in urban environments: the *bolero ranchero* and the *banda norteña*, for example, both represent reinterpretations of esthetic codes formulated in the early 20th century. The creative borrowing of unfamiliar musical genres – the result of specific social changes as well as commercial imperatives – has added further twists to the play of identities.

AN ENDURING ICON: THE 'RANCHERA'

Ranchera songs emerged from the *ranchos* (farms), so dear to the hearts of the nationalists of the early 20th century, as the countryside, and rural life in general, was endowed with new significance by the mythology of the 1910 Revolution. These passionate tales of treachery and nostalgia for the land, sung to the accompaniment of a guitar, found a new, texturally richer level of expression in the mariachi ▲ 322 (*right*), and in the voices of giants of the music scene: Lucha Reyes in the 1930s, Pedro Infante in the 1950s, Lola Beltrán and Vicente Fernández more recently. The decor associated with the *ranchera* – cacti, rivers, huts – has become increasingly lost in the mists of time, but this form of popular music has survived and still produces major figures, such as José Alfredo Jiménez, known as 'El Rey' ('Life is worthless', he sings, but 'I'm still its king…').

The electric group Nortec uses rhythms taken from the popular music of Tijuana, while Mono Blanco has recovered the sounds of the Afro-Indian communities of the Atlantic coast. The process of *mestizaje*, profoundly marked by the urban experience, finds common ground in the poetry of Lila Downs (*bottom right*), the derision of Café Tacuba and the ska of Maldita Vecindad. Finally, the appropriation of foreign elements such as *cumbia* and hip hop distinguish the experiments of El Gran Silencio and Control Machete.

NORTEÑO MUSIC

In northern Mexico, as in Texas, the accordion was introduced during the 19th century, along with the mazurka and the polka dance styles, by immigrants from western and central Europe.

Throughout the 20th century, *norteño* music accompanied the workers trying to cross over to the United States. The predominant style here is the *corrido*, a sung description of regional heroes and striking personalities. (*Above*, musicians in Catemaco.)

... AND ITS VARIATIONS

In the 1950s, the popularity of this genre made it worthwhile to add instruments such as a drum kit and electric keyboards. This music, which has gradually strayed from its origins, has now incorporated Afro-Caribbean rhythms, as well as drawing on the brass bands characteristic of the Pacific coast – the *bandas*. This new style is called *grupero* (played by groups). Straddling the border, this cultural mix is slowly penetrating into the heart of Mexico, giving rise to a host of new forms: *tecnobanda*, *quebradita* and *narcocorrido*, spearheaded by artists such as Los Tigres del Norte, Los Cadetes de Linares, Ramón Ayala y Cornelio Reyna, El Recodo, Los Tucanes de Tijuana, El Mexicano, Los João, Los Flamers and Los Bukis.

The Mexican bullfight: a play of mirrors

Although both the bull and the horse were unknown in the Americas before the Conquest, it did not take long for the Spanish to introduce bullfighting into their colonies. After the 19th-century wars of independence, some nations, such as Argentina, rejected this symbol of Spain; others, such as Mexico, transformed it into an emblem of their own identity.

THE 'CHARREADA'

The *charreada*, now considered the 'Mexican national sport' but practiced by its elite, features displays in which fillies and bull-calves are dominated and lassoed. At first sight, this seems little more than a demonstration of traditional techniques used in livestock farming; a closer analysis from an anthropological angle, however, reveals a subversion of the Spanish bullfight. The ungainly picador is replaced by a stylish virtuoso, while the bull-calves are never exalted or put to death, nor do they come from a 'wild race' (*raza brava*), but from livestock reared for meat. Their aggression is only exploited in the *jineteo de toros*, a bull-riding exhibition which, by supplanting the horse, seems ironically to heap scorn on the horse-riding and bullfighting techniques championed by the Spanish colonizers.

BREEDING AND THE 'CHARRO' COSTUME

Bull-breeding has become a specialty of the central states of Mexico. The enterprise follows the same lines as in Spain, except that, instead of wearing the Andalusian costume typical of the Old World, the ranch hands adhere to the tradition of the *charro* costume. This quintessentially Mexican costume embodies all the ambiguity of a nation that unites opposites, such as luxury, which is symbolized by the luxurious *haciendas* of livestock farmers, and revolutionary fervor (both Villa and Zapata are idolized by the *charros*). This outfit owes as much to Spanish history as it does to the indigenous peasants, and as much to the memory of Moctezuma as to that of the Emperor Maximilian, who established the model during his tragicomic reign in Mexico ● *27*.

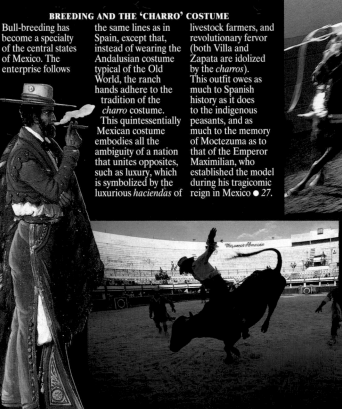

THE DANCE OF THE 'TORITOS'

The dance of the *toritos* is an essential ritual in village carnivals and patronal celebrations. On this occasion, the animal is not real, but a dummy of a bull borne on the head and shoulders of a dancer who plays at charging the onlookers. The idea is of Spanish origin but it is undoubtedly most widespread in Mexico. The most spectacular *toritos* are found in Michoacán, where they are emblems of city neighborhoods and villages, and resemble carnival floats, featuring a wealth of pre-Hispanic motifs.

THE CORRIDA

The arenas in Mexico City (*left*) are the biggest in the world, with a seating capacity of 50,000. These are obviously part of the Spanish heritage, but certain details counteract this influence. For example, the preliminary procession of the *toreros* is preceded by a *charro* horseman derived from local tradition, who rides alongside the baroque *alguacil* (an official in 17th-century costume customarily seen in Spain), as if to control it. Another interesting detail: after a successful killing, the lap of honor is undertaken in a counter-clockwise direction, while the posthumous lap of the valiant bull goes in the other direction; in Spain, the opposite is the case.

RIDING THE BULL: THE 'JARIPEO RANCHERO'

Although the iconoclastic El Cordobés once jumped on top of a bull he was fighting, this dangerous practice is not normally seen in Spanish bullrings. It first appeared on the colonial *haciendas* of Mexico and Peru, as if the indigenous and mestizo farmhands wished to defy the law forbidding them to ride a horse. Symbolically speaking, this upturned the Spanish canons of riding and established the identity of Mexican bullfighting. Nowadays, in the popular *jaripeo ranchero* – a spectacle similar to the rodeo, itself of Mexican origin – indigenous and mestizo bull-riders (*jinetes*) risk their lives by mounting champion animals that can weigh up to 1,800 pounds (800 kg), in the hope of escaping the poverty that ensnares a good part of the Mexican population.

3a. CORRIDA
EL TOREO DE PUEBLA
Temporada 1958
420
SOMBRA
GENERAL
ENTRADA
A LA LOCALIDAD
SOMBRA GENERAL
ENTRADA
A LA PLAZA

From 1935 to 1955, the Mexican movie industry reached new heights as it won over audiences at home and abroad to become the most important film business in the Spanish-speaking world. At first, filmmakers, in search of a national identity, favored narratives that reflected popular national concerns, but they then succumbed to the temptation to imitate the productions of Hollywood. Two constant themes during these twenty years were the *rancho* and the family, and these gave rise to genres that were exploited – or overexploited – to the full by the Mexican studios. Other formulas that were used to provide local color were rural and knockabout comedies, family melodramas, religious and urban dramas and adaptations of classic novels.

MOVIES OF THE MEXICAN REVOLUTION

These tended to exalt national sentiments: *Vámonos con Pancho Villa* (1936) by Fernando de Fuentes is the best illustration, still standing as the most important fictional work dealing with the Mexican Revolution.

THE STARS

In the silent era, Mexico started to develop a female star system based on the model of Hollywood. After a career in the United States, Dolores del Río (1905–83) played the leads, in 1943 and 1944, in major films by 'el Indio': *Flor Silvestre*, *María Candelaria*, *Las Abandonados*, *Bugambilia*. María Félix (*Doña Bárbara*, *Enamorada*, *La Diosa arrodillada*, *Río Escondido*) embodies the erotic myth. Her fame led her to play opposite Jean Gabin, Yves Montand and Gérard Philipe. A legend of the silver screen, she coined the image of the femme fatale who defied the prevailing machismo, destroying men's lives in the process. The dancing talents of Ninón Sevilla guaranteed her a starring role in movies about Mexican nightlife: *Revancha* (1948) and *Aventura en Río* (1949) by Alberto Gout, and *Víctimas del pecado* (1950) by Emilio Fernández.

Top left: poster for *La Pasionara* by Roberto Gavaldón (1955)
Top right: Dolores del Río in *In Caliente* by Lloyd Bacon (1935)
Left: María Félix, aka 'la Doña' ('Madame')

Right: *Enamorada*, with María Félix
Below right: *María Candelaria*, with Dolores del Río

MOVIES WITH LOCAL COLOR

Emilio Fernández, also known as 'el Indio' (1903–86), was the embodiment of cultural nationalism and one of Mexico's most important directors in the 1940s. His movies about persecuted lovers and marginalized Indians, with their highly personal style, were successful overseas: *El Huracán* (1943), *María Candelaria* (1944), *Salón México* (1949) and *Siempre Tuya* (1952).

KNOCKABOUT COMEDY

Two stars of Mexican comedy and Spanish-speaking cinema, Cantinflas (*Ahí Está el Detalle* by Juan Bustillo Oro, 1940) and Tin Tan (*El Rey del barrio* by Gilberto Martínez Solares, 1950), created popular characters in this field.

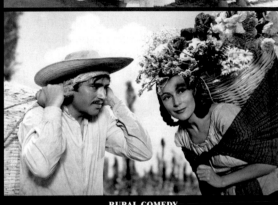

RURAL COMEDY

The *ranchera* comedy, distinguished by its folkloric songs and bucolic scenery, was the first specifically Mexican genre. The *ranchero*, picturesque peasant – funny, goodhearted and naïve – was portrayed by figures such as the comedian Carlos López 'Chaflán', the actor-singer Jorge Negrete and Pedro Infante, an authentic national idol. *Allá en el Rancho Grande* (1936) by Fernando de Fuentes, the epitome of the genre, idealized rural life as a lost paradise.

URBAN FAMILY MELODRAMA

The mother (morality) and the whore (immorality) were the archetypes here. *Santa* (1918) by Luis Gerardo Peredo, remade by Antonio Moreno in 1932 (the first Mexican talkie) codified the genre and became its prototype. The cabaret melodrama, with its parade of tropical dancers, prostitutes, gigolos and gangsters, was the inspiration for over 200 movies.

THE STUDIOS

The golden age corresponded with the industry's commercial apogee: 80 movies per year were made on 56 sound stages. The Churubusco Studios, opened in 1944, were on a par with those of Hollywood, as well as the most prolific in Latin America. After World War II, American cinema became all-pervasive and swamped the Mexican movie industry, which went on to be nationalized.

Left: the comedian Cantinflas (1911–93), relaxing between takes

61

● Popular art

Right: Pottery pineapple
from Tlaquepaque

Craftwork is not only the mirror of the artistic creativity of the Mexican people, but also a testament to the country's ethnic and cultural diversity. It comes out of various social, economic and cultural contexts in both rural and urban areas and, since pre-Hispanic times, from indigenous communities. Craft goods – widely available in markets and specialty stores, as well as by roadsides – can serve utilitarian, decorative or ritual purposes. Loaded with symbolism, they help to reinforce communal identities. Although the demands of the tourist market and the effects of social upheavals have tended to reduce quality, many craftspeople keen to perpetuate techniques from the past are still producing works of startling beauty.

STONE

Just like their forefathers, today's stonemasons continue to work volcanic rock to create millstones (*metates*), pestles and ashtrays. Whereas obsidian (colored black, green and brown) was used in the pre-Hispanic era to make arrowheads, it is now a choice material for chess pieces and statuettes depicting pre-Columbian deities. Alabaster, limestone, onyx and pumice are also sculpted, while semi-precious stones such as turquoise are used for intricate pieces of jewelry.

Below: 'Fridas' (models of Frida Kahlo) made of clay (Ocotlán de Morelos, Oaxaca)

POTTERY

Some techniques perpetuate centuries-old traditions (firing at low temperature, polishing, modeling, molding, appliqué, polychrome designs), while others were introduced by the Spanish in the 16th and 17th centuries (high-temperature firing, glazing, ceramics, enameling). The results can be simple or highly sophisticated, serving a utilitarian function (pitchers, cooking pots, dishes) or destined for ritual use, such as the censers of Santa Fe Laguna and Puebla. Apart from the miniatures so beloved by Mexicans, among the most attractive items are the jars from Tonala (Jalisco), trees of life from Metepec (State of Mexico), candleholders from Azúcar de Matamoros (Puebla), black clay objects from San Bartolo Coyotepec (Oaxaca), dolls from Atzompa and pineapples from San José de Gracia, Michoacán. (*Above*, working with clay.)

TEXTILES

The techniques have barely changed for 3,000 years: weavers still make clothes for their family on a belt loom ▲ *260* of pre-Columbian origin. The pedal loom, introduced by the Spanish, is used to weave woolen rugs. The most highly regarded textiles come from Oaxaca, the Sierra de Puebla and Huaxteca. *Rebozos*, shawls worn by Indian women all over the country, can be made of silk (Santa María del Río, San Luis Potosí) or cotton or synthetic fibers (Tenancingo, State of Mexico, Uruapan and Pátzcuaro, Michoacán).

PAPER

Although the pre-Columbian era has bequeathed us pictographic documents, it was the Spanish missionaries who taught the Indians how to use paper to make decorative objects – the most popular today being fantastic animals, skeletons, dolls and toys in the form of death. These items can be made of papier-mâché or paper strips.

● Popular art

SILVER
Taxco, Zacatecas and
Oaxaca are the cities
most renowned for their
silverwork ▲ 178 (below).

VEGETABLE FIBERS
Mexico's geographical
and climatic diversity
provides an infinite
source of plants,
and the original
inhabitants took
advantage of this
abundance to weave
baskets and obtain
the fibers needed to
make clothes, even
before they mastered
the technique of
terracotta. Even
today, the fibers of
sansevieria and agave
are used to make
hammocks, while
others are used for
hats (*above left*),
bowls (*coritas*), mats,
ropes, toys, and
similar products.

COPPER
Hammered and
chiseled copper
articles are a
traditional craft
product of Santa
Clara del Cobre,
Michoacán ▲ 317
(*left*).

METALWORK
Copper was already being used in the pre-Hispanic era,
while goldsmiths had mastered the lost-wax technique.
The Spanish taught the Indians the arts of enameling,
filigree, embossing, chiseling and engraving.
Hammered wrought iron, a legacy of the Spanish,
serves to make balconies, grills, crosses and
decorative accessories. Colorful objects and highly
original mirrors are manufactured from aluminum
sheets (*hojalatas*) salvaged from cans for beer
and food (Oaxaca).

WOOD

Woodwork was encouraged by the missionaries and applied to religious art in the colonial era ▲ *168*. It also gives rise to utilitarian objects, such as carved, polished spoons (Pátzcuaro, Michoacán) and chocolate bowls

(Mérida, Yucatán), as well as essentially decorative items: lacquered coffers and boxes, adorned with incised or painted designs; plates with encrusted lacquer; lacquered

gourds finished with gold leaf or silver (*right,* Olinala Guerrero); inlaid chests (Santa María del Río, San Luis Potosí) and boxes incorporating abalone shells. Multicolored carved masks, used for dances, display references to myth and religion (*above,* Ocozocoautla). The 'iron-wood' sculptures of the Seri Indians (Sonora) and the carved, painted

*alebrijes (*animals) of Oaxaca (*left*) have earned some of their creators an international reputation.

AND ALSO...

In Chiapas, amber (a fossilized resin), serves to make jewelry ▲ *257*. Tiny *chaquiras* (beads) are used by the Huichol Indians ▲ *328* (*below*). Coconuts are sculpted and inlaid with silver to create

delightful decorative objects, while cow horns are sculpted and engraved to obtain miniature caskets and pictures. Conches are carved in Lower California. Finally, blown glass, introduced by the Spanish in the 16th century, rounds off traditional dishware.

SKINS

Pre-Hispanic frescos and vases depict people dressed in jaguar skins. Deer skin served to make percussion instruments and sandals (the Kikapoo Indians in the State of Coahuila perpetuate this tradition by producing deerskin moccasins embroidered with multicolored beads). With the introduction of cattle by the Spanish, leatherwork, most evident nowadays in boots, embroidered saddles and embossed leather chests, has also become a traditional Mexican craft.

● A multicultural cuisine

No table in a restaurant or *taquería* is without these small bowls of chili sauce, used to season all dishes. Left to right: *salsa roja*, *salsa verde* and *salsa chipotle*.

Mexican food is not only hot, spicy and invitingly colorful, it is also extremely varied: even in the time of the Aztecs, the Emperor Moctezuma had the choice of 78 dishes at each meal. The arrival of the Spanish expanded this culinary wealth still further, as indigenous ingredients – corn, tomato, avocado, red bean, chilies – were complemented by ingredients imported from Europe: rice, wheat, onion, garlic, pork, spices and oil of Moorish origin.

CORN:
A SACRED PLANT
According to a Mayan legend, man was created from a grain of corn ● *106*. This cereal, which has been present in Mexico for over 7,000 years, played a key role in feeding all the pre-Columbian peoples and is still the staple foodstuff today.

TORTILLAS:
MEXICAN BREAD
These corn pancakes are an essential part of any meal. In the countryside, women still make them by hand; in the towns, they are sold in *tortillerías*.

TACOS
Smaller than tortillas, these are folded in two or rolled and cooked on a metal plate. They are sold by street vendors, who fill them with meat, onions and spicy sauces.

QUESADILLAS
These are tortillas made with corn (or wheat in the north) and stuffed with cheese (*queso*).

ENCHILADAS
Tortillas stuffed with chicken, meat or vegetables, topped with a red pepper sauce, sprinkled with cheese and then grilled (*below*). An *enchilada suiza* has green sauce and fresh cream.

'FRIJOLES NEGROS' (BLACK BEANS)
One of Mexico's staples, along with corn and chilies. They can be eaten alone in their broth, as *refritos* (sautéed with onion and *epazote*, an aromatic local herb) or as a purée to accompany all types of dishes.

MEAT, FROM NORTH TO SOUTH
In the cattle-rearing lands of the north, red meat is extremely popular, either grilled (*asada*) or dried, cut in thin strips and then fried with onions (*machaca* or *cecina*). In the center of the country, the traditional festival dishes are *moles*: poultry (turkey or chicken) accompanied by a sauce made with spices, three types of chilies, peanuts, almonds and cacao. The *mole* from Puebla (*mole pueblano*) is the most famous ▲ *289*, but *moles* are also widespread in Oaxaca. Lamb is either stuffed (*birria*, Zacatecas and Jalisco) or steamed (*mixiote*, State of Mexico). In Yucatán, meat (particularly pork) is steamed in banana leaves (*cochinita pibil*).

FISH
When marinated in lime juice with coriander, spices, chili and olive oil, fish is known as ceviche (Yucatán) ● *69*. In Veracruz, it is baked (*à la veracruzana*) in the oven with olives, chilies, tomatoes and onion. Also common are delicious seafood cocktails, such as *vuelve a la vida* (start to feel alive again): oysters, shrimps, crabs and periwinkles, which are mixed together and doused with oyster broth, lemon juice and a spicy sauce.

THE AVOCADO

Mexicans call this *aguacate* (from the Nahuatl *ahuacatl*, meaning testicles).
It accompanies Tampico-style meat dishes and forms part of the *sopa azteca* and the
caldo tlalpeño – without forgetting the famous guacamole ● 68, *ahuacamolli*.

DRINKS

Beer (*cerveza*) is a very popular drink, both to wash down a meal and to enjoy with friends. The mildest brands include Sol and Corona; the tastiest, Superior and Dos Equis; the strongest, Bohemia and Negro Modelo (a dark variety). The quintessential Mexican liquor is tequila, extracted from a bluish agave ▲ 324, while mescal comes from the heart of maguey, an agave plant that is particularly common in Oaxaca ▲ 303.

Aguas frescas, drinks based on fruit or flowers mixed with water, replace water at all meals: melon, papaya, watermelon, tamarind, pineapple and hibiscus (*agua de Jamaica*) are common flavors. *Horchata* is a tasty sugared rice water flavored with cinnamon.
Atole, a thick, hot drink, is based on *masa* (corn dough), mixed with milk and sometimes flavored with chocolate, vanilla and cinnamon.

'NOPAL'

This cactus ▲ 388, eaten by Mexico's earliest hunter-gatherers, is grown not only for its fruits (*tunas*) but also for its succulent leaves (the prickles are removed first!). The *ensalada de nopalitos* is a very popular dish, widespread in the markets of Mexico City (fried cactus with tomatoes, onions and coriander).

'TAMALES'

Made with corn dough (as used to make tortillas), supplemented with lard. When savory, they are stuffed with meat and vegetables; when sweet, with ground almonds. They are wrapped in banana leaves or corn husks and then steamed.

● Recipe: guacamole

INGREDIENTS FOR 6 PEOPLE

3 tomatoes	3 ripe avocados
1 medium onion	2 limes (or lemons)
4 sprigs of fresh	2 spoonfuls of olive (
coriander	Salt, pepper

Tortillas and judicious use of chilies are primordial in Mexican cooking. That said, however, a few delicious, and no less typical, dishes are the exceptions that prove this golden rule (which would otherwise bar European aficionados from preparing *enchiladas* or a *mole*).

We present two that are colorful and simple to prepare. Served in a *molcajete* (bowl made of volcanic stone), guacamole stands alongside the chili sauces on the tables of *taquerías* and is served alone or as a garnish to other dishes. As for ceviche, extremely popular on the coasts and the Yucatán Peninsula, this is usually made with fatty fish – bass, barracuda, mackerel or tuna – but this can just as easily be replaced by fillets of ling or pollack. The most important thing, of course, is to ensure that the fish is fresh.

1. Cut the tomatoes and onions into small pieces and chop the coriander.

2. Remove the flesh of the avocados with a spoon and crush it roughly with a fork, while sprinkling it with lime juice to stop it turning black.

3. Mix all the ingredients together, sprinkle on the remaining lime juice, season and add the olive oil.

4. Serve chilled, accompanied by *totopos* (leftovers of tortilla cut into triangles and fried) or their commercial equivalent (*nachos*).

INGREDIENTS
FOR 6 PEOPLE
1 lb (500 g) of filleted fish
(pollack or black ling)
Juice of 4 large limes (or lemons)
1 large onion
3 plump tomatoes, seeded
4 sprigs of fresh coriander,
chopped
Green olives (to taste)
Capers
2 spoonfuls of olive oil
Salt and pepper
2 avocados
Oregano

1. Cut the fish into
small cubes, removing
any bones.

2. Put the fish into a deep bowl,
pour the lime juice on top,
cover and leave in the refrigerator
for 4 hours.

3. Once the fish has been 'cooked'
in the juice, cut the onions and tomatoes
into small pieces and add the chopped
coriander.

4. Drain the fish. Add the
mixture of tomatoes, onion
and coriander.

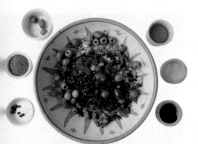

5. Add the olives,
capers and olive oil.
Season.
Mix gently.

6. Put the entire mixture on a
plate, adding slices of avocado
(previously sprinkled with a few
drops of lime juice). Dust with oregano.

● Chili

Chili is the star of Mexican cooking. The Aztecs first gave it its name and greatly appreciated it, both for its nutritional (Vitamin C) and medicinal (antiseptic and digestive) qualities. This fiery plant is found in countless recipes and serves to make the red or green salsa that is an essential condiment on all Mexican dining tables. There are more than 150 varieties of chilies.

CHILIES EATEN FRESH

JALAPEÑO CHILI
(Gulf of Mexico) Fairly strong, green. Used in sauces, *pescado a la veracruzana*, *picadillo* (beef stew), *guacamole* and *frijoles* (**1**). Often confused with *chili serrano*, less plump but stronger.

GÜERO CHILI
(South) Yellow, curved. Eaten pickled, as an aperitif and with eggs (**5**).

VERDE CHILI
(North) Bright green, about 6 inches (15 cm) long, and fairly mild. It is best eaten stuffed, as a substitute for *chili poblano* (**6**).

CHILACA CHILI
(North) Large, green. Cooked in strips and accompanied with fresh cream to make *rajas de chile* and *chilacas con queso* (**2**).

POBLANO CHILI
(Center) Green or dark red, as big as a pepper. The basis of *chiles rellenos* (stuffed chilies) and *chili en nogada* (with walnut sauce).

HABANERO CHILI
(Yucatán) This orangey-red chili is the strongest of all. Used in sauces and *cochinita pibil*.

CHILIES EATEN DRIED

ANCHO CHILI
(*chili poblano* dried) Used in *mole*, sauces for *enchiladas* or *pipián* sauce with zucchini seeds (**3**).

CHIPOTLE CHILI
(large *jalapeño*, dried and smoked). Similar to the *chili ancho* but smaller. Very aromatic, used in sauces, *caldo tlalpeño*, *sopa Xochitl*, *tamales* and *albóndigas* (meat balls).

GUAJILLO CHILI
(North) Deep red. Used in *mole*, *birria* (lamb stew) and *barbacoa* (beef) (**7**).

PASILLA CHILI OR NEGRO CHILI
(Center) Dark brown, aromatic. Used in *mole*, *caldo tlalpeño* and *sopa de tortillas*.

PIQUÍN CHILI OR CHILTEPÍN
Small, red, round and very strong. Crushed in sauces and soups such as *sopa de frijoles* and *sopa de ajo* (**4**).

MULATO CHILI
(Center) Brownish, similar to the *chili ancho*, but with a smokier flavor. Used in *mole* (**8**).

THE CHILI SCALE

The Scoville scale evaluates the concentration of capsicum – the tasteless substance with no aroma found on the inner sides and seeds of chilies – and so establishes a classification of chilies, from the mildest to the strongest. 0 unit: sweet pepper; 1,000–1,500 units: *chili pasilla* and *chili ancho*; 50,000 units: *chili piquín*; finally, the strongest of all, the *habanero*, contains 100,000–300,000 units!

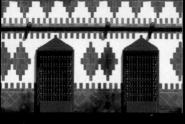

Architecture

Mesoamerican cities

At its height (around AD 500) ● *24*,
Teotihuacán (see map, *below*) had a population of between 75,000
and 125,000, spread over an expanse of 8 sq. miles (20 sq. km).

Mesoamerican cities vary enormously, depending on their origins
and history, period and location. Whether their population was
dispersed or concentrated, these cities acted as centers of power
– political, military, administrative and
religious. The populace included
the higher ranks of society – the
people who held these powers –
and their entourages, as well as
merchants, farmers and
specialist craftsmen.

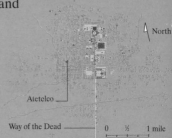

North

Atetelco

Way of the Dead

0   ½   1 mile

CITY PLANNING
(Teotihuacán ▲ *162*)
The city (facing 15°25 eastward) followed a
strict grid scheme. Of the two main areas (the
north and south), the
former contained most of
the monumental
structures and
residential
complexes.

MURAL PAINTING
Allegorical compositions and processions of
animals representing the warrior orders were
painted on the inner walls of the
residential complexes in
Teotihuacán.

THE RESIDENTIAL COMPLEX
Teotihuacán included about 2,000 residential complexes,
sometimes occupied by craftsmen working in the same trade (potters,
stone carvers, shell artists, and so on). These complexes housed 60 to
100 people from the same lineage. Communal worship was carried out
in their courtyards, which often had a central altar.

The Atetelco
complex in
Teotihuacán

THE MAIN SQUARE
(Monte Albán ▲ *299*)

Around 500 BC, the
villages of the Oaxaca
Valley were under
threat, so they built
the fortress of Monte
Albán on a group of
hills. The seats of civic
and religious power
were spread around a
square measuring 990
feet (300 m), north to
south, by 330 feet
(100 m). The group of
buildings to the north
(**1**) seems to have
been residential,
possibly royal. The
southern platform (**2**)
bore a temple. The
steles and sculptures
in the square, from
the building known as
the Danzantes (**3**)
and the pointed
Observatory (**4**),
celebrated military
victories (shackled
prisoners, lists of
conquered cities, and
so on). The court for
the ball game was also
here (**5**).

Infill   Stucco   Wall

THE 'SACBEOB'
These were raised causeways with a primarily ceremonial purpose: they linked the Mayan settlements to each other, or connected groups of buildings within a city.

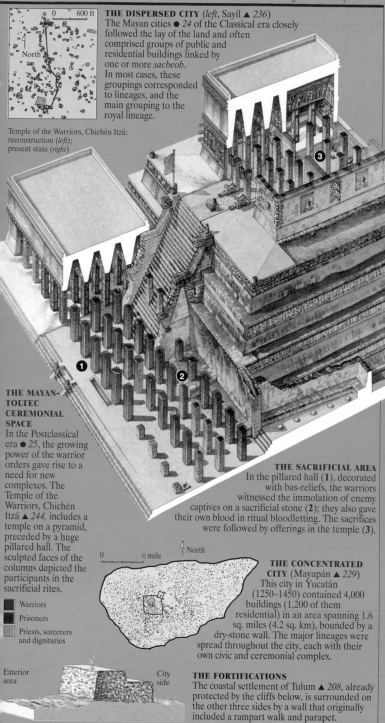

THE DISPERSED CITY (*left*, Sayil ▲ *236*)
The Mayan cities ● *24* of the Classical era closely followed the lay of the land and often comprised groups of public and residential buildings linked by one or more *sacbeob*. In most cases, these groupings corresponded to lineages, and the main grouping to the royal lineage.

0   600 ft

North

Temple of the Warriors, Chichén Itzá: reconstruction (*left*); present state (*right*)

THE MAYAN-TOLTEC CEREMONIAL SPACE
In the Postclassical era ● *25*, the growing power of the warrior orders gave rise to a need for new complexes. The Temple of the Warriors, Chichén Itzá ▲ *244,* includes a temple on a pyramid, preceded by a huge pillared hall. The sculpted faces of the columns depicted the participants in the sacrificial rites.

■ Warriors
■ Prisoners
■ Priests, sorcerers and dignitaries

THE SACRIFICIAL AREA
In the pillared hall (**1**), decorated with bas-reliefs, the warriors witnessed the immolation of enemy captives on a sacrificial stone (**2**); they also gave their own blood in ritual bloodletting. The sacrifices were followed by offerings in the temple (**3**).

0   ½ mile   North

THE CONCENTRATED CITY (Mayapán ▲ *229*)
This city in Yucatán (1250–1450) contained 4,000 buildings (1,200 of them residential) in an area spanning 1.6 sq. miles (4.2 sq. km), bounded by a dry-stone wall. The major lineages were spread throughout the city, each with their own civic and ceremonial complex.

Exterior area   City side

THE FORTIFICATIONS
The coastal settlement of Tulum ▲ *208*, already protected by the cliffs below, is surrounded on the other three sides by a wall that originally included a rampart walk and parapet.

73

● Mesoamerican buildings

THE BALL-GAME RING. Contrary to popular belief, the rings must have served as markers, because the balls were far larger than the rings.

Mesoamerican buildings were constructed on a base that could range from merely a low platform to a tiered pyramid over 200 ft (60 m) high. Whether simple or colossal, the buildings were generally arranged around squares or patios. In comparison to the monumental architecture intended for political or religious purposes, even the most noble residences were often relatively modest.

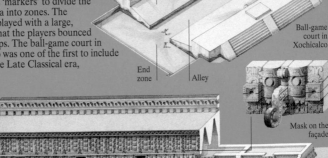

Side marker

Terrace

THE BALL GAME (Xochicalco ▲ *176*)
The courts used paving stones fixed to the ground or sculptures in the masonry as 'markers' to divide the playing area into zones. The game was played with a large, solid ball that the players bounced off their hips. The ball-game court in Xochicalco was one of the first to include rings (in the Late Classical era, 800–1000).

End zone

Alley

Ball-game court in Xochicalco

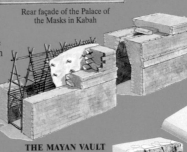

Mask on the façade

THE 'PALACE' (Kabah ▲ *236*)
Mayan Puuc architecture boasts buildings akin to palaces, with two wings divided into several rooms. The rear façade of the Palace of the Masks in Kabah is totally covered with masks of monsters (stone mosaic in relief). Statues of the king adorn the main façade, which is crowned by an openwork ridge.

Rear façade of the Palace of the Masks in Kabah

Tablud-tablero
▲ *162*

THE MAYAN VAULT
Held up with mortar and blocks of stone, this rested on two walls thicker at the base; the top was closed off with a horizontal slab. To raise the vault, a frame supported the blocks from each course while the cement was applied. The facing served as formwork.

BASES
Both simple and pyramidal bases were made of embankments held in by external walls; when these were very bulky, they were stabilized by a network of internal walls.

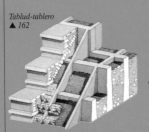

STONE FACING
The rear part of the stones that formed mosaic decorations (here, at Teotihuacán) was not sculpted but was solidly embedded in the embankment.

STUCCO WALLS
To support a thick stucco adornment, a preparation of mortar encrusted with stones was applied to the wall and left protruding to serve as an armature in relief.

DYNASTIC CULT
Some pyramids were built around a grave. The Temple of the Inscriptions in Palenque is particularly elaborate, with funereal décor, long staircases and a vaulted tomb designed to receive the body of King Pacal ▲ 268. The temple's façades display images of the king as the

Temple of the Inscriptions, Palenque

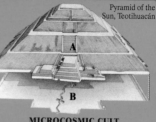

Pyramid of the Sun, Teotihuacán

MICROCOSMIC CULT
The Pyramid of the Sun in Teotihuacán (1st century) is one of the most imposing buildings in Mesoamerica. Built above caves (**B**) that are partly man-made ('the underworld'), the pyramid (**A**) sits over a place considered the birthplace of the world.

personification of thunder, a symbol of power.

1. Stone sarcophagus with a large sculpted lid
2. Steps leading to the tomb
3. Temple: this recalls a primitive hut; its interior spaces are extremely confined in comparison to the proportions of the masonry
4. Ridge tile

DIVINITY CULT
From the start, the Tenayuca pyramid supported twin temples dedicated to two gods (probably Tlaloc and Huitzilpochtli ▲ 133). This type of twin-temple pyramid only appeared in the later Postclassical era ● 25.

Tenayuca pyramid

SUPERIMPOSITIONS
One characteristic of Mesoamerican architecture is the frequent construction of sanctuaries on earlier temples. So, the great temple of the Chichimecs, in their capital Yenayuca, was periodically rebuilt right up to the final days of the Aztec world. There were eight successive structures.

POLYCHROMY
All except the most modest Mesoamerican architecture is embellished by stucco (a mixture of fine sand and lime) and painted in bright colors (predominantly red). The walls, pillars, flooring of the squares and stucco or stone sculptures were periodically refurbished and repainted. Only hints of this flamboyant decoration can be seen today.

Colonial city planning

Over three hundred years – from the beginning of the 16th to the end of the 18th century – Spain founded more than one thousand cities in the Americas, including several hundred in Mexico. The city was an instrument of control, as well as a cultural and religious model for the Indians to observe and learn from. The main point of reference is imperial: the colonial orthogonal layout was inherited from the Romans, and it can be found not only in Hispanic cities but also in remote Indian villages. The city is the fruit of colonial ideology. Its façades reflect religious or political precepts, its spaces establish hierarchies: so, in Mexico City, the Indians were excluded from the *traza* (Spanish city) and consigned to indigenous suburbs.

THE NEW CITY AND THE MIXED CITY

Some cities (such as Puebla, Guadalajara, Morelia and San Cristóbal) were created from scratch after 1521 ● *26*; others have evolved as part of the indigenous heritage, although their appearance changed with colonization (Tlaxcala, Cholula). Most are of mixed origin, as indicated by their names – Oaxaca, for example, constitutes the Indian part and Antequera the Spanish part of the same city. Mexico City is a special case: the colonial city rose up after the Spanish razed an indigenous site.

INDIGENOUS VILLAGES

Indians live in *barrios* or *parcialidades* (suburbs) or in pueblos (villages). In the early days of colonization, the indigenous population was often grouped in new villages, on plains close to cities. These provided their larger neighbors with manpower and extra lines of defense.

SAN CRISTÓBAL DE LAS CASAS ▲ *252* (*right*)

1. *Ejidos* (communal territories)
2. Indian territory
3. Pueblos (Indian communities)
4. Marshland serving as defensive trenches
5. Hispanic city with grid layout
6. Monasteries

San Cristóbal (here, in the 17th century) is the archetypal colonial city. At an altitude of 6,560 feet (2,000 m), it enjoyed a temperate climate, with wide open spaces around it that permitted cavalry maneuvers, and forests to meet its requirements for wood. The city was built and maintained by the Indian population (under Spanish supervision), which not only supplied forced labor but also tax revenues.

PLAZA MAYOR IN MÉRIDA
1. Cathedral and bishopric
2. Municipal palace
3. Government palace and
residence of governors and
captain generals
4. Residence of the *Conquistador*

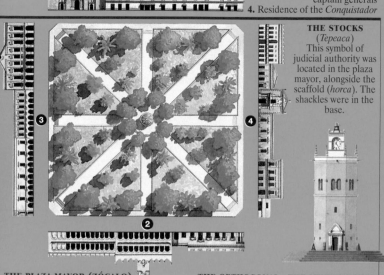

THE STOCKS
(*Tepeaca*)
This symbol of
judicial authority was
located in the plaza
mayor, alongside the
scaffold (*horca*). The
shackles were in the
base.

THE PLAZA MAYOR (ZÓCALO)
The main streets converged on
the plaza mayor, which was
bordered by various seats of power and
patrician residences; troops might drill on its
paving stones. In the center was usually a
fountain bearing heraldic symbols,
which stood as further testimony
to the power, luxury and
nobility flaunted by
this space.

THE ORTHOGONAL URBAN LAYOUT
The checkerboard
layout, imposed
systematically by the
Spanish urban
planners, was a
response to the
need for rationality
and efficient
workmanship. Its
monotony was broken
up over time by a
proliferation of
squares.

THE MINING TOWN
Mining towns such as
Zacatecas and
Guanajuato sprung
up by chance, out of
simple camps, and
were often located on
rugged terrain in
semiarid regions.
Their growth was not
controlled by any
planning, with only
the gradients of the
valleys governing
their organization.

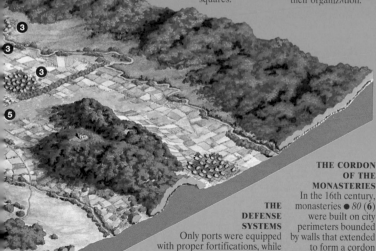

THE CORDON OF THE MONASTERIES
In the 16th century,
monasteries ● *80* (**6**)
were built on city
perimeters bounded
by walls that extended
to form a cordon
around the cities.
They maintained
contact with the
indigenous peoples,
and played a
supervisory role.

THE DEFENSE SYSTEMS
Only ports were equipped
with proper fortifications, while
on the high plateaus, settlements
would sometimes benefit from protective
marshlands (**4**). In the 16th century, several
conquistadors' houses were built with defense
towers. The religious buildings could also
serve as defensive spaces.

● The urban colonial house

Below: a window from the Tamayo Museum in Oaxaca ▲ 297
Bottom: the doorway in the house said to have belonged to
Cortés in Oaxaca ▲ 294

The design of the urban house during the colonial era was Mediterranean in origin but was adapted to fulfill various functions: the accommodation of a large and varied household (including servants and slaves), the protection of privacy, the display of wealth and position and diverse economic activities (semi-rural, commercial, craft-based). This type of house survived until the late 19th century. Its façade is pierced by vertical openings, enclosed by ironwork. It was fitted with a doorway (*portada*) topped, in the most lordly examples, by an elaborate balcony adorned with shields. The entrance hall (*zaguán*) opened onto the banquet room, behind which the patio could be glimpsed, flooded in light. The domestic space was organized around this patio, bounded by the private rooms (*recámaras*).

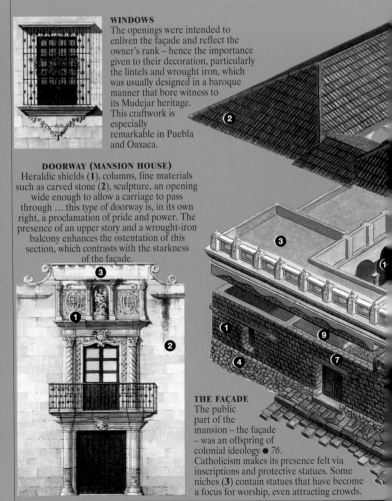

WINDOWS
The openings were intended to enliven the façade and reflect the owner's rank – hence the importance given to their decoration, particularly the lintels and wrought iron, which was usually designed in a baroque manner that bore witness to its Mudejar heritage. This craftwork is especially remarkable in Puebla and Oaxaca.

DOORWAY (MANSION HOUSE)
Heraldic shields (**1**), columns, fine materials such as carved stone (**2**), sculpture, an opening wide enough to allow a carriage to pass through … this type of doorway is, in its own right, a proclamation of pride and power. The presence of an upper story and a wrought-iron balcony enhances the ostentation of this section, which contrasts with the starkness of the façade.

THE FAÇADE
The public part of the mansion – the façade – was an offspring of colonial ideology ● 76. Catholicism makes its presence felt via inscriptions and protective statues. Some niches (**3**) contain statues that have become a focus for worship, even attracting crowds.

A SINGLE STORY

(*Above*, Oaxaca-style house)
When the construction materials used for a house are modest, the façade is coated with colored paint (ocher, red). Decoration is concentrated on the openings, with white stone frames left entirely or partially bare. Traces of the Spanish origins of these buildings are ever-present, as in the false crenellations on the roof.

AZULEJOS

The Spanish tradition of enameled tiling (*azulejos*) took root in the colonial cities and towns in the 16th century, especially in Puebla and Guanajuato.

Mexican tiles draw on regional resources and are made from volcanic or carved stone, or dried, unfired bricks mixed with straw (*adobe*).

THE RESIDENCE OF HIGHER RANKS: 'CASAS PRINCIPALES' AND 'ACCESORIAS'

In the grander residences, the domestic space (*casa principal*) adjoined buildings that were rented out (lodgings, shops, workshops). These *casas accesorias* marked the boundaries of social segregation.

PATIO AND 'CORRAL'

The patio was a space reserved for leisure and conviviality. The work was done in the *corral* (rear courtyard), where the stables, farmyard, haystacks and kitchens could be found. It had its own entrance (known as a 'false door') at the rear of the house.

THE RESIDENCE

1. Adobe
2. Roman tile
3. Roof terrace
4. Rubble stone
5. Coat of whitewash
6. Cladding to protect against damp
7. Doorway
8. *Casa principal*
9. *Zaguán* (hall)
10. *Sala* (ceremonial hall)
11. Patio
12. Covered gallery
13. Column with capital
14. *Recámaras* (private rooms)
15. Tiled roof
16. Window with ironwork
17. Sidewalk
18. *Casa accesoria* (workshop or shop)
19. Entrance to the *casa accesoria*

● The 16th-century mission

THE ATRIUM CROSS. This was made of wood at first and later of carved stone (*right*, Huejotzingo; the plinth represents the Crown of Thorns).

The missions built by the mendicant orders (Franciscans, Dominicans and Augustinians) number among the most original architectural complexes in the history of art. They were conceived as bases for evangelization – an undertaking that not only involved converting the Indians to the Christian faith but also introducing them to European culture. The missions' most striking characteristics are their fortress-like appearance and their monumentality, intended to convey the superiority of the Christian God over pagan deities. The main features are the church, the ✝ cloister and the atrium, where the cross was planted, surrounded by the corner chapels and the 'Indian chapels'.

Huejotzingo, chapel of repose

Below: open chapel of Tlalmanalco, and a reconstruction of the façade, which was originally whitewashed.

THE FORMAL RESPONSES TO A SPECIFIC EVANGELIZATION

The atrium, or enclosed courtyard, is found with two types of layout: quadrangular in front of the church (Izamal, *right*), or L-shaped (Tlalmanalco, *below*). In the center stood the atrium cross, with symbols of Christ's Passion. The *capilla abierta* (open chapel, **1**), also known as the Indian chapel, served as the *presbiterio* (chancel) during the open-air religious services, while the atrium acted as the nave, particularly during ceremonies attended by the Indians en masse. Small buildings in the corner of the atrium, the *capillas posas* (chapels of repose) provided a stopover for the holy sacrament during the processions round the courtyard; they were often given two entrances so that people could leave and enter with greater ease.

Tlalmanalco
A. *Sotocoro* or *coro bajo* (narthex)
B. Nave
C. *Presbiterio* (chancel)

The *tequitqui* consisted of a fusion of pre-Hispanic elements and a clumsy misinterpretation of European models by indigenous craftsmen, although some observers have defined it as cultural syncretism.

THE CHOICE OF DÉCOR: A MIXTURE OF STYLES

Each building combined elements taken from various European styles, most importantly GOTHIC (Gothic arches with curved moldings, ribbed vaults) and MUDÉJAR (bilobate, mullioned windows, moldings and archivolts (in Franciscan monasteries this was often made up of cord).

The Renaissance styles drew above all on elements from the PLATERESQUE idiom (baluster or bulging columns) and from MANNERISM (composition of doorways, use of the orders of Classical art). These elements were complemented by *tequitiqui* (*above*).

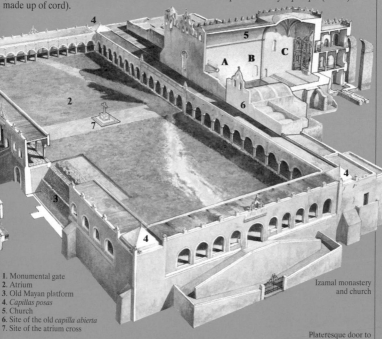

1. Monumental gate
2. Atrium
3. Old Mayan platform
4. *Capillas posas*
5. Church
6. Site of the old *capilla abierta*
7. Site of the atrium cross

Izamal monastery and church

Plateresque door to the Tepoztlán church

SYMBOLIC ORNAMENTATION

The iconography in evidence on the doorways and altarpieces, in the open chapels, the chapels of repose and on the walls of the cloisters played a crucial role in the evangelization process. The Last Judgment, the torments of Hell, the consoling presence of the Virgin Mary … but there are also moral, ethical and doctrinal messages dear to the friars depicted in these visual sermons.

THE CHOICE OF SITE

The monasteries were usually built on platforms or high places, often occupied by pre-Hispanic temples. This undoubtedly reflected the need to assert the superiority of the new religion over indigenous beliefs, for reasons of faith but also, and above all, for political ones. Nevertheless, the strategic thinking of the *conquistadores* and the symbolic criteria of the friars also exerted a strong influence, as lofty places could be linked to the holy mountain of Zion and the temple of Solomon.

● The baroque church

1. Huejotzingo

2. Oaxaca

Cherub with an Indian head, complete with
headdress; detail from the multicolored wooden
altarpiece in the Church of Santa Teresa in Morelia

Baroque architecture in New Spain developed with
relative autonomy. Although the basic models provided
by architectural treatises or major buildings like Saint
Peter's in Rome were taken into account, they served only
as a starting-point for original and imaginative creations.
In order to better understand the development of this artistic
style in the neo-Hispanic architecture of the 17th and 18th
centuries, it is helpful to use classification by formal categories,
particularly for the supporting elements (*see opposite*). These
categories are often complemented by two varieties of artistic
expression inextricably linked to materials: plaster and mortar
(stucco baroque) and the *azulejo* (Talaveresque baroque).

TOWERS AND BELL
These come in various
types. Areas
vulnerable to
earthquakes opted for
resistant bell towers
of a single level;
elsewhere, the bell
towers soared to two
levels, crowned by a
lantern (*above*,
Zacatecas Cathedral
▲ *342*).

THE DOME
Baroque domes are
characterized by an
octagonal drum,
which can have a
circular form inside.
(*below*, San Cristóbal,
Puebla).

THE DOORWAY: AN 'ALTARPIECE IN THE STREET'

Following the
cultivation of
representational
depiction in Roman
and Gothic art, the
culture and society of
the time needed a
symbolic outward
expression, on the
façade, of what lay
inside a church (that
is, nothing less than
heavenly Jerusalem
on Earth) – unless, of
course, the proud
Creole society had
merely wished to
show off its wealth
and status (*below*,
Santuario de Ocotlán,
Tlaxcala ▲ *285*).

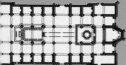

TYPES OF LAYOUTS
1. Single-nave layout (convents)
2. Latin-cross layout (parish churches and
monasteries). *Camarín* (**a**)
3. 3- or 5-nave basilica layout
4. Centered layout (this emerged in the late
17th century; Pocito dates from the 18th c.)

THE NAVE AND THE 'CAMARÍN'
The dome of the nave floods the transept with a shaft of light, symbolic of the axial pillar joining the earth to the sky. Many churches dedicated to the Virgin contain, behind the high altar, a *camarín* that stands for her chamber. This room is topped with a dome, while its stucco walls are adorned with altarpieces.

Above: *camarín* of the Santuario de Ocotlán; below: details of *yesería*, Tonantzintla (*left*) and the Virgin of Anguish in multicolored wood, Taxco (*right*)

STUCCO ('YESERÍA')
Both inside and outside, *yesería* (treated plaster and mortar) was an important element in the embellishment of buildings and gave rise to a highly original iconographic language. This was especially evident in the regions of Oaxaca, Puebla, Tlaxcala and Veracruz.

ALTARPIECES
Whether stone, wood or stucco, altarpieces are often multicolored and lavishly decorated, with additional formal solutions peculiar to Mexico, such as niches and canopies. The altarpiece reveals the heightened expression of the baroque (*left*, the high altar of Tepotzotlán ▲ *167*).

THE FORMS
Supports (columns and pilasters) define classifications of the baroque forms. The main ones are as follows:
– **Solomonic** (**A**) (wreathed, wavy or zigzag appearance);
– **Estípites** and **anástilo** (**B**, also known as Churrigueresque). These two styles are often identical visually, but the former applies to a supporting body like a column or pilaster, while the latter is just an adornment.
– **Tablerado** (**C**)
– **Neóstilo** (**D**) This autochthonous style draws on all the other forms with the exception of *estípites*.

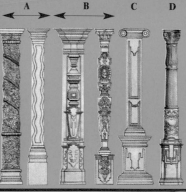

A   B   C   D

● The hacienda

Right: The *troje* constitutes a beautiful decorative element in its own right (San Miguel Barrientos, Cuyoaco, Puebla)

Left: Silos are common features (Palo Alto, Aguascalientes)

The *haciendas*, which appeared in the second half of the 16th century, were enormous estates devoted to farming, forestry or mining that were the heart of rural life and played a key role in the country's economic prosperity for over three centuries. Although their architecture did not establish any recognizable archetype, their particular purpose did give rise to specific forms and spaces suited to the way people lived and worked: the master's house, the chapel, the sleeping quarters, the administration offices, and the areas for production or processing and storage. To these must be added the infrastructures that allowed the *haciendas* to exploit their resources profitably (aqueducts, roads, bridges, railroads, and so forth).

The *casco* ('kernel') refers to the complex of buildings intended as living quarters and for agricultu the house, the barn, the corral and the water supply point (San Antonio Limón, Veracru

PRODUCTION

The first *haciendas* diversified their agricultural production, as both crops and livestock were required to secure the dietary self-sufficiency of the Spanish. Later, as the *haciendas* increased in number, some estates began to specialize according to their location and climate, as well as to period and demand (regional, national or international) – hence the rise of *haciendas* devoted to cereals, livestock, mining, sugar and logging, as well as the

The sugar *haciendas* were the first to develop greater complexity, which came in the form of specific buildings for processing cane. The *casco* very quickly took shape, with a boundary wall punctuated by sentry

THE 'CASCO'

boxes and towers, designed for overseeing the workers and, if necessary, for defense. Inside were the buildings that comprised the heart of the plantation: the master's house, workers' quarters and

the church; the barns, granaries, stables and corrals; the workshops for processing raw materials, the warehouses, the offices for administrative work, and, sometimes, the railroad station.

'TROJE' AND SILO

Corn, wheat and barley were the first crops to be grown. These precious cereals were stored in *trojes* (granaries) or silos, often endowed with vaults. These veritable strong-boxes served both to protect and to conserve the crops, to take advantage of any future increase in their value.

The *troje* above is exceptional in its form, with its two levels and defensive elements (San Nicolás el Grande, Lázaro Cardenas, Tlaxcala).

production of fibers (cotton, sisal ▲ *201*), drinks (*pulque* and *mescal* ▲ *325*, coffee, cacao and tobacco).

CORRAL AND STABLES

The corral that enclosed animals is often the only structure, along with the stable, to distinguish a *hacienda* devoted to livestock. Its high walls give it the appearance of a fortress (*above*, Tenexac, Terrenate, Tlax).

4. Eclectic style (19th century), San José Ozumba, San José Chiapa (Puebla)

It was only in the late 19th century that living quarters, albeit very humble, were built. These family units sometimes had their own small private courtyards. Below: the *calpanería* in the Mimiahuapan *hacienda* (Tlaxcala)

THE 'CALPANERÍA'

In the early days, the numerous workers living on the *hacienda* slept in improvised dormitories in galleries (inherited from the missions ● 80). The insalubrious conditions led, however, to the allocation of a specific section in the *casco*; the Indians put up their huts there, in chaotic fashion.

THE AGE OF STEAM

The arrival of steam changed the *hacienda*, as machines led to the mechanization of work and, above all, revolutionized transport as a result of the railroad. The huge plantations' private lines were linked to regional and national networks, facilitating the transportation of harvests and deliveries.

The architecture of the sugar *hacienda* is distinguished by the high *chacuacos* (chimneys) that dominate its façades (often neoclassical in style). The tower served as a lookout post for supervising work. Above: Uayalceh hacienda ▲ *231*, Abalá (Yucatán); below: railroad station in Venta de Cruz *hacienda*, Nopaltepec (State of Mexico).

THE CHURCH

Smaller than a town church, this was put up alongside the master's house, which also had its own chapel or oratory. The church clock marked out the hours for the workers, and before the liberal reform of 1848 the church also served as a mausoleum for its owners.

The Church of San José dates from 1900. (Carpizo, Champotón, Campeche).

THE STATION AND TRADE. The *haciendas* had their own railroad station on the premises as well as their warehouses in towns.

1 THE MASTER'S HOUSE

1. Colonial style (16th century), San Pedro Ovando, Acatzingo (Puebla)
2. Baroque style (17th–18th century), Los Espinos, Zamora (Michoacán)
3. Neoclassical style (19th century), San Juan Tlacatecpan, Otumba (State of Mexico)

If the *casco* reflects the power of the *hacendados* (● 28, 36), the house is its 'pearl'. Its layout and austere décor, organized from the beginning around a central patio, drew on Spanish traditions, and some colonial features would linger on: the ground-level living space and the defensive elements such as corner watchtowers and sentry posts, as well as slit holes protecting the entrance. In the 18th century, the houses were enlarged or rebuilt, often turning into veritable palaces adopting contemporary styles. The predilection for towers and defensive elements, albeit now merely decorative, was the only constant feature, symbolizing the power of the landowning aristocracy.

● The Porfiriat in Mexico City (1877–1920)

Detail of the stylized pre-Hispanic capital in the Palace of Arts

From 1877 to 1910, the government of Porfirio Díaz established social progress and the modernization of the country as priorities, now that independence had been consolidated. The development of the infrastructures, roads and railroads, and the transformation of the major cities – with Mexico City becoming the 'most beautiful city in America' – were important parts of this process, which largely focused on the importation of European academic models (mainly from Paris, London and Rome), while foreign architects, such as the Italians Adamo Boari and Silvio Contri, were responsible for most of the large-scale projects. The 1910 Revolution did not modify these architectural tastes, which prevailed until the early 1920s.

THE BEAUX-ARTS STYLE: THE CLASSICAL CANONS

(Above: the Palace of Communications 1904–1911, now the National Museum of Art, ▲ *139*)

Architects trained in the late 19th century in Europe, particularly in the École des Beaux-Arts in Paris, introduced the nobility of the classical canons to Mexico. This style, known as Beaux-Arts, reflected the sophisticated tastes of Porfirian society and spread rapidly with the launching of the project for the celebration of the centenary of independence in 1900 ● *28*. Supremely extravagant buildings were put up, turning the capital into 'the City of the Palaces'. THE PALACE OF COMMUNICATIONS, designed by Contri, juxtaposed the classical purity of its façade with an ornate interior: a grand staircase with twin loops and a rotunda combining wrought iron and glass. At the same time, a more eclectic style was emerging, best exemplified by the POST OFFICE PALACE, built by Boari (1902–07).

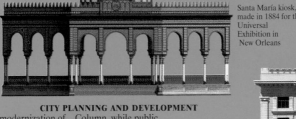

Santa María kiosk, made in 1884 for the Universal Exhibition in New Orleans

CITY PLANNING AND DEVELOPMENT

The modernization of the capital manifested itself in new amenities and the creation of large avenues. The refurbished Avenida Reforma ▲ *144* was adorned with statues of famous figures and commemorative monuments, such as the Independence Column, while public gardens such as the Alameda de Santa María ▲ *142* were spruced up. A kiosk installed there in 1910 (*above*) bears witness to this embellishment; entirely made of wrought iron, it boasts remarkable Moorish-style decoration.

1. Street
2. Carriage entrance
3. Garden
4. Terrace
5. Living areas
6. Servants' patio
7. Servants' room

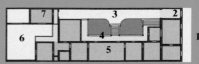

MODERNITY

(Above: Chopo University Museum, 1903–5, ▲ *145*) Metal architecture, a symbol of progress and the desire to match European standards, found its supreme expression in the Palacio de Cristal. This building, made in 1902 for the Düsseldorf industrial fair, then dismantled and rebuilt in Mexico City in 1903 under the supervision of Luis Bacmeister, bares its metal structure as a decorative motif.

URBAN EXPANSION: THE 'COLONIAS'

During the Porfiriat, the capital's surface area increased fivefold, while its population doubled. The upper classes, along with foreigners, abandoned the historic center, with its nucleus of offices and stores, to occupy the new residential neighborhoods: the *colonias*. Their one- or two-story houses were organized around interior patios. Their façades displayed a wide range of styles, from neoclassicism to art nouveau.

Colonia Roma, Mexico City
Above: house in neoclassical style, Puebla, no. 191
Below: house in art nouveau style, Chihuahua, no. 78

THE NATIONAL ART SCHOOL

(The Palacio de Bellas Artes, former National Theater, 1904–34, ▲ *142*)

The Academy of San Carlos became the National Art School in 1867. Although engineering courses were eliminated in favor of architecture, the two disciplines remained closely linked. The best reflection of the school's ideas was the National Theater, designed by Boari in 1904. This building still stands as the masterpiece of its age, on account of both its construction techniques – metal structure and cement roofs – and its refined ornamentation. Although the imposing composition of volumes, underlined by sculpted groups and crowned by a triple dome, is in the Beaux-Arts style, its details draw on the floral elements of art nouveau (ironwork, canopies, friezes). Federico Mariscal's art deco interior was completed in 1934.

The art deco Monument to the Revolution ▲ *145*, 1933–8, was conceived by Carlos Obregón Santacilia, a prolific architect who skillfully synthesized his various sources of inspiration.

At the end of the Revolution, in 1920, the new nationalist movement sought to affirm the Mexican identity. Encouraged by the muralists, architects abandoned the models that had prevailed during the Porfiriat to explore their own heritage. The neo-colonial and neo-indigenous approaches had a significant impact until the early 1930s, but they have left few traces today; meanwhile, the new European trends – first art deco, then functionalism – quickly took root. These styles, supported by ceaseless research, enriched the country's architectural language.

NEO-COLONIAL STYLE

Californian-style house, Colonia Polanco, Mexico City

The historicist revisionism of Federico Mariscal and Carlos Obregón Santacilia sought to reflect the Mexican identity through one particular idiom: the neo-colonial style. This complex mix of Plateresque and baroque influences found its fullest expression in the Californian style, when applied to individual houses, particularly those built in the Colonia Polanco or around the Parque México ▲ *152*. These had profuse decoration framing the doors and windows, tiled roofs and a garden onto the street; the traditional distribution axis – the patio – was discarded.

THE NEO-INDIGENOUS STYLE (The Anahuacalli, Mexico City, 1935–40, ▲ *154*)

The first attempts to integrate pre-Colombian elements into modern architecture date from the late 19th century, such as the Mexican pavilion presented at the Universal Exhibition in Paris in 1889. In the 1920s, most commemorative monuments and a few buildings copied indigenous pyramidal forms and geometrical décor; Diego Rivera, therefore, designed the Anahuacalli on pre-Hispanic lines, a temple designed to house his art collection.

Bank of Mexico, Carlos Obregón Santacilia, 1926–8

THE ART DECO STYLE

The 1925 exhibition of decorative arts in Paris and the silhouettes of New York skyscrapers triggered a craze for the art deco style in Mexico. From 1925 to 1935, many commercial and residential buildings, including the first 'skyscrapers' – albeit with only seven floors – adopted the geometrical lines and symmetrical arrangements characteristic of art deco. La Nacional, with its tiered façade, and the Bank of Mexico HQ, with its opulent interior replete with marble, mirrors and brass, bear witness to the far-reaching effects of this influence.

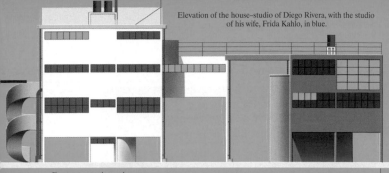

Elevation of the house–studio of Diego Rivera, with the studio of his wife, Frida Kahlo, in blue.

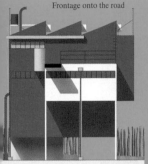

Frontage onto the road

FUNCTIONALISM

(House of Diego Rivera, Juan O'Gorman) O'Gorman, steeped in the theories of Le Corbusier, designed the first Functionalist buildings. This house-studio, put up in 1932, is nothing less than an architectural manifesto, an indispensable reference: simple and colorful geometrical volumes, roof terraces, highlighting of technical, functional and circulation elements.

Side façade

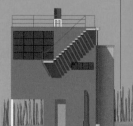

Rear façade

'BUILD MORE AND BETTER, WITH LESS MEANS'
(Revolución scholastic center, Antonio Muñoz, 1932–5)

Functionalism gave Mexico a long-sought image of modernity from 1930 to 1940 by striving to adapt to local materials and settings. To confront the population explosion, numerous complexes – offices and homes, hospitals and schools – were put up under the government slogan of 'Build more and better, with less means'.

TOWARD THE INTERNATIONAL STYLE

UNAM library, Mexico City, Juan O'Gorman, 1952 ▲ 155

The project for the National University (UNAM), launched in the late 1940s, was the crowning glory of functionalism in Mexico. Under the supervision of Mario Pani and Enrique del Moral, sixty architects came up with twenty buildings and sports complexes using state-of-the-art techniques. The library, a blind parallelepiped set on a transparent horizontal volume (the reading rooms), decorated with mosaics on all four façades (left), has become the university's most emblematic building and a model for the visual integration of décor and architecture.

● Luis Barragán
(1902–88)

Gilardi House, Mexico City

Tlalpan Chapel, suffused with light from the amber-glass windows

Luis Barragán, the Mexican architect with the greatest international reputation, is famous for his austere, enigmatic spaces, dominated by light and color. He created his first buildings in Guadalajara in a regionalist style, influenced by the local architecture as well as by the Mexican monasteries and *haciendas* of the 16th century. Deeply impressed by the beauty of the Alhambra and the gardens of Ferdinand Bac in 1925, he started to integrate water and nature into his architectural vocabulary.

BARRAGÁN'S HOUSE ▲ *151*
Around 1930 Barragán settled in Mexico City, where he worked in the then fashionable functionalist style, until he turned his back on it to build his own house; the interior spaces are separated from the exterior by leafy façades, only interrupted by small openings. Its layout follows a complex orthogonal floor plan.

TLALPAN CHAPEL (1952–63)
Distinguished by the contemplative atmosphere created by the light pouring through its amber-glass windows.

SAN CRISTÓBAL STABLES (1966–8)
Barragán's mature style: simple, geometric volumes in a symphony of pink and orange, arranged around a fountain/drinking trough.

GILARDI HOUSE (1975–7)
Barragán's crowning achievement in his handling of color.

Mexico
as seen by painters

In the second half of the 19th century, artists began to take an interest in nature and everyday life. The following generation was mainly attracted by indigenous realism and the ideological aspects of the so-called Mexican School, although a rebellious splinter group focused on the act of painting itself and steered clear of excessive nationalism. SATURNINO HERRÁN (1887–1918), steeped in humanist values, was greatly influenced by symbolism and modernism; he admired Greece and Spain, but he was fascinated by the new Mexican man born of racial mingling. His realist paintings are marked by a popular religiosity, and sometimes imbued with mysticism. *La Ofrenda* (*The Offering*, 1913) (**2**), is one of his most important works and crystalizes the transition from modernism to an intrinsically Mexican vision, as it alludes to the cult of the dead ● 48. The line of boats loaded with flowers and the foreground scene allow us clearly to identify the Xochimilco canals to the south of Mexico City. Despite the orangey glow of the *cempoalxochtil* (French marigolds ● 49), the members of the family look weighed down and resigned, and the sadness they exude is only heightened by the omnipresent water and the absence of a horizon. ANTONIO RUIZ (1897–1964), a trained architect, was an eclectic artist who worked as both a stage designer and a caricaturist. He left only some fifty paintings, most of which draw on the tradition of Mexican altarpieces. Ruiz painted for pleasure, but his mundane scenes reveal a sharp critical acuity and a highly personal surrealistic stamp. *El Verano* (*The Summer*, 1937) (**1**), is a key work, both for its pictorial qualities (the precision of line and detail, the vivid colors) and the atmosphere it emanates. This theatrical scene, built around oppositions and contrasts, depicts the confrontation between two social groups, two cultural models, two countries out of step. The Indian couple in the thrall of a display akin to a Hollywood-style scene acts as a metaphor for a new and subtly observed social reality. The career of ROBERTO MONTENEGRO

figures from high society and Indian women. His quadruple portrait, entitled *Mujeres mayas* (*Mayan Women*, 1926) (**3**) is stylistically similar to the murals he painted when he was younger. The profiles of the women are strongly accentuated, recalling the sculpted faces of Mayan statues. In an almost empty setting, the influences of both Surrealism and Cubism merge to create a powerful, distinctive body of work that uses repetition to great effect.

(1887–1968), initially marked at home by art nouveau, was later influenced in Paris by Pierre Puvis de Chavannes and Cubism, albeit seen through the prism of Aubrey Beardsley. Back in Mexico, Montenegro was drawn to the new emphasis on popular and pre-Columbian art, and the subsequent exploration of the world of the Indians. In 1926, he published a book entitled *Máscaras mexicanas* (*Mexican Masks*). He was also a poster designer and magazine illustrator, as well as a painter of portraits of both

Mexico as seen by painters
Volcanoes

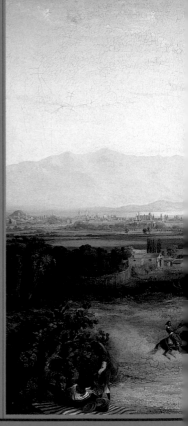

A flamboyant idealist, a researcher into new techniques, an amateur volcanologist and a long-time committed activist, GERARDO MURILLO (1875–1964), known as DR ATL (meaning 'water' in Nahuatl), is primarily famous for his paintings of volcanoes, although he also produced many portraits. More than any other subject, landscape seemed to allow him to record his strongest emotions and discover his true personality. In *Arenales del Paricutín* (*Sands of Paricutín*, undated) (**1**), the eruption of a volcano, drawn from life, is dramatized by the darkness of the mountains, dimly lit by the white fumaroles and the fire burning in the distance. Dr Atl created his own colors from resins and worked from aerial photographs that he took himself in order to pursue his unremitting passion for natural phenomena. The English landscape artist DANIEL THOMAS EGERTON (1797–1842) stayed in Mexico from 1829 to 1836. Attracted by the country's exoticism, he set about capturing typical scenes by means of countless drawings, watercolors and paintings in the Mexico Valley. In *Vista del Valle de México* (*View of the Mexico Valley*, 1837) (**2**), Egerton united in a single picture his two main interests in Mexico: landscape – here, a valley dominated by a majestic volcano – and genre painting – everyday scenes in which both the figures and the settings are painted in luminous colors and with meticulous attention to detail.

JOSÉ MARÍA VELASCO (1840–1912) is considered the greatest Mexican landscape painter of the 19th century. Trained in the Academy, with its heavy European influence, he was drawn to Impressionism and gradually developed a highly personal approach to color. He settled in the countryside and painted rural settings, in particular the volcanoes around Mexico City, in a series of monumental landscapes, such as *Valle de México* (1875), (**3**). Attempting to convey the effects of natural light, Velasco sought the reality of nature rather than any idealization.

Juan O'Gorman
(1905–82), the
creator of the famous
mosaic in the
university library in
Mexico City ▲ 155,
was also an architect,
painter and muralist.
A skilled draftsman
and sophisticated
colorist, he was by
nature a perfectionist
who paid meticulous
attention to the
detail in his work.
Ciudad de México
(1947) (**3**), reflects
the construction
boom in the capital
and pays homage to
those responsible,
particularly the
worker to the left.
This painting is
just teeming with
information; the
canvas encompasses
the city's three
historical and esthetic
ages, crowned by
the symbols of the
foundation (the eagle
and the serpent) and
the nation (the flag),
with a plan of

Tenochtitlán shown
in the foreground.
Following the lead of
Rufino Tamayo ● 98,
RONALDO MORALES
(1925–2001) took
painting down a path
that was strongly
influenced by the
culture of Oaxaca.
His worldview, fed by
his childhood
memories, is marked
by the presence of
women, religion and
baroque art. He
superimposes various
periods from his own
life story, and cuts up
space and reorganizes
it in perspectives,
arcades and empty
squares. *El Velo del
ángel* (*The Angel's
Veil*, 1989) (**2**),
illustrates this
microcosm, in which
the flow of life is
punctuated by rites of
passage: births,
marriages and funeral
vigils. Morales' art,
from his sources to
his formal inventions,
is impregnated with a

nostalgia and love for
his people. The
pictorial work of
MARISA LARA (b.
1960) is inspired by
popular Mexican art,
posters, advertising
and the movies. A
member of the so-
called Neo-Mexican
school ● 102 of the
1980s, Lara uses
painting to question
the values and myths
of everyday reality
and probe life and
death, but also to
exalt love. In her
work *Terremoto de
amor* (*Earthquake of
Love*, 1988) (**1**), the
two lovers are alone
in the world, oblivious
to chaos and disaster.

OLGA COSTA (1913–93) was born in Leipzig and arrived in Mexico in 1925. She went on to form part of Mexico City's artistic set by working in theater and ballet. Her particular style of painting belongs to the pictorial movement, which emphasized the world of the imagination and the senses to express deep emotional attachments. *Vendedora de frutas* (*Fruit Seller*, 1957) (*above*), captures the friendly, colorful atmosphere of modern market stalls. RUFINO TAMAYO (1899–1991), who very early on in his career assimilated European modernity and rejected the esthetic doctrines of the Mexican School, opted for a style that used vibrant colors and subtle monochrome variations in a fluid space where outlines are blurred. In his paintings and prints, Tamayo declared his love for Oaxaca by painting animals, fruit, female figures, musicians and cosmic landscapes. His work can also evoke the solitude of an artist who had to struggle to impose his 'solar splendor' on Mexico. Watermelons were a recurring subject in still-lifes that were almost musical variations celebrating Tamayo's Mexican identity (*Sandías*, 1968, *below*).

The Mexican School and the ruptures of the 20th century

The birth of the Mexican School of painting, between 1920 and 1924, triggered by the groundbreaking Muralist Movement, was a unique phenomenon with no equivalent in the world at the time. Unlike Socialist Realism, which was codified and regulated, Mexican Muralism developed a diversity of styles, in keeping with the ideals of the 1910 Revolution, and allowed painters to explore their ideas about history and nature with total freedom. The movement began to falter after two decades of intense and brilliant production (more than 1,000 paintings, on public and private buildings throughout the country between 1922 and 1969). The narrative murals of DIEGO RIVERA (1886–1957) reveal an encyclopedic eloquence that fuels a didactic interpretation of history and an idealization of the Indian. The Revolution lies at the heart of his visual approach. In his frescos for the Cortés Palace in Cuernavaca (1929), (1), Rivera

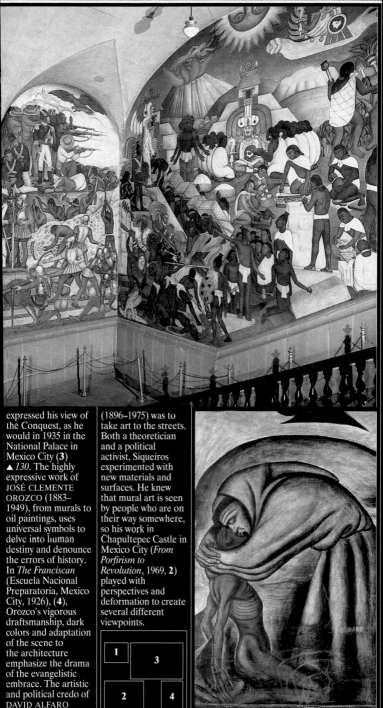

expressed his view of the Conquest, as he would in 1935 in the National Palace in Mexico City (**3**) ▲ *130*. The highly expressive work of JOSÉ CLEMENTE OROZCO (1883–1949), from murals to oil paintings, uses universal symbols to delve into human destiny and denounce the errors of history. In *The Franciscan* (Escuela Nacional Preparatoria, Mexico City, 1926), (**4**), Orozco's vigorous draftsmanship, dark colors and adaptation of the scene to the architecture emphasize the drama of the evangelistic embrace. The artistic and political credo of DAVID ALFARO SIQUEIROS

(1896–1975) was to take art to the streets. Both a theoretician and a political activist, Siqueiros experimented with new materials and surfaces. He knew that mural art is seen by people who are on their way somewhere, so his work in Chapultepec Castle in Mexico City (*From Porfirism to Revolution*, 1969, **2**) played with perspectives and deformation to create several different viewpoints.

1	3
2	4

Like other artists of his generation who stood apart from the Mexican School, RUFINO TAMAYO ● 98 rejected the idea of any fixed, stereotyped or caricatured identity. Whether portraying the earth (people, fruits, animals) or the cosmos (planets, constellations), he gave precedence to visual rather than thematic considerations, without ever indulging in form for form's sake. Each painting encourages an all-embracing interpretation, for which only he had the key. The 1940s ushered in new themes, which were explored through sophisticated, velvety textures and subtle color schemes. Man was depicted confronting infinity and his own destiny, and elongated figures reaching for the stars reflected these new existential ideas. In *La Gran Galaxia* (1978), (**1**), the metaphor of day and night calls to mind the more human opposition of life and death.

By dwelling on the obsessive accumulation of objects, Vargas recalls the lavishness of baroque altarpieces and their fascination with the beauty of craftsmanship. JULIO GALÁN (b. 1950) explores his archaic fears by creating a world that is seductive on the surface but terrifying (and terrified) when examined closely. The self-portrait is his favorite genre. Galán is not a painter of dreams – he offers an interpretation of his own reality, seeking truth in a narcissistic vertigo in which both his face and body are often costumed. In *Tehuana* (1985), (**3**), the recourse of wearing a woman's dress while standing in front of the Tehuantepec Isthmus is a disturbing echo of his own search for identity. JOSÉ LUIS CUEVAS (b. 1934), essentially a draftsman and printer, broke away from the Mexican School in 1957. The self-portrait is his preferred means of giving form to his obsessions (disease, old age, madness, loneliness, despair).

The figure in the lithograph *The Giant in Matisse's Studio* (undated), (**4**) embodies, in his physical monstrosity and immoderation, the violence of the world, which Cuevas never ceases to denounce.

Feria (1988), (**2**) by ISMAEL VARGAS (b. 1945) illustrates the new sensibility of the 1980s, which postulated another approach to Mexican identity. After the pugnacious nationalism and assertive indigenism of the Mexican School, the 'Neo-Mexicans' expressed their cultural and personal identities in a wide range of styles. One of their iconographic leitmotifs was the incorporation into their work of signs and icons borrowed from pre-Columbian and popular art.

The work of
GABRIEL
OROZCO (b. 1962),
the figurehead of
contemporary art,
draws from Marcel
Duchamp as much as
from Arte Povera or
Minimalism. Orozco
explores everyday life
by focusing on
manufactured or craft
objects, fragments of
the natural world and
materials such as
metal, paper and
terracotta (*My Hands
Are My Heart*, 1991,
right). His playful
approach reconstructs
worlds – both real
and virtual – by
establishing a number
of incongruous
associations. His
protean work,
distinguished by a
great freedom of time
and place, defies all
categorization.
FRANCISCO TOLEDO
(b. 1940), a leading
light on the Mexican
scene since the 1960s,
is a painter, sculptor,
printer, potter and
photographer.
An accomplished
draftsman and
colorist, he has
a carnal, erotic
relationship with

his wide range of
subjects. Steeped in
childhood stories,
nourished by his land
of Oaxaca ▲ *306*, he
metamorphoses

myths and legends in
a fabulous, playful
ritual that mingles,
through free
association, images
that he has taken

from his cultural
storehouse with those
he has created from
scratch (*Mujer sobre
dos sillas*, 1963),
(*below*).

Mexico as seen by writers

EARLY HISTORY AND MYTHOLOGY

THE CREATION OF MAN

The ancient Mayan book Popol Vuh *describes how the sky and earth were formed, then divided into different parts, as told by the Creator of all things. At the beginning of Part I there is only empty sky; the following section is from Part III, and it explains how men come to be on the earth.*

❛Here, then, is the beginning of when it was decided to make man, and when what must enter into the flesh of man was sought.

And the Forefathers, the Creators and Makers, who were called Tepeu and Gucumatz, said: "The time of dawn has come, let the work be finished, and let those who are to nourish and sustain us appear, the noble sons, the civilized vassals; let man appear, humanity, on the face of the earth." Thus they spoke.

They assembled, came together and held council in the darkness and in the night; then they sought and discussed, and here they reflected and thought. In this way their decisions came clearly to light and they found and discovered what must enter into the flesh of man.

It was just before the sun, the moon, and the stars appeared over the Creators and Makers.

From Paxil, from Cayalà, as they were called, came the yellow ears of corn and the white ears of corn.

These are the names of the animals which brought the food: *yac* (the mountain cat), *utiú* (the coyote), *quel* (a small parrot) and *hoh* (the crow). These four animals gave tidings of the yellow ears of corn and the white ears of corn, they told them that they should go to Paxil and they showed them the road to Paxil.

And thus they found the food, and this was what went into the flesh of created man, the made man; this was his blood; of this the blood of man was made. So the corn entered [into the formation of man] by the work of the Forefathers.

And in this way they were filled with joy, because they had found a beautiful land, full of pleasures, abundant in ears of yellow corn and ears of white corn, and abundant also in *pataxte* and *caco*, and in innumerable *zapotes, anonas, jocotes, nantzes, matasanos,* and honey. There was abundance of delicious food in those villages called Paxil and Cayalà. There were foods of every kind, small and large foods, small plants and large plants.

The animals showed them the road. And then grinding the yellow corn and the white corn, Xmucané made nine drinks, and from this food came the strength and the flesh, and with it they created the muscles and the strength of man. This the Forefathers did, Tepeu and Gucumatz, as they were called.

After that they began to talk about the creation and the making of our first mother and father; of yellow corn and of white corn they made their flesh; of corn-meal dough they made the arms and the legs of man. Only dough of corn meal went into the flesh of our first fathers, the four men, who were created.❜

POPOL VUH – THE SACRED BOOK OF THE ANCIENT QUICHÉ MAYA,
trans. from the Spanish by Adrián Recinos.
English version by Delia Goetz and Sylvanus G. Morley
pub. William Hodge & Co. Ltd, London, 1951

MOCTEZUMA

The Spanish conquistador Bernal Diaz de Castillo (1496–1584) wrote an account of the conquest of Mexico as he witnessed it during the years 1517 to 1521. Here he relates what he has heard about the Aztec emperor.

❛The Great Montezuma was about forty years old, of good height and well proportioned, slender and spare of flesh, not very swarthy, but of the natural colour and shade of an Indian. He did not wear his hair long, but so as just to cover his ears, his scanty black beard was well shaped and thin. His face was somewhat long, but cheerful, and he had good eyes and showed in his appearance and manner both

tenderness and, when necessary, gravity. He was very neat and clean and bathed once every day in the afternoon. He had many women as mistresses, daughters of Chieftains, and he had two great Cacicas as his legitimate wives. He was free of unnatural offences. The clothes that he wore one day, he did not put on again until four days later. He had over two hundred Chieftains in his guard, in other rooms close to his own, not that all were meant to converse with him, but only one or another, and when they went to speak to him they were obliged to take off their rich mantles and put on others of little worth, but they had to be clean, and they had to enter barefoot with their eyes lowered to the ground and not to look up in his face. ... For each meal, over thirty different dishes were prepared by his cooks according to their ways and usage, and they placed small pottery braziers beneath the dishes so that they could not get cold. They prepared more than three hundred plates of the food that Montezuma was going to eat, and more than a thousand for the guard. When he was going to eat, Montezuma would sometimes go out with his chiefs and stewards, and they would point out to him which dish was best, and of what birds and other things it was composed, and as they advised him, so he would eat, but it was not often that he would go out to see the food, and then merely as a pastime. I have heard it said that they were wont to cook for him the flesh of young boys, but as he had such a variety of dishes, made of so many things, we could not succeed in seeing if they were of human flesh or of other things, for they daily cooked fowls, turkeys, pheasants, native partridges, quail, tame and wild ducks, venison, wild boar, reed birds, pigeons, hares and rabbits, and many sorts of birds and other things which are bred in this country, so numerous that I cannot finish naming them in a hurry; so we had no insight into it, but I know for certain that after our Captain censured the sacrifice of human beings, and the eating of their flesh, he ordered that such food should not be prepared for him henceforth.'

BERNAL DIAZ DE CASTILLO,
THE DISCOVERY AND CONQUEST OF MEXICO,
trans. A. P. Maudsley,
pub. Da Capo Press, New York, 1996

TREASURE IS COLLECTED BY THE SPANIARDS

General Cortés wrote to his king, Carlos V, describing the progress of his troops, and in particular his meetings with an increasingly worried Moctezuma.

'I spoke to Montezuma one day, and told him that your Highness was in need of gold, on account of certain works ordered to be made, and I besought him to send some of his people, and I would also send some Spaniards, to the provinces and houses of those lords who had there submitted themselves, to pray them to assist

Your Majesty with some part of what they had. Besides Your Highness's need, this would testify that they began to render service, and Your Highness would the more esteem their good will towards your service; and I told him that he should give me from his treasures, as I wished to send them to Your Majesty, as I had done with the other things. ... Thus it was done, and all those lords to whom he sent gave very compliantly, as had been asked, not only in valuables, but also in bars and sheets of gold, besides all the jewels of gold and silver, and the featherwork, and the stones, and the many other things of value which I assigned and allotted to Your Sacred Majesty, amounting to the sum of one hundred thousand ducats and more. **'**

HERNÁN CORTÉS, *LETTERS OF CORTÉS – THE FIVE LETTERS OF RELATION FROM FERNANDO CORTÉS TO THE EMPEROR CHARLES V,* trans. and ed. Francis Augustus MacNutt, pub. G. P. Putnam's Sons, New York, 1908

THE LAND

FERTILITY AND ABUNDANCE

*F*rancisco Cervantes de Salazar (1514–c. 1575) was a professor of rhetoric who wrote this description of New Spain as an aid to the study of Latin languages. It was first printed in 1554.

'Many regions are mountainous, but not unfruitful; the rest is an extensive plain, with many, though not large, perennial springs and rivers. It is well populated and extremely rich in gold, silver and other metals. ... For Indians and Spaniards alike, the land abounds in fruits, though unproductive of the grape or the olive, and produces wool, cotton, cochineal, sugar, and honey more than moderately, as well as cattle and herds from which many hides are transported to Spain. It teems with every kind of game, and not alone for fowlers and hunters – eagles, herons, nightherons, wild geese; and the quadrupeds, hares, coneys, antelopes, deer, bears, lions, and tigers are found here and there. Indeed, the whole region is pleasing with woodlands and groves. To be brief, what Cicero wrote about Asia, consider written about New Spain; for, as he said, "it easily excels all other lands in the fertility of its fields, the variety of its products, the extent of its grazing, and in the multitude of things for export". **'**

FRANCISCO CERVANTES DE SALAZAR, *LIFE IN THE IMPERIAL AND LOYAL CITY OF MEXICO IN NEW SPAIN*, trans. by Minnie Lee Barrett Shepard, pub. Univ. of Texas Press, Austin, 1953

TROUBLE WITH MOSQUITOES

*M*iles Philips, a 16th-century sailor and pirate, was shipwrecked and forced to make his way through the jungle in search of food. He was captured by a warlike Spanish force and became slave to a Spanish master for five years. This is a description of the terrain he traversed before capture.

'We travelled on westward, sometimes through such thick woods that we were enforced with cudgels to break away the brambles and bushes from tearing our naked bodies: other sometimes we should travel through the plains, in such high grass that we could scarce see one another, and as we passed in some places, we should have of our men slain, and fall down suddenly, being struck by the Indians, which stood behind trees and bushes, in secret places, and so killed our men as they went by, for we went scatteringly in seeking of fruits to relieve ourselves. We were also often greatly

annoyed with a kind of fly, which the Spaniards call mosquitoes. They are scarce so big as a gnat; they will suck one's blood marvellously, and if you kill them while they are sucking, they are so venomous that the place will swell extremely: but if you let them suck their fill, and to go away of themselves, then they do you no other hurt, but leave behind them a red spot somewhat bigger than a flea-biting. **'**

MILES PHILIPS, 'A DISCOURSE...', in Richard Hakluyt,
Voyages and Discoveries, pub. Penguin Books, Harmondsworth, 1972

PYRAMIDS OF TEOTIHUACAN

American historian William Hickling Prescott (1796–1859) was committed to the study of ancient literature, especially of Spain and South America. He wrote books about The History and Conquest of Peru*, and Spanish monarchs, as well as* The History and Conquest of Mexico *(1843), from which the following extract is taken.*

'The monuments of San Juan Teotihuacán are, with the exception of the temple of Cholula, the most ancient remains, probably, on the Mexican soil. They were found by the Aztecs, according to their traditions, on their entrance into the country, when Teotihuacan, the habitation of the gods, now a paltry village, was a flourishing city, the rival of Tula, the great Toltec capital. The two principal pyramids were dedicated to Tonatiuh, the Sun, Meztli, the Moon. ... In fact, time has dealt so roughly with them, and the materials have been so much displaced by the treacherous vegetation of the tropics, muffling up with its flowery mantle the ruin which it causes, that it is not easy to discern at once the pyramidal form of the structures. The huge masses bear such resemblance to the North American mounds that some have fancied them to be only natural eminences shaped by the hand of man into a regular form, and ornamented with the temples and terraces the wreck of which still covers their slopes. But others, seeing no example of a similar elevation in the wide plain in which they stand, infer, with more probability, that they are wholly of an artificial construction.... According to tradition, the pyramids are hollow; but hitherto the attempt to discover the cavity in that dedicated to the Sun has been unsuccessful. In the smaller mound an aperture has been found on the s o u t h e r n side, at two-thirds of the elevation. The largest of these is about fifteen feet deep, and the sides are faced with unbaked bricks, but to what purpose it is devoted, nothing is left to show. ...

The summit of the larger mound is said to have been crowned by a temple, in which was a colossal statue of its presiding deity, the Sun, made of one entire block of stone, and facing the east. Its breast was protected by a plate of burnished gold and silver, on which the first rays of the rising luminary rested. An antiquary, in the early part of the last century, speaks of having seen some fragments of the statue. It was still standing, according to report, on the invasion of the Spaniards, and was demolished by the indefatigable Bishop of Zumárraga, whose hand fell more heavily than that of Time itself on the Aztec monuments.

Around the principal pyramids arc a great number of smaller ones, rarely exceeding thirty feet in height, which, according to tradition, were dedicated to the stars and served as sepulchres for the great men of the nation. They are arranged symmetrically in avenues terminating at the sides of the great pyramids, which face the cardinal points. The plain on which they stand was called Micoatl, or "Path of the Dead". The labourer, as he turns up the ground, still finds there numerous arrowheads, and blades of bosidian, attesting the warlike character of its primitive population.'

WILLIAM PRESCOTT, *HISTORY OF THE CONQUEST OF MEXICO*,
pub. George Allen & Co., London 1913

TRAVELING BY TRAIN

*K*atherine Anne Porter (1890–1980) was born in Texas and made several trips across the border to Mexico. She wrote one novel, but is best known for her short stories. The following extract comes from a story called 'Hacienda'.

'Now that the true revolution of blessed memory has come and gone in Mexico, the names of many things are changed, nearly always with the view to an appearance of heightened well-being for all creatures. So you cannot ride third-class no matter how poor or humble-spirited or miserly you may be. You may go second in cheerful disorder and sociability, or first in sober ease; or, if you like, you may at great price install yourself in the stately plush of the Pullman, isolated and envied as any successful General from the north. "Ah, it is beautiful as a pulman!" says the middle-class Mexican when he wishes truly to praise anything. ... There was no Pullman with this train or we should most unavoidably have been in it. Kennerly traveled like that. He strode mightily through, waving his free arm, lugging his

> 'MEXICO HAS A FAINT, PHYSICAL SCENT OF HER OWN, AS EACH
> HUMAN BEING HAS. AND THIS IS A CURIOUS, INEXPLICABLE SCENT,
> IN WHICH THERE ARE RESIN AND PERSPIRATION, AND SUNBURNED
> EARTH, AND URINE, AMONG OTHER THINGS.'
>
> D. H. LAWRENCE, *MORNINGS IN MEXICO*

portfolio and leather bag, stiffening his nostrils as conspicuously as he could against the smell that "poured," he said, "simply poured like mildewed pea soup!" from the teeming clutter of wet infants and draggled turkeys and indignant baby pigs and food baskets and bundles of vegetables and bales and hampers of domestic goods, each little mountain of confusion yet drawn into a unit, from the midst of which its owners glanced up casually from dark pleased faces at the passing strangers. Their pleasure had nothing to do with us. They were pleased because, sitting still, without even the effort of beating a burro, they were on the point of being carried where they wished to go, accomplishing in an hour what would otherwise have been a hard day's journey, with all their households on their backs. ... Almost nothing can disturb their quiet ecstasy when they are finally settled among their plunder, and the engine, mysteriously and powerfully animated, draws them lightly over the miles they have so often counted step by step. And they are not troubled by the noisy white man because, by now, they are accustomed to him. White men look all much alike to Indians, and they had seen this maddened fellow with light eyes and leather-coloured hair battling his way desperately through their coach many times before. There is always one of him on every train. They watch his performance with as much attention as they can spare from their own always absorbing business; he is a part of the scene of travel.'

KATHERINE ANNE PORTER, *FLOWERING JUDAS AND OTHER STORIES*,
pub. Harrison, Paris, 1934

AN ARTIST'S WORK

One of Mexico's leading novelists, Carlos Fuentes (b. 1928) often writes about his homeland. His first novel, Where the Air Is Clear *(1958), describes the history of Mexico from the Aztecs to the mid-20th century. The following extract is from* Terra Nostra *(Our Land), where an old woman describes a traditional tapestry she is creating and the significance of the threads.*

"The color of each field indicates the kind of bird that can be hunted there. In addition, these are the actual feathers of the birds that inhabit each sector of the jungle. The quetzal, the hummingbird, the macaw, the golden pheasant, the wild duck, and the heron. Each area is irregular, do you feel it?, except for the center. That is regular; it has a perfect circumference. That is the forbidden part of the jungle. There are no feathers there; no one can derive sustenance there; there nothing can be hunted or killed to satisfy the hunger of the body; there dwell the masters of words, signs, and enchantments. Their kingdom is the field of dead spiders that I join with glue to the object you call cloth. And the limits of the cloth are those of the known world. One can go no farther. The tips of the arrows all point outward. Toward the unknown world. They are a limit; they are also invitation. The frontier between the hearth and the marvelous." This is what the Indian woman told me in her tongue as she handed me this offering the first time I came to this land.'

CARLOS FUENTES, *TERRA NOSTRA*,
trans. Margaret Sayers Peden,
pub. Secker & Warburg, London, 1977

OAXACA

Aldous Huxley (1894–1963) is best remembered for Brave New World *(1932), a fable in which the world has been reorganized according to a scientific caste system. His other novels also mix satire with a deep humanity.*

In spite of three major earthquakes, in spite of seven sieges, including one by a French army under Bazaine, in spite, above all, of four centuries of Mexican existence, Oaxaca remains a stately city, full of impressive buildings. Santo Domingo has been repeatedly pillaged, but is still, none the less, one of the most extravagantly gorgeous churches in the world. The cathedral has been shaken and

● The Day of the Dead

cracked, yet continues to stand, enormous, at the centre of the town. The monks have fled, the clergy is without power or money; but strolling through the streets you find yourself at the portals of what were once magnificent monasteries, now transformed into warehouses and workshops and Indian dwellings; you come upon handsome churches, in which the baroque saints still gesticulate above the altars and the gilded plaster still writhes in a tripe-like luxuriance over vault and ceiling. Yes, Oaxaca is a fine place. Fine and, as gaiety is reckoned in the provinces of Mexico, positively gay. There are two or three cafés in the plaza; and at night a band discourses from the kiosk at the centre. The Indians squat on the pavements to listen, their dark faces melting into the night – invisible. High-heeled, in every tender shade of artificial silk, the flappers stroll giggling under the electric light. There is a rolling of eyes, a rolling of posteriors. The young men stroll in the opposite direction. In the roadway, the most correct of the correctos circulate very slowly in their automobiles – round and round and round. **'**

ALDOUS HUXLEY,
BEYOND THE MEXIQUE BAY,
pub. Chatto & Windus, London, 1934

THE DAY OF THE DEAD

FEASTING
Anita Brenner (1905–74) was a Mexican-born writer, translator and journalist, who lived in the country all her life apart from a brief period spent in Texas during the Mexican Revolution. Idols Behind Altars, *her famous study of Mexican culture, was first published in 1929.*

' The Day of the Dead was fixed by the missionary friars according to the Christian calendar, but it was a habit long before. This holiday comes on the first and second of November. All Saints' Day is all adult ghosts' day, and All Souls' Day belongs to the children. The spirits return according to their ages, on the first and second eve, to dine with their living relatives. The table is set on the altar. There are beans, chili, tortillas, rice, fruit, other daily dishes, and the specialities of the season: pumpkins baked with sugar-cane, pulque or a bluish maize-brew with a delicate sugar film, and Dead Mens' bread. For the children, candy skulls, pastry coffins, ribs and thigh-bones made of chocolate and frosted sugar, tombstones, wreaths, and pretentious funerals.

The living do not eat of the feast until the dead have left. The sit up all night 'with the little dead ones' (affectionate term for invisible beings) as if at a wake – a Mexican wake; singing, praying, drinking, making a little love. And it is a wake, except that the prayers are said not for the dead, but to them. Everybody "weeps the bone" picnicking in the graveyards. The tombs are turned into banquet tables similar to those at home. The food is put upon them, on banks of flowers, heavy purple wild blossoms and the yellow pungent cempoalxochitl, ancient and sacred bloom. Little flags fly from the mounds; sometimes arcades and booths are raised over them, as upon holiday canoes. The recently bereaved or the especially punctilious really may shed a few tears for the honoured "bones". But somehow these tears are like the flowers and skulls, simply part of the gesture. One's respected relatives, who "have moved their sleeping mats" come to call. They must be treated courteously. A ceremonious gaiety is the proper tone. **'**

ANITA BRENNER, *IDOLS BEHIND ALTARS*,
pub. Chapman & Hall, London 1939

Photos by Manuel Álvarez Bravo
Left: *Day of the Dead*, 1932
Below: *Fireworks for the Baby Jesus*, 1980

ON LOCATION

John Steinbeck (1902–68) writes to actor Max Wagner from the set of the movie The Forgotten Village, *expressing his frustrations about the impossibility of filming during the annual festivities.*

❛The days of the dead are here and our village is drunk to a man and a woman. They have been gradually picking up their binges for three days and they have two days to run. They mix pulque and agardiente and it flops them beautifully. Herb [Kline, the director] cannot learn that a Mexican answers what you want to hear. He asked if the October sky was clear and of course they said yes. I could have told

him that there is rarely a cloudless afternoon in October. You see, this is not like a studio picture. We have to wait for light and catch it as we can.❜

LETTER TO MAX WAGNER, NOVEMBER 1, 1940, FROM *JOHN STEINBECK: A LIFE IN LETTERS*, ed. Elaine Steinbeck and Robert Wallstein, pub. Heinemann, London, 1975

LOCAL PRODUCE

MEMOIRS OF A CHOCOHOLIC

Thomas Gage (1603–56) was an English Dominican friar with a taste for travel and, it appears, a liking for his food.

❛The cinnamon and the long red pepper are to be first beaten with the aniseed, and then the cacao, which must be beaten by little and little, till all be powdered, and in the beating it must be turned round that it may mix the better. Every one of these ingredients must be beaten by itself, and then all be put into the vessel where the cacao is, which you must stir together with a spoon, and then take out that paste, and put it into the mortar, under which there must be a little fire, after the confection is made. If more fire be put under than will only warm it, then the unctuous part will dry away. The achiote also must be put in at the beating that it may better take the colour. ... The manner of drinking it is divers. The one most used in Mexico is to take it hot with atole, dissolving a tablet in hot water, and then stirring and beating it in the cup where it is to be drunk with a molinet, and the scum taken off and put into another vessel, the remainder be set upon the fire with as much sugar as will sweeten it, and when it is warm, then to pour it upon the scum which was taken off, and so to drink it.... I have heard physicians of the Indias say of it, and I have seen it by experience in others, though never I could find it in myself, that those that use this chocolate much grow fat and corpulent by it. Which, indeed, may seem hard to believe, for considering that all the ingredients except the cacao do rather extenuate than make fat because they are hot and dry in the third degree.'

THOMAS GAGE, *THOMAS GAGE'S TRAVELS IN THE NEW WORLD*,
ed. J.E.S.Thompson, pub. Univ. of Oklahoma Press, Norman, 1969

LUNCH IN MEXICO CITY

Sybille Bedford (1911–2006) described her travels in Mexico in A Sudden View, *published 1953, which was later reissued as* A Visit to Don Otavio *(1960).*

'There is a wait of twenty-five minutes, then a succession of courses is deposited before us in a breathless rush. We dip our spoons into the soup, a delicious cream of vegetable that would have done honour to a private house in the French provinces before the war of 1870, when two small platefuls of rice symmetrically embellished with peas and pimento appear at our elbows.

"Y aquí la sopa seca." The dry soup.

We are still trying to enjoy the wet one, when the eggs are there: two flat, round, brown omelettes.

Nothing is whisked away before it is finished, only more and more courses are put in front of us in two waxing semicircles of cooling dishes. Two spiny fishes covered in tomato sauce. Two platefuls of beef stew with spices. Two bowlfuls of vegetable marrow swimming in fresh cream. Two thin beefsteaks like the soles of children's shoes. Two platters of lettuce and radishes in an artistic pattern. Two platefuls of bird bones, lean drumstick and pointed wing smeared with some brown substance. Two platefuls of mashed black beans; two saucers with fruit stewed in treacle. A basket of rolls, all slightly sweet; and a stack of tortillas, limp, cold, pallid pancakes made of maize and mortar. We eat heartily of everything. Everything tastes good, nearly everything is good. Only the chicken has given its best to a long and strenuous life and the stock pot, and the stewed fruit is too sticky for anyone above the age of six. The eggs, the stew, the vegetables, the salad, rice and beans are very good indeed. Nothing remotely equals the quality of the soup. We are drinking a bottled beer, called Carta Blanca, and find it excellent. At an early stage of the meal we had been asked whether we desired chocolate or coffee at the end of it, and accordingly a large cupful was placed at the end of the line with another basket of frankly sugared rolls. This pan dulce and the coffee are included in the lunch. The bill for two of us, beer and all, comes to nine pesos, that is something under ten shillings.'

SYBILLE BEDFORD, *A VISIT TO DON OTAVIO*,
pub. William Collins, Glasgow, 1960

TARAHUMARA HERBS

Mexican poet Alfonso Reyes (1889–1959) compiled an anthology of Mexican poetry shortly before his death that was translated into English by Samuel Beckett. This piece tells of the Tarahumara Indians ▲ 376 *coming to town to sell their herbs, because of a poor harvest in the mountains.*

Sometimes they bring gold from their hidden mines
and all the livelong day they break the lumps
squatting in the street,
exposed to the urbane envy of the whites.
Today they bring only herbs in their bundles,
herbs of healing they trade for a few nickels:
mint and cuscus and birthroot
that relieve unruly innards,
not to mention mouse-ear
for the evil known as "bile";
sumac and chuchupaste and hellebore
that restore the blood;
pinesap for contusions
and the herb that counters marsh fevers,
and viper's grass that is a cure for colds;
canna seeds strung in necklaces,
so efficacious in the case of spells;
and dragon's blood that tightens the gums
and binds fast the roots of loose teeth ...

With the silent patience of the ant
the Indians go gathering their herbs
in heaps upon the ground –
perfect in their natural science.

ALFONSO REYES, 'TARAHUMARA HERBS',
FROM *AN ANTHOLOGY OF MEXICAN POETRY*,
trans. Samuel Beckett,
pub. Thames & Hudson, London, 1959

THE MEXICANS

WALK TO HUAYAPA

*B*ritish poet and novelist D. H. Lawrence *(1885–1930) traveled to Mexico with his wife Frida in 1922, and there he began work on* The Plumed Serpent *(1926) and completed many stories and poems. He loved the country but was forced to return to England the following year to try and save his marriage. This extract shows his passion for the Mexican landscapes.*

❝The morning is perfect; in a moment we are clear out of town. Most towns in Mexico, saving the capital, end in themselves, at once. As if they had been lowered from heaven in a napkin, and deposited, rather foreign, upon the wild plain. So we walk round the wall of the church and the huge old monastery enclosure that is now barracks for the scrap-heap soldiery, and at once there are the hills.
"I will lift up my eyes until the hills, whence cometh my strength." At least one can always do that in Mexico. In a stride, the town passes away. Before us lies the gleaming, pinkish-ochre of the valley flat, wild and exalted with sunshine. On the left, quite near, bank the stiffly pleated mountains, all the foot-hills, that press savannah-coloured into the savannah of the valley. The mountains are clothed smokily with pine, ocote, and, like a woman in a gauze rebozo, they rear in a rich

115

blue fume that is almost cornflower-blue in the clefts. It is their characteristic, that they are darkest-blue at the top. Like some splendid lizard with a wavering, royal-blue crest down the ridge of his back, and pale belly, and soft, pinky-fawn claws, on the plain.

Between the pallor of the claws, a dark spot of trees, and white dots of a church with twin towers. Further away, along the foot-hills, a few scattered trees, white dot and stroke of a hacienda, and a green, green square of sugar-cane. Further off still, at the mouth of a cleft of a canyon, a dense little green patch of trees, and two spots of proud church. **'**

D.H. LAWRENCE, *MORNINGS IN MEXICO*,
pub. Martin Secker, London, 1930

TEMPLE OF THE AZTECS

F rances Calderon de la Barca (1804–82) was the Scottish wife of the Spanish minister to Mexico and she lived there for two years, during which time she wrote many letters to friends back home, describing her experiences.

'The carriage drew up in front of the cathedral, built upon the site of part of the ruins of the great temple of the Aztecs; of that pyramidal temple, constructed by the Ahuitzotli, the sanctuary so celebrated by the Spaniards, and which comprehended with all its different edifices and sanctuaries, the ground on which the cathedral now stands, together with part of the plaza and streets adjoining. We are told that within its enclosure were five hundred dwellings, that its hall was built of stone and lime, and ornamented with stone serpents. We hear of its four great gates, fronting the four cardinal points of its stone-paved court, great stone stairs, and sanctuaries dedicated to the gods of war; of the square destined for religious dances, and the colleges for the priests, and seminaries for the priestesses; of the horrible temple, whose door was an enormous serpent's mouth; of the temple of mirrors and that of shells; of the house set apart for the emperor's prayers; of the consecrated fountains, the birds kept for sacrifice, the gardens for the holy flowers, and of the terrible towers composed of the skulls of the victims – strange mixture of the beautiful and the horrible. We are told that five thousand priests chanted night and day in the Great Temple, to the honour and in the service of the monstrous idols, who were anointed thrice a day with the most precious perfumes, and that of these priests the most austere were clothed in black, their long hair dyed with ink, and their bodies anointed with the ashes of burnt scorpions and spiders; their chiefs were the sons of kings.

It is remarkable, by the way, that their god of war, Mejitli, was said to have been born of a woman, a Holy Virgin, who was in the service of the temple, and that when the priests, having knowledge of her disgrace, would have stoned her, a voice was heard, saying "Fear not, mother, for I shall save thy honour and my glory," upon which the god was born, with a shield in his left hand, an arrow in his right, a plume of green feathers on his head, his face painted blue, and his left leg adorned with feathers! Thus was his gigantic statue represented. **'**

FRANCES CALDERON DE LA BARCA,
LIFE IN MEXICO,
pub. Chapman & Hall, London, 1843

TYPICAL INCIDENTS

E velyn Waugh (1903–66) was known for his caustic travel journalism, so the following piece is high praise indeed.

'Various small incidents stand out as typical, if not of the country, at least of my trip there:–

The Indian chambermaid at the simple inn at Tenancingo who, as we left, pursued my wife into the street with a 20 peso bill which she had found on the floor of our room.

The little janitor at the museum in Oaxaca who was learning English; he had transcribed in pencil, in an awkward hand, the verses of the hymn "All things bright and beautiful" and asked our Mexican companion to explain some of the words to him in Spanish; I see them now against the glass cases full of Mixtec gold construing the poem together.

A drunk mestizo at the hotel in Oaxaca. The dining-room was the former patio of the house, now roofed with glass, the floor bare tiles; every sound swelled and echoed monstrously; he sat with a friend shouting, spitting and singing uproariously and glaring round the room as if he expected someone to start a fight. He was quite mirthless and curiously lonely in his cups. His sober friend sat opposite him eating impassively. Presently he made the plain and slatternly waitress sit at the table with him. She tried to make him take her to the cinema; instead he took her up to his room where he sang and shouted most of the night. I asked who he was. "He must be a politician," they said. "Otherwise he would not behave like that." Further enquiry discovered that he was a commercial traveller.❜

EVELYN WAUGH, *ROBBERY UNDER LAW:*
THE MEXICAN OBJECT LESSON,
pub. Chapman & Hall, London, 1939

MEXICAN SOCIETY

*A*ll the Pretty Horses *(1992), part of Cormac McCarthy's* Border Trilogy, *is a modern-day morality tale of two cowboys traveling in Mexico, speculating about the nature of the universe and the meaning of life. In the following piece, a grandmother tells them of her experiences and opinions.*

● Revolutionaries

❝"I am not a society person. The societies to which I have been exposed seemed to me largely machines for the suppression of women. Society is very important in Mexico. Where women do not even have the vote. In Mexico they are mad for society and for politics and very bad at both. My family are considered gachupines here, but the madness of the Spaniard is not so different from the madness of the creole. The political tragedy in Spain was rehearsed in full dress twenty years earlier on Mexican soil. For those with eyes to see, nothing was the same and yet everything. In the Spaniard's heart is a great yearning for freedom, but only his own. A great love of truth and honor in all its forms, but not in its substance. And a deep conviction that nothing can be proven except that it be made to bleed. Virgins, bulls, men. Ultimately God himself. When I look at my grandniece I see a child. And yet I know very well who and what I was at her age. In a different life I could have been a soldadera. Perhaps she too. And I will never know what her life is. If there is a pattern there it will not shape itself to anything the eyes can recognize. Because the question for me was always whether that shape we see in our lives was there from the beginning or whether these random events are only called a pattern after the fact. Because otherwise we are nothing."❞

CORMAC McCARTHY, *ALL THE PRETTY HORSES*
pub. Pan Books, London, 1993

REVOLUTIONARIES

BEFORE AND AFTER
*M*alcolm Lowry (1909–57) lived *in Mexico with his first wife Jan from 1936 to 1938. His novel* Under the Volcano, *which is considered his best work, is a complex description of Mexican history in the first half of the 20th century, seen through the eyes of an alcoholic British ex-consul.*

❝It spoke of the Mexico of Juan' childhood, of the year Hugh was born. Juarez had lived and died Yet was it a country with free speech, and the guarantee of life liberty, and the pursuit o happiness? A country of brilliantly muralled schools, and where ever each little cold mountain villag had its stone open-air stage, an the land was owned by its people free to express their native genius? A country o model farms: of hope? – It was a country of slavery, where human beings were sol like cattle, and its native peoples, the Yaquis, the Papagos, the Tomasachics exterminated through deportation, or reduced to worse than peonage, their land in thrall or the hands of foreigners. And in Oaxaca lay the terrible Valle Naciona where Juan himself, a bona-fide slave aged seven, had seen an older brother beate to death, and another, bought for forty-five pesos, starved to death in seve months, because it was cheaper this should happen, and the slaveholder bu another slave, than simply have one slave better fed merely worked to death in year. All this spelt Porfirio Díaz: *rurales* everywhere, *jefes*, *políticos*, and murder, th extirpation of liberal political institutions, the army an engine of massacre, a instrument of exile. Juan knew this, having suffered it; and more. For later in th revolution, his mother was murdered. And later still Juan himself killed his fathe who had fought with Huerta, but turned traitor. Ah, guilt and sorrow had dogge Juan's footsteps too, for he was not a Catholic who could rise refreshed from th cold bath of confession. Yet the banality stood: that the past was irrevocably past. And conscience had been given man to regret it only in so far as that might change the future. For man, every man, Juan seemed to be telling him, even as Mexico, must ceaselessly struggle upward. What was life but a warfare and a stranger's sojourn? Revolution rages too in the *tierra caliente* of each human soul. No peace but that must pay full toll to hell.'

MALCOLM LOWRY, *UNDER THE VOLCANO*,
pub. Jonathan Cape, London, 1947

MEXICAN POLICE

Graham Greene (1904–91) visited Mexico in 1938. The Power and the Glory (1940) describes the wanderings of a whisky-sodden priest during the dangerous years of the Revolution.

'The squad of police made their way back to the station: they walked raggedly with rifles slung anyhow: ends of cotton where buttons should have been: a puttee slipping down over the ankle: small men with black secret Indian eyes. The little plaza on the hill-top was lighted with globes strung together in threes and joined by trailing overhead wires. The Treasury, the Presidencia, a dentist's, the prison – a low white colonnaded building which dated back three hundred years, and the steep street down – the back wall of a ruined church: whichever way you went you came ultimately to water and to river. Pink classical façades peeled off and showed the mud beneath, and the mud slowly reverted to mud. Round the plaza the evening parade went on: women in one direction, men in the other: young men in red shirts milled boisterously round the gaseosa stalls.

The lieutenant walked in front of his men with an air of bitter distaste. He might have been chained to them unwillingly: perhaps the scar on his jaw was the relic of an escape. His gaiters were polished, and his pistol-holster: his buttons were all sewn on. He had a sharp crooked nose jutting out of a lean dancer's face: his neatness gave an effect of inordinate ambition in the shabby city. A sour smell came up to the plaza from the river and the vultures were bedded on the roofs, under the tent of their rough black wings. Sometimes a little moron head peered out and down and a claw shifted. At nine-thirty exactly all the lights in the plaza went out.'

GRAHAM GREENE, *THE POWER AND THE GLORY*,
pub. William Heinemann Ltd, London 1940

THE BLUE HOUSE

British novelist and journalist Rebecca West (1892–1983) writes of the strange juxtaposition when the exiled Leon Trotsky stayed in the vibrant, dramatic Blue House created by Frida Kahlo.

'The Trotskys stayed there for two years. It must have been an ambiguous experience. At first they were intoxicated by Mexico ... "even with its fruit and vegetables." Why not, indeed? In no other place I have ever been are the peppers flashing green like emeralds, or the tomatoes red as a coral but brighter. Impermanent jewels, and the impermanence does not matter, there are so many high piles of them on the tables before the Indian women sitting quietly in the markets. Also the taste is often new. But it was Trotsky's nature not to dwell on such pleasures, though he was capable of recognising them; he was like a camera which rejects colour films and insists on photographing in black and white. For that very reason, the new phase of his exile must soon have struck him as not at all the proper, classic thing.

It cannot be exaggerated how blue the Blue House is. It is a theatrical set ... littered with objects, organic and inorganic. It was as if the woman who had made this house, having been born perfect in form and lost that perfection by gross surgical assaults, tried to put back her lost perfection into her life by assembling as many beautiful works of art as possible around her. But Trotsky also had his chosen theatrical set, and its distinctive characteristic was that it was so far as possible destitute of objects. There he was following a European convention of long standing. ... Trotsky obeyed this convention to a degree which delighted those that followed it and disconcerted those to whom lowly birth had given the privilege of being as comfortable as if they had not been saved. His houses were always Saharas. His theatrical set was designed to serve a bleaker performance than has yet been seen....

In the wrong setting, mimosa blossom drooping over him in uncontrollable and overscented luxury and tickling his neck, Indian ceramics and Aztec idols of terrible frangibility hemming him in, Trotsky faced less material and more complicated hardships. The sword of his power rusted in him. **'**

REBECCA WEST, 'SURVIVORS IN MEXICO', ed. Bernard Schweizer, pub. Yale University Press, New Haven, 2003

SACRED STONE

AN EXPERT'S OPINION

Henry Moore (1898–1986), one of the foremost British sculptors of the 20th century, gives his seal of approval to the work of Mexican artists.

'Mexican sculpture, as soon as I found it, seemed to me true and right, perhaps because I at once hit on similarities in it with some eleventh-century carvings I had seen as a boy on Yorkshire churches. Its "stoniness", by which I mean its truth to material, its tremendous power without loss of sensitiveness, its astonishing variety and fertility of form-invention and its approach to a full three-dimensional conception of form, make it unsurpassed in my opinion by any other period of stone sculpture. **'**

HENRY MOORE, QUOTED IN *HENRY MOORE ON SCULPTURE*, ed. Philip James, pub. Macdonald, London, 1966

DIVINE GEOGRAPHY

The last word goes to distinguished American travel writer Paul Theroux (b. 1941).

'The pyramids of Mexico ... are clearly the efforts of people aspiring to make mountains; they match the landscape and in places mock it. The god-king must demonstrate that he is capable of duplicating divine geography, and the pyramids were visible proof of this attempt. **'**

PAUL THEROUX, *THE OLD PATAGONIAN EXPRESS*, pub. Mariner Books, 1979

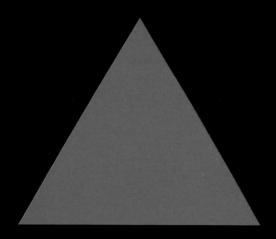

Itineraries

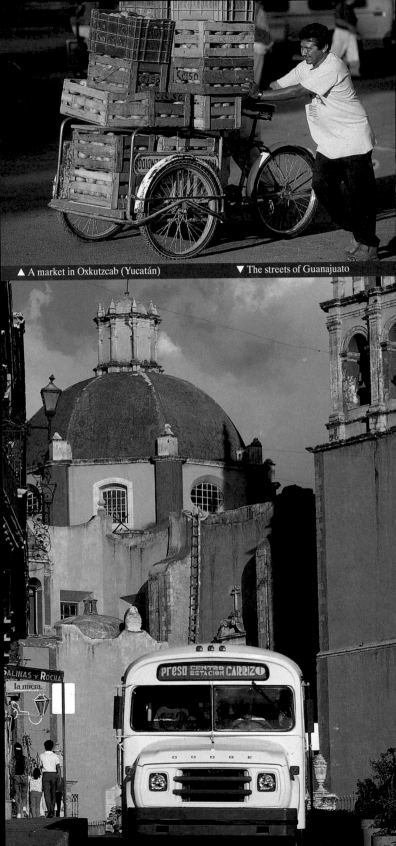

▲ A market in Oxkutzcab (Yucatán)　▼ The streets of Guanajuato

▲ Baja California   ▼ Doorway, church of San Francisco in Querétaro

▲ Puebla

▼ Cathedral of San Cristóbal de las Casas

▲ Mural depicting the Virgin of Guadalupe

▼ Canal boats (*trajineras*), Xochimilco

▲ Pico de Orizaba   ▼ Atrium of the Tilaco Mission (Sierra Gorda)

Mexico City

THE FIGHT AGAINST POLLUTION
Mexico City, set in the bottom of a basin enclosed by a circle of volcanoes ● *20*, is subject to heavy pollution. Since 1990, the local authorities have closed factories, refineries and cement works, reclaimed green spaces and introduced the alternating driving program '*Hoy no circulo*', reducing automobile traffic by one fifth.

THE 1985 EARTHQUAKE
On September 19, 1985, an earthquake of a magnitude of 7.5 on the Richter scale brought down a large number of buildings ● *20*. The tragedy led to acts of heroism, however, as volunteers pulled the injured from the rubble and distributed aid packages in the parks used to accommodate the rescued citizens. The reconstruction, undertaken in accordance with new anti-earthquake regulations, took ten years to complete.

Mexico City emerged from an aquatic landscape. It could only be built after an inland sea was filled in (a vast expanse of water covering the bottom of the Anáhuac basin). Over the course of its chaotic expansion, its heaviest buildings have sunk into the mud under the surface, giving the central streets a crooked look, with curving horizontal lines and verticals at angles. Remains of Tenochtitlán, once capital of Mesoamerica, are embedded in this unstable land.

THE COLONIAL CITY: TENOCHTITLÁN BECOMES MEXICO CITY. The city boasted 300,000 inhabitants just before the Conquest, but only 30,000 remained by 1524. Tenochtitlán was discarded in favor of Castilian palaces, churches and convents, made with stone recovered from the huge demolition site that had once been Aztec temples. The 16th century took on the color of tezontle, the red volcanic rock that set off the entablature of the gray stone. Mexico ceased to be an island in the early 18th century. The insalubrious conditions created by flooding prompted engineers to excavate a tunnel under the mountain to drain and cleanse the area. The last vestiges of the lake could be seen in the network of waterways that earned the city the epithet of 'the Venice of the Americas'.

MEXICO IN THE BELLE ÉPOQUE. In 1862, Maximilian, the emperor imposed by Napoleon III ● *27*, decided to settle in Chapultepec Castle, far from the tumultuous Zócalo, and laid the Paseo de la Reforma through the marshes to link the two. This boulevard is lined with villas and private hotels. The city center moved westward as, inspired by the progress of science, the 'enlightened dictatorship' of Porfirio Díaz ● *28* proclaimed the advent of the industrial era. The new palaces were steel structures covered with carved stone ● *86*. The 1910 Revolution interrupted such large-scale construction projects but, once things had settled in the 1920s, the monuments of the Porfiriat were turned into institutional headquarters, schools and ministries, which the muralists ● *100* were commissioned to adorn with revolutionary imagery.

THE TWENTIETH CENTURY. Mexico City's population passed the half-million mark in the 1920s and over the course of the 20th century, it multiplied by 35. A new north–south thoroughfare, the Avenida de los Insurgentes, was the axis of urban development. The flexibility derived from reinforced concrete enabled housing to proliferate on the peripheries: to the north, workers' districts and factories; to the south, the elegant suburbs of Condesa and Roma. The car took on a leading role: in 1940, the Río de la Piedad was filled in to create a highway; in 1960, it was the turn of the last remaining waterway, the Río Churubusco. Tlatelolco, once the Aztec market, was turned into a large complex, drawn up by the architect Mario Pani. The lava fields to the south now provide the setting for the tower blocks of the National University. To the west, the ring road winds along the old banks of the lake to the suburb of Ciudad Satélite. Audacious architectural creation have appeared (Museo Nacional de Antropología, 1964; Basílica de Guadalupe, 1976, and so forth ● *88*). Seen from the air, the city is an ocean of lights at night, glittering right to the edges of the Anáhuac basin. The suburbs bear the names of old lakeside towns: Ixtapalapa, Ecatepec, Nuacalpán, Tlanepantla, Atzcapozalco. The city has sucked up the lake, climbed the mountains, spilled on to the Chalco Valley and the State of Mexico, and branched out along the Puebla and Pachuca freeways. Both old and ultramodern, the world's biggest city is fed by European immigration and the constant influx from the rural hinterland, making it at once cosmopolitan and indigenous.

View of the megalopolis, with Ixtaccihuatl in the background

The Zócalo ◆ J E4

The story of the city began here, on the original islet (the 'Belly of the Moon'), the heart of the Aztec city. Its foundation stone is the center of both the *traza* (the first map of the Spanish city in 1524) and, later, the perfect circle of the Federal District after independence. The PLAZA DE LA CONSTITUCIÓN, also known as the ZÓCALO, is a magical place. A historical showcase and a permanent market, a forum and a fair, this square, with sides 788 ft (240 m) long, is invariably buzzing with music and the banter of artists displaying their work, children flying kites, vendors setting up stalls and protest groups pitching their camps. Every political and social movement has ended up in the Zócalo; its buildings have resounded to revolts and *pronunciamientos*, demonstrations and repressions, patriotic processions and mass meetings. On each side it is bounded by the country's institutions, monuments to its power, both past and present.

PALACIO NACIONAL. The executive authorities occupy the entire eastern side of the square. This was the site of Moctezuma's old palace, before it was knocked down to make way for that of Cortés. In 1562, it became the residence of the viceroys. In 1624, the Creoles and the archbishop tried to burn it down, in revolt against the governor sent from Spain. In 1692, it was once again the target of firebrands, during riots protesting against food shortages. Since independence, the restored building has served as the headquarters for both the presidency of the republic and the Ministry of Finance. The façade made of volcanic granite was raised by one story in 1928. From 1929 to 1935, Diego Rivera ● *100* raised his scaffolding here to paint his *Epic of the Mexican People*, a 4,800-sq.-foot (450-sq.-m) fresco that created a link between Quetzalcóatl and the class struggle in a panorama that puts trade unions alongside gods. On the walls of the main staircase, Marx, Madero, Zapata and Cortés confront Rockefeller, Vanderbilt and Morgan: heroes of independence, jaguar-warriors, Indians and workers are pitted against *conquistadores*, inquisitors and capitalists.

Detail of one of Rivera's frescos in the Palacio Nacional

ZÓCALO
This Spanish word of Arab origin, related to both the souk and the socle (base of a pyramid), has given its name to Mexico City's main square. By extension, *zócalo* has become the word that customarily designates the central square in any Mexican town.

THE BELL OF INDEPENDENCE
The bell hanging above the main door of the Palacio Nacional comes from the town of Dolores. Father Miguel Hidalgo rang it in 1810 to announce the uprising against Spain ▲ *356*. Every September 15, the eve of Independence Day, the president chimes it in celebration.

CATEDRAL METROPOLITANA. Built between 1573 and the early 19th century, the cathedral stands on the north side of the Zócalo. Its baroque façade is 17th-century, and the two pinnacles were added in 1793. In 1813, the architect Manuel Tolsá drew up the central dome and the clock tower, adorned with the virtues of faith, hope and charity. Fourteen richly decorated chapels are arranged around the triple nave. The baroque altar of the Capilla del Perdón was sculpted in the 17th century by Juan de Rojas, also responsible for the choir stalls. The altarpiece in the Kings' Chapel was created by Jerónimo de Balbás, from Seville, in 1737. *The Church Triumphant* by Cristobal de Villapando ▲ *169* and *Christ's Entrance into Jerusalem* and *Saint Michael Overcoming the Dragon*, both by Juan Correa, can be seen in the 16th-century sacristy. The SAGRARIO METROPOLITANO – a sacristy with a remarkable 18th-century façade bedecked with statues – leans markedly to one side. Behind the church, vendors on the Calle del Sagrario and the Pasaje Catedral sell devotional objects, not to mention iguanas, devil fish and ginseng roots which are used as traditional medicines.

THE ZÓCALO ★
To obtain a view of the Zócalo in its entirety, the best plan is to go and have a drink on the roof terrace of one of the big hotels around the square.

AN IRRESISTIBLE SLOPE
The imposing cathedral is tilted: the plumb line hanging in the nave reveals the extent of its incline, which amounted to 20 feet (6 m) at the start of the new millennium.

Lowering the flag on the Zócalo

THE TEMPLO MAYOR ★
Embedded in what
has become the
colonial heart of the
city, it powerfully
evokes the clash
between two worlds.

Below: details from
the *Codex Sahagún*
Bottom: neo-Aztec
dancers on the Zócalo

The Templo Mayor ◆ J E3

RAZED, HIDDEN THEN REDISCOVERED. After the
Conquest, the Avila brothers, colleagues of Cortés, built
their house on this old ceremonial site. After their eviction in
1566, it was razed to the ground and the land deliberately
sullied by being put to use as a garbage dump. In the 19th
century, the Porrua bookshop was built on this site, on top of
ramps decorated with sculpted dragons. In 1900, a canal was
bored through the buried pyramids to expel sewage from the
city center. Numerous pre-Columbian remains were dug up,
but the temple continued to go unnoticed. In 1978, a
laborer's pickax struck a sculpted 8-ton disk 7 feet (2 m)
below Calle Argentina depicting the goddess Coyolxauhqui.
The find triggered the clearing and excavation of an entire

**DANCERS;
ORATORS AND
HEALERS**
The area between the
cathedral and the
Palacio Nacional
reverberates with the
heavy rhythms of
drums and the
moaning of conches,
like the sound of a
distant battle, as
dancers wearing
ankle-bells, feathered
headdresses and
tunics embellished
with golden motifs
gyrate on the
cobblestones ● 46.
In front of the ruins
of the Templo Mayor,
orators protest at
length about the
injustices of history,
while healers submit
their clients to a
purification ceremony
(*limpia*) involving
smoke from copal
resin and herbal
plants.

block of houses in the heart of the city. The dig now spans an
area of 2,000 by 2,600 feet (600 by 800 m) which is still
expanding, encroaching on the nearby buildings.
THE NEST OF TEMPLES. The excavations
yielded more riches than expected: a total of 7,000
items have been retrieved. Not just one but seven
PYRAMIDS ● 75 were discovered, built one on top of
the other between 1375 and 1502. The *conquistadores*
destroyed the biggest (130 ft/40 m); its base, along with the
older pyramids, was left intact, however, when they raised the

Above left: detail of the great disk of Coyolxauhqui
Above: a general view of the Templo Mayor
Left: sacrificial knives

level of the city and covered the site with an embankment. The sewage canal of 1900 made a cross-section that unveiled the passing of time layer by layer right into the heart of Phase 3: the twin temples of Huitzilopochtli and Tlaloc, dating from 1450, have remained impeccably preserved amidst the stones piled around them. Another area that escaped destruction was the RECINTO DE LOS GUERREROS ÁGUILA, from the final period, a sanctuary decorated with colored bas-reliefs that contained numerous statues.

The excavations continue to this day, particularly on the western side, a veritable treasure trove: in the spring of 2005, sculpted floor from Phase 4 was found here. One unanticipated effect of the elasticity of the muddy subsoil is that, while the palace and the Cathedral are sinking, the pyramids – freed of the weight that previously buried them – have started to rise and now peer out above street level.

MUSEO DEL TEMPLO MAYOR. The GREAT DISK OF COYOLXAUHQUI takes pride of place in the site's museum, which also has clay statues of eagle-warriors, SACRIFICIAL KNIVES made of flint and obsidian (with stone eyes added to form a face), masks and delicate terracotta objects left as offerings at the various tombs. Other treasures include a host of animal figures – dogs, crocodiles, sea turtles, jaguars, fish – and jewelry incorporating exotic materials (shells, corals) that bear witness to the extensive trading and traveling of the Aztec merchants (*pochteca*). Models and drawings of Tenochtitlán explain how it reclaimed territory from the water by creating artificial islands (*chinampas*); their alluvial soil was held in by underwater enclosures and used to plant trees ▲ *128*. In a room devoted to the Conquest, illustrations and texts of the FLORENTINE CODEX, compiled by the monk Sahagún from accounts by the Indians of Tlatelco, provides an indigenous view of the arrival of the Spanish.

TLALOC AND HUITZILOPOCHTLI
The twin temples bear the name of two important divinities in the Aztec pantheon: Tlaloc was the god of rain, Huitzilopochtli a tutelary warrior deity (of Chichimec origin).

In 1300, a group of nomads coming from the north – later to be known as the Aztecs – arrived in the Anáhuac Valley, a basin between volcanoes filled by a lake. Several peoples had already made their home on its banks. The newcomers initially settled in Chapultepec, then in Culhuacán, but their brutish customs upset their neighbors....

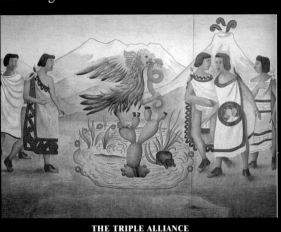

THE FOUNDATION
Chased off the banks, they headed for an island washed by brackish water: Mexico, the 'Beast of the Moon'. It is said that they encountered an eagle on a *nopal*, devouring a serpent. The saw this as a sign that their wandering had come to an end and founded their capital, Tenochtitlán. The first temples were built with bamboo and clay. Game was scarce and the land infertile. The Aztecs lived on fish, snakes, the fruit and leaves of the *nopal* and the insects' eggs that formed a froth on the surface of the water.

THE TRIPLE ALLIANCE
In 1372, the Aztecs decided to place themselves under the tutelage of a local lord, thereby protecting themselves within the network of power that was being forged by the lakeside cities. They came under the protection of the stronghold of Azapotzalco, but later turned against it, besieging and capturing it in 1428 as a result of the Triple Alliance with the cities of Texcoco and Tacuba. They went on to conquer the Huastec and Totanac regions of Veracruz, and, after fierce fighting, the Mixtecs and Zapotecs of Oaxaca and Puebla, thereby extending their influence from coast to coast. The Triple Alliance had become the 'Empire'.

THE CITY ON THE WATER

When Cortés discovered Tenochtitlán in 1599, its pyramids loomed over the lake. The highest – those of the Great Temple – had been opened in 1487 with the sacrifice of thousands of captives. They were surrounded by enormous palaces, libraries, astronomical observatories, zoos, fishponds and gardens with exotic plants. The Temple Island was linked by neighborhoods on piles to the Tlatelolco Island, with its big market. The city's 300,000 inhabitants were protected from the brackish water by a dike 10 miles (16 km) long, the work of the prince, engineer and poet Nezahualcóyotl (*below*), allowing them to profit from the fresh water to bathe, gain sustenance from the *chinampas* (raft gardens) and move about in canoes. Tributes from subjugated towns poured in via the causeways linking the city to dry land. The southern road led to Iztapalapa, Coyoacán and Xochimilco; the western embankment served as an aqueduct (also providing access to Tacuba, Popotla and Azcapotzalco), while the northern one stretched to the sanctuary of Mount Tepeyac.

AT THE MERCY OF THE CONQUISTADORES

The Aztec Empire proved fragile, however. It had no horses or means of transport to control a vast territory with a hundred different languages. The peoples it conquered were not colonized, merely required to pay for protection, while the rebellious strongholds of Tlaxcala, Huejotzingo and the Purépecha of Michoacán caused endless wars. The Spanish dismantled the Aztecs' alliances as they advanced, then, in 1521, they cut off the flow of the aqueducts and used cannons to destroy the Nezahualcóyotl dike. The island was once again washed with brackish waves; its inhabitants grew thirsty, their floating gardens were ruined and the influx of extorted tributes ceased. Facing an adversary governed by logistics different from their own, the Aztec defenses fell. Tenochtitlán, a mirage on a watery horizon, suddenly became vulnerable in the midst of this totally flat theater of war, where their canoes were easy targets. Cortés was able to coordinate at first hand the movements of his ships and the final assault via the three causeways.

Calle Correo Mayor

PERFUMES
20 Y 30

To the east of the Zócalo

Between the Palacio Nacional and the Templo Mayor, the CALLE DE LA MONEDA – thus named because coins were once minted here – runs between palatial façades, votive statues tucked in corner niches and carriage entrances that open onto quiet patios shaded by palms, oblivious to the hubbub of the street. You can sample one at no. 13, belonging to the MUSEO NACIONAL DE LAS CULTURAS. The street is crossed by CALLE LICENCIADO VERDAD, the site of New Spain's first printing house, as well as the old bishopric, convent and church of SANTA TERESA LA ANTIGUA, sloping at an astonishing angle (now the Santa Teresa Cultural Center). Behind the Presidential Palace, the CALLE CORREO MAYOR is distinguished by clothes drying on balconies, flowerpots decorating windows boarded up with plywood, and plants growing in the walls of this old working-class neighborhood. Despite efforts to crack down on unlicensed traders, the thoroughfare is invaded by vendors hawking plastic jewelry and other cheap goods.

MUSEO JOSÉ LUIS CUEVAS ◆ **J** F3. (*Calle Academia, at the junction with Calle de la Moneda*) The patio of the museum devoted to José Luis Cuevas ● *103,* an old convent restored by the artist himself, is dominated by his huge sculpture *The Giantess*. Cuevas, the leader of the generation that turned its back on Muralism, has assembled a fine overview of his career, along with prints by Picasso, work by contemporaries such as Lila Carillo and Arnaldo Cohen, and the biggest collection of erotic art in Mexico.

IGLESIA DE LA SANTÍSIMA ◆ **J** F4. (*Calle de la Moneda, beyond Calle Loreto*) The carved door of the Church of the Santísima (17th c.), several feet below street level, reveals the level of the ground at the time of its construction.

SANTA TERESA LA NUEVA. Heading north, Calle Loreto passes another baroque church, Santa Teresa la Nueva, before reaching a square with a fountain that is dominated by the neoclassical Iglesia de Loreto.

SAN ANTONIO TOMATLÁN. One street north, Calle San Ildefonso leads, at its third junction, to one of the most touching religious buildings in the city center: the small and simple Church of San Antonio Tomatlán (early 17th c.).

PAINTING AND THE REVOLUTION
The decadent bourgeois figures of Orozco's frescos on the first floor of San Ildefonso exasperated students so much that they defaced them in 1923, giving rise to one of the first university conflicts affecting the regime born out of the Revolution. Sixty-five years later, the 1968 movement was attacked here by the army.

RIVERA, HIS FRIENDS, HIS FRESCOS
The construction site of the SEP was the meeting point for a generation, as friends, assistants and celebrities milled round and often served as models. Diego met Frida Kahlo here, and Tina Modotti photographed its progress. The two women appear on the final fresco – *The Arsenal* (1929), on the second floor – alongside Modotti's lover, the Cuban revolutionary Julio Antonio Mella, who was killed that year. Rivera included José Vasconcelos, seen from behind on an elephant, among the ethereal intellectuals: an epilogue to a friendship that had turned sour.

To the north of the Zócalo

SAN ILDEFONSO ◆ J E3. (*Calle Justo Sierra, 16*) Opposite the Templo Mayor, the Museo San Ildefonso, a Jesuit school in the 17th century and then the preparatory school for the university, was the birthplace of the Muralist Movement in the early 1920s ● *100*. Anxious to recover the lost art of the Italian Renaissance fresco, Rivera produced his first mural here, with wax polish: *The Creation.* The panels in the entrance hall illustrating the life of Bolívar are the work of Fernando Leal. Fermín Revueltas depicted religious festivals on the walls of the large patio, while the Frenchman Jean Charlot re-created *The Conquest of Tenochtitlán* on the staircase. The mural painted by Siqueiros in the small patio is a rousing call for revolution.

Below: detail of a fresco by Orozco in San Ildefonso

SECRETARÍA DE EDUCACIÓN PÚBLICA ◆ J E3. (*Calle Argentina, 28*) The Secretariat of Public Education (SEP) was another breeding ground for Muralism. The education minister, José Vasconcelos, was responsible for its creation and its decoration reflects his far-reaching aspirations. The four corners of the first neoclassical courtyard are marked by sculpted effigies of Athena and Buddha, a caravel bearing the Christian cross and an Aztec deity. In 1923, Vasconcelos unleashed the muralists in the two huge patios. Amado de la Cueva and Jean Charlot painted part of the north wall of the second courtyard, but very soon the site was taken over by Diego Rivera: his FRESCOS – 235 panels spread over three floors, covering 17,200 sq. feet (1,600 sq. m) – run everywhere, even in the stairwells and elevator shafts, and use striking trompe l'œil effects to integrate the building itself into his paintings. Peasants in meetings sit on the lintels of the doors, and even the electric switches seem to form part of workers' tools or the bourgeoisie's strong boxes. There is an abundance of Masonic and Communist symbolism (red stars, hammers and sickles), Indian laborers, miners and other workers. Zapata, Villa and leading social figures are prominent, but bullfighters, poets and stars from the world of entertainment are also featured.

MURAL PAINTINGS ★
The area around the Zócalo is one of the best places to discover Mexican Muralism.

PLAZA SANTO DOMINGO ◆ J DE2-3. Alongside the SEP the Calle Cuba leads to the lively Plaza Santo Domingo. To the north, the IGLESIA SANTO DOMINGO is flanked by an elegant building that forms a bridge above Calle Leandro Valle, while to the west, under the old wooden portico, public scribes write letters for lovers who are short of inspiration.

Casa de los Azulejos

VILLA'S NIGHTSPOT
♦ J C3
To the right of Calle
Madero, Calle
Filomeno Mata cuts
across Calle 5 de
Mayo by the famous
cantina (bar and
restaurant) LA
OPERA, distinguished
by its gilded baroque
jigsaw decor. It was
here that Pancho
Villa broke into a
dance on the roof to
celebrate his arrival in
the city in 1914.

**THE VESTIGES OF
THE AZTEC CITY**
At the base of the
façade of the Museo
de la Ciudad, the
mouth of the plumed
serpent Quetzalcóatl,
recovered from a
pagan temple, serves
as the cornerstone.

To the south of the Zócalo

AYUNTAMIENTO ♦ J E4. The south side of the Zócalo is
occupied by the center of municipal power: the city hall, an
enormous building with neocolonial arcades. Its incumbent
was always a delegate appointed by the president, but since
1997 the populace has been allowed to elect its own mayor,
and the city has been run by the PRD, a center-left party.
MUSEO DE LA CIUDAD DE MÉXICO ♦ J E5. (*Avenida
Pino Suárez, 30*) The former residence of the Counts of
Santiago houses the City Museum, where prints and models
trace the progress of the capital. A plaque, further to the left
on this avenue (once the southern causeway of Tenochtitlán),
marks the meeting-place of Cortés and Moctezuma in 1519.
THE BELLE ÉPOQUE IN MEXICO CITY ♦ J E4. (*Calle 20
de Noviembre*) The steel-and-glass domes of the department
stores EL PUERTO DE LIVERPOOL and EL PALACIO DE
HIERRO (built by a 'Barcelonnette'), inspired by the great
Parisian stores, dates from the city's French period in the late
19th century. At the junction of the Zócalo and Calle 16 de
Septiembre, the GRAN HOTEL DE MÉXICO, with its
impressive art nouveau foyer, wrought-iron elevator and
glass roof, was built in the same era.

To the west of the Zócalo

The arcades of the western side of the Zócalo are occupied
by goldsmiths, silversmiths and jewelers, while a state-owned
pawnshop stands further north, with long lines of borrowers
outside on the days prior to festivals.
THE STREETS OF THE REVOLUTION ♦ J CD3-4. Along
the streets running westward from the Zócalo, the colonial
façades alternate with 19th-century neoclassical buildings,
their decor almost unchanged since the famous photographs
of the 1910 Revolution. The PHOTOGRAPHY BAZAAR on
Calle Madero, on the corner of Calle Bolívar, allows viewers
to relive those heady days through the archives of the
Casasola brothers. At no. 17, after the Calle Bolívar, the
Banamex Bank has restored the sumptuous colonial palace
of the Marquis of Jarral, the residence of the Emperor
Iturbide in 1822. Continuing along Calle Madero, two

THE CITY SEEN FROM ABOVE
On the corner of Calle Madero, the terrace restaurant at the top of the
HOTEL MAJESTIC offers a panoramic view of the Zócalo and the
Centro Histórico. The bar-restaurant on the 44th floor of the TORRE
LATINOAMERICANA also provides an ideal vantage point.

churches at no. 7 – SAN FRANCISCO, from the 18th century,
and SAN FELIPE DE JESÚS, built in 1780 – set up an arresting
contrast with the TORRE LATINOAMERICANA, a scaled-
down replica of the Empire State Building that was the city's
highest skyscraper from 1953 to 1976.

CASA DE LOS AZULEJOS ◆ J C3. Across the road, this old
18th-century residence covered with blue tiles is now
occupied by the Sanborns restaurant. The Zapatistas stopped
here when they occupied the city in late 1914, and a famous
photo shows them in their sombreros, lined up along the bar
in front of the coffee percolators. The fresco on the staircase,
Omniciencia, was painted by José Clemente Orozco.

PLAZA MANUEL TOLSÁ ◆ J C3. This square bears the
name of a sculptor and architect who helped shape the

'BARCELONNETTES'
The epic journey of
the group of French
immigrants known as
the Barcelonnettes
began in the 19th
century. The dire
economic situation
back home forced
these mountain
people to seek their
fortune elsewhere.
The new arrivals
stayed together and
soon became
prosperous. Starting
off as street traders,

appearance of the city in the 19th century. He was
responsible for the EQUESTRIAN STATUE OF CHARLES IV
OF SPAIN and, on the southern side, the PALACIO DE
MINERÍA (1813), a neoclassical masterpiece.

MUSEO NACIONAL DE ARTE ◆ J C3. This completes the
symmetry of the Plaza Manuel Tolsá and adheres to the
tenets of classicism, even though it was built almost a century
after the Palacio de Minería. The stucco shafts of the
twinned pillars in the hall mask a steel armature. The
building combined state-of-the-art engineering with opulent
luxury in a fervent proclamation of modernity: allegories of
Progress painted on the ceilings, suspended metal staircase,
outsize windows. The exhibition halls reveal surprising facets
of 19th-century Mexican painting: academic depictions of the
Conquest by Leandro Izaguirre and landscapes in the Mexico
Valley at the time of the *haciendas* by José María Velasco
● 95. Notable sculptures include *Despite Everything*, a
sensuous white marble by Jesús Ocampo. To the museum's
west, the Avenida Lázaro Cardenas (1934) marks the limits
of the Centro Histórico; after this, the streets become wider.

they gradually built
up a thriving financial
and industrial empire
(especially in the field
of textiles). After the
fall of Porfirio Díaz
● 28, some of them
decided to return to
France, where the
wealthiest built
fabulous mansions.
Some 50,000
descendants of
Barcelonnettes are
still living in Mexico
today.

Above: Calle Madero
seen from the Zócalo,
with the Torre
Latinoamericana in
the background

In Mexico City, the site of one of the world's biggest urban sprawls, various periods, places, cultures and peoples mingle and merge. History and diversity are reflected in elements found in everyday life, in the gastronomic, social and cultural practices and customs of the city's population. By creating a dynamic series of connections, these elements allow visitors to perceive a city – with all its paradoxes, archetypes and customs – that blends tradition and modernity in a constant process of renewal.

THE BALLROOMS ('SALÓN DE BAILE')

In the last few years, Mexico City has seen a proliferation of huge ballrooms, in which up to 2,000 people can be found twirling around, without stimulation from alcohol or cigarettes (both forbidden). They were originally patronized by the working class, but they now attract aficionados of all ages, from all different backgrounds – proof that the rumba, cha-cha-cha and merengue are establishing an increasingly eclectic fan base.

THE 'CABAS'

The nylon-fiber *cabas* is an indispensable shopping companion, as well as often being the only receptacle available for countless other purposes. Hard-wearing (although deformable), it comes in a range of colors and sizes. It has recently even had the impertinence of appropriating sacred icons, by reproducing images of the Virgin of Guadalupe and Frida Kahlo.

THE BIRTHDAY CAKE

In the city center, the store windows on Avenidas 16 de Septiembre and 5 de Mayo are crammed with pyramids of cream, sugar and multicolored plastic decorations. Each cake seeks to outrival the next in inventiveness, whether for weddings and birthdays. Both sexes and all ages will find something to their taste here, from Cinderella to the Little Mermaid, from the Simpsons to a soccer pitch, from Mickey Mouse to mangas (Japanese comic strips).

THE BEETLE, AN ECOLOGICAL TAXI

Not a single street or neighborhood (however humble or chic) or traffic jam in the Mexican capital is without a small green and white Beetle. It is always there when you need it, does not require any coaxing and runs, slightly out of breath, for distances now almost beyond its age Sixteen years after its launch, however, the *bocho*, a non-polluting taxi, is threatened with extinction. As Volkswagen has decided to stop making its most emblematic model, it is gradually giving way to a bigger car that will continue the city's ambitious attempts to combat the smog problem.

THE SOMBRERO

Whether made of reinforced straw or canvas, whether unbleached or dyed the color of ivory, the hat is the essential attribute of the Mexican man. In all weathers, in the country but also in the city – where it migrated with its rural owners – the sombrero is a cultural marker and social symbol. It allows a man to affirm his virility and so provides a seductive power that brings together elegance and machismo.

THE PROTECTIVE AMULET

Superstitions and ritual practices, often inherited from the countryside, lurk within many of the city's inhabitants. Every household requires protection and this can take on a number of forms; the most common include garlic, aloes and thyme, used to venerate the patron saint, Ignatius of Loyola. Today's amulets, glittering with gilt and sequins, can be more than a little kitsch!

THE 'TELENOVELA'

Every day, around ten *telenovelas* (soap operas) – craftily assembled blends of money, luxury, sex, deceit and intrigue – brashly proclaim their litanies of clichés. Nobody is immune from the emoting of secret lovers, the remorse of treacherous or betrayed women and the rage of cheated husbands.

THE CANDLE ('VELA')

Religious fervor in Mexico City is not confined to churches. A small shrine can be set up anywhere, particularly in markets, on street corners, in restaurants and stores, or inside homes. Apart from the plastic flowers, it is the flame of these small candles that breathes new life into the venerated saints.

THE COMIC STRIP ('HISTORIETA')

The *historieta* is usually pocket size, containing around a hundred pages. Their drawings are crude, their narratives stereotyped, their characters predictable and roughly delineated, but nevertheless these small magazines sell in the millions every single day. Once they have been read, they pass into the second-hand market, so that other readers can benefit, at discount prices, from these distillations of life, which invariably have a comforting conclusion.

Interior of the Correo
Mayor

The Palacio de Bellas Artes and the Eastern Alameda

PALACIO DE BELLAS ARTES
◆ **J** C3. (*Corner of Avenidas Lázaro Cárdenas and Juárez*) As this building has sunk into the ground, its patrons descend to cross its threshold. The work of the Italian architect Adamo Boari, this national opera house clad with Carrara marble and topped with a triple dome in bronze was intended to be the cultural showpiece of the regime of Porfirio Díaz ● *28* but the Revolution interrupted construction. Although begun in 1904, it was not opened until 1934, after an audacious transformation of its decoration. Its romantic nymphs and odalisques made way for jaguar-warriors on the keystones and serpents on the friezes underlying the arches. Its resolutely art deco interior, with geometrical red marble and futuristic lamps, is straight out of the movie *Metropolis*, casting diffuse light on the neo-Aztec copper masks on the staircase. Siqueiros, Orozco, Rivera, O'Gorman and Tamayo painted the frescos on the upper floors.

PALACIO DE CORREOS ◆ **J** C3. (*Corner of Calle 5 de Mayo and Av. Lázaro Cárdenas*) The central post office, built in 1908, is a palace with a metal structure that blends the Venetian Renaissance, English Gothic and Mudejar (Hispano-Moorish) styles. Its interior architecture and the staircases crossing its enormous lobby are well worth a look.

MUSEO FRANZ MAYER ◆ **J** B3. (*On the other side of Avenida Lázaro Cárdenas, by Av. Hidalgo*) Two charming churches – SANTA VERACRUZ, with a Churrigueresque door, and SAN JUAN DE DIOS, with a leaning bell tower – flank a small square tucked below the street. Between the two stands the FRANZ MAYER MUSEUM, set in a 16th-century hospital building. The two stories around its pillared patio contain rooms displaying magnificent pottery from Delft and China, crockery from Puebla, traditional shawls and costumes, fine pieces of silverware, colonial furniture and 16th-century Flemish and Spanish paintings. On one side, the MUSEO DE LA ESTAMPA traces the rich history of Mexican engraving.

The Alameda Central and the area to its west ◆ **J** B3

To the west of the Palacio de Bellas Artes, shady alleys run through THE ALAMEDA PARK, once surrounded by canals. In the 16th century, it served as the execution ground where the sentences of the Inquisition were carried out. In 1791, the viceroy converted this infamous spot into an elegant promenade. This was knocked down in 1868, when the canal were filled in. Diego Rivera painted the glory days of the

MARKETS ◆ **J** AB5
From the Balderas subway station, Avenida Balderas runs to the north along the Ciudadela – now the Mexico City Library, with its walls still riddled with shrapnel, a vestige of Huerta's counter-revolutionary victory over Madero in 1913 – then reaches the MERCADO DE LA CIUDADELA, devoted to jewelry and hand-woven textiles. Turning right from Avenida Balderas, the Calle Ayuntamiento runs to another crafts market three blocks further east, the MERCADO SAN JUAN, which is also one of the city's best stocked and most varied food markets.

park in his fresco *Dream of a Sunday Afternoon in the Alameda*, featuring a host of historical figures, including himself and Frida Kahlo ▲ *156*. This has been preserved in the MUSEO MURAL DIEGO RIVERA, in the far west of the Alameda, next to the baroque Church of San Diego. On the other side of Avenida Hidalgo, on the corner of the Paseo de la Reforma, the baroque door of the HOTEL CORTÉS (1780) opens on to an inviting colonial patio with a restaurant.

To the north of the Alameda

PLAZA GARIBALDI ◆ J C2. (*Via Avenida Lázaro Cárdenas*) Mariachi bands on the avenue's sidewalk entice drivers to pay for a song. They increase in number going north to Plaza Garibaldi, where their blaring trumpets can be heard at night accompanied by lyrical declarations of love. The square is lined with *cantinas*, including the famous Tenampa, where the atmosphere recalls the movies of Pedro Infante ● *61*.

PLAZA DE LAS TRES CULTURAS ◆ G B1. The Avenida Lázaro Cárdenas leads northward to this aptly named square, which is steeped in history. The old market of Tenochtitlán, where Cuauhtémoc was captured by the Spanish, became an enormous public housing project in 1964, and it was here that a massacre of students took place on October 2, 1968. In its center, unearthed Aztec ruins stand opposite the Church of Santiago and the monastery where, in 1553, the Franciscan Sahagún compiled the *Florentine Codex*.

Details of the Palacio de Bellas Artes

THE STAGE CURTAIN
The stage curtain in the opera and concert hall of the Palacio de Bellas Artes is made of multicolored glass pieces arranged to depict the volcanoes Popocatépetl and Ixtaccihuatl. It was designed by Dr Atl ● *94* and created by the Tiffany workshops in New York.

The Tenampa *cantina* on Plaza Garibaldi

Above: The Paseo de la Reforma, with Sebastián's *Caballito* (*left*) and the Stock Exchange (Centro Bursatil)(*right*)
Below: Independence Column, topped by a golden angel

Le Paseo de la Reforma ◆ I A1-B2-B3

To the west of the Alameda, the statue of the CABALLITO, a giant horse forged out of yellow steel by the sculptor Sebastián, marks the junction of Avenida Juárez with the Paseo de la Reforma. This broad promenade was laid by the Emperor Maximilian as a link from the Old City to Chapultepec Castle. Under Porfirio Díaz, it acquired gardens, fountains and statues of leading figures of the republic. A cluster of small hotels are vestiges of that era, now dwarfed by steel-and-glass skyscrapers. The huge traffic circles adorned with monuments are used as landmarks by tourists and locals alike: from east to west, EL CABALLITO, the statues of CHRISTOPHER COLUMBUS and AZTEC EMPEROR CUAUHTÉMOC, the INDEPENDENCE COLUMN, and the fountain of DIANA THE HUNTRESS (DIANA CAZADORA).

Basílica de Guadalupe

(*About 3 miles/5 km north of the Alameda, via the Paseo de la Reforma and the Calzada Misterios*) The top of Mount Tepeyac, on the north bank of the lake, was once the site of the sanctuary of the Aztecs' mother goddess, Tonantzin. It was here that the brown Virgin appeared to Juan Diego ▲ *146*, leaving her likeness imprinted on his tunic. The sacred image was put on display and venerated by the Indians, first in an oratory then, in 1709, in the first basilica (now deconsecrated). It is now set in the modern basilica built in 1976. A devotional path decorated with tiles leads to the top of the hill, where a chapel commemorates the apparition. It receives pilgrims from all over the country, who arrive in procession on the particular day allotted to their guild (taxi drivers, builders and so forth). On December 12, several million worshippers flock here for the Festival of La Guadalupe, which arouses many expressions of faith on the esplanade, particularly the dances of the *concheros* in Aztec costumes.

Insurgentes Norte ◆ I A1

When the Paseo de la Reforma reaches the statue of Cuauhtémoc, it crosses Avenida Insurgentes, a road over 30 miles (50 km) long that crosses the city and leads northward to the MONUMENTO A LA REVOLUCIÓN, a soaring copper dome on four pillars that forms a familiar silhouette on the horizon. Intended to be the central dome of the Legislative Palace commissioned by Porfirio Díaz, the metal structure of this enormous arch was left to rust until the 1930s, when it finally acquired its cladding, along with the sculptures that turned it into a monument to the Revolution. Beyond Av. Puente de Alvarado, on the left on Calle Orozco y Berra, there stands the bizarre-looking lacy metal structure, topped with two spikes, of the MUSEO DEL CHOPO, imported from Germany in 1900, now a hall for exhibitions and live music. Behind the Museo del Chopo, the Calle Dr Atl links up to the north with Santa María la Ribera, a peaceful old neighborhood surrounding a park with a pretty Moorish kiosk, on the corner of Calle Díaz Mirón.

La Zona Rosa ◆ I B2

To the south of its junction with the Paseo de la Reforma, Avenida Insurgentes runs alongside the Zona Rosa, a touristy neighborhood with pedestrian streets bordered by countless hotels, restaurants, bars with terraces, trendy boutiques and jewelry stores. It also has a crafts market, in Calle Londres (*near the crossroads with Calle Amberes*). One of the surviving villas from the 19th century, the former French Embassy is now the CASA DE FRANCIA (*Calle Havre, 8*). In the middle of the Zona Rosa, the Calle Genova runs from the Independence Column to the Insurgentes subway station, which marks the boundary between the Zona Rosa and the neighborhoods of Roma and Condesa.

THE BOOTBLACK ('EL BOLERO')
Whether seasoned professionals or young beginners, the *boleros* clean, wax and shine shoes with unrivaled dedication and meticulousness. When they set up shop outside hotels or on the corners of shopping streets, they provide a comfortable armchair, protected from the sun, and may even supply a newspaper and cigarettes. When the bootblack has no such

facilities, his clients remain standing, while he firmly plants their foot on his box of polishes and rapidly brings out the shine in their shoes.

EL CHOPO MARKET
On concert days, the *tiangui* – the street market selling records and T-shirts outside El Chopo – is a meeting place for punks and heavy metal fans.

▲ The Virgin of Guadalupe

The cult of the Virgin found fertile soil in New Spain. It appears in a number of different guises, but its most popular manifestation – and the one most representative of indigenous and Creole Mexico – is undoubtedly Our Lady of Guadalupe, which has absorbed the Virgins of los Remedios and Carmen, among others. La Guadalupe is a symbol of the entire country, marking the union between Christian devotion and Aztec earth-mother cults, and in particular that of the goddess Toci, who was once worshipped on the same spot where the Virgin's sanctuary was built.

THE APPARITION

The apparition on Mount Tepeyac was said to have occurred in 1531. According to legend, the Indian Juan Diego witnessed this sacred visitation and found a swath of Castilian roses and the image of the Virgin miraculously imprinted on his tunic (*tilma*). The cult of the Virgin of Guadalupe did not really take root until two centuries later, when it caused other images with less symbolic impact to fall out of fashion. Juan Diego was canonized during Pope John Paul II's visit to Mexico in 2002.

VIRGINAL ICONOGRAPHY

Guadalupe was first popularized by devotional images borne by pilgrims to the Tepeyac sanctuary, but she now also adorns domestic shrines, calendars and T-shirts. She is the indispensable lucky charm of all bus drivers, protecting them, for example, on dangerous mountain tracks. Her image can be seen in churches, chapels, ossuaries, oratories and at springs.

THE VIRGIN AS STANDARD BEARER

Among the Mexican emigrés and Chicanos ● *42* in the United States, the Virgin represents a transnational patriotism and is the foremost symbol of their Mexican identity.

THE FESTIVAL OF LA GUADALUPE

Every year, December 12 and the days leading up to it give rise to fervent devotion throughout the country, not to mention the grueling pilgrimages made by devotees, but the atmosphere is most intense at La Guadalupe's basilica, on Mount Tepeyac in Mexico City. Crowds converge on the sanctuary and stalls selling pious images spring up in the surrounding area. Traditional Indian dances are performed in their Christianized version – while, typically, Christian dances are presented in their Aztec version, as in the *palo volador* ▲ 193.

LA GUADALUPE IN THE INDIAN COSMOLOGY

The immense popularity of the cult of the Virgin of Guadalupe must be seen within the context of the cosmology of the Indians from Central Mexico, in which the Sun is contrasted with a range of lunar and earthly deities for which the Virgin has become the symbol. Hence her consolatory, cathartic and miraculous function, which she now shares with saints and Virgins of regional devotion, such as the Virgin of San Juan de los Lagos (Jalisco).

THE EMPEROR'S BATH

Chapultepec Wood was once famous for its springs, which provided the Aztec city with water. On the path going up the hill, engraved stones mark the spot where the Emperor Moctezuma came to bathe.

Chapultepec Wood

Beyond the traffic circle known as Diana Cazadora (the Huntress), the Paseo de la Reforma continues westward to Chapultepec ('the hill of crickets' in Nahuatl), where families from the city come on Sunday to visit the museums and the zoo, or to row on the lake.

CHAPULTEPEC CASTLE ◆ ❙ BC4. This fort, which stands on the top of a hill, was built in 1785 and has served as a residence for viceroys, the Emperor Maximilian (whose apartments are on display), Porfirio Díaz and, after the Revolution, all the presidents up to Lázaro Cárdenas, who turned it into the MUSEO NACIONAL DE HISTORIA in 1940. Its paintings and documents illustrate the colonial period, the struggle for independence and the Porfiriat. It also features

Street vendors on the shores of Lake Chapultepec

outstanding frescos by O'Gorman, Siqueiros and José Clemente Orozco. The sumptuous glassed gallery provides a view of the Paseo de la Reforma stretching to the city center.

MUSEO DE ARTE MODERNO ◆ ❙ B3. (*At the entrance to the park off the Paseo de la Reforma*) The Modern Art Museum is dedicated to 20th-century sculpture, photography and painting. Apart from temporary exhibitions of contemporary art, it also offers a fresh insight into the Muralists by way of their oil paintings (particularly portraits by Rivera, Orozco, Siqueiros and O'Gorman). The museum also owns paintings by José María Velasco, Dr Atl and Frida Kahlo, as well as photos by Manuel Alvárez Bravo.

MUSEO RUFINO TAMAYO ◆ ❙ B4. (*On the other side of the Paseo de la Reforma*) This was built in 1984 to display the collections built up by Tamayo ● *98, 102* as well as subsequent acquisitions. The fresco *La Raza*, on the right in the entrance, was painted by Tamayo himself. There are other works on display by Francis Bacon, Giorgio de Chirico, Salvador Dalí, Willem de Kooning, Jean Dubuffet, Max Ernst, Alberto Giacometti, Fernand Léger, René Magritte, Joan Miró, Victor Vasarely, Andy Warhol and Pablo Picasso.

Museo Nacional de Antropología ◆ I B4

On the right-hand side of the Paseo de la Reforma, the statue of the god Tlaloc heralds the Anthropology Museum, a marble palace designed in 1964 by the architect Ramírez Vázquez. Aztec culture has pride of place here.

SALA PRECLÁSICA. (1800 to 200 BC) This demonstrates the extent of the interrelationships between the cultures of the altiplano and the subtlety of their figurines, among them a man holding a dog, and a reclining woman with infants. The TOMB OF A TLATILCO SHAMAN, reproduced at the end of the room, yielded *The Acrobat*, a superb piece made of gray clay depicting a state of ecstasy and trance.

SALA TEOTIHUACANA. The period described as Classical (AD 300–900) was distinguished by the creation of cities, or

Reconstruction of a frieze from the Temple of Quetzalcóatl in Teotihuacán

MUSEO NACIONAL DE ANTROPOLOGÍA ★
A trip to this museum provides the perfect introduction to pre-Hispanic Mexico, but the breadth and richness of its collections can be overwhelming. It is advisable to visit (or return) after traveling elsewhere, with the benefit of your observations.

rather ceremonial centers. In the Teotihuacán room, monumental art makes a dramatic entrance via two reproductions – the FRIEZE FROM THE TEMPLE OF QUETZALCOÁTL and the Tlalocán Gate (an enclosure representing Paradise) – and, in the center of the room, the monolith of the goddess of water, Chalchiutlicue. Display cases show impeccable obsidian knives and a turquoise mask.

SALA TOLTECA. This opens on to the BLUE-GREEN FRESCOS OF CACAXTLA and the steles of Xochicalco. Tula, which inherited Teotihuacán, occupies center stage with a warrior-column (*atlante*) and a CHACMOOL ▲ 245. On the right, before the exit, a delicate coyote head, made with a mosaic of mother-of-pearl, holds a human mask in its mouth.

SALA MEXICA. An ocelot made of black stone guards the imposing Tenochtitlán room and, on the building's axis, the AZTEC CALENDAR, discovered in 1790 during construction work in the Zócalo, with COATLICUE, the goddess of serpents, to its left. The fresco showing the lake city, with models of the Templo Mayor and the Tlatelolco Market, effectively conjures up the splendors of the period. The perfect sculpture of a gourd, a jar in the form of a rabbit,

▲ Mexico City
Museo Nacional de Antropología

ETHNOGRAPHIC FLOOR
The first floor of the museum is devoted to a reconstruction of the current lifestyle of sixty Indian peoples from Mexico.

Above: the 'Piedra de Sol' Aztec calendar
Below: the goddess of corn

figurines of old men and the face of a drunk with red coral eyes all evoke the everyday life of the Aztecs. To the right of the exit, there are gold jewels – the few that escaped the clutches of the *conquistadores* – a copy of the headdress that Moctezuma sent Cortés (who passed it on to Carlos V), and a monkey vase of polished obsidian of breathtaking purity.

SALA OAXACA. The STELES OF DANCERS reveal the Olmec influence on Monte Albán. A CLAY JAGUAR and a delicate JADEITE MASK OF THE BAT GOD illustrate Zapotec art. The Mixtecs, or Nusabi ('people of the clouds'), drew up codices recording their lineages, worked with bronze, gold, amber, jet and alabaster (a serpent-head vase with three feet), and played music: here are *teponaztli* (wooden drum with vibrating strips), a water whistle in the form of a coyote, and a flute carved out of a femur. The weaponry on display is a reminder that they were also warriors.

SALA GOLFO DE MÉXICO. Olmec culture presents some mysteries, as the COLOSSAL HEAD from La Venta has African features and the STATUE OF A WRESTLER looks Asian. The influence of this mother culture extends from the Totonacs of El Tajín to the Huastecs of the North (statue of an adolescent boy, alabaster monkey vase). The figurine of a dog with rollers is astonishing, as it is the product of a world that did not use the wheel.

SALA MAYA. This contains the STELES from Palenque that allowed us to decipher Mayan writing, the engraved LINTELS of Yaxchilán and the superb CEREMONIAL DISKS incrusted with turquoise from Chichén Itzá. The figurines include a turkey, an iguana, an old man emerging from a snail and another from a flower. The garden displays a reproduction of the multicolored temple of Bonampak. In the basement, there is the magnificent SARCOPHAGUS OF KING PAKAL, just as Alberto Ruiz discovered it in 1952.

SALA CULTURAS DEL NORTE. This room chronicles exchanges between hunter-gatherer nomads and the sedentary farmers, who mixed with the Toltecs. Here you will find painted textiles, a double-faced vase, copper disks and mother-of-pearl necklaces.

SALA CULTURAS DEL OCCIDENTE. This room offers recent discoveries: the presence of the Olmecs in

Guerrero, and the importance of the Tarascs of Michoacán and the Amazi, a frontier people similar to the Navajo.

Casa Museo Luis Barragán ◆ I C5

(Calle Francisco Ramírez, 14. To the south of the park.) The home and studio of Luis Barragán ● *90*, built in 1947 and listed by UNESCO as a world heritage site in 2004, is well worth a detour. The architecture of this 'house-clock' crystallizes the meeting of time and volume. Following the principle of pre-Columbian monuments, Barragán aligned the building so that the sun would create interplays of light and shade at precise moments. According to the angle of its rays, the colors vibrate, the water in the pond reflects or glimmers, the openings in the thick walls are lit or muffled and the bare terrace turns into an abstract painting. Stretches of yellow highlight the geometric angles and set off the paintings specially created for the building, such as the golden monochromes by Mathias Goeritz.

Below: roof terrace of the Casa Museo Luis Barragán

CASA MUSEO LUIS BARRAGÁN ★ Unmissable for anybody with the slightest interest in modern Mexican architecture, this unique sanctuary can only be visited by appointment.

▲ Mexico City
The Colonias Roma and Condesa

Colonia Roma, left to right and top to bottom:
Av. Álvaro Obregón, 163; Calle Flora, 3; Av. Valladolid, 31; Calle Querétaro, 109

THE COLONIAS ROMA AND CONDESA ★
An architectural laboratory, with well-spaced neighborhoods, ideal for strolling and very fashionable (see the bars and restaurants on Avenida Michoacán).

THE UPS AND DOWNS OF TINA MODOTTI
An Italian immigrant in California, a Hollywood starlet, and a nude model for photographer Edward Weston, Tina Modotti dazzled the Mexico City of the 1920s with her audacity, and with the fervor of her commitment to the anti-Fascist cause. In 1929, after the murder of her lover Julio Mella, the newspapers dragged her through the mud and in 1931 she was expelled from Mexico for her Communist allegiances. She went on to become an undercover Stalinist agent in the Spanish Civil War, but returned to Mexico City in 1938 as 'Camarada María', remaining faithful to her convictions ● 39.

The Colonia Roma ◆ I C2

Av. Álvaro Obregón moves away from Av. Insurgentes to penetrate eastward into the Roma neighborhood. On the right, after Calle Monterrey, an old market, the PASAJE PARIÁN, stands out on account of its pinnacles and stucco heads of devils. The neighborhood boomed in the 19th century, as evidenced by the luxurious houses (originally country homes), such as the CASA LAMM, at no. 99. Later on, the emergence of reinforced concrete led to a proliferation of *vecindades* (apartments built around a patio) with original, cleverly designed forms; small houses from the 1930s and 1940s can also be seen – modest jewels of art deco decorated in pink, green and blue. Avenida Álvaro Obregón crosses lively shopping streets, including the Calle Orizaba, which opens on to two charming squares, the PLAZA RIO DE JANEIRO and the PLAZA LUIS CABRERA. An old house in this shady street was home to William Burroughs and acted as a magnet for members of the Beat Generation in 1951.

The Colonia Condesa ◆ I C3

In the late 1920s, the *hacienda* belonging to the Countess of Escandón was divided into plots, giving rise to this elegant neighborhood the other side of Avenida Insurgente. Six streets to the south of Avenida Álvaro Obregón, Calle Michoacán leads westward to the PARQUE MÉXICO, the *hacienda*'s old hippodrome, surrounded by the double oval of Calles Amsterdam and México. The property developers of the time conceived this park, dotted with palms, jacarandas and bougainvilleas, as an Eden reserved for the new leisured classes. Its Greek-cum-Hollywood porticos, adorned with friezes and multicolored cement statues, lead to the open-air Lindbergh Theater, inaugurated by the aviator after his Atlantic crossing in 1927. Calle México, to the north of the park on the right, leads to the Basurto building, a daring futuristic creation from the 1930s, then on to the Modernist

Mexico City ▲
Coyoacán

Colonia Condesa, left to right and top to bottom:
Parque México; Av. Nuevo León; Plaza Popocatépetl; Av. México, 63; Av. Amsterdam, 154

fountain in PLAZA POPOCATÉPETL. To the east of Parque
México, Calle Parras crosses the PARQUE ESPAÑA and runs
into Avenida Veracruz. At no. 42, on the corner of Calle
Tampico, stands the house where Tina Modotti lived and
produced much of her work; its triangular shape and round
windows led her to christen it 'El Barco'. In 1924, its roof
terrace provided the backdrop for Edward Weston's nude
pictures of her, which caused a scandal in Mexican society.

Coyoacán ◆ H

(*About 5 miles/8 km to the south of the historic center*) Once a
village on the southern shore of the lake, Coyoacán has now
been swallowed up by the city. Cortés withdrew to this spot
the day after the Conquest.
PLAZA CENTRAL ◆ Z Z0. With its theaters, restaurants and
galleries, this square is a permanent cultural attraction. The
building in which Cortés tortured Cuauhtémoc to get him to
hand over his imagined hidden treasure stands here. To the
south, the PARROQUIA DE SAN JUAN BAUTISTA (16th c.)
and its monastery overlook the JARDÍN CENTENARIO.

**SOUVENIRS OF
CORTÉS AND LA
MALINCHE**
Calle Higuera, to the
east of the Zócalo,
leads to the CASA DE
LA MALINCHE, at no.
57, on the corner of
the Plaza de la
Conchita, which also
boasts a delightful
baroque chapel of the
Conception. To the
west of the Zócalo,
Calle Francisco Sosa
leads to a square
enlivened by the
bright yellow Church
of Santa Catarina. At
the end of the street,
on the corner of
Avenida Universidad,
the CHAPEL built by
Cortés is tucked away
on the bank of an old
canal.

COYOACÁN ★
The friendly market
that takes over the
main square of
Coyoacán on Sunday
is ideal for a
weekend stroll.

San Ángel and the University City

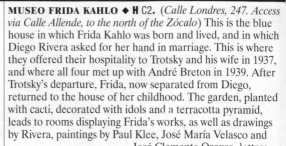

Below: Museo Frida Kahlo
Opposite top: Plaza San Jacinto, garden of the church cloisters
Opposite bottom: fresco by Siqueiros in the UNAM

MUSEO SOUMAYA ◆ **H** A3 (*Plaza Loreto, to the south of San Ángel, on the corner of Avenidas Revolución and Río Magdalena*) The museum, founded by the owner of the Telmex corporation, has seventy works by Rodin, and paintings by Renoir, Matisse, Degas and Tamayo.

MUSEO FRIDA KAHLO ◆ **H** C2. (*Calle Londres, 247. Access via Calle Allende, to the north of the Zócalo*) This is the blue house in which Frida Kahlo was born and lived, and in which Diego Rivera asked for her hand in marriage. This is where they offered their hospitality to Trotsky and his wife in 1937, and where all four met up with André Breton in 1939. After Trotsky's departure, Frida, now separated from Diego, returned to the house of her childhood. The garden, planted with cacti, decorated with idols and a terracotta pyramid, leads to rooms displaying Frida's works, as well as drawings by Rivera, paintings by Paul Klee, José María Velasco and

José Clemente Oroxco, letters, photos and pre-Hispanic objects. The décor is completed by the Indian costumes Frida loved so much, along with her *judas* (giant dummies) and *piñatas* ● 51. The old-fashioned kitchen gives on to the dining room, where she installed two grandfather clocks, one stopped at the time of her divorce with Diego in 1939, the other at that of their remarriage in late 1940. The staircase, decorated with 2,000 naive

ANAHUACALLI (*2 miles/3 km south of Coyoacán*) This unsettling pyramid of black volcanic rock designed by Diego Rivera served as his last studio, and it was here that he decided to display his archeological relics and modern art collection. The first floor has four Aztec sculptures: the gods of wind (Ehecatl), rain (Tlaloc) and fire (Huehueteótl), and the goddess of corn (Xilonen).The second floor contains Rivera's work tools, his charcoal studies for his murals, several of his oil paintings – including the portrait he left uncompleted on his death in 1957 – and figurines from Jalisco, Michoacán, Nayarit and Colima; the next story presents masks and terracotta pieces, while the view from the roof terrace takes in the southern part of the Mexico Valley.

commemorative, metal plaques, goes up to her bedroom and her studio, where her wheelchair remains in front of her easel, complete with her unfinished portrait of Stalin.

MUSEO DE TROTSKI ◆ **H** C2. (*Calle Viena*) After breaking off relations with Rivera, Trotsky moved two streets farther north in 1939. The former head of the Red Army, ever watchful, had chosen this site because of the protection provided to the rear by the Churubusco River. The waterway has since been covered by Avenida Churubusco, and it is from there that visitors enter the museum. Here, time seems to have stood still. The windows are shuttered, the lookout posts remain intact on the corners. Documents and photos bear witness to the everyday life of the militants around Trotsky in this fortified villa. The walls of the bedroom bear the marks of the attack on him by Siqueiros, the muralist, disguised as a policeman. In the office lie newspapers dated August 20, 1940, the day on which Stalin's envoy, Ramón Mercader, killed Trotsky with a blow from an icepick.

San Ángel ◆ **H**

(*About 2 miles/3.5 km west of Coyoacán, via Avenida Miguel Ángel de Quevedo*) On Avenida Revolución, the CONVENTO DEL CARMEN, with its massive 17th-century vaults, is famous for the mummies on display in its crypt. To the right, Calle Madero, paved with shingle, rises between the old stone façades toward the PLAZA SAN JACINTO, the site of the Bazar del Sábado, the Saturday souvenir market. On the right, at no. 15, the 17th-century CASA DEL RISCO is laid out around an elegant fountain. At the back of the square, the garden of the CHURCH AND CLOISTER OF SAN JACINTO invites passersby to take time out.

CASA ESTUDIO DIEGO RIVERA ◆ H A2. (*From Av. Revolución, take Calle Altavista*) On his return from the US in the early 1930s, Rivera built identical functional studios, for himself and for Frida Kahlo, suspended above the trees and linked by a walkway. Some of his canvases are on show, along with his pre-Hispanic figurines and two *judas*, brightly colored papier-mâché dummies.

The University ◆ **H** AB3

The Ciudad Universitaria is the biggest campus in Latin America. Built in the 1950s on the lava deposits of El Pedregal de San Ángel, the National Autonomous University of Mexico (UNAM) is a town in its own right, with over 300,000 students, teachers and employees and around one hundred buildings spread over 990 acres (400 ha). In the FACULTY OF SCIENCES, Chávez Morado is responsible for both the glass mosaic in the auditorium, *The Conquest of Energy*, and the fresco in the courtyard, *The Return of Quetzalcóatl*. The FACULTY OF MEDICINE is decorated with mosaics of pre-Columbian inspiration by Francisco Eppens Helguera, while the south wall of the RECTORATE TOWER, built by the architect Mario Pani, is adorned by a fresco in relief, created by Siqueiros ● *96*.

A TRULY AUTONOMOUS UNIVERSITY
The statute of the UNAM, granted in 1929, declares it an autonomous territory – although this did not prevent the repression of the protest movement in 1968. Ever since it was founded, the UNAM has applied the principle of free education. In 1999, the dean attempted to introduce enrollment fees. The ensuing strike lasted a year and resulted in a revocation of this policy. In the spring of 2000, the police raided the campus at dawn and put an end to the strike by arresting a thousand students.

Bottom: *Self-portrait as a Tehuana* (*Diego on my mind*), 1943
Opposite top: *Henry Ford Hospital*, 1932
Opposite center: *The Embrace of the Universe, the Earth (Mexico), Diego, Me and Sr. Xólotl*, 1949
Opposite bottom: *The Shattered Spine*, 1944

The work of Frida Kahlo (1907–54) is inextricably linked to the painful destiny that governed her life. Stricken by polio as a child, and seriously injured in a bus accident at the age of 18, she saw painting as a sublimation of suffering. Her life, punctuated by operations and spells in hospital, interspersed with fruitful periods marked by traveling, was transcended by the love and creativity that prevented her from succumbing to madness or suicide. Although, in the midst of this never-ending torment, her relationship with Diego Rivera enriched her both as a woman and as an artist, it was her strong personality that forged a body of work imbued with fantasy. Self-portraits were the dominant element, but they were complemented by small paintings that are like autobiographical tales, evoking, through metaphor, her blood ties with the earth, her pride in her Mexican identity, her mutilated body, her frustration at not being able to have children and her love for Diego.

DIEGO RIVERA, A LOVE WITHOUT LIMITS
Although her love for the painter Diego Rivera – whom she met in 1922, married in 1929, divorced in 1939 and remarried in 1940 – was at the center of her life and work, Frida Kahlo did not hide her attraction to other men (including Trotsky) and also to women. The relationship between Frida and Diego was chaotic but deeply marked by an emotion on her part that combined daughterly love, friendship and passion. Frida saw Diego – her senior by 21 years – as the incarnation of a strong, protective Mexico as much as an unfailing support in her worst moments of doubt and despair.

A DISTINCTIVE SENSE OF FANTASY

In Frida Kahlo's painting, the discordant juxtaposition of different objects and images is the basis for an intellectual and iconographic world that parallels the mental and visual landscape of the Surrealists – Breton said that her art was like 'a ribbon around a bomb'. Frida Kahlo herself rejected any affiliation with Surrealism, however. Her fondness for Mexican popular art, along with the passion that she shared with Rivera for commemorative plaques and pre-Columbian art, takes her painting into the realm of a distinctively Mexican form of fantasy.

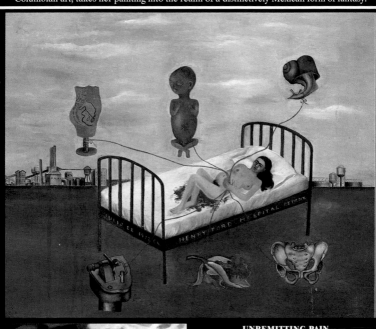

UNREMITTING PAIN

Frida Kahlo's physical suffering was permanent, but she used her everyday experience of pain as food for her painting. Whether viewed as a kind of art therapy or as exhibitionist autobiography, her creativity was both an outlet for the burdens of her tragic destiny and an inner space in which she could crystalize her obsessions. Her autobiographical or fantastic images, which were often distinguished by a raw realism, tell stories but also transcend the pain she always had to endure.

THE ICON OF MEXICAN IDENTITY

In an age when a number of artists and intellectuals of the Mexican avant-garde were looking toward Paris, the Rivera-Kahlo partnership developed a social and cultural life within a strongly local context, valuing both the art of the past and contemporary Indian life. With her clothes borrowed from the women of Oaxaca and Chiapas, her extravagant hairdos bedecked with flowers and ribbons and her jewelry (whether antique or of pre-Columbian inspiration), Frida Kahlo continually emphasized her Mexican identity by cultivating a seductiveness that perhaps allowed her to transcend the pain of her everyday life.

Xochimilco ◆ G B3

MUSEO DOLORES OLMEDO.
From the Taxqueña subway station, take the *tren ligero* to La Noria station. Two streets from there, on the Antiguo Camino a Xochimilco, the Museo Dolores Olmedo is a beautiful 16th-century *hacienda*, once occupied by a close friend of Diego Rivera, and it exhibits the 137 works that she bought from him – the largest collection of his paintings anywhere. Also on show are pre-Columbian pieces and the silver dining set of the Emperor Maximilian, as well as 25 paintings by Frida Kahlo and 43 by the painter Angelina Beloff.

THE CANALS OF XOCHIMILCO. (*17 miles/28 km from the center via the Calzada de Tlalpan or via the tren ligero from Taxqueña subway station*) From the central square, facing the 16th-century Church of San Bernardino, Calle 16 de Septiembre leads southward to a market with plants, flowers and pottery. The landing stages are 440 yards (400 m) from the market, via Calle Galeana. The boats, decorated with paper flowers, go down the main canal and its offshoots, past *chinampas* (floating market gardens) anchored to the silt by the poplar trees reflected in the still waters. Dolores del Río paddled here in a classic of the golden age of Mexican movies, *María Candelaria* ● *60*. The boats' passengers soon attract other vessels: orchestra boats loaded with mariachis or marimba players, a photography boat, a canoe with a rose seller, a floating kitchen with pans bubbling on hotplates. This favorite haunt of Mexican families at festival times also represents a return to their roots, a living image of the old lakeside culture on this last vestige of Lake Xochimilco.

MUSEO DOLORES OLMEDO ★
Although this museum is off the beaten track, the charming house and fascinating collections fully justify the time spent getting there.

CUICUILCO PYRAMID
(*Avenida Insurgentes, at the junction with the ring road*) The oldest pyramid in Mexico City and the only round one (442 ft/135 m in diameter) bears witness to the Olmec presence in the valley several centuries before Tenochtitlán. The statues that have been unearthed from recent architectural digs are on display in the small museum.

The central plateau (around Mexico City)

▲ The central plateau (around Mexico City)

1. Teotihuacán and the
   surrounding area
   ▲ 162
2. North of Mexico City
   ▲ 167
3. The monastery route
   ▲ 172
4. Southwest of
   Mexico City ▲ 174

**EL NEVADO DE
TOLUCA**
From this volcano
(14,954 ft/4,558 m)
there is a stunning
view of the Anáhuac
volcanoes and the
mountains of
Michoacán. (*RF 134
heading to Tejupilco.
In Santiago, turn left
on to Route 3. After
the barrier, a track [out
of bounds in fog]
climbs to the peak.*)

Below: the volcanoes Popocatépetl and Ixtaccihuatl
stand guard over the Anáhuac Valley

After the overthrow of the Aztec Empire, the agricultural system was severely disrupted. The *hacienda* made its first appearance around Tenochtitlán, but the Spanish quickly understood that, in order to feed the city, they had to intensify farming and extend it to several climatic zones. This need gave rise to small colonial towns, clustered around the *haciendas* and their churches.

THE STATE OF MEXICO. The state occupies most of the belt and encircles practically all of Mexico City. Its many fertile valleys, rivers and mountains of 6,000 to 18,000 feet (1,800–5,400 m) have endowed it with a pleasant, healthy climate and made it popular for getaways from the city. Four massifs give the region its special character: El Nevado de Toluca (14,954 ft/4,558 m), Popocatépetl and Ixtaccihuatl (17,887 ft/5,452 m and 17,343 ft/5.286 m, respectively) and, to the southeast, the Monte Alto and the Monte Bajo, the capital's green lungs. The state's 12 million inhabitants mainly live in the industrial cities of Toluca, Satélite, Tlanepantla, Naucalpan, Cuautitlán Izcalli and Ecatepec. Although Toluca is still separated from Mexico City by a few acres of forest, the other towns have been absorbed into the megalopolis. The state was long known as the country's main silver-producing province ▲ *178*, thanks to the fabulous mines of Temascaltepec, El Oro, Zacualpan and, on the foothills of the Sierra Madre Oriental, Real del Monte. Its current prosperity, however, is derived from the economic growth of the capital. It is at once the market garden of the Distrito Federal, the dormitory of the middle classes and the headquarters of thousands of industries and businesses, whose taxes bring in substantial revenue.

THE LEGEND OF THE VOLCANOES
A young army captain and the princess Xochiquetzal fell in love. Her father promised him her hand on condition that he brought him the head of his cruelest enemy. Several years later, the captain, with the enemy's head on his spear, set out to claim his bride. Meanwhile, the father, giving him up for lost, had married Xochiquetzal to another, and she had died of a broken heart. The desolate captain had an enormous mountain built, facing the sun. He laid the body of his loved one on the summit, covered it with white flowers and lit a censer. Ever since, Popocatépetl ('the crouching warrior') has been watching Ixtaccihuatl ('the sleeping woman')…

▲ The central plateau Teotihuacán

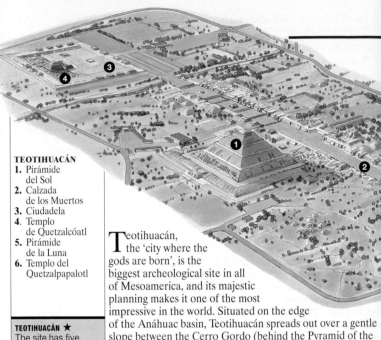

TEOTIHUACÁN ★
The site has five entrances, each one with its own parking lot. If you come by bus from Mexico City, it is advisable to enter by Gate 1 (south) and leave by Gate 3 (north) to catch the return bus. Another way of reaching your vehicle is by boarding the small train that connects the main points of interest.

THE 'TALUD-TABLERO'
This decorative architectural feature, widespread in the Mesoamerica of the Ancient Classical era (AD 300–600), is part of the tiered arrangement of a pyramid: a wall in the form of an embankment (*talud*) is topped by a vertical wall delimited by projecting edges (*tablero*) ● 74.

Teotihuacán, the 'city where the gods are born', is the biggest archeological site in all of Mesoamerica, and its majestic planning makes it one of the most impressive in the world. Situated on the edge of the Anáhuac basin, Teotihuacán spreads out over a gentle slope between the Cerro Gordo (behind the Pyramid of the Moon) and the Cerro de Patlachique. The dry San Juan riverbed crosses the site alongside the Ciudadela. (*Leave Mexico City via Insurgentes Norte. A 32-mile/50-km trip on the freeway.*)

History

We know little about Teotihuacán, the people who lived there or the language they spoke. Archeologists distinguish three periods: Teotihuacán I (200 BC–AD 1) is characterized as the Age of Obsidian. Teotihuacán II (AD 1–350) saw the construction of the pyramids and the Temple of Quetzalcóatl. At its apogee, Teotihuacán III (350–750), it boasted 200,000 inhabitants and occupied 20 sq. miles (50 sq. km), making it the biggest city in the world. The city was divided into neighborhoods occupied by thousands of craftsmen drawn from remote provinces. At this time, Teotihuacán's outreach extended as far as Guatemala, but it seems that the city, which was a peaceful and militarily vulnerable theocracy, had great problems in resisting invaders from the north. Then, around 600, Teotihuacán was ravaged by a catastrophic fire, which triggered its decline; in a way it never fully recovered from the disaster. Between 650 and 750, the city mysteriously disintegrated and the sanctuaries visited by pilgrims and traders from all over Mesoamerica were destroyed. A whole world vanished, and the shockwave was so strong that other thriving settlements, such as Cantona ▲ 190, disappeared in its wake, giving rise to a general economic collapse. Fortified towns sprung up and new centers such as Cholula, Tula and Xochicalco took on an increasing importance. There was a proliferation of warrior gods and human sacrifices. We know that between 1350 and 1521 the Mexicas, better known as the Aztecs, came to Teotihuacán every three weeks to worship the old gods. When the Spanish passed through, after the episode of the Noche Triste ● *33*, they saw only hills covered with earth. It was not until after the 1910 Revolution that the ethno-archeologist Manuel Gamio unearthed the pyramids of the sleeping city; they have since become a symbol of Mexican identity.

The site ◆ **D** B2

THE MUSEUM. (*Enter by the central gate [no. 1] and cross the width of the site.*) A large model of the site, set under a glass floor, offers a superb overview and provides a good general introduction to the history of Teotihuacán.

THE PYRAMID OF THE SUN. This rests on a base measuring 728 by 738 feet (222 by 225 m) and stands 213 feet (65 m) high (for reference, Kheops measures 459 ft). A staircase of 242 steps and five landings leads to the top, which was undoubtedly once crowned with a temple and perhaps even a soaring stone statue. This pyramid, built using the talud-tablero technique, is not a necropolis and so has no tombs inside. At its base, a small iron door at the foot of the central staircase

THE CREATION OF THE FIFTH SUN
The gods met in Teotihuacán to decide which of them would be the Fifth Sun, as the four previous worlds had been destroyed by terrible natural catastrophes. Tecuciztécal, the Lord of the Snails, and Nanahuatzin the Pustular were chosen for the sacrifice. The former represented the exaltation of beauty, the latter imperfection and ugliness. They both wanted to be the Fifth Sun but, to achieve this goal, they first had to purify themselves by jumping into the cosmic fire. Tecuciztécal tried four times to immolate himself but fear held him back every time. Seeing this hesitation, Nanahuatzin the Pustular leapt straight into the brazier, quickly followed by the Lord of the Snails. The Pustular became the Sun and Tecuciztécal, the Moon. The gods, irritated by the latter's indecision, threw a rabbit in his face so that the moon would not shine as brightly as the day star. The Fifth Sun is due to come to an end in December 2012.

The Square of the Moon, at the foot of the Pyramid of the Moon

▲ The central plateau Teotihuacán

Below: the Way of the Dead

PRIESTS AND WARRIORS
The Ciudadela was the center of political and religious power. Thirteen skeletons, presumed to be of priests, were found here with their teeth encrusted with jade and their hands and feet tied, along with 113 other skeletons, thought to be of warriors, with

opens on to a tunnel 328 feet (100 m) long (discovered in 1971) that leads to a cavity in the form of a four-leaf clover with a gushing spring. This womblike symbol of creation lies exactly perpendicular to the summit of the pyramid. The archeologist Ruben Cabrera, the leader of the Teotihuacán project, is investigating the site's underground network to try to decipher its importance in the ceremonial complex. A subterranean tour will soon be available to the public.
CALZADA DE LOS MUERTOS. The Way of the Dead (*2½ miles/4 km long and 148 ft/45 m wide*) is the main axis, leading north to the Pyramid of the Moon and south to the Ciudadela. Remains of sculptures and polychrome stucco

pendants made of coyote teeth and bones around their heads.

suggest that it was entirely colored red, yellow, green and blue. Clay reproductions hawked by vendors fall far short of evoking the likely reality of the scene: thronged with people, with each building bearing a small temple with a palm-leaf roof, sheltering a priest sitting cross-legged, fanned by slaves
CIUDADELA. (*Follow the road southward and pass in front of the Viking group.*) The area known as the Citadel is a huge quadrilateral with sides 1,312 feet (400 m) long, a veritable fortress embedded in the ground, reached by a single staircase on the western façade. The Ciudadela can be circled by following the ring road to the left. It is immediately apparent that power was concentrated here: the left side of the quadrilateral contained the military headquarters and warriors' barracks, while the right held the spacious lodgings of dignitaries. In between, the TEMPLO DE QUETZALCÓATL is preceded by a large esplanade, also accessible via the western staircase. This pyramid, currently closed for excavations, is hidden by another pyramid half as old which you must climb to admire the sloping expanse of the other one. This is adorned with superb sculptures featuring two alternating motifs: a serpent with its head surrounded by a necklace of petals and feathers, and a body decorated with shells, symbolizing water; and a mask representing the god of storms (the ancestor of Tlaloc, the Aztec god of rain).

ROMANTIC RUINS
The magnificent view from the top of the Pyramid of the Moon has inspired numerous artists, including the landscape painter José María Velasco ● 95, who was moved to produce huge works on the subject even before the first digs had been undertaken.

Below: the Pyramid of the Moon
Bottom: bas-relief depicting Quetzalcóatl on a
pillar in the Palacio del Quetzalpapalotl

PYRAMID OF THE MOON. This provides the best vantage point for admiring the Pyramid of the Sun. Although the latter is higher, the two peaks are at the same altitude due to a slight slope (the Pyramid of the Moon measures 151 feet/ 46 m). Major excavations are currently in progress and, contrary to received wisdom, they have revealed a necropolis. The digs undertaken by the archeologist Ruben Cabrera since 1998 have brought to light several funeral chambers with sumptuous offerings, such as obsidian knives and a jade masque of Mayan origin (to the bewilderment of the experts). In 2004, however, the discovery of an offering consisting of sacrificed children, puma bones and various

THE NEW AGE IN
TEOTIHUACÁN
On March 21, over a
million people from
all over Mexico
congregate in
Teotihuacán, dressed
in white, to celebrate
the festival of the
spring equinox.
They climb the
Pyramid of the Sun,
which is considered
to be endowed with
energy comparable to

obsidian objects suggests that the tomb of a senior dignitary is hidden somewhere under the Pyramid of the Moon. Unearthing such graves is proving a complicated task: once the corpse had been placed inside with its offerings, the funeral chamber was completely filled with earth, to prevent pillagers from profaning it. At the foot of the pyramid, the large, symmetrically proportioned SQUARE OF THE MOON, with an altar in the middle and several four-story platforms around it, is proof of a highly sophisticated approach to city planning.

that of Lhasa, Tibet.
This ceremony is
accompanied by the
dances of the neo-
Indians ● 46.

PALACIO DEL QUETZALPAPALOTL. The Palace of Quetzal-Butterfly, on the west side of the Square of the Moon, was a residence for high priests. Its staircase is decorated with serpents' heads, while its courtyard reveals sculpted pillars encrusted with obsidian. A tunnel leads to one of the oldest parts of Teotihuacán, the PLUMED SNAIL STRUCTURE, replete with astonishing bas-reliefs of green parrots. The middle building is the PALACIO DE LOS JAGUARES, where fragments of frescos show jaguars with human heads blowing into shells (a pictogram representing music).

TEPEXPAN MAN
The State of Mexico can be considered the country's oldest population center, as it is close to the Sierra Tlachique (6 miles/10 km from Teotihuacán), where the 12,000-year-old Tepexpan Man was found. A small museum has been built on the spot, 2½ miles (4 km) from the Acolman Monastery, where the fossilized remains of this man, aged about 55, were discovered. He would have hunted mammoths in the swamps of the Anáhuac Valley long before the emergence of agriculture.

The area around Teotihuacán

CONVENTO AGUSTINO DE ACOLMAN ◆ D B2.
(*Turning after 6 miles/10 km, on the way back to Mexico City*)
This fortified 16th-century church has undergone many transformations over the centuries, resulting in an extraordinary juxtaposition of styles. Its splendid façade, typical of the Plateresque style, is marked by the contribution of indigenous craftsmen (floral motifs). The altarpieces on the lower left side of the Gothic nave opt for Churrigueresque baroque, while the frescos of Spanish inspiration were undoubtedly based on models brought by friars from the Old Continent. The columns in the Renaissance cloister bear sculpted plant motifs – another example of the indigenous influence. The impact of Spanish Roman art is also evident in the way in which the doors are framed by broad carved stones. A beautiful Renaissance CROSS with a pre-Columbian feel stands opposite the atrium.
CHAPINGO ◆ D B2. (*2 miles [3 km] southeast of Texcoco*)
On the campus of the autonomous university of Chapingo, in the grounds of a 19th-century *hacienda*, the Escuela de Agricultura (agricultural school) hides, amidst a clump of high trees, a CHAPEL decorated with superb frescos by Diego Rivera (1923–25) ● *100. The Song of the Earth* is the best known. On the right-hand side, the famous muralist traced

Above and above right: the Acolman Monastery

the biological evolution of human life; this is complemented by an exploration of historical and social development on the opposite wall. The two come together in a large frontal composition showing Man as the master of socioeconomic development. Other frescos decorate the school's patios and staircases, including the Burial of the Revolutionaries Emiliano Zapata and Otilio Montaño: their bodies convey the vigor of their legendary exploits to the crops, and the light of their spirits brightens the petals of a fiery sunflower.

Interior of the Church of
San Francisco Javier

**THE INTERIOR OF
THE CHURCH OF SAN
FRANCISCO JAVIER ★**
This summit of Jesuit
baroque art in
Mexico is guaranteed
to take your breath
away...

The road that leads north of the capital toward Tula passes the extraordinary monastery complex of Tepotzotlán, before reaching the Mezquite Valley: semidesert landscapes dotted with gray-green agaves, which the Aztecs used to make *pulque* ▲ *325.*

Tepotzotlán ◆ **D** A2

(8 miles/13 km from Mexico City, on the Querétaro road. Turn right just before the toll booth and continue under the bridge.) In the 16th century, Franciscans and Augustinians were intent on evangelizing and instructing the Indians, while the Jesuits concentrated on training the elite of New Spain and promoting a Creole clergy with a high intellectual level. To do this, they created a network of twenty-two schools, richly endowed with buildings and land by the owners of the major silver mines. These schools taught Nahuatl, Spanish and theology, along with geography, cartography, ethnology, botany and architecture. The four most important schools were in Mexico City, Morelia, Zacatecas and Tepotzotlán. Tepotzotlán, founded in 1582 (but not finished until 1682), now contains the Church of San Francisco Javier, a museum of colonial art in the old school and a domestic chapel. The buildings – most built in the 17th and 18th century – cover a surface area of 645,000 sq. feet (60,000 sq. m). The interior and exterior decorations of the church are a matchless example of *estípite* baroque ● *82*, and it has not been subject to any modifications since the expulsion of the Jesuits in 1767. Seven years later, it was converted into an ecclesiastical reformatory. Since 1964, this jewel of Mexican baroque has housed the National Museum of New Spain.

**THE MEXICAN ART
OF FEATHER
DECORATION**
The ancient art
of ornamentation
with feathers was
discovered by the
Spanish during
the course of the
Conquest, and went
on to find great
success in Europe.
It was widely used by
the Catholic Church
throughout the
colonial period. The
feathers were usually
tied or glued;
although the former
technique is common
in the Americas, the
latter is almost
exclusively confined
to Mexico. Feathers
are cut with rigorous
precision, assembled
and then glued to
create veritable
mosaics. The feather
decoration of colonial
Mexico was the
epitome of mestizo
art, as it combined
indigenous techniques
with Western
iconography. Some
sixty feather
compositions can still
be seen in various
parts of the world.
The Tepotzotlán
church contains a
Christ Pantocrator
created with this
technique.

The evangelizing friars founded art and craft schools in Indian villages to respond to the need for images of Christianity. It was here that the 'natives' discovered European artists and traditions, but they also preserved some of their own traditions, which they adapted to new subjects and new uses. The Indians had mastered techniques and materials unheard of in Europe, such as feather mosaics and sculpture with paste made from corn stems; the Europeans, for their part, brought metal tools and printing equipment. At the same time, artists and craftsmen settled in the cities, where they formed European-style guilds. As in the rest of Iberian America, they developed their own versions of European styles, with the support of the clergy and the leading Creole families. Toward the end of the 17th century, and even more so in the 18th century, a host of secular subjects – events, portraits, landscapes, local objects and characters – began to supplement the predominantly religious iconography. The Royal Academy of San Carlos, founded in Mexico City in 1785, was the last artistic endowment that Spain made to its colony.

SCULPTURE
Just like oil painting, the sculpting of figures in gilded or multicolored wood was something new to the indigenous population. In only a few generations, however, a large part of the production was in the hands of autochthonous studios. The solemnity of the Renaissance gave way, in the 17th century, to figures with angular drapery and expansive poses. In the 18th century, the clothing took on a greater fluidity, while the movements of the body became more complex and the proportions more elongated. Although most of the sculptures decorating the colonial altars were gilded and multicolored, the most important cultural figures were dressed with real clothes from the 16th century on, and in the 18th century some were specifically adapted to wear clothes. The Academy of San Carlos reintroduced sculpted clothes. (*Left: Saint Michael*, alabaster, 18th century).

ALTARPIECES
Many of the paintings and sculptures produced in New Spain were designed for altarpieces. When all the pieces of an altarpiece have been kept together, it is easier to understand the special character of Mexican baroque, which transforms walls and interior spaces into multiform surfaces embellished with gold and bright colors. Altarpieces are classified according to the types of architectural supports framing the paintings and sculptures. In chronological order, these categories are Renaissance, with wreathed columns (*salomónico*), with *estípites* (pilasters in the form of a cut-off pyramid turned upside-down), with no apparent support (*anástilo*), autochthonous neoclassical (*neostilo*) and neoclassical ● 82.

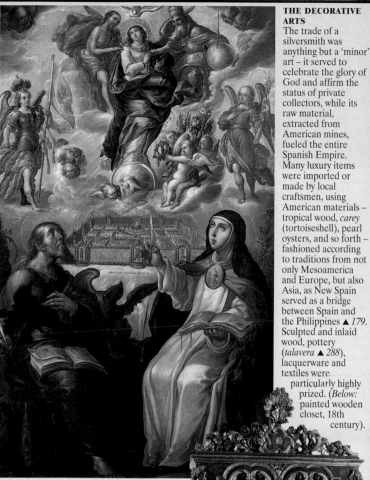

The trade of a silversmith was anything but a 'minor' art – it served to celebrate the glory of God and affirm the status of private collectors, while its raw material, extracted from American mines, fueled the entire Spanish Empire. Many luxury items were imported or made by local craftsmen, using American materials – tropical wood, *carey* (tortoiseshell), pearl oysters, and so forth – fashioned according to traditions from not only Mesoamerica and Europe, but also Asia, as New Spain served as a bridge between Spain and the Philippines ▲ 179. Sculpted and inlaid wood, pottery (*talavera* ▲ 288), lacquerware and textiles were particularly highly prized. (*Below:* painted wooden closet, 18th century).

PAINTING

The most significant paintings from the 16th century are the frescos in monasteries and the Italian-style canvases by Spanish, Flemish or home-bred artists. The following century witnessed the emergence of dynasties of local painters, such as the Echaves and the Juárez. Cristóbal de Villalpando (c. 1645–1714), the great master of the baroque and a student of the last Echave, produced huge allegorical paintings for the cathedrals in Puebla, Mexico City and Guadalajara, where his familiarity with Rubens and contemporary Spanish painting is evident. The works of Miguel Cabrera (1695–1768), the most talented 18th-century painter in New Spain, combined neoclassical sensibility with pale colors and great delicacy of expression. (*Above:* Villalpando, *Mystic Vision of the City of God [Jerusalem]*)

BAROQUE TO DAZZLE THE EYES
The façade of San Francisco Javier rivals those of Santa Prisca (Taxco) and La Valenciana (Guanajuato) in spectacle. Niches adorned with statues, medallions and beautifully harmonized bas-reliefs transpose, with evangelizing zeal, the lines of an altarpiece on to the surface of a façade. Note the cascades of fruit, flowers and foliage that run along the flanks of the tower's campanile.

IGLESIA DE SAN FRANCISCO JAVIER. The Churrigueresque façade (1760 ● 82) of this jewel of Mexican baroque is made up of two bodies: the porch, with its crown, and the five-level clock tower. The decoration develops three main themes: the glory of the first Christian martyrs; the Jesuits' founding fathers; and an invocation of the Virgin and the Archangel Gabriel (protector of the order). The central niche contains a statue of the church's patron saint; as on the main altarpiece inside, he has the Virgin Mary as his intercessor. At his feet, two Indian figures symbolize the evangelization achieved by the Society of Jesus in the Americas. The interior (through the museum) is awash with gold and cherubs. Seven magnificent altarpieces of elaborately carved, gilded wood punctuate the nave. On the high altar, the statue of Francisco Javier is flanked by the Immaculate Conception on the right and Saint John the Baptist on the left. Particularly worthy of note among the other altarpieces are those of Saint Ignatius of Loyola, the order's founder, the Virgin of Luz and, above all, the Virgin of Guadalupe – evidence of the Jesuits' special devotion to this mestiza Virgin. The saints around her are Isidoro the Laborer; Catherine, the patron of the millers; Barbara, the mediator of storms; and Juan Fandilas, the mediator of floods. The fresco on the central vault, representing the apparition of the Virgin of Guadalupe to the shepherd Juan Diego, was painted by Miguel Cabrera (1756) ▲ 168. Next to the chapel of Our Lady of Loreto, the CAMARÍN (octagonal room where the statue of the Virgin was dressed) is another masterpiece of Mexican baroque. Under the celestial vault of its dome, the altarpieces and paintings depicting the Evangelists are, once again, the work of Miguel Cabrera. The decoration is completed by *azulejos* (tiles) and a mural, with the coronation of the Virgin Mary as its main subject.

THE MONASTERY. There is a striking contrast between the sumptuousness of the place of worship and the sobriety of the spaces reserved for study and reflection. The stark corridors of the former school now lead to the MUSEO NACIONAL DEL VIRREINATO (Museum of the Viceroyalty). Its collections of Chinese art evoke Mexico's relationship with Asia ▲ 179. The CLAUSTRO DE LOS ALJIBES (Cloister of Fountains) displays several paintings, including some by the great baroque painter Cristóbal de

Left: *camarín* of San Francisco Javier in Tepotzotlán
Below left: ivory Crucifixion from the Philippines,
owned by the museum
Below: atlantes from Pyramid B in Tula

Villalpando ▲ *168*. Next door, the CAPILLA DOMÉSTICA contains paintings by Miguel Cabrera and an altar that is remarkable for its mirrors. The coats of arms of New Spain's six main religious orders are lined up along the vault.

Tula ◆ D A2

(50 miles/80 km from Mexico City, via the Tepeji del Río exit)
The city of Tollan, the old Toltec capital, perched on a hill, not only dominated central Mexico up to the Postclassical era (c. 1100) but also influenced Meosamerica as a whole, particularly the Mayas of Yucatán. The Toltecs were an autochtonous people who, like the Chichimecs, emigrated from Nayarit over the course of a long peregrination between the 7th and 9th centuries. Another aboriginal group was the Nonoalco, native to Tabasco. The Axtecs (or Mexicas), who would later come to dominate the Anáhuac, considered themselves the descendants of the Toltecs, and they borrowed some elements of their culture and religion.
THE SITE. The central altar of this major ceremonial center, the Coeatepantli ('Wall of Serpents'), and the Palacio Quemado ('Burnt Palace'), a ball-game ground and a *tzompantli* ● *75*, still survive. All that remains of the Pyramid of Tlahuizcalpantechuli ('Morning Star') is the platform, adorned with the famous ATLANTES, basalt statues 16 feet (5 m) high, that represent Quetzalcóatl as a heavenly warrior.

MYTH AND REALITY
According to legend, Mixcoatl ('Cloud Serpent'), the chief of the Nonoalco, married the princess of Tepotzotlán, who brought Acatl-Topiltzin ('One-Reed') into the world. The latter, after extensive astronomical studies in Xochicalco ▲ *176*, returned to found the capital, Tollan ('Place of the Reed'), which he placed under the protection of Quetzalcóatl, the god of good and of agriculture. At this point, reality merges with myth: the son of Mixcoatl became Quetzalcóatl, a living god, the spiritual master of the Toltecs, who brought back to life the myth of the Plumed Serpent. Twenty years later, his rival Tezcaltipoca ('Smoking Mirror') picked a fight with him. Quetzalcóatl had to leave Tollan. He headed for Cholula, then went down the Tabasco to reach Yucatán. He brought Toltec culture to the Mayans (Chichén Itzá), who acknowledged him as Kukulkán (the Plumed Serpent of the Mayans).

A circular arc running round the edge of the Altiplano Central, between Tepozteco and Popocatépetl, joins the monasteries of Tepoztlán, Tlayacapan, Totolapan, Atlatlahuacan, Yecapixtla, Ocuituco and Tetela del Volcán. These fortified complexes were built between 1530 and 1580 by the mendicant orders, on the sites of indigenous temples and pyramids, using materials taken from their ruins. Their extremely thick walls, often reinforced by side buttresses to support the vaults, convey an awareness of the potential danger of the nearby volcanoes, as well as a desire to defend themselves against Indians and demonstrate the power of the new Church. Their high, narrow (and usually sparse) windows recall the Roman or early Gothic styles. One side of their nave is endowed with a porch halfway up, leading to the cloister (invariably austere but often decorated with religious scenes) with a cross or well in the center. The open chapels ● *80* on the exterior welcomed the Indians. Most of these villages have retained a certain charm, and several still boast small baroque chapels.

Entrance to the Tepoztlán monastery

Tepoztlán ◆ **D** B3

(45 min. from Mexico City on the Cuernavaca highway) Tepoztlán, the 'place of copper', is tucked in the Tepozteco Valley, where copper may be the dominant color but is not in fact present. Perched on a rock with sheer walls, 1,970 feet (600 m) above the village, stands the Pyramid of Tepoztécal, the god of harvests. Tepoztlán is a getaway for wealthy Mexicans fleeing the pollution, noise and traffic of the capital – so its population doubles at weekends.

TEMPLO DE TEPOZTÉCATL. *(Access via a steep track and a 1½-hour walk)* The Tlahuica – who were subjugated by the Aztecs in 1486 and conquered by the Spanish in 1521 – built a platform here to support a pyramid next to the rock face. The arduous walk is rewarded by an extraordinary view of the village and valley, enclosed by the 'sugar-loaf' mountains of Amatlán.

DOMINICAN MONASTERY. This superb example of the colonial Plateresque style was built between 1559 and 1588, following the plans of the Spanish architect Francisco Becerra. On the façade, the Virgin is surrounded by two saints and medallions depicting the sun, moon, stars and

THE BRINCO FESTIVAL
The Tepoztlán carnival features dancing by *cinelos* (*above*), dressed in velvet robes, masks depicting bearded Spaniards and hats embroidered with *chaquira* (tiny beads).

Dominican cross. The single-nave church is completed by a semicircular apse. The upper floor of the extremely simple cloister provides a magnificent view of the Tepozteco Valley. The small museum contains a collection of pre-Hispanic objects bequeathed by the poet Carlos Pellicer.

Tlayacapan ◆ D B2

(*Take the Oaxtepec exit from the Cuautla highway.*) Tlayacapan is a large village hugging the opposite slope of Tepozteco Valley. The CONVENTO DE SAN JUAN was one of the first monasteries built in Mexico by the Augustinians (1534). An imposing fortress-church stands on a large esplanade planted with eucalyptus and Indian laurels. The elegant cloister leads to the De Profundis Hall, with its frescos in black and white (the only color permitted by the Augustinians, to mark the mourning of Christ's death). Outside, the Municipal Palace and the Cerería, an old candle factory, have served as settings for dozens of films, including *The Magnificent Seven* and *The Old Gringo*.

Toward Tetela del Volcán ◆ D B2

The monastery in TOTOLAPAN (*6 miles/10 km from Tlayacapan on the RF 160, in the direction of Xochimilco*) has features in common with that of Tlayacapan. Farther along the same road, the ATLALAHUACAN monastery has two fine procession chapels in its atrium. (*Farther on, turn right toward Cuautla, then left in the direction of Tetela del Volcán.*) In Yecapixtla, the monastery recalls the fortresses of the Middle Ages, with its outer walls crowned with pointed battlements. Next come Ocuituco and Tetela del Volcán, whose churches were built from the same architectural plans, brought from Spain by the Augustinian Father Jorge de Ávila. Tetela del Volcán, the last village on the monastery route, hugs the foothills of the volcano Popocatéptl, which regularly makes groaning noises. You can round off the excursion by going back down the valley by a winding road, passing volcano crests, up to the town of Cuautla, and the highway to Cuernavaca, Mexico City or Puebla.

Cloister of the monastery in Ocuituco

The architectural site
of Malinalco

The southern end of the Mexico Valley is blocked by
Mount Ixtle, a volcano that erupted at the beginning of
the modern era, spreading a vast layer of lava as far as
Cuernavaca. The latter was not isolated by this occurrence,
however, as the Aztecs always considered that the region –
despite being divided by the volcanic massif – depended on
Cuernavaca, the power center of the Aztec world:
Moctezuma had his palace in the 'City of Eternal Spring'.

Malinalco ◆ **D** A3

(*It is advisable to do the Mexico City–Malinalco return trip in
daylight. Reckon on 64 miles/104 km, via Tenancingo.*) A
magnificent road crosses the woody countryside before
reaching this unusual ceremonial center. The 'Hill of Idols' is
a monolithic structure built by the Matlazincas. The
construction work began in 1501, in the reign of Ahuitzotl.
At the top of the broad staircase leading to the entrance to
the temple, visitors are confronted by an enormous forked
tongue, protruding from a serpent's mouth that serves as the
entrance to the circular pyramid. Inside, a half-moon cavity
has been carved into the rock, encircled by a bench and
embellished with sculptures of a jaguar and two eagles. On
solstice days, the sun enters through the serpent's mouth and
lights up the entire space within. This temple was used for
the initiation of the eagle and jaguar warriors who belonged
to the nobility; they were charged with guarding the
ceremonial centers and spilling their blood as an offering
to the gods. Monument II is a truncated pyramid, while the
other buildings are very dilapidated, as the site was used as a
quarry for the Augustinians when they built their Plateresque
MONASTERY, endowed with a beautiful Renaissance cloister
(*The mountain chain separating Malinalco from Cuernavaca
prevents easy travel between the two.*)

IN THE CATHEDRAL
Note the frescos tracing the life of Saint Felipe de Jesús, a
Mexican missionary martyred in Japan.

Cuernavaca ◆ D B3

(50 miles/80 km from Mexico City on the highway)
Cuernavaca's perfect climate made it the getaway of choice
for the Aztec emperors, while Cortés built a palace here in
1527. Much later on, the town concealed the trysts of the
Emperor Maximilian with his Indian mistress, Bonita, in the
cool Casa Olinda. In the 1950s, American jet-setters built
splendid houses, their high walls shielding idyllic parks,
shaded by tropical trees and dotted with brilliantly colored
flowers. The Shah of Iran selected Cuernavaca for his exile.
The philosophers Ivan Illich and Erich Fromm pondered
here, while Dom Hélder Câmara and Sergio Mández Arceo
were laying the foundations of liberation theology.

Nowadays, however, the 'City of the
Eternal Spring' increasingly resembles
an eternal bottleneck. The beautiful
houses are becoming rarer, too, as
many have been parceled out and their
gardens turned into parking lots for
supermarkets. Its population now a
million, the city has been taken over by
pharmaceutical laboratories, factories
(Renault, Nissan) and multinationals
that have fled Mexico City.

PALACIO DE CORTÉS. *(On the
zócalo)* This austere fortress is one of
the few surviving examples of 16th-
century civil architecture. The building,
now a regional museum, has three
loggias, one of them decorated by
Diego Rivera in 1920 ● *100*. His fresco
portrays the meeting of two worlds: the
pre-Hispanic sacrifices, the birth of
civil architecture, the exploitation of
the land and the Indians, and the
violence of the *conquistadores*.

**REVOLUTIONARIES
FROM THE SOUTH**
Emiliano Zapata ● *36*
(born in San Miguel
de Anenecuilco)
formed his renowned
revolutionary bands
in his home region of
Morelos, and went on
to lead them to the
gates of Mexico City.

Below: fresco by
Rivera in the Palacio
de Cortés and its
patio (*bottom*)

XOCHICALCO, CITY OF ASTRONOMERS
The chimney of the observatory is 28½ feet (8.70 m) high, offering the possibility of observing with great precision the position of the sun with respect to the Tropic of Cancer. On May 14–15 and July 28–29, the sun lights up the entire cave at its zenith. This enabled the astronomers to check their equations and

Xochicalco ◆ **D** A3

(*24 miles/38 km from Cuernavaca, taking the highway to Alpuyeca*) The 'Place of the House of Flowers' is set in a beautiful spot, on hills with eroded peaks. This dynamic and well-protected city controlled a rich agricultural region – it is considered to have been the most important fortified city in Mesoamerica after the fall of Teotihuacán. The Mexican archeologist Jaime Litvak King believes that Xochicalco, like El Tajín and Cholula, contributed to the decline of Teotihuacán (600–900) by preventing the distribution of essential items to the big city. Once the latter disappeared, however, Xochicalco lost its military role and, therefore, its power. It was also an important center for the study of the heavens, as astronomers gathered here to make the religious and civil calendars coincide. The city disintegrated suddenly around 900, for unknown reasons: maybe it was the victim of internal power struggles, a great fire or an armed raid. It was subsequently abandoned.

THE ACROPOLIS. This raised complex contains several patios, bounded by granaries and *temazcal* (steam baths ▲ *195*). The main square (measuring 32,300 sq. ft/3,000 sq. m) is dominated by the PYRAMID OF QUETZALCÓATL, whose *tableros* (vertical panels) are decorated with eight plumed serpents accompanied by headdresses and snails (*left*). Figures resembling Mayans and the symbol of the new fire (Fifth Sun) can be seen between the snakes' sinuous forms, which create semicircles around the glyphs of the calendar. A disk divided into segments is thought to represent an eclipse that would have been visible in 743. An altar with a stele adorned with two glyphs stands in the center of the square.

calculations. Archeo-astronomers have worked out that the first rays of the sun penetrated on April 30 and then disappeared on August 12, after 105 days. A further 260 days therefore remained without light – the equivalent of a *tonalpohuali* (a measure of 260 days in the sacred calendar). This observatory also offered views of Jupiter and Venus.

OBSERVATORY CAVE. To the north of the main square and two levels down, the observatory (one of the best preserved in all Mesoamerica) was built inside an artificial cave around 700 BC.

BALL-GAME GROUNDS. The northern ground, below the observatory, is unusual for its absence of seats along the sides, while the eastern ground has only one seat, with a hoop of sculpted bats and parrots. To the south of this area, a mysterious ramp arises, made up of 252 stones sculpted in the form of animals.

Taxco ◆ **D** A3

In the 18th century, José de la Borda discovered the fabulous silver seam of San Ignacio, which quickly turned Taxco into one of the main mining centers in New Spain. Borda made

The city's inhabitants used the space on the basis of a strict hierarchy. At the top, surrounded by defenses, stands the acropolis, home to the dignitaries and their families. Further down, on a big square, the political, economic and financial area was organized around the pyramid of the Plumed Serpent. On a third level, the Square of the Stele with Two Glyphs was dominated by the great pyramid, the site of the religious ceremonies that the population were obliged to attend.

an immense fortune and built the SANTA PRISCA CHURCH, one of the glories of Mexican baroque architecture. In 1930, Taxco found a second wind, thanks to the American William Spratling, who opened the first silversmiths' workshops – there are now over 250. Taxco (*above*) is a charming town on the slopes of Atachi, which is gashed by dizzying canyons. The whiteness of its houses, reminiscent of an Andalusian town, has bewitched a host of foreign visitors, including Alexander von Humboldt ▲ *180*, D. H. Lawrence ▲ *115*, Malcolm Lowry ▲ *118* and Leon Trotsky.

THE CITY. The *zócalo*, adorned with a small kiosk, lies in the shadow of Santa Prisca. Narrow streets with no sidewalks lead off it to reveal the charms of Taxco, their cobblestones winding round the hill through a chain of tiny squares, embellished here and there by exuberant bougainvilleas. Around the Plaza Toril (*below the Santa Prisca Church*), the delightful market, a veritable maze spread over several levels, offers superb vantage points.

BUYING SILVER IN TAXCO ★
Make sure that all jewelry or other silver items you buy bear the stamp of the Mexican eagle, the MCA grade and the maximum content ('925' means that 92.5% of the metal is silver). Beware! Some articles are made of nickel silver, an alloy softer than pure silver. Compare the price of a gram from one store to another.

▲ Gold, silver and cacao beans

Mixtec shield made of gold, silver and copper, found in a shipwreck near Veracruz

The indigenous civilizations used cacao beans rather than metal coins for trading. Metal – particularly gold and copper – was only used to make jewelry. In 1540, a report by the Franciscan Marcos de Niza on the riches of the uncharted territory encouraged the Spanish *conquistadores* to venture farther north. The discovery of the Zacatecas mines in 1546 set their pulses racing. The 'Camino de Santa Fe', the silver road that linked the mines to each other and to the capital, began to take shape. The prosperity of New Spain would now depend on these mines.

Plan of the mines in Oaxaca, 18th century

A NEW EXTRACTION PROCESS

An immigrant from Seville, Bartolmé de Medina revolutionized mining in 1593 with an amalgam process using mercury, which was patented by the King of Spain. The output increased by 80%, and the silver mines of the New World experienced a boom.

'COZTIC' AND 'IZTAC'

According to the indigenous codex, *Coztic and Iztac* – gold and silver, but also the sun and the moon in Nahuatl – were gleams from the eyes of the gods. In pre-Hispanic cultures, gold taken from riverbeds was more widely used than silver, even though the latter was more abundant – imprisoned in its shell of quartz, it was inaccessible to the Indians, who were unfamiliar with crushing and fusion techniques.

SILVER MINES IN THE BAROQUE PERIOD

The Silver Road coincided with the baroque period, and the mine owners built countless churches to thank the heavens for their generosity.

THE SILVER ROAD

Mexico's silver deposits are situated along the Sierra Madre Oriental and on the Altiplano. The first silver boom took place between 1550 and 1630. The seams were epithermal, that is, close to the surface. The second occurred between 1767 and 1810, triggered by an increased demand for metal in Europe. The most prosperous seams – and the purest in the world – are those of La Valenciana, in Guanajuato, and Real del Monte, in Pachuca.

Opposite: cacao tree and the gods of *pulque* and cacao doing a deal, 16th century

THE 'NAO DE CHINA'

Right up to independence (1821), silver was exported to Asia, where it served as currency. Every year, a galleon called the *nao de China*, staunchly defended by the Spanish Armada, sailed to the Philippines with its holds crammed with silver. It returned, again under heavy escort, with gold, spices and porcelain, which were then sent on to Europe.

Map of the Pacific by Abraham Ortelius, geographer to the King of Spain, 16th century

CACAO, AN UNUSUAL CURRENCY

The Spanish discovered the hard way that the Indians exchanged bitter-tasting beans as a kind of currency. When they got their hands on Moctezuma's treasure, they found, instead of the anticipated gold, 40,000 cases of cacao beans.

The viceroys nevertheless decided to retain this autochthonous currency: on the one hand, it proved very reliable; on the other, and more particularly, its usage enabled the entire output of silver to be exported to Europe and Asia. The cacao bean also found favor in the Vatican because it prevented avarice (it could not be hoarded, as it kept for two years at most). Its use therefore continued throughout the three hundred years of colonization. The few silver coins minted in Mexico were used only by the Spanish.

'CACHUACHICHUIUA'

From the time of the Aztecs, *cachuachichuiua* was the term used for forged money, made by filling the outer casing of cacao beans with earth. Counterfeiting was punished by forced labor.

179

In 1798, the German Baron von Humboldt and the French naturalist Aimé Bonpland embarked on a long tour of the Spanish possessions in the Americas. Humboldt recounted this expedition in his *Voyage to the Equinoxal Regions of the New Continent*, a lengthy record of his scientific observations. Taxco preserves a relic of his presence, as the Casa Humboldt can still be admired (now the Museo de Arte Sacro Virreinal).

EASTER WEEK IN TAXCO

For centuries, the brotherhoods and congregations that organize the Easter celebrations have assembled hundreds of penitents and devotees. The most striking procession takes place on Holy Thursday, the day on which Christ is paraded through all the city's colonial neighborhoods: some penitents tie bundles of cactus to their bodies, so that the thorns penetrate the skin of their shoulders and back. Sergei Eisenstein filmed this powerful spectacle in his film *¡Que Viva México!* Others flagellate their bare torso to obtain pardon for their sins. Women follow the procession, walking in chains, almost crouching, for hours on end in intense heat, under the *andas* (palanquins) of the saints. At nightfall, a silent procession brings together the entire population, dressed in black. On Good Friday, there is a reenactment of the three Falls, the Crucifixion and the Entombment of Christ.

CHURCH OF SANTA PRISCA. In 1750, members of the Catholic bourgeoisie sought social prestige through pious works that enabled them to enter the Establishment. It was a Spaniard, Diego Durán Berrueco, who drew up this pink jewel of Mexican baroque, as well as supervising the construction – begun in 1748 and completed a mere ten years later. This rapidity largely explains its stylistic unity and formal harmony. José de la Borda made sure that the Church authorities, whom he considered overly conservative, had no say with respect to the lavish baroque decoration he was planning. The highly elaborate façade of pink limestone is marked by its sophistication and exuberance, although the stark lower sections of the two side towers provide visual relief and balance. Above the portal, a bas-relief crowning the papal tiara depicts the baptism of Christ. Every single niche and space between the pillars seems to be filled with cherubs, plant motifs, shells and escutcheons. This lavish decor is echoed by the upper bodies of the towers, replete with carvings. Inside, the walls are adorned with nine gigantic Churrigueresque altarpieces, made by Vicente Balbas with gold-leaf wood alternating with pink stone pilasters. Also noteworthy are the paintings by Miguel Cabrera ▲ *169*,

Church of Santa Prisca

Below: Acapulco Bay
Bottom: the diver of La Quebrada, built as a symbol of the city

particularly in the sacristy and on the tympanum on the door to the Capilla del Padre Jesús (or the Capilla de los Indios), with its depiction of the martyrdom of Saint Prisca (beheaded in the 3rd century).

Acapulco ◆ **D** A5

(*Via the Mex 92 highway*) The country's most famous resort is now just half an hour from Mexico City by plane, or 4 hours on the freeway, making it practically an annex of the capital. The most fashionable beach, LA CONDESA, also bears the name of the trendiest neighborhood. This splendid bay was the port used by the galleon from the Manila route, also known as the *nao de China* ▲ *179*. Once every year, this ship set off with an imposing escort to take silver from Mexico, Chile and Peru to the Philippines, to exchange it for gold, spices, precious wood and pottery. All that remains of these adventures is the FUERTE DE SAN DIEGO, a pentagonal fortress that defended the bay against pirates. Apart from September and October, the weather is always fine in Acapulco, attracting some 4 million tourists per year. A range of pleasures are on offer: along the Costera Miguel Alemán, the beaches made fashionable by the American jet set in the 1950s have now been taken over by 20-floor international hotels, which dominate the bay. The rock that cuts the latter in two is a popular meeting place; here, visitors make friends and swim in the sea, before meeting up again to go dancing, as Acapulco is also a paradise for night owls. In the last few years, the resort has extended toward the airport: the new hub of tourism, the ACAPULCO DIAMANTE, boasts three golf courses, including Tres Vidas, considered the most elegant in North America. The fine sands of the beach,

THE ANGELS OF ACAPULCO
(*The cove of La Quebrada is linked to the center by the avenue of the same name.*) No visit to Acapulco is complete without taking a look at the famous divers of La Quebrada. These young people plunge from a height of 115 feet (35 m) into a deep but narrow creek, having first commended their life to the Virgin of Guadalupe. The best view of this spectacle is from the terraces of the Mirador Hotel. Also in this old neighborhood of Acapulco, fans of Tarzan can enjoy a night in the Flamingo Hotel, once home of Johnny Weissmuller.

Below: Ixtapa

ISLA GRANDE
(*2 miles/3 km from Ixtapa in the direction of Lázaro Cárdenas*) This rocky islet, connected to the mainland by a continuous stream of small fishing boats, offers two attractive beaches – one for observing beautiful tropical fish, the other for enjoying calm and shallow waters. Stalls shaded by *palapas* sell cold drinks and grilled *huachinangos*.

BARRA DE POTOSÍ
(*Take the turning 9 miles/15 km before Zihuayanejo.*) The long beach in this fishing village, sheltered by a rugged spur, is a peaceful spot for a swim – followed by superb fish served in the shade of a coconut grove.

stretching for 18 miles (30 km), are lined with classy hotels but provide an oasis of calm, ideal for strolling or sunbathing. It is possible to walk right to LA BARRA, at the end of the road, to sample, in the small beachside restaurants, delicious *huachinangos a la talla*: enormous Pacific sea breams split in two, brushed with achiote (a sweet pepper) and cooked over a charcoal grill.

Pie de la Cuesta ◆ **D** A5

(*A few miles northwest of Acapulco*) Pie de la Cuesta, the perfect place for admiring the sunset or escaping the hubbub of Acapulco, is popular with the locals and the beach is packed on Sundays. You can rent a hammock and *palapa* by the day and revel in the shrimp cocktails and grilled fish. The sea is spectacular, but often so rough that it is only possible to bathe in the foam of the waves that break a hundred yards from the beach. Another alternative is a boat trip in the Coyuca Lagoon, fringed with mangroves and coconut trees. The village of La Barra, at the far end, has lost none of its authenticity.

Ixtapa–Zihuatanejo ◆ **C** E6

(*207 miles/331 km west of Acapulco*) Ixtapa or Zihuatanejo? Big hotels and American-style package deals, or the charm of an old fishing village? A rocky spur separates the two poles of this resort spread over 6 miles (10 km). In Ixtapa the sea is warm and transparent, and the sand is reddish-brown; the sea in Zihuantanejo, enclosing the bay, is less crystalline and there is more of a family atmosphere. These resorts offer pleasure cruises, underwater diving and big-game fishing.

The Gulf coast

VANILLA
According to legend, vanilla – a tropical climbing orchid – was first cultivated by the Totonacs near El Tajín. Its name in Totonac and Nahuatl means 'black flower'.

In bygone days, seafarers called this coastal region Sotavento ('land protected from the wind').

The Gulf of Mexico is bordered by the states of Tamaulipas, Veracruz and Tabasco. This coastal region is well watered by the abundant rains from the Gulf; the rich soil produces rice, green beans, mangoes, pineapples and bananas. The luxuriant vegetation, with its tall tropical trees and multicolored orchids – including vanilla, coffee, *maracujas* (passion fruit) and rubber trees – is gradually disappearing as free-range cattle farming requires more and more land to be cleared for grazing. The landscape of Sotavento is often rather whimsical with its strange cattle, a cross between Swiss cows and Brazilian zebus, chewing the cud beneath the coconut trees.

HISTORY. Early in its history, the Gulf coast was occupied by the Olmecs, the founding civilization of Mesoamerica, whose monolithic legacy includes some amazing colossal heads ▲ 196. Much later, the Totonacs of El Tajín appeared on the northern Gulf coast, and their influence spread across the Anáhuac Plateau. Veracruz, the port open to the Caribbean, was founded in 1519 by the Spanish explorer Hernán Cortés. This white town, which suffered numerous pirate attacks, became a major port during the 19th century as trading links were developed with Europe, the Caribbean and the Spanish colonies. Veracruz was subject to all kinds of influences, including that of nearby Cuba, which gave it its own individual character known as *jarocho* (Veracruzan) – an indefinable tropical quality that combines sensitivity with a touch of poetry, nonchalance and the gentle art of living.

GULF OF MEXICO

an Andrés Tuxtla
Catemaco
LAGUNA DE
SONTECOMAPAN
GO DE
MACO
Acayucan
[5]

Coatzacoalcos La Venta **TABASCO**

COMALCALCO

Jalpa de
Méndez

Heroica
Cárdenas Villahermosa
[6]

VERACRUZ

AUGUSTÍN LARA
El Flaco de Oro (the
'Golden Streak of
Lightning', *flaco*
meaning thin, or
skinny) was born in
Tlacotalpan in 1897
and died in 1970. He
composed and sang
boleros and romantic
songs, acquiring
international renown
after the Revolution.
He was married for a
while to actress María
Felix ● *60*, for whom
he wrote María
Bonita. During his
career, he wrote over
700 songs, including
the famous 'Granada',
'Solamente Una Vez',
'Gotas de Amor',
'Veracruz', and
'Noche de Ronda',
and appeared in thirty
or so movies. He was
the most prolific
writer and singer of
popular Mexican
music and his songs
have become part of
the national culture.

Veracruz ◆ **D** E3

When Hernán Cortés landed on
this coast in 1519, he founded the
Villa Rica de la Vera Cruz ('rich
town of the Truc Cross') in the
little bay protected by the island of
San Juan de Ulúa. Since 1589, it
has stood opposite the offshore
Island of Sacrifices. Today,
Veracruz is a delightful town
whose charm lies in its tropical
scents, its exquisite cuisine and its
festive atmosphere. The townsfolk
seem to spend the day on the café
terraces under the arcades of the
ZÓCALO (main square), the Plaza
de la Constitución, or on the
MALECÓN, the main waterfront
promenade that runs along the
port to the harbormaster's office.
The dazzling white cathedral
and coconut palms filled with
chattering black birds invite you to
take a break, all the more so since
it is often very hot in the town, the
most tropical and most sensual in

185

'EL DANZÓN'
'...Hasta la Reina
Isabel baila el danzón
Porque es un ritmo
muy dulce y sabrosón.'
('Even Queen Isabel
dances the *danzón*
Because its rhythm is
very gentle and
delightful.') In the
1950s, the Marina del
Puerto band, led by
Camerino Vázquez,
established the twice-
weekly *danzón* on the
zócalo of Veracruz.
Since then, it has
become a tradition.
Originally from Cuba,
the *danzón* is danced
to a four-beat rhythm,
with the steps
describing a small
rectangle. It is
an elegant, subtle
and sensual dance.
Each piece of music
includes three pauses
so that the women
can fan themselves
and the men can mop
their brow. The first
pause, the *coqueteo*,
allows the man to
hold his partner as
she fans herself. The
best dancers say that
the secret of the
danzón lies in the left
hand and that a
woman well led will
dance the night away.

Mexico. Twice a week, the locals gather on the Cathedral Square for an evening *danzón* to the sound of local bands. Beneath the arcades, cafés serve *mojitos* (rum flavored with mint leaves), *cubas libres* (rum and Coke with a squeeze of lime) and beer. Marimba bands play *són*, merengue, bossa-nova and fandango on their wooden xylophones ▲ 277.

SLOWING THE PACE. Veracruz is best enjoyed at the slower pace of the local inhabitants – by relaxing on the Plaza de la Constitución, lingering in the cafés, shelling shrimps bought from street vendors, watching the world go by or strolling along the Malecón. The FUERTE DE SAN JUAN DE ULÚA, which once housed an arsenal, a prison and a chapel, has been transformed into a museum. Today, you can see the weapons used to defend the city against foreign invaders and pirates. Visitors seeking the old Veracruz, or simply wanting a swim, should go to the beach of the Hotel Mocambo, about 5½ miles (9 km) from the *zócalo*. Here you can enjoy a drink or eat to the sound of marimbas (wooden xylophones).

ACUARIO DE VERACRUZ. (*On the waterfront, toward Mocambo*) The circular oceanic gallery of this aquarium contains the fish that live in the Gulf – rays, turtles, groupers, coral fish and sharks. The freshwater section houses fish of the rivers, marshes and mangroves. The crocodiles, piranhas and *pejelagartos* (longnose gar) are the undisputed stars.

THE COAST AROUND VERACRUZ. At BOCA DEL RÍO and ANTÓN LIZARDO (*20 minutes from Veracruz*), you can enjoy

delicious fish and huge shrimp at one of the waterfront restaurants, while listening to musicians who sing and play harps and *jaranas* (small guitars).

Veracruz to Xalapa

LA ANTIGUA ◆ D E2. (*17 miles/28 km north of Veracruz on the RF 180*) This strange town, seemingly overrun by luxuriant vegetation, conceals the ruins of ancient dwellings built by the *conquistadores*. The walls and two huge fig trees are all that remain of the house where Cortés once lived, and an eroded tree trunk on the river bank is where he is supposed to have moored his boat. Linger awhile and enjoy freshwater shrimp or grilled fish in the local restaurants.

Opposite top: fortifications of Veracruz
Opposite bottom: *el danzón*
Below: La Antigua

CEMPOALA ◆ D D2. (*27 miles/43 km north of Veracruz on the RF 180*) This small but delightful Totonac archeological site consists of a broad, grassy esplanade, planted with a few coconut palms, a truncated pyramid with a large flight of steps, and a strange circular structure. A high wall known as AMURALLADO IV once enclosed the administrative center of the site. In 1519 the Totonacs decided to join the Tlaxcalans and form the native infantry of Hernán Cortés in his conquest of Tenochtitlán (Mexico) ● *32*. Following this unfortunate alliance, Cempoala was abandoned, and later transformed into South America's first sugar-cane plantation by the *conquistador* Rodrigo de Albornoz.

XALAPA ◆ D D2. (*2 miles/100 km north of Veracruz, on the RF 180 to Cardel, then the RF 140*) Xalapa (also spelt Jalapa) lies on the slopes of the Cerro de Macuiltepec, opposite the Cofre de Perote, which can be seen from the town when there isn't too much mist or when there is a break in the virtually daily rainfall known locally as *chipichipi*. The state capital, this busy agricultural center and university town is nicknamed the 'Atena Veracruzana' ('Athens of Veracruz'). The many parks and gardens offer pleasant respite from the heat, but the main attraction is the Museo de Antropología.

FILOBOBOS NATURE RESERVE (*near Tlapacoyan, on the road to Martínez de la Torre*) Veracruz is a rafter's paradise. The 'Aventurec' camp offers a choice of three routes on the Río Bobos – the Encanto-Palmilla with its spectacular gorge over 650 feet (200 m) deep; the Pirámide, which includes a visit to the Filobobos archeological site; and the Alto Fino which follows a long section of the river as it runs between two high cliffs.

Museo de Antropología, Xalapa

(*Above the old town, on the road to Mexico City*) This prestigious museum, one of the finest in Mexico, showcases each of the main Gulf cultures, in three main sections – the Olmecs, the Central Veracruzan cultures, and the Totonacs and Huastecs. Using a simple but very effective layout, the rooms are connected by a broad, well-lit marble gallery that encircles the building. The most beautiful pieces are displayed in three large covered patios, in a setting of regional plants and flowers.

OLMEC SECTION. Visitors are greeted by COLOSSAL HEAD NO. 5 from San Lorenzo, a helmeted warrior with large, slightly crossed eyes, and full, parted lips. There are seven of these heads in the museum. In the nearby garden, HEAD NO. 1 – known as 'The King' – is badly eroded. At over 9 feet (2.85m) high, it is the largest of the colossal heads found at San Lorenzo. The display cases contain magnificent Olmec artifacts – yolks, figurines, stone palm leaves, masks made of jadeite, malachite and basalt, and monumental basalt thrones. In the gallery area, MONUMENT 2 from Potrero Nuevo represents two small telamons wearing the characteristic helmets of the Olmec heads, their raised arms supporting an entablature. In Room 1, EL PRINCIPE DE LA CRUZ DEL MILAGRO ('Prince of the Cross of the Miracle') adopts a catlike posture, typical of the part-human, part-animal composite pieces. In Room 2, visitors can see COLOSSAL HEAD NO. 7 from San

Opposite top: gallery of the Museo de Antropología
Opposite bottom: Olmec head
Below left: hollow Totonac ceramic figure from El Zapotal
Below right: *Señor de las Limas*
Bottom right: seated Totonac man from El Zapotal

Lorenzo, and STELE NO. 4, depicting a seated man holding a copal (incense) ball.

CENTRAL VERACRUZAN CULTURES. The Central Veracruzan cultures have bequeathed some magnificent ceramic pieces. These include the 'Caritas Sonrientes', the 'smiling children' figurines found in numerous tombs, which belong to the Remojadas culture. In the display cases, figurines whose mouths and feet have been highlighted with touches of *chapopote* (crude oil) represent Tlazoltéotl, the goddess of vitality. In the same section are the Cihuateteos, life-size terracotta sculptures of female warriors who were deified because they died in childbirth. Exhibits from the Pinome-Popoloca culture (12th–16th century) include *La Dualidad (Duality)*, an extraordinary sculpted human head associated with death, effigies of Tlaloc, and a zoomorphic figure from Nopiloa. One of the most striking pieces in this room is the statue known as the SEÑOR DE LAS LIMAS, sculpted from a single block of jadeite, which represents a seated shaman holding a feline child. In the gallery area there is a model of the Totonac site of El Tajín ▲ *191*. In the

▲ *191*

MYSTERIOUS PIECES
In the Totonac and Huastec section, a series of small figurines in yellowish-red terracotta, decorated with splashes of *chapopote* (crude oil), have puzzled the experts. Their features are certainly not Mexican. One theory suggests that they could represent Europeans shipwrecked on the Gulf coast long before the Conquest.

ARCHEOLOGICAL REPLICAS
Archeological replicas are beginning to find their way into museums. These are not so much copies as 'authentic replicas', crafted by the descendants of each civilization. Brigido Lara, who spent several years in prison for 'counterfeiting', has since been employed by the Instituto Nacional de Antropología y Historia (INAH) as an expert. He has made many pieces at the museum but only he knows which ones.

adjacent room, wall paintings from the town of Las Higueras, near El Tajín, depict dancers, priests holding incense balls, and gods, such as the god of thunder and lightning.

TOTONAC AND HUASTEC SECTION. In the gallery area, the display cases contain beautiful plant and animal vases made from ceramic and alabaster (showing the influence of Teotihuacán). In the main room, fifteen or so steles and large stone statues represent women dressed in long robes. One of the finest sculptures, OZULUAMA (the Rising Sun of the Huastecs), stands 1.85 meters (6 feet) high and has a splendid horseshoe pectoral. Last but not least, there is a series of CODICES (manuscripts) from the time of the Conquest.

GRILLED FISH ON THE BEACH
From El Tajín you can rejoin the coast at
Tecolutla (*right*). This popular resort,
famous for its delicious grilled fish, is best
avoided during the Mexican holiday period.

Above: coffee shop in
Coatepec

**TIME OUT IN
CUETZALAN ◆ D** C2
In the nearby Sierra
Norte del Pueblo,
Cuetzalan de
Progreso, the region's
coffee capital, is well
worth a visit. In this
traditional village
with its steep, paved
streets, the houses
have overhanging
roofs to protect
passers-by from the
rain that falls for a
few minutes nearly
every day. In early
October, a major
huipil and *rebozo* ● *63*
festival is celebrated
with processions,
dancing, and
voladores ('fliers').
Don't miss the
archeological site of
Yohualichan about
4½ miles (7 km) from
Cuetzalan. It is
regarded as the twin
city of El Tajín, with
which it was closely
linked.

EL PICO DE ORIZABA
At 8,405 feet
(5,610 m), the volcano
– also known as
Citlaltépetl – is
Mexico's highest
point. Although
it has not erupted
since 1687, it is not
classified as extinct
and is still carefully
monitored. Climbers
scale the north or
south face to reach
the crater.

Xalapa and around

COATEPEC ◆ D D2. (*10 miles/16 km south of Xalapa*) Deep
in the hot and humid tropical forest, this former Indian
village is today a major center for the cultivation of coffee
and orchids. The Casa María Cristina, on the street leading
to the *zócalo*, opens its garden to the public at weekends. You
can sample *mole* and lemon sorbet, two regional specialties,
at one of the cafés on the attractive square.

HACIENDA DEL LANCERO. (*7½ miles/12 km along the road
to Veracruz*) This beautiful *hacienda*, built by one of Cortés'
lieutenants, later became the residence of Mexican president
General Santa Anna ● *26*. Its magnificent grounds are
regularly used for shooting romantic or period movies.

CANTONA ◆ D C2. (*Just past Perote, take a track on the left
toward El Frijol Colorado – best avoided on rainy days.*) This
mysterious city was built on a basalt outcrop, in an arid
region where the only plants are cacti and yuccas. And yet
the remains, which cover an area of 4½ square miles (12 km²)
suggest it had a population of around 100,000. This would
make it one of the largest cities in Mesoamerica, which
enjoyed its golden age between 650 and 900. The many stone
workshops attest to the fact that the city's wealth was based
on the obsidian sold to Teotihuacán, so the latter's decline,
before AD 1000, led to a reversal of Cantona's fortunes.
Cantona (so-called by the Swiss archeologist Henri de

Saussure in 1855, because it reminded him of the Chinese city of Canton) was built in haphazard manner. In fact, its layout is like that of a maze. Streets, buildings and pyramids are all asymmetrical, and only 12 of its 26 ball courts have a pyramid, a square, a building and a sacrificial altar.

El Tajín ◆ D C1

(*Reached via the RF 130 and 180*) The former Totonac capital, with its famous niched pyramids and angelically smiling statues, is the only example of urban society on the lowlands of the Gulf coast, at the foot of the Sierra Papanteca. Unlike other civilizations of the Classic era, the principal god of this society was not Tlaloc, god of rain, but the god of thunder and lightning, probably because of the proximity of the ocean and the hurricanes that ravage the region. This city-state was at its height at about AD 950, when it had close links with Teotihuacán, which it survived, and then Xochicalo, Cholula and Cacaxtla. Discovered in the 18th century, El Tajín covers an area of more than 356 acres (144 hectares) and has some 180 structures. It was not cleared of the luxuriant rain forest until 1938.

PIRÁMIDE DE LOS NICHOS. On the main square (PLAZA DEL ARROYO) stands the spectacular and beautifully proportioned pyramid that symbolizes El Tajín. Its seven tiers are punctuated by 365 niches, one for each day of the solar

MUSEUM OF EL TAJÍN
The beautiful pieces discovered during the excavations of El Tajín include the bas-relief from Structure 4, which shows two intertwined, feathered serpents surrounded by dignitaries associated with the rituals of *pulque* and sacrifice. Also worthy of note is a sculpture from the Pyramid of the Niches depicting two more feathered serpents in a solar disk with a dignitary seated on a throne, and three sculpted columns from the Building of the Columns.

EL TAJÍN ★
In view of the region's hot and humid climate, it's best to avoid the hottest hours of the day when visiting El Tajín.

FRET MOTIF
This is a recurrent motif at El Tajín. It represents Xicalcoliuqhui, the feathered serpent, also known as Quetzalcóatl.

Left: Pirámide de los Nichos, El Tajín

Right: Tlacotalpan
Below: dance of the *voladores*
Bottom: bas-reliefs from the South
Ball Court at El Tajín

THE SOUTH BALL COURT
According to archeologist Felipe Solis, the first bas-relief panel of the South Ball Court, showing the players all dressed alike, depicts preparations for the ceremony. The next panel shows preparations for the sacrifice, with musicians and priests holding knives. The third panel, picturing two players in confrontation, symbolizes the movement and union of opposite forces (life and death). On the fourth, the player who has opposed the destiny of the sun is decapitated, and his blood spatters onto the sacred ground. The last two panels concern the fertilization of sacred liquids. On one, *pulque* ▲ *325* is celebrated with a sacrifice. On the other, the rain god performs a self-sacrifice by piercing his own penis to fertilize the land.

year, that create a delicate interplay of light. You have to imagine that each of the niches was painted in cinnabar and outlined in blue. The fact that they were all empty suggests their function was purely decorative. On the east side, a broad flight of steep steps, flanked by two ramps decorated with fret motifs, leads to the top of the pyramid where the temple once stood. The Pyramid of the Niches was El Tajín's most important political and religious building. Ritual ceremonies, such as the ritual dance of the *voladores*, were held in the main square, at the foot of the steps.

THE SOUTH BALL COURT. (*Immediately behind Structure 5, south of the Plaza del Arroyo*) The most interesting of El Tajín's ball courts has a series of six panels sculpted in bas-relief on its long sides. They describe the way in which the ritual, the symbolic struggle between life and death, should be carried out in order to satisfy the gods.

THE GREAT XICALCOLIUQHUI. From the North Ball Court (*behind Structure 3*), follow the enclosure wall (*on the right*) that separated the ceremonial and residential areas. The Great Xicalcoliuqhui is a strange platform, 1,180 feet (360 m) square, whose spiral structure has earned it the name 'mother of all scrolls'.

EL TAJÍN CHICO. Beyond the wall lies El Tajín Chico, built on the hillside. A dozen or so buildings have been restored, but the rest are still lost in the forest. The nobles and high priests who lived here enjoyed an unrestricted view and cool sea breezes. The residential buildings were built using *pozzulana*, a sort of cement made from porous volcanic ash, shells and lime. Archeologists have discovered elegant verandahs constructed with slender columns that made the structure lighter and allowed air to circulate. Some of the palaces in El Tajín Chico even had windows, elements that were almost unknown to the architects of Mesoamerica. STRUCTURE C was probably an

administrative building, a sort of check-point between the two parts of the city. It consists of three superposed tiers, and has eighteen niches and a cornice decorated with a finely sculpted fret motif. The porticoed building opposite has some beautiful polychrome murals. On STRUCTURE A, the most important building in El Tajín Chico, a narrow flight of steps leads to a sort of balcony that encircles the building and opens onto rooms whose walls still have traces of paintings.

EDIFICIO DE LAS COLUMNAS. At the top of the site, the Building of the Columns (which once supported the roof of a vast palace), must also have been one of the buildings reserved for priests and the nobility. Some columns are decorated with bas-reliefs depicting the victories of the ruler 13 Rabbit, who can be seen seated in front of his people.

South of Veracruz: two charming ports

ALVARADO ◆ D E3. (*45 miles/72 km south of Veracruz on the RF 180*) This typically *jarocho* (Veracruzan) port, on the lagoon of the same name, has retained its 18th-century architecture. It is famous for the stalwart character of its inhabitants, the beauty of its women, its traditional music and its cuisine. Overwhelmed by heat, corroded by salt and rust, Alvarado is a sleepy port, where you wouldn't be at all surprised to bump into a swashbuckling pirate or two....

TLACOTALPAN ◆ D E3. (*10 miles/16 km south of Alvarado*) For a long time Tlacotalpan was the main Gulf port and rival of Veracruz. Its location on the banks of the Papaloapan River meant that steamships from Europe could berth there when the *norte* was blowing, a cold northerly wind that prevented them from docking at Veracruz. This charming, colorful town with its Caribbean atmosphere has been classified as a UNESCO World Heritage Site. In the late 19th century, it invested in education and culture as its means of development. It has an opera house-cum-theater and a Moorish pavilion, and its Candlemas celebrations are truly unforgettable. Agustín Lara ▲ *185*, the region's famous son, is Tlacotalpan's pride and joy.

EL PALO VOLADOR
This pole dance ● *52*, traditionally performed for the festival of Corpus Christi, is becoming a great tourist attraction at El Tajín, Papantla and Cempoala. Even so, it is spectacular. The dancers are attached by their feet to long ropes wound round the top of a 50-foot (15-meter) pole. As the pole turns, the ropes unwind and the dancers are spun lower and lower, while the circles they describe become larger and larger. A musician, who obviously has a head for heights, plays the flute and drum on top of the pole.

193

Above: the flora and fauna of the Tuxtlas, the Cascades of Eyipantla, and the Lagoon of Sontecomapan.

THE 'HEALERS OF THE LAKE'
The Catemaco region is famous for its *curanderos* (healers), *yerberos* (herbalists) and *brujos* (witches). These are much sought after by the local population and visitors to cure their ailments and ward off bad luck and negative thoughts. The healers use potions made from curative plants, as well as *limpias* – a method of spiritual and physical purification that combines the use of medicinal plants and copal (incense) ● 54.

The Tuxtlas ◆ D F3

The Tuxtlas, named after a yellow-and-green parrot known as the *totzli*, lie 93 miles (150 km) south of Veracruz. It is a hot and humid mountainous region, characterized by a series of 300 volcanic cones – the highest are San Martín (5,427 ft/1,650 m) and Santa Marta (5,592 ft/1,700 m). It was from these mountains, at a time when they were covered with dense tropical vegetation, that the Olmecs extracted the basalt for their colossal heads ▲ *196*. The Tuxtlas is also a region of lakes, rivers, waterfalls and mineral springs. Although only a fifth of the original primary forest remains, it still harbors an amazing diversity of plants – 1,300 different species, including 800 vascular plants and 270 medicinal plants. The wildlife is also extremely varied, with 128 species of mammal and 561 bird species. Today, much of the tropical forest is protected due to the creation of a biosphere reserve that covers an area of 383 acres (155 hectares).

SANTIAGO TUXTLA ◆ D F3. (*44 miles/71 km from Alvaredo*) The town was founded in 1525 by Hernán Cortés, who also introduced the cultivation of sugar cane into the region. Nestling in a fertile valley, Santiago still has some beautiful colonial buildings, while its square is dominated by 'El Negro', a colossal Olmec head. Other Olmec pieces can be seen in the MUSEO TUXTECO. The Olmec site of TRES ZAPOTES, about 8 miles (13 km) from the town, can be reached via a track suitable for motor vehicles.

SAN ANDRÉS TUXTLA ◆ D F3. (*13 miles/21 km from Santiago*) The town is a hive of commercial activity and its large daily market sells a wide range of agricultural produce.

LAGUNA ENCANTADA.

(1½ miles/2 km northeast of San Andrés) The 'Enchanted Lagoon' occupies a small volcanic crater and is so called because the water level rises in the dry season and drops during the rainy season. Local healers draw water from a sacred cave on the lake shore.

SIHUAPAN. *(Between San Andrés and Lake Catemaco)*

Tobacco has been grown in this hot, humid region since the late 19th century. The local cigar *(puros)* factory is open to the public. From there, a narrow road leads to the SALTO DE EYIPANTLA, a spectacular 164-foot (50-m) waterfall in a beautiful natural setting.

LAGO DE CATEMACO ◆ D F3.

According to legend, the town on the edge of Lake Catemaco was founded by a local fisherman, Juan Catemaizca, when Nuestra Señora del Carmen appeared to him at the cave known as 'El Tegal', where today water is drawn from a sacred spring. The lake covers an area of 7 by 5½ miles (11 by 9 km) and has its own fleet of fishing boats. Visitors can hire a *lancha* (motor boat) and visit the ISLANDS. The largest, AGALTEPEC, is a reserve, and home to seventy black howler monkeys. Olmec remains include zoomorphic figures, ceramics and a small shrine. TANAZPILLI ('Island of the Monkeys') has a population of macaques imported from Thailand for observation by the University of Veracruz. More archeological remains were discovered on TANAZPÍN, while TOTOGOCHIO is the chosen nesting site of egrets and white herons. The NANCIYAGA NATURE RESERVE is an area of tropical forest where visitors can enjoy mud baths and bathe in a mineral spring.

LAGUNA DE SONTECOMAPAN. *(12½ miles/20km from Catemaco)*

Boats take visitors along narrow waterways, through the mangroves that provide refuge for aquatic birds, turtles and red crabs, to LA BARRA, a wild, unspoiled beach.

THE 'TEMAZCAL'
The *temazcal* was a form of steam bath popular with the Aztecs and the Maya before them. It was hygienic, therapeutic and spiritual (it purified the body and soul through the alliance of water and fire). The entrance to the semicircular structure is via a small, low door that opens to the east. In the center red-hot stones are placed on a burning fire. A collective *temazcal*, such as those at Nanciyaga (about 4½ miles/7 km east of Catemaco) can hold about fifteen people. A shaman conducts the ceremony with drums ● 54 and songs sung in Nahuatl.

▲ Olmec sculpture

A ceremonial jade ax in the form
of a jaguar head

The term 'Olmec' defines a style – distributed unequally across Mesoamerica between 1200 and 300 BC – rather than a civilization. However, the major political and ceremonial centers (San Lorenzo, La Venta and Tres Zapotes) are all located on the Gulf coast. These centers are extremely well designed and are the result of vast collective undertakings that involved excavations, the construction of pyramids and earthworks, and the burial of gigantic offerings. Monumental sculpture played a key role in this man-made landscape.

SCULPTURE IN THE ROUND
More than any other Mesoamerican culture, the Olmecs produced sculptures in the round – seated figures of kings and chieftains ('The Wrestler', *left*), entire jaguars, supernatural beings wearing a jaguar mask, jaguar masks and heads with a horizontal tenon.

COLOSSAL HEADS
The famous colossal heads, which date from the early Olmec period (1200–1000 BC), stand up to 6½ feet (2 m) high. They are thought to be representations of the severed heads of enemies defeated on the ball courts, rather than portraits of reigning kings or their ancestors, as was traditionally believed. In fact, they are wearing helmets and the 'jewels' in their ears are false, made from wood or paper, and are not the jade ornaments worn by people of rank.

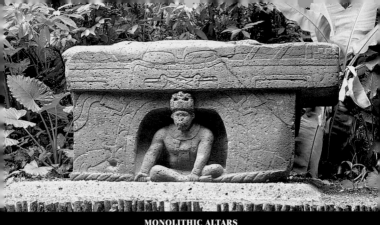

MONOLITHIC ALTARS

These were crafted soon after the colossal heads and represent an apparition – the king emerging from a niche hollowed out of the front surface to represent the gaping jaws of a jaguar, symbol of the terrestrial monster. This image compares the birth of the king, or his accession to the throne, to the rising sun emerging from the earth. The solar metaphor applied to the Olmec kings was echoed in Mayan iconography.

TRANSPORTING RAW MATERIALS

Basalt blocks weighing up to 40 tons were transported overland on sleds, and by river on rafts, from the mountains of the Tuxtlas ▲ *194* to where they were sculpted – a distance of more than 30 miles (50 km).

STELES

Steles are long, vertical monuments sculpted in high or low relief. Their subject is usually a royal personage, alone or with other mortals, or sometimes with the ancestors who confer his legitimacy. The scene may be depicted within the gaping jaws of a jaguar. Stele C from Tres Zapotes is inscribed with one of the earliest dates in the 'Long Count' system, the equivalent of 32 BC.

▲ The Gulf coast
Tabasco

THE OLMEC REGION
The Olmec territory extended along the Gulf of Mexico between the lagoons of Alvarado and Términos, in the State of Tabasco. The seventeen colossal heads that typify Olmec art were discovered on the sites of San Lorenzo, Tres Zapotes and La Venta. Because the last two sites are difficult to reach and badly eroded, the sculptures are preserved in the museums of Xalapa and Villahermosa.

CHOCOLATE
The huge trees to the left of the site of Comalcalco (*below left*) belong to the cocoa plantation of La Herencia, which is open to the public. The Padrón Murillo family are delighted to explain their cultivation methods and the traditional process used for making chocolate, before offering you a sample – it is drunk cold, mixed with water.

Below right: the site of Comalcalco

Villahermosa ◆ E D3

The only thing of interest in this hot and humid oil town, capital of the State of Tabasco, is the La Venta archeological park, the showcase of Olmec art and civilization.

PARQUE-MUSEO LA VENTA. (*Av. Ruíz Cortines*) This open-air museum on the Laguna de las Ilusiones ('Lagoon of the Illusions') was designed by local poet and anthropologist Carlos Pellicer to provide a setting for thirty-three archeological pieces from the Olmec site of La Venta. The monumental statues are presented in an area of forest that re-creates the location in which they were discovered. Four COLOSSAL HEADS, the symbol of Olmec art, are the pride of the collection, which also includes steles, historiated altars and more modest sculptures characterized by the purity of their lines, the attention to proportion and the delicacy of their ornamentation. This includes a number of zoomorphic designs inspired by the jaguar, as well as by birds and serpents. The park also has a zoo.

Comalcalco ◆ E C2

(*56 miles/90 km from Villahermosa. Follow the Paseo Tabasco toward Cardenas, then turn off to the right toward Comalcalco.*) The originality of this major Mayan city, built between 800 and 1250, lies in the fact that it was constructed in brick. On the lowlands of Tabasco, which were prone to flooding, freestone was hard to come by. Mortar – made from a mixture of earth, sand and crushed seashells – is clearly visible at the base of the buildings. Comalcalco is arranged in three main sections in which only a few structures have been excavated. The rest is left to the imagination under mounds covered with neatly cut grass that blends harmoniously with the dark red of the brick. The absence of raw materials in the region led this Mayan community to turn to commerce, exchanging cocoa, feathers and cotton for obsidian, hematite, volcanic stone, jade, serpentine and copal. Don't miss the STUCCO MASK OF THE MAYAN SUN GOD KINICH AHAU, in Temple VI, or the BURIAL CHAMBER OF LOS NUEVE SEÑORES ('nine lords of the night') whose frescos depict the lords of the nine regions of the underworld, in TEMPLE VII.

The Yucatán peninsula

▲ Yucatán peninsula

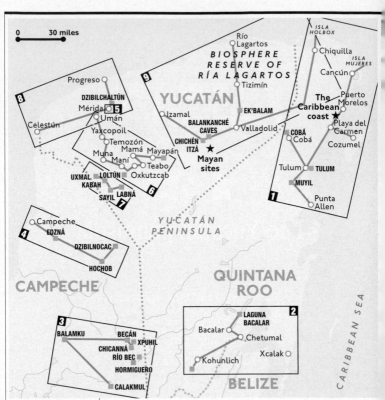

The Yucatán peninsula is a low-lying limestone plateau whose arid, karstic landscape contrasts with the highlands ● *16* that constitute the rest of the country. Throughout its history, the peninsula – today divided into the states of Yucatán, Campeche and Quintana Roo – has had closer ties with the Caribbean than with highland Mexico. Before the Conquest, its east coast, washed by the Caribbean Sea, underwent a remarkable development that has only been equaled by the modern tourist boom. The region was situated on the long-haul trade routes between present-day Honduras and Guatemala, on the one hand, and northern Yucatán, bounded by the Gulf of Mexico, on the other.

PRE-HISPANIC PERIOD. During the Classical era (300–900) the main urban centers were located in the forests of Petén, in what is now Guatemala, and along the rivers Motagua and Usumacinta. Northern Yucatán was less developed at the time and did not enjoy its golden age until the Recent Classical and especially the Postclassical eras, after the collapse of the great cities. In eastern Yucatán, Cobá ▲ *211* was the only major commercial center from where salt, in particular, but also shells, honey, wax and cotton were transported to the coast of present-day Belize and Honduras. When these centers of consumption disappeared, large-scale migrations changed the region's cultural, economic and demographic balance, and other major centers developed in the highlands of Guatemala, northern Yucatán and on the coast of Tabasco. From here, navigators organized new river and trading routes, and controlled the areas of cocoa production in Guatemala, Honduras and the coast of Belize by setting up trading counters along the Caribbean coast. Many towns sprang up, such as Tulum and Cozumel, as well as small sanctuaries that served as refuges for traders (who could also make offerings to the gods), where merchandise could be exchanged and distributed inland.

THE EUROPEAN CONQUEST. The Spanish not only dispossessed the Indians of their commercial activities, but they also decimated the population with imported epidemics. Although the villages of Polé (Xcaret), Cozumel and Zama (Tulum), survived for some time, they were abandoned after being plundered by pirates, and the east coast remained virtually deserted for almost two centuries. Only the English came, to cut dyewood and replenish their freshwater supplies.

THE CASTE WAR. During the second half of the 19th century, the Yucatán peninsula was rocked by a violent conflict between the Maya and Europeans (*below*, a drawing of the war). The Indians were being heavily taxed by the government and also saw their ancestral lands seized and given to large estates. Their chiefs, whose privileges were being threatened by liberal laws and European abuses of power, launched a violent rebellion that intensified from 1874 onward. The rebels controlled much land until the end of the 19th century, but were eventutally defeated by the Europeans.

SISAL, THE GREEN GOLD OF YUCATÁN
The west of the Yucatán peninsula is the home of sisal (*Agave sisalana*, or *henequen* in Spanish), cultivated since pre-Hispanic times for the fiber that made the region's fortune in the 19th century. It was made into ropes and rigging which supplied 90% of world demand.
The dispersal of the plant, which is today cultivated in Brazil and Tanzania, and the competition from artificial fibers such as nylon, have decreased the profitability of this crop. The temporary wealth that it brought to the region is reflected in the mansions of the aristocracy in the center of Mérida and the old *haciendas* ● 84.

PIRATES AND CORSAIRS
The Yucatán peninsula was constantly under attack by pirates, buccaneers, corsairs and enemy warships seeking refuge on this deserted coast and plundering the villages for supplies. Campeche, founded in 1540 and the only port on the coast, was plundered six times by corsairs and pirates between 1559 and 1685, when a wall was finally built around the town.

MAGNIFICENT
BEACHES
The beaches of
Quintana Roo are
remarkable both for
the color of the sea –
which is transparent
to a depth of 130 feet
(40 m) and changes
from emerald green
to sapphire blue –
and for their fine
white sand, which is
always cool, even
beneath the blazing
sun of the Tropics.
This is because the
microscopic shells
that form the sand are
calcareous and do not
retain the heat as
siliceous sand does.
However, strong
currents and sudden
changes in wind
direction can make
these beaches
treacherous for
swimmers and
windsurfers.
In summer,
temperatures are
around 104° F (40° C)
with humidity levels
between 70 and 80 %.

Cancún ◆ F F1, ◆ L

A MODERN RESORT. In the 1970s a vast project was
launched to transform this deserted coastline, trapped
between jungle and sea, and until then devoid of
communication routes. The idea was to build a series of
tourist centers that could compete with the over-saturated
resort of Acapulco. Bounded by the sparkling waters of the
Caribbean, and with an ideal climate (except in the hurricane
season, between July and October), the tiny island of Cancún
was linked to the mainland and a vast tourist complex built
that has made it one of the most popular resorts in the world.
Cancún attracts large numbers of visitors from the United
States, versed in the art of all-inclusive package deals (*todo
incluido*), who are accommodated in large hotel-clubs strung
out along the beach. Today Cancún's population is 300,000.
TWO TOWNS IN ONE. There are in fact two Cancúns. The
zona hotelera occupies the original extended island, with its
hotels lining the Avenida Kukulcán facing the sea, and the
restaurants and shopping centers overlooking the lagoon.
The town center, whose inhabitants staff and service this vast
tourist town, is crossed north-to-south by the Avenida Tulum.
THE LAGOON. Between the island and mainland lies a vast
lagoon bordered by mangroves and linked to the sea by the
Nizuc Canal, to the south, and the Nichupté to the north.
THE ANCIENT SITE OF EL REY ◆ L C3. This discreet
Maya site, the last remaining pocket of pre-Hispanic culture
in the midst of the *zona hotelera*, is today populated by large
iguanas. It consists of a main plaza surrounded by three
platforms, a pyramid, two small temples and a vaulted
structure. A second plaza consists of two platforms and a
vaulted building with a small shrine in the center.

Isla Mujeres ◆ F F1

A few miles north of Cancún lies the Isla Mujeres ('Island of
Women'). It was probably discovered in 1517 by Francisco
Hernández de Córdoba who noticed several female idols in
one of its temples. The island is 4½ miles (7 km) long and
between 330 and 875 yards (300–800 m) wide.
VILLAGE. The fishing village (1,400 inhabitants) at the
northern end of the island has retained its traditional

Above: Cancún, a
string of hotels
between sea and
lagoon
Opposite: Isla
Mujeres

character. To the north of the village, the PLAYA DE LOS COCOS, with its fine sand and transparent waters, is the best beach on the island.

VISITING THE ISLAND. *(There's a road suitable for vehicles and you can hire bicycles or golf buggies in the village.)* In the 19th century, the HACIENDA DE MUNDACA was used as a base by Fermín Mundaca, a smuggler who fell in love with a beautiful Spanish woman and built her a palace and a fort to protect it. But she married another, and he died of a broken heart. The ruined fort and gardens can still be seen today. The BEACHES (Garrafón, Indios, Lancheros and Pescador) lie along the southwest coast of the island, washed by the calm, transparent waters of a blue sea. GARRAFÓN is the

JARDÍN BOTÁNICO ALFREDO-BARRERA-MARÍN
(20 miles/32 km from Cancún, on the road to Chetumal) The gardens offer visitors an opportunity to discover a wide range of regional plants, spot the spider monkeys in the tall trees and explore archeological remains (El Altar).

most interesting as it teems with tropical fish and is an ideal spot for divers (extra care should be taken near the coral reef). At the south end of the island is the ANCIENT TEMPLE OF IXCHEL, damaged by Hurricane Gilbert in 1988. Four openings facing the four points of the compass suggest it was originally an observatory. Between the lighthouse and the temple, perched on the limestone rock, a garden has been laid out where visitors can admire several modern monumental sculptures. Each morning, this headland is the first piece of Mexican soil to be touched by the sun's rays.

Cancún to Playa del Carmen

The stretch of coast between Cancún and Punta Allen has recently been named the 'Mayan Riviera'. The first village you come to, PUERTO MORELOS, is a former fishing village and port for precious tropical hardwoods and *chicle* (latex from the *chicozapote*, the sapodilla used to produce the natural component of chewing gum ▲ 279). Along the coast between Cancún and Puerto Morelos, a number of hotels and resorts have been developed around tourist attractions, such as the crocodile farm at Croco Cun Acamaya Ecopark.

A PIRATE HAVEN
For centuries, the Isla Mujeres provided a safe haven for pirates and smugglers. In 1821 Pierre Lafitte was mortally wounded here by the Spanish. He died at sea and was buried at Dzilam in northern Yucatán. But his memory lived on and Lafitte became a legend in the region.

ISLA CONTOY ◆ F F1
(*Trips from the Isla Mujeres*)
The Isla Contoy, 15 miles (24 km) north of the Isla Mujeres, was made famous by the French underwater explorer Jacques-Yves Cousteau, and is a popular spot with divers. It also attracts bird-watchers, since it is a major nesting site.

Playa del Carmen ◆ F F2

Among the palm trees of the residential district of this small town, which has become a wealthy tourist resort, the remains of small temples bear silent witness to the presence of the Maya who once sailed along these coasts from Honduras in dugout canoes. The port of Xaman-Há (Playa del Carmen) was in fact one of the boarding points for pilgrims on their way to Cozumel to consult the oracle of the goddess Ixchel. It has a magnificent beach of fine sand, a large number of hotels and an airport, and is still a departure point for nearby Isla Cozumel. All this, combined with a lively night life and excellent diving and shopping facilities, make it a more popular choice than Cancún for most European tourists.

PUNTA BETE ◆ F F2
(*Between Puerto Morelos and Playa del Carmen*)
A rough dirt track leads through the jungle for about 3 miles (5 km) to the beaches of Punta Bete, protected from the open sea by a coral reef. The beaches have restaurants, chalets, a campsite and *palapas* – open-sided, wooden structures with palm roofs.

Isla Cozumel ◆ F F2

Isla Cozumel is the largest of the Mexican islands. It is 33 miles (53 km) long and 8½ miles (14 km) wide, and has a population of 50,000. Its Mayan name Cuzamil means "Island of the Swallows". It was occupied by the Maya for two thousand years and has a number of archeological remains.
A TRADING HISTORY. The important trade network between Guatemala, Honduras, the Gulf of Mexico and northern Yucatán ended at the island of Cozumel, which was protected by the sea. The intermediate ports were open to attack and, like Tulum ▲ *209*, had defensive walls. The temple of Cedral, one of the thirty-five Mayan sites discovered on the Isla Cozumel, was used as a prison in the 19th century.

ARRIVAL OF THE EUROPEANS. In 1518, Juan de Grijalva was the first Spaniard to visit the island where Hernán Cortés stayed for some time before embarking on his conquest of Mexico. The Spanish occupation of Yucatán destroyed the Mayan trade network, and the ruined Caribbean ports were gradually abandoned by their inhabitants. In the 16th century, French pirates plundered the remaining villages, including Cozumel (also known as San Miguel and El Pueblo). In the 17th century, the Islas Cozumel and Mujeres were used as bases by English pirates who exploited the region's tropical hardwoods. The island of Cozumel was subsequently abandoned until the Indian uprising of 1874 ▲ *201*. The coastal fishermen used to take shelter there, but the population never exceeded five hundred.

UNDERWATER TREASURES
The 25 miles (40 km) of reefs surrounding Isla Cozumel, at varying depths, are guaranteed to give divers an unforgettable experience. The most beautiful dives do not exceed 100 feet (30 m), so you don't have to be highly experienced to enjoy the underwater treasures of the Isla Cozumel. The waters are clear throughout the year (except in the hurricane season), and have an average temperature of 77–82° F (25–28° C). The most attractive reefs lie to the west of the island – Palancar, the best known, was filmed by Jacques Cousteau. Then there's the impressive wall of Santa Rosa, the fairly shallow, coral-covered Colombia reef, and Paso del Cedral, inhabited by huge green moray eels.

Far left: Playa del Carmen
Left: coral reef off the Isla Cozumel

INCREASING PROSPERITY. The *chicle* (chewing-gum) ▲ *279* boom transformed the village of Cozumel into a trading port. During World War II it became the site of an American military airport and was then forgotten until underwater explorer Jacques Cousteau explored the Palancar Reef and brought this beautiful site to the world's attention.
SAN GERVASIO. (*There's a road that takes you round the island.*) Inhabited up to the time of the Conquest, this major site included the sanctuary of Ixchel, goddess of pregnancy, medicine and the fertility of the moon. Her oracle attracted Mayan pilgrims, who landed at Xamancab, present-day Cozumel, which is the only town on the island.
THE BEACHES. The PLAYA SAN FRANCISCO and PLAYA PALANCAR, about 9 miles (15 km) south of the town, are a true paradise for divers. The lighthouse on the PUNTA CELARÁIN offers magnificent views.

STONE BASS, OR WRECKFISH
If threatened, the wreckfish
changes color – the lower part
of its body turns white and
the upper part almost black.

The coral reefs of the Caribbean are barely 20,000 years old
and have evolved on the fossilized remains of older corals
destroyed during the last Ice Age. Since then, the sea level has
risen, forming numerous lagoons. The corals continue to form
slowly in the warm, clear waters and, as they do so, create a
barrier that shelters an incredibly richly stocked marine
'oasis'. However, the fragile ecological balance of this
natural environment – consisting of corals, sponges,
calcareous algae and several hundred species of fish – is
under threat from the damage caused by tourism and
the intensification of commercial fishing.

BLACK-TIPPED SHARK
This coastal shark lives in groups of six to
eight individuals. It is renowned for its
agility and amazing leaps out of the water.

Sand star

Fan coral,
or sea fan

Moray

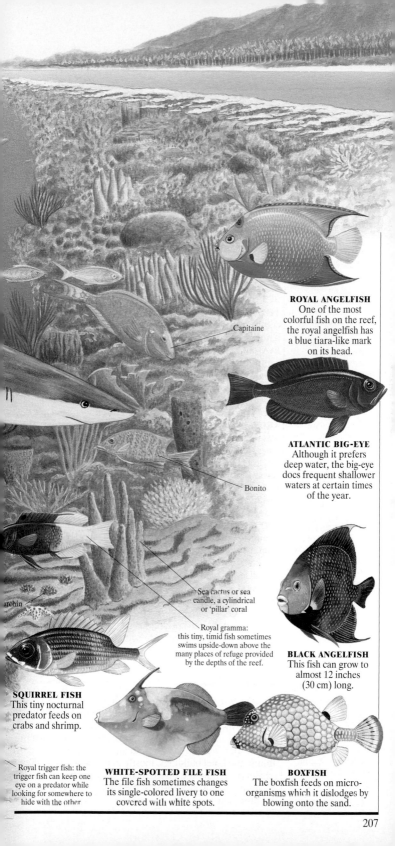

Capitaine

Bonito

Sea cactus or sea
candle, a cylindrical
or 'pillar' coral

Royal gramma:
this tiny, timid fish sometimes
swims upside-down above the
many places of refuge provided
by the depths of the reef.

rchin

Royal trigger fish: the
trigger fish can keep one
eye on a predator while
looking for somewhere to
hide with the other

ROYAL ANGELFISH
One of the most
colorful fish on the reef,
the royal angelfish has
a blue tiara-like mark
on its head.

ATLANTIC BIG-EYE
Although it prefers
deep water, the big-eye
does frequent shallower
waters at certain times
of the year.

BLACK ANGELFISH
This fish can grow to
almost 12 inches
(30 cm) long.

SQUIRREL FISH
This tiny nocturnal
predator feeds on
crabs and shrimp.

WHITE-SPOTTED FILE FISH
The file fish sometimes changes
its single-colored livery to one
covered with white spots.

BOXFISH
The boxfish feeds on micro-
organisms which it dislodges by
blowing onto the sand.

TURTLES
Like certain
Californian and
Pacific shores, the
Caribbean coast is
one of the places
where turtles come
to lay their eggs.
Between May and
September, these
reptiles – which can
weigh up to 310 lbs
(140 kg) – leave the
water at nightfall and
find a quiet, dark
place where they can
dig their nest and lay
their eggs. About 45
days later, the eggs
hatch and the baby
turtles scuttle toward
the sea. Many are
eaten by sea birds and
fish and never reach
maturity. The turtle is
also the object of an
illegal trade, hunted
for its shell, flesh and
especially its eggs,
which are supposed to
have aphrodisiac
qualities. No wonder
the turtle is an
endangered species.

Between Playa del Carmen and Tulum

THE BEACHES. XCARET, on the road to Tulum, is a tourist
complex with beaches and underground rivers offering safe
bathing, *cenotes* (sinkholes) ▲ *238* and a dolphin aquarium.
PAAMUL has a small, quiet beach with chalets and a
campsite. Giant turtles come to lay their eggs here in
summer. PUERTO AVENTURAS has a marina, luxury hotels, a
golf course, stores and a museum. Further south, at
KANTENAH, you can hang your hammock between the palm
trees lining the beach, and eat fried fish under a *palapa*.
AKUMAL ◆ F F2. (*62 miles/100 km south of Cancún*) Akumal
was made famous by the discovery of a Spanish galleon,
Nuestra Señora de los Milagros, which sank off the reef in
1741. The objects recovered are on display in the local
MUSEUM. Popular for the blue-green waters of its tiny bay
and its reef, Akumal was one of the first beaches to offer
diving and surfing facilities. In summer, giant turtles come
here to lay their eggs on the beach.
CHEMUYIL AND XCACEL ◆ F F2. CHEMUYIL and its
beautiful beach are ideal for diving or just relaxing. On
Sundays, giant iguanas hide as the beach is invaded by
weekend bathers. At XCACEL, another forgotten corner of
paradise, you can visit a *cenote* and dive to a sunken wreck.
TANKAH ◆ F F3. The area was transformed into a coconut
plantation, which was replaced by *chicle* ▲ *279* during the
first half of the 20th century. Its beach doesn't have tourist
facilities but the offshore reef is stunning. The archeological
remains seen here are an extension of the site of Tulum,
2½ miles (4 km) away.

Tulum ◆ F F3

(*81 miles/131 km south of Cancún*) Tulum is the most
important archeological site on the Caribbean coast. Its ruins
overlook the sea, giving it a particular charm which is
enhanced by 6 miles (10 km) of unspoiled beaches that
stretch southward to the Sian Ka'an Biosphere Reserve. At
Tulum, the hotel buildings, mostly in the form of *cabañas*
(chalets), are low and discreet, and use local materials. This
makes it a relatively well-preserved resort that is at its best
out of season.

XEL-HA
(*Between Akumal and
Tulum*) Tropical forest
surrounds a lagoon, a
beautiful natural
aquarium fed by the
sea and the fresh
water of the *cenotes*
(sinkholes). Xel-ha
has been transformed
into a leisure park
and is an ideal place
for a family outing.

The ancient city of Tulum ◆ F F3

Tulum was an important city and port during the century preceding the Spanish Conquest. The cliffs on which it stands formed a natural protection. Like Mayapán ▲ *229*, the site was surrounded by walled defenses which originally had a rampart walk and parapet. The fortifications protected the port – a simple cove between the rocks – and the sanctuary against attack and enabled major commercial activity to take place all year round. Stone causeways (*sacbeob*) ● *72* led through the jungle toward the interior. Tulum was founded c. 1200 as a commercial port on the east coast of the Yucatán peninsula. It had close links with Mayapán and enjoyed its golden age after the latter's decline from 1400 onward. Most of the ruins that can be seen today date from this period. The city was still occupied when the Spanish landed in 1518.

THE CARIBBEAN COAST ★
In spite of the tourist boom of recent years, there are still little corners of paradise to be found on the so-called 'Mayan Riviera'.

TULUM
1. The 'Castillo'
2. Grand Palace
3. Temple of the Frescos
4. Temple of the Diving God
5. Enclosure wall

BUILDINGS IN MINIATURE
The architects of Tulum used poor-quality masonry and concealed any faults with a thick layer of stucco. They tended to favor miniature structures, which were sometimes so small that they made any form of human activity difficult, if not impossible. A small sanctuary in the center of an only

ARCHEOLOGY. Frederick Catherwood and John Lloyd Stephens visited the site in 1841, but the first scientific excavations were carried out in the 1920s by American and Mexican archeologists. They drew a plan of the site and studied the architecture and ceramics, placing great emphasis on preserving the paintings and dating the various styles. For example, the center of the site, where the buildings are grouped around a plaza, is clearly Mayan. However, the structures built along a street orientated 17° East attest to a Mexican influence since this orientation is widely found in central Mexico, especially at Teotihuacán ▲ *162*. The columned edifices date from the middle of the Postclassical era, while most of the other buildings are Late Postclassical.

EL CASTILLO. The largest structure on the site overlooks

the Caribbean to the east and a courtyard surrounded by small buildings on the landward side.

TEMPLO DE LAS PINTURAS. The Temple of the Frescos is in fact two superposed Late Postclassical temples. The first is covered by a second whose wide entrance is divided by four columns. The interior walls of both structures are covered with well-preserved frescos, in which the 'cosmic' construction of the decoration is a constant element – the figures are represented with the sky above their heads and the underworld beneath their feet – and the scenes are divided into panels by coiled serpents. In the inner sanctuary, the central iconographic theme is corn, with which the divinities represented are all connected: the so-called *Dios descendiente* ('Diving God') has two plants in his headdress, a

slightly larger temple, such as the Templo de las Pinturas (Temple of the Frescos) is one of the most typical forms. There are also miniature structures on the shores of the Caribbean which are thought to have been used as landmarks by sailors.

kneeling goddess is grinding corn on the upper register, while above her and to the right, the seated god K (Kauil) ▲ *217* is presenting a small corn god to a standing goddess.

TEMPLO DEL DIOS DESCENDIENTE. On the back wall of the Temple of the Diving God, the celestial frieze includes one of the sun's rays and possibly a symbol of Venus. It is surmounted by a band terminated at either end by the top half of an image of the sky in the form of a two-headed serpent. The earth is also depicted as a two-headed serpent, the counterpart of the celestial monster. Two groups of figures are shown, including a woman giving an object to a man, probably a god. Below the earth, a central panel depicts the aquatic underworld.

Top: El Castillo
Above: Templo de las Pinturas
Right: a Diving God

Cobá ◆ **F** E2

Cobá

This archeological site covers an area of 19 square miles (50 km²). Cobá was founded in the early 7th century and occupied, more or less continuously, until the 15th century. Its architecture is reminiscent of that of Tikal (in Guatemala) and, like Tikal, it enjoyed its golden age between the 7th and 10th centuries, when it was the most important city in the northeast of the Yucatán peninsula. This is evidenced by the many steles and the impressive network of raised causeways (*sacbeob*) radiating from the city. An alliance between Tikal and Cobá made the latter an important trading center with products from the coast, especially salt, being delivered there before being sent on to Petén in Guatemala.

MAIN GROUP. Located in the northeast section of the main group, STRUCTURE 1 – also known as the 'Tallest Pyramid' (Nohoch Mul) – reflects the city's long occupation. A Late Postclassical structure, similar to those at Tulum, was built on top of the 79-foot (24-m) Late Classical pyramid. STELE 20, discovered at its base, dates from AD 684 and is one of the best preserved on the site. From the top of the pyramid of the Castillo, there is a stunning view across the forest and the five lakes (including Lake Macanxoc) surrounding the site.

RAISED CAUSEWAYS. *Sacbeob* leading in five directions link the main group of structures to other architectural groups on the site. Raised causeways also linked Cobá to other sites – Ixil, about 12½ miles (20 km) to the southwest, and Yaxuná, 62 miles (100 km) to the west (the longest known Mayan road). This causeway was probably made during the Late Classical era.

'SACBEOB'
Sacbeob (singular, *sacbe*) are raised causeways (sixteen have been recorded), and are between 1½ and 8 feet (0.5–2.5 m) above the ground and about 4¾ feet (4.5 m) wide. Their sides are rough stone walls, filled with rubble and covered with sascab, a natural limestone cement which hardens when wet and compressed ● *73*.

**FELIPE CARRILLO
PUERTO AND THE
CASTE WAR**
Driven back by the
federal troops of
Yucatán in 1849, the
insurgent Maya ▲ *201*
regrouped around a
cenote ▲ *238* in the

The Sian Ka'an Biosphere Reserve ◆ **F** E4

A sandy track, suitable for all types of vehicles, runs from
Tulum to Punta Allen, a distance of 35½ miles (57 km). It
passes through the Sian Ka'an Biosphere Reserve (*below*)
where only the coastal strip is accessible to the public. At
BOCA PAILA, the chalets are particularly popular with
visitors from Cozumel and Cancún. The track runs between

jungle. And then a
miracle occurred – a
'talking cross'
appeared and
promised the Maya a
decisive victory. The
'little Sacred Cross'
became 'Chan Santa
Cruz' and its
sanctuary the center
of a new power – a
huge church, the
Balam Na, was built
on the spot. Today, on
May 3 (Santa Cruz),
the Maya still visit the
small *cenote* of Felipe
Carrillo Puerto where
the cross first spoke
to them.

the sea and the LAGUNA DE CHUNYAXCHÉ and then across
a wooden bridge, where there is a nearby camping facility.
The lagoon is part of the reserve and is a sanctuary for
migratory birds, such as flamingos, herons and egrets. There
are more than three hundred bird species in the reserve, and
two species of tropical crocodile (*Crocodylus moreletti* and
Crocodylus acatus). In PUNTA ALLEN, a tiny fishing village at
the end of a sandspit at the north end of the Bahía de la
Ascensión, fishermen catch lobsters with their bare hands.

Toward Muyil ◆ **F** E3

From Tulum, a road heads south toward the former Mayan
capital, Chan Santa Cruz, present-day Felipe Carrillo Puerto.
For about 62 miles (100 km), the road runs through what was
until about twenty years ago, thick jungle. Today it is an
uninteresting expanse of vast, deforested areas, *ranchos* and
grazing cattle. About 15½ miles (25 km) south of Tulum, the
ruins of MUYIL (also known as Chunyaxché) stand on a rocky
promontory overlooking the Laguna de Chunyaxché. Early
surveys indicated that the site was occupied continuously from
the 1st century AD to the time of the Conquest. A *sacbe* ▲ *21*
links the ceremonial center with the lagoon 3 miles (5 km)
away. Six structures are still standing along the *sacbe*. The
CASTILLO, situated midway along the causeway and almost 69
feet (21 m) above the level of the lagoon, supports a circular
tower which is the only one of its kind in Mayan archeology.

Laguna Bacalar ◆ F E5

Bacalar Lagoon (*above*), 31 miles (50 km) long and with an average width of 1⅓ miles (2 km), is linked to the Bahía de Chetumal. This long ribbon of shallow, picture-postcard water is known locally as the Laguna de Siete Colores ('Lagoon of Seven Colors'). About 20 miles (33km) before Chetumal, a turning leads to the CENOTE AZUL which, with a depth of 295 feet (90 meters), is one of the most impressive sinkholes after Chichén Itzá ▲ *244*. Today, a pleasant family restaurant stands on its edge. The road continues along the lake to the village of Bacalar. This once densely populated region declined rapidly after the Conquest. The village of Salamanca de Bacalar, founded in 1544 by Gaspar Pacheco, was abandoned after an Indian uprising. It was rebuilt during the 17th century but remained under constant threat from pirates, who plundered it several times, and was eventually abandoned once again. During the first quarter of the 18th century, Antonio Figueroa, the governor of Yucatán, built a FORT there (now a museum) to keep an eye on the English who were in the process of settling in what was to become Belize. During the Caste War ▲ *201*, the village was captured by the Maya who massacred the population. It was not recaptured until 1901. Bacalar is not on the main tourist route and has fairly basic hotel facilities, but its relaxed, family atmosphere is characteristically Mexican.

Chetumal ◆ F E5

This modern commercial town was founded in 1898 following the signing of the Spencer-Mariscal Treaty, according to which Mexico recognized the borders of British Honduras (now Belize). A pontoon was anchored in the bay opposite the village of Payo Obispo, from where a watch could be kept on the illegal trade in arms and tropical hardwoods being brought down the Río Hondo. When the refugees from the Caste War returned from Honduras, the village of Payo Obispo flourished. In 1915, it became the state capital and was renamed Chetumal. It lies in the hurricane zone, and was ravaged in 1916 and 1942, and again, most violently, in 1945 by Hurricane Janet.

MUSEO DE LA CULTURA MAYA. The exhibits are on three levels linked by a huge silk cottonwood tree ▲ *279*, the cosmic tree of the Maya, as if linking the underworld, mortal world and heaven.

XCALAK
Midway between Felipe Carrillo Puerto and Chetumal, a road leads to the Xcalak peninsula. Beyond Majahual, a track follows the coast north to Puerto Herrero and south to Xcalak. The region has a number of unexplored archeological sites. During the colonial period, it served as a refuge for the Maya fleeing Spanish domination.

TRADITIONAL DRESS
Yucatecan women still often wear white dresses with brightly colored embroidery around the hem and neck.

Mayan writing, calculation and calendar

CODICES

Only three Mayan manuscripts, traditionally referred to as codices, have survived to the present day. One of these, the *Dresden Codex*, is a treatise on divination and astronomy.

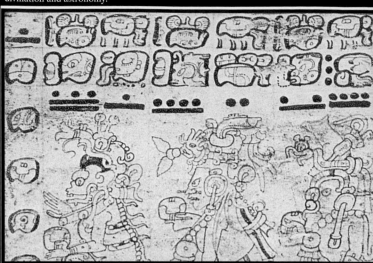

The Maya are the only ancient civilization on the American continent to have developed a form of writing that could express all types of thought and language through a combination of signs and symbols. As early as the Classical era, the Maya had books (codices) in the form of long strips of bast paper folded in a 'concertina', on which the scribe painted texts and images. As regards calculation, the Maya perfected the discoveries of their post-Olmec predecessors in the fields of positional arithmetic and the calendar. Their mastery of the calculation of time enabled them to write history and, above all, to predict the future by means of a cyclical conception of chronological units.

READING ORDER

Mayan writing is presented in the form of blocks of glyphs arranged either in rows or columns and usually read from left to right and from top to bottom. These glyphic blocks are made up of various symbols or glyphs – a principal symbol with affixes.

THE LANDA ALPHABET

In the 16th century, Diego de Landa, Bishop of Yucatán ▲ *231*, attempted to transcribe the European alphabet into Mayan symbols (*below*) – an impossible task since Mayan writing is syllabic.

VERB-OBJECT-SUBJECT

In the example taken from the *Dresden Codex* (*above*), each figure is accompanied by a text of four glyphic blocks. The first block, the verb, denotes the action – presenting an offering. The second, the object, denotes the offering itself (the same glyph appears in the hand of each figure). The third, the subject, names the figure, and the fourth is the prophecy for the period in question – good or bad depending on the divinity.

A DUAL SYSTEM OF SYMBOLS

About 800 different symbols have been recorded in Mayan texts. The number is too great for an alphabetical or syllabic form of writing but too small for a purely logographic form. A study of the texts has revealed that certain symbols express concepts while others are a transcription of syllables.

'KATUN' CALENDAR ROUND
Diego de Landa reproduced the *katun* cycle on this calendar round.

TIME CYCLES
Years were calculated from an initial date corresponding to 3114 BC. The units were the day (*kin*), the 20-day month (*uinal*), the 360-day year (*tun*), the period of 20 *tuns* (*katun*) and the period of 20 *katuns* (*baktun*). Time was divided into independent cycles. The principal cycles were the divinatory cycle or *tzolkin* (260 days), the solar year or *haab* (365 days) and the Great Cycle of 5,200 tuns (5,200 × 360 days) or 'Long Count'.

NUMBERS
In the Mayan vigesimal system (that is, based on units of twenty) of positional arithmetic, the value of the numbers increased in vertical columns from bottom to top – first the value of the units (0–19), then by 20s, then by 400s, and so on. Figures were written by combining bars (which had a value of 5) and dots (which had a value of 1), sometimes with glyphs in the form of a head, as on the right-hand side of this panel from the 'Palacio' at Palenque (*below*).

GLYPHS IN THE FORM OF A COMPLETE FIGURE
Complete figures were used to represent numbers and periods in certain early series, which feature at the beginning of many inscriptions and indicate the time that has elapsed since the initial date of the Mayan calendar.

For numerical notations the Maya used a system of bars and dots.

| 1 | 2 | 5 | 6 | 9 | 12 |

Image from the *Dresden Codex* – a celestial monster with two heads (one at either end).

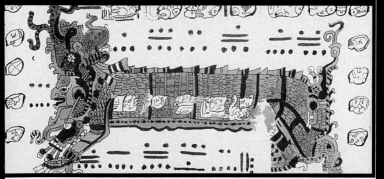

215

During the Preclassical and Classical eras, the Maya represented natural forces (earth, sky, death, lightning) in the form of hybrid creatures or symbols whose images changed according to what they were required to embody. During the Postclassical era, these images became fixed, and the creatures acquired a personality and became immutable divinities who were part of a hierarchical pantheon. Bloody rituals, such as human sacrifice, were a tribute that had to be paid to natural and supernatural powers to obtain favors such as rain, a good harvest, victory and universal harmony.

THE COSMIC MONSTER
This creature from the Classical era (stylized at Bonampak, *above*) inhabits both celestial and terrestrial realm. The world of natural and supernatural powers is centered on the basic duality that is illustrated by the contrasting heads of the two-headed monster. The living head at the front of the creature represents life, moisture, fertility and day, while the shriveled head at the back is invested with the opposite qualities – death, drought, infertility and night.

A MULTIPLICITY OF CREATURES
An entire population of creatures associated with humidity, fertility and the fecund earth, with features suggesting reptilian or froglike origins, developed alongside the cosmic monsters. Another group of grotesque figures, whose features are more feline, are represented as solar creatures, the spirits of sacrifice, war and death. Thus, they pass from one extreme to the other, just as life ends in death, and death in rebirth.

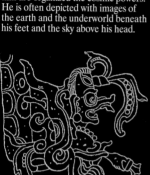

THE KING WITHIN THE COSMOGONY
In the official monumental art of the city-states, the figure of the king represents the center of the universe. Around him are organized the cosmic powers. He is often depicted with images of the earth and the underworld beneath his feet and the sky above his head.

THE GOD CHAC
Because of their long noses, the masks on the façades of Yucatecan sites (*above*) tended to be identified as those of the rain god Chac, who was not really well established as a divinity until the Late Postclassical era. In fact, they are the masks of the cosmic monster, usually in its terrestrial form.

THE GOD K
The creature of the Late Classical era traditionally known as the god K (Kauil) is represented with a smoking ax embedded in its forehead, and symbolizes lightning (*left*).

HUMAN SACRIFICE
There are a great many scenes depicting human sacrifice by tearing out the heart, mostly dating from the 11th century onward. The recipients of the sacrifice were probably the sun, which was thereby invested with the power to be reborn the next morning, and the earth, which was made fertile. As well as this method, decapitation and sacrifice by arrows were also practiced. The Maya also performed a double sacrifice which involved tearing out the heart for the sun, and decapitation to release a flow of blood that would slake the earth's thirst.

CHANGING BELIEFS
In the Postclassical era changes in beliefs and rituals came about through 'Mexican' influences (Toltec, Zapotec, Totonac) and the weakening of political structures. By the beginning of the Early Postclassical era, monumental art no longer celebrated royal power but two orders of rival warriors. From then on, worship focused on war and human sacrifice. At the same time, an authentic pantheon of gods invested with a physical personality began to appear.

217

MASKS ON STEPS 2 AND 3
The faces have the symbol *kin* (sun) in their eyes, and T-shaped incisors. They are contained within the jaws of a serpent, probably representing the sky, formed by two vertical jaws joined by a celestial band (the symbol *lamat*, meaning 'star', can be seen below the left-hand mask on Step 3). Each face is framed by two masks, one on its head and the other beneath its chin. The ear ornaments are surmounted by a fish mask and extended below by a serpent mask.

Top: Plaza Mayor at Kohunlich
Above right: mask representing the sun

Kohunlich ◆ **F** D6

(*About 43½ miles/70 km west of Chetumal, on the main Escárcega road, a turning on the right leads to the ruins of Kohunlich, 5 miles/8 km further on.*) The site, occupied from the Preclassical to the Postclassical era, was the subject of major excavations during the 1990s.

PLAZA MAYOR. Three smooth steles stand on the entrance steps to this great Late Classical plaza, and below them lies a stone altar. At right angles to the plaza is a long platform, lined by various buildings whose doors are framed by twin columns.

TEMPLE OF THE MASKS. The Temple of the Masks was constructed at the far end of the site, and lies beyond a number of other structures, one of which is a large ball court. Painted stucco masks line both sides of the four steps of an Early Classical pyramid. They have been protected by the construction of a later pyramid, and this still covers the base of the first building. The masks on Steps 2 and 3 have human faces, while on the fourth step the human face is replaced by that of a jaguar. The masks adorning this pyramid are thought to represent the ceremonial aspects of the sun – the star itself and the king with whom it was identified.

The Río Bec region lies at the center of Maya territory, midway between Chetumal and Francisco Escárcega. Among the many discoveries in the region is that of a remarkable architectural and ornamental style. These Mayan sites, which flourished between AD 600 and 830, remained undiscovered by such explorers and archeologists as John Lloyd Stephens, Frederick Catherwood, Désiré Charnay and Alfred Maudslay, who did not investigate the region. The French explorer Maurice de Périgny was the first to visit central Yucatán in 1907. Like the Chenes style (Hochob, Dzibilnocac) found farther north, Río Bec is characterized by temples whose doors represent the jaws of the terrestrial monster. The pyramidal towers crowned by non-functional 'temples' are usually only found in Río Bec architecture.

Xpuhil ◆ F C5

(*The region's main archeological sites can be reached via the RF 186. Xpuhil is about 76 miles/123 km west of Chetumal.*)
EDIFICE 1. The central body of the edifice (*below*) consists of three adjoining elements. Each of the outer entrances is

RÍO BEC AND HORMIGUERO
◆ F C6
Río Bec is less easily accessible than Xpuhil or Chicanná. The site, which gave its name to the Mayan architectural style typical of the region, has one of the most romantic ruins in Central America. Although very badly damaged, Group N has some beautiful remains invaded by creepers and flowering trees. Hormiguero is the strangest and most excessive of the Río Bec sites, but getting there is also something of an adventure.

surmounted by a frontal mask of the terrestrial monster, with the opening corresponding to its jaws. Stylized masks of the same creature, usually in profile and bas-relief, are superposed on either side of each entrance to emphasize the fact that the edifice represents the earth. The staircases of the structure's three pyramidal towers slope at an angle of 70° and can therefore have served no practical purpose. In the center of each of the staircases, huge frontal masks of the terrestrial monster break the monotony of the vast expanse of stonework. The dummy pyramids are surmounted by dummy temples, whose central doorways also represent the terrestrial monster's jaws. But here, the false doors are surmounted by a frontal mask and flanked by two masks in profile. Each temple was extended by a decorative roof comb.

DZIBANCHÉ
(*18½ miles/30 km north of Kohunlich*)
The ruins of Dzibanché, situated in a region that was clearly well populated during the pre-Columbian era, have been intensively excavated since 1992. Some spectacular tombs have been discovered in the large pyramids forming part of the main group.

Below left: Structure 9 at Becán
Bottom: Structure 2 at Chicanná

Becán ◆ F C5

(*3 miles/5 km from Xpuhil*) The center of the largest of the Río Bec sites is surrounded by a ditch, originally 16 feet (5 m) deep and 52½ feet (16 m) wide. The earliest recorded buildings date from the end of the Early Classical era.

MONUMENTS. The considerable architectural activity that took place during the five or six centuries of Becán's existence is reflected in the additions, superpositions and modifications made continuously up to and during the Early Postclassical era. The decorative repertoire of the Río Bec style is well illustrated on the buildings of this regional capital – groups of small, engaged columns, 'checkerboards', crosses and superposed masks are scattered liberally across the façades. STRUCTURE 8 is something of an enigma. Nine completely dark, interconnecting rooms were found within the main body of the pyramid, with only a narrow passageway connecting them to the outside. One theory is that the complex may have been used for ritual ambulations in an environment designed to represent the underworld.

INTO THE JAWS OF THE MONSTER...
In the huge monster mask at Chicanná (*below*), the broad snout is drawn back to reveal a row of impressive-looking teeth. The eyes have hook-shaped pupils. Two spirals emerging from the corners of the mouth probably represent the breath of life. A U-shaped cavity on the forehead indicates access to the underworld.

Chicanná ◆ F C5

(*7½ miles/12 km from Xpuhil*) The façade of STRUCTURE 2 consists of three sections – a central building with two adjoining wings. The cornices above the lateral entrances are in the form of simple peasant dwellings with thatched roofs, whose empty niches once contained statues. Below the cornices, the smooth walls were covered with stucco and painted with glyphs, a few of which are still visible today.
GIANT MONSTER MASK. In contrast to the soberness of the wings, the façade of the central building is completely sculpted. Above the entrance, the main motif is a frontal

The funerary mask and jadeite pectoral ornaments (*below*) discovered at Calakmul can be seen in the Museo Arqueológico in Campeche ▲ 222.

mask of the terrestrial monster whose lower jaw is represented by the projecting platform that forms the threshold. Behind the great profile masks that frame the entrance are two sculpted panels of superposed, stylized, terrestrial masks. The great two-headed serpent arching above the frontal mask probably represents the sky.

Balamku ◆ F B5

(*37 miles/60 km from Chicanná*) Balamku, discovered by chance in 1990, is today famous for its HOUSE OF THE FOUR KINGS. The façade of this edifice dates from the Early Classical era and bears a stucco frieze 55 feet (17 m) long. The decoration is extended upward by four masonry blocks added to the roof, so that the roof level represents the earth's surface separating the underworld from the mortal world. The image of the king emerging from the jaws of the terrestrial monster (symbolizing accession) alternates with that of a seated or kneeling jaguar bound as a sacrificial victim.

Calakmul ◆ F C6

(*About 1½ hours south of Balamku, along a track suitable for vehicles.*) Situated near the Guatemalan border, Calakmul is one of the largest Classical Mayan sites. Early on, its development enabled it to assert its domination over the other city-states in the region, although it vied with its great rival Tikal to achieve and retain political supremacy within the Mayan world. While Calakmul gained the upper hand in the 7th century, it was Tikal that dominated the lowlands during the 8th century. Its monumental architecture – a thousand or so buildings – is located in an area of ¾ square mile (2 km²). Beyond that, another 6,250 structures are scattered over an area of 7¾ square miles (20 km²). The ruins are surrounded by a network of canals and reservoirs. The monumental architecture dates from the Preclassical era, as evidenced by Structure II-sub-C. The structure, which stands 42½ feet (13 m) high, is decorated with a huge stucco frieze showing the dead king falling from the sky, by analogy with the setting sun. It was later covered with a series of pyramids, the last of which reached a height of almost 197 feet (60 meters). Calakmul is famous for its many monuments (120 steles) which are unfortunately badly eroded due to the poor quality of the local limestone. It is one of the few sites to possess a pair of steles representing the king and queen.

SCENES OF EMERGENCE
On the frieze at Balamku a terrestrial monster mask is surmounted by a toad and a crocodile with their heads thrown back. The king is depicted emerging from their open jaws, seated on a jaguar-skin cushion and wearing his 'chin' and 'headdress' masks. This decoration is a celebration of royalty and stresses its close relationship with the cosmos. The frieze represents the king's accession to the throne (symbolizing rebirth) from the bowels of the earth, which associates him with the sun and corn.

221

Below: Puerta del Mar

VAUBAN IN AMERICA
Following the sacking of the port in 1685, the idea of building a wall around the town, like those of Havana and Santo Domingo, was accepted by the Spanish king and work was begun under the direction of the German architect, Johannes Franck. The peace treaty signed between France and Spain at Ryswick, in 1697, made collaboration between the two nations possible. The French engineer Louis Bouchard de Bécourt suggested certain modifications as well as additional protective measures. The Vauban-style fortress was thus introduced to America.

Campeche, founded in 1540 by Francisco de Montejo, alias El Mozo ('the young man'), is the oldest Spanish town on the Yucatán peninsula and the only import and export point for the region's products. Situated on a flat coastline, with no natural land or sea defenses, it was an easy target for pirates, so a defensive stone wall was built around the town. The wall was opened up in the late 19th century to allow the city to expand more freely. Since then, vast areas of land have been reclaimed outside the old wall and modern buildings have totally altered the landscape of Campeche's golden age. Classed as a UNESCO World Heritage Site in 1999, the town's historic center has been carefully restored.

Fortifications ◆ F B3-4, ◆ M

Although the fortification of the port began in the 16th century, when a tower was built and equipped with a small artillery, work was not completed until the 19th century. Despite being captured and burned by pirates during the 17th century, Campeche remained without any effective defenses until the fortifications proper were built in the 18th century. They formed an irregular hexagon with a bastion at each corner, another in the center of the rampart overlooking the sea, and another in the center of the landward-facing rampart. The wall, which was over 1½ miles (2½ km) long and 26 feet (8 m) high, later became redundant and was gradually demolished from the 19th century onward. Today, only the bastions (*baluartes*) remain and have been converted into museums.

MUSEUMS AND GARDENS.
The Puerta del Mar ('Sea Gate'), overlooking the harbor, was protected by the Baluarte de la Soledad, now the MUSEO DE LAS ESTELAS, an archeological museum containing Mayan steles. To the west, the Baluarte de San Carlos has been transformed into the town museum, the MUSEO DE LA CIUDAD. On the landward side, the *baluartes* Santa Rosa and San Juan guarded against attacks from the south, as did the Baluarte de San Francisco, near the

PUERTA DE TIERRA ('Land Gate') – where *son et lumière* events are organized – and the Baluarte de San Pedro. The partly ruined Baluarte de Santiago is now occupied by the JARDÍN BOTÁNICO XMUCH HALTÚN. The FUERTE SAN MIGUEL was built to keep watch over the beaches and sea, but today houses the MUSEO ARQUEOLÓGICO, which has beautiful pieces from the Isla Jaina ▲ 223 and Calakmul ▲ 221. The 18th-century Polvorín (powder magazine), a fine example of this type of military architecture, is not only interesting to visit but also offers a splendid view of the town

Around the Plaza Mayor ◆ **M** B1

COLONIAL MANSIONS.
Behind Campeche's cathedral
(17th–19th century), the
MANSIÓN CARBAJAL, which has
been converted into an office and
craft shop, is a fine example of a
wealthy colonial mansion, with its
marble floor, columns and
Mozarabic arches. Other colonial
mansions are open to the public,
including CASA NO. 6 (opposite
the cathedral), which has been
partly renovated in 19th-century style; the 18th-century CASA
DE ARTESANIAS 'TUKULNA' (Calle 10, between *calles* 59
and 61); and the CASA DEL TENIENTE DEL REY (18th
century). They all have the same layout with the rooms
opening onto a central courtyard surrounded by arcades.
There was a well in the center of the courtyard and a second
service courtyard.

MONASTERIES AND CHURCHES. According to tradition,
the FRANCISCAN MONASTERY OF SAN FRANCISCO was
built (1546–98) on the spot where the first Mass was
celebrated in the New World. It was also where the grandson
of Hernán Cortés was born and baptized. The façade of the
Iglesia de San José, whose construction was begun by the
Jesuits in the early 18th century, is covered with enameled
tiles known as *talaveras* ▲ *288*. The construction of the
college was interrupted in 1767 when the Jesuits were
expelled from the Spanish colonies. The IGLESIA DEL DULCE
NOMBRE DE JESÚS, the town's oldest church, was originally
used as a place of worship by Blacks and mulattos.

**THE STATUETTES
OF JAINA ◆ F** B3
The Isla Jaina,
famous for its ancient
cemetery dating
from the Classical
era, was originally a
coral reef. The Maya
raised its surface
by transporting
limestone to the
island as a base for
their architectural
structures. The first
account of the island
was written by Désiré
Charnay in 1886.
Jaina lies about 18½
miles (30 km) north
of Campeche and is
separated from the
mainland by a narrow
channel. Among the
offerings found there
were the magnificent
polychrome
statuettes, often
referred to as
'American *tanagras*',
for which the island is
famous. They
represent various
types of figures,
clothed and armed,
and provide firsthand
information on the
costumes and ritual
objects of the
Classical era.

SMALL ACROPOLIS
A small acropolis, to the south of the Great Acropolis, consists of a platform 246 feet (75 m) square on which four structures surround a central courtyard. At the foot of a ruined temple on the west side of the courtyard, steles dating from AD 627–810 were discovered on the platform.

Edzná ◆ F B4

(*38 miles/61 km from Campeche, along the road to Hopelchén. Turn off to the right at Cayal.*) Edzná is a fine example of Mayan urban organization. In 600 BC, a group of Maya settled in this valley, isolated from other population centers, where they lived until the 10th century. In the 3rd century AD, an urban center developed, which provided a focal point for the region's surplus agricultural products. These were traded with the region of Petén, in present-day Guatemala, the source of the ritual objects, traditional crafts and cultural influences that characterize the art of Edzná. The local aristocracy controlled the valley's rural population, exacting tributes and commandeering their labor to build magnificent temples and palaces. After the 6th century, neighboring provinces (Río Bec, Chenes and Puuc) developed to the east and north, opening up new commercial possibilities. Edzná appears to have retained a certain autonomy and individuality, but was not altogether impervious to the influence of its powerful neighbors. After the collapse of the great Maya civilization in the 9th century, Edzná declined in importance and was abandoned like other towns and cities of the Classical era. The peasants retreated, probably in the interests of safety, to the foothills of the valley.

Temple of the Five Stories, Edzná.

GROUP OF THE CEREMONIAL CENTER. The group around the vast Plaza Mayor is dominated by the partly restored Great Acropolis, the Nohol Na, facing the Annex of the Knives (Cuchillos), to the north, and the Temple of the House of the South (Casa del Sur). A *sacbe* ▲ *211* leads from the Great Acropolis toward a group of dwellings situated between the Annex of the Knives and the Nohol Na, and surrounded by other structures. This complex is based on those of Petén.

PLAZA MAYOR. The rectangular Plaza Mayor – 186 by 105 yards (170 by 96 m) – was once covered in stucco. It slopes slightly southward to allow rainwater to drain into the canal.

GREAT ACROPOLIS. The impressive complex of the Great Acropolis stands on a vast platform measuring 175 by 162 yards (160 by 148 m). Each of the first four pyramidal tiers of the TEMPLE OF THE FIVE STORIES consists of rows of cells, while the temple on top is surmounted by a roof comb that brings the overall height to 102 feet (31 m). A central staircase (some of the steps bear glyphs) leads from the Plaza Mayor to the temple, which is reached via a courtyard. At the entrance to the seven first-story rooms (one beneath the

entrance to the seven first-story rooms (one beneath the staircase) are the remains of Río Bec-style cement stone pillars, while the monolithic columns on the fourth story are in the Puuc style ▲ *234*. The five-story temple-pyramid partly covers an older, Petén-style temple. To the south of the courtyard, a temple reached via a staircase stands on a platform measuring 132 by 99 feet (40 by 30 m). This edifice also covers an older structure. At the southwest corner stands a temple that shows the influence of the Petén style, and a later annex that partly blocks the central staircase. A similar structure existed at the other side of the staircase, leaving a narrow access to the courtyard. Other structures include the Temazcal (steam bath ▲ *195*), the northwest temple, the Puuc platform and the north platform.

INDIAN HOUSES
In these forested regions, houses are often little more than basic huts (*above*) with openwork walls made from planks or plant stems, and roofs thatched with palm leaves. Modern materials (half-round tiles, corrugated iron, roofing felt) are tending to replace traditional materials, even though they are often less comfortable and more expensive. However, they do give the houses a longer lease on life, and make them better able to withstand bad weather and earthquakes.

Hochob and Dzibilnocac ◆ **F** C4

(*About 77½ miles/125 km southeast of Campeche. Take the road to Hopelchén and then turn right to Dzibalchén. Hochob lies to the south, and Dzibilnocac to the north of Dzibalchén.*) These two virtually unexplored sites reflect the splendor of the Chenes style. HOCHOB, to the south of Dzibalchén, is the better restored of the two. The façade of the temple, to the right of the plaza, represents the terrestrial monster. Most of the ruins on this vast site are unexcavated and as yet have not revealed the secrets of the people who once inhabited this forested region. Beyond Dzibalchén and Vicente Guerrero, a track leads to the site of DZIBILNOCAC. Although the first two temples are disappointing, the delicacy of the architecture and fineness of the frescos and sculptures of the third make the journey worthwhile. The top of this temple also offers a spectacular view of the surrounding ruins.

Above: a doorway in the temple at Hochob

ERMITA DE SANTA ISABEL
The Hermitage of Santa Isabel is situated on the outskirts of Mérida, on the old Campeche road. This modest but elegant, single-nave structure, which stands alone in its garden-plaza, is a refuge for walkers.

Ancient Tiho, or Ichcanziho, was one of the principal towns of the Mayan province of Chacán. On January 6, 1542, Francisco de Montejo confirmed the Spanish occupation of the region by founding the town of Mérida on this ancient site – the Mayan ruins reminded him of the Roman ruins of Mérida in Spain. The town's layout, with its attractive central square and parallel streets intersecting at right angles, is based on the blueprint for all colonial towns built in America. Today, this busy cultural capital still has a strong colonial identity, albeit attenuated by time and modernity, and a few 19th-century architectural gems.

Plaza Mayor ◆ N B2-3

Plaza Mayor and Mérida Cathedral

The CATHEDRAL and BISHOP'S RESIDENCE were constructed on the east side of the Plaza Mayor. The Palacio

Montejo, built for Francisco de
Montejo, originally occupied the
entire south side. To the west is
the Palacio Municipal and, to the
north, the Palacio del Gobierno
and the governor's and
commander-in-chief's residence
● 77. These buildings have been
modified over the years, with the
bishop's residence being replaced
by the offices of the federal
authorities, which have in turn
been replaced by the MUSEO DE
ARTE CONTEMPORANEO ATENEO
DE YUCATÁN (MACAY), while
other 'modernizations' were made
in the late 19th century. However,
the plaza has retained its parklike
atmosphere where visitors and
inhabitants can walk or sit in the
shade of the weeping figs.

THE CATHEDRAL ◆ N B2-3.

The town's cathedral, built
between 1562 and 1598, was the
first to be completed on the
American continent. It was based
on a basilican layout, with three
naves and twelve pillars, and its
distinctive dome is the oldest in Mexico. In the center of the
austere FAÇADE, with its two Renaissance-style towers and
three entrances, a huge blazon originally bore the Spanish
coat of arms. After Independence, these were replaced by the
Mexican eagle. Its layout and decoration were partly
modified as a result of the damage sustained during the
Revolution. The two lateral chapels on the south side were
destroyed, while venerated sculptures such as the *Christ of
the Blisters*, the altar, the organ and other works of art and
furnishings were burnt. The cathedral houses important
archives and a collection of ancient paintings.

CASA DE MONTEJO ◆ N B3. Built between 1543 and 1551,
the Casa de Montejo is one of the oldest residences in
Mérida. All that remains of the original building is the
sculpted Plateresque façade, one of the finest in America.
The entrance depicts the Montejo coat of arms flanked by
two armed *conquistadores* with their feet resting on grimacing
heads, a symbol of the Conquest. The scene is completed by
several other figures and motifs. Today it is a bank.

PALACIO MUNICIPAL ◆ N B3. The original 17th-century
structure, which stands on the site of the ancient pyramid
that provided building materials for the cathedral and the
Casa de Montejo, has undergone several transformations,
including the addition of a tall tower completely out of
harmony with the architectural style of Mérida.

PALACIO DE GOBIERNO ◆ N B2. The present Palacio del
Gobierno was opened in 1892. It contains works of one of the
last great Mexican mural artists, Fernando Castro Pacheco
(1886–1966), which trace the region's history.

Top: a toy-seller in
Mérida
Above: statues of
conquistadores on the
doorway of Casa de
Montejo

**TEATRO JOSÉ PEÓN
CONTRERAS**
With the boom in
the production of
sisal ▲ *201*, Mérida
experienced a
remarkable period
of development
during the second half
of the 19th century.
The colonial
mansions with their
austere façades were
either demolished or
renovated. A new
wave of European-
style buildings
appeared and
changed the face of
the town. A new
'European' theater,
with lots of marble
columns, a large
dome and frescos,
was built on the
university campus.

227

SAN JUAN BAUTISTA DISTRICT
The old colonial town lay between the south side of the Plaza Mayor and the district of San Juan Bautista where, in the sacristy of the church of San Juan, the first liberals (a group known as the 'Sanjuanistas') met on the eve of Independence to develop a political system more favorable to the Indians. The archway overlooking the Plaza de San Juan is one of three that once marked the boundaries of the old Spanish town. San Juan lay at one end of the Camino Real that led to the port of Campeche.

Around the Plaza Mayor

IGLESIA DEL TERCER ORDEN ◆ N B2. (*Corner of calles 59 and 60*) On the tiny Plaza de los Hidalgos, the Iglesia de Jesús, known as the Iglesia del Tercer Orden, stands on land that belonged to the Jesuits until 1767.

THE UNIVERSITY ◆ N B2. The modern university occupies the site of the former Colegio de San Pedro (1711), which was part of the Real y Pontifica Universidad de San Francisco Javier, founded in 1624. In 1984, it became the Autonomous University of Yucatán. The old Jesuit building was transformed by the addition of the upper story and the entrance porch on the corner of Calles 60 and 57.

EX-CONVENTO DE LAS MONJAS ◆ N A2. Behind the Palacio Municipal are the ruins of the monastery of Nuestra Señora de la Consolación, known today as Las Monjas (The Nuns). It was founded in 1633 as a residence for the Sisters of the Immaculate Conception and closed down in 1867. Today the monastery, which has a distinctive arcaded tower, is occupied by a store selling traditional crafts, a cultural center and the Museo de la Canción Yucateca (Museum of Yucatecan Music). Further west, the IGLESIA DE SANTIAGO dominates the plaza of this former Mayan district.

CONVENTO DE LA MEJORADA ◆ N C2. (*Corner of Calles 59 and 50*) Built in the 17th century, the monastery is today occupied by an architectural college and the MUSEO DE ARTE Y CULTURA POPULAR (Museum of Popular Art).

MERCADO CENTRAL ◆ N B3. (*To the southwest of the zócalo*) The central market was built on the site of the ruined monastery of San Francisco. Calles 65 and 67, opposite Calle 65, are reserved for local crafts. Beneath the arcades, the old corn exchange (*Calles 65 and 56*) has retained all the atmosphere of the colonial markets.

Paseo de Montejo ◆ N B1

The town expanded rapidly and, from the early 20th century, the main avenue – the Paseo de Montejo – was enhanced by palatial residences as a result of the boom in the production

Below left and right: residences on the Paseo de Montejo
Below center: the Mercado Municipal

of sisal. One of those remaining contains the MUSEO DE ARQUEOLOGÍA (*on the corner of Calle 43*), which traces the development of Mexico's pre-Hispanic cultures, and in particular the Maya, showcasing some of the most important pieces found in Yucatán. At the end of the avenue, an impressive monument by the Colombian sculptor Romulo Rosso relates the country's history in bas-relief.

The archeological site of Mayapán ◆ F C3

(*About 25 miles/40 km southeast of Mérida, on a minor road [no. 18]*) The Mayapán chieftains belonged to the Cocom lineage, descended from a certain Hunal Ceel who captured and destroyed Chichén Itzá ▲ *244* in the early 13th century. Mayapán took over from Chichén Itzá and underwent significant changes due to a new wave of Mexican influence. Just before 1450, one of the noble houses of Mayapán rebelled against the Cocoms. Shortly afterward, Mayapán was plundered and abandoned, leaving the way open for a number of 'warring kingdoms' in perpetual conflict.

REMAINS. Mayapán has a temple similar to the 'Castillo' of Chichén Itzá, complete with serpent columns, serpent handrails, flagpoles and small telamons. However, the *chacmool* ▲ *245*, ball courts, *tzompantli* and all evidence of the worship of jaguars and eagles have disappeared. The terrestrial monster masks and moldings inherited from the Puuc tradition ▲ *234* can still be seen on some of the façades.

RELIGIOUS BUILDINGS. There are two types of ceremonial complexes found in Mayapán. One has a hypostyle hall, a sanctuary and an oratory; while the other has a temple with a hypostyle hall, an oratory on the right-hand side of the temple, a sanctuary opposite the oratory and, between the two, a platform for statues. Many of these buildings had a religious function, as evidenced by the large number of associated altars, caches, burial places and ossuaries for sacrificial victims. Each complex corresponded to a particular lineage, consisting of several families who practiced a private form of worship as well as the official form.

THE CENSERS OF MAYAPÁN
Some of the effigies on these ceramic censers (*below*), dating from 1300 to 1450, represent Mexican gods. Others represent the Mayan gods who appear on the wall paintings of Tulum and the pictographic manuscripts of the *Madrid* and *Dresden Codices*. The development of a religious pantheon, and a decentralized form of worship of individual deities, corresponded to a weakening of centralized political power.

Opposite: Convento de Man

As soon as the Franciscans arrived in Yucatán, they set about converting the Maya and, to this end, built a great many monasteries. These centers were also used for the dissemination of European culture. Indian children were taught how to keep cattle and grow new crops, and also learned crafts such as wrought-iron work, cabinet-making and how to make musical instruments. As it winds its way through the heart of rural Yucatán, the monastery route takes you past a number of *haciendas* and through peaceful villages with colorful markets.

The entrance to the church in Mamá is decorated with extremely elaborate naive motifs carved by Mayan craftsmen.

From monastery to monastery

MAMÁ ◆ F C2. The name of this village means 'no, no'. The 17th-century CHURCH, dedicated to the Assumption of the Virgin, is crowned by a bell tower. The sober façade is offset by an elaborate entrance carved by Mayan sculptors.

TEABO ◆ F C3. The frescos in the sacristy of the 17th-century basilican CHURCH OF SAN PEDRO AND SAN PABLO are clearly of European inspiration and are among the most beautiful in Yucatán. In the ruined cloister, fragments of frescos have survived the eroding effects of the weather.

MANÍ ◆ F C3. The province of Maní (meaning 'all is past' in Maya) was the first to form an allegiance with the Spanish, and a treaty establishing Indian territorial borders was signed here in 1557. Maní was also the first province to welcome Franciscan friars. In 1550, Fray Juan de Mérida oversaw the construction of the MONASTERY, which took six thousand Indians seven years to complete. The complex consists of the monastery, the church, the great atrium, the school and the hospital. Fray Juan de Herrera, accompanied by the French monk Jacobo (Jacques) de Testera, who invented a writing system that enabled him to give religious instruction to the Indians, took charge of the school, which became famous throughout Yucatán. Herrera also had a great open-air chapel built, the first of its kind on the peninsula. The stones used to construct the complex, built on a pre-Hispanic platform, came from ancient Mayan temples. In the 18th century, the original façade of the church was demolished, the nave extended forward and a new façade built. Only one of the original corner chapels still exists.

OXKUTZCAB ◆ F C3. The town of Oxkutzcab ('land of three tobaccos', in Maya) has an important, early 18th-century basilican church, the IGLESIA DE SAN FRANCISCO DE ASIS. The sober façade is pierced by a portal with lateral pilasters supporting a classic pediment.

LOLTÚN CAVES
◆ F C3
(*About 4 miles/7 km south of Oxkutzcab*)
The Loltún Caves – whose name means 'stone flower' in Maya – are a stone fairyland of vast underground chambers. Bones found in the caves provided the earliest evidence of human habitation in Yucatán.

TICUL ◆ F C3. Ticul is famous for its terracotta craftwork and is also an important agricultural center. The 17th-century IGLESIA DE SAN ANTONIO has a sober façade and an entrance decorated with twin columns, niches for sculptures and a Franciscan coat of arms. The church was once part of a monastery of which only a few elements have survived.

MUNÁ ◆ F C3. The 16th-century MONASTERY dedicated to the Assumption of the Virgin stands in the center of a large plaza and, like most Yucatecan monasteries, is partly preserved. The area in front is a public square.

UMÁN ◆ F B2. The CONVENTO DE SAN FRANCISCO DE ASIS was demolished and only the annexes and church have survived. The church was rebuilt in the 18th century, except for the only tower on the façade. Unusually for Yucatán, the nave has a transept, while the dome, visible from some distance away, looks out of place in the landscape. The 16th-century open-air chapel (now dedicated to San Pedro and San Pablo) opens onto the church and monastery.

Haciendas

On the way back to Mérida, it is worth stopping at the small Hacienda de Ochil (now a restaurant), or the impressive Hacienda de Temozón, a luxury hotel (*signposted off to the right on the Muná–Umán road*).

HACIENDA DE YAXCOPOIL ◆ F C2. (*Between Muná and Umán, on the Mex 261*) This 18th-century *hacienda* was converted for the production of sisal and extended at the end of the 19th century. It has since been transformed into a museum reflecting the glory of the famous *haciendas* that made Yucatán's fortune up to the 1920s.

DIEGO DE LANDA
In 1562, Diego de Landa, a missionary and future Bishop of Yucatán, ordered an *auto-da-fé* at Maní during which many images and codices were destroyed in front of the monastery walls. The incident, at which a large number of people were killed, terrified the Maya and disturbed Spanish consciences. Apparently stricken by remorse, Landa wrote a history of the Maya and their customs in his *Relación de las Cosas de Yucatán*. However, while acknowledging their wisdom, he still would not renounce his religious dogmatism.

Below: Hacienda de Uayalceh, beyond Temozón

▲ 'Milpa'

Agricultural techniques are the same in the highlands and lowlands, but the calendar is different.

Milpa – a Mexican word derived from Nahuatl, meaning 'freshly cleared ground' – is an area of cultivated forest. In Maya tradition trees are ancestors and cutting them down would be tantamount to committing murder. To ensure that the forest regenerates, land must be cleared according to precise rules and rituals based on the Mayan peasant's excellent knowledge of the environment and the different species of plant life. Corn is not the only crop grown on the plot. A number of different crops are cultivated using a remarkable combination of archaic techniques and highly complex systems of irrigation, drainage, terracing and soil classification, all adapted to the particular region.

Coa

LAND CLEARANCE Land is cleared using the ax (*bat*) and the machete-like *coa* or *lotche*, usually in August when the wood is at its most tender. A hardworking peasant can clear 2–3 *mécates* in a day (8,729–12,884 sq. feet/800–1,200 sq. m).

BURNING. The Maya walk round their plots lighting fires with a torch at regular intervals and whistling to invoke beneficent winds – this is regarded as vital for a successful harvest.

SOWING. Corn is sown 'between the stones' with a sort of dibble (*choul*), a traditional tool that has only been modified once since prehistoric times – the wooden point, originally hardened by fire, has been replaced by a steel tip.

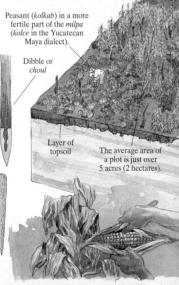

Peasant (*kolkab*) in a more fertile part of the *milpa* (*kolce* in the Yucatecan Maya dialect).

Dibble or *choul*

Layer of topsoil

The average area of a plot is just over 5 acres (2 hectares).

Gadget for extracting the corn from its husk

WEEDING. In the 1970s, weedkillers began to replace the use of the *coa* for weeding. However, farmers are becoming increasingly aware of their disadvantages and are adopting more eco-friendly methods.

HARVEST. The women and children help with the harvest and, sometimes, other farmers who in turn enlist help for their own harvest. The average yield is in the order of 660 lbs (300 kg) of corn per acre (0.5 ha).

Corn

The stems of the cobs are 'broken' in September–October to prevent the cobs being pecked by birds or rotting through rainfall.

Beans

Squash

VARIETIES OF CORN
The several varieties of this starch-rich cereal crop are classified according to color and ripening period (2–5 months). Corn is almost always grown with beans and squash, whose seeds are sown in the same holes as the corn seeds.

POLYCULTURE

Red and black beans

Squash   Gourd   Sweet potato   Tomatoes   Bananas

Chilies

In the richer areas of soil, usually located in small, damp depressions known as *k'op*, the peasants plant various food crops – pulses, tubers, fruit and vegetables and, of course, chilies ● 70.

Stony ground where the corn is grown 'between the stones'   *Storage hut*

Forest canopy

Sinkhole or *cenote*

Permeable karstic layer

Palm tree left during clearance

MILLING
After the harvest, the corn has to be turned into flour. Today the millstone has been replaced by a hand- or motor-operated mill.

MAKING TORTILLAS
The rhythmic sound of women slapping corn pancakes into shape can be heard late in the morning in any Maya village.

233

'RUTA PUUC'
(*Allow a full day*)
The route, marked
Via ruinas ('route of
the ruins'), links the
sites where visitors
can admire the finest
examples of Puuc
architecture. From
Mérida, take the RF
180 to Umán, then
the regional road
(Mex 261) to Uxmal.
From there the sites
of Kabah, Sayil and
Labná are easily
accessible. A 'Ruta
Puuc' coach leaves
Mérida daily at
8.00 am, stopping at
Uxmal for 2½ hours.

The Puuc region, south of Mérida, had its political and economic center at Uxmal. Its influence spread to the north of the peninsula, reaching Chichén Itzá, Tiho and present-day Mérida. In Yucatán, the Puuc style of architecture represented a transition from the Classical to the Postclassical, the period during which Chichén Itzá was built. These sites, today largely restored, flourished in the Late Classical era, in about AD 800–900. They are characterized by large, elongated structures with sculpted decorations. The Puuc cities collapsed when the Toltecs arrived in Yucatán, particularly at Chichén Itzá.

THE PUUC STYLE. The Puuc style takes its name from the range of hills running northwest–southeast across the north of the peninsula. It is distinguished by certain technical features (masonry cladding) and decorative techniques (mosaics in relief on the upper part of façades). The Puuc style often used sculpted stone mosaics composed of

UXMAL
1. Nunnery Quadrangle
2. Pyramid of the Magician
3. Ball Court
4. Cemetery Group
5. Governor's Palace
6. The Turtle House
7. The Pigeon House
8. Great Pyramid

prefabricated elements. The decorative elements included openwork, multiple columns, step-and-fret motifs and frontal masks on façades or superposed on the corners of buildings, all geometrically arranged and repeated. Terrestrial monster masks formed doors and ran riot over façades.

Uxmal ◆ F B3

Uxmal is one of the best known of the Mayan sites due to its relatively good state of preservation and the quality of its Puuc-style stone mosaic decorations. Little is known about the origins and development of this important center, which was at its height between AD 800 and 1000. However, the site has revealed the existence of Lord Chac, who appears to have ruled in the early 10th century. The city is characterized by its quadrangles in which large, elongated, multi-roomed buildings form a closed complex around a courtyard.

PIRÁMIDE DEL ADIVINO.
The temples that are visible
correspond to the two final
stages in the construction of
the Pyramid of the Magician.
On the west side is a Chenes-
style temple, an imitation
of an earlier Puuc-style
structure. The most recent
temple was built at the top of
the pyramid, at a height of 85
feet (26 m), on a new tier. The

sculpture, dating from the first stage of construction, shows a
king of Uxmal emerging from a serpent's jaws.

CUADRÁNGULO DE LAS MONJAS. The Nunnery
Quadrangle was so called by ancient travelers who compared
the closed complex to that of a convent. The courtyard
measures 249 by 201 feet (76 x 61 m) and each of the
buildings has a double row of rooms. The building on the
north side, standing on a higher platform, appears to be the
most important. The eleven-doored façade is decorated with
superimposed masks of the terrestrial monster and a pseudo-
Tlaloc mask, which alternate with images of huts surmounted
by two-headed serpents. The decoration of the east building
consists of several groups of rigid two-headed serpents which
decrease in length toward the base. The south façade is
decorated with huts surmounted by a mask of the terrestrial
monster. The façade decoration becomes more complex on
the west side where, as well as superimposed masks, there
are enthroned figures beneath a dais and warriors in haut-
relief, the whole framed by feathered serpents.

CASA DE LAS TORTUGAS. The Turtle House is
remarkable for its proportions and simplicity. The frieze
consists of an uninterrupted decoration of small, engaged
columns between two Puuc-style dovetail moldings with a
central cordon. On the upper cordon is a row of realistically
carved turtles (symbolic of the earth in Maya culture).

**ARCHEOLOGICAL
RESEARCH**
In 1836, Jean-
Frédéric de Waldeck
● *264* published a
brief description of
the site, which he had
visited a few years
previously. Although
extensive restoration
work was begun in
1928, and again in
1938, the site has
never been
systematically
excavated.

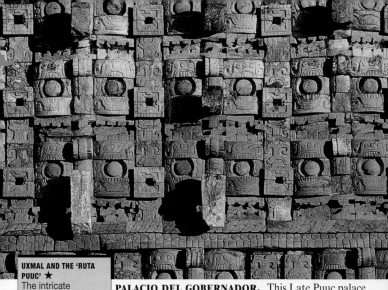

UXMAL AND THE 'RUTA PUUC' ★

The intricate stonework of the Puuc sites is at its most beautiful in the golden light of evening.

Above: detail of the Codz Pop at Kabah

DEVELOPMENT OF THE PUUC STYLE
Early monumental columns enabled doors to become wider, with a simple lower molding. Then engaged columns and masks appeared. Finally, after 870, mosaic decorations triumphed over a limited area, and combined engaged columns with openwork and fret motifs.

PALACIO DEL GOBERNADOR. This Late Puuc palace (9th–10th century) consists of a main building and two wings. It is almost 330 feet (100 m) long by 39 feet (12 m) wide, and 28 feet (8.6 m) high. It has been estimated that the stone mosaic decoration of the façade required some 20,000 sculpted elements. The two largest rooms, aligned in the central building, are connected to the outside by three doors. The main entrance to the Governor's Palace is surmounted by an image of the king seated on his throne against a background of two-headed serpents decorated with celestial symbols, which suggests that he is the founder of a dynasty. Other dignitaries are represented emerging from the open, upturned jaws of the terrestrial monster. The decoration is completed by step-and-fret motifs and frontal masks against a background of latticework.

EL PALOMAR. This residential palace was built between AD 700 and 800 in a style that predates that of the Nunnery Quadrangle. Its poor state of preservation belies the fact that the exterior walls were once covered in stucco ornaments. It was nicknamed the 'Pigeon House' because the many openings that pierce the long roof comb are reminiscent of European dovecotes.

Other Puuc sites

KABAH ◆ F C3. The CODZ POP ('Palace of the Masks') ● 74 at Kabah has ten rooms arranged in two parallel rows. The west façade is completely covered with masks of the terrestrial monster in relief. One row covers the platform on which the building stands, three more decorate the lower part of the façade below a central cordon, and the last three decorate the top part of the building between the central cordon and the roof. In the Palace of the Masks, the concept of a teratomorphic building (that is, representing a monster) whose main body is defined by superimposed masks is taken to the extreme. On top of the east façade, eight statues of the same king (identified by his facial scarifications) stand against a background of feathers. An arch almost 16 feet (5 m) wide stands at the end of the *sacbe* that runs from Kabah to Uxmal.

SAYIL ◆ F C3. (*4½ miles/7 km south of Kabah*) Sayil is famous for its 'three-story' PALACE. In fact the 'stories' are

not superimposed but are arranged in terraces on the three tiers of a stone base. The first two include two rows of rooms. On the upper frieze, a mask of the terrestrial monster alternates with a figure diving vertically into the jaws of another mask flanked by two lizardlike creatures in profile, against a background of small columns. The third consists of a structure with a single row of rooms ● 72.

LABNÁ ◆ F C3. Labná has two juxtaposed quadrangles linked by a monumental vaulted arch flanked by two rooms. The decoration on the west side includes a miniature hut above the door to each room. The huts, which once contained stucco statues, are framed by latticework panels. On the east side, the decoration consists of two opposed step-and-fret motifs against a background of small engaged columns. The motifs form the tiered jaws, extended by spirals, of a terrestrial monster mask. The structure is crowned with a small roof comb pierced by a number of rectangular openings.

Above: Palace of Sayil
Below: Arch of Labná

THE MAYA AND WATER
In this karstic region where there is no surface water, the Maya survived by building underground cisterns (*chultunes*) to collect rainwater. They also obtained water from the region's natural sinkholes, or *cenotes* ▲ 238.

'CENOTES'

The word *cenote* is derived from the Maya word *dzonot*. *Cenotes* are the natural holes in the surface of the limestone that makes up the Yucatán peninsula, which once formed part of the sea bed. As the slightly acid water drained from the surface, it eroded the limestone and created natural reservoirs of varying sizes whose 'roof' finally collapsed. These open wells, which sometimes plunge to great depths, are the only source of drinking water in this karstic region. Today, they are still regarded as a gift from the gods, the dwelling place of spirits and a route to the underworld.

Toward Progreso

DZIBILCHALTÚN ◆ F C2. *(7½ miles/12 km north of Mérida)* The Maya city of Dzibilchaltún was founded in 600 BC but was inhabited inconsistently until the 9th century, when it enjoyed its golden age, probably due to the salt trade. At the time, the population stood at almost 25,000 and the city center was made up of a hundred or so stone buildings, some of which had vaulted roofs and were supported by step pyramids. A total of 8,000 houses were recorded in the vicinity, over an area of 7⅓ sq. miles (19 sq. km). Most were simple huts but 2,000 had part-masonry walls. The center of the site was linked to other groups of dwellings by *sacbeob*. Built c. 700, the TEMPLO DES LAS SIETE MUÑECAS ('Temple of the Seven Dolls') is one of the most unusual on the site. It is perched on top of a pyramidal base with four staircases and has four doors which open onto a corridor surrounding a central room. The room is surmounted by a vault in four sections which appears to be a sort of tower dominating the rest of the building. The upper section of the walls was decorated with an aquatic frieze celebrating underground water, the source of the earth's fertility. During the Late Classical era, the temple was covered by another, larger pyramid. Centuries later, during the Late Postclassical era, a passage was opened into the temple and an altar was built. The temple is named for an offering of seven clay dolls placed before the altar. Some 30,000 Mayan objects were found in the *cenote* of Xlacah, over 165 feet (50 m) deep.

PROGRESO ◆ F C1. *(22 miles/36 km north of Mérida)* The port of Progreso was founded in the mid-19th century to replace the port of Sisal, which had been used since the Spanish Conquest. The new port was better protected from winds and currents, and was equipped to handle exports of sisal ▲ *201* and imports such as paving stones from England and tiles from Marseilles, which are still used today in Mérida and the neighboring villages. Progreso beach attracts thousand of visitors.

Celestún ◆ F B2

(57 miles/92 km west of Mérida) The fishing port of Celestún lies within an impressive nature reserve. Although the beach is unremarkable, the lagoons bordered by mangroves ▲ *240* are well worth a visit, with their flocks of flamingos, herons, anhingas, ibises, pelicans and frigate birds. Its 146,135 acres (59,139 ha) constitute a very special biosphere reserve and provide sanctuary for migratory birds from Canada and the northern United States, which come to overwinter in the warm regions of the Tropics. The marshes, bordered by mangroves, have an abundant supply of the fish and small crustaceans on which these birds feed. Some 234 species of mammals have been identified in the reserve, in particular the ocelot, jaguar, spider-monkey and other endangered species, as well as three types of turtle and two species of crocodile. There are organized trips in motorboats.

CELESTÚN BY BOAT. Trips usually begin with flamingos (the best time to see them is between May and August) and continue along the coast in search of other birds. After a dip in an *ojo de agua* (freshwater basin), visitors are transported through the mangroves to the *bosque petrificado* (petrified forest), an amazing expanse of fossilized tree trunks.

LOST HACIENDAS
From Celestún, you can return to Mérida via Maxcanú and admire the *haciendas* of Chunchucmil, Kochol, Santo Domingo and Santa Rosa (now a hotel), in a quiet and relatively unknown part of Yucatán.

Below: cormorants in the mangroves
Bottom: the *bosque petrificado* or petrified forest

Only a few very well adapted trees can cope with the high salt levels and tidal waters of the mangroves. However, the lack of variety in plant species is more than made up for by the wealth of animal life. At high tide, the forests of submerged mangrove roots provide shelter for many species of fish and crustaceans, while flocks of birds nest in their branches and feed on the muddy deposits teeming with aquatic life.

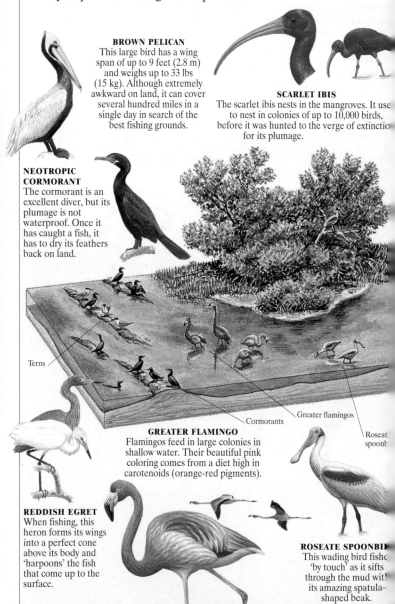

BROWN PELICAN
This large bird has a wing span of up to 9 feet (2.8 m) and weighs up to 33 lbs (15 kg). Although extremely awkward on land, it can cover several hundred miles in a single day in search of the best fishing grounds.

SCARLET IBIS
The scarlet ibis nests in the mangroves. It use to nest in colonies of up to 10,000 birds, before it was hunted to the verge of extinctio for its plumage.

NEOTROPIC CORMORANT
The cormorant is an excellent diver, but its plumage is not waterproof. Once it has caught a fish, it has to dry its feathers back on land.

Terns

Cormorants

Greater flamingos

Roseat spoont

GREATER FLAMINGO
Flamingos feed in large colonies in shallow water. Their beautiful pink coloring comes from a diet high in carotenoids (orange-red pigments).

REDDISH EGRET
When fishing, this heron forms its wings into a perfect cone above its body and 'harpoons' the fish that come up to the surface.

ROSEATE SPOONBI
This wading bird fishe 'by touch' as it sifts through the mud wit its amazing spatula-shaped beak.

BIRTH OF A MANGROVE
Mangrove seeds germinate on the tree, forming a long root that hangs down beneath the leaves.

These post-like seedlings fall at low tide and take root in the mud. In this way, they are not washed away by the tide.

Magnificent frigate birds

Mangrove

LOGGERHEAD TURTLE
Their sex is determined by the temperature at which the eggs are incubated: at 75°–84°F (24°–29°C), only male turtles are born, while at 86°–93°F (30°–34°C) females are produced.

White ibises

FIDDLER CRAB
This crab, with its unequally sized claws, is a common sight in the mangroves.

MANATEE, OR SEA COW
The manatee grazes on aquatic plants in the fresh waters of estuaries and coastal lagoons, which has earned it the nickname 'sea cow'. This discreet and peaceable sirenian is very sensitive to any form of disturbance in its natural habitat, and is today on the verge of extinction.

Male performing a mating display

MAGNIFICENT FRIGATE BIRD
The frigate bird's forked tail and long wings, with their slow, sweeping movements, enable it to make some surprising aerial maneuvers.

FORGIVENESS AT IZAMAL
During his visit to Yucatán in 1993, Pope John Paul II celebrated a Mass at Izamal which was attended by tens of thousands of Indians from regions throughout Mexico and Central America. The pope asked their forgiveness, in the name of the Roman Catholic Church, for the suffering caused by the Spanish Conquest and the Christianization of their people.

IZAMAL ★
Most visitors pass through Izamal without stopping. And yet an evening spent there would offer a unique opportunity to enjoy the effects of the evening light playing on the ocher buildings, far from the hustle and bustle of Mérida.

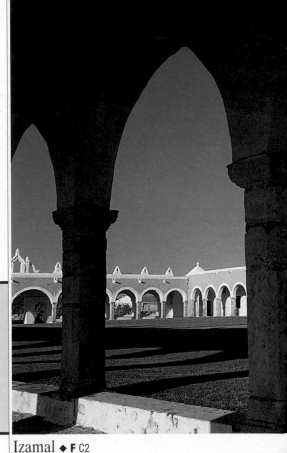

Izamal ◆ F C2

(*12 miles/19 km from Kantunil, toward Cancún*) Izamal, the most beautiful colonial town in Yucatán, stands on the site of a prosperous pre-Hispanic city that had the largest pyramids on the peninsula. These temples were dedicated to the worship of Itzamná – patron of learning and inventor of writing – and to Kinich Kakmo, the sun god. Several pyramids remain and are currently being restored, including the small pyramid behind the arcaded plaza built by the Spanish (*above*), and the pyramid dedicated to the sun.
BUILDING THE MONASTERY. Izamal was a place of pilgrimage for the Maya and, when the Spanish occupied the region, the friars saw it as their religious duty to convert the Indians to Christianity. Diego de Landa ▲ *231* demolished one of the temples, the Popolchac, dedicated to the rain god so that a monastery could be built on its vast platform – 1,71 feet (520 m) long by 1,410 feet (430 m) wide and 40 feet (12 m) high. Work on the monastery began in 1553, under the architect Fray Juan de Mérida, who designed and built the most important monasteries in the region. The monastery,

church and atrium were finished by 1561, and the additional buildings and arcades in the first half of the 17th century.

AN IMPRESSIVE COMPLEX. The Izamal complex, the largest of its kind in America, is reached via three ramps on the sides of the atrium. The principal ramp is surmounted by a magnificent triumphal arch which opens on either side onto arcades surrounding the atrium. A chapel with a pyramidal roof was built in each of the four corners (CAPILLAS POSAS). In 1880 a small, rather unprepossessing tower was added to the original façade of the church, simple but robust, while the FORMER OPEN-AIR CHAPEL ● *80*, was converted into the chapel of La Tercera. The venerated statue of the Virgin of Izamal, the patron saint of the town and Yucatán, still stands behind the chancel, in the CAMARÍN DE LA VIRGEN. The statue, as well as a copy, were commissioned in Guatemala and destined for Mérida and Valladolid but, on leaving Izamal, the bearers felt that the statue was getting heavier the further they got from the town. They were obliged to return to Izamal and place the statue in the chapel which soon became a place of pilgrimage. The original statue, destroyed by fire in 1829, was replaced by a copy.

The impressive atrium of the monastery

CAMARÍN DE LA VIRGEN
This chapel, situated behind the chancel, is dedicated to the Holy Virgin ● *82*. The Virgin of Izamal, the oldest in Yucatán, has been worshipped here since the mid-17th century.

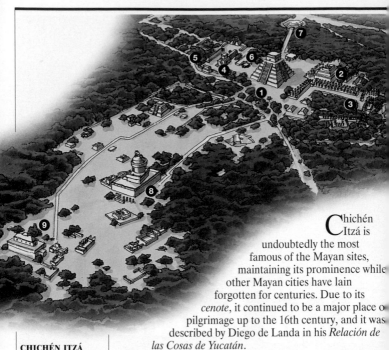

'MEXICAN' INFLUENCES

This is the term used to designate certain characteristics found in central Yucatán, especially those of Toltec origin, which mark the northern part of the site – hypostyle halls, serpent columns, the feathered serpent so widely used in architecture and sculpture, *chacmools*, *tzompantli* ▲ *247*, ● *75*, entablatures supported by telamons, and flagpoles.

Chichén Itzá is undoubtedly the most famous of the Mayan sites, maintaining its prominence while other Mayan cities have lain forgotten for centuries. Due to its *cenote*, it continued to be a major place of pilgrimage up to the 16th century, and it was described by Diego de Landa in his *Relación de las Cosas de Yucatán*.

History

Beginning as a small Puuc-style town, from the 10th century onward, Chichén Itzá developed into a cosmopolitan city – the only major city in Yucatán for the next 250 years. This unprecedented ascendancy was achieved through a spirit of openness and reciprocity rather than by authority and force. The originality of Chichén Itzá ('well of the Itzas') lies in the use of 'Mexican' architectural and iconographic features hitherto unseen on Mayan sites. Some of these innovative features had already appeared in the Puuc region ▲ *234*; while others seem to have come directly from Tula, the Toltec capital of the Mexican basin ▲ *171*. Although centuries-old practices – such as the erection of steles and writing – appear to have been abandoned, there were areas of continuity with the Classical world, especially with regard to cosmology. The most radical change was the weakening of royal power in favor of an elite class of nobles, priests and warriors. The federative role of Chichén Itzá was favored by the sacred *cenote*, into which thousands of pilgrims threw offerings. The city remained an important place of pilgrimage until it was conquered in 1221 and Mayapán ▲ *229,* built shortly afterwards, became the new regional center.

EXCAVATIONS. The first archeological research, undertaken in 1841–42 by John Lloyd Stephens and Frederick Catherwood ▲ *265* was continued in the late 19th century by Teobert Maler, Alfred Maudslay and William Holmes. Circa 1900 Edward Thompson, the United States consul in Yucatán bought and took up residence in the

Chichén *hacienda* (now a hotel), from where he carried out excavations and dragged part of the *cenote* on behalf of the Peabody Museum at Harvard University. Excavations were begun in 1924 by a team from the Carnegie Institution of Washington under the direction of Sylvanus Morley. The principal buildings were excavated and restored, but the cultural chronology of the site still has to be established and various structures have not yet been dated precisely.

The site ◆ F D2

The Puuc-style buildings attributed to the Late Classical era are located in the southern section of the site, while those of the Early Postclassical era, characterized by 'Mexican' influences, are situated in the northern section.

EL CASTILLO. The Castillo stands in the center of the great plaza in the northern part of the site. It consists of two superposed temple-pyramids (Early Postclassical era). The first pyramid (*access via the north face*), consisting of nine sloping terraces and a single staircase, was surmounted by a two-roomed temple with vertical walls and a single entrance to the north. The Mexican decorative elements are interspersed with jaguars in bas-relief, round fringed shields and a *chacmool*. The second pyramid also has nine sloping terraces with reliefs – whose height diminishes toward the top to emphasize the impressive nature of the structure – and four staircases, each with 91 steps, with handrails in the form of serpents. The 364 steps plus the step of the temple entrance symbolize the 365 days of the solar year.

Above: the Castillo at Chichén Itzá is one of the most symbolic – as well as one of the most vertiginous – Mexican pyramids.

THE 'CHACMOOL'
The *chacmool* is a sculpture in the round representing a reclining man, holding an offerings vessel or tray. It is thought that the hearts torn from sacrificial victims were placed in the vessel or on the tray.

Below: the *chacmool* of the Temple of the Warriors gazes toward the Castillo.

CHICHÉN ITZÁ ★
Chichén Itzá is probably the most visited site on the Yucatán peninsula. The best times to avoid the crowds are the first hour after opening or the last hour before closing.

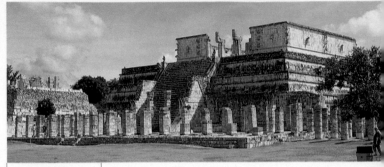

**BALANKANCHÉ
CAVES ◆ F** D2
*(4½ miles/7 km from
Chichén Itzá toward
Valladolid)*
The Balankanché
Caves were
discovered in
1959. These dark,
mysterious caves were
an important Mayan
ritual site, and secret
acts of worship still
take place here today.
A rocky passageway
leads to a series of
chambers where
offerings from the
Toltec period can be
viewed just as they
were left by the
Toltecs. At the end of
the passageway is an
underground pool,
lost in the darkness.
When they resurface,
visitors can enjoy the
botanical garden near
the entrance.

WALL PAINTINGS
Wall paintings once
decorated the interior
walls of the Temple of
the Warriors and the
Temple of the
Jaguars. They were
discovered by John
Lloyd Stevens ▲ *264*
in 1841, but only
traces remain today.
In the first temple,
scenes of battles
fought by the sea
have been identified,
while the paintings in
the Temple of the
Jaguars include a
battle or a war dance
with a great many
participants. There
is also a village on
the edge of a forest
populated with
animals.

TEMPLO DE LOS GUERREROS. The Temple of the
Warriors, whose layout is very obviously inspired by Structure
B at Tula, is named for the sculptures of Toltec warriors on
the pillars of the front portico and those that supported the
temple roof ● *73*. At the top of the great staircase, in front of
the temple entrance, is a *chacmool*, a sculpture in the round
depicting a reclining man, holding an offerings vessel or tray.
GRUPO DE LAS MIL COLUMNAS. The Group of a
Thousand Columns is the remains of a series of vast
hypostyle meeting halls. The bonded columns have rounded
drums and the square pillars are sculpted in bas-relief. The
exact nature of the roof they supported is not known – it may
have been a flat roof made of beams and covered with
mortar or thatch, or possibly a corbeled vault.
BALL COURT. The ball court – 540 feet (166 m) long by 225
feet (68 m) wide – is not only the largest of the thirteen
courts ● *74* discovered at Chichén Itzá but also the largest in
the whole of Mesoamerica. It has markers on the vertical

Left: Temple of the Warriors and
Group of the Thousand Columns
Below right: detail of the Puuc style
in the Nunnery Complex and *tzompantli*

walls on either side of the central aisle. At the
foot of the walls, a sloping bench is covered with
bas-reliefs showing two teams witnessing the
decapitation of the captain of the losing
team. The ball court, which dates from the
Postclassical period, reflects influences from
central Mexico (walls and rings) and the Gulf
coast (bas-reliefs in the style of El Tajín ▲ *191*).

TEMPLO DE LOS JAGUARES. Behind the
vast ball court, this low temple, decorated with
warriors in bas-relief, was partially covered by
the pyramid of the upper temple. The latter's
façade is decorated with Toltec-inspired friezes,
depicting shields and a procession of jaguars.

CENOTE SAGRADO. The *cenote* is reached
along a specially built causeway or *sacbe* 990
feet (300 m) long. Archeological excavations
have confirmed the account of Diego de Landa
concerning the human sacrifices and offerings
of precious objects that were thrown into the
large *cenote* ▲ *238* at the north end of the site,
where some fifty skulls and numerous long
bones have been discovered. Contrary to the
persistent belief that the Maya threw only
maidens into these sinkholes, bones from
skeletons of both sexes and all ages have been
retrieved. Rustic pots were also found that still
contained incense, but the most beautiful
objects were in copper and gold – disks with
repoussé decorations, necklaces, masks,
pendants, rings, ear ornaments, bells and beads.
While most came from Central America,
Oaxaca and the Mexican Valley, the repoussé
disks were made locally and illustrate scenes of
battle and sacrifice. Fragments of burnt cloth,
jade beads, sacrificial knives, and bone and shell
ornaments were also found.

EL CARACOL. This circular structure, which stands on two
superimposed, rectangular platforms, was built during
different periods – the actual 'Caracol' is more recent than its
platforms. Round structures, which appeared in Yucatán
(there is one at Uxmal) during the Recent Classical era, were
'imported' from central Mexico where they are traditionally
associated with Quetzalcóatl in his manifestation as the wind
god. In the center, a spiral staircase (*caracol* in Spanish
means 'snail') leads to a small room pierced with square
openings, whose directions appear to have had some
astronomical significance.

CONJUNTO DE LAS MONJAS. Next to the impressive
building nicknamed the 'Nunnery' by the Spanish (*monja* in
Spanish means 'nun') because its many rooms reminded
them of a convent, are two small Puuc-style temples – the
'nunnery annex' and the church. Above the entrance to the
nunnery annex, the jaws of the terrestrial monster are
represented by a single row of teeth above the lintel. Higher
up, in the space of the open jaws, is an image of a seated
king. The rest of the façade is covered with frontal masks.

'TZOMPANTLI'
The sides of this vast
platform are
decorated with a
broad frieze of several
rows of skulls impaled
on stakes (*above*).
The platform
therefore represents a
tzompantli, a sort of
palisade on which
victims' skulls were
displayed. The large-
scale display of trophy
heads is a feature of
Postclassical Mexican
society that was
adopted by the Aztecs
● *75*.

Top: the former monastery of San Bernardino
Above: Calzalda de los Frailes

A BEAUTIFUL COLONIAL COMPLEX
The former monastery of San Bernadino is reached via the beautiful Calzalda de los Frailes, whose colonial façades have been tastefully restored. The monastery and great atrium, planted with shady trees, make for a beautifully proportioned complex.

Valladolid ◆ F E2

After Mérida, Valladolid is the most important town in Yucatán. It was founded in 1543 by Francisco de Montejo on the ruins of ancient Zaci, and, with Mérida, Campeche and Bacalar, was one of the four main Spanish towns on the Yucatán peninsula. Valladolid was badly damaged by fire during the Caste War ▲ *201*, and never regained its former splendor. Even so, it has a delightful colonial center. The *zócalo* is filled with the intoxicating sound of birdsong emanating from the Madeira bay trees, while the streets are lined by tall, brightly colored façades.

EX-CONVENTO DE SAN BERNADINO (SISAL).
When the Spanish occupied the ancient town of Zaci, they built a church and monastery on the outskirts of the town, in the neighborhood of Sisal, to convert the Indians to Christianity. Designed by the architect Juan de Mérida, the monastery, church and open-air chapel were completed in 1560. Unusually, the open-air chapel was built onto the side of the church rather than the façade of the monastery. At the end of the single-nave CHURCH, the vaulted apse is adorned with Gothic-type ribs. The CLOISTER is 66 feet (20 m) square and the largest in Yucatán after the cloister of Izamal ▲ *242*. Of the seven surviving retables, that of San Antonio is one of the most beautiful altarpieces, dating from the first half of the 18th century. The CHANCEL RETABLE is still attached to the wall of the apse with reeds (18th century).

'CENOTE' DE ZACI. Like all the villages in Yucatán, Valladolid had its own *cenote* ▲ *238*. Partly covered by a huge stone vault, its dark and mysterious waters still inspire the same feeling of respect that led the Indians to regard it as the entrance to the underworld. The nearby garden, with its

indigenous plants and wildlife, has a small restaurant where visitors can relax and enjoy this oasis of peace. Drawings and prints of the ancient *cenote* appear in the works of such 19th-century travelers and explorers as Désiré Charnay ▲ *265*.
CENOTE DE DZITNUP. (*13½ miles/22 km southwest of Valladolid*) The tiny village of Dzitnup was built around the X-Kéken *cenote*. With its stalactites and stalagmites, and its deep blue waters bathed by the light from a hole in the vault, this is one of the most beautiful *cenotes* in Yucatán.

Toward Río Lagartos

EK'BALAM ◆ F E2. (*About 15½ miles/25 km from Valladolid toward Tizimín*) Excavations begun in 1994 focused mainly on the center of the site. The most impressive structures cover an area of half a square mile (1.25 sq. km) and are surrounded by a double enclosure wall pierced by five entrances each reached via a *sacbe* ● *73*. Most of the visible monuments date from the Late Classical era. The ACROPOLIS or STRUCTURE 1, which measures 525 feet (160 m) long by 231 feet (70 m) wide and 102 feet (31 m) high, is formed from a number of superimposed structures and constitutes the main attraction of the site. Just below the summit, there is a large temple in Río Bec style, flanked by two annexes. The amazingly well-preserved stucco façade bears a huge mask of a terrestrial monster, whose gaping jaws form the entrance – the uprights and lintel are positively bristling with teeth. The platform in front of the entrance, also armed with teeth, represents the monster's lower jaw. Above the platform, an aquatic frieze depicts the waters of the underworld, the source of all life. The statues on the monster's forehead and at the corners of the building are probably of ancestors. The temple once contained the lavish royal tomb of Ukit Kan Le'k Tok. The two small, shallow annexes flanking the temple have simulated thatched roofs.

THE VIRGIN OF GUADALUPE
The Iglesia de San Bernadino has a statue of the Virgin of Guadalupe and was the first church in Yucatán to worship the Mexican Virgin.

MAYA CEMETERIES
The tombs are surmounted by small monuments representing pyramidal churches and other objects. They are painted blue, green or pink, and decorated with multicolored flowers – a symbol of the respect and love of the living for those who have gone before them to the hereafter.

Below: Maya cemetery near Río Lagartos

BETWEEN MÉRIDA AND DZILAM

Conkal is famous for its magnificent Convento de San Francisco de Asis. Motul, once the center of sisal production. It has a 16th-century monastery dedicated to San Juan Bautista, which still has its open-air chapel, *posas* chapels and two-story cloister. A small museum honors the memory of Felipe Carrillo Puerto, the socialist governor assassinated in 1924. At Cansahcab, the road forks north toward Dzidzantún, which has one of the most majestic monasteries in Yucatán, built in the 16th century by Fray Francisco de Gadea. The church's single nave – 255 by 36 feet (78 by 11 m) – is the largest in Yucatán. It has been very badly damaged and its sculptures and frescos are poor reflections of its former glory. Along the mangroves of Dzilam de Bravo, the canals fed by the fresh water of the *cenotes* attract thousands of flamingos, while beautiful, fine white sandy beaches make this an ideal place to relax. Boats take visitors to Bocas de Dzilam.

RÍO LAGARTOS ◆ F D-E1. The biosphere reserve of Río Lagartos was established in 1999, at the same time as the Celestún reserve ▲ *239*. It welcomes a wide variety of birdlife, including the colonies of flamingos (*above*) which, from May to July, build their nests on the sandy beaches and feed in the shallow waters of the coastal marshes. From the small fishing port of Río Lagartos, boats take visitors along the coast to San Felipe or the natural salt pans of Las Coloradas, in search of the most beautiful inhabitants of the mangroves. This uninhabited and protected strip of coast is the site of America's largest sanctuary for migratory birds.

Isla Holbox ◆ F F1

(*Turn north off the Mérida–Cancún road – the RF 180 – at Nuevo X-Can. The last part of the journey is made by boat from Chiquila.*) The Isla Holbox is in fact a peninsula and the village a former shark-fishing port. Today it focuses more on lobster-fishing and tourism. Unknown to tourists until a few years ago, Holbox, with its delightful palm-fringed beaches, is fast becoming the more peaceful alternative to Cancún. In spite of the development of waterside chalets, it has retained the relaxed atmosphere of a tiny pueblo and is an ideal coastal resort. However, it is best visited during the drier months, between December and April. During the rest of the year, currents can disturb the waters of the Gulf and deposit foul-smelling seaweed on the beach (*below*).

Chiapas

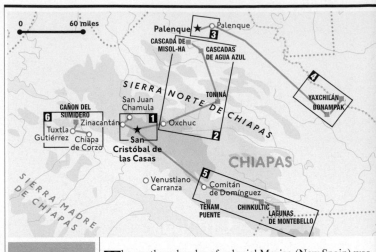

The southern border of colonial Mexico (New Spain) was formed by the Isthmus of Tehuantepec. Until Independence in 1821, Chiapas was the gateway to a less important border province, the Captaincy General of Guatemala (or Kingdom of Guatemala), which corresponded to modern Central America and whose capital was Antigua. The Sierra Madre, whose highest point – the Tacaná volcano 13,450 feet (4,100 m) – marks the beginning of the long volcanic chain running along the Pacific coast, is a fragment of the American continental shield. The rest of Chiapas is a karstic region – the highlands (Jurassic), with their highest point at the Cerro Tzontehuitz (9,840 feet/3,000 m), extend into the Sierra de los Cuchumatanes whose foothills are formed by the great arc of middle-range mountains in the north and east (Cretaceous). The Lacandón Forest marks the start of the tropical forest of Petén (Guatemala) and Belize.

San Cristóbal de las Casas ◆ E D4

San Cristóbal lies at an altitude of 6,955 feet (2,120 m), in a deep depression bounded by three extinct volcanoes. It was founded during the early days of colonial rule, and is one of the oldest Spanish towns in South America. The idea of building a town was first conceived in 1524 by Bernal Díaz del Castillo during his long battle against the rulers of Chamula, who occupied the territory at the time. The idea was turned into a reality in 1528 by Captain Diego de Mazariegos, who only lived there for a few months. Torn between the fear of Indian uprisings and the need to come to terms with its Indian inhabitants (who today account for almost half the population), the town developed within the human shield of its *barrios* of loyal Indians. The inhabitants were slowly 'de-Hispanicized' and the new Creole population severed ties with Spain in 1821, initially hesitating between the statute of a free and sovereign country and allegiance to Mexico. They finally voted to join Mexico in 1824, but had to fight frequent battles to maintain their federal status. In fact Chiapas has fought constantly to retain its identity within the

SAN CRISTÓBAL DE LAS CASAS ★
San Cristóbal has a good hotel infrastructure, with accommodation to suit every purse. It makes an ideal base for exploring Chiapas.

FROM 'CHÍA' TO CHIAPAS
Chía is a sort of sage whose seeds are used to make a refreshing drink (*chía fría*) and to produce the oil used to make lacquer ▲ 281.

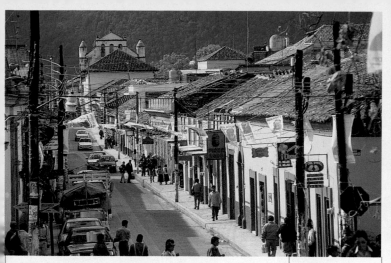

Mexican Constitution. Under the leadership of Joaquín Miguel Gutiérrez until 1838, and then Angel Albino Corzo, it struggled to resist the centralism advocated by the Conservatives and then Maximilian I. Later, under Miguel Utrilla, it pressed for free elections. Armed struggle was involved in each case. The choice of San Cristóbal by Zapata's National Liberation Army as the seat of the uprising of January 1, 1994, ● 29 was partly due to this tradition of insurgence. The town's stockbreeders and landowners – who had blocked the 1910 Revolution – perpetuated the marginalization of San Cristóbal, with the majority of the population reaping no benefit from the wealth generated by the region's agriculture, hydroelectric dams, oil, coffee or tourism. The anarchists built new towns to the north and south, in the shadow of the historic town. Between 1980 and 1990, the population of San Cristóbal de las Casas doubled and today stands at more than 100,000.

Central Plaza ◆ P B2

THE CATHEDRAL. The Mudejar bell tower, whose height has been reduced by several earthquakes, was once a separate structure. The WEST FAÇADE was completed in 1696. The restoration (in 1993) of its original colors (using natural colorings) has re-created the effect of an architectural *huipil* – yellow ocher from the soil of Chamula ▲ 260 and red ocher from Cuxtitali, colors once used for the

THE FIRST CHAMPION OF INDIAN RIGHTS
Fray Bartolomé de las Casas, the son of one of Columbus's caravel pilots, became Bishop of Chiapas in 1543. He had already denounced the *encomiendas* – a system that subjugated the Indians to the Spanish – in Hispaniola (present-day Cuba) and Venezuela. He sent a report in the form of an indictment to Charles V – the *Brevísima relación de la destrucción de las Indias* – and was an instigator of the new laws that made cruelty illegal and prepared for the abolition of slavery. He failed to get the laws adopted in Chiapas and returned to Spain, bequeathing his name to the town.

'CARACOLES ZAPATISTAS'
The five autonomous Indian capitals of Chiapas – whose name derives from *caracol*, the 'snail' or spiral shell that is an omnipresent motif in Mayan glyphs – are constantly visited by militants from Mexico and other countries. In recent years, the EZLN ● 29 has undertaken the construction of an alternative society in these cities.

**HISTORICAL
TESTIMONY**
The cathedral has been the scene of historic events that have marked the history of Chiapas – the declaration of Independence (1812), the alliance with Mexico (1824) and the dialog between the government and representatives of the EZLN ● *29* (1994), which transformed an armed rebellion (now a thing of the past) into a political conflict that is as yet still unresolved.

**LAYOUT OF
THE TOWN ● *76***
San Cristóbal is built along a north-south axis that incorporates three architectural complexes – the monumental complex of Santo Domingo in the north, the square in the center, and El Carmen in the south. They are linked by the former Calle Hidalgo, which has been restored and pedestrianized. The secondary centers that developed around this axis were interspersed with beautiful residences. Beyond these lie the *barrios* (former Indian districts). Further out still and in line with the four points of the compass are the mills that once supplied the town.

town's façades. The white 'embroidery' is rendered by the stuccowork (lime, sand and egg-white moldings) and highlighted by two black panels and columns representing Chamula wool. The baroque interior has cedar altarpieces, made and assembled during the reign of the Indian bishop Moctezuma (1754–66), a descendant of the last Aztec king.

IGLESIA DE SAN NICOLÁS. San Nicolás has served successively as the church of the town's Negro slaves (when the Indian population was in decline due to epidemics), a canonical church (chapter house), a prison during the Reform wars, and finally a parish church. It stands next to the cathedral and has a typically Mudejar façade.

'PORTALES'. Rebuilt after the conflict of 1836, the *portales* (arcades) on the east side of the square are a popular place to relax. An 18th-century manuscript tells how messengers from the great haciendas came here to conduct business. They would sing out: 'So much for a black slave, for each of my donkeys, my mares or my plots of land.'

RESIDENCES. The east façade of the 17th-century Hotel Santa Clara has Plateresque motifs, the Hotel Ciudad Real is neoclassical, and the French-style façade of the Banco Bancomer dates from the days of Porfirio Díaz ● *28*.

PALACIO MUNICIPAL. Built as the governor's palace by local engineer Carlos Flores, the Palacio Municipal was intended to familiarize masons with the designs and proportions of the neoclassical style. After its completion in 1895, the elements of this composite example of cornices, pediments and Tuscan, Doric and Ionic windows were frequently reproduced as part of a new urban design trend.

Grand residences

The 18th-century Hotel Mazariegos (*on the corner of Calles 5 de Febrero and General Utrilla*) has a magnificent broad, wooden *corredor* in its east wing. On the other side of the street, the west annex – the former residence of Bishop Moctezuma – has stucco moldings and friezes. In the 19th century, the Hotel Fray Bartolomé (*Niños Heroes, 2*) housed the bishop's court. It still has an attractive patio surrounded by a beautiful *corredor*. On the corner of the Calles Belisario Domínguez and Adelina Flores, 'La Enseñanza' is an experiment in neoclassical adobe by Carlos Flores.

Santo Domingo district ◆ **P** B1

Today, the monuments of the church and monastery of Santa Domingo in the northern part of the town stand in the gardens of La Alameda, whose terraces are a reminder of the fortifications built in 1863 during the Reform wars. The two-headed eagle of the Austro-Hungarian monarchy on the façade encouraged the supporters of Maximilian I to seek refuge in the fortress-like church overlooking the town.

MONASTERY. The monastery was founded in 1546 by Dominican monks who turned it into an 'Indian mission'. Its most famous prior was Fray Matías de Córdoba, author of the text of the 'Cry' for Independence (1821). Restructured just before 1712, the monastery has an interesting MUSEUM OF REGIONAL HISTORY and a beautiful cloister.

CHURCH OF SANTO DOMINGO. The construction of the church adjoining the monastery began at the end of the 17th century with the façade – a remarkable piece of pink stuccowork, sculpted in a baroque style belonging to an esthetic of the Counter-Reformation and predating the extravagant Churrigueresque style

● 82. Punctuated by lines and cabled columns, the three registers are covered with stucco reliefs of vine branches, flowers, objects, figures and abstract motifs. On the upper register, Santo Domingo is flanked by two-headed eagles, while the coat of arms of the Order of the Holy Ash forms the pinnacle. The damaged statues in the niches are a reminder of the violent clashes during the Reform wars, when General Utrilla opened fire on Maximilian's supporters from the Calle Real de Mexicanos. The interior walls of the church were literally lined with gold, silver and the paintings of thirteen 18th-century altarpieces (only eight are still intact). To create an effect of continuity, the altarpieces in the nave are set between vertical carved gilt wood panels whose motif repeats to produce an overall effect of rhythm and unity.

Above: San Cristóbal is encircled by mountains
Opposite: San Cristóbal Cathedral

Interior of the church of Santo Domingo

MUSEO DE TRAJES REGIONALES SERGIO CASTRO
◆ **A** A2
(*Guadalupe Victoria, between Calles Matamoros and 12 de Septiembre*)
Sergio Castro devoted his life to providing medical treatment for the Indians of Chiapas, especially those suffering from burns, and built up a detailed knowledge of life in these communities. In the rooms of an old house, he put together a collection of *huipiles* and other objects from the villages he visited, all carefully labeled. A visit to the museum (by appointment and accompanied by Sergio himself) is a fascinating way to find out about the traditions of each village through the materials and motifs of its *huipiles*, which form a series of codes to be deciphered.

Outside the Iglesia de la Guadalupe

SAN JOLOBIL. (*To the left of the entrance to the monastery of Santo Domingo*) The 'house of weaving' is a Tzotzil-Tzeltal cooperative established in 1996 to preserve and showcase the traditional skills of the Maya. You can buy authentic *huipiles* ▲ 259 woven by Mayan women from the surrounding villages.

IGLESIA DE LA CARIDAD ◆ **P** B1. On the lower south terrace, the Iglesia de la Caridad (Charity), built in 1714, is a memorial to the suppression of the Indian uprising of Cancuc (1712), when Tzeltal's patron saint, Our Lady of the Rosary, led the Indians against her Spanish equivalent, Our Lady of Charity (or the Presentation). After the victory of San Cristóbal on November 21 (the festival of the Presentation), Our Lady of Charity was proclaimed 'general' (a field-marshal's baton was added to her statue) and protectress of the town. The church's façade is a more sober but equally animated expression of colonial baroque architecture.

CAPILLA DEL SÓTANO. Adjoining the Iglesia de la Caridad, the Chapel of the Sótano (Christ in the Dungeon) was built between 1831 and 1839 by local Indians in response to the construction of the rebellion memorial. The masons had restored San Cristóbal's Cathedral in 1815 and they imitated its gargoyles and two neoclassical entrances here.

El Carmen district

IGLESIA DEL CARMEN ◆ **P** B3. The church of El Carmen was damaged by fire in 1993, when its altarpieces and paintings were destroyed, but has retained its double, right-angled façade (1744 and 1764) which stands at the end of the monumental axis that crosses the old town north-to-south. Currently being restored, the building is a fine example of vernacular, polychrome baroque architecture. Nearby is the ruined nunnery of the Franciscan Sisters of the Incarnation. The sisters played an important part in the life of the town's – much larger – female population during the colonial era, and supported the rebels in the struggle for Independence.

Below: patio of the Casa Na Bolom
Bottom: the Mercado Municipal

TOWER-PORCH ◆ **P** B3. An anarchic restoration of the roof of the church of El Carmen mistakenly attached it to the tower-porch of 1677 – San Cristóbal's only surviving town gate – and obscured the church's west façade. The tower's former status and its style (geometric Mudejar, stucco arabesques and naive polychromy) are a valuable reminder of the early urbanization of San Cristóbal.

Casa Na Bolom ◆ **P** C1

(At the top of Calles Chiapa de Corzo and Comitán) This beautiful late 19th-century residence was owned by Frans Blom and his wife, Gertrude Duby. Today it houses the headquarters of a foundation that continues their research and work for the Lacandón cause. The library has a collection of more than 8,000 books and 55,000 of Gertrude's photographs. At the end of the garden is a Lacandón Indian refuge – *Na Bolom* in Maya means 'shelter of the jaguar'. The museum traces the history of the Lacandón people through ritual objects and costumes. There is also an interesting neoclassical chapel (1903).

Mercado Municipal ◆ **P** B1

(Calle General Utrilla, north of Santo Domingo) Each morning, the highland Indians come down to the town to sell their fruit, vegetables and flowers, and fill the sidewalks with this huge, noisy open-air market. It reveals a very obvious urban dichotomy – the white population tend to frequent the covered market, which has a wider range of merchandise.

AMBER
Amber is a transparent, honey-colored fossilized resin that is both hard and brittle. The Greeks called it *electron* because it became static when rubbed. In Chiapas, it was formed during the marine encroachments and regressions that gradually opened up the Atlantic during the Cretaceous period, as Africa became separated from America. This geological phenomenon, resulting from the fragmentation of the ancient landmass known as 'Pangaea', explains two of Chiapas' resources – oil (a sedimentary formation) and amber (the petrification of submerged pine trees). A small museum, the Museo del Ambar, occupies the former Convento de la Merced (on Calle Diego de Mazariegos).

FRANS BLOM AND GERTRUDE DUBY
While traveling in Mexico for an oil company, Danish-born Frans Blom became passionately interested in the archeology and landscapes of the Indian territory. Gertrude ('Trudy') Duby was an anti-fascist Swiss militant. As a journalist and photographer, she became interested in the Mexican Revolution. The couple met in Chiapas where they devoted their lives to the study and protection of the Lacandón Indians. At the time, it took ten days on horseback to reach the Lacandón Forest.

During the pre-Hispanic period, weaving was placed under the patronage of the moon goddess Ixchel, since it was closely associated with the myth of the Creation, the renewal of vegetation and the symbolism of childbirth. Today, it is still regarded as a sacred activity that is essential to the reproduction of the mythical universe of the Maya. The Mayan cosmogony is represented by – stylized or figurative – plant, animal and geometric motifs. The brocaded or embroidered designs, the product of a continuous process of creation, not only refer to pre-Columbian elements but also to elements of local and colonial history. The makeup of the designs decorating a Mayan garment (*huipil*) can be read like a text whose content varies according to the ethnic group, community, social status, age and sex of the person wearing it.

LOZENGE
The lozenge or 'diamond' symbolizes the universe conceived as a cube with three planes – the sky, the earth and the underworld. The four sides delimit the boundaries of time and space. Each lozenge has twelve motifs relating to the four corners of the *milpa* ▲ *232*, to the angle formed by the solstices indicating the dates of the sowing and harvest, and to the four points of the compass.

GERMINATION
The brocaded motifs on the sleeves of this *huipil* describe the complete growth cycle of corn and beans. From top to bottom, the yellow and black seeds germinate, flower and reach maturity under the protection of the Lord of the Earth and toads, believed to be the harbingers of rain. They are also decorated with an inscription of the Mayan agricultural calendar (365 days) and the ritual calendar (260 days) ▲ *214*.

VULTURE, BEES AND STARS
Below the rows of lozenges in the central motif, the brocaded vulture motifs recall a tragic episode in the history of the village of Magdalenas, the bee motifs refer to a myth related to the weaver's own lineage, while the work is signed with a variation on star motifs.

MONKEYS
Monkeys are synonymous with disaster and evoke a previous creation. On the *huipiles* of Chenalhó, the body of the monkey, represented by three vertical lines, is surrounded by curves forming the arms and legs. The motif reminds mortals of their obligation to worship the gods.

THE 'HUIPIL' OF SANTA MARÍA MAGDALENAS

The women of Magdalenas believe that Mary Magdalene taught their ancestors to weave and brocade garments. Every year, they weave a *huipil* to offer to Santa María Magdalena so that she will help them perpetuate the art of weaving. This *huipil*, a 'detailed image of Mayan cosmology and local mythology', can be interpreted as a prayer in which the weaver describes the relationship between the gods and the growth of plants. In this way, she hopes that the gods invoked will ensure that the earth is given new life.

On Lintel 24 (AD 719) at Yaxchilán, the Mayan queen, Lady Xoc, is wearing a *huipil* decorated with lozenge motifs similar to those found today on the *huipiles* of Magdalenas.

CORN

The Maya had an almost physiological relationship with plants. The Tzotzils cut the umbilical cord of a newborn baby on a corn cob and sowed the child's first *milpa* ▲ *232* with the bloodstained seeds. The women of Venustiano Carranza brocade corn plants on their *huipiles*, and the women of Chamula embroider *milpas* on their blouses.

ZIGZAGS

Zigzags are the symbol of the god of lightning, the dispenser of rain, and are a popular motif on the textiles of many villages. The women of Pantelhó use zigzags to decorate the sleeves of their garments, which are dotted with stylized toads (the harbingers of rain).

FERTILITY

The hem of the skirts worn by the Tzotzil women of Venustiano Carranza are embroidered with cactus, flower and scorpion motifs. The scorpion, a symbol of fertility, is believed to bring rain by invoking lightning.

▲ Chiapas
Indian villages around San Cristóbal

BELT-MAKING
On the *telar de cintura* (the loom on which belts are made, *below*), the vertical threads of the warp are stretched between two rollers. The top roller, whose ends are attached to a cord in the shape of an inverted Y, is fixed to a tree. The bottom roller is attached to a belt that the weaver, who kneels on the ground, fastens around her waist to control the tension. Straw hats decorated with multicolored ribbons (*bottom*), whose shape varies from region to region, are still found throughout Chiapas.

The 'barrios'

This adobe town is best appreciated in the old Indian districts – Mexicanos (northwest); Cerillo (north); San Antonio with its hill (south); Cerrito, the *mirador* of the town and its valley (west); Cuxtitali, where the colonial toll bridge has a tiled roof and benches (northeast); El Peje de Oro and the 'Miguel Utrilla' mill. The identity of these districts derives from their ethnic origin (Aztec, Tzotzil, Zapotec, Quiché), the religious order in charge (Dominicans, Franciscans) and their traditional specialty (wood, wrought iron, firecrackers, dyeing, cooked meats). The walls facing onto the streets are often windowless since the traditional houses usually only open onto a patio. The streets of the *barrios* are very different from those of the 'enlightened' town center where neoclassic modernization has opened up impressive windows with adobe aedicules.

Tzotzil villages

Chamula and Zinacantán, in the immediate vicinity of San Cristóbal de las Casas, are two of the most visited Tzotzil villages.

In an attempt to limit tourism, the local authorities have introduced such severe measures as entrance fees for churches, and permits and charges to photograph certain ceremonies. These include the performance of important rituals, ceremonies for the transfer of power within the brotherhoods (January 1), saint's day festivals (San Juan, San Lorenzo and Santo Domingo) and carnival (*k'in tajimoltik*), and also serve to strengthen weakened ties between the parent community and its dispersed members (settlers in the Lacandón Forest), whose numbers have greatly increased in recent years. These villages were and are still the scene of bitter conflicts between Catholics and Protestants, especially in the village of Chamula, where many Protestants have been forced to leave for the new shanty towns around San Cristóbal. These communities have always developed amid conflict, either as the victims of regional or national politics, or because the religious and administrative pressures exerted by the colonial authorities became an unbearable assault upon their very existence ● *40*.

CARNIVAL OF SAN JUAN CHAMULA

The carnival corresponds to the five transitional days of the ancient Mayan calendar. It includes the ritual presentation of a series of historical events involving all kinds of invaders and enemies, who represent the disorder of the world and the threat to Mayan society.

Left: San Juan Chamula

A LAND OF REBELLIONS
The major rebellions that broke out during the early 18th century were a reaction against the extortionate tributes exacted by the Spanish and the efforts of their clergy to eradicate idolatry and destroy the power of *nagualista* priests (or shamans) who perpetuated traditional Indian practices. With their idols condemned and destroyed by the Church, the Indians turned to the Catholic Christ, Virgin and saints to represent their claims and defend their concept of a more just and equitable society. The appearance of the Savior-Virgin at Zinacantán in 1708, and again at Santa Marta in 1711, were the early signs of the great 1712–13 uprising that spread across a large part of Chiapas from Cancún. A total of thirty-three Tzotzil, Tzeltal and Chol communities rebelled and swelled the ranks of the 'soldiers of the Virgin', but they were soon subjected to the most terrible repression followed by years of poverty and famine. Even so, their hopes of an alternative society were not entirely destroyed – they merely took other, less spectacular forms of expression. In January 1994, they suddenly reemerged in the more organized form of the EZLN and, for the first time in history, attracted international attention ● *29.*

SAN JUAN CHAMULA ◆ E D4. This small but busy market town, where a huge open-air market stands opposite the church on the *zócalo*, is the hub of a community of 60,000 inhabitants and a melting pot for the strange mixture of influences that has forged the Maya religion. An indefinable atmosphere emanates from the church where statues of saints stand alongside a syncretic Maya pantheon, where prayers are said kneeling on a floor covered with pine needles, before rows of candles whose numbers and color depend on the request made, and in the presence of a few chickens brought as offerings. In the atrium outside, Maya crosses made from green wood are attached in threes (the Trinity) to the branches of trees (the tree of life).

ZINACANTÁN ◆ E D4. Zinacantán nestles in a valley where vast amounts of flowers, fruit and vegetables are grown in fields and greenhouses. The main church, which serves both the Catholic and Maya communities, is surrounded by textile stores selling woven articles, from good-quality Maya embroidery to the less authentic creations for tourists.

Right: the site of Toniná
Below: excavations in 1992

THE TEREBINTH
The terebinth is widely found in Chiapas above 2,625 feet (800 m), and its Spanish name (*ocote*) forms the basis of a number of place names throughout the state, for example, Ocosingo. Its superior quality wood is used to make much of the region's furniture and altarpieces, while its needles are scattered on the ground at festivals to create a scented carpet. The ink used for the codices was made from a sort of pitch produced from the sap of this conifer.

THE STATUARY OF TONINÁ
The life-size (or smaller) statues in the round have a vertical tenon designed to be set into a masonry socket. The altars of Toniná are thin disks, usually sculpted with inscriptions. Sovereigns are depicted wearing a long cloak and either holding a ceremonial staff or with their hands resting on their belts. Their headdresses consist of superimposed masks.

The first part of this route runs through the Ocosingo fault, which separates two tectonic plates – the Central American plate (highlands) to the south, and the North American plate (northern mountains) to the north. These plates move about ¾ inch (2 cm) each year. Beneath the fertile pastures of the valley floor are the alluvial deposits of the fossil meanders of a river whose course has often been altered by earth tremors.

Oxchuc ◆ **E** D4

This Tzeltal village is the focal point for an agricultural pilgrimage held on the festival of Santo Tomás (December 21), which is also attended by the Tojolabal Indians. Its church is one of the few whose atrium still has two of its four *capillas posas* (repository chapels ● 78), where traces of paintings can be seen. In the chancel, a sculpture with a pre-Hispanic motif was discovered embedded in the wall. It represents three shells, the distinctive symbols of both the name of the village in Tzeltal and of Quetzalcóatl. In 1687, Bishop Nuñez de la Vega confiscated all Mayan calendars and codices and demanded that worshippers repeat the *credo*. Today, Oxchuc is still a seat of Maya resistance.

Toniná ◆ **E** E4

(*7½ miles/12 km east of Ocosingo*) Toniná is situated at 2,950 feet (900 m), in pastureland enclosed by mountains that combines tropical and high-altitude vegetation. As well as occupying a delightful situation, the site is also well worth a visit for the originality and quality of its sculptures.
HISTORY. The Ocosingo Valley and site of Toniná were occupied from the Late Preclassical era, but Toniná enjoyed its golden age during the Late Classical. This border town probably survived the collapse of the Maya civilization longer than most due to its geographical position, and it was here that the most recent Mayan stele was erected, in AD 909. The ruined city was inhabited intermittently and its tombs reused, but its statues and inscriptions were destroyed. The center of

Toniná was built on a specially prepared hillside site with seven terraces, reproducing the form of a pyramid. The site was briefly described and some of the statues illustrated by an expedition from the University of Tulane in the 1920s. During the 1970s a team of French researchers devoted several campaigns to its excavation.
SCULPTURES. A naked and decapitated captive in haut-relief, a colossal trophy head and numerous panels of scenes depicting capture and sacrifice decorated the temples and pyramids. The sculptures on the stuccowork structures were also based on the themes of war and sacrifice. A huge relief, discovered at the foot of the sixth terrace, presented one of the most terrifying images of the Mayan world – scenes of a hellish underworld with skulls, severed heads and mythical creatures.

MUSEUM. The museum does justice to the exceptional variety of stone sculpture, in two and three dimensions. Captives about to be sacrificed are much in evidence, shown kneeling, their arms bound behind their backs, and covered with marks that attest to their humiliating condition.

Agua Azul Cascades ◆ **E** E3

(98 miles/158 km northeast of San Cristobál on Mex 199) An impressive series of broad, low waterfalls cascades through the jungle, creating a string of pools over a distance of several hundred yards. A path runs alongside the river, giving access to the different levels of this natural phenomenon, and the surrounding area has been specially adapted for tourists. The Agua Azul Cascades are named after their turquoise-blue waters, but this unusual color only occurs in April–May, during the dry season.

Misol-Há Waterfalls ◆ **E** E3

(115 miles/185 km northeast of San Cristobál on Mex 199) This powerful 115-foot (35-m) waterfall plunges into the jungle at the junction of the Río Paxilhá and the north-flowing Río Tuliá. You can bathe at the foot of the falls.

CHOL TERRITORY
Before the Spanish Conquest, the vast lowland territory between the River Usumacinta and Lake Izabal was occupied by Chol communities. In the 16th century, they were deported to the highlands where they were decimated by disease and the cold, or assimilated into other ethnic groups. Other members of this linguistic group are found in Tila, Tumbalá (north of Ocosingo) and several villages near Palenque, where they settled as a result of tradition or coercion during the Conquest ● 40.

Agua Azul Cascades

After their conquest of Central America, the Spanish – with a few notable exceptions – showed little interest in the region's history, and the mysteries of the Mayan civilization remained largely unsolved. It was not until the rediscovery of cities buried deep in the forest, in the 18th and particularly the 19th century, that the Maya became the subject of many investigations and the Europeans and Americans began to explore their civilization (a study known as 'Mayanism') in much greater depth. Adventurers and travelers were followed by professional archeologists and photographers, all passionate and resolute in their attempts to solve the mysteries of Mayan culture.

DIEGO DE LANDA, CONQUISTADOR AND MISSIONARY

The first Franciscans landed in South America in 1535. Diego de Landa (1524–79), the future bishop of Yucatán, persecuted the Maya in the name of the 'true faith', at the same time taking a keen interest in their history and customs. He was the first to describe Mayan cities ▲ *231* in his *Relación de las Cosas de Yucatán*.

Above and above right: two profiles, a study in comparative physiognomy by Waldeck.

WALDECK, A ROMANTIC VISION In 1832, the artist and adventurer Jean-Frédéric de Waldeck (*right*) arrived at Palenque to draw the site. He painted 'picturesque views' of ruins and forest landscapes inhabited by imaginary figures (*above*). Convinced that the Mayan civilization had its origins in Europe, he searched for evidence that could have been left by the Hebrews, Greeks or Hindus. He didn't ever hesitate to invent a few missing facts in order to support his firmly held romantic and mythical vision of the world of the Maya.

Désiré Charnay (1828–1915) was the first to photograph the Mayan sites in 1859. His pictures were used to illustrate *Les Anciennes Villes du Nouveau Monde* (1863). (*Below*, Chichen Itzá.) Charnay met Alfred Maudslay, a young English photographer who introduced him to the technique of molding (layers of damp newspaper applied to bas-reliefs and dried).

PROGRESS IN THE STUDY OF MAYAN TEXTS

In 1864, the Abbé Brasseur de Bourbourg (1814–74) discovered Landa's *Relación de las Cosas de Yucatán*, which reproduced Mayan glyphs. Brasseur (*right*) noticed that they were different from those used in Aztec manuscripts, and the notion of an independent Mayan civilization was born. Another breakthrough occurred in the 1960s, following critical appraisal of the well-preserved paintings of Bonampak ▲ 272. Their depiction of torture and human sacrifice challenges the view of a peaceable Mayan society.

STEPHENS AND CATHERWOOD

With the American writer John Lloyd Stephens (1805–52), the age of romantic studies came to an end. His travels with Frederick Catherwood (1799–1854), an English architect and artist produced his *Incidents of Travel in Central America, Chiapas and Yucatán* of 1841, a work that is characterized by its restrained descriptions and cautious interpretations. It was illustrated by Catherwood, who used the latest photographic techniques – especially the camera lucida – to make his drawings as precise as possible. (*Above right*: Uxmal, by Catherwood.)

MAUDSLAY, THE PRAGMATIST

Alfred Maudslay (1850–1931) understood the importance of reliable documentation. To this end he used three techniques – photography, molding and drawing. In 1882, he was able to use a newly invented photographic technique – the dry-gelatin negative – that was not available to Charnay. His four volumes devoted to the archeology of Mayan sites in the collection *Biologia Centrali-Americana* (1889–1902) are a fine example of the genre.

THE FIRST PROFESSIONAL EXCAVATIONS

The first professional excavations were carried out in 1891 by Harvard's Peabody Museum. From 1914 to 1958, the Carnegie Institution of Washington was at the forefront of Maya archeology, in particular at Chichén Itzá.

Above: Palenque

PALENQUE ★
Palenque is best
visited as soon as
the site opens, but
don't go without a
mosquito repellent…

Above: Palenque
Below: *U Paka
k'inich*, a bas-relief –
11½ feet (3.5 m) high
– in the Museum of
Palenque

Like a stone mirage emerging from the tropical forest, the magnificent site of Palenque rises in tiers on a hillside draped in the mists of Chiapas. It is one of the earliest Mayan sites to be discovered, and one of the best preserved, with a remarkable royal sepulcher. Palenque had access to the most famous and imaginative architects of the day, and used the most gifted scribes. Visitors can therefore admire some of the most beautiful examples of Mayan calligraphy.

History

Although the site was occupied in 100 BC, the city whose remains we admire today did not expand until the 7th century. By the early 9th century, its golden age was over, and no new buildings or inscriptions were commissioned. The first sovereign of the Palenque dynasty, Chaacal I, acceded to the throne in 501, while the reign of the last sovereign, Kuk, ended sometime after 784. The most recent inscriptions date from the very end of the 8th century.

Excavations

In 1735, Father Antonio Solis, who had been sent to Palenque by his bishop, was surprised to find 'stone houses' in the forest. But it wasn't until 1784 that the governor of Guatemala commissioned a series of individuals to investigate the truth of these rumors of 'stone houses' hidden deep in the forest at first hand. In 1785, surveyor and architect Antonio Bernasconi drew a plan of the site and, in 1787, after spending some time at Palenque, Captain Antonio del Río concluded that these ruins, like those of Yucatán, predated the Spanish Conquest and were the work of the same 'nation'. In 1832, Jean-Frédéric de Waldeck ▲ *264* spent over a year in the ruins of Palenque, studying the architecture, drawing sculptures and carrying out several excavations. The results of his research were not published for another thirty years, and it was John Lloyd Stephens who revealed Palenque to the world in 1841. In 1952, Alberto Ruiz Lhuillier discovered a trap door in the floor of one of the temples, and spent the next three years excavating a staircase leading to the center of the pyramid and to an underground crypt that housed an extraordinary sculpted sarcophagus containing the remains of the Mayan king Pacal.

'The ancient city stands on a hillside, on a fairly small plateau, which was cleared to free the ruins from the invasive vegetation that constantly threatens to engulf it. In fact, if it were allowed to grow unchecked, it would not be many years before the pale and slightly yellowish gray stone was once more covered by green foliage.'

André Pieyre de Mandiargues
Deuxième Belvédère

Museum of Palenque

(*Below the site, ½ mile/1 km before the main entrance, at the side of the road*) Opened in 1994, the museum has three hundred original pieces from the archeological site. Visitors can admire a number of sculpted panels of glyphic texts and/or dynastic scenes. The fineness of the limestone used has enabled the scribe and artist to express their talent fully. A major collection of tubular ceramic incense holders, decorated with modeled figures, illustrates the complexity of the Mayan cosmology. The delicate terracotta figurines are another of the treasures from this magical site.

PALENQUE
1. Palace
2. Temple of the Inscriptions
3. North Group
4. Temple of the Cross
5. Temple of the Sun
6. Temple of the Foliated Cross
7. Ball court

PALENQUE, THROUGH THE FOREST
Palenque is linked to the museum by a pleasant footpath. It starts from the east of the site, behind the ball court, and runs beside a series of small waterfalls on the Río Otulum.

Above: Palenque
Below: bas-relief, patio of the Palacio

The archeological site ◆ E E3

Palenque was built at the foot and on the sides of a specially prepared hillside site. It has three levels: the plain at sea level, an intermediate level at about 330 feet (100 m) and an upper level at 390–490 feet (120–150 m). The Maya took advantage of these levels to construct terraces and, with relatively little effort, transform the hill into a step pyramid. The site covers an area of 6 sq. miles (16 sq. km). Only the Principal Group, which covers an area of 37 acres (15 ha), has been cleared and is accessible to the public.

TEMPLO DE LAS INSCRIPCIONES. The Temple of the Inscriptions ● 75 is the funerary monument of Pacal, the first great sovereign of Palenque. The tomb, which lies beneath the temple at the foot of a long staircase, was discovered in 1952. Prior to this, it was thought that the pyramids were merely foundations for temples. Also discovered in the pyramid were three panels carved with glyphs that constitute one of the longest known Mayan inscriptions (617 glyphic blocks). It recounts the dynastic history of the city from the early 6th century to the time of Pacal (615–83), whose royal remains were contained in the SARCOPHAGUS, surrounded by a rich collection of jade jewelry. It was covered with a huge sculpted slab showing the dead sovereign falling into the fleshless jaws of the terrestrial monster. On the mask representing the underworld is one of the sacred trees (the *ceiba* ▲ 279) from the four corners of the universe. The two-headed serpent represents the sky, while the quetzal bird at the top of the tree symbolizes the diurnal sun at its zenith. The ten half-figures emerging from the earth, sculpted on the sides of the sarcophagus, represent some of Pacal's royal ancestors.

EL PALACIO. The so-called Palace of Palenque consists of a platform – 246 feet (75 m) long by 180 feet (55 m) wide and almost 33 feet (10 m) high – supporting about fifteen structures (referred to as 'houses' and designated by a

letter of the alphabet) arranged around three courtyards. The complex is the result of almost two centuries of architectural activity which covers at least six reigns. The first structures were built in the 7th century by Pacal. In spite of its name, this was not a royal residence but a religious complex reserved for the king and his appointed priests, in which the various buildings were dedicated to the celebration of different ritual ceremonies. This intricate complex of rooms, corridors, underground galleries and patios is decorated with a great many stone and stucco bas-reliefs – sculpted pillars and handrails, grotesque figures, medallions, steles and panels. The east courtyard with its sculpted flagstones is well worth a look. Unusually, the complex also has a three-story tower, the only one of its kind in Mayan architecture, that was probably used as an astrological observatory.

Stucco mask of the Mayan king Pacal

GRUPO DE LA CRUZ. The reference to mythical creatures is clearly expressed in the so-called Cross Group. The complex consists of three pyramid-temples built around a square open to the south. The TEMPLO DE LA CRUZ is the largest and occupies the most elevated position, while the TEMPLO DEL SOL occupies the lowest, on a four-step pyramid. The third is the TEMPLO DE LA CRUZ FOLIADA. They were built during the reign of King Chan Bahlum between 683 (the date of the death of his father, Pacal) and 692, and represent a three-stage cosmic journey, with each stage defined by a specific orientation and environment. The Temple of the Cross symbolizes the first stage, the origin of the supernatural and mortal world. From the Temple of the Sun, the next stage of the journey emulates the journey of the nocturnal sun – symbolized by the jaguar – through the underworld. The final stage, represented by the Temple of the Foliated Cross, celebrates fertility and rebirth.

GRUPO NORTE. The North Group consists of five temples, each different in layout, which stand on pyramidal platforms. During the 8th century, in response to the demands of an expanding population, these buildings were restructured and transformed into dwellings. The space was divided up with new walls, and old blocks inscribed with glyphs were reused.

'As evening approaches, the peaks are shrouded in mist and, in the light of the setting sun, the different greens of the vegetation merge into a single dark-green mass, verging on black. Against this backdrop, the strange, squat forms of the pale-gray temples stand as if on stilts above the large leaves and mosses, like huge baroque elephants beneath their howdah and caparison.
André Pieyre
de Mandiargues,
Deuxième Belvédère

▲ Chiapas
The Lacandóns

ANIMAL SPIRITS
The little terracotta
figurines made by the
Lacandón Indians
represent the animal
spirits of the forest.
They are both
worshipped and
feared, like the forest
itself, which is a
source of both life
and danger for those
who live there.

In the region of eastern Chiapas that projects into Guatemala, the Lacandón Forest (Selva Lacandona) covers an area of some 1,930 sq. miles (5,000 sq. km) to the south of Yaxchilán and Bonampak. Only recently has this territory, now the Montes Azules Biosphere Reserve, been protected against the forestry companies that have been plundering the forest for tropical hardwoods, especially mahogany, since the 19th century. The four hundred or so surviving Lacandóns who live in the forests have found themselves, unwittingly, at the center of a scientific controversy which has not yet been entirely resolved. For a long time they were thought to have been the direct descendants of the Maya of the Classical era, the legitimate heirs of the architects of Yaxchilán and the artists of the temple frescos of Bonampak. Ethnological and historical studies have shown, however, that the Lacandóns are in fact descended from populations who migrated from the south of the Yucatán peninsula and Petén in the 18th century. Although they refer to themselves as 'Hach Winik' (the 'true men'), they have also been labeled somewhat pejoratively as 'Caribes' (cannibals) and 'Lacandones'. This

THE 'BALCHÉ' RITUAL
Balché is a fermented
drink made by
soaking strips of bark
from the *balché* tree
(*Lonchocarpus
longistylum*) in sugar-
cane sap or honey
diluted in water for
24 hours. It is
prepared in a dugout
canoe. The *balché*
ritual is performed
to entreat or thank
the gods, individually
or collectively, and
as such it provides
regular opportunities
for the men of the
caribal (Lacandón
community) to get
together without their
womenfolk and talk,
drink and sing all day
long. This conciliatory
and communal
ceremony is also seen
as a test for those who
may have infringed
certain common rules
or codes of conduct.
Vomiting as a result
of drinking too much
is not only regarded
as an indication of
guilt, but is also
believed to be a
process of
purification.

Bonampak,
Structure 17

last term is probably derived from Acam Tun, the name of an island in Lake Miramar applied, in the 16th century, to the whole of the forested region of eastern Chiapas. At the time, this region was inhabited by communities who remained free from Spanish control and were feared by the Christianized Indians of the highlands ● *40*.

THE LACANDÓNS: TOWARD OBLIVION? Whole areas of Lacandón mythology and ritual have been forgotten, and only a few fragments of their complex pantheon, dominated by Hachakyum the Creator, the worship of censers, the ritual use of the fermented *balché* drink, and their traditional hunting and fishing skills, have survived. These Indians in their long white tunics are mere shadows of their ancestral selves, and today exploited by a lucrative tourist trade. In only a few years, the fervor of evangelical missionaries, the greed of hardwood extraction companies, and the brutal colonization of the Lacandón Forest by thousands of landless peasants have got the better of this traditional culture.

Bonampak ◆ **E** F4

It is likely that the interior walls of the more prestigious buildings on all Mayan sites were covered with paintings that complemented the carved or sculpted decoration of the exterior. The humid, tropical climate has meant that most of these paintings have not survived. Bonampak, however, discovered in 1946, has preserved a most comprehensive collection of Mayan art. It lies a few miles south of the Usumacinta River and Yaxchilán, on the edge of the Lacandón Forest. At its center is an acropolis – a terraced hill with several small temples that dominates a square bordered by buildings on three sides. The stone sculpture, in the form of steles and lintels, is very well preserved. The building that contains the paintings (STRUCTURE 1), on the first terrace, has three rooms whose walls and vaulted ceilings have retained most of their original paintings ▲ *272*.

CENSERS
Only the Nahá Lacandóns still practice this form of worship. The clay censers bear the modeled effigy of a god and are kept in a sanctuary that stands apart from people's houses. They are considered to be the permanent representatives of the gods among mortals. During ceremonies, they are placed in a row on a mat of palm fronds and offerings of incense and *balché* are made to support a request or give thanks for a beneficent act on the part of the gods concerning agriculture, health or a birth.

Structure 1 at Bonampak consists of three non-connecting rooms, each with a single door and a vault bearing most of the decoration. The triangular partition walls are also painted. The paintings in the three rooms illustrate three stages in the same narrative (from left to right) – before, during and after a battle that took place during the reign of Chaan Muan, who came to the throne in 776 and was still in power in 790.

ROOM 2
The painting (*above*) opposite the entrance to Room 2 depicts a battle in which the warriors of Bonampak, armed and richly attired, triumph over their disarmed and almost naked enemies. The judgment and torture of the prisoners appears above the door.

The vaulted ceilings of rooms 1 and 3 are decorated with images of the celestial cosmic monster (*below*). These are replaced in Room 2 by images of captives and symbols of constellations.

COLLECTIVE SELF-SACRIFICE
The battle is over but not the offering of blood. The king and his entourage, seated on the bench which serves as a throne, offer their blood (and their pain) by passing a cord through their tongue. Their self-sacrifice automatically complements the sacrifice of the prisoners (*right*).

> 'The frescos of Bonampak compel us to revise the generally accepted idea that the Mayan civilization of the first millennium was of a more or less permanently peaceable nature.'
>
> Jacques Soustelle

ROOM 1

In Room 1 (*below*), dignitaries are depicted standing inside a building (against a red background), at the foot of the royal throne. Above the door, the king is being dressed in preparation for a dance, which is taking place in the center of the lower register, in the open air (against a blue background). To the left of the dancers is a procession of musicians and masked figures while, to the right, a group of dignitaries watches the ceremony.

JUDGMENT OF THE PRISONERS

The battle ends with the defeat of the enemy, their judgment (*above*) and torture. Chaan Muan appears in the center of the composition, at the top of the pyramid, accompanied by dignitaries, captains and courtiers, both male and female. The conquered enemy have been stripped of their jewelry and clothing (except for a loincloth) and their hair is loose. A dead prisoner lies at the king's feet. Everywhere tortured prisoners awaiting execution hold out bloodstained hands. On the far left, an executioner holds his victim by the wrist. A severed head rests on a bed of leaves. Other warriors look on at the foot of the pyramid.

DANCE PREPARATIONS

In the detail above, the king is wearing a jaguar skin, jaguar-skin sandals and a necklace decorated with pearls. The central motif of his impressive headdress is a water lily being nibbled by a fish, a symbol of fertility. A framework of feathers is attached to the dancer's back. While one servant fastens a bracelet, another offers him jewelry.

ROOM 3

After the battle and the capture and torture of prisoners, the story painted on the walls of Structure 1 at Bonampak comes to an end with a great dance (*left*). The king and his two acolytes take part at the top of the pyramid, while other dignitaries crowd around its base.

Ceiba (silk cottonwood tree ▲ *279*)
on the Río Usumacinta

SCEPTERS OF YAXCHILÁN

The sovereigns of Yaxchilán and sometimes their lieutenants hold the scepter-figurine traditionally known as god K ▲ *217*: an image of lightning and the symbol of power and fertility. The shaft of the scepter is a serpent that forms one of the legs of a small figure with a human body and the head of a reptile. The electrical charge of the lightning is represented by a smoking ax planted in his forehead. Other scepters held by the sovereign and his acolytes during ceremonies include directional trees surmounted by a bird, long rods extended by a wickerwork structure, and others which are wider and decorated with partly mobile crosses, jaguar paws and torches.

Yaxchilán ◆ E F4

(*100 miles/160 km southeast of Palenque, on a good road to Frontera Corozal, then by boat*) From Frontera Corozal, a boat takes visitors to Yaxchilán, which lies a little farther along the same bank of the Río Usumacint. The site is enchanting, mainly due to its impressive vegetation – silk cottonwood trees, gum trees and many other trees with massive trunks and visible roots – and the sounds of the jungle – all kinds of bird calls and the roar of the howler monkeys.

HISTORY. Nestling in a bend of the Río Usumacinta, which marks the Chiapas–Guatemala border, Yaxchilán was the region's principal urban center in the early 6th century. It enjoyed its golden age during the Late Classical era with the Jaguar dynasty, whose reigns and conquests appear on the site's steles, altars and lintels. The most recent inscriptions date from the early 9th century.

MONUMENTS. Some of the structures are built on a terrace bordering the left bank of the river, others occupy the slopes above, while the majority are gathered together in two acropolises reached via long, steep staircases. They are predominately elongated, rectangular buildings with a single or double row of rooms and three entrances in the façade. Their foundations are relatively low and they have large, openwork roof combs.

SCULPTURES. The upper section of the façades is often very elaborately decorated with stone mosaics set off by sculptures in the round and stucco motifs. For example, the frieze of STRUCTURE 33 included statues of dignitaries seated on terrestrial monster masks or appearing at inverted

Structure 33,
Yaxchilán

MAYAN PROFILE
The characteristically
flattened forehead
was obtained by
compressing the skull
of newly born babies
between two planks of
wood, held in place
for several days.

T-shaped window openings, while the center of the roof
comb was occupied by a colossal stucco statue of the seated
sovereign. The LINTELS of the three doors were entirely
sculpted, and a stele and altar stood before the central door.
The sculptural style of the Usumacinta, and especially

Stele 35
of Temple 21

Yaxchilán, is justly famous for its
freedom of expression. The
architectural sculpture and
exterior monuments (steles and
altars) are often damaged, whereas
most of the detail on the lintels has
been preserved. The iconography
highlights the rituals performed by
the sovereign and members of his
immediate entourage – his wife,
mother, sons or a lieutenant. The
scenes of self-sacrifice – in one, a
woman is passing a cord of thorns
through her tongue – are explicitly
portrayed. In some cases the ritual
is represented by a basket of
sacrificial instruments (stingray
spines, sharp knives and cords of
thorns), accompanied by strips of
bast paper on which the victim's
blood was offered to the
beneficiaries of the sacrifice. The
sculptures also show scenes in
which the names of the victor and
vanquished are inscribed,
sometimes on their thigh.

▲ Chiapas
The southern highlands

Below: Finca Santa María
Bottom: Comitán

To the southeast of San Cristóbal and beyond Comitán, a long plateau slopes gently toward the lakes at an average altitude of 4,920 feet (1,500 m). It is bordered in the northwest by the Meseta Central de Chiapas, the central mountains of Chiapas, and in the southeast by the hills running along its southern edge before the land plunges down into the jungle and the central depression. All the tracks on this plateau lead to historical *fincas* (today mostly communal land) which initially belonged to the first inhabitants of San Cristóbal, and then in some cases to the Dominicans, and finally to Comitán in the 19th century. They are situated in a key area, on the edge of the Lacandón territory and the Guatemalan border. Several of these estates were the scene of battles fought either to occupy a strategic position or replenish supplies of agricultural products and livestock.

FINCA SANTA MARÍA
(*On the road to Montebello National Park about 18 km/ 11miles before the park entrance, signposted on the right*) This former finca, 20 km/ 12 miles from La Trinitaria, has been converted into a hotel – the Posada Museo Santa María. It consists of a main building (casa grande and restaurant), a chapel that houses an attractive collection of religious art, stables (with horses for hire), a large courtyard, a kitchen garden and an orchard. All the rooms have 18th- and 19th-century furniture and paintings.

Comitán de Domínguez ◆ E E4

Comitán stands at an altitude of 5,150 feet (1,570 m), at one end of this undulating plateau carpeted with fields of corn. Only 50 miles (80 km) from the Guatemalan border, it has seen its population swollen by the rural exodus of Tojolabal Indians from southeastern Mexico. It has some beautiful reminders of its colonial past and a number of fine *haciendas* in the surrounding area. The town's MAIN CHURCH – built in the 16th century and later renovated – stands in the *zócalo* opposite the neoclassical TEATRO DE LA CIUDAD which dates from the time of Porfirio Díaz ● *28*. An ancient arcature decoration was found at the foot of the bell tower.

The MUSEO BELISARIO DOMÍNGUEZ occupies an attractive colonial house that was once the home of one of Chiapas's famous sons, after whom so many of the state's streets have been named. Dedicated to helping the poor of Chiapas and defending their rights, and an ardent supporter of the Revolution, he was assassinated by order of the dictator Victoriano Huerta ● 28 after making a radical speech.

The site of Tenam Puente

The site of Tenam Puente ◆ E E5

(6 miles/10 km south of Comitán, a road on the right leads to the site 3 miles/5 km farther on.) Excavations have revealed a site on one of the hills bordering the plateau of Comitán that offers a spectacular view of the Cerro Tzontehuitz and the Sierra de los Cuchumatanes. This Mayan city is built on three levels, each with a ball court and several pyramids, often arranged around a sunken patio (*patio hundido*). Its architecture represents two successive stages of the Late Classical era, sometimes superimposed. With the exception of one dated stele in bas-relief (which can be seen in the museum of Tuxtla Gutiérrez), all the steles discovered at Tenam Puente were smooth. Beyond the site, an unsurfaced road continues across the mountain and down the other side to a surfaced road leading to Comitán. En route there are some magnificent views of the central valleys of the Sierra Madre, with small sulfur pools dotted across the pastureland.

The site of Chinkultic ◆ E E5

(Turn left about 4½ miles/7 km before the Montebello Lakes. A track leads to the ruins about ⅔ mile/1 km farther on.) The site covers a long period of history, since there is evidence of a connection with Toniná ▲ 262 (whose most recently dated stele is AD 909) and colonial manuscripts seem to refer to its occupation in the 16th century. The most interesting sculptures, which are in a poor state of repair, are near the ball court. They are decorated with Mayan symbols for war and death. Higher up the mountain, beyond the stream, is a monumental complex with a small platform at the foot of the pyramid and another on the edge of a deep *cenote* ▲ 238 which, when explored, revealed several cavities containing mortuary offerings. The top of the pyramid offers a stunning view of the Montebello Lakes and Lake Chinkultic.

THE MARIMBA
The marimba is the traditional and symbolic music of Chiapas, and also the name of the instrument used to play it – a sort of xylophone derived from the African *balafon* introduced to South America by Negro slaves. It is also the national instrument of Guatemala. It consists of strips of rosewood of varying lengths, connected to a series of resonators enclosed by a piece of gold-beater's skin (a thin membrane from the internal organs of an ox) or pig-gut membrane that serves as a vibrating tongue or reed. The marimba is played by at least three musicians at once who strike it using wooden sticks with hard rubber ends.

▲ The tropical forest

MORPHO
The erratic flight of these large, metallic-blue butterflies adds splashes of light to the dark undergrowth of the forest.

Mexico's richest ecosystem continues to evolve in the hot and humid atmosphere of the tropical forest. In the past, it covered much of the south and east of the country and represented over 10% of its total surface area. Today, the pressure of human activity has reduced this to a mere 0.5%. Even so, there are thousands of plant species and many animal species that have not yet been identified. Mistakenly regarded as hostile, these forests still represent a world waiting to be explored.

RESPLENDENT QUETZAL
The quetzal was highly prized and imported by the lowland Maya. Its feathers are still the subject of an ancestral trade.

BOA CONSTRICTOR
Hunted for their skin or captured to be sold as pets, these nonpoisonous snakes are an endangered species. They can grow up to 13 feet (4 m) and live for 25–30 years.

AMAZON PARROT
Amazon parrots fly rapidly through the forest in small, noisy bands.

GREAT CURASSOW
This large, flightless, solitary bird is under threat from hunting and deforestation.

KEEL-BILLED TOUCAN
Its beak enables it to feed on fruit at the end of the most slender branches.

SCARLET MACAW
Macaws are popular pets and have become extremely rare in the wild.

AGOUTI
This rodent helps to disseminate the seeds of tropical trees.

NINE-BANDED ARMADILLO
The armadillo is hunted for its meat and decorative shell from Argentina to the United States.

JAGUAR
The largest of the American cats is a formidable hunter. featured in the mythology of many pre-Hispanic civilizations.

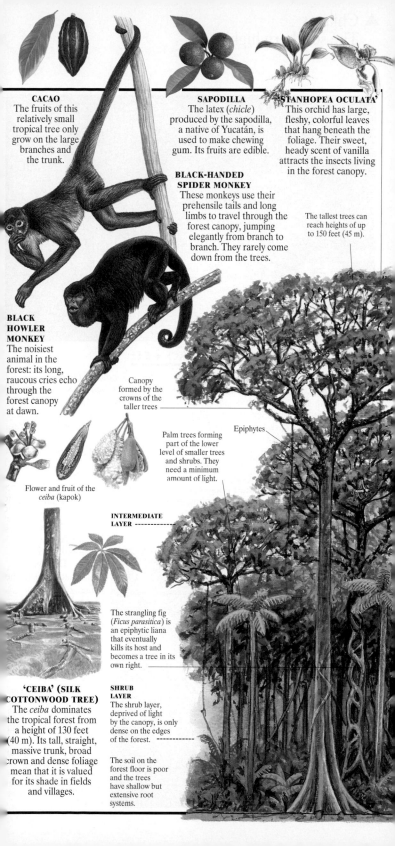

CACAO
The fruits of this relatively small tropical tree only grow on the large branches and the trunk.

SAPODILLA
The latex (*chicle*) produced by the sapodilla, a native of Yucatán, is used to make chewing gum. Its fruits are edible.

'STANHOPEA OCULATA'
This orchid has large, fleshy, colorful leaves that hang beneath the foliage. Their sweet, heady scent of vanilla attracts the insects living in the forest canopy.

BLACK-HANDED SPIDER MONKEY
These monkeys use their prehensile tails and long limbs to travel through the forest canopy, jumping elegantly from branch to branch. They rarely come down from the trees.

The tallest trees can reach heights of up to 150 feet (45 m).

BLACK HOWLER MONKEY
The noisiest animal in the forest: its long, raucous cries echo through the forest canopy at dawn.

Canopy formed by the crowns of the taller trees

Flower and fruit of the *ceiba* (kapok)

Palm trees forming part of the lower level of smaller trees and shrubs. They need a minimum amount of light.

Epiphytes

INTERMEDIATE LAYER

The strangling fig (*Ficus parasitica*) is an epiphytic liana that eventually kills its host and becomes a tree in its own right.

'CEIBA' (SILK COTTONWOOD TREE)
The *ceiba* dominates the tropical forest from a height of 130 feet (40 m). Its tall, straight, massive trunk, broad crown and dense foliage mean that it is valued for its shade in fields and villages.

SHRUB LAYER
The shrub layer, deprived of light by the canopy, is only dense on the edges of the forest.

The soil on the forest floor is poor and the trees have shallow but extensive root systems.

A WALK THROUGH THE RAIN FOREST
In the region of the Montebello Lakes, the early morning jungle mists lift as the sun rises and fall again during the afternoon as the air temperature cools. The eastern exposure of the site and its altitude – 4,600 feet (1,400 m) – form a barrier against the trade winds and create the conditions necessary for high-altitude rain forest. The most common species of trees are sweet-smelling conifers, oaks – with bromeliads (*right*), epiphytes and orchids – and sweet gums with their maplelike sap and leaves, which grow above a dense undergrowth of flowers, aromatic plants, giant ferns and shrubs. There is also a wide variety of wildlife, including deer, armadillos and all kinds of birds.

Montebello Lakes ◆ **E** E5

THE NATIONAL PARK. (*About 35 miles/57 km from Comitán, a few miles east of where the road forks to Chinkultic*) The lakes (*above*) act as an 'overflow' for the water sinks of the endorheic valley of Comitán – 'endorheic' means its river system doesn't flow into a trunk river. The color of the lakes varies according to the composition of their floor – sand (blue-green) or rocks (chalky) – and whether they are in shadow (deep blue-black) or sun (opal-blue). A series of pools begins about 12 miles (20 km) before the lakes. The water pours beneath the rocks (water sinks) and then plunges into the jungle, which begins near La Cañada. The road forks as you enter the park. The left road leads to several lakes, including Esmeralda, La Encantada and

Bosque Azul, which are popular for picnics. The right-hand road leads to the village of Tziscao through some spectacular scenery – lakes nestling in more mountainous terrain, their rocky shores adapted here and there as viewpoints, surrounded by dense forest. There is basic accommodation available at the Indian village of Tziscao, and visitors can hire cycles, boats and horses – but be wary of the quicksand on the beach.

Tuxtla Gutiérrez ◆ E D4

This colonial town was relatively unimportant until 1892, when it became the capital of Chiapas. A REGIONAL MUSEUM traces the region's pre-Columbian history. The town became a liberal center under the influence of Joaquín Miguel Gutiérrez (1796–1838). Born here, into a family of Spanish immigrants, Gutiérrez became a militant federalist and then a representative, a governor and finally a *guerillero*. With its 460,000 inhabitants, Tuxtla is the only town in Chiapas with modern urban developments – parks, bypasses and 20th-century monuments built by famous contemporary Mexican architects. The ZOOMAT (Zoológico Miguel Álvarez del Toro), to the south of the ring road, is regarded as one of the most beautiful zoos in Latin America. The zoo was completely redesigned in 2003, and only keeps species endemic to Chiapas – jaguars, ocelots, quetzals, monkeys, crocodiles, snakes and butterflies – living in semi-liberty in surroundings similar to their natural environment.

PARQUE MARIMBA
Every evening, a free marimba concert is held beneath the kiosk of the Parque Marimba, in Tuxtla. Young and old gather to dance, chat, sip a soda or nibble a *taco*.

Main plaza,
Tuxtla Gutiérrez

Chiapa de Corzo ◆ E D4

An Olmec engraving dating from 36 BC was found on this site, which was occupied in c. 1000 by the Chiapanecs and, in the 16th century, by the Aztecs. It was the first town in the region to be conquered by the Spanish and remained the most important town in the province until the 18th century.
COLONIAL FOUNTAIN. The fountain of Chiapa de Corzo was the result of the extensive hydraulic work carried out during the colonial period. The monumental Mudejar fountain with its diamond-shaped bricks was built in 1562 by the Dominican friar Fray Rodrigo de Léon.
EX-CONVENTO DE SANTO DOMINGO. The monastery's two cloisters represent two successive structures. On the first floor, the Dominican order is evoked by a stucco mural (Dominican shields and pairs of hounds) that plays on their Latin name – *domini-cani* or the 'hounds of God'. The 'Lacquer Room' upstairs has a display of decorative objects.

LACQUER
Lacquer is a hard waterproof varnish made from cochineal (a red dye extracted from the cochineal insect that feeds on cactus plants), whitening and *chía* oil (a sort of sage ▲ 252). It is applied with a brush made from cat's hairs inserted into the quill of a chicken feather.

**GRAN FIESTA
DE ENERO,
CHIAPA DE CORZO**
The Gran Fiesta de
Enero, or Festival of
Saint Sebastian
(January 20), partly
religious and partly
secular, is one of
Mexico's finest
popular festivals. It is
associated with the
legend of Doña María
de Angulo, a wealthy
Spanish woman who
came to Chiapas, at
an indeterminate time
in the past, to find a
cure for her sick son.
The boy was saved.
When, sometime
later, the region was
devastated by a
plague of locusts, she
showed her gratitude
by helping the local
people with generous
gifts in the name of
her son – *para el chico*
(for the boy). This
was the origin of the
parachicos, the
carnival figures who
parade through the
streets wearing
colored masks and
hats decorated with
multicolored ribbons.
Throughout most of
January, the town is
alive with colorful
floats, firework
displays on the river
and processions.

Cañon del Sumidero ◆ **E** D4

The Río Grijalva is Mexico's second largest river. Its waters
are harnessed by several hydroelectric dams located
upstream from the Cañon del Sumidero (*above*), an
impressive fault over 18½ miles (30 km) long, whose rocky
walls reach heights of up to 3,280 feet (1,000 m). The
vegetation varies according to the orientation of the canyon
walls – a thick layer of tropical vegetation in the shade and a
carpet of small cacti in the sun. The Cañon del Sumidero was
the scene of a historic battle in which the Spanish defeated
the local population. According to legend, the Indians
preferred to jump into the depths of the gorge rather than be
subjugated by the *conquistadores*. Because of its symbolism
for the inhabitants of Chiapas, the canyon appears on the
state coat of arms. There are two ways to explore the canyon
– by road from Tuxtla Gutiérrez or by boat from Chiapa de
Corzo or Cahuaré.

THE ROAD OF BELVEDERES. (*From Tuxtla, take the
Avenida Central toward Chiapa de Corzo, then turn left onto the
Calle del Sumidero.*) The road winds steeply through the
Granja district, then on up the mountainside, before entering
the park and following the western edge of the canyon. A
series of viewpoints offers vertiginous views of this deep
gorge. The road comes to a dead end at an altitude of 4,265
feet (1,300 m).

TRIPS ON THE RÍO GRIJALVA. (*There are two starting-
points for these river trips – the Embarcadero Cahauré on the
road to Chiapa de Corzo [turn right after the bridge over the
Grijalva] and the Embarcadero Malecón near the zócalo in
Chiapa de Corzo. Both return trips last about 2 hours.*) Ten-
seater motor boats (*lanchas*) take visitors through the narrow
fault as far as the Chicoasén reservoir, the furthest point on
the route. There's plenty to see on the way, including a cave,
rock formations, waterfalls and the amazing vegetation on
the rocky walls of the canyon.

Puebla–Oaxaca–Pacific coast

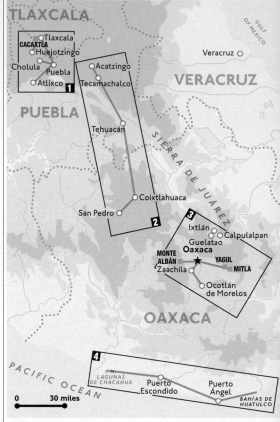

0   30 miles

🚶 **THE ASCENT OF
LA MALINCHE**
◆ **D** C3
*(20 miles/32 km from
Tlaxcala, via Apizaco
and then the RF 136)*
You can climb to the
top of the volcano –
14,635 feet (4,461 m)
– from the Centro
Vacacional Malintzín.
Allow 3–4 hours to
get to the top and 2
hours for the descent.
You can hire the
services of a guide.

S outheast Mexico was the home of the great pre-Hispanic
rival civilizations of the Mexica: the Cholula and above all
the Monte Albán. During the colonial period, the towns built
in the region – the Spanish town of Puebla and the Indian
town of Oaxaca – were unrivaled for their baroque splendor.
The relief and terrain change toward the south as the high
plateaus planted with corn become much more arid, with the
exception of a few oases of greenery such as Tehuacán. The
landscape changes abruptly on the road to Oaxaca, near the
Cerro Verde, as you approach the purple mountains of the
Sierra Madre, covered with 'chandelier' cactuses (so called
because of their branching stems). The land becomes
increasingly barren and devoid of vegetation, often verging
on the apocalyptic, especially in the rainy season (August and
September) when torrential tropical storms threaten to wash
away the roads. The seemingly endless descent toward the
coast makes the beaches seem all the more desirable.

Tlaxcala ◆ **D** C2-3

Tlaxcala (meaning 'the place where the corn grows' in
Nahuatl) is the smallest state in Mexico, and much of it is
occupied by La Malinche, a volcano named for Cortés'

Indian consort and interpreter ● *32*. This delightful colonial town has two architectural gems that are absolute musts.

CONVENTO DE SAN FRANCISCO. In the historic center, a paved lane shaded by old *ahuehuetes* (bald cypresses) leads to the first colonial monastery (1525–27) built by the Franciscans in New Spain. In the older CHURCH OF THE ASSUMPTION, the Mudejar style of the flat cedarwood ceiling, decorated with gilt stars, attests to the influence of the Arab culture via Spanish architecture. In the CAPILLA DEL TECER ORDEN is the original font where four Tlaxcalan chiefs were baptized in 1520. The monastery has been transformed into the Museo Regional de Tlaxcala. On the lower level the CAPILLA DE LOS INDIOS has some beautiful Gothic vaults. The bullring is next to the monastery, whose cellars serve as a *toril* (bullpen), especially during the *feria* held in Tlaxcala in late October–early November.

SANTUARIO DE OCOTLÁN. (*Above the town. Reached by car or on foot via the Calle Zitlalpopoca – follow the signs. About 1 mile/1.5 km.*) The church, which stands high above the town, is one of the most beautiful baroque buildings in Mexico. It was built between 1536 and 1539 by the Franciscan friar known as 'Motolinia' ('Poor one'), and is fascinating for its sheer exuberance. The church entrance is framed by hexagonal, brick-colored *azulejos* (ceramic tiles) that provide a striking contrast with the brilliant white stucco motifs that decorate the FAÇADE and the TWIN TOWERS. All that remains of the original INTERIOR, which was refurbished in the 19th century, are the lateral altars, the high altar and the *camarín* (the hexagonal room where the statue of the Virgin was dressed ● *82*), decorated with eight paintings by the artist Juan de Villalobos. The legend of Our Lady of Ocotlán, who is said to have appeared to a young Indian shepherd, is similar to that of the Virgin of Guadalupe ▲ *146*.

Desert region between Puebla and Oaxaca

Santuario de Nuestra Señora de Ocotlán

Frescos in Cacaxtla: battle scene (*left*) and warrior in eagle costume (*right*)

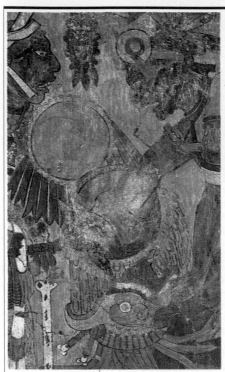

Cacaxtla ◆ D B2-3

(*Take the expressway A 150 to the toll at San Martín Texmelucán, then follow the signs to Tepetitla for 3 km/1⅔ miles. Turn left as you leave San Rafael Atoyatenco and continue through three small villages. The site access is on the left, 1⅓ miles/2 km before Santa María Nativitas.*) The sites of Cacaxtla and Xochitécatl stand on a hill near Tlaxcala. They were built by migrant populations from the Gulf and, during their golden age, appear to have maintained close relations with the Maya and Zapotecs ▲ 299 (650–850). Following the collapse of Teotihuacán ▲ 162, these populations assumed great importance due to their strategic position in the border regions of the Anáhuac basin. Cacaxtla became the administrative center that controlled the surrounding domains, and Xochitécatl an important ceremonial center of a fertility cult. Today, Cacaxtla is

XOCHITÉCATL
(*15 minutes' walk from Cacaxtla*) The Cerro de Xochitécatl is an ancient volcano that was transformed into a ceremonial center and necropolis. The nine-story Pyramid of the Flowers was dedicated to the gods of fertility. It offers a spectacular view of Cacaxtla and La Malinche, and the volcanoes of the Anáhuac plateau.

famous for its MURALS, whose colors have retained much of their original splendor and in which the features of certain figures are clearly reminiscent of the Mayan style.

BUILDING A. In the TEMPLO DE VENUS, with its recurrent motif of the morning star, it is still possible to make out part of a female figure with a blue body (her breast, waist and the jaguar skin around her hips) against a red background. On the next column, her male counterpart, also painted in blue, is wearing a necklace, feathers and a jaguar-skin loincloth. He has the tail of a scorpion emerging from his buttocks.

BUILDING B. The most spectacular mural is the MURAL DE LA BATALLA, whose forty-six life-size figures in full regalia tell the story of the terrible battle that reportedly took place between the Olmeca-Xicallanca (the victors) and the Maya (the vanquished). It was painted c. 650 on a slightly sloping limestone embankment divided in the center by a flight of steps. On one side it shows groups of warriors dressed as eagles and jaguars. The jaguar-knights are armed with spears, obsidian knives and shields decorated with feathers, while the eagle-knights – naked and without weapons – adopt submissive postures. On the other side, it depicts the sacrifice as a jaguar-knight plunges his obsidian knife into the heart of his defeated victim. On PORTICO A, two more extraordinary paintings represent an eagle-knight and a jaguar-knight surrounded by an aquatic frieze that features crabs, turtles and shells.

TEMPLO ROJO. The figure of an old man, with only one tooth and very long hair, probably represents a merchant: he

MAYAN BLUE
This unique blue, almost turquoise, is still not fully understood. It is made from a mixture of clay and indigo heated to high temperatures, but its intensity and resistance remain something of a mystery. Certain chemists have suggested that the pigments used may contain minute particles of iron that affect the optical properties of the paint.

THE BATTLE OF PUEBLA (MAY 5, 1862)
Following their victory at Las Cumbres (Veracruz), the only town likely to block the advance of the French into Mexico was Puebla which, at the time, had a population of only 70,000. It was defended by the two forts of Loreto and La Guadalupe held by 1,200 soldiers under the command of General Negrete. The French thought they would make short work of the town, but Negrete had sent for reinforcements and General Ignacio Zaragoza surrounded the French troops with 3,000 men. The Mexicans, now superior in number and commanded by Colonel Porfirio Díaz, launched a final offensive against the invaders, who were routed on May 5, 1862. Today, the Cinco de Mayo is a national holiday and gives rise to all kinds of celebrations throughout Mexico and even in the United States, where the date has been recognized as a day of national importance for Mexico.

has a very large pack filled with various types of merchandise that he is carrying on his back. Opposite the merchant, a cacao tree – surmounted by a quetzal ▲ *278* – and several maize plants celebrate local agriculture and the fertility of the earth.

Huejotzingo ◆ **D** B3

(*On the RF 190 Mexico–Puebla, 18 miles/29 km beyond Cholula*) Between 1554 and 1570, the Franciscans built a MONASTERY in this town, which had chosen to join Cortés against the empire of Moctezuma ● *32*. The exterior of the church is a strange mixture of Plateresque and Mudejar styles. The first is expressed in the contrast between the very sober façade of the church and the overextravagance of the flowers and plants decorating the porch. The second is reflected in the form of the porch – an ogee arch. The INTERIOR houses one of the few 16th-century altarpieces remaining in Mexico. The fresco in the SALA DE PROFUNDIS depicts the first Franciscans arriving in Mexico. The ATRIUM still has its corner chapels – *capillas posas* or repository chapels ● *78* (1550). The carnival at Huejotzingo attracts large numbers of visitors. It commemorates the victory over the French troops of Napoleon III on May 5, 1862, the legend of Agustín Lorenzo, a sort of 18th-century Mexican Robin Hood, and the celebration of the marriage of Calixto, the first Indian from Huejotzingo to convert to Roman Catholicism.

The ornate tiles of Puebla – known as *talaveras* by association with Talavera de la Reina, a major center of production in Spain – have their roots in the culture of Andalusia. Introduced into Mexico in the 16th century, this glazing technique reflects a number of cross-cultural influences. In the Mexican *talavera*, for example, it is possible to identify Moorish, Spanish and even Chinese influences. The two most beautiful collections of *talaveras* are to be found in the Museo de Arte José Luis Bello y Gonzalez in Puebla, and in the Museo Franz Mayer ▲ 142 in Mexico City.

For a long time, Puebla has competed with Mexico City, remaining as traditional and conservative as its rival is liberal and progressive. Founded in 1531, the influence of the regional capital of southeast Mexico extends into Yucatán. It occupies an impressive site bounded by three, often snow-capped volcanoes – Popocatépetl, Ixtaccíhuatl and La Malinche – and has a rich architectural heritage and very mild climate, with average temperatures of 61–68°F (16–20°C). Puebla's other delightful features include the polychrome tiles that decorate most of its old colonial buildings and its gastronomy (the famous *mole poblano*).

The Cathedral district ◆ 0 B3

CATHEDRAL. (*Plaza de la Constitución*) Thought to be the oldest cathedral in Mexico, the main entrance, the Puerta del Perdón, is flanked by the statues of four saints: Joseph and James (above the entrance) and Peter and Paul (below). The NORTH ENTRANCE has statues of the kings of Spain (Carlos V, Filippo I, II and III) who reigned during its construction. With a height of 216 feet (66 m), the north tower is the highest bell tower in Mexico. All that remains of the original colonial interior is the CAPILLA DEL OCHAVO, with it Mudejar-style hardwood pews, at the southwest corner.

BIBLIOTECA PALAFOXIANA. (*Calle 5 Oriente*) The only complete colonial library (17th century) in Latin America contains almost 43,000 works, including some rare books and manuscripts. It is the collection of the famous bishop of Puebla, Don Juan Palafox y Mendoza, and has been enriched over the years by donations.

Capilla del Rosario ◆ 0 A-B2

(*In the Iglesia de Santo Domingo, Calle 5 de Mayo*) The chapel (*left*) – one of the most dazzling examples of Mexican baroque architecture – was built by the Dominicans to teach the Indians how to worship the Virgin, and to introduce them to esthetic principles that were different from their own. Its richly extravagant and symbolically charged decor attests to the influence of popular Indian art and techniques: the artisans coated the stuccowork with flour mixed with egg-white before covering it with gold leaf. The three vaults present the Three Virtues – faith (carrying a cross and chalice), hope (with an anchor) and charity (a mother and her two children) – which lead to Divine Grace embodied by the

Left: Casa de los
Muñecos, covered
with *talaveras*
Below: Capilla del
Rosario

'MOLE POBLANO'
The most famous
Mexican *mole* (sauce)
● 66, is made with
cocoa, pumpkin
seeds, almonds,
peanuts and a dozen
more or less spicy
chilies, and is usually
served with a piece of
turkey or chicken.
According to legend,
when the Bishop of
Puebla was invited to
dine in a local
convent, the cook –
Sister Andrea de
Asunción – was so
nervous at the
thought of preparing
a meal for a bishop
that that she knocked
the entire spice rack
into her sauce. It was
too late to make
another but a quick
prayer to Saint Jude
(aka Thaddeus), who
intercedes on behalf
of those in desperate
straits, did the trick –
the sauce was
exquisite.

Virgin, crowned with palm and laurel leaves. Another dome
depicts the seven gifts of the Holy Spirit. Among the
secondary decorative elements, pelicans symbolize Christ,
while angels, birds and flowers represent praise, music and
offerings respectively.

Museo Amparo ◆ ❶ B3

(*Calle 2 Sur, 708, between calles 7 Oriente and 9 Poniente*)
This is one of Mexico's finest museums of colonial and pre-
Hispanic art, housed in the former hospital of the Purísima
Concepción.

THE PRE-HISPANIC COLLECTION. The objects on
display in the first three rooms showcase artistic techniques,
while those in the next four follow a chronological and
cultural presentation, highlighting the influences between the
six great cultures of Mesoamerica. A final room brings
together the finest pieces in the museum. These masterpieces
include some very beautiful Mayan stone masks, the lid of a
Mayan tomb from the Isthmus of Tehuantepec, decorated
with a strange figure holding another person in its hands, and
a Mayan stone censer sculpted with the face of a dignitary.
The museum's pride and joy is an altar frieze in white
limestone (from the late Maya period), probably from Dos

**SWEETMEATS
OF PUEBLA**
Camotes, delicacies
made from sweet
potato, are eaten hot
or warm with a piece
of cheese.

Below left: San Francisco district
Below right: Casa del Alfeñique
Bottom: *La China Poblana* by Edouard Pingret (1852)

LA CHINA POBLANA
In 1621, the viceroy of Mexico let it be known that he wanted a young Chinese girl to add a touch of exoticism to his court. Captain Miguel de Sosa of Puebla bought Catalina, a twelve-year-old slave girl and daughter of the Great Mogul, who had been captured and brought to Mexico on the *nao de China* ▲ 179 by Portuguese pirates . However, instead of offering her to the viceroy, the captain adopted her. She was very beautiful, and cooked and sewed admirably, but refused to learn to read or write. When Don Miguel died in 1624, she was taken in by a priest and began to live the life of an ascetic, having visions that made her famous. Thousands of people came to see her, and women began to wear embroidered aprons like hers. After her death, in 1688, 'La China Poblana' was venerated like a saint and became a national emblem.

Pilas (*on the Río Usumacinta*). It depicts a man and a woman in conversation, sitting cross-legged and wearing the headdresses of dignitaries. The glyphs have not yet been deciphered.

THE COLONIAL SECTION. The works are presented in the artistic, political and social context of the period. Thus, an interesting room of religious art is centered on representations of the Virgin of Guadalupe. Another, devoted to polychrome sculptures, relates to the ideological conquest of New Spain. Secular art is also showcased via the baroque exuberance of Indian artists working in wood, ivory, bone and shell. Gold- and silverwork, ceramics, wrought iron and freestone are shown in relation to the techniques used.

East of the 'zócalo' ◆ **0** B-C2

IGLESIA DE LA COMPAÑÍA. (*Av Camacho, corner of Calle 4 Sur*) 'La China Poblana' is buried beneath the dome of this church, whose blue and white *azulejos* are characteristic of Puebla.

CASA DEL ALFEÑIQUE. (*Corner of 4 Oriente and 6 Norte*) So called because the frothy white decorations on the façade look like sugar paste (*alfeñique*), this house contains the MUSEO DEL ESTADO. Exhibits include 16th-century Indian codices, Spanish armor and coaches.

Markets

The MERCADO DEL PARIÁN (*Calle 2 Oriente*) is picturesque, but good quality Pueblan crafts are few and far between. On Sundays, the secondhand market, on the Plazuela de los Sapos, is a good place to track down a few bargains.

Cholula ◆ **D** B3

(*8 miles/13 km from Puebla. Take the Av Juárez, then the Av Teziutlán Norte to the main Puebla–Cholula road.*) 'We have found two thousand magnificent buildings flanked by towers and as many temples as there are days in the year!' (Cortés). The ancient ceremonial site and sacred city of Cholula had already existed for 2,500 years when it was captured by Cortés, in 1519, after a terrible battle that claimed 3,000 lives. The Spanish built 365 chapels on top of Cholula's 365 temples, and Carlos V invested the town with its own coat of arms in 1540. Today, visitors can enjoy a local *mole* under the 17th-century porticos of the town's pleasant *zócalo*.

SANTUARIO DE LOS REMEDIOS. The Pyramid of Quetzalcóatl (or Tepanapa), thought to be the largest in the world, is 1,395 feet (425 m) square at the base and stands 203 feet (62 m) high. It was rebuilt seven times, but is today almost entirely buried. Archeologists have excavated a long tunnel that cuts through the pyramid and which is open to the public. It is surmounted by the TEMPLO DE NUESTRA SEÑORA DE LOS REMEDIOS, built in 1594 and entirely rebuilt in 1864–74 after an earthquake. On a clear day, there is a spectacular view of the volcanoes and the Puebla Valley.

AFRICAM
(*10 miles/16 km from Cholula. Take the Calle 9 Sur to the Periférico Ecológico, turn left onto it and continue until you reach the turnoff to Valsequillo and Africam. It's well signposted.*) This 495-acre (200-ha) safari park was founded in 1972 by Carlos Camacho, an eccentric aviator and animal lover, who was killed by one of his lions. Africam, whose 256 species include monkeys, elephants, ostriches, a white rhinoceros and some Bengal tigers, is open to the public 24 hours a day.

Below: Cholula

Below left: detail from Santa María Tonantzintla
Below right: façade of San Francisco Acatepec

South of Cholula

TONANTZINTLA ◆ D B3. (*3 miles/ 5 km from Cholula*) Santa María Tonantzintla is a jewel of baroque architecture, a fantasy created by the 18th-century Indian craftsmen who sculpted its amazingly extravagant decor. The inside of the dome represents Paradise with the nine orders of angels and a wealth of fruit and flowers. Before the Conquest, the Indians worshipped Tonantzín, mother of the gods and the protectress of corn. The Spanish allowed them to model the stuccowork in accordance with their own traditions, to avoid offending their ancestral beliefs – the angels are coffee-colored, the children have plumed headdresses and the decoration is interspersed with vigorous ears of corn ● 82. On the pillars, the telamons are plumed Indians. The façade combines red brick and faience tiles.

SAN FRANCISCO ACATEPEC ◆ D B3. (*⅔ mile/1 km to the south*) The chapel is another example of Puebla's baroque art, with its façade of green, yellow and blue *azulejos*, and an interior decor resplendent with gilt stuccowork.

CAPILLA DE TLAXCALANCINGO ◆ D B3. (*1¾ miles/3 km from Acatepec*) The chapel has a beautiful red-brick façade and a bell tower faced with *azulejos*.

ATLIXCO AND AROUND ◆ D B3. (*25 miles/40 km from Cholula via the Avdas Juárez and Atlixco*) This delightful town at the foot of Popocatépetl was a major center for the production of corn. Its *zócalo* looks more like a public garden, with its bandstand shaded by leafy old Madeira bays, eucalyptus and Chile pines (monkey-puzzle trees). Don't miss nearby TOCHIMILCO, the former headquarters of Emiliano Zapata. It has a beautiful old Franciscan monastery

THE SCENIC ROUTE BETWEEN PUEBLA AND OAXACA
From Izúcar, the old Oaxaca road takes you to Acatlán, famous for its black ceramics, and Chila, whose houses cluster around a Baroque church with a yellow dome. The mountain road twists and turns through an extremely wild landscape to HUAJUAPAN DE LEÓN, renowned for its onyx, and then on to Nochixtlán and the freeway to Oaxaca.

with a remarkable Plateresque entrance. On the road to
Izúcar de Matamoros, the village of HUAQUECHULA has a
fortified church whose side entrance, inspired by 16th-
century engravings, depicts the Last Judgment.

Between Puebla and Oaxaca

Although it's best to take the freeway between Puebla and
Oaxaca, several villages are well worth a detour.

ACATZINGO ◆ D C3. (*30 miles/49 km from Puebla*) The
FRANCISCAN MONASTERY has some magnificent gilt
altarpieces and a very beautiful 'Christ on the Cross'. The
Capilla de la Virgen de los Dolores combines paintings on
wood, onyx and *talaveras* ▲ 288.

QUECHOLAC. (*6 miles/10 km beyond Acatzingo, on the same
road*) On the main square, the façade and sculpted stone
peristyle are all that remain of a FRANCISCAN CHURCH
badly damaged in the earthquake of 1973. On the other side
of the square, the convent church, with its two impressive
towers, houses gilt altarpieces, baptismal fonts, a stone
architrave and an interesting San Sebastián bound to a
cactus, which serves as an instrument of torture.

TECAMACHALCO ◆ D C3. (*Continue along the same road,
which takes you under the freeway, and follow the signs to
Tecamachalco, 9 miles/15 km farther on.*) On the
outskirts of the village, a road on the right leads up to
the austere church which has frescos by Juan
Gerson – 28 medallions, painted in 1562, inspired
by the Wittenberg Bible. They attest to the 16th-
century vision of the Old Testament. (*Retrace your
steps for 3 miles/5 km and take the freeway*)

TEHUACÁN ◆ D C3. A clean, well-organized little
town – an ideal place to stop and take a break in its
pretty *zócalo*. The modern frescos under the
arcades of the Palacio Municipal trace the
history of the town. The MUSEO DEL VALLE DE
TEHUACÁN has specimens of the earliest type of
corn (3,000 years old) found in nearby dry caves. The
road to Oaxaca offers an extraordinary spectacle. For
a distance of 25 miles/40 km, the only vegetation that
can survive under the burning tropical sun are
chandelier cactuses (prickly pears), interspersed
with agaves, golden ball cactuses ('mother-in-
law's cushions') and other spiny plants. There
are special viewpoints along the road ▲ 388.

COIXTLAHUACA ◆ D D4. (*77 miles/124 km
before Oaxaca*) This village has a wonderful
Renaissance-style monastery which still has its
open-air chapel. You enter the church through a
beautifully sculpted Plateresque entrance. Inside, the
wooden altarpieces were carved, painted and gilded by
the great Sevillian master Andrés Concha.

TEPOSCOLULA ◆ D C4. (*Take the right-hand fork at
Asunción/Noxichtlán*) The open-air chapel is one of
the most beautiful in Mexico ● 80. Built in 1550–75,
its imposing appearance comes from the harmony of
its fluted columns, flying buttresses and abutments.

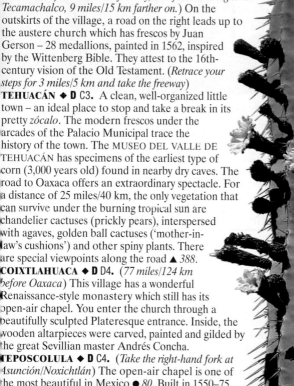

**CACTUS
CONSERVATORY,
ZAPOTITLÁN ◆ D** C4.
(*From Tehuacán,
follow the signs to
Huajuapán de León
for about 12½ miles/
20 km. On the right, a
road suitable for
vehicles leads to the
'Jardín Botánico y
Vivero de Cactaceas'.*)
The road winds past
marble and alabaster
quarries into the
heart of the Sierra de
Zapotitlán, where you
can walk among the
giant cactuses. Some
species, such as the
'elephant's foot'
cactus, are thought to
be more than 2,000
years old, while others
are 65 feet (20 m) tall.

Mixtec turquoise necklace
and gold pendant found in
Tomb 7 at Monte Albán

FIESTA OAXAQUEÑA
To celebrate the
Fiesta del Rabano
('night of the radish'),
held on December 23,
the people of Oaxaca
carve figures out of
radishes, eat *buñuelos*
(jam fritters) and
throw terracotta
bowls into the air. If
they break, it means
they can look forward
to a good year.

The beautiful region of Oaxaca, the cradle of the Zapotec and Mixtec cultures, constitutes one of the earliest centers of population in Mesoamerica. Hernán Cortés was so captivated by its attributes that, until 1910, his descendants bore the title the 'Marquis of the Valley of Oaxaca'. The greenish limestone (*cantera verde*) used to build its churches gave rise to its Indian name, 'City of Jade', which the English poet and novelist Malcolm Lowry (1909–57) described as the 'most beautiful city in the world'. In spite of its amazing colonial architecture it has also retained a strong Indian identity, even though the Indians have been gradually

OAXACA ★
Oaxaca is a
UNESCO World
Heritage Site and it's
worth allowing
several days to enjoy
its light, invigorating
air and take time out
to visit the 'central
valleys' around the
town.

pushed toward the outskirts. A large community of retired North Americans, attracted by the purity of the air and amiability of the inhabitants, has contributed to the restoration of the beautiful residences that they occupy. As well as being the ultimate retirement and holiday resort, Oaxaca also boasts a dynamic artistic community, inspired by such local artists as Rufino Tamayo, Rodolfo Morales and Francisco Toledo.

The 'zócalo' ◆ **D** D5, ◆ **Q** B3

The *zócalo*, the heart of the town, is a beautiful tree-filled space where children play and local residents meet to catch up on the latest news and gossip. What could be better than sipping a coffee or a beer under the arcades that border the square, watching the endless comings and goings? The town band plays on the central bandstand, and marimba players sometimes set up their instruments in front of the terraces. The nearby square of the Alameda is dominated by the CATEDRAL DE LA ASUNCIÓN, whose baroque façade is punctuated by niches containing saints. The beautiful residences along the pedestrianized and attractively paved streets leading to the Iglesia Santo Domingo (Calles Macedonio Alcalá, 5 de Mayo, Reforma) are occupied by stores that invite you to while away a pleasant hour or two.

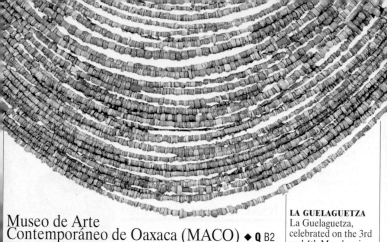

Museo de Arte Contemporáneo de Oaxaca (MACO) ◆ Q B2

Although this residence is known as the 'Casa Cortés', he neither stayed nor lived here. It is nonetheless a fine example of 17th-century civil architecture ● *78*, with its sober façade embellished by an entrance flanked by sculpted columns, a wrought-iron balcony on the upper story and a protective figure of the Archangel Rafael at the top of the pediment. Inside, three patios house exhibitions by local artists.

Ex-Convento de Santo Domingo ◆ Q B1

This magnificent monastery houses the MUSEO DE LAS CULTURAS DE OAXACA, opened in 1998. It is arranged around two cloisters – the extremely austere Patio de Lectores and the admirably proportioned Renaissance-style Patio de Procesiones, whose murals are illuminated by the light shining through the arches of the peristyle. This second cloister, where the friars washed their hands at the central medieval-type fountain on their way to the refectory, opens onto a palatial vestibule with two monumental staircases that led to the prior's cells. On the upper floor, two vast corridors intersect, and end in large windows that create pleasant vanishing points. In 1770, the monastery had 91 cells; these have been refurbished to house the museum collections.

COLLECTIONS. On the first floor, the ETHNOGRAPHIC COLLECTIONS offer an overview of local Indian cultures; also here is the PRE-COLUMBIAN ART. On display in Room 3 is the MIXTEC TREASURE from Tomb 7 at Monte Albán – take time to enjoy the array of gold, jade, turquoise and mother-of-pearl jewelry, and funerary masks (the highlight is a gold pectoral in the form of a finely carved human skull). The adjacent rooms are post-Conquest, and also look at the role played by Oaxaca in the struggle for Independence and after. THE BIBLIOTECA FRAY FRANCISCO DE BURGOA has eleven books printed before 1500, including *Comentarios a la filosofía de Aristóteles*, by Juan Versor.

LA GUELAGUETZA
La Guelaguetza, celebrated on the 3rd and 4th Mondays in July, on a hill called the Cerro de Fortín, is undoubtedly Mexico's oldest folk festival. It not only brings the people of Oaxaca and the surrounding area together in an annual celebration of music, dance and traditions, but it also plays a major role in terms of political and cultural integration. The origins of the festival have long been forgotten but it is almost certainly rooted in the traditions of the Olmecs. The 'Dance of the Feather', a strong cultural element in Zapotec communities, is the high point of the fiesta.

DOMINICAN GENEALOGY
Near the entrance to the church of Santo Domingo, beneath the organ chancel, a vine branch modeled in polychrome and gilt stuccowork represents the genealogy of the Dominicans, the order founded by Domingo de Guzmán.

EX-CONVENTO DE SANTA CATALINA
◆ **Q** B1-2
(*Calle 5 de Mayo, at the intersection with Abasolo*) This former 16th-century convent of Dominican nuns has been converted into a hotel (the Camino Real). Today, you can enjoy a drink in the Bar Novicias.

Parvis of Santo Domingo

JARDÍN HISTÓRICO ETNOBOTÁNICO. Today a botanical garden occupies the former vegetable gardens of the Dominican friars. In an area of 5 acres (2 ha), all the varieties of plants that grow in the region are tastefully presented.

Iglesia de Santo Domingo

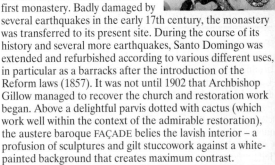

In 1529, Fray Domingo de Betanzos, the first Dominican provincial of New Spain, ordered his community to establish a Dominican presence in Oaxaca. A vast area was reserved for the order in the town's grid layout and, in 1552, twelve friars were sent to oversee the construction of the first monastery. Badly damaged by several earthquakes in the early 17th century, the monastery was transferred to its present site. During the course of its history and several more earthquakes, Santo Domingo was extended and refurbished according to various different uses, in particular as a barracks after the introduction of the Reform laws (1857). It was not until 1902 that Archbishop Gillow managed to recover the church and restoration work began. Above a delightful parvis dotted with cactus (which work well within the context of the admirable restoration), the austere baroque FAÇADE belies the lavish interior – a profusion of sculptures and gilt stuccowork against a white-painted background that creates maximum contrast.

CAPILLA DEL ROSARIO ◆ **Q** C1. The most beautiful of the church's eleven chapels was added to the right-hand side in

Below left: detail of the vine-branch genealogy
in the Iglesia de Santo Domingo
Below right:detail in the Capilla del Rosario

1731. Decorated with gold leaf, it has a magnificent
altarpiece whose white-robed Virgin was brought from Italy
in 1725. It is regarded as the most rococo altar in the whole
of Mexico. Beneath the dome, 104 medallions depict
Dominican martyrs.

Museo Rufino Tamayo ◆ Q A-B2

(*Av Morelos 503*) The museum, which occupies a beautiful
colonial residence ● 78, houses a collection of pre-
Columbian art bequeathed by the artist to his native town.
The collection is beautifully presented in small showcases
painted in traditional colors, as if they too were works of art.

La Soledad ◆ Q A2

IGLESIA DE LA SOLEDAD. (*Calle Independencia, between
Mier y Terán and Morelos*) Legend has it that, in 1617, a mule
carrying a chest containing an image of the Virgen de la
Soledad appeared mysteriously in a merchant caravan en
route to Guatemala. The worship of the Virgen de la Soledad
became so popular that the tiny hermitage of San Sebastián
had to be transformed into a sanctuary. On the sober
baroque FAÇADE, the twenty-one sculptures and bas-reliefs
of religious images and the foliage of the niches and columns
respect the esthetic principles of European architecture. The
neoclassical INTERIOR was imposed by Archbishop Gillow in
preference to the baroque style. The Virgen de la Soledad,
the patron saint of Oaxaca, is richly adorned with precious
stones and garments of gold thread. The annex of the church
houses a small museum of popular religious imagery.
ON THE HILLS ABOVE OAXACA. Opposite the Iglesia de
la Soledad, a former Capuchin convent houses the School of
Fine Arts. The Calle Mier y Terán leads up the hillside to the
FORTÍN (now an observatory) which offers a panoramic view
of the town.

**THE COLORS
OF TAMAYO**
Rufino Tamayo,
one of the greatest
contemporary
Mexican muralists
● 98, is renowned
internationally for his
work on Mexican
roots and colors –
blue, red, green, pink
and especially his
characteristic white,
known as 'Tamayo
white'.

A STRONG INDIAN PRESENCE
Along with neighboring Chiapas, the state of Oaxaca has the highest Indian population, with 16 of Mexico's 52 ethnic groups represented. The most important groups, numerically, historically and culturally speaking, are the Zapotecs, Mixtecs, Huaves, Chontals, Zoques, Mixes and Amuzgos. Of the 590 Indian communities, 169 live in the kind of extreme poverty that gives rise to violence over land distribution and religious conflicts. This poverty is driving people out of the rural areas to the outskirts of the towns and cities, the first stage in the illegal and dangerous migration toward the United States ● 42.

OAXACA CHEESE
Queso de Oaxaca (or *queso asadero*) is made throughout Mexico, but its name derives from the province where it originated. Made from cow's milk, with a consistency similar to that of mozzarella, it is sold on the markets in long strips that form 'skeins'. It is one of the tastiest Mexican cheeses and can be eaten fresh or melted. It is ideal for *quesadillas* ● 66.

Markets ◆ Q B3

(*Corner of Calles Miguel Cabrera and Las Casas*) The Mercados Centrales occupy the area behind the *zócalo*.

MERCADO BENITO JUÁREZ (CRAFTS). The State of Oaxaca has some 500,000 artisans – a figure that gives some idea of the richness of its popular art – whose techniques and secrets have been handed down for generations and who practice their crafts in the valleys around Oaxaca. Here visitors can buy glazed ceramics from Atzompa, black pottery from Coyotepec, metalwork from Tlaxiaco and Tlacolula, chased gold from Tehuantepec, textiles from Jalieza, Mitla and Teotitlán del Valle, wickerwork from Etla, and *alebrijes* (fantastical wooden animals ● 65) from Tilcajete.

MERCADO SAN JUAN DE DIOS (FOOD). One of the most exciting, inspiring and colorful Mexican markets may be explored like a huge, smoky kitchen where you can sample regional specialties at one of the many makeshift restaurants. Try traditional *moles* ● 66, *nopal* (prickly pear) soup, *enchiladas* (soft tortillas filled and covered with red or green chili sauce), *chiles rellenos* (stuffed chilies), *tamales* (corn meal and meat steamed in a corn husk) and all kinds of snacks and appetizers – grilled bugs, fried grasshoppers, sauces made from the slightly acidic white agave worms, *queso de Oaxaca* (Oaxaca cheese), chorizos, and fox, armadillo, squirrel and coypu meat.

At an altitude of 6,560 feet (2,000 m), the impressive site of Monte Albán (*above*) dominates the region from the top of a hill that was leveled and terraced (*6 miles/10 km southwest of Oaxaca*).

History

Construction began on the Zapotec city of Monte Albán in 500 BC. The ceremonial center, palaces and tombs were grouped together on the plateau, while the population (100,000 at the city's height) lived on the hillside. After being closely linked to the Olmec centers of La Venta during the Preclassic period, Monte Albán subsequently came under the Maya influence from the 5th to 10th centuries. It reached its height during the golden age of Teotihuacán, a city with which it maintained strong commercial ties. Circa 900–1000, the Zapotecs abandoned Monte Albán and the site was occupied by the Mixtecs ('people from the land of the clouds'), who had settled in northwest Oaxaca but were driven out by the Toltecs in the 10th and 11th centuries. Wars and intermarriage enabled them to seize power from the Zapotecs by taking over 200 major cities. They made Mitla their capital and transformed the city of Monte Albán ● 72 into a necropolis for their royal tombs.

The archeological site ◆ **D** D5

ESPLANADE. Two platforms stand on a vast esplanade that measures 819 by 984 feet (250 by 300 m). The remains of four structures, including an altar, are aligned along the center. At one end stands an asymmetrical mound in the form of an arrowhead, its staircase representing the shaft. Its alignment suggests that it was probably an observatory.
EL PALACIO. The palace, reached via a monumental staircase, was probably where the priests lived.

'TIANGUIS'
AROUND OAXACA
Tianguis are weekly markets held on set days, when the Indians from the surrounding villages come to buy and sell produce – Mondays in Ixtlán, Wednesdays in San Pedro y San Pablo Etla, Thursdays in Zaachila, Fridays in Ocotlán de Morelos, and Sundays in Tlacolula.

JADE MASK
The mask of the bat god, known to the Zapotecs as Piquitezina, was found in a tomb in the Palacio and dates from the second phase of Monte Albán's history, Monte Albán II (200 BC–AD 250). This god with human features, a long nose and three jade tongues beneath his chin, is often associated with Pitao Cozobi, the corn god. This was also the name of the fourth month of the Zapotec year.

▲ Zapotec 'funerary' urns

The so-called funerary urns – discovered in the tombs of Monte Albán in the late 19th century by the American archeologist Marshall H. Saville – are well known to art historians and collectors, and constitute a reference point for the Zapotec civilization. They are in the form of cylindrical receptacles with an effigy attached to the front. These effigies are usually sitting cross-legged with their hands resting on their knees, and most have a complex headdress and animal mask. They are often naked and asexual but some are wearing garments and jewelry and holding attributes – objects of great iconographic significance.

GENUINE AND REPLICA URNS

Between the late 19th century and the end of the 1920s, the success of the funerary urns on the international art market triggered what can only be described as the most prolific production of fakes in the field of pre-Columbian art. Of the 4,000 Zapotec urns recorded worldwide, at least 20% must be regarded as fakes. None of the major ethnographic museums seems to have been spared. Research carried out in recent years has identified twenty-three types of fakes. Made by local craftsmen, possibly at the instigation of collectors, these fake urns have little in common with Zapotec art, which really only began to be appreciated in the 1930s. And because counterfeiting tends to be a reflection of its own time, many are in fact influenced by such contemporary trends as art nouveau and art deco.

False urns: the 'Napoleon' type (*below*) and the 'Chamberlain' type (*bottom*)

STYLES

EARLY PERIOD
During the early period of the Zapotec civilization, the urns were usually small – under 10 inches (25 cm) – and round. The receptacle was incorporated into the body of the often naked figure. The faces commonly had animal snouts (mostly serpents), while headdresses were still few and far between and relatively small. Attributes and ornaments were rare. In short, urns from this period appear to be highly individualized, with a very varied iconography. (*Left*: urn no. 3 from Tomb 109, Monte Albán)

300

A   B   C

Left: the development of the glyph 'C' recorded on the urns
Below: reconstruction of the chamber of Tomb 104 at Monte Albán (c. 600), National Museum of Anthropology, Mexico City

SYMBOLISM

Because the first urns were discovered in tombs, they were described as 'funerary' urns, which is in fact incorrect. They were not always found in a funerary context (many come from foundation deposits) and never contained ashes or human remains. In fact, they probably contained perishable offerings such as perfumes or food. Although they bear divine attributes (especially masks), the effigies do not represent gods but are more likely to be important figures (chiefs, princes, ancestors) taking part in terrestrial ceremonies. Their function could well have been more political than religious.

STYLES

LATE PERIOD
During the late period of the Zapotec civilization, the 'funerary' urns became much larger. The figures were also distinct from the receptacles and were intended to be seen from the front. They wore rich garments and jewels and their spectacular headdresses were sometimes as tall as the figures themselves. They were usually male and had human faces, as on this urn from the Monte Albán IV era (*right*). These urns appear to adhere to strict iconographic rules that give them a hieratic and 'standardized' appearance.

301

In a cruciform tomb, the famous jade mask representing the Zapotec bat god Piquitezina ▲ *299* was discovered.

SOUTH PLATFORM. The 130-foot- (40-m-) high platform has steles arranged against the retaining wall. One represents a captured warrior, castrated and covered in blood. The top of the pyramid offers a spectacular view of the sunset across the rest of the site and the valley.

TEMPLO DE LOS DANZANTES. The famous 'temple of the dancers' dates from the 4th–5th century BC. Its two structures, which have been rebuilt several times, correspond to the apogee of the Zapotec civilization (300–800). A series of stone tablets, between 6½ and 10 feet (2 and 3 m) high, are decorated with fine low-reliefs representing negroid figures.

'LOS DANZANTES'
The facial features and glyphs on these reliefs are similar to those on the reliefs found at the Olmec site of La Venta, on the Gulf of Mexico. These images attest to the fact that, at the time, the Zapotecs were familiar with writing, the calendar and calculation. The 'moving' figures were for a long time thought to be drunken dancers. However, more recent interpretations suggest that they are in fact slaves expressing their suffering.

NORTH PLATFORM. The platform is reached via a staircase 123 feet (38 m) wide. At the top of the steps are the remains of two rows of columns, 6½ feet (2 m) in diameter, that once supported the roof. Another staircase leads to the Patio Hundido (sunken plaza), the setting for a stele that can now be seen in the National Museum of Anthropology.

TOMBS 104 AND 107. Behind the pyramid of the North Platform, a path leads northwest to the famous Mixtec tombs 104 and 107. Unfortunately, they are no longer open to the public. In the magnificently decorated Tomb 104, discovered in 1937, the remains of an adult male and a rich offering were discovered beneath a stone slab covered with glyphs. The 'funerary' urn represents the corn god, Pitao Cozobi. Tomb 107, excavated by Alfonso Caso five years earlier, contained one of the richest archeological treasures found in the Americas – 500 objects carved in gold, silver, jade, turquoise, quartz and alabaster. Today, most of this treasure can be seen in the Museo de las Culturas de Oaxaca ▲ *295*.

Tlacolula Valley ◆ **D** D-E5

(*East of Oaxaca, on the RF 190*)
SANTA MARIA EL TULE. (*7½ miles/12 km from Oaxaca*)
The main attraction of this village is its huge *ahuehuete* (bald
cypress, *below*), said to be 2,000 years old. It is 130 feet (40
m) high and its trunk is 42 meters (138 feet) in diameter.
SAN JERÓNIMO TLACOCHAHUAYA. (*5 miles/8 km farther
on, the road forks to San Jerónimo.*) This 17th-century
Dominican monastery is well worth a visit, especially for the
floral motifs of its murals, painted by Indian artists. The
chancel has a beautiful organ, dating from 1739, that has
recently been restored. Enjoy a stroll through the paved
streets and unwind on the *zócalo* of this charming pueblo.
DAINZÚ. (*12½ miles/20 km from Oaxaca*) This unrestored
Zapotec site (600 BC–1400) has Olmec-inspired BAS-
RELIEFS depicting ballplayers, priests and jaguars.
LAMBITYECO. (*14 miles/23 km from Oaxaca*) All that can
be seen of the PALACIO DE LOS CACIQUES that once stood
on this largely unexcavated, late Zapotec site (600–900) is a
frieze depicting its royal rulers .
TLACOLULA ◆ D D5. (*20 miles/32 km east of Oaxaca. Take
the right fork 6 miles/10 km before Mitla.*) In this beautiful
baroque monastery, the Dominicans used the figures of four
Christian martyrs to convert the local population. The village
is one of the centers for the production of mescal.

MESCAL
This strong alcohol
(43%) made from the
maguey (agave) plant
in the state of Oaxaca
is a type of eau de vie.
It is produced from
the *maguey espadin*
(sword agave), the
blue-green variety
that reaches maturity
after 8–12 years
(*above*). When the
tlachiquero has
removed its leaves,
the agave looks like a
large pineapple that
can weigh up to 220
lbs (100 kg). It is then
cut into four sections
and placed on white-
hot stones in a rock-
lined conical pit
known as a *palenque*.
The pit is covered
with *maguey* leaves,
stones and earth, and
the agaves are slow-
cooked for about 72
hours. Then they are
crushed by a huge
millstone turned by a
donkey and the pulp,
separated from the
fibers, is fermented
before being placed
in the still. After
distillation, the
mescal is aged in
wooden vats. Most of
the distilleries are
found in four villages
– Santiago Matatlán
del Mezcal (100
distilleries for 6,000
inhabitants), San
Dionisio Ocotepec,
Santa Ana del Río
and San Luis del Río.

HUAUTLA, MISTS AND MAGIC MUSHROOMS ◆ **D** D4
(*Via the RF 135 from Oaxaca, the road forks at Teotitlán.*)
Travelers still go to Huautla de Jiménez in search of the spirit of Doña Sabina, a famous shaman of the 1970s, whose cures involved the consumption of

YAGUL ◆ **D** D5. (*24 miles/39 km from Oaxaca*) The site only assumed importance after the decline of Monte Albán, c. 800. Of particular interest are the PATIO DE LA TUMBA TRIPLE, the complex of four temples surrounding the plaza, the ball court (the largest in the Oaxaca Valley) and the PALACIO DE LOS SEIS PATIOS, a real labyrinth that probably constituted the residential district of the aristocracy. The Palacio offers a magnificent view across the valley.

MITLA ◆ **D** E5. (*32 miles/51 km from Oaxaca*) Mitla, with its spectacular architecture, was the political capital of the

hallucinogenic mushrooms. Doña Sabina is no longer there but, in the wet season, certain visitors still seek out the mushrooms and also consult local healers and witches for purifications (*limpias*) and other traditional cures. Twenty minutes away, the road and villages of Santa Cruz and San Andrés are well worth the detour. As the warm air of the Gulf of Mexico meets the cooler air of the high plateaus, mists are formed that festoon the tropical trees. You can return to Veracruz via Tuxtepec and a series of Indian hamlets.

Mixtecs c. 900, but most of the buildings date from the 14th century. It became the Zapotec capital after the abandonment of Monte Albán, which explains why Zapotec chiefs and high priests were buried in the beautiful tombs decorated with mosaics of the north and west structures. The two most famous buildings on the site are the GROUP OF THE COLUMNS and the PATIO OF THE MOSAICS. The walls surrounding the courtyard of this patio are faced with 100,000 tiny mosaics assembled to form fourteen classic geometric motifs – crosses, interlaced bands, chevron friezes, fret patterns – that create an interplay of light and shade depending on the position of the sun. A large MARKET is held daily at the entrance to the site, where you can find a complete range of crafts produced in the region. Sadly, the quality of the items has deteriorated in recent years.

HIERVE EL AGUA. (*4⅓ miles/7 km from Mitla, toward Zacatepec, fork right through San Lorenzo Albarradas, where two Indian communities charge a modest entrance fee.*) Two hot springs saturated with limestone and sulfur form huge, dazzlingly white, petrified waterfalls that plunge into a green valley. You can bathe in the hot-water basins and swimming pool (72–77° F/22–25° C). The Mixtecs diverted water from these springs along a series of shallow canals (still visible today) so that the sun separated the sulfur from the water. I this way, they obtained water that could be used to irrigate their crops 985 feet (300 m) below. A footpath skirts round the waterfalls.

Zimatlán Valley ◆ **D** D5

(*South of Oaxaca, on the RF 175*)

CUILAPÁN. (*6 miles/10 km from Oaxaca*) In this Mixtec village, the Dominican friars began to build a church and monastery dedicated to Santiago Apostol (Saint James the

Apostle) (1555). The unfinished building – it doesn't have a roof, doors or windows – has an undeniably romantic charm. The FAÇADE is in Renaissance style, and the elegant CLOISTER still has traces of murals. Diego Aguilar and Joana Cortés, a Zapotec prince and princess who converted to Roman Catholicism, are buried in the monastery. A small MUSEUM reminds visitors that President Vicente Guerrero spent his last hours here before facing a firing squad in 1831. **ZAACHILA ◆ D** D5. (*10 miles/16 km from Oaxaca*) The Zapotecs transferred their capital to Zaachila at the time of the Mixtec invasion ▲ *299*. The site's main attraction is its two FUNERARY CHAMBERS. The decor in Tomb 1 depicts two fleshless human figures, two figures with glyphs (Flor 5 and 9), and another with a turtle shell and an obsidian knife.

OCOTLÁN DE MORELOS ◆ D D5. (*10½ miles/17 km further on*) This is the native village of artist Rodolfo Morales ● *96*, whose foundation occupies an old 18th-century house. It contains collages, fabrics and a number of canvases and is well worth seeing. He devoted the last years of his life to restoring several churches in the region, including the 16th-century EX-CONVENTO DE SANTO DOMINGO which is reached via an elegant walkway planted with cypresses.

ZIMATLÁN, AN ARTISANS' VALLEY
Arrazola
(*6 miles/10 km from Oaxaca*) is famous for its *alebrijes* ● *65*, small multicolored animals carved from copal wood. The local artisans often work on the threshold of their houses and invite visitors to take a closer look at their work. The village of San Bartolo Coyotepec (*6¾ miles/11 km from Oaxaca*) is the home of the famous *barro negro*, shiny black earthenware pottery (*below*). Some workshops produce extremely beautiful modern pieces. The artisans of San Martín Tilcajete (*15½ miles/25 km from Oaxaca*) make a variety of *alebrijes* in the form of fantastical animals – dragons, unicorns, winged horses. Some famous artisans, such as Paula Sanchez and Miguel Ortega, exhibit their work in the galleries of Oaxaca. Teotitlán del Valle, once a center for Zapotec oracles, is today famous for its rugs, blankets and serapes, traditionally woven using natural colors and pigments.

FRANCISCO TOLEDO, OAXACA CLOSE TO HIS HEART
Influenced by all the great Mexican artists, Francisco Toledo ● *104* is the most representative of the Oaxaca school. He has created his own distinctive pictorial language, drawing on pre-Hispanic sources and using natural colors and pigments. Through his foundation PRO-OAX, he is also an ardent defender of the cultures and traditions of his native region. He successfully gained international support to prevent a world-famous fast-food chain from opening an outlet on the *zócalo* of Oaxaca, on the grounds that this type of food had no place in a town renowned for its gastronomy.

Sierra de Juárez

Etla Valley

(*Northwest of Oaxaca, on the RF 190*)

SAN JOSÉ MOGOTE. (*10 miles/16 km from Oaxaca*) This is one of the oldest archeological sites in the central valleys. In Building 1, the stele of the captive bears the date 1200 BC.

SAN PEDRO AND SAN PABLO ETLA. (*11¾ miles/19 km from Oaxaca*) This village is famous for its chocolate, which is drunk cold, mixed with water, and its cheese. Its massive, two-story monastery still has traces of murals. In the nearby VILLAGE OF SAN AGUSTÍN, the PRO-OAX foundation was founded by Francisco Toledo to defend the cultural heritage of Oaxaca. One of his workshops, which occupies the former power station of La Soledad, produces paper using the plants and natural fibers, aromas and pigments of the region. The Day of the Dead is still celebrated in the village.

YANHUITLÁN ◆ D C4. (*93 km/58 miles from Oaxaca*) This impressive Renaissance-style church was built by the Dominicans on the site of a pyramid. Behind the Plateresque façade, the interior has some beautiful baroque altarpieces.

Sierra de Juárez ◆ D D4-5

North of Oaxaca, in the Sierra de Juárez, a profusion of villages perched at an altitude of 9,865 feet (3,000 m) provide a series of viewpoints across the central valleys. This range, where nature has remained wild and untamed, is popular with ramblers, climbers and potholers. The Indian communities, known as the 'people of the clouds', jealously guard their traditions (festivals, gastronomy, music) and protect this unique natural environment. Excursions are

organized by agencies in Oaxaca. **ITINERARY.** First stop HUAYAPÁN (*8¾ miles/14 km from Oaxaca*), whose baroque church has a beautiful altarpiece and some amazing hollow Solomonic (twisted barley-sugar) columns. The little 17th-century church of LACHATO (*30 miles/48 km further on*) has a sober baroque façade and gilt altarpieces. The paved streets and adobe houses with their tiled roofs give the village a very provincial atmosphere. GUELATAO (*3¾ miles/6 km away*) was the birthplace if Benito Juárez, ● *27*, and his death mask is in the museum. Nearby IXTLÁN has a Churrigueresque church with beautifully executed wood and stone sculptures. Finally, CALPULALPAN (*5½ miles/9 km further on*) nestles amid mountains clad in tropical forest. The ceiling of its church like the inverted hull of a ship.

Below: Puerto Escondido
Bottom: surfers on the Playa de Zicatela

To reach the beaches of the Pacific coast, you have to cross the Sierra Madre del Sur from Oaxaca. The shortest route is via the RF 175, but it has lots of twists and turns. The RF 190 is less tortuous but longer – it takes you to Salina Cruz and you have to travel back up the coast for 125 miles (200 km). However, you would be ill-advised to take the RF 135 which, although it takes you direct to Puerto Escondido, is in a poor state of repair and relatively unstable. The Oaxaca–Pacific freeway is currently under construction.

Puerto Escondido ◆ **D** D6

This little port nestling in a sheltered bay (*escondido* means 'hidden') has been a popular retirement resort for Canadians and North Americans since the 1960s, and has changed very little over the years. Although family hotels and *cabañas* have sprung up, the absence of a waterfront development policy has deterred international investors from laying waste the landscape. The resort has clear waters and breathtaking underwater landscapes, but its waves can be quite formidable and attract surfers from all over the world. As well as restaurants and bars, where you can sit and sip generous margaritas, there are plenty of stores and boutiques on the Andador Público, the main pedestrianized street. You can swim in the bays on the far side of the lighthouse – Puerto Angelito, Carrizalillo and Manzanillo (*reached on foot or by boat from the port*). The Playa de Bacocho, with its luxury hotel, is certainly the most romantic at sunset.

WARNING
Don't walk on the beach at night, and above all don't carry identity papers or jewelry. Thieves are known to prowl.

SURFING ON THE PLAYA DE ZICATELA
Surfers pit their skills against the waves of the Playa de Zicatela. Puerto Escondido is a favorite spot with tanned, well-muscled young surfers and hosts an annual world surfing championship in October.

LAGUNAS DE CHACAHUA ◆ D C6
(*Head north along the coast on the RF 200 for 53 miles/85 km to San José del Progreso, just before the Río Verde.*)
This ecological reserve consists of several lagoons, opening into the Pacific and bordered by mangroves, which can be explored by boat – but don't forget your mosquito repellent! The peace and tranquility of the site (except in the

holiday period) makes it an ideal place to relax and unwind. There are several deserted beaches and some basic accommodation, ideal for meditation.

Top: Chacahua lagoon
Above: Mazunte

Puerto Escondido to Puerto Ángel

MAZUNTE. (*41 miles/66 km east of Puerto Escondido*) You can swim in the clear, calm waters of this delightful little bay in safety, provided you don't venture beyond the small rocks, toward the Punta Mita, which is pounded by extremely strong currents. The village, which has developed in less than ten years, has a basic yet delightful hotel infrastructure – *cabaña* on the beach or perched on the hillside.

ZIPOLITE. (*Between Mazunte and Puerto Ángel*) Playa Zipolite was discovered by hippies in the 1960s and '70s. It is still very relaxed, and campers and nudists are welcome. But beware: even when it is calm, the sea is extremely dangerous

PUERTO ÁNGEL ◆ D D6. (*50 miles/80 km from Puerto Escondido*) Puerto Ángel was a quiet little cove before hippies made it fashionable in the 1970s. Today, this large town, occupied by a Mexican naval base and a naval college, has lost much of its charm. The Playa del Pantéon (next to the cemetery with its colored tombs) is the most attractive of the beaches. It is linked to the main beach by a paved pathway.

Bahías de Huatulco ◆ D E6

(*25½ miles/41 km from Puerto Ángel, east of Pachuca*) The nine bays of Huatulco, washed by beautifully clear waters, are bounded by a 4,940-acre (2,000-ha) 'eco-friendly' tourist complex financed by the government. Sadly, it is completely soulless. To make way for the international hotel chains, the fishermen and inhabitants of Santa Cruz were moved to the town of Santa María, 9 miles (15 km) to the east, and their fish restaurants replaced by air-conditioned fast-food outlets. The fish, however, are still swimming amongst the corals of its coastal waters. They can be see in the bays of Tangolunda, Santa Cruz, Chahuté and San Agustín, which can be reached by water taxi from the new dock of Huatulco or by footpaths

Occidente

1. Morelia to Meseta Tarascán (Michoacán) ▲ 311
2. Guadalajara to Tequila (Jalisco) ▲ 320
3. Tepic to San Blas (Nayarit) ▲ 326
4. Colima to Manzanilla (Colima) ▲ 330
5. Manzanilla to Puerto Vallarta (Pacific coast) ▲ 332

Landscape between Zamora and Quiroga

The region of Occidente forms a quadrilateral that covers an area of 65,640 sq. miles (170,000 sq. km) and has a population of 15 million. It consists of four states – Jalisco, the largest, with an area of 30,940 square miles (80,137 sq. km); Nayarit; Michoacán; and Colima, the smallest, with an area of 2,106 sq. miles (5,455 sq. km).

GEOGRAPHY. The region is crossed by two intersecting mountain ranges – the imposing mass of the Sierra Madre Occidental, which runs north–south and rises to more than 6,560 feet (2,000 m) in Nayarit, and the east–west range of recent volcanic mountains ● 20. Occidente lies just below the Tropic of Cancer (23°N) and therefore has a tropical climate, but its mountainous relief gives rise to a wide range of regional variations, from the heat and humidity of the coast (northern Nayarit) to the semiarid grassland of the canyons (northeastern Jalisco). Only Michoacán has tropical forest. The valleys of Zamora, Guadalajara and Tepic are extremely mild, with average temperatures of 66°F (19°C).

IDENTITY. The region's unity derives from its intermediate position between the two extremes that dominate Mexican life – the Federal District (capital Mexico City) and the North, the border region with the United States. Occidente has always striven for independence. As early as the colonial period, the kingdom of New Galicia (whose capital was Guadalajara) and the diocese of Valladolid (modern-day Morelia) were separate entities from Mexico City. In the 20th century, their peasants rebelled (1926–29) in the name of the Christ-King against the agrarian (and antireligious) revolution of Central Mexico. But, more fundamentally, Occidente is a patchwork of states that reflects the many facets of Mexican life and culture. For example, MICHOACÁN is heir to the brilliant kingdom of Purépecha (renamed Tarascán by the Spanish), which resisted Mexica (Aztec) expansion and whose identity was reinforced by the figure of its first bishop, Don Vasco de Quiroga ▲ *314*, known as 'Tata' (father) Vasco. In JALISCO, which is closer to the pioneer (or 'dollarized') front, Guadalajara asserts its Hispanic heritage. NAYARIT juxtaposes, but doesn't really integrate, the mestizo (Tepic) and Indian (Sierra del Nayar) cultures. COLIMA, wedged between Jalisco and Michoacán, demonstrates an amazing vitality for such a small state.

Morelia ◆ C E4 ◆ R

(*250 km/155 miles from Mexico City on the Mexico City–Guadalajara freeway*) Valladolid was renamed Morelia in honor of the anti-Spanish insurgent José María Morelos who was born here in 1765 ● *26*. Founded in 1541 by order of Antonio de Mendoza, Viceroy of New Spain (1530–50), it lies in a valley running north–south, at an altitude of 6,235 feet (1,900 m), and its city center was constructed to an impeccable grid layout ● *76*. For a long time Valladolid was the rival of the Indian town Pátzcuaro ▲ *314*, where Vasco de Quiroga established the seat of his bishopric. In 1571 the seat was transferred here, and for more than 200 years it became

WINGED MIRACLE
◆ C F4
(*Santuario Sierra el Campanario, via Angangueo. Leave the Mexico City–Morelia freeway at Maravatío and follow the signs to Angangueo, 30 miles/ 50 km to the south.*)
A miracle of nature occurs each year in Michoacán, as monarch butterflies complete their long migration from Canada, a distance of some 2,500 miles (4,000 km). Flying at a rate of 15–20 miles (25–35 km) per day, they come to over-winter in the forested

highlands in the east of the region. Along the road, you'll see some fairly unusual signs – 'Beware! Monarchs crossing!' – and you may even witness the sudden appearance of an orange-colored stream as it flies out of the forest and across roads and open countryside, on its way to the nearby sanctuary. There are five sanctuaries, two of which are open to the public. In the SANTUARIO SIERRA EL CAMPANARIO, in the last two weeks of February and early March (the reproductive period), it is quite common to see the firs and pines in the forest entirely covered by whole swarms.

Below: Morelia, view to the Cathedral
Bottom: frescos in the Palacio del Gobierno

FRESCOS OF THE PALACIO DEL GOBIERNO
The Palacio del Gobierno (*almost opposite the Cathedral*) was originally built as a seminary, in 18th-century baroque style. It provides the setting for three large murals by the Michoacan artist Alfredo Zalce (1908–2003), in the stairwell and along the exterior corridor of the upper story. These historic works (especially *La Reforma* and *La Revolución*) are the counterparts of Diego Rivera's great mural in the Palacio Nacional in Mexico City. They are less grandiloquent and more colorful, but perhaps it is wrong to compare such spectacular works painted thirty years apart. These frescos are merely one facet of the artistic personality of Zalce, who was a sculptor, painter and graphic designer. Some of his paintings are preserved in the Museo de Arte Contemporáneo in Morelia.

an episcopal, even clerical, city. Morelia has been the political capital of Michoacán since 1824. Lázaro Cárdenas (born in Jiquilpan, northern Michoacán), state governor and then a great revolutionary president (1934–40), increased the city's influence, especially in respect of its university. With its beautiful pink stone, Morelia is one of the most stunning colonial cities in Mexico. Its architectural heritage, very well preserved, is a marvel of balance and harmony.

PLAZA DE ARMAS AND AROUND ◆ R B2. On the east side of the Plaza de Armas, set off by delightful gardens and surrounded by beautiful residences, stands the monumental CATHEDRAL (1660–1744) whose restrained baroque style is reinforced by later neoclassical elements. Its two elegant towers and mosaic-covered dome dominate the urban landscape. The triple-naved interior is no less impressive with its gold- and silverwork and much-venerated image of Christ made from corn. The building is best seen from the arcades of Los Portales, on the opposite side of the square (*Avenida Francisco Madero*). Here, you can relax at one of the restaurants or café terraces before strolling through the nearby streets and gardens, lingering in some of the shady patios filled with flowers, fruit trees and whispering

fountains. Many of the city's beautiful residences have been transformed into inviting hotels (particularly in the streets behind the Avenida Francisco Madero).

CONVENTO DE SAN FRANCISCO ◆ R C2. Many of the city's religious buildings have also been converted, encompassing a wide range of activities and styles. Built in Plateresque style, the Convento de San Francisco, on the square of the same name, today houses the CASA DE LAS ARTESANÍAS, which doubles as a gallery and craft market.

BIBLIOTECA PÚBLICA ◆ R A2. The library is housed in the former Jesuit church, built in 17th-century baroque style (*corner of Calle Nigromante and Avenida Madero*). Its austerity can be offset by a visit to the nearby Mercado de Dulces (candy market) (*Calle V. Gomez Farias*), where the candied fruits are another of Michoacán's specialties.

CONVENTO DEL CARMEN ◆ R B1. (*Avenida Morelos Norte*) This austere, quadrilateral building, with its central paved patio, was begun in 1596 in the east part of the city. Today, a busy cultural center (Casa de la Cultura) is housed in the labyrinth of high rooms and monumental staircases.

PLAZA VILLALONGÍN ◆ R C2. On the plaza stands THE TARASCANS, a bronze statue and fountain that has become a symbol of the city. The statue, which shows three Tarascan Indian women holding aloft a large basket of fruit and vegetables, represents the generosity of the Michoacán character. In the distance, the AQUEDUCT, over a mile long, and supported by 253 arches, was built (1785–89) by a philanthropic bishop.

Two convents to the north of Morelia

CUITZEO ◆ C E4. (*18⅔ miles/30 km from Morelia*) The AUGUSTINIAN CONVENT of Cuitzeo, on the far side of the shallow, reed-filled Lake Cuitzeo, provides an excellent introduction to Michoacán architecture. The Augustins were great builders and Cuitzeo offers some fine examples of their sense of esthetics – a 16th-century Plateresque façade, inspired by Hispanic architecture but executed by the Indian architect Francisco Juan Metl, some remarkable animal sculptures (especially eagles), frescos, an open-air chapel and a garden.

YURIRIA ◆ C E3. (*22 miles/ 35 km farther north*) THE CONVENTO DE SAN PABLO YURIRIA (State of Guanajuato), founded in 1548, displays the same architectural characteristics as Cuitzeo but looks more like a medieval fortress. The cloister, with its beautiful Gothic ribs and frescos, is simply delightful, as is the parvis and the busy market town that clusters around it.

THE MUSEUMS OF MORELIA
The MUSEO DE ARTE COLONIAL (*Calle Juárez*), housed in an 18th-century residence, has a remarkable collection of images of Christ made from corn. The collections of the MUSEO DEL ESTADO (*Prieto, 176*) are presented in three sections – archeology, ethnology and history – and there is also an old pharmacy (1868). In a baroque residence there is a MUSEO REGIONAL MICHOACANO (*Allende, 305*).

Yuriria monastery

DON VASCO DE QUIROGA

Don Vasco de Quiroga (1470–1565) was a lawyer and *oidor* (judge) at the court of Mexico City – offices that enabled him to demonstrate his remarkable talents. He was also a humanist who greatly admired Thomas More, and gave concrete expression to his ideals by founding a hospice (Santa Fe) near Mexico City. The hospice took care of the poor, both physically and spiritually, and taught them manual skills. He founded a similar institution at Tzintzuntzan. In 1533, Carlos V made him the first bishop of Michoacán. He brought great energy to his new position – as a missionary, architect, promoter of traditional crafts and a staunch opponent of Indian slavery. Guided by faith and reason, he was responsible for entire areas of today's Michoacán identity.

Pátzcuaro ◆ C E4

(*35 miles/56 km from Morelia*) Pátzcuaro is the Indian counterpart of Morelia and, although only a few miles away, it is like entering a different world. Situated at an altitude of 7,020 feet (2,140 m), at the south end of Lago de Pátzcuaro in the Michoacán highlands, the town has a particularly invigorating climate. This is especially true in the rainy season when the cool dampness does wonders for the old stones, patios … and visitors. Time seems to have stood still here: Pátzcuaro is still very conscious of its prestigious past a the first Purépecha capital, and is pervaded by the memory o 'Tata' Vasco, who established the seat of his bishopric here in 1540. Its urban development is less regular than Morelia's grid layout – it radiates outward from an area of high groun in the east, occupied by an Indian temple and then by the Basilica de Nuestra Señora de la Salud. What could be more picturesque than the low, ocher-and-white houses, with thei overhanging eaves, leading up to the church on its acropolis Another difference between the two towns is the building materials – adobe (sun-dried brick) and wood in Pátzcuaro, as opposed to *cantera* (freestone) in Morelia.

BASILICA DE NUESTRA SEÑORA DE LA SALUD. Don Vasco de Quiroga dreamed of making this his cathedral, envisaging a radial layout with four converging naves. However, his overambitious project was never realized and all that remains of the edifice is the central nave, which has been badly damaged by successive earthquakes.

PLAZA VASCO DE QUIROGA. Below the Basilica, the tow attempts to observe the colonial grid layout around two plazas. In the center of the main plaza, one of the most delightful in Mexico, is a statue of the bishop after whom it i

PÁTZCUARO AND LAGO DE PÁTZCUARO ★
The nights are cool (the hotels rarely have heating) and the summers are often stormy. But this in no way detracts from the extraordinary charm of the town and its lake – on the contrary. Just remember to pack suitable clothing.

named. Formal and shady, it is surrounded by the town's main civil buildings, hotels and stores under the porticoes.

PLAZA GERTRUDIS BOCANEGRA. The plaza is bounded to the north by the former CONVENTO DE SAN AGUSTÍN, now converted into a library (don't miss the evocative mural of the history of Michoacán by Juan O'Gorman ● *96*) and to the northwest by a popular market. Indian crafts (textiles, lacquer) represent one of the attractions of Pátzcuaro, while foodstuffs, traditional crafts and various kinds of produce attract local inhabitants and visitors alike.

CASA DE LOS ONCE PATIOS. (*Southeast of the Plaza Vasco de Quiroga*) This former Dominican convent has been converted into a two-story showcase for regional crafts. Beneath vaults and magnificently sculpted arches, the patios and cells are simply overflowing with colorful and original merchandise. It is all delightfully anarchic – somewhere between archaism and casualness, rather like the town.

Tarascan Indian women at Pátzcuaro market

315

Lago de Pátzcuaro and around

Fisherman on Lago de Pátzcuaro using one of the famous butterfly nets

DAY OF THE DEAD IN THE PÁTZCUARO REGION
Balanced syncretism, generosity of spirit and the tragedy of the Conquest (the ghost of Michoacán's last king of walks on November 1) are some of the reasons that underlie the celebration of the Day of the Dead in the Pátzcuaro region. From Tzintzuntzan to Pátzcuaro, via the islands of Jarácuaro and especially Janitzio, the tolling of the church bells summons the dead to the feast and other ceremonies organized by the living. The encounter takes place on the night of November 1–2, among the tombs. Those for the children, with their floral decorations and tissue-paper cut-outs, are particularly moving. The dead (*muertitos*) of each family are guided to the family altar – where their photos stand amid mauve, green, yellow and orange objects – along a path of saffron-colored *cempaxúchil* (French marigolds ● *49*).

Lago de Pátzcuaro

As you enter Pátzcuaro, opposite the statue of Lázaro Cárdenas, the lake forms the backdrop for a magnificent view of the town. Outside the town, the Convento de San Francisco on the Cerro El Estrivo (*2½ miles/4 km to the west*) offers a unique view of the lake and its sprinkling of a dozen or so islands, in a setting of forest-clad volcanoes – El Tzirate, to the north, rises to 10,826 feet (3,300 m).

TZINTZUNTZAN ◆ **C** E4. (*On the northeast shore*) Tzintzuntzan ('Place of the Hummingbirds') was the capital of the Purépecha (Tarascán) Indians before the Conquest. At the time, the pine forests were much more in evidence, the mists more diffuse and the lake more extensive, especially along its eastern shore. Pre-Hispanic, especially ceremonial, REMAINS are strung out along the upper shore. In the center of the site, a platform is surrounded by six *yácatas*, original circular monumental structures. As well as palaces and various residential, commercial and manufacturing zones, the city also had a ball court, a zoo and public baths. Many of the beautifully crafted objects discovered in the tombs were made from metal (jewelry, votive axes, bells). This capital was an authentic Mesoamerican city, unique in a world that was even more rural than the Altiplano. This makes it most conducive to meditation, especially in the setting provided by the atrium of the CONVENTO DE SAN FRANCISCO, planted with ancient olive trees and a beautiful cross bearing the instruments of the Passion. An impressive Plateresque entrance forms part of an open-air chapel. Remarkable, too, is chapel of San Lorenzo, decorated by an Indian artist.

THE ISLANDS. JANITZIO, with its 132-foot (40-m) Monument to Morelos, is the most spectacular of the islands and the easiest to get to (from the main *embarcadero* in Pátzcuaro), so it is the most exploited and spoiled by tourism. Some of the others are no longer islands since the drop in the water level has linked them to the shore (Urandén, Carián, Jarácuaro). URANDÉN DE MORELOS and URANDÉN DE MORALES (reached by boat from Huecorio, west of the *embarcadero*) offer some unrivaled views of the lake.

Around Pátzcuaro

SANTA CLARA DEL COBRE (OR VILLA ESCALANTE)
◆ **C** DE4. (*10½ miles/17 km south of Pátzcuaro*) This dynamic and inventive craft center specializes in the manufacture of beaten copper in all its forms ● *64*. The MUSEUM (*Calle Morelos*) traces the development of this technique since it was first introduced during the colonial period. In the workshops, the craftsmen are always on the lookout for new trends and innovations, which they adapt – more or less successfully. Visitors who are not too laden with purchases may want to walk through pine forests to the LAGUNA DE ZIRAHUÉN (*6 miles/10 km to the west*), a beautifully preserved miniature version of the Lago de Pátzcuaro.

TUPATARO. (*9 miles/15 km from Pátzcuaro, on the road to Morelia, via a short detour 2½ miles/4 km to the south*) This picturesque village has an attractive *zócalo*, where the wooden columns of the porticos are in perfect harmony with the red tiles of the roofs. The church houses an architectural jewel – a magnificent 18th-century wooden vault painted with eighteen scenes from the life of the Virgin. The gilt altarpieces are also remarkable.

THE PURÉPECHA INDIANS
Like the Mexica (Aztecs), the Purépecha civilization was destroyed at its height. It covered the entire northern half of present-day Michoacán, around the region of the lakes and, in 1519, had a population of almost 800,000. Archeologists have traced two original characteristics – the widespread use of metals (copper, gold, silver) among the elite, and the circular form of monumental structures (*yácatas*). Both were widely found at Tzintzuntzan which, at the time, had a population of 25,000.

Porticos of Santa Clara del Cobre

Right: Guitar-maker's workshop in Paracho
Below right: Purépecha women preparing tortillas

EATING IN MICHOACÁN
The best eating experience involves sitting at a table covered with a single-colored tablecloth, preferably white with lace openwork or dark blue, highlighted by the reflections of the *aguas frescas* (fruit-flavored waters) in the pitchers – *aguas de alfalfa* (alfalfa), *de Jamaica* (hibiscus), *de tuna* (prickly pear), *de guayaba* (guava). The meal begins with a few *antojitos* (appetizers), ranging from the classic (cheese from Cotija) to the more obscure (*cueritos de chicharrán*, pork rind marinated with chili), followed by fish soup flavored with chili and garlic to whet the appetite. When it comes to the main dish, you are simply spoiled for choice – the region has any number of *birrias* (lamb stews) and at least two dozen different *moles* (sauces) – while some recipes are more like pieces of pre-Hispanic archeology. Desserts tend to be milk-based, although a pumpkin cooked for hours in a cooking pot becomes as smooth and sweet as honey. And what better to round off the meal than coffee from Uruapan? Eating in Michoacán is a minefield of temptations.

TIRIPITIO ◆ C E4. (*9 miles/15 km farther east*) The Augustinian monastery, founded in 1537, has a number of claims to fame. In 1540, it became the first center for advanced studies in America. It was subsequently regarded as 'the first wonder of Michoacán' with its cloister, church, hospital and open-air chapel. Today, the predominantly 17th-century complex houses a museum.

Meseta Tarascán

The Meseta Tarascán has two gateways – opposites in every respect except the mildness of their climate – Zamora (in the north) and Uruapan (in the south), whose valleys lie at an altitude of 4,920 feet (1,500 m). The term *meseta* (plateau) is misleading since this is in fact a series of volcanoes and high-altitude depressions, which reaches its highest point in the southwest with the Pico de Tancitaro at 12,470 feet (3,800 m) It has three very distinctive characteristics – its volcanoes, forests and Tarascán communities.

URUAPAN ◆ C D4. Uruapan ('Place of Flowering' in Purépecha) has been regarded as the 'paradise of Michoacán' because of its many tropical charms. Visitors ca discover the richness of the region's crafts in the MUSEO HUATÁPERA, which occupies the former Franciscan monastery (and hospital) founded by Fray Juan de San Miguel in 1533, in the early years of Christianization. Don't miss the magnificent lacquers that cover an infinite variety o wooden objects, including *bateas* (trays). The same diversity

The twin towers of the Iglesia de San Juan
emerging from the lava of the Paricutín volcano

and richness of color can be found in the market and the PARQUE NACIONAL.

⚡ THE PARICUTÍN VOLCANO ◆ C D4. In only nine years of activity, this young volcano, which first erupted in 1943, formed a cone 1,445 feet (440 m) high and engulfed the village of San Juan Parangaricutiro in lava – today, only the church's twin towers are visible. This surreal landscape can be reached on foot or horseback from Angahuán (22 miles/35 km northwest of Uruapan), while the more intrepid visitors can continue to the crater of the volcano. Since its first eruption, the inhabitants have resettled in Pueblo Nuevo San Juan, dominated by an impressive new church which their religious devotion enabled them to build in only a few years (8 miles/13 km west of Uruapan).

BETWEEN URUAPAN AND ZAMORA. The road passes through mixed forest (conifers and broad-leaved trees) which, although increasingly sparse, is still at the heart of local traditions. There are some interesting wooden structures – houses (*trojes*), carved doors and columns – in the most modest villages (Cherán, Angahuán, Charapán), which have given rise to a whole range of crafts – *bateas*, cooking utensils and musical instruments – and some dynamic communities, such as Ocumicho (22 miles/35 km south of Zamora). A few decades ago, the women began to make burlesque ceramic caricatures which proved extremely successful worldwide.

ZAMORA ◆ C D3-4. This industrious town exports the fruit grown in its rich, black soil to the United States, while its *aguas frescas* (fruit-flavored waters ● 67) and *chongos zamoranos* (very sweet milk desserts) are famous throughout Mexico. It is also the outlet for the region's ceramic production (Patámban, *to the south*). All these products are previewed in its COVERED MARKET. The SANTUARIO DE NUESTRA SEÑORA DE GUADALUPE, near the town center, is more than a curiosity. In the early 20th century, an enterprising bishop began to build a huge cathedral, but work was interrupted by the Revolution and the building was still without a roof by the end of the century. Circa 1990, another equally dynamic bishop restarted work on the cathedral, which is today nearing completion. In terms of its size, it is the sixteenth largest Roman Catholic building in the world – in a town with less than 300,000 inhabitants.

PARICUTÍN ★
It's only a thirty-minute walk from Uruapan national park to the buried village of San Juan, but it takes about 6 hours to walk to the top of the volcano and back. Ride on a horse, if you prefer.

LAGO DE CHAPALA ◆ C C3
(*23½ miles/38 km south of Guadalajara*)
This once delightful lake is unfortunately a classic example of the detrimental effects that a large metropolis such as Guadalajara can have on an idyllic but fragile environment. Each year, the water level recedes and pollution increases. These effects are less noticeable to the west of the town of Chapala, in the direction of Ajijic, where visitors can catch a glimpse of the lake as it used to be.

THE 'CHARRO'
The *charro*, like the mariachi, is one of Guadalajara's traditional figures. They wear the same embroidered costumes and wide-brimmed sombreros (*below*), and are in their element at the famous *charreadas* ● *58* held on Sunday afternoons (*Lienzo Charro de Jalisco, Avda. Dr. R. Michel, 577*).

A REGION OF ARTISTS
Two of Mexico's greatest 20th-century writers hail from the region of Guadalajara – Agustín Yáñez (who was governor of Jalisco) and Juan Rulfo. Two of the most significant painters from the first half of the 20th century – José Clemente Orozco ● *101* and Dr Atl ● *94* – are Guadalajarans. Finally, the great architect Luis Barragán was also born in the region ● *90*. Guadalajara has examples of his early works – the futuristic Casa Cristo (1929) (*Calle Pedro Moreno, 1671*), a sort of Moorish fantasy – and from his later years – the Capilla del Calvario (1958) (*Calle del Sol, reached via the Av. de los Arcos*).

Guadalajara ◆ C C3

In 1530, the Spanish found the situation to the north of the Lerma–Chalapa–Río Grande de Santiago river system much less satisfactory than to the south. A fringe of stable but relatively undeveloped kingdoms incorporated most of the population from Tonala to Nayarit. Beyond that, a formidable nomadic people known as the Chichimecs were feared even by the Mexica (Aztecs). It was this territory that Nuño Beltrán de Guzmán, the would-be rival of Hernán Cortés, conquered in less than two years. He set out on what proved to be a fruitless search for the legendary kingdom of the Amazons, pushing as far as Culiacán. He established the kingdom of New Galicia on the way, which foreshadowed the region of Occidente, and also founded Guadalajara, which he named for his hometown in Spain. However, faced with the intransigence of the population, and lacking the political skills of Cortés, he conducted a bloody campaign. Guadalajara was established on its definitive site in 1541, in the broad Atemajac valley at an altitude of 5,050 feet (1,540 m), surrounded by volcanoes rising to 6,560 feet (2,000 m). It benefited from the workforce of nearby Tonala and a mild, springlike climate. The capital of New Galicia, it was endowed with prestigious buildings but, as well as suffering a series of earthquakes, it was continually exposed to the rivalry of Zacatecas and the proximity of Mexico City. However, by c. 1800, it had a population of 24,000 and had achieved the status of a city that was unequaled north of Mexico City. It was the main redistribution center for a large area (from the Pacific to Aguascalientes) and was opening up to a textile industry that would develop throughout the 19th century. In 1824, it became the capital of the powerful state of Jalisco, which then included Nayarit. Following a population explosion in the second half of the 20th century, the *tapatio* megalopolis today has 3.6 million inhabitants and presides over the entire northwest sector of Mexico. The layout of the city center is less harmonious than those of other colonial towns and cities and it doesn't have a *zócalo* around which the principal constituent powers are assembled.

THE CATHEDRAL DISTRICT ◆ T AB2. The Plaza de Armas, the city's oldest square, provides an ideal setting for the PALACIO DEL GOBIERNO (whose main staircase is dominated by a huge mural by José Clemente Orozco ● *101*). The square is neither too big nor surfaced with concrete, and has a beautiful iron bandstand (made in the Jura mountains in the late 19th century).

THE CATHEDRAL ◆ T AB2. The Cathedral, which was consecrated in 1618, is one of the oldest in Mexico. The first thing that strikes you is its massive size. It has a composite appearance, with the Renaissance harmony of the façade

broken, to the south, by the neoclassical CAPILLA DEL SAGRARIO and by the two 'sugar loafs' atop the two towers, which replaced the domes damaged by the 1818 earthquake. Inside, another unexpected feature are the pointed Gothic arches of the three naves, which can be explained by the fact that Guadalajara was on the outer limits of the Spanish empire during the decline of the 16th century.

MUSEO REGIONAL ◆ T B1. (*Opposite the Rotunda de los Hombres Ilustres*) The museum is housed in a former Jesuit seminary whose austere exterior belies its beautiful patios and rich collections of historical pieces and religious art.

TEATRO DEGOLLADO AND AROUND ◆ T B1-2. The theater occupies the site of one of the city's oldest plazas, where *tianguis* (Indian markets) were held in the 17th century. Although many of Guadalajara's religious buildings were badly damaged following the introduction of the Reform laws (1857), the CONVENTO (monastery) DE SAN AGUSTÍN and its female counterpart, the CONVENTO (nunnery) DE SANTA MARÍA DE GRACIA (16th–17th century) are two of the best preserved.

TWO BAROQUE CHURCHES ◆ T A1-B3. One of Guadalajara's most beautiful churches is the IGLESIA DE SANTA MÓNICA (*corner of Calles San Felipe and Santa Mónica*). Its elaborate 18th-century baroque façade is decorated with almost Romanesque sculptures (the effect of provincialism on art), as is its magnificent *San Cristóbal*. Equally delightful are the remains of the huge CONVENTO DE SAN FRANCISCO (with its church and Capilla de Aránzazu), dating from the late 17th and early 18th century, with their beautiful Solomonic (twisted barley-sugar) columns ● *82*.

Bandstand on the Plaza de Armas

LOS 'TAPATIOS'
This term has been used to refer to the inhabitants of Guadalajara since the 17th century. Derived from the Nahuatl word *tlapatiotl* (meaning 'cocoa bean'), it is a reference to the locals' business skills.

Religious devotion in the Cathedral

321

Below: Instituto Cabañas
Bottom: mariachis in Tlaquepaque
Right: Tonala earthenware and market in Guadalajara

MARIACHIS

The term mariachi (which refers to both the music and the musicians) is in fact derived from Mexican Spanish. The music originated on the borders of Nayarit and Jalisco in the 19th century, and was influenced by the musicians from central Europe who accompanied Maximilian I – some of the polkas from Nayarit are truly remarkable. But things have changed and, in the flashy Mexican movies made in the 1950s ● *60*, the harp was replaced by the trumpet. The music is still just as popular, however, and no family celebration would be complete without the cheeky humor and joyful resonance of the couplets sung by the mariachi musicians and echoed by the assembled company *'alegrados por sus sones'* ('cheered up by its sounds'). José Alfredo Jiménez ● *56* is ranked as one of the best Mexican composers.

INSTITUTO CULTURAL CABAÑAS ◆ T C1. This former early 19th-century orphanage is today the city's most symbolic monument, thanks to the generosity of Bishop Cabañas and the genius of Spanish architect Manuel Tolsá. The beautifully proportioned and impressive neoclassical structure is built around twenty-three patios. In 1936–9, the muralist José Clemente Orozco ● *101* became involved, and decorated its disused chapel with disturbing frescos. Painted in grisaille, which makes these tragic scenes of urban life even more somber, the walls are in stark contrast to the brilliant and liberating colors of the dome, which offers an escape for the huge, hovering figure of flame known as the 'Man of Fire'.

PLAZA TAPATÍA ◆ T C1. The Instituto Cabañas stands at the eastern end of the vast Plaza Tapatía, which stretches a third of a mile (500 m) from the Teatro Degollado. Its construction, in the euphoria of the 1980s, destroyed much of 19th-century Guadalajara. What little remains – houses and patios transformed into restaurants – can be discovered as you stroll around this pedestrianized area. Almost without knowing it, you will find yourself at the Mercado Libertad (or San Juan de Dios), immediately south of the institute.

MARKET DISTRICT ◆ T C2. According to the *tapatios*, who have a tendency to exaggerate, this is the largest market district in Mexico. After exploring this vast array of products (especially leather), it is impossible to enjoy a glass of tequila at one of the cafés on the Plaza de los Mariachis without being approached by the mariachi musicians, who are, in the words of the song, *en [su] tierra* ('on home ground').

Around Guadalajara

Urban development has meant that these former artisans' villages have become suburbs of Guadalajara.

TLAQUEPAQUE ◆ C C3. For a long time Tlaquepaque was the favorite resort of wealthy Guadalajarans. These rich *tapatios* built deliciously cool residences whose magnificent porches opened onto patios where water gurgled between flowers and fruit trees. All this has been preserved and today serves as a setting in which to display and sell regional crafts, especially along the pedestrianized Avenida Independencia. As well as blown glass, visitors will find sheets of beaten metal (*repujado* in pewter, aluminum, bronze), and exotic birds and various types of monsters made from papier-mâché. Ceramics are also very much in evidence, and the MUSEO REGIONAL DE LA CERÁMICA (*Av. Independencia*) provides a good introduction.

TONALA ◆ C C3. Tonala is the true home of ceramics. As early as the 17th century, Spanish officials were sending *loza* (earthenware) back home, and colonial earthenware jars made in Tonala can still be found in some Mediterranean palaces. The most traditional are *barro bruñido* or polished earthenware, and *petatillo* (the most sought after) whose fine striations imitate *petate* (rush matting).

Tequila ◆ C B3

(*35 miles/56 km west of Guadalajara, on the road to Nayarit*)
The town of Tequila, named after the spirit made from the blue maguey (*Agave tequilana*), lies at the foot of the volcano of the same name. *El tequila* (the spirit) is a hybrid, since it is produced from an American plant using a Spanish still. Both can be found before you get to Tequila, at Amatitán, which lies at an altitude of 3,610 feet (1,100 m), in a volcanic valley tinged blue by agave plants. Here the HACIENDA SAN JOSÉ DEL REFUGIO – with its 19th-century distillery – is open to the public.

CHOOSING CERAMICS
It's best to visit Tonala on a Thursday or Friday, when the ceramics are displayed in the streets. Don't hesitate to go into the back of stores, but avoid those that try to attract customers with photos of visiting celebrities. Although the goods can look spectacular, the most expensive *petatillo* is not always the most authentic.

THE VIRGIN OF ZAPOPAN
In the 17th century, a small statue of the Virgin performed miracles in this Indian district in the north of the town. Creoles and Indians both laid claim to its virtues until an agreement was reached. And so the statue spends the summer in various churches in the capital and returns to its Franciscan home of Zapopan on October 12. These comings and goings attract thousands of spectators along streets carpeted with flowers, amid dancing and serenades.

323

▲ Tequila

First stage –
cutting the agave

Mexico is so closely associated with the maguey (agave) – of which it has some 200 species – that the plant appears at every stage of the country's history, and even in the black-and-white movies of the great era of Mexican cinema ● *60*. In the north, the inhabitants have always drunk its juice while, in the south, they still extract and use its fibers. In the west, the Spanish *conquistadores* had the idea of distilling it. In this region of *charros* and mariachis, tequila, which has become the symbolic drink of any self-respecting Mexican male, has in fact contributed to the success of Mexican culture throughout the world.

LAND OF THE AGAVE
The blue maguey (*Agave tequilana*) grows at an altitude of 6,560 feet (2,000 m). It is found throughout Jalisco, where the Spanish made their *haciendas* pay by planting it in the arid soil of the hillsides. Since distillation requires a great deal of water, the first distilleries were built below the village of Tequila, where there is a plentiful supply. Tequila brands bear the names of the region's former great families – Cuervo, Herradura, Orendain, Rojas and Sauza.

Left: agave hearts (*piñas*) stripped of their leaves

TEQUILA REPOSADO

THE AGAVE PLANT

The blue maguey is so called because of the slightly blue tinge to its thick, spiky leaves. It takes two years to prepare the ground for planting and the plants have to be tended for another seven before the hearts (*piñas*) can be harvested. It is estimated that there are currently 150 million plants with a *denominación de origen* (guarantee of quality) – tequila is protected by the free-trade agreements with Canada and the United States.

HOW TO DRINK TEQUILA

Tequila should be served in a small glass known as a *caballito*. Before taking a mouthful, you lick the salt sprinkled into the

SANGRITA AND MARGARITA

Sangrita, so called because of its blood-red color, is a very spicy tomato juice made with *piquín chili* ● *70*. It is served in a *caballito* alongside another of tequila. You drink a mouthful of one followed by a mouthful of the other – that's a *tequila*

hollow of the left hand, between the thumb and index finger, and suck half a lime. *Tequila rapido*, mixed with lime and soda, is drunk in one go after raising the

sangrita. A margarita is a cocktail made with white tequila and lime. It is served in a cocktail glass whose edges have been sprinkled with salt, accompanied by a wedge of lime, and so is a more elegant way of observing tradition. Mexicans regard it as a ladies' drink.

glass (covered by the palm of the hand) and tapping the base on the counter. *Tequila reposado* and *añejado* are drunk slowly and respectfully.

OTHER PRODUCTS FROM THE AGAVE

In the Oaxaca region, another species of agave is used to produce the colorless alcoholic spirit known as mescal ▲ *303*. Before the Conquest, the Indians drank *pulque* (fermented agave juice) which is still sold on the markets of the central plateau today. After removing the heart of the plant, the sap is extracted by draining it into a calabash (bottle gourd). The viscous liquid is renowned for its nutritive and medicinal qualities, and is good for stomach ulcers. Sold as aloe, the sap is also a famous cosmetic.

FROM AGAVE TO TEQUILA

Once stripped of their leaves, the agave hearts (*piñas*) are trimmed, cut into sections and cooked in a rock-lined conical pit that is known as a *palenque*. Decoction and cooling take four days, after which the plants are shredded and milled. The pulp is mixed with water in fermentation vats. After three days, the liquid is transferred to the still.

TYPES OF TEQUILA

The most widely found type of tequila is white and contains methanol. *Tequila reposado* has been left to settle for three months in an oak barrel, while *tequila añejado* has been aged for 18 months and acquires its amber color from the wood.

Below: Playa de los Cocos, San Blas
Center: transporting drinks to Tepic

A LOCAL SPECIALTY
Zarandeado, a fish served in many of the region's restaurants, is a local specialty.

Terracotta figurine from Nayarit

Nayarit: Tepic to San Blas

When Nuño Beltrán de Guzman ▲ *320* reached here, he forced its people into slavery, and the Indians who escaped – the Coras and Huichols ▲ *328* – sought refuge in the Sierra del Nayar and the surrounding area. Despite its 217 miles (350 km) of Pacific coastline, Nayarit was not a maritime region until San Blas was founded in 1768. Before that, the inhabitants merely watched the Manila galleon sailing by in the distance, or staved off intermittent attacks by English or Dutch pirates. In the early

19th century, the fortunes of San Blas seemed guaranteed, with the port extending its activities (in foreign hands) from Peru to the Californias. This is why, after the 1824 Constitution of the United Mexican States, Guadalajara refused to be separated from this maritime access that ensured its prosperity. In the end, it was a combination of circumstances – the Indian rebellion, led by the *caudillo* Manuel Lozada (1853–66), the influence of the Tepican bourgeoisie in Mexico City and the fall of Maximilian I – that finally separated Nayarit from Jalisco in 1867.

TEPIC ◆ C A2. Tepic, situated between the mountains and the ocean, has a very provincial charm. It occupies a warm, tropical setting, at an altitude of 3,250 feet (990 m), in the foothills of the sierra which rises to over 6,560 feet (2,000 m). It has an impressive sugar refinery, which envelops the town in ashes and the smell of molasses during the *zafra* season (sugar-cane harvest). It has some lovely gardens (Amado Nervo) and parks (La Alameda and La Loma) and a fascinating MUSEO REGIONAL DE ANTROPOLOGÍA E HISTORIA (*corner of Avs. Mexico and José María Morelos*). The Convento Franciscano de la Cruz de Zacate houses a miraculous cross made of grass (Cruz de Zacate), which appeared in 1619 and is one of the sacred objects that symbolizes the region's identity (*Av. Ejército Nacional in the southern part of the town*).

SAN BLAS ◆ C A2. (*43 miles/70 km northwest of Tepic*) Today San Blas is a simple fishing port and small coastal resort; there is little evidence of its former activity. It has some romantic ruins – the IGLESIA DE LE VIRGEN DEL ROSARIO and the former Contaduría (counting house), whose position on the CERRO DE LA CONTADURÍA affords good views. As well as the semi-deserted beaches (Los Cocos, Bahía de Matanchén, Las Islitas), deep-sea fishing and whale-watching (December–March), the mangroves are one of the town's main attractions. From the *embarcaderos* of El Conchal (San Blas) and La Aguada (Matanchén), boats take visitors to the PARQUE NATURAL LA TOBARA – 5 miles (8 km) further up the river – where the tangled roots and branches of the mangroves provide refuge for all kinds of tropical birds, iguanas and crocodiles.

MEXCALTITÁN DE URIBE ◆ C A1. (*68 miles/110 km north of Tepic, via Santiago Ixcuintla*) The 'Venice of Nayarit' lies on a circular island in the middle of a lagoon. Passenger ferries leave from the *embarcadero* of La Batanga, near Santiago Ixcuintla. The layout of Mexcaltitán, and the fact that its streets are transformed into canals at high water, have led some ethnologists to believe that the Aztecs stopped here during their long march to Tenochtitlán, and that Mexcaltitán may be an early example of the latter.

A STRONG HUICHOL PRESENCE
In Tepic and San Blas, there is no shortage of regional crafts for sale. Some of the most striking items are made by the Huichol Indians using *chaquiras*, colored glass beads that are embroidered or attached to various garments and accessories ▲ 328.

LOS TORILES ◆ C B2 (*1¾ miles/3 km east of Ixtlán del Río, on the RF 15 Guadalajara–Tepic*) Los Toriles, Nayarit's main archeological site (4th century BC–AD 7th century), is situated 50 miles (80 km) south of Tepic. A total of 7½ acres (3 ha) have already been excavated, revealing half a dozen platforms and an original circular temple. A number of extremely interesting objects have been discovered in the *tumbas de tiro* (tombs with funerary chambers) characteristic of Occidente's pre-Hispanic culture. (*Left*, terracotta figurine)

▲ The Huichol Indians

The Huichols occupy a place apart in the Mexican ethnic landscape: they have fascinated generations of ethnologists, starting with Norwegian explorer Carl Lumholtz, who 'discovered' the Huichol culture over 100 years ago. With their neighbors, the Coras of the Sierra del Nayar, the Tepehuas and the Mexicaneros, the Huichols form a cultural group whose religions are mutually comprehensible, especially via the *mitote*, one of the most elaborate fertility rituals – based on battles between the stars – in Mexican Indian culture. Their supposed primitivism has meant that the Huichols, like the Lacandóns of Chiapas ▲ *270*, have for a long time been regarded as 'living fossils' who have made it possible to study ancient Mexican societies via the present. As the only Mexican Indians to wear feathers, they conform to the Western stereotype of the American Indian.

Below: *Tatéi Nécha*, the festival of the drum

THE GREAT PEYOTE PILGRIMAGE
The Huichols are famous for the ritual and esthetic extensions of their 'visions', experienced during the great annual pilgrimage to Wirikuta, the sacred peyote grounds in the state of San Luis Potosí, more than 186 miles (300 km) from their territory. The pilgrims are placed under the leadership of a *mara'akame*, a shaman and officiant who, through trancelike experiences and visions, makes contact with the ancestral figure Tatewari, god of fire and master of the peyote (*peyotl* in Nahuatl), a cactus containing the alkaloid mescaline ▲ *388*. This species – endemic to the desert of San Luis Potosí, whose use is strictly limited by the authorities to the Huichols – induces complex optical hallucinations. Today, the ritual pilgrimage to Wirikuta is made by road but remains central to the ritual structure that ensures the cohesion of Indian society.

CARL LUMHOLTZ

In his classic work *Unknown Mexico* (1902), Norwegian explorer Carl Lumholtz (1859–1922) gave the first description of the material culture, beliefs and symbolism of the people of northwest Mexico, in particular the Tarahumaras and Huichols. His account of these people, who were still regarded as 'barbarians', inspired anthropological research throughout the Sierra Madre Occidental that is still going on today.

THE HUICHOL WAY OF LIFE

Since the pre-Hispanic period, the Huichols have occupied one of the most mountainous regions in the Sierra Madre Occidental, crossed by deep, almost inaccessible canyons. Today there are over 10,000 Huichols, some of whom have moved to the large towns and cities where they make and sell traditional crafts. The Huichols live in adobe houses with thatched roofs, in very dispersed communities. They still practice subsistence farming and raise cattle.

HUICHOL ART

Traditional Huichol art is extremely ornate, whether in the form of dazzlingly patterned colored wools or votive dishes decorated with beads (*jícaras*) ● *64*. The elaborate designs of these artistic compositions reproduce the central themes of Huichol mythology, including solar motifs and zoomorphic images in which the deer is the ultimate sacred animal. They reflect a very vivid vision of the Amerindian world, which is echoed in its shamanistic rituals and chants.

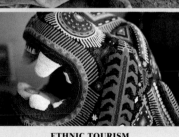

ETHNIC TOURISM

The extensive commercialization of Huichol objects has created a dichotomy between articles with a domestic function and those intended for ritual purposes or as a form of exchange. A real commercial art has developed, in complete harmony (which explains its success) with the principles of Indian esthetics. The increasing number of 'mystic' tourists, who go in search of esoteric knowledge and the meaning of ritual practices, has encouraged the Huichols to identify with the image of primitivism imposed by the Western world, and to negotiate the sale of their artistic skills with art galleries in the United States and Europe.

The Colima Volcano sent
out warning tremors in 199[

UNIVERSITY OF COLIMA

The university is a major power within the State of Colima, and has found its vocation as an urban research center on the shores of the Pacific. As well as specializing in the very latest data processing technology, it also controls most of the state's cultural activities. Many of the museums and art galleries in the town of Colima are owned by the university.

'IZCUINTLI'

The ancient Tomb Culture of Colima is characterized by the *tumbas de tiro* (tombs with funerary chambers) which contained a wealth of ceramics, including the delightful *izcuintli* (*below*). These little ceramic dogs, in all kinds of different poses, were thought to represent the dogs that led the dead into the underworld. Replicas can be seen in store windows throughout the town.

Colima ◆ C B4

The sleepy appearance of this tropical town nestling at the foot of its volcano belies the strength and violence of the natural forces at work in Colima: the hurricanes from the Pacific, the active volcano and, above all, the brutality of the earthquakes, which have not spared a single colonial building. The present cathedral, built between 1875 and 1894, was practically destroyed by the tremors of 1900, 1932 and 1941. Architecturally, the best the town has to offer is a rather severe neoclassical style. Its attractions lie in the vitality, generosity and variety of the natural environment. From the ocean to the volcano, an entire range of ecosystems are represented in this pocket-handkerchief state.

HISTORY OF THE STATE OF COLIMA.

The ancient cultures of Colima belong to the politically fragmented cultures of Occidente, at their height between 300 BC and AD 600. After conquering the region in 1523, Cortés founded the Spanish town of Colima in the hope of making this distant territory a bridgehead for his conques[of Asia… The project came to nothing and Colima remained distant and inaccessible, which preserved the region's identity and strengthened the influence of the ruling elite, with their cocoa and sugar-cane plantations, and later coffee and *vino de coco* (palm wine). The region became more accessible in the second half of the 19th century, via the coastal town of Manzanillo, which took advantage of the decline of San Blas ▲ *326* and Mazatlán. German steamships berthed here regularly and there is still a strong German presence today. In 1900, the railroad reached Colima, while in the 1980s the process was completed due to the construction of the expressway between Colima and Guadalajara, a Mexican president who was a *colimense*, and the influence of the university.

CASA DE LA CULTURA. (*Calle Ejército Nacional*) Colima's most important museum is the MUSEO DE LAS CULTURAS DEL OCCIDENTE. Devoted to archeology (there's a large Tomb Culture display), it is part of the Casa de la Cultura, a very modern space within an old building.

Around Colima

THE SITE OF EL CHANAL. (*2½ miles/4 km from Colima*) Before the Conquest, El Chanal covered an area of 495 acres (200 ha) and was the stronghold of a military power. Remains include two pyramids, various platforms and altars.

MUSEO ALEJANDRO RANGEL. (*5 miles/8 km north of Colima*) The museum, which occupies the former *hacienda* of a sugar-cane plantation (HACIENDA DE NOGUERAS), contains a collection (45 pieces) of ceramic dogs, which are owned by the university.

COMALA ◆ C B4. (*About 7½ miles/12 km north of Colima*) This former Indian village, today overrun by intellectuals and tourists, could be the Comala in Juan Rulfo's compelling novel *Pedro Páramo*. However, opinions are divided ... A relaxed atmosphere pervades its *zócalo* and porticos, opposite the delightful church. If you don't look up, you can almost forget you are already on the slopes of the looming Colima Volcano.

Manzanillo ◆ C B5

(*68 miles/110 km from Colima, via an expressway bordered by palm groves*) The expressway runs along the shores of the Laguna de Cuyutlán and its salt marshes. CUYUTLÁN has a salt museum – the Museo Comunitario de la Sal – which occupies a former salt silo. The lagoon also attracts some of the region's bird life. Manzanillo is a busy commercial port and tourist resort that spreads along the beaches of Manzanillo and Santiago bays. If you're looking for peace and quiet, head for the edge of the port area. South of Cuyutlán, the half-dozen little resorts, from Torugaria to El Chupadero, are ecological centers and turtle sanctuaries.

🏔 AROUND COLIMA
The dormant, snow-capped Nevado de Colima – 13,910 feet (4,240 m) – and the active Colima Volcano – 12,530 feet (3,820 m) – are situated in the PARQUE NACIONAL VOLCÁN DE COLIMA (*23½ miles/38 km north of Colima on highway no. 1*). But don't set out into the park's 54,363 acres (22,000 ha) of pines and oak trees without checking that it is safe to do so at that time. Alternatively, the beautiful lakeside setting of LAGUNA DE MARÍA (*13½ miles/22km north of Colima on highway no. 16*) – is ideal for hiking and camping enthusiasts, while the village of SUCHITLÁN (*6 miles/10 km northeast of Colima*) has some well-preserved traditions.

Manzanillo

Puerto Vallarta

La Costalegre

DAY TRIP TO YELAPA ◆ A C3
At the southern end of the Bahía de Banderas is the delightful, well-preserved fishing village of Yelapa with its palm roofs (*palapas*) – although these are beginning to be replaced by tiles. It can only be reached by boat but makes a pleasant day trip, with the options of swimming, horseback riding and excursions into the nearby jungle.

BARRA DE NAVIDAD ◆ C A4. (*60 km/37 miles from Manzanillo*) It was from this little port that the expedition led by Miguel Lopez de Legaspi and Fray Andres de Urdaneta set out to conquer the Philippines in 1564.

LA COSTALEGRE ◆ C A4-5. Further north, the strip of land between the Bahía de Navidad and Bahía de Chamela (*88 miles/142 km south of Puerto Vallarta*) offers some captivating glimpses of the biosphere, with its sea birds, crustaceans, and humpbacked and gray whales, which come to calve in its warm waters between November and March. The 43 miles (70 km) of coastline currently being developed for tourism do not yet have the frenetic atmosphere of the Puerto Vallarta region and visitors can still enjoy the beautiful landscapes and the amazing sunsets for which the Pacific coast is famous – especially in the BAHÍA DE CHAMELA with its scattering of islands whose white and red cliffs provide refuge for sea birds. On the mainland, swathes of mangroves harbor their characteristic fauna – pelicans, herons and crocodiles. The southern part of this stretch of coast, between the BAHÍA DE TENACATITA AND BAHÍA DE NAVIDAD, is the most welcoming and the most accessible (via the Barra de Navidad). Tenacatita, nestling in its bay, has only two hotels while CUASTECOMATES, to the south, has just one. Visitors can linger under the palm roof of one of the many traditional restaurants and enjoy grilled fish.

TURTLES
In the place names of La Costalegre, the word *carey* ('turtle') is very much in evidence – Bahía de Careyitos, Playa Careyes and so on. It is a reference to the marine turtles that frequent the many sanctuaries along this stretch of coast and, between June and September, come to lay their eggs on the beaches.

Puerto Vallarta ◆ C A3

Since 1964, when John Huston chose it as the setting for his legendary movie *The Night of the Iguana*, starring Richard Burton and Ava Gardner, this little fishing village has become a tourist town with a population of 30,000 – it is particularly popular with Canadians in winter. The development of the 15½-mile (25-km) Bahía de Banderas included a new port at its northern end – Nuevo Puerto Vallarta – with a marina for 270 boats, opposite the Islas Marías (a federal ecological reserve), yet the town center has preserved its friendly atmosphere. The town itself is divided in two: the luxury hotels and yachting marinas to the north, and, to the south, the beaches and natural sites.

The colonial cities of northern Mexico

▲ The colonial cities of northern Mexico

THE LAST DAYS OF EMPEROR MAXIMILIAN
The Cerro de las Campanas, now a national park adjoining the university campus, was the scene of the last battle between the imperial forces and the republican army. It was here that Habsburg emperor Maximilian I ● 27 and his generals Miguel Miramón and Tomás Mejía made their last stand, before surrendering to the liberal troops of President Benito Juárez. This marked the end of the so-called 'French intervention'. The Empress Sophie had a small chapel built on the spot where the three men were executed by firing squad on June 19, 1867.

After consolidating the conquest of Mexico–Tenochtitlán, the Spanish found themselves in control of a truly vast area. Their thirst for riches and the news of the discoveries made by Alvar Nuñez Cabeza de Vaca, who had reached Sinaloa via Florida after an epic journey (1527–36), inspired more expeditions to explore the unknown north.

RICH MINERAL RESOURCES. The discovery of rich silver deposits at Zacatecas, Guanajuato and San Luis Potosí provided a powerful incentive to explore the northern regions – a systematic progression that entailed the foundation of garrisons (*presidios*) to secure routes and guarantee supplies to the mining communities ▲ 178. The urban landscape of northern Mexico was therefore built around two types of town, one based on the exploitation of mineral deposits and the other on the fertility of the land and a plentiful supply of manpower around the staging posts.

FERTILE LANDS. With the establishment of the *haciendas* ● 84, models of agricultural production that had long been forgotten in Europe were improved and updated. Impressive towns grew up around these family mansions, whose beauty rivaled that of the mining centers. Thus Querétaro, San Juan del Río, San Miguel el Grande, Irapuato, Celaya, Salamanca, León, Aguascalientes and San Luis Potosí, in the agricultural region of the Bajío, became increasingly important, either through mineral resources or the fertility of the land.

Querétaro ◆ C F3 ◆ S

Jardín Zenea and the Convento de San Francisco, Querétaro

(*124 miles/200 km north of Mexico City*) During the colonial period, Querétaro – situated on the route linking Mexico City to the mining centers of Guanajuato, San Luis Potosí and Zacatecas – was the third largest city in Mexico. Its name, which means 'ball court' in Purépecha, is a reminder of its pre-Hispanic origins and its proximity to an ancient Toltec site. Santiago de Querétaro was founded in 1532 by the Otomi Indian chief Conín, following his surrender and baptism as Don Hernando de Tapia. During the 17th and 18th centuries, the town's development was gradual and harmonious, and it soon became renowned for the importance of its *haciendas*, its commerce and its industry. In the 19th century, it was the scene of some decisive historic events – the beginning of the armed struggle for independence (1810), the collapse of the empire of Maximilian I (1867) and the promulgation of the present Mexican constitution (1917) ● *26*. Due to the proximity of the federal capital, Querétaro experienced an unprecedented expansion, as evidenced by its major industrial corridors, its development in the fields of commerce and education, and its residential areas, serviced by an excellent network of expressways. Today, Querétaro has all the charm of a modern city that has successfully preserved its rich historical heritage as an eloquent reminder of its past splendor.

PLAZA DE INDEPENDENCIA ◆ S BC1-2. What better place to begin a visit to the city's historical center than this delightful plaza, refreshed by a beautiful fountain fed by the waters of the aqueduct and dominated by a statue of the aqueduct's architect, Don Antonio de Urrutia y Arana, Marqués de la Villa del Villar del Águila? At its north end stands the CASA DE LA CORREGIDORA DE QUERÉTARO (now the Palacio del Gobierno), from where the *corregidora* (wife of the chief magistrate), Doña Josefa Ortiz de Domínguez, warned Miguel Hidalgo, leader of the independence movement ▲ *356,* that their conspiracy had been discovered. Also bordering the plaza is the CASA DE ECALA, a mansion that belonged to the *regidor* (alderman) Tomás López de Ecala. Its impressive and finely sculpted 18th-century freestone façade is highlighted by the most beautiful wrought-ironwork in Querétaro, as well as a rather anachronistic detail – the two-headed Habsburg eagle.

SUNDAY IN THE PARK
On Sundays, between 7 and 9 o'clock in the evening, the inhabitants of Querétaro gather in the Jardín Zenea to listen to the local band, sometimes accompanied by dancers.

335

Above: San Agustín
Above right: a square in Querétaro

THE AQUEDUCT
This impressive monument is a compelling part of Querétaro's urban landscape. Its purpose was to provide the town and especially the Franciscan Convento de la Cruz, on the heights of Sangremal, with water, but its construction presented something of a challenge. It was made possible by the patronage of Don Antonio de Urrutia y Arana, Marqués de la Villa del Villar del Águila, who also directed the entire project (1726–38), which involved erecting 74 arches that reached a maximum height of 75 feet (23 m). The aqueduct also made it possible to install a series of fountains and reservoirs throughout the city, which added to its charm and its beauty.

In the streets around the plaza are the PORTAL (portico) DE SAMANIEGO (*corner of Calles 5 de Mayo and Pasteur*), the CASA DEL CONDE DE RAYAS (*Pasteur, 21*) and the mansions of the Marqués de la Villa del Villar del Águila (*Hidalgo, 19*) and the Conde de la Sierra Gorda (*Hidalgo, 18*).

COLEGIO AND TEMPLO DE SAN IGNACIO Y SAN FRANCISCO JAVIER ◆ S C1. (*Corner of Calles 16 de Septiembre and Vega Norte*) The philosophical influence of the Jesuit colleges of Querétaro and the State of Michoacán played a key role in the early stages of the struggle for independence. It is expressed here via the consistent and innovative language of Creole esthetics, illustrated by the moldings of the door and window openings and by the baroque patio. Today the building is the seat of the Autonomous University of Querétaro.

CONVENTO DE SAN FRANCISCO ◆ S B2. (*Jardín Zenea*) Built by the Franciscans in the second half of the 16th century, the monastery tells the story of its day. The FAÇADE is decorated with a relief of Saint James the Apostle according to the traditional Spanish representation of the saint as the slayer of Moors, who later became the slayer of Indians (in other words, pagans), to symbolize the alliance with the Christianized Indians. The CLOISTER is basically Renaissance in style but with some noticeably baroque elements. Today, the monastery is occupied by the MUSEO REGIONAL DE QUERÉTARO, whose collections include paintings by famous Mexican artists and some beautifully representative pieces of Mexican art and history.

TEMPLO DE SANTA CLARA ◆ S A2. (*Corner of Calles Madero and Allende*) The nunnery of Santa Clara, built in 1605, was founded by the cacique Don Diego de Tapia, son of Don Hernando, for his daughter Doña Luisa, who took holy orders. According to art historian Francisco de la Maza, its CHANCEL is 'the most important in [the history of] Hispanic

Part of one of the gilt wood altarpieces in the Templo de Santa Clara

Baroque'. The richly decorated altarpieces that line the walls bear witness to the various formal stages of 18th-century baroque. The building has a rectangular layout, as did most nunneries. Here, the nuns entered via the little door on the left that opened onto the lower chancel (*coro bajo*), opposite the window through which they received communion. The upper chancel (*coro alto*) is enclosed by a huge screen. There is also a GALLERY, which echoes the Moorish tradition, from where the nuns could see the interior of the church without being seen. Near Santa Clara is the CASA DE LA MARQUESA (*Calle Madero, 41*), with its remarkable ornate 18th-century decoration and beautiful entrance door.

CONVENTO DE SAN AGUSTÍN ◆ S B2. (*Allende Sur, 14*) The monastery's relatively late construction (the complex was completed in 1745) reflects the changes that took place in traditional Augustinian architecture – it had moved from the austere Plateresque style of the 16th century, to a more urbane form of expression reflected by the richness and sophistication of baroque. The CLOISTER (Museo de Arte de Querétaro), undoubtedly the richest in Mexico in terms of its sculpture, is particularly interesting – while the friars, always sympathetic to the Renaissance style, had used a classic iconography, the fountain, parapets, figurative motifs (plants, human figures, animals) reflect a sense of the baroque.

TEMPLO DE SANTA ROSA DE VITERBO ◆ S A3. (*Corner of Calles Arteaga and Ezequiel Montes*) The convent of Santa Rosa was founded (1752) to take the 'overflow' of novices from the Templo de Santa Clara. Like Santa Clara, the walls of the church are lined with altarpieces covered with 18- or 24-carat gold leaf, which are among the richest in Mexico. The chancels and gallery are also remarkable, while the PULPIT – inlaid with tiny pieces of colored tortoiseshell, ivory and exotic wood – is a masterpiece of marquetry. The SACRISTY has an unusual *Last Supper* with movable figures, and a strikingly beautiful *Portrait of Sister Ana María de San Francisco y Neve* painted by an anonymous artist.

San Luis Potosí ◆ **C** E1

Templo de Santa Rosa de Viterbo

STONE SCROLLS
Scrolls are a favorite motif used in the architectural decoration of Querétaro. The thrust of the dome counterbalanced by two flying buttresses attached by a huge stone scroll is a feature of the churches of Santa Rosa and San Ignacio y San Francisco Javier.

On March 4, 1592, Pedro de Anda discovered silver deposits on the site, which he named San Pedro del Potosí hoping it would prove as rich as the Potosí silver mines in Bolivia. The local Huachichil population became more static under the influence of Fray Diego de Magdalena and the mestizo captain Miguel Caldera. The hillside site was abandoned due to lack of water, and a new settlement was established on what is now the Plaza de Fundadores. This was named San Luis Minas de Potosí and, c. 1631, it became the capital of San Luis Potosí, Coahuila, Texas, Tamaulipas and Nuevo León, bordering Louisiana. Apart from the period known as the 'Troubles' – the popular reaction to the expulsion of the Society of Jesus in 1767 – the 18th century proved most prosperous for San Luis Potosí due to the exploitation of the mines. This prosperity is reflected in the city's architectural heritage. In the 19th century, the modernization of the mines and the development of the *haciendas* gave the city a new lease on life, especially during the presidency of Porfirio Díaz ● *27*, when it acquired a number of new buildings.

THE CATHEDRAL. In 1855, the diocese of San Luis was created and the former parish church (completed in 1730) was consecrated and given the basilican layout that it has today. The Carrara marble sculptures on the neoclassical façade are copies, by the Italian Biagi brothers, of those on the basilica of Saint John Lateran, in Rome. The nearby PALACIO MUNICIPAL stands on the site of the Casas Reales, destroyed during the 'Troubles'. The authorities moved into the building opposite – the NUEVAS CASAS REALES.

STROLLING THROUGH SAN LUIS POTOSÍ
Don't miss the splendid mansions in the CALLE DE ZARAGOZA, with their ornate balconies, and the attractive PLAZA DEL CARMEN, where the inhabitants gather in the evening to chat and eat ice cream.

TEMPLO DEL CARMEN. (*Plaza del Carmen*) An extraordinary DOME covered with ceramic tiles crowns the city's most remarkable building, whose construction was overseen by the self-taught Indian master mason José Lorenzo (1713–1800). On the lower part of the FAÇADE, two original Solomonic (twisted barley-sugar) columns, decorated with pendentive motifs reminiscent of scapulars,

Templo del Carmen (*left*) and Convento de San Francisco (*right*), both in San Luis Potosí

frame the central bay and its multifoil door. Between the columns are statues of the prophets Elijah and Elisha, traditionally regarded as the founders of the Carmelite order. The upper part of the façade, whose supporting elements are *estípites* pilasters ● *82*, has statues of the Spanish Carmelite reformers Saint Teresa of Avila and Saint John of the Cross (San Juan de la Cruz). On the pediment, beneath sweeping folds of sculpted stone, Our Lady of Mount Carmel offers her protection while, on the top of the bell tower, in stone filigree, the cross is held by Saint Teresa. The sculptures are the work of Francisco Eduardo Tresguerras (1827), who also produced the magnificent high altar. The LATERAL ENTRANCE dedicated to Saint Joseph has the same decorative profusion. The TRANSEPT and interior façade of the CAMARÍN ● *82*, with their gold leaf-covered stonework, represent the apotheosis of the popular style known as *tequitqui*, or 'Indo-Christian'. On a profusion of ridges and moldings is a glorification of the Eucharist, surrounded by seven archangels and a host of angels reminiscent of Santa María Tonanzintla ▲ *292*.

PLAZA DEL CARMEN. In a beautiful neoclassical Porfiriato ● *86* building that once housed the telegraph office, the MUSEO DE LAS MÁSCARAS presents an extraordinary collection of 2,500 Mexican masks. Opposite is the PORFIRIATO TEATRO DE LA PAZ by architect José Noriega (1894). The façade, with its classical pediment on a high colonnade, creates a monumental but harmonious effect.

CONVENTO DE SAN FRANCISCO. (*Plaza de San Francisco*) In the sacristy of the CHURCH, there is an exceptional decorated stone relief – representing Saint Francis receiving the stigmata – on the rear vault of the door leading to the washroom. Inside the monastery, the 18th-century CAPILLA DE ARANZAZÚ is also an excellent example of popular baroque. Today, the monastery houses the MUSEO REGIONAL POTOSINO.

IPIÑA BUILDING
Francisco Madero stayed in this building (*opposite the Plaza de los Fundadores*) and in the building belonging to the Meade family, also known as the Palacio Monumental (*at Francisco Madero, 125*), while he wrote the Plan de San Luis ● *28* on the eve of the Mexican Revolution. The two buildings are both grandiloquent examples of late 19th-century Potosino architecture. The Meade family's country house, which today houses the Casa de la Cultura (*Av. Venustiano Carranza, 1815*) is another fine example of this style.

The journey to Real
de Catorce is like
traveling back in time.
From Matahuela,
which makes an
excellent base, you
take the road to the
village of CEDRAL
whose oasis once
supplied water for the
mine. A thirty-minute
drive along a paved
road gives a good idea
of what it must have
been like in the past.
POTRERO was where
the pack animals used
to transport the ore
were corralled.
The panoramic view
from DOLORES
TROMPETA is very
instructive as you
realize the full extent
of the wasteland that
was so rich in mineral
resources. After
that, you come to
MINERAL DE LA LUZ
and the excavations of
El Refugio – well
worth a visit on the
way back.

PLAZA DE LOS FUNDADORES O DE LA COMPAÑIA.
Today, the Plaza de los Fundadores occupies the original site
of the settlement of San Luis Potosí ▲ 338. Circa 1623, the
Jesuits established themselves in the first church to be built,
the hermitage of La Santa Vera Cruz, where they received
the Indian community. Later, they built the annex of the
IGLESIA DE LORETO, a masterpiece of finely sculpted
stonework with floral and animal motifs. The façade with its
Solomonic columns dates from the early 18th century. Today,
the courtyard of the former Jesuit college is occupied by the
AUTONOMOUS UNIVERSITY OF SAN LUIS POTOSÍ.

Real de Catorce ◆ B D5

(*About 160 miles/257 km north of San Luis Potosí. Take the
freeway to Matehuala, then highway 62. Turn left 6¾ miles/
11 km beyond Cedral.*) The history of the Real de Minas de la
Limpia Concepción de Nuestra Señora de Guadalupe de los
Alamos del Catorce (the royal mining establishment of the
Immaculate Conception of Our Lady…) is petrified in its
ruins. Today, Real de Catorce is nothing but a ghost town –
it takes time to get there, but it's well worth the effort, even
negotiating the 1¾-mile (3-km) road tunnel (the OGARRIO)
just outside the town. Real de Minas, which has an irregular

View from the
hillside above
Real de Catorce

layout, like all mining towns, nestles in the hollow of a small valley. The most interesting of its typically 18th- and 19th-century buildings is the PARROQUIA, with its statue of San Francisco known affectionately as El Charrito ('the little peasant who tames horses'). Each year, the statue is presented to thousands of Huichol Indians ▲ *328* during the course of a procession on October 3. Also worth seeing are the CASA DE LA MONEDA (mint), with its grilles, bars, bolts, locks and other defensive paraphernalia, and the PALENQUE or pit used for cockfighting.

Zacatecas ◆ C D1 ◆ U

(*118 miles/190 km from San Luis Potosí via the Mex 49*) Zacatecas is situated in the middle of a desert region, at the foot of a range of mountains known as the '*bufas*'. The climate is continental and the landscape dominated by cactuses and *mezquites* ▲ *382*. From an archeological point of view, it is virtually on the borders of Mesoamerica, midway between the great sedentary cultures and the region of nomadic cultures. Zacatecas is one of the richest and most elegant towns in the Mexican cultural heritage – baroque and neoclassical architecture blends harmoniously, offering beautiful proportions and great unity in the materials used.

'TOMA [CAPTURE] DE ZACATECAS'
This epic battle – fought on June 23, 1914 – resulted in a victory for the famous División del Norte ('Division of the North'), commanded by Pancho Villa, over the federal troops. At the same time, it gave the revolutionary forces ● *28* access to the capital. The fall of the dictator Victoriano Huerta would, however, stir up disagreements between the constitutionalist army of President Venustiano Carranza and the dreaded División del Norte.

▲ The colonial cities of northern Mexico
Zacatecas

Below: the cathedral
Right: view of the cathedral and the Mercado Gonzáles Ortega
Far right: maze of narrow streets on the hillsides

THE 'MORISMA'
The city has preserved certain mestizo traditions, especially dances and festivals such as the *morisma* – a re-enactment of the struggle between Moors and Christians in which the whole town takes part. The three-day festival is held in the last week of August.

ZACATECAS ★
Relatively unspoiled by tourism, quiet, never too hot, and very pleasant to stroll around – visitors often stay in Zacatecas longer than planned.

THE CATHEDRAL ◆ U B3. As well as being the city's most precious architectural jewel, the Cathedral is also one of the most striking examples of Mexican baroque ● 82. The lavish ornamentation of the MAIN FAÇADE, built between 1730 and 1760, has left no space undecorated. It observes the Renaissance tradition of three bays and three registers with a pediment. In this instance, the supporting elements are Solomonic columns. Although the round window above the main entrance tends to be a Gothic feature, its heavily sculpted execution places it firmly within the baroque tradition. The decoration is dominated by the figure of Christ (in the center of the upper register, flanked by the twelve Apostles), while the elaborately decorated square containing the round window includes the four Doctors of the Latin Church. The magical effect of the pink stone of the façade is even more pronounced at sunset. The LEFT LATERAL ENTRANCE depicts Christ's martyrdom, in late Plateresque style, while the right-hand entrance, dedicated to Nuestra Señora del Rosario, is closer to the baroque tradition.
AROUND THE CATHEDRAL. The PALACIO DEL GOBIERNO, which occupies the former mansion of the Condes de Santiago de la Laguna, has an elegant façade highlighted by elements in pink sandstone. The former

Mercado Gonzáles Ortega (*on one side of the cathedral*) is a fine example of the intrusion of Porfiriato ● *86* in this baroque city (1903). The combination of freestone and modern materials (steel, glass, concrete) gives it an original hybrid appearance that respects the dimensions and proportion of the bays that characterize the city's architecture. The building has been transformed into a shopping mall with restaurants and craft stores. Opposite the market, the TEATRO CALDERÓN was built in eclectic style (1891–97) on the site of a theater destroyed by fire during the Revolution.

COLEGIO DE SAN LUIS GONZAGA (MUSEO PEDRO CORONEL) AND TEMPLO DE SANTO DOMINGO ◆ U B2. (*Plaza de Santo Domingo*). In 1574, Don Vicente Saldívar y Mendoza – a knight of the Order of Saint James of Compostela, local peacemaker and husband of Doña Ana de Bañuelos, daughter of the city's *conquistador* – became founder and protector of the Jesuit church for which he commissioned paintings by Luis Juárez. Not to be outdone, Doña Ana launched the construction of the college in 1616. After the expulsion of the Jesuits in 1767, the Dominicans took over the church and college, which was subsequently used as a military headquarters, a hospital and a prison. Since 1983, the restored building has housed the magnificent and amazing collections of art from Mexico and other countries put together by local artist and collector PEDRO CORONEL – etchings, lithographs and serigraphs by the most famous 20th-century European artists (Rouault, Tápies, Picasso, Van Dongen, Bonnard, Chagall, Braque, Léger), etchings by earlier artists (in particular Goya and Daumier) and various objets d'art. The triple-naved CHURCH has the most beautiful altarpieces in Zacatecas, with part of the original statuary, and paintings by Miguel Cabrera ▲ *169* and Francisco Antonio Vallejo.

MUSEO ZACATECANO ◆ U B3. (*Dr Ignacio Hierro, 301*) In the former CASA DE LA MONEDA (1810), this small museum of popular arts showcases Huichol embroidery, early photographs by Lumholtz ▲ *329* and more recent ones of the Huichol peyote pilgrimage ▲ *328*. It also has an interesting collection of 19th-century popular sacred objects.

THE 'HIGHS AND LOWS' OF ZACATECAS
A miniature railway takes visitors on a guided tour of the 400-year-old MINA DEL EDEN, where silver, copper, zinc, iron and gold were mined. After the tour, you can take the Teleférico, the panoramic cable car that runs from the top of the Cerro de Grillo to the CERRO DE LA BUFA, on the far side of the city. This 525-foot (160-m) peak was once used as a lookout post and defensive position. The CAPILLA DE NUESTRA SEÑORA DEL PATROCINIO (patron saint of miners), with its beautiful baroque façade, was built here in 1548 and renovated in 1728. Down below in the city, on the PLAZA DE LA REVOLUCIÓN MEXICANA, three equestrian statues were erected in 1989 in honor of the local revolutionary generals Pancho Villa, Felipe Angeles and Pánfilo Natera.

343

Top: collection of masks at Museo Rafael Coronel
Above: the ex-Convento de San Francisco

MUSEO DE ARTE ABSTRACTO MANUEL FELGUÉREZ ◆ **U** B1 (*Calle Colón, corner of Calle Seminario*) Manuel Felguérez (b. 1928 in Zacatecas) is an internationally renowned artist. He has bequeathed part of his work to the city and helped to create a space devoted to Mexican abstract art within the walls of a massive 19th-century building which has been used, among other things, as a prison. The interior architecture is beautifully executed and the large, uncomplicated dimensions offer a welcome respite from the city's baroque extravagance.

EX-TEMPLO DE SAN AGUSTÍN ◆ **U** B3. (*Dr Ignacio Hierro*) In the 17th century, the Augustinian order decided to redefine the form of its architectural expression within the baroque model. Zacatecas was part of this transition, since the construction of the church and monastery began in 1617 and was not completed until the 18th century. The church, which has a Latin cross layout with a dome, was partly destroyed when Juárez's liberal government sold it to the Presbyterian Church. The LATERAL ENTRANCE, decorated with the *Dream of Saint Augustine*, was fortunately blocked up rather than destroyed, and has recently been cleared and preserved. In the cloister, semicircular, ogee and bilobate arches combine in a harmonious blend.

EX-CONVENTO DE SAN FRANCISCO (MUSEO RAFAEL CORONEL) ◆ **U** B1. (*Calle Abasolo*) Although the Franciscans were the first to arrive in Zacatecas, the Convento de San Francisco, located slightly outside the colonial town center, conceals architectural elements dating from the 17th century and later. Its ruins attest to the original grandeur of the building, which was bombarded during the capture of Zacatecas ▲ *341*. On the FAÇADE of the church, the first register represents a classic Roman triumphal arch with fluted columns. The second has an octagonal window, Solomonic columns and two niches which, together with the niche on the high pediment, form an equilateral triangle. The gatehouse has been rebuilt. Beyond the roofless nave and some romantic ruins invaded by luxuriant vegetation, lies the part of the monastery that houses the MUSEO RAFAEL CORONEL and the largest collection of masks in the world. This extraordinary collection consists of more than 5,000 pieces, from a wide range of different cultures, all as colorful as they are stunning. There is also a priceless collection of terracotta figurines from the colonial period, and a large part of the Rosete Arand marionette collection.

La Quemada

Around Zacatecas

GUADALUPE ◆ C D1. Guadalupe is only a few minutes from the historic center of Zacatecas. Once a town in its own right, it is today a suburb of the city. In the late 17th century, the Convento de San Francisco was founded here as the College for the Propagation of the Faith, which contributed to the town's glorious reputation as the supreme city of northern Mexico. Adjoining the building of the viccroyalty, the CAPILLA DE NÁPOLES, built by the brilliant self-taught stonemason José Refugio Reyes, is one of the most successful examples of Mexican neoclassicism. Today it is occupied by the MUSEO VIRREINAL, which has one of the richest art collections both in terms of the quantity and quality of its works, including paintings by the most prestigious names in Mexican colonial art ▲ 168. The TRANSPORT MUSEUM is housed in an annex.

LA QUEMADA ◆ C D1. *(35 miles/56 km south of Zacatecas)* Possibly once an Aztec settlement, the site consists of a complex of stone structures built against the hillside after which it is named. The ruins, especially a pyramidal altar and ceremonial platforms, suggest an association between its builders and the Mesoamerican cultures, as well as various fluctuating links, between AD 300 and 1200, with the inhabitants of Teotihuacán and the Tarascán, Toltec and Mexica Indians. The north side of the site is dominated by a 13-foot (4-m) wall which seems to place the site within the northern boundaries of Mesoamerica ● 30.

Aguascalientes ◆ C D1-2

The small but important State of Aguascalientes provided major economic support for Zacatecas agriculturally. Today it has one million inhabitants and a modern infrastructure. Its capital, Aguascalientes, is famous for its *feria*.

José Guadalupe Posada:
Death in festive mood

Arrested and imprisoned as a young man for his political views, José Guadalupe Posada (1852–1913) was the first politically committed Latin American artist. In the turbulent social and political climate of the early 20th century, at a time when the rural exodus was gathering pace and the working classes were becoming more powerful, he produced drawings and caricatures for such opposition newspapers as *La Patria* and *El Ahuizote*, and illustrated the works of poets and writers with his etchings and engravings. As well as being amusing, sad and even frightening, his images were also meant to be informative and to prick people's social and political conscience. His chronicle of the life of the Mexican bourgeoisie and lower classes, and his critique of the privileged and ruling elite are invaluable in understanding these years of deep-rooted upheaval in Mexican society.

Top: *Vendedora de mole* (sauce-seller) Above: *El jarabe tapatio* (Mexican hat dance)

A POLITICALLY COMMITTED ENGRAVER
José Guadalupe Posada was the son of a baker. As an apprentice printmaker, he studied etching and engraving before going on to set up his own studio. As an independent artisan, he produced most of his etchings and engravings (some 20,000 prints) in the publishing house of Antonio Vanegas Arroyo, in Mexico City. From ballads to songs and tales, from prayers to news items, from calendars to recipes, this prolific engraver created a language that was personal, popular and politically committed. However, Posada – the rebel who never betrayed his origins – died forgotten and alone. The Muralists ● *100* laid claim to his artistic heritage. His influence, thanks to a reevaluation of the engraver's profession, will be perpetuated by enabling the print to be regarded in Mexico as a form of artistic expression in its own right.

LA CATRINA
La Calavera Catrina ('Death Dressed up to the Nines') was a flamboyantly realistic figure that became the symbol of the period. In the mural *Sueño de una tarde de domingo en la Alameda* ▲ *142* (1947–48, Mexico City), Diego Rivera represented himself, with Posada, as children holding the hand of *La Calavera Catrina*.

'CALAVERAS', POLITICS AND HISTORY

While historians attribute the idea of skeletons and skulls to Posada's contemporary, Manuel Manilla, it was in Posada's hands that the depiction of *calaveras* (skeletons, *below*) achieved its most sophisticated form of expression and its true identity. At once archetypal and allegorical, this image of death is found throughout the engraver's work as he flirts with it in various situations and contexts, making fun of it the better to exorcise it.

CHRONICLE OF DAILY LIFE AND SOCIAL CARICATURE

Posada was a keen analyst of the actions of the society in which he lived. He pinpointed its contradictions by depicting the main protagonists, especially the pawnbrokers who exploited the misery of its weakest members and the nouveaux riches, whose ridiculousness he emphasized. Petits-bourgeois, bureaucrats, priests and the military all passed under the microscope of his sarcastic humor, while the working classes were treated with tenderness and affection.
(*Below: Las Gracias* [the Three Graces])

PORTRAITS OF THE REVOLUTION

Although 1910 marks the official start of the Revolution, Mexican society had been the chaotic scene of demonstrations and strikes for several decades, an expression of the growing opposition to the regime of Porfirio Díaz ● 28. It was within this context that Posada forged and refined his incisive and satirical style in order to examine moments of tenderness (*right*) as well as the violence of the events he was witnessing. His keen eye and profound critical awareness enabled him to express the fiery spirit of Emiliano Zapata, the weakness of Francisco Madero and the courage of the female soldier.

**FERIA DE SAN
MARCOS,
AGUASCALIENTES**
At the end of April,
the Feria de San
Marcos – the region's
most famous festival –
changes the face of
this peaceful capital.
The *feria* was first
held c. 1882 in the
old covered market
(Parián) and moved,
twenty years later,
into a specially
constructed garden
in the east of the city.
This magnificent
garden, enclosed by a
beautiful neoclassical
balustrade, has
become a symbol of
Aguascalientes. As
well as the essentially
commercial activity of
the cattle market, and
the industrial and
craft exhibition, the
festive element adds
international cultural
events, folk music,
cockfighting, firework
displays and
bullfighting (*right*)
in the recently
renovated bullring.
Over the years,
the aptly named
'monumental' bullring
has welcomed the
cream of the
bullfighting world.

THE CATHEDRAL. Its slender outline is reminiscent of a
regional style whose best examples are found in Lagos, San
Juan de los Lagos and Incarnación. Built in the early 18th
century, its ornate façade has Solomonic columns ● *82* and
hieratic sculptures of the four Doctors of the Latin Church.
IGLESIA DE GUADALUPE. (*Corner of Guadalupe and
Nicolás Bravo*) The influence of the Iglesia de San Diego in
Guanajuato ▲ *350* is very much in evidence, especially in the
excellent stonework. This is due to the avant-gardism of
Guanajuato's baroque architecture, at a time when the
region had not developed its own form of expression.
IGLESIA SAN ANTONIO. (*Corner of Pedro Parga and
Zaragoza*) This hybrid product of romantic architecture,
which borrows elements from the neoclassical and neo-
Gothic styles, was built in the 19th century by the great

master mason José Refugio Reyes, who was more successful
here than in San Miguel Allende or Guanajuato. It has an
impressive dome whose drum surmounts a circular gallery
that adds height and luminosity. Opposite the church, the
seminary, with its pure classical lines, today houses the
Museo de Aguascalientes. Its two patios are designed in a
different style, in accordance with the tradition of the time.
OTHER 'MUST SEES'. The Iglesia de San Diego
(1651–1767) has the beautiful Camarín ● *82* de San Marcos
(1763), while the many scrolls of the Palacio del Gobierno
attest to the influence of Querétaro. In the Triana district, a
small museum is devoted to the work of José Guadalupe
Posada ▲ *346*, one of the city's famous sons.

Guanajuato ◆ C E2-3 ◆ V

Cunax-huato ('mountainous place with frogs') was the town's first Chichimec name. It was founded between 1526 and 1550, in line with the exploitation of the San Juan de Rayas Mine. Its irregular topography has produced a haphazard urban layout that climbs and twists according to the demands of the terrain. The city is divided into four districts: Marfil, Tepetapa, Santa Ana and Santa Fe. The rush to settle near the water courses, to protect the ownership of the deposits, meant that the original town was flooded and destroyed a number of times before a more controlled urban development managed to channel the water toward the river bed. This is one of the most beautiful cities in Mexico but, although it was founded in the 16th century, what you see

today dates from the 18th century, when the city was at its height. With flooding, and the extensive development that preceded independence, virtually nothing has survived from the city's early history. In 1746, Filippo V of Spain invested it with the title 'Santa Fe y Real de Minas de Guanaxuato'. At the time, when Mexico City had some 120,000 inhabitants, the population of Guanajuato was already in the region of 80,000. In the 19th century, it acquired a number of elegant buildings, such as the Teatro Juárez, the Mercado Hidalgo and the Palacio Legislativo. Although nowadays Guanajuato is quite a small city, it is well serviced by a network of streets below ground level that follow the lines of the river bed and the old mining tunnels, and give it a distinctive character.

FESTIVAL CERVANTINO, GUANAJUATO
This is one of Mexico's most important cultural events. For two weeks during October, Guanajuato welcomes top international artists and young designers who offer a fascinating view of modern art in the participating countries via a wide range of displays and events – dance, theater, music, cinema and the visual arts. It's essential to book accommodation well in advance.

MUSEO-CASA DIEGO RIVERA
(*Calle de Pócitos, 7*)
Diego Rivera was born in Guanajuato in 1886 ● *100*. His house has been transformed into a small museum.

Top: panoramic view of Guanajuato
Above: poster for the Festival Cervantino, Guanajuato

PLAZA DE LA PAZ
To the west of the Jardín de la Unión, this triangular square is dominated by the impressive BASÍLICA COLEGIATA DE NUESTRA SEÑORA DE GUANAJUATO, which houses a polychrome statue of the Virgin. The statue was a gift to the town from Fillippo II of Spain, a token of his appreciation for the tons of silver sent to the Spanish Crown.

TEMPLO DE SAN DIEGO ◆ V C2. (*Jardín de la Unión*) The Franciscans settled in mining communities to collect funds for their missions in the Philippines and China. Following the expropriation of its parvis to create a small plaza and its monastery to build the Teatro Juárez, the church's privileged situation left it standing in the center of the city. This remarkable building (1784) was made possible by the generosity of Don Antonio de Obregón y Alcocer, Conde de la Valenciana.

TEATRO JUÁREZ ◆ V C2. (*Next to the Templo de San Diego*) The building (1892–1903) is a fine example of the eclecticism that characterized the tastes and outlook of an entire age – the age of Porfirio Díaz who, after the armed struggles of the 19th century, was a prodigious and grandiloquent builder

GUANAJUATO ★
Although the city's network of alleys (*above and right*) and underground streets has a certain charm, it's a nightmare for drivers. You are advised to leave your car in a parking lot (*there's one behind the Teatro Juárez*).

● *28*. The harmoniously proportioned neoclassical façade is surmounted by beautiful statues of the Muses. New materials – steel and glass – also have their place. The architect Antonio Rivas Mercado also created the Monument to Independence in Mexico City ▲ *144*.

TEMPLO DE LA COMPAÑÍA ◆ V C1. (*Calle de Pócitos*) The outline of the Compañía dominates the urban landscape. The church and college (1732) belong to the artistic and economic renaissance of Guanajuato. Within the context of *estípites* and Churrigueresque baroque ● *82*, the church's façade presents a variation since the *estípites* are decorated with geometric rather than vegetal motifs. However, the presence of inter-*estípites*, which leave no undecorated space reasserts its affinity with Churrigueresque baroque. The open cornices create the impression of flight, while the balconies add a civil element to the building. The absence of most of the church's interior decoration is due to the neoclassical fervor and zeal of the great architect Francisco Eduardo Tresguerras. The college was modified by a governor who destroyed the original building and replaced it with a copy which he attributed to the university.

CASA DE LOS MARQUESES DE SAN JUAN DE RAYAS
◆ **V** B1. (*Calle de Pócitos, 7, next to the university*) This
charming mansion is the result of a concept of space specific
to a city where, because of the topography, patios are
difficult to fit. It has a private chapel (1776) and today
houses the MUSEO DEL PUEBLO DE GUANAJUATO.
ALHÓNDIGA DE GRANADITAS ◆ **V** A2. (*Mendizábal, 6*)
This beautiful structure, built as an *alhóndiga* (public
granary), is among the last achievements of the viceroyalty.
Its construction was the decision of the *intendente* (provincial
governor) Juan Antonio de Riaño y Barcena, who died
defending the building when Miguel Hidalgo captured
Guanajuato in 1810 ▲ *356*. Riano had chosen the solidly built
granary, with its small openings to ensure good ventilation, as

**AROUND
GUANAJUATO**
(*On the road to León*)
On the outskirts of
Guanajuato, the
former HACIENDA
DE SAN GABRIEL DE
BARRERA, in its
magnificent garden
setting, has been
transformed into a
museum. Beyond lie
the ivory mine of
MINERAL DE
MARFIL and the well-
preserved village of
MINERAL DE LA
LUZ, where the first

a place of refuge for the wealthy citizens and their property
during the rebel attack. The courtyard reflects the elegance
and proportions with which Don Manuel Tolsá invested the
Academia de San Carlos – the mother of neoclassicism in
Mexico – in Mexico City ● *86*. Today the building houses the
MUSEO REGIONAL, with murals by José Chávez Morado.
AROUND THE MERCADO HIDALGO ◆ **V** A2. (*Via the Calle
de Mendizábal*) The Mercado Hidalgo is worth a visit for its
neoclassical architecture and craft stores. From the market,
the Calle Juárez leads to the small plaza and the IGLESIA DE
SAN ROQUE, a delightful square where there are regular
performances of Miguel de Cervantes' *Interludes*. From here
you can rejoin the PLAZA DE SAN FERNANDO and the
Palacio Legislativo.
CALLEJÓN DEL BESO ◆ **V** B2. The labyrinth of the old
town is like a vast open-air museum. Legend has it that in the
delightfully picturesque and extremely narrow 'Alley of the
Kiss', two lovers were able to kiss from opposite balconies. At
night, the streets, which are still pervaded by the atmosphere
of colonial Mexico, are the preserve of groups of students
and musicians.

silver deposits were
discovered and the
first mine established.
About 28 miles
(45 km) from
Guanajuato, LEÓN is
Mexico's shoemaking
capital.

**THE CENTER OF
MEXICO**
(*15½ miles/25 km
from Guanajuato,
toward Silao*) The
geographical center
of Mexico is located
on the Cerro del
Cubilete, where a
national monument
has been erected to
Christ the King.

MUSEO
DE LAS MOMIAS
(*Camino a las
Momias*)
Guanajuato's best-
known and most
popular museum was
created when more
space was needed in
the nearby cemetery,
and naturally
mummified bodies
were exhumed. The
phenomenon is
explained by the dry
air and mineral
content of the soil – it
would have taken five
or six years to
mummify the bodies.
The museum contains
over a hundred
mummified bodies,
most dating from the
19th century.

**BETWEEN
GUANAJUATO AND
SAN MIGUEL**
(*Via the freeway*)
Beyond IRAPUATO,
the Mexican
strawberry capital,
the town of
SALAMANCA is
worth a detour for
the Augustinian
monastery of San
Juan de Sahún
(1615), named for
the friar Saint John
of St. Facond. The
interior is a single
altarpiece, a
scenography in gilt
wood that extends
into the nave. The
artist Pedro de Rojas,
commissioned in
1768 after working
on Our Lady of
Mount Carmel in
San Luis Potosí
▲ *338*, was dedicated
to the point of
obsession and had to
mortgage his house
to finance his work.
The baroque style
and grandeur of the
courtyard of the
college attest to
the continuity of
Augustinian
architectural tastes
in the 18th century.

Around Guanajuato ◆ C E2-3

(*Via the Carretera Panorámica to the south of the city*)
MINA DE LA VALENCIANA. (*2½ miles/4 km from the city
center*) The La Valenciana Mine has one of the region's
most beautiful churches, the TEMPLO DE SAN CAYETANO
(*below*), built by the Conde de Valencia (1765–88).
Its principal and lateral façades are masterpieces of pink
stonework on which there is no shortage of the lambrequins
and *estípites* that characterize Churrigueresque baroque
● 82. The interior has three monumental altarpieces, all
beautifully executed in the same style, dedicated to San
Cayetano, the Virgin of Guadalupe and the Assumption of
the Virgin. The pulpit is exquisite, with its inlay of horn and
exotic woods, while the baptismal fonts are some of the fines*
examples of their kind bequeathed by the 18th century.

MINA DE CATA. A little further on, the Cata Mine also has
a beautiful CHURCH, whose *estípites* façade is incomplete bu*
nonetheless exquisitely executed. The mine was owned by
Don Alonso de Villaseca, the richest man in New Spain. In
1618, Don Alonso made a gift of the figure of Christ that stil*
adorns the church, which is known as 'Our Lord of Villaseca*
OTHER INTERESTING PLACES. This itinerary includes
the MINA DE MELLADO, the MINA DE RAYAS, the BARRIO
DE PASTITA and the PRESA ('reservoir') DE LA OLLA. The
opening of the sluices, to replenish the water of the reservoir
and clean up the Guanajuato river bed, is celebrated by a
popular festival that has been held since the 18th century.
The itinerary ends at the MIRADOR DEL PÍPILA, which
offers an unforgettable view of the town.

San Miguel de Allende ◆ C E3

In 1542, Fray Juan de San Miguel, a great builder of colonia*
establishments and subscriber to the utopian ideals of Vasco
de Quiroga ▲ *314*, founded a hospital at Izquinapan. He
called it 'San Miguel' in honor of his patron saint and, with
the agreement of the local Huachichils, encouraged Otomi
and Purépecha groups to settle there. These *presidios*, or
garrisons, were used to strengthen the routes and positions

established by the Spanish in their bid to conquer the Chichimecs and explore northern Mexico. Although the traditional crafts and work carried out by the Indians enabled the establishment to be self-sufficient in the 16th century, it was *guanajuatense* gold that transformed the surrounding area, whose fertile soil could feed the uncultivated mining regions. The flatlands of the Bajío ▲ *334*, with their wonderful climate, were ideal for agriculture and stock farming, and became the 'larder' of the mining communities. They were at their height in the 18th century. The town of San Miguel has preserved the charm of its considerable historic heritage, in a peaceful yet cosmopolitan atmosphere, since large numbers of foreign retirees have settled here.

PARROQUIA SAN MIGUEL ARCÁNGEL ◆ W B3. (*Plaza Principal*) The unusual outline of the church – perfect neo-Gothic – has become a symbol of the town. It was the work (begun in 1880) of master mason Zeferino Gutiérrez, who built it against the sober 17th-century portal.

Above: *zócalo* of San Miguel de Allende
Below: mariachis in San Miguel

♿ **JARDÍN BOTÁNICO EL CHARCO DEL INGENIO**
(*From San Miguel, take the road to Querétaro and turn left at the equestrian statue of Allende, opposite a shopping mall.*) This magnificent botanical garden devoted to the preservation of Mexican flora, especially its many hundreds of species of cactus, occupies an area of 247 acres (100 ha) and includes a canyon which has several walks lasting between 30 minutes and 3 hours.

Above: back of the Parroquia San Miguel Arcángel
Opposite above: patio in the cultural center of El Nigromante
Opposite below: door of the Casa del Mayorazgo de la Canal

TEMPLO DE SAN FRANCISCO ◆ W B2. (*Corner of Calles San Francisco and Juárez*) The church forms an angle with the 17th-century Franciscan monastery of San Antonio. The complex is enhanced by one of the most beautiful façades in the Guanajuato region, by the same architect, or at least the same school, responsible for those of Dolores and La Valenciana ▲ *352*. The neoclassical bell tower was completed (1799) with the proceeds from bullfights. Its *estípites* ● *82* are extremely finely crafted and its iconography represents Christ's martyrdom. It houses paintings by Rodríguez Juárez, Juan Correa and Baltasar Gómez.

ORATORIO DE SAN FELIPE NERI ◆ W B2. (*Corner of Calles Insurgentes and Pepellanos*) In 1712, the priest of Pátzcuaro ▲ *314*, Juan Antonio Pérez de Espinosa, managed to found the church by promising to care for the mulattos who built it. The details of its execution in fact attest to Indian influences, since the style is somewhat outmoded compared with the date of its construction. The church is interesting, but it is above all the CAPILLA DE LORETO (1736) that captures the attention. Like other remarkable Mexican chapels, it was built thanks to the generosity of the town's richest man, in this instance Don Manuel Tomás de la

Canal and his wife, who both worshipped Our Lady of
Loreto, a cult introduced to Mexico by Italian Jesuits. It is a
jewel of baroque architecture, from the FAÇADE to the
octagonal CAMARÍN ● *82*, whose intersecting Mudejar
arches support the lantern, in the form of a papal crown. The
sacristy and its annexes house a rich art collection. In the
sacristy, the door is covered with polychrome embossed
leather in accordance with the Mudejar tradition.

CIVIL ARCHITECTURE. An eloquent testimony to the
standard of living attained by Mexican high society on the
eve of independence, the town's most
beautiful mansions were occupied by
promoters or sympathizers of the
libertarian movement, for example the
CASA DE DON IGNACIO ALLENDE
(*Museo Histórico, Cuna de Allende, 1*),
the leading light of the 1810
revolution, who persuaded Miguel
Hidalgo to join his cause. The façade,
with its lambrequins and neoclassical
entrance surmounted by the motto
'*Hic natus ubique notus*' ('This is
the birthplace of someone who
became universally known'), marks
a stylistic transition. The CASA DEL
MAYORAZGO DE LA CANAL (*corner of
Plaza de Allende and Calle de la Canal,
4*) is one of the most impressive
mansions in the whole of Mexico. Its
door, framed by four lambrequins,
represents a sort of farewell to
baroque, with the rest of the building
belonging to an elegant neoclassical
tradition. In the Calle de la Canal, the
mansion has three floors, with latticework above the windows decorating
the space between the stories. The
entrance is reminiscent of an
altarpiece, surmounted by a huge
sculpture of Our Lady of Loreto. A
portico runs along the façades on the
Plaza de Allende, echoing the tradition
of arcaded plazas. Also worth a visit
are the CASA DE LOS PERROS ('House
of the Dogs') (*Umarán, 4*); the CASA
DEL CONDE DE LOJA (*Diez de
Sollano, 1*); the CASA DE
LANZAGORTA (*Correo, 4*), which
belonged to the revolutionary
Francisco Lanzagorta; the CASA DEL
CONDE DE JARAL DE BERRIO
(*Correo, 17*), with its equally
remarkable exterior and interior; the
CASA DEL INQUISIDOR (*Cuadrante,
18*), with its interesting baroque façade
decorated with lambrequins; and the
CASA DE LA INQUISICIÓN (*corner of*

**OTHER 'MUST
SEES'**
The IGLESIA DE
LA SALUD, the
CONVENTO DE LA
CONCEPCIÓN, with its
impressive dome and
vast cloister, and the
HOSPITAL DE SAN
JUAN DE DIOS.

MIGUEL HIDALGO Y COSTILLA
The 'Father of the Country' was born on the Hacienda de Corralejo, in the present-day state of Guanajuato, on May 8, 1753. He studied at the Jesuit college of Valladolid (Morelia). After his expulsion from the Society of Jesus (1767), he entered the Colegio de San Nicolás, where he was a teacher and then dean. When the Napoleonic army entered Spain in 1808, he took part in a revolutionary movement that was intended to provoke an armed uprising from Querétaro. The conspiracy was discovered and Hidalgo anticipated the rebellion by issuing a call to arms from the Iglesia de Dolores where he was curate, on the morning of September 16, 1810. The incident is referred to as the 'Cry of Dolores', which announced the beginning of the armed struggle for Mexican independence. Hidalgo was to declare independence in Guadalajara and form a provisional government, but he was executed by firing squad on July 30, 1811. His head, along with those of other revolutionary leaders, was hung in the Alhóndiga de Granaditas in Guanajuato ▲ *351*.

ATOTONILCO ★
The monastery, which still attracts hundreds of pilgrims, has been classified as a UNESCO World Heritage Site.

Quadrante and Hernández Macias), with its green cross and its 18th-century ceramic tiles. Above the entablature of the entrance to the INSTITUTO ALLENDE (*Ancha de San Antonio, 21*), the family home of Don Manuel de la Canal (1735) is a niche with a rear vault. It contains a statue of Our Lady of Loreto surmounted by the cross of Caravaca. The PARQUE DE LOS BERROS is ideal for a quiet stroll.

Santuario de Atotonilco ◆ **C** E2

(*About 6 miles/10 km from San Miguel on the road to Dolores Hidalgo*) The church's nickname of the 'Mexican Sistine Chapel' is well deserved. Between 1746 and 1748, the pious Oratorian Luis Felipe Neri y Alfaro founded a house of 'spiritual exercises'. In the church are representations of the 'compositions of place': scenes conducive to meditation from the famous book of exercises according to the treatise of the Jesuit priest Father Jerónimo Nadal. The paintings are the work of the *tlacuilo* ('painter') Miguel Antonio Martínez Pocasangre, whose name (which means 'little blood') is in stark contradiction to the wealth of bloody images, in both Spanish and Mexican tradition. His artistic devotion kept him busy for at least thirty years, since he did not leave a single unpainted space or surface on the walls of the church (*below*). His pictorial images extend from the drum of the entrance to the church – also known as the Santuario de Jesús Nazareno – to the Camarín de los Santos Apóstoles, the sacristy, the choir, the Capilla de 'La Gloria Escondida' ('hidden glory'), the Capillas de Nuestra Señora del Rosario, de la Virgen Loreto, de Belén, del Santo Sepulcro and the Capilla del Calvario. The continuous stream of pilgrims carrying scourges and wearing hair shirts gives the church a medieval atmosphere. It was here that Miguel Hidalgo, asking for divine help as he launched the struggle for independence, took possession of a banner of the Virgin of Guadalupe, making it his battle standard.

The Missions of the
Sierra Madre Oriental

▲ The Missions of the Sierra Madre Oriental The Sierra Gorda

1. The Sierra Gorda ▲ *358*
2. Xilitla and Huasteca Potosina ▲ *362*
3. The Sierra Madre of the Augustinians ▲ *364*

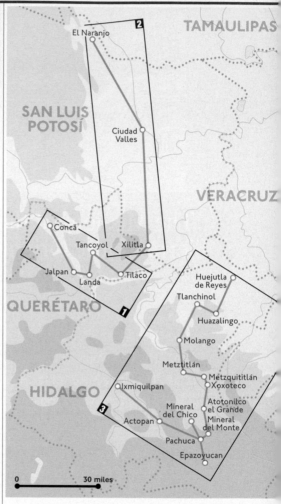

Arugged landscape that moves from the starkness of a desert to the lushness of a tropical forest marks the way into Huasteca. When approached from Querétaro, the massive mountains are known as the Sierra Gorda, but they go under the generic name of the Sierra Madre Oriental for travelers from Pachuca. The two itineraries meet up in Huejutla. Both sierras offer extraordinary views that more than make up for the arduous roads, and they also present a fascinating contrast, as they reveal two different worlds, in terms of period and style: the Sierra Gorda of Querétaro revels in the delirium of the Franciscan baroque of the second half of the 18th century, but the Pachuca–Huejutla route reflects the evangelizing adventures of the Augustinian friars in the more austere 16th century. In both cases, the indigenous sensibility shines through in architectural carving and ornamentation. This land of missions, so different from the civilization on the plains, provided a refuge for liberty.

From Querétaro, the first stop is Jalpan, an ideal base and the site of the first of the extraordinary missions on the Sierra Gorda. Jalpan can be reached by two routes. The road via San Juan del Río offers a stopover in Tequisquiapan, a delightful and lively village that sells craft goods at reasonable prices. The other option involves a shortcut through El Bernal, a village huddled round the foot of an impressive basalt monolith (*above*). (*This shorter route, via secondary road no. 4, will take you to Jalpan in 2½ hours.*)

HISTORY. The meandering road makes it easier to see why this region resisted the advances of missionaries and *conquistadores* alike. Although attempts were made to conquer it in the time of Cortés, the Sierra Gorda was not subdued until 1743, two centuries after the Augustinians had made inroads into the Sierra Madre Oriental. After fending off competition from both the Augustinians and the Dominicans, the Franciscans from the school of San Fernando de México succeeded in establishing five missions. The conversion and domestication of the Pame and Jonace Indians, who until then had lived in the most 'idle, complete and barbaric freedom' – in the words of the 'pacifier' of the Sierra, José de Escandón – was not achieved without a substantial reduction in the indigenous population, despite the Franciscans' efforts to create a Utopia here.

Jalpan ◆ **B** E6

Although laid out in the form of the Latin cross characteristic of the time, the SANTIAGO MISSION presents some highly distinctive features, such as an octagonal apse and a slender clock tower, set on two levels and also octagonal. The atrium, out of favor elsewhere in the 18th century, was revived in the Sierra Gorda, although the corner chapels in Jalpan have disappeared (if ever they existed). The façade is typical of the baroque of the time, with its rich phytomorphous decoration, its drapes and its pilasters in the style of *estípites*, but local ingredients have been added to the standard recipe. The bases of the columns and pilasters, for example, bear an element found in other missions: a double-headed eagle with each head devouring a serpent – unlikely to be the blazon of the House of Austria, so more fittingly interpreted as an allegory of cultural fusion (the union of the Mexican eagle and the Spanish eagle).

LANDSCAPES OF THE SIERRA GORDA
At first sight, the Sierra Gorda appears stark and rocky, but in fact this protected natural area has few rivals in Mexico for ecological richness and diversity. The initial desert is only one of no less than fourteen different types of climate and vegetation on view. The landscape can sometimes change with startling abruptness. From one side of a mountain bend to another, cacti can give way to poplars and firs, which in turn hand over to pines, before the heat and the aridity reclaim their rightful due. The majesty of the kapok trees along the road presages the high canopies and exuberate lushness awaiting on the descent toward Huasteca.

Below: Jalpan mission

**BROTHER
JUNÍPERO SERRA**
Born in Majorca,
Spain, in 1713, Serra
joined the Franciscans
at the age of sixteen.
He arrived in Mexico
in 1749 and was sent
to the Sierra Gorda.
His disciplined but
generous character
quickly marked him
out as a missionary.
He established close
relationships with
the Indians, as
shown today by
the magnificent
monuments on the
Sierra. Later, after a
long spell in Mexico
City (where he was
responsible for
training novices),
Father Serra took
over the Californian
missions that the
recently expelled
Jesuits had left
vacant. It was in
California that he
spent his final years
before his death in
1784. San Diego and
San Francisco are just
two of the nine
missions that he
founded in Upper
California. He was
beatified in 1988 by
Pope John Paul II.

The main entrance is crowned by a dais in the form of a shell
that symbolizes baptism. The small niches in the embrasure
of the arch contain statues of Saints Peter and Paul. On the
same level, the side sections house saints Dominic and
Francis, while the niches higher up hold the Virgin of
Guadalupe and the Virgin of Pilar, emblems of Mexican and
Spanish devotion, respectively.

Concá ◆ **B** E6

(*24 miles/38 km north of Jalpan*) This is the smallest of the
five churches. The gigantic Franciscan blazon above its
entrance is flanked by Saint Ferdinand and Saint Roch: the
presence of the former can undoubtedly be read as an
acknowledgment of the house of the founding friars in
Mexico. Here, the supporting elements are not *estípites*, but
fluted columns on the first register and Solomonic ones on
the second ● *82*. The entire façade is covered with enormous
clusters of flowers, symbolizing the Eucharist. The striking
figure of Saint Michael trampling a diabolical monster
underfoot reveals a touching, almost medieval naiveté. The
depiction of the Holy Trinity in the form of three men on a
globe – an image forbidden by the Council of Trent – crowns
the façade. The top parts of the buttresses are adorned with a
rabbit, the local symbol for the moon, and an eagle, the
symbol for the sun. These motifs probably refer to a syncretic
version of Christ as the alpha and the omega, although they
could also refer to Jesus and Mary. The INTERIOR is worth a
visit for the superb octagonal dome, the baroque openings
and the decorated festoon of the lower choir.

Landa ◆ **B** E6

(*11 miles/18 km from Jalpan*) The iconographic decor of this
church's façade is without question the most extravagant of
all those on the Sierra Gorda, and its construction marked

Mission façades on the Sierra Gorda, from far left to below right: Jalpan, Concá, Landa, Tilaco. All are adorned with the emblem of the Franciscans, showing the arms of Christ and Saint Francis intertwined.

the end of the spiritual conquest of the area. On the eve of their departure, the Franciscans left behind their favorite devotional figures. So, as in Jalpan, the founding saints, Dominic and Francis, occupy the niches in the side sections of the first level. Those in the *estípites* contain the four Franciscans responsible for reforming the order in the 15th century: Bernardin de Sienne, Jean de Capistran, Jacques de la Marche and Albert de Sarteano. A statue of the Immaculate Conception stands between the door and the rose window overlooking the upper choir. The Virgin is flanked by two of her most staunch defenders, the theologian Duns Scot and Maria of Ágreda. Above them, the Franciscan blazons are linked by Saint Francis's cord, which winds round the rose window. The pediment bears the three deacon martyrs, Saints Sebastian, Lawrence and Vincent. Landa has preserved its open chapel or 'Indian chapel' ● 78, with its cherubs frolicking amongst the pillars in the interior.

Tilaco ◆ B E6

(*Around 28 miles/45 km from Jalpan*) Surrounded by lush mountains and bounded by a baroque enclosure, this is the most complete monastic complex in the Sierra Gorda, as it has conserved not only its monastery but also its atrium, with its *capillas posas*, *capilla abierta* and cross. The dais on the FAÇADE recalls that of Jalpan; it is set under the sign of Saint Francis, here accompanied by musicians of Plateresque inspiration. The adjoining columns on the first level are transformed, along their axis, into *estípites* on both the second level and the pediment. The side sections of the first level bear statues of Saints Peter and Paul. On the entablature, mermaids (symbols of temptation) support the bases of the *estípites* on the second level; their reversed hands are irrefutable evidence of their dual Indian-Christian origin. The diamond-shape opening is elegantly embellished with drapes held up by attentive cherubs.

A MEETING OF CULTURES
The prosperity of the newly founded congregations between 1750 and 1758 must undoubtedly be credited to Junípero Serra. He learned the Indians' language very quickly and succeeded in persuading them to build churches that incorporated elements from their own culture. Although he was only involved personally in Santiago de Jalpan, his missionary colleagues followed his example when they went on to build the four other churches with the creative complicity of the local people. This is evident in their extraordinary façades, which alone make this itinerary unforgettable.

Tancoyol ◆ B E6

(24 miles/38 km from Jalpan: turn left to La Vuelta, on Route 120.) This is reached via a hair-raising but magnificent descent lined with cacti. The beautiful square in front of the town church contains the remains of two *capillas posas*. The pinnacles of the clock tower and the roof are echoed on the enclosing wall. The façade, dedicated to Our Lady of the Light, is adorned with *estípites* and plant motifs. The niches on the first level are occupied by Saints Peter and Paul, while those of the second level house the Virgin, accompanied by Saint Anne and Saint Joachim, and those on the third, Saint Roch and Saint Anthony of Padua. Above the opening of the choir, Saint Francis is depicted receiving the stigmata. The façade is surrounded by angels bearing symbols of the Passion.

Below: baptismal font at Tancoyol church
Opposite: the garden of Las Pozas, Xilitla

Xilitla ◆ B E6

(40 miles/65 km from Landa, via Route 120) Xilitla's tropical vegetation and legendary climate make it an ideal introduction to the distinctive culture of the enormous region known as Huasteca. The food, typical craft goods and indigenous embroidery sold by street vendors are the first signs of the region's distinct identity – even now, it is not unusual to see both men and women wearing their traditional costume with pride. The area is dotted with caves, but the main attraction in Xilitla, however, is its extraordinary Surrealist garden.

LAS POZAS. *(A little way from the town; follow the track indicated by the signposts)* A visit to this garden is full of surprises that more than compensate for the detour. Las Pozas represents a dream come true in the midst of the forest. Begun in 1949, it is the folly of a fabulous wealthy Englishman enamored of both Surrealism and nature. In this seeming endless garden, Edward James started building an enthralling architectural decor that merges into the exuberant vegetation of the forest to become an integral part of it. The constructions, deliberately and joyously anti-utilitarian, create stunning spaces and views that appeal to all five senses: staircases that soar out of sight, doors that cannot be opened, paths that lead nowhere, waterfalls, pillars shrouded in plants, a permanently empty swimming pool in the form of an eye. It is advisable to obtain a map at the entrance to the garden.

MISSIONS OF THE SIERRA GORDA ★
The isolation of this region – however beautiful the access road may be, its winding bends are very daunting – has made it a veritable treasure trove that can often be enjoyed without ever encountering another tourist. If possible, make the effort to continue to Xilitla, in order to prolong this unique experience far from the madding crowd.

Ciudad Valles and Huasteca Potosina

CIUDAD VALLES ◆ B E6. *(54 miles/87 km north of Xilitla)* Anybody looking for ecotourism tinged with adventure will find Ciudad Valles, considered the 'main gate' to Huasteca Potosina, a particularly fruitful stopover. The town itself provides a survey of the rich local culture via the collections

EATING IN HUASTECA
Apart from the unmissable *cecina*, or dried meat, and the local *enchiladas*, which are also available in Jalpan, Huasteca offers other traditional dishes, such as *bocoles* (pies made with corn and beef fat), *zacahuil* and huge *tamales* – sometimes several pounds in weight – stuffed with pork, beef and chicken.

of the MUSEO REGIONAL HUASTECO and the MUSEO TAMUANZAN, while the many rivers running through the lush wooded landscape create scenes of breathtaking beauty.

PUENTE DE DIOS ◆ B E6. (*Not far from Tamasopo, 34 miles/55 km west of Ciudad Valles, on the Río Verde road*) The forest and the river combine their charms to offer travelers the opportunity of a refreshing swim in an enticingly tranquil natural setting. Also worth a visit are the TAMASOPO AND TRAMPOLÍN WATERFALLS.

AQUISMÓN ◆ B E6. (*32 miles/50 km south of Ciudad Valles, on the Tamazunchale road*) There is plenty to explore on the way out of this town: the SOURCE OF THE RÍO TAMBAQUE, the impressive TAMUL WATERFALL, THE RAPIDS OF THE RÍO SANTA MARÍA, THE CAVERN OF LAS GUAGAS and the MONTEZUMEL GROTTOS.

EL NARANJO ◆ B E5-6. (*About 53 miles/85 km from Ciudad Valles; take Route 85 toward Ciudad Mante, then, continuing westward, take Route 80.*) In summer, the SALTO WATERFALL crashes from a height of 230 feet (70 m), creating a series of natural pools (ideal for swimming); in the dry winter season, the water is less abundant and is channeled to a hydroelectric plant. Another waterfall, EL MECO, plunges 115 feet (35 m), while the WATERFALL and POOLS OF MINAS VIEJAS are even more spectacular.

EDWARD JAMES
Born in Scotland in 1907 into a family of immense wealth (which he went on to inherit), this patron of the Surrealists counted among his friends Dalí, who made the famous lobster telephone for him and designed his New York apartment, and René Magritte, who painted him in *The Forbidden Reproduction*. James discovered Xilitla on a trip in the company of his close Mexican friend Plutarco Gastélum Esquer. Impressed by the splendor of the landscapes, he saw an omen in a cloud of monarch butterflies ▲ *311* that set the forest alight with a flaming mass of yellow: he decided to build the house of his dreams on this spot. From 1949 until his death in 1984, he poured millions into the project, sometimes employing as many as 150 workers at any one time.

▲ The Missions of the Sierra Madre Oriental
The Sierra Madre of the Augustinians

STONE ANGELS
The richly decorated façade of Molango church is topped with a superb Gothic rose window and is replete with ornaments from the roof to the door (*below*), including charming sculptures of angels bearing crosses (*bottom*).

The Augustinians arrived in Mexico in 1533 and quickly set out on the trail to the Sierra Madre Oriental, reaching Huejutla between 1540 and 1544. The Augustine buildings of the 16th century reveled in their splendor, encouraging the natives to abandon their pagan traditions through 'the glory of buildings, the richness of temples, the solemnity of festivals and divine worship' – in the words of Brother Alonso de la Vera Cruz. Although elsewhere the Augustinian excesses would be brought down to size by the rival ambitions of other religious orders, or by the prerogatives of secular power and the scarcity of indigenous labor, the isolation of the northeastern missions removed them from any kind of ecclesiastical competition, or from interference by pedantic civil administrations. Furthermore, the Augustinians could always count on an abundant supply of manpower in these parts, as can be seen today by their legacy of grandiose buildings – one of the most impressive architectural expressions of spirituality bequeathed to us by the 16th century.

From Mission to Mission: via the Sierra Madre

HUEJUTLA DE REYES ◆ D B1.
Although the successive interventions in the courtyard and the cloister have altered much of its original appearance (1544), the dimensions of this monastic complex are still remarkably eloquent. The arched vault and the belltower arcade with three bells add original touches to the church. Some impressive baptismal fonts in sculpted stone have been conserved in the interior.

HUAZALINGO ◆ D B1. (*On Route 105, at the same level as Tehuetlán*) The approach route is taxing but is worth the effort, for the church is interesting, and boasts a magnificent baroque altarpiece decorated with excellent paintings. It offers a stunning view of the sierra that makes it impossible not to wonder exactly what force was driving the missionaries in their desire for conquest.

MOLANGO ◆ D B1. (*Farther south, on Route 105*) Here again, there is a breathtaking panoramic view of the sierra, as well as the region's oldest Augustinian mission. The complex was built on a colossal pre-Hispanic ceremonial platform under the supervision of Antonio de la Roa, who was responsible for spreading the

Gospel in this area. The church contains just one nave, in a Spanish Plateresque style, embellished by profuse ornamentation of a markedly indigenous character. The PULPIT, made of sculpted stone, is impressive, as are the elegant colonnades in the monastery's cloisters. The six bays of the immense belltower arcade open up on to the enchanting landscape of the sierra, which from now on is covered by ferns and pines.

SANTA MARÍA XOXOTECO ◆ **D** B1. (*1⅓ miles/2 km from Metzquititlán via a dirt track*) The arid southeast side of the sierra hides a delightful valley whose lushness contrasts with the dryness of the surrounding landscapes. It boasts a modest chapel that attracts few tourists but is well worth a detour on account of its magnificent frescos. These depict a *Last Judgment* remarkable for the capricious fantasy of its treatment of the creation of Eve, the learning of Good and Evil and the expulsion from Paradise – not to mention the startling interpretation of Hell.

Above: *Last Judgment* of Santa Maria Xoxteco

METZTITLÁN ◆ **D** B1. (*Continuing southward, on Route 105, take the left-hand turn to Metztitlán.*) The 15 miles (23 km) separating this village from the main road are made up of a fertile valley under towering ridges – an appropriate preamble to the monastery that stands starkly in the midst of the wild landscape like a fortress embedded in the mountain. The CONVENTO DE LOS SANTOS REYES was built between 1539 and 1560 by Juan de Sevilla and Antonio de la Roa. Its Plateresque façade is crowned by a belltower arcade with seven bays that looms over a complex with an atrium of imposing dimensions. The nave in the church is adorned by five altarpieces with some fine paintings. In the monastery itself, the remains of the original frescos are on display; they rival those of Actopan and Epazoyucan as prime examples of 16th-century Augustinian art.

ATOTONILCO EL GRANDE ◆ **D** B1. (*31 miles/51 km south of Metzquititlán*) The frescos conserved on the stairwell in the convent are unique in Mexico, as they show Saint Augustine surrounded by the leading figures of Greco-Roman philosophy: Socrates, Plato, Aristotle, Pythagoras, Seneca and Cicero – an intriguing collection, in the light of the religious culture of the period.

TLANCHINOL ◆ **D** B1 (*Between Huejutla de Reyes and Molango*) The Tlanchinol church, shrouded in mist, boasts a magnificent belltower arcade with six openings that overlook the wall of the atrium.

MINERAL DEL CHICO
(*about 9⅓ miles/15 km
north of Pachuca*)
◆ **D** B1 is a small
mining town with
paved alleys, situated
in the heart of the
Parque Nacional
Mineral del Chico,
created by Porfirio
Díaz in 1898. The
surrounding area
offers numerous
possibilities for
walks in the cool,
wooded countryside.
MINERAL DEL
MONTE (*7½ miles/
12 km east of
Pachuca*) ◆ **D** B2, also
known as El Real, is
lost in the middle of
the forest. It was built
over a seam of silver
long considered the
richest in the world.
Now spruced up
for tourists, it is
somewhat lacking in
soul, except in its
evocative English-
style cemetery on
the Cerro del Judío.
The owner of this
mine, the Count of
Regla, dug out forty
galleries and built an
underground church.
The silver produced
here was so pure that
the London Stock
Exchange accepted
the seal of Real del
Monte as a guarantee
of 100% silver.

The area around Pachuca

ACTOPAN ◆ **D** B1. (*22 miles/35 km from Pachuca, via Route
85*) SAN NICOLAS DE TOLENTINO is undoubtedly the most
magnificent of all Mexico's monastic complexes, and it
is also the most complete. Its sumptuous architecture is
characterized by finely balanced proportions (*above*).
Particularly striking are the church's belltower (evidence of
a Mudejar influence), the sacristy, the patio and the kitchen
staircase, the pergola in the garden, the water tank and the
refectory, with its coffered vault decorated in Renaissance
style. The extremely varied forms of the windows of the
different structures deserve special mention. The stairwell of
the cloister is adorned with frescos in excellent condition, as
is the open chapel, one of the biggest in Mexico.

IXMIQUILPAN ◆ **D** B1. (*28 miles/44 km further on*) The
Plateresque façade of the IGLESIA DE SAN MIGUEL
ARCÁNGEL is distinguished by paired columns on the lower
level and an attractively decorated opening overlooking the
upper choir. The belltower annex is integrated into the
complex by means of its crown and openings, reminiscent of
a bell tower with arcades. The church contains an interesting
painted frieze mural (1572) showing knights in the form of
eagles and tigers fighting against fantastically shaped
centaurs. In the cloisters in the MONASTERY, which are
topped by a ribbed vault, some frescos still remain.

EPAZOYUCAN ◆ **D** B2. (*Approx. 40 miles/25 km southeast of
Pachuca*) This splendid fortified monastery was built by the
Augustinians (c. 1550–70). There are beautiful carvings on
the arch of the chapel, and stunning 16th-century frescos
(*below*) attributed to Juan Gerson ▲ 293 in the cloisters.

The North

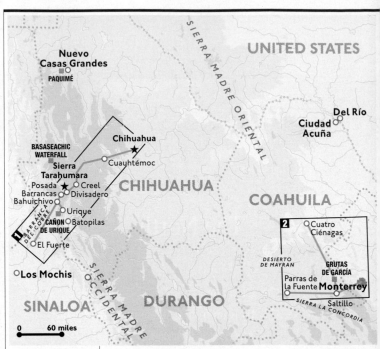

POLITICAL CONFLICTS

It was in the north that Miguel Hidalgo ▲ 356, 370 was finally captured and executed. In the mid-19th century, Benito Juárez ● 27 took shelter in Chihuahua and Ciudad Juárez, from where he organized the resistance to French intervention. Finally, several leading lights of the Revolution ● 36 came from the north and started their struggle there: Madero, Carranza, Villa, Obregón, and others.

The vast northern region of Mexico is crossed diagonally by the country's two biggest mountain ranges: the Sierra Madre Occidental and the Sierra Madre Oriental. This rugged landscape is complemented by a semiarid or desert climate and vegetation – hardly surprising, as, like most deserts on earth, it is close to the Tropic of Cancer. The only exceptions are the few mountainous areas where the altitude permits the growth of coniferous forests and lakes (Sierra Arteaga, in the State of Coahuila to the east, Sierra Tarahumara in Chihuahua and Sierra Sombrerete in Zacatecas, to the west).

DISTINGUISHING FEATURES. Marked as it is by these geographical and climatic characteristics, northern Mexico is radically different from the rest of the country, not only because of its landscapes, flora and wildlife, but also because of its history, population, music and customs. Archeologists make a firm distinction between Mesoamerica and Aridoamerica (the cultural region that embraces the north of Mexico). The ethnic groups in northern Mexico are closer to the 'Redskins' of the United States (on account of their nomadic lifestyle and their physical appearance) than the groups from Mesoamerica. They also live in landscapes that have been used to shoot numerous American and Mexican Westerns (Durango region). Apart from the archeological site of Paquimé ▲ 371, however, the ancestors of the Yaqui, the Seri, the Pima, the Mayo, the Tarahumara, the Tepehua and the Cochimi barely left any traces.

STATES BOTH RICH AND IMMENSE. The north is home to the biggest states in the country: Chihuahua, Sonora, Coahuila, Durango, Nuevo León and San Luis Potosí. These

> 'Mexico! The great, precipitous, dry, savage country,
> with a handsome church in every landscape,
> rising as it were out of nothing.'
>
> D. H. Lawrence, *The Plumed Serpent*

large virgin territories – lacking in indigenous towns, because their population was extremely dispersed and largely nomadic – were the last to be colonized. The Aztecs preferred to extend their empire southward, because they were uninterested in mining and, above all, because they found the peoples there easier to subjugate. Nowadays the northern states number among the most developed in the whole country, on account of not only the richness of their subsoil but also their agricultural and fishing resources and their production and distribution of gas and electricity. As a result, the capital of Nuevo León, Monterrey, has grown into an urban and industrial hub that is expanding at a phenomenal rate. Manufacturing industry (the famous *maquiladoras* ▲ *379*) is also contributing to this acquisition of wealth, and, furthermore, Mexico shares over 1,800 miles (3,000 km) of border with the United States.

THE AMERICAN INFLUENCE. This privilege – or historical tragedy – has given rise to mutual influences on both sides of the border that affect people's way of speaking, dressing and eating. So Mexicans in the north prefer their tortillas made with wheat flour rather than corn, and they also eat more meat. Generally taller than their compatriots, the *norteños* (northerners) also have a paler skin and are enthusiastic wearers of cowboy boots, checked shirts and ten-gallon hats.

THE MYSTERIES OF A UNIQUE NATURAL WORLD. Northern Mexico may show little trace of its ancient cultures but its extraordinary landscapes are fascinating showcases for the inexplicable caprices of nature. NASA trained its astronauts in the Pinacate Desert (Sonora) in 1969 before the Apollo landing, so close are the similarities between this wilderness and the moon. Even more intriguing is the 'Zone of Silence', straddling Durango, Coahuila and Chihuahua, where radio waves cannot be transmitted normally and fragments of meteorites fall with startling regularity.

LOS TIGRES DEL NORTE
This group, with its trademark boots, belts and hats (*below*), has earned unprecedented success with its interpretations of *norteñas*, traditional cowboy songs from northern Mexico ● *57*. The 'Tigers of the North' have toured continually since 1968 and are stars all over the country, with 55 albums (including the 1987 Grammy Award winner *América sin fronteras*), 500 songs and record sales of 30 million to their credit. Their first big hit, the evocatively titled *Contrabanda e Traición* ('Contraband and Treachery') from 1973, fell within the subgenre of the *narcocorrido*, which deals with drug smuggling and other problems associated with the border.

AQUEDUCT
At the junction of Calle Allende and Calle 56, in southeast Chihuahua, an aqueduct built by the Jesuits in the 18th century still stands almost intact.

The capital of Mexico's biggest state is important not only for agriculture and livestock but also for industry and commerce. It is a treasure trove for history lovers: Miguel Hidalgo was executed here, Benito Juárez came here to recruit soldiers and, above all, Pancho Villa established his HQ here during the Revolution. On the architectural front, impressive buildings from both the colonial era and the 19th century bear witness to the wealth of the city, which was founded in 1709 close to the Santa Eulalia mines. There is a tribute to their original owner, Don Antonio Deza y Ullóa, on the Plaza de Armas, opposite the Cathedral.

Historic center ◆ A F4

CHIHUAHUA GATE
This monumental sculpture in the south of the city was created by Sebastián, one of Chihuahua's most remarkable artists, also responsible for the famous yellow metal horse ('El Caballito') on the Paseo de la Reforma ▲ 144).

THE CATHEDRAL. Built between 1726 and 1795, it displays a FAÇADE of pink stone carved in the Churrigueresque style ● 82, flanked by two immense towers. Amid a profusion of sculpted leaves, fruit and flowers, biblical characters look

down from their niches onto the picturesque kiosk on the Plaza de Armas. The INTERIOR, divided into three naves, boasts two superbly realized high altars, one carved from stone and the other from Carrara marble. Chandeliers made with Venetian glass throw light on the massive organ, imported from Germany, and the chapel, with its intriguing Black Christ produced by Mapimí. The MUSEUM OF SACRED ART (in the crypt) displays some fine canvases by Miguel Cabrera ▲ 169 and other major painters of the colonial area.

PALACIO DE GOBIERNO. Built in 1881 but since restored, this occupies part of what was once the Loreto school built by the Jesuits in 1717. Miguel Hidalgo ▲ 356, was shot here on July 30, 1811. A few years later, the SHRINE OF THE MOTHERLAND, complete with an eternal flame, was erected on the exact spot of the revolutionary priest's execution. In the central courtyard, FRESCOS painted by Aarón Piña Mora trace the history of

CASA REDONDA
(*On the outskirts, at the corner of Colón and Escudero, near the Centro de Convenciones*)
An abandoned semicircular railroad shunting yard has been imaginatively converted into a space for contemporary art.

Opposite center: the door of Chihuahua cathedral
Opposite bottom: statue of Pancho Villa
Below: the Quinta Gameros

the region since the Conquest. Opposite the palace, the Plaza Hidalgo revolves around a monument in honor of the hero.

CALABOZO DE HIDALGO. (*In the Federal Palace; entrance in Av. Juárez*) The jail in which Hidalgo was held from April to July 1811 has been preserved under the Federal Palace and turned into a tiny museum displaying documents and eyewitness accounts, but above all the hero's personal possessions – a modest bed, a small table, a candlestick and a crucifix. On the wall, there is a touching farewell in the form of the verses he wrote just a few hours before his execution to thank his jailers for their care.

Bullets and art nouveau

MUSEO DE LA REVOLUCIÓN. (*Calle 10a, 3010*) This museum is set in the house lived in by Pancho Villa at the end of his life, before he was assassinated in 1923 in Hidalgo del Parral. His last wife, Doña Luz Corral de Villa, founded the museum and lived here until her own death in 1981. Visitors can see Villa's office and other rooms opening onto the patio. The highpoint, however, is the 1922 Dodge car in which he was shot, with bullet holes still visible in the rear. Another building is dedicated to the history of the Revolution in the north of the country.

QUINTA GAMEROS. (*Corner of Paseo Bolivar and Calle 4a*) This large European-style middle-class house, topped with a green roof studded with pinnacles, was built by a wealthy mine owner, Don Manuel Gameros, who intended it as a gift for the woman he loved. She became his wife but did not live to see the completion of the building in 1910. During the Revolution, it was requisitioned by the troops of the División del Norte to serve as their HQ. Its interior, with its stained-glass windows, elaborate moldings and a majestic staircase, conceals several art-nouveau rooms (including a fully-fitted bathroom) as well as a furniture collection.

EXCURSION TO PAQUIMÉ ◆ A E2
(*A few miles from Casas Grandes, in the northeast of the State of Chihuahua*)
The most important archeological site in northern Mexico was a flourishing town from the 10th to the early 13th centuries but it was pillaged and burned c. 1340. Little is known of the people who lived here. The remains suggest that it was a crossroads for the Mesoamerican civilizations (there are two ball courts and burial mounds in the form of a serpent) and the cultures of the southeastern United States. The distinguishing features of Paquimé are its colorful pottery and its adobe houses with low T-shape doors to keep out the cold (*below*).

A series of majestic canyons, known by the name of one of them – the 'Barranca del Cobre' (Copper Canyon) – cuts across the Sierra Madre Occidental in an area inhabited by the Tarahumara Indians (hence its other name: 'Sierra Tarahumara'). A conjunction of volcanic and seismic phenomena occurring in the Tertiary era has resulted in a rugged landscape cloven by rivers weaving their way through the foothills of the escarpments. The famous Chihuahua-al-Pacífico train crosses the sierra, connecting Chihuahua with Los Mochis – a journey of over 408 miles (653 km) punctuated by no less than 37 bridges and 86 tunnels. An awesome spectacle is guaranteed by the dizzying views down the plunging rock faces, but it is worth dividing the trip into several stages in order to enjoy the natural beauty of the sierra.

Creel ◆ A F4

(*185 miles/297 km from Chihuahua*) At around 7,545 feet (2,300 m), Creel is both the main town in the Sierra Tarahumara and the best base for exploring the region. It owes its name to the Mexican-American Governor

CONQUERING THE MOUNTAIN
In the 19th century, a railroad was intended to link Chihuahua with Los Mochis (Sinaloa). The first track was laid in the period of the Porfiriat ● *28*, but the work was interrupted by the Revolution. The most difficult section – that of the Sierra Tarahumara – had yet to be finished. Construction was only resumed decades later and the line was finally opened in 1961 by President López Mateos.

of the State, Enrique Creel, who built several sawmills in the region in the early 20th century. A huge white Christ, arms outstretched, watches over the wooden houses, while winding paths disappear into the pine forests, home to several Tarahumara communities. The MUSEO TARAHUMARA outlines the town's historical and ethnographic context.

Excursions from Creel

LAGO ARARECO ◆ **A** F4. (*3 miles/5 km from Creel, heading toward Guacochi*) The shoreline of gray-brownish rocks backed by pines and holm oaks is mirrored in this lake's crystalline waters, and the rugged islets that peep out from the depths seem to form part of the reflection. It is possible to camp by the water; boats, horses and bikes can be hired.
MANANTIAL TERMAL (THERMAL SPRINGS) DE RECOHUATA ◆ **A** F4. (*19 miles/30 km southwest of Creel, at the bottom of the Tararecua Canyon*) The water at the source of the spring is 127°C (185°F), but it runs into a river and cools, creating a warm area ideal for swimmers.

> 'The Tarahumara country is full of signs, forms and natural effigies that do not seem to have been born by chance, as if the gods, whose presence can be felt everywhere here, had wanted to manifest their powers.'
>
> Antonin Artaud, *The Tarahumaras*

CUSÁRARE WATERFALL ◆ A F4. *(9⅓ miles/15 km of road suitable for vehicles and a walk of approx. 2 miles/3 km along a path by the river)* In Rarámuri, the language of the Tarahumaras, *Cusárare* means 'place of eagles'. The waters here plunge 90 feet (28 m) down an escarpment in various shades of ocher, yellow and pink. Not far away, at the foot of a rock formation, a cave contains white wall paintings of hunters with bows and arrows pursuing deer. Much later pictures were painted on top in red, showing a village and its people, domestic animals and a church.

BASAEACHIC WATERFALL ◆ A E4. *(3–4 hours from Creel)* The highest waterfall in Mexico soars up to 1,000 feet (310 m). Its name means 'place of the waterfall or the coyotes'. The waterfall can be seen from the road from Creel, but another road *(more difficult to find; enquire at the site)* leads right to the top, where a 1⅓-mile (2-km) path provides a means of descent; halfway down is the spot known as the 'Ventana' ('window'), with a spectacular side view of the falls.

BATOPILAS ◆ A F5. *(72 miles/115 km from Creel, 5–6 hours in a bus or jeep)* This excursion is worth a detour, both for the journey itself (6,000 ft/1,800 m to the bottom of the canyon) and for the old mining town *(below)*. On the side of the mountain, the road has vantage points over the canyons, before giving way to an interminable but spectacular track hugging the rocks. On this descent into the huge abyss, the pines are replaced by cacti and dry shrubs, while the heat becomes suffocating. Mango and papaya trees, acclimatized to Batopilas , compete with bougainvilleas on the banks of the small river that feeds this oasis. In the late 19th century, the town had a population of 10,000 (now down to 800). Batopilas has preserved the remains of its colonial past: houses with patios, the façade of the Palacio Municipal and the elegant 18th-century church. At the entrance to the town, on the other side of the river, the EX-HACIENDA DE SAN MIGUEL, an imposing ocher-colored brick building, now in ruins, was once the home of a rich American mine owner.

THE MENNONITES IN CUAHTÉMOC *(63 miles/100 km southwest of Chihuahua)* These dissidents of the Reformed Church, followers of the Dutchman Menno Simons (1496–1561), took refuge in the United States (now the Amish of Pennsylvania) and Latin America after being chased out of Prussia, Russia and Canada. The 50,000 Mennonites thought to be in Mexico are divided into fifteen colonies, mainly situated in the north. The most important of these communities is Cuahtémoc. The Mennonites are white and blonde; the men wear dungarees, the women, a dress and a hat with a band. They keep to themselves, speak an archaic German and have their own land and schools. Their lifestyle is based on a rejection of progress inspired by Saint Paul: 'Be content with what they have taught you and with what you are capable of doing.'

🗺 BATOPILAS-URIQUE ON FOOT
You can make the journey between these two canyons on foot in three or four days, accompanied by a guide. It is also possible to hire donkeys or horses in Batopilas to carry your provisions and camping equipment. This hike is only advisable between November and April (the cooler dry season). Pack some warm clothes, as part of the route is at altitude.

MISSION OF THE SANTO ÁNGEL CUSTODIO DE SATEVÓ ◆ A F5. (*4 miles/6 km beyond Batopilas*) This mission's white façade stands out against a striking red-ocher landscape rich in minerals. This 'place of sand', sometimes known as the 'cathedral of the Sierra' or 'the lost Sierra' was built in brick in the 18th century. Behind the wooden door, the interior is austere and in bad condition, but the blue altar and handful of colored statues imbue it with a special atmosphere. The mission was abandoned for decades but is now maintained by the Tarahumara.

Divisadero/Posada Barrancas ◆ A EF4

(*About 1¼ hours from Creel*) The train stops at Divisadero, the junction of three canyons (Cobre, Urique and Tararecua) to allow passengers to enjoy a view that is hard to beat for spectacle. It has often been compared to the Grand Canyon, but the Barranca del Cobre is believed to be deeper. It is possible to stay the night in a hotel in Divisadero, where you will be visited by Tarahumara Indians selling craft goods and regional produce. The canyon provides various possibilities for short hikes, leading to the MESA DEL DIVISADERO, PIEDRA VOLADA, LA ESCALERA or Tarahumara houses and uninhabited caves. The train stops again at POSADA BARRANCAS, 2½ miles (4 km) down the track, where there are more views and plenty of accommodation available (there's a hotel near the station or lodgings in a private house in the nearby village of Areponápuchi).

Below: the Satevó Mission

THE SIERRA TARAHUMARA ★
The train takes 15 hours to cross the Sierra, but the main pleasure lies in interrupting the journey to go on excursions. Reckon on a minimum of 5–6 days.

Bahuichivo/Cerocahui ◆ A E4-5

At the train's next stop, Bahuichivo (*28 miles/46 km from Divisadero*), you can visit (*30 min by pickup truck*) the sleepy village of CEROCAHUI, founded in 1680 by the Jesuit Juan María de Salvatierra, who later built the first mission in Lower California in Loreto ▲ *397*. The exquisite little CHURCH is distinguished by its perfect symmetry: observe

the balance between the masses of its bell tower and its yellow dome. Its cramped interior is adorned with large statues and a fascinating stained-glass window depicting the death of Saint Francis-Xavier off the shores of China. The Jesuit mission stands close to a Tarahumara boarding school. The YEPARÁVO WATERFALL makes a fine setting for a stroll.

The area around Cerocahui

CAÑON DE URIQUE ♦ A E5. (*Access in 4-wheel-drive car only; 2-hr trip. A driver can be hired in the village.*) This canyon (*above and below*), with a drop of 6,165 feet (1,879 m), is the most breathtaking of all. Its proportions can be appreciated before you reach ground level merely by driving along the dizzying road that winds its way along the wall, under the watchful gaze of the vultures circling overhead. As you descend, the heat sets in and coniferous forest gives way to tropical vegetation, replete with banana, avocado and orange trees. At the bottom, the village of Urique, with its tiny square, is engulfed by the natural scenery. As in the case of Batopilas ▲ *373*, its mining industry was developed in the late 19th century; its old windmills can still be seen on the river.

El Fuerte ♦ **A** E5

One of the most spectacular parts of the journey lies between Bahuichivo and Temoris: from the top of a canyon, the train almost imperceptibly follows a 180° curve, going through tunnels all the while, to continue its descent toward the plain of EL FUERTE. This town is an attractive place to stop over at either the beginning or end of the trip. It was founded in 1564 by Don Francisco de Ibarra, the first explorer of the high mountains of the Sierra Madre Occidental. In 1610, a fort was built here to protect the site from raids by the Zuaque and Tehueco Indians. In the 19th century, its mining activity brought prosperity, made evident by its old houses, pretty central square and cathedral.

THE TARAHUMARA AT THE OLYMPICS
The stamina of the Tarahumaras has amazed even the organizers of the Olympic Games! Two Tarahumara, José Torres and Aurelio Terrazas, represented Mexico in the Olympic marathon in Amsterdam in 1928. Even though they crossed the finish line several minutes after the medal winners, they went on running, until an official informed them that the race was over. They could not believe their ears: the 26 miles 385 yards of the marathon struck them as being far too short!

EXCURSION TO ÁLAMOS ♦ A E5 (*130 miles/210 km from Los Mochis, via Navojoa*) This charming little colonial town has largely been restored by Americans, who have turned it into a getaway that offers a respite from the heights of the Sierra Madre.

▲ The Tarahumara Indians

The southeast of the State of Chihuahua, in the heart of the Sierra Madre Occidental, is home to the Tarahumara Indians, or Rarámuri ('feet that run'), as they call themselves. Set apart from the Mesoamerican culture ● *30*, they form part of the Uto-Nahuatl linguistic group ● *40*, like the Huichol ▲ *328*, with whom they share many distinguishing traits. Once nomadic hunter-gatherers, they became more or less sedentary with the arrival of the missionaries (1607), although the increasing scarcity of prey was also a contributing factor. Today they number about 70,000 and mainly live in *rancherías* (hamlets with five to ten families) scattered in the mountains.

THE 'RARAHIPA', A RACE THROUGH THE MOUNTAINS

Each participant must kick a wooden ball the size of a grapefruit, known as a *gomakari*. The runner projects it about 100 feet (30 m) ahead, then catches it up and kicks it again. When the Indians decide to run, it is always the consequence of a challenge thrown down by one runner, or one *ranchería*, to another. The capacity for endurance is at stake here – the longest races can cover distances of around 60 miles (100 km)! Runners repeat the same circuit several times; lines of small stones near the start indicate the number of laps remaining.

CLOSE TO SELF-SUFFICIENCY

The Tarahumara gather edible wild plants, fish in the small rivers (catfish and sardines), hunt deer (now increasingly rare), hares, squirrels and wild turkeys, and grow corn, red beans, squash and chili. In addition, there is a bartering of goods between the high plains and the canyons, particularly with the mestizos: chili, corn, the skins of goats, badgers and raccoons, and small baskets woven with cactus fibers are exchanged for textiles, sugar, salt, coffee and tires (for making sandals).

CLOTHING

The men wear a *zapeta*, a piece of white cotton held around the waist by a thick woolen belt, and a baggy shirt, often white, with a *coyera* (white bandanna) around their forehead and *akaka*, sandals made with tire rubber and leather thongs, on their feet. The women wear a similar type of shirt (but with a narrow cuff) and several flounced, roomy skirts, one on top of the other.

THE PEYOTL CULT AND ANTONIN ARTAUD ● *113*

The Tarahumara refer to *peyotl* ▲ *388*, the little cactus that yields the
strong hallucinogenic extract of mescaline, as *hikuri* or *jikuri*. For them,
it is a sacred plant to be venerated like a god. Its power is feared, and
peyotl is only used by the *sukuruames* (shamans) in the context of
healing rituals. Antonin Artaud, who went to live in the Sierra
Tarahumara in 1936, wrote: 'Peyotl takes the I back to its true sources:
there are no more emotions or outside influences that can lead you
astray from them.'

HOUSING

On the high plateaus,
with their harsh
winters, most of the
houses are made of
pine wood or stone.
In the canyons, the
Tarahumara build
adobe houses, using
unfired earth bricks,
but these structures
are mainly used to
store food: the
majority of the
Indians prefer to
sleep outdoors,
around a log fire.

THE EASTER FESTIVAL

The most important festival of the year was introduced
by the Jesuits in the 18th century, then perpetuated and modified
by the Indians. Its durability can be explained by the fact that it
coincided with the indigenous spring festivals, in which the gods
were asked to bring rain before the sowing season.
On Easter Thursday, families go down into the abandoned missions
in the valleys, where the *tesgüino* (beer made from fermented corn)
flows freely for three days. To the rhythm of drums, the Indians
perform the frenetic 'dance of the devils': the struggle between
Good and Evil, symbolized by their black and white body paint.
Evil is represented by the *fariseos*, who are covered with white clay.

TARAHUMARA TERRITORY

This is spread over 19,000 sq. miles (50,000 sq. km) of the Sierra
Madre Oriental and divided into two distinct geographical areas: the
cold lands of the high plateaus covered with pines and oaks and the
semidesert flanks of the *barrancas* (canyons), whose bottoms
welcome tropical vegetation. Their territory is continually being
eaten away by the lumberjacks and mixed-race *vaqueros* who are
encroaching on their ancestral lands, so the Tarahumara take
refuge in the most inaccessible areas.

**THE SALÓN
DE LA FAMA**
(*Northeast of the
Macroplaza*)
This late-19th-century
bar in Cuauhtémoc
has assembled an
entertaining and
important collection
of souvenirs, writings
and photographs
related to baseball,
which is very popular
in Mexico,
particularly in the
north.

**THE CERRO
DE LA SILLA**
Monterrey's
geographical
situation is striking:
the city is tucked
away in a basin with
a hot, sticky climate,
bordered by the
dry and rugged
mountains of the
Sierra Madre
Oriental. The
Cerro de la Silla
('Hill of the Chair'),
a beautiful craggy
peak visible almost
everywhere, has
become the emblem
of the city.

With its 3.2 million inhabitants, Monterrey is the third
biggest city in Mexico and, obviously, the industrial and
urban nucleus of the region. Founded in the last quarter of
the 16th century, it was the birthplace of the first Mexican
constitution (1824–25) but later fell into the hands of the
Americans for two years (1846–48). It has climbed to second
place in the country's economic league as a result of its
factories, its exports – some of the world's leading glassware
and cement companies are based here – and its state-of-the-
art technology. One indicator of Monterrey's increasing
importance is its designation as the venue for the Forum of
Civilization and Culture in 2007. Monterrey, like most of the
northeast, largely takes its cues from its Texan neighbor and
its lifestyle is highly Americanized. The locals, known as
'Regiomantanos', tend to look down on other Mexicans – the
feeling is often mutual – and are fiercely proud of their
region and their modern city.

La Macroplaza ◆ B D3

HISTORY OF THE SQUARE. Much of the historic colonial
city was knocked down to make way for this square during
the 1980s as part of a typical urban renewal program; 427
buildings were demolished, entire neighborhoods were
declared a danger to public health and countless narrow
streets and small businesses were swept away. The resulting
65-acre (44-ha) expanse is far bigger than Red Square, Saint
Mark's Square or even the Zócalo in Mexico City ▲ *130*. This
monumental space has, however, preserved many of the
distinguishing traits of Latin American city planning: the
concentration of power round a single square and the

marked contrast between the old
and the new. At one end of the
north–south axis stands the
PALACIO DE GOBIERNO of the
state (Nuevo León); at the other
the CITY HALL, built in a
contemporary style in the early
1980s and embellished with
official frescos inside.
MONUMENTS. From one end
to the other, the square boasts
a succession of symbols of
religious, political, financial and
juridical power, passing from the
colonial style to postmodernism.
Particularly outstanding, on the
west side, is the LATIN
AMERICAN TOWER, which rivals
that of Mexico City ▲ *139*, with
its huge Coca-Cola bottle. Near
the PALACIO DE GOBIERNO, a
cobbled section contains statues
of the 19th-century heroes of the
construction of the Mexican
nation (including Juárez ● *27*).
They are overshadowed, further

Opposite: view of the Beacon of Commerce
and Monterrey Cathedral
Below, left and right: the Contemporary Art
Museum (MARCO)

in to the left, by the totemic BEACON OF COMMERCE, a
strip of red wall measuring 220 by 39 feet (70 by 12 m) that
was designed in 1984 by architect Luis Barragán ● 90 for the
centenary of Monterrey's Chamber of Commerce. It is
crowned by a green laser that pinpoints city landmarks at
night. It was declared a national artistic monument by the
National Institute of Fine Arts (INBA) in 2001.

Contemporary Art Museum (MARCO)

The square's main center of interest owes its design to
Ricardo Legoretta, a disciple of Barragán ● 90 who has
become one of the most highly regarded architects in the
whole country. Conceived in a geometric style that draws
inspiration from vernacular themes and color schemes, this
building is made up of a series of interlocking areas that
bestow a feeling of spaciousness on the exhibitions of
contemporary art (which include architecture, decoration,
photography, cinema and literature) by Mexicans as well as a
host of international names (Mies van der Rohe, Josef
Koudelka, Frank Lloyd Wright, Fernando Botero, Pierre
Alechinsky, etc.). It also has a permanent collection of eight
hundred works by local artists. The museum is organized
around a central patio embellished by a fountain and white
balloons that float about, dreamlike, in the air.

Barrio Antiguo

The remains of this historic center lie to the east of the
Macroplaza. Several dozen *cuadras* (blocks) have benefited
from an energetic restoration program that has chased out
most of the former residents. The area is now packed with
trendy bars, restaurants and art galleries. Every Sunday, the
Calle Mina plays host to the 'Corridor of Art', a craft market
with live music, featuring the work of local artists.

REGIONAL CUISINE
Cabrito (kid) is one of
the most typical
dishes in the
northeast. Apart from
eating the *pierna* (leg)
and the *paleta*
(shoulder), intrepid
gourmets can also
sample the *cabeza*
(head) and the
machitos (testicles).

'MAQUILADORAS'
Most of these
factories (*below*),
set up by foreign
groups to assemble
imported parts, are
based in the north of
the country. As they
require a great deal of
manpower, they are
important sources of
jobs: the General
Motors plant in
Saltillo, for example,
employs 4,000 people,
3,800 of them manual
laborers.

**UNIVERSITY OF
THE FUTURE**
The Institute of
Technology and
Higher Education
or TEC (*below*)
takes its inspiration
from the liberal,
entrepreneurial
philosophy of the
American MIT.
The select few who
attend have to pay
a fortune to study
law, engineering,
marketing or political
science in this ultra-
modern setting: state-
of-the-art computer
technology, long-
distance courses live
on screen, and so
forth. The TEC has
thirty-three branches
spread across the
country, with 100,000
students in all (60,000
in Monterrey).

Around Monterrey

Continuing southward, it is possible to ascend the Sierra
Madre Oriental by car, right to the summit of Chipinque.
The road winds some 10 miles (16 km) through the
mountains before reaching a belvedere with a restaurant and
hotel. The view of the city from this height is breathtaking.
THE SIERRA MADRE ORIENTAL ◆ B D3. With its
escarpments (particularly those of the Cumbre de Monterrey
Park, with spectacular sites such as the Tatewari and the
Guitarritas), its canyons and its rapids (which can be
negotiated in a kayak), the Sierra Madre Oriental has won an
international reputation for adventure tourism. Monterrey is
a good starting point for the array of circuits on offer. Hardy
souls can opt for the Matacanes route (12 hours) or the
Hidrofobia circuit (2½ days), which pass through narrow
canyons by skirting their walls and navigating their rivers.
Between Monterrey and Saltillo (*an hour's trip*), a 25-mile
(40-km) excursion leads to the VILLA DE GARCÍA CAVES
(*reached by a funicular train*), which are famous for their
abundance of stalagmites and stalactites, as well as fossils
dating back 60 million years.

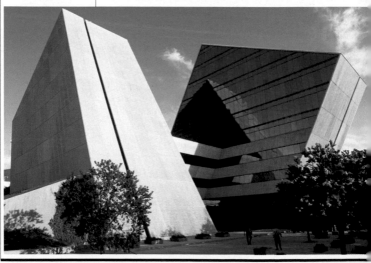

Saltillo ◆ **B** D4

Saltillo, which has a cooler climate than
Monterrey, makes an ideal base for excursions
into the desert. This large industrial city, capital
of the State of Coahuila, has one of the country's
biggest concentrations of *maquiladoras*, especially
in the municipality of Ramos Arizpe. The city has
many customs in common with Texas, which is
hardly surprising since its American neighbor
formed part of Coahuila until 1845.

THE HISTORIC CENTER. Although modest in
size, it is highly attractive, especially above the
PLAZA DE ARMAS (to the south). The city is
thought to have been founded in 1574. The late-
18th-century CATEDRAL DE SANTIAGO (*right*),
dedicated to Saint James, was built with local limestone
and white rock. It mixes three styles: the frontispiece is
unadulterated Churrigueresque baroque ● *82*, while the bell
tower is neoclassical, albeit with Moorish embellishments.
Across the square, the PALACIO DE GOBIERNO, also
neoclassical, is built entirely with imported pink stone.
Saltillo's ALAMEDA (promenade) is considered one of the
prettiest in the whole of Mexico.

BIRD MUSEUM. (*South of the square*) This museum
possesses the biggest collection of stuffed birds in North
America. It is housed in the old Jesuit colonial mission,
which was renovated in the 19th century.

DESERT MUSEUM. The exhibits cover most of northern
Mexico, focusing on the Chihuahua Desert. The cactus
gardens offer a dizzying view of the city sprawl.

The 'desert route'

The region bounded by Saltillo, Monclova and Torreón forms
an arid triangle linked to the Chihuahua Desert, tracing what
is known as the 'desert route'. The RESERVA DE CUATRO
CIÉNAGAS ('four swamps') lies at the foot of the Sierra de la
Fragua, to the west of Monclova, 3–4 hours from both Saltillo
and Monterrey. This 125,000-acre (85,000-ha) protected area
is humid and presents an unusual ecosystem in the heart of
the arid mountains, where the temperature can drop to
17.6°F (–8°C) in winter and reach 113°F (45°C) in summer.

'PAN DE PULQUE'
Pan de pulque is sold
in various forms
(*empanadas, molletes*
and, above all,
semitas); the flour
used for its pastry
contains agave. It is
available from the
Megapan bakeries in
Saltillo and in the
neighboring town of
Ramos Arizpe, where
it originated.

**THE 'POZAS' DE
CUATRO CIÉNAGAS**
These natural
waterholes ▲ *382*
have attracted the
attention of NASA
and various scientists
from all over the
world, as they contain
stromatolites,
fossilized corals made
of cells millions of
years old. They could
be the origin of life on
earth, as they produce
oxygen.

THE CONQUEST OF THE DESERT
The indigenous populations were almost completely exterminated between the 16th and the 19th centuries, during the course of the 'conquest of the desert' initiated by the Spanish and completed by the Mexican government. The Chichimeques, nomads from the north of the country, were never subjugated, however. At the end of the 16th century, the Spanish, despairing of doing away with these cruel 'savages', imported 87 families of Tlaxcalteca Indians – considered far more civilized – from central Mexico to found the village of San Esteban de la Nueva Tlaxcala. The Tlaxcalteca have left numerous marks on the cultural life of Saltillo, particularly their serapes, brightly colored scarves that now form part of the clichéd vision of Mexico.

THE 'POZAS' DE CUATRO CIÉNAGAS ◆ B D2. The *pozas*, around five hundred in number, are natural cavities filled with freshwater, set in soil with a high gypsum content and interlinked by an underwater drainage system. A few of them, on the way out of the village, are filled with warm water and can be used for swimming: LAS PLAYITAS and, further out, LA POZA DE BECERRA, where you can snorkel amid the fish. Two other *pozas* close to the information center are protected but open to visitors: the POZA DE LAS TORTUGAS, with its turtles, and, above all, the stunning POZA AZUL, resembling a Caribbean beach, with its shades of green and blue. The plant and animal life is astonishingly diverse, and some of it is exclusive to this area. Guided tours to the mountains, complete with rock paintings, are also available. By the POZA DE BECERRA, a path leads to the gypsum dunes.

THE GYPSUM DUNES ◆ B D2. Spread over 1,200 acres (800 ha), these dunes (*above*) alongside the Churinze Lagoon are considered the biggest in the world. Here, a rich display of plant and animal life reveals itself: palms, *mezquites* (type of acacia), *huisaches*, *gobernadores*, *zotoles* and cacti; crows, vultures, *aguilillas* (small eagles), ibis and, if you are lucky, wildcats, coyotes, foxes and *mapaches* (wolverines).

Parras de la Fuente ◆ B C4

(*1½ hours west of Saltillo, via Highway 40*) Parras de la Fuente is a delightful little town that seems unchanged since the 17th century. It is set in the heart of an oasis of vines and walnuts that stands out from the desert all around it. Baroque art makes its presence felt in the IGLESIA DE SANTO MADERO, perched on a rock, and the JESUIT COLLEGE OF SAN IGNACIO DE LOYOLA. Many people find that bathing in the crystal-clear yellow *estancos* (pools) – particularly the Estanco de La Luz – is a perfect way to relax.

Baja California

▲ Baja California

UNITED STATES

San Diego
Tijuana
Rosarito
Ensenada
1
DESIERTO
DE ALTAR
Tucson

GULF OF CALIFORNIA

San Quintín
2
Cataviña
San Luis
Gonzaga
3
BAJA
CALIFORNIA
NORTE
BAHÍA DE
LOS ANGELES
Bahía de
los Angeles
San
Borja
Hermosillo
SONORA
SIERRA DE SAN FRANCISCO
Guerrero Negro **4**
LAGUNA
OJO DE
LIEBRE
5 San
Ignacio
Santa
Rosalía
6
Mulegé
DESIERTO DE
VIZCAÍNO
Laguna
San Ignacio
BAHÍA
CONCEPCIÓN
GULF OF CALIFORNIA (MARE DE CORTÉS)

BAJA
CALIFORNIA
SUR
ISLA
CORONADOS
7 Loreto
San Javier
ISLA
EL CARMEN

PACIFIC OCEAN

Ciudad
Insurgentes

ISLA
PARTIDA
ISLA
ESPÍRITU
SANTO
8 Pichilingue
La Paz
9
Todos
Santos
San José del Cabo
Cabo San Lucas
CABO
SAN LUCAS

0   60 miles

A LAND APART
For a long time, the
peninsula was isolated
from the rest of the
country: it only
acquired the status of
a federative state in
1952 (until then it
had been no more
than a territory of the
Mexican Republic
divided into two
districts) and went on
to be split into two
states in 1974. The
long road that runs
along the peninsula
only began to be
paved in 1965 and it
was not until 1973
that the south was
finally connected to
the north.

Baja California was inhabited by various indigenous societies of hunter-gatherers when Cortés – who had heard of a mysterious island abounding in precious pearls – tried to explore it in 1535, starting from the bay that today encloses the city of La Paz. The extreme aridity of the area drove him back. Further expeditions in the 16th and 17th centuries were similarly unproductive.

THE FIRST COLONIALISTS: THE JESUITS. The Jesuits founded their first mission in Loreto in 1697 and went on to establish eighteen more before their expulsion in 1767. The Franciscans and Dominicans then took up the reins in the north of the peninsula and also in Upper California. Many of these missions were short-lived, either because their attempt at self-sufficiency failed, or because of conflicts with the indigenous population.

THE FIRST CIVIL COLONIZATIONS. These were brought about by means of land grants to private citizens, starting in the 19th century; to foreign companies, such as the copper-mining firm El Boleo in Santa Rosalía ▲ 393, and British and American companies in Ensenada; and, in the 20th century, to the saltworks of Guerrero Negro ▲ 391.

Tijuana in 1926

THE PARTITION OF CALIFORNIA. Loreto was the historic capital of California, before the administration divided it into Upper and Lower (Baja) California, and before La Paz subsequently became the capital of the latter. The war with the United States led to the loss of territories in northern Mexico ● *26*, and the new frontier separated the two Californias: the upper part went to the United States, which also coveted the lower part and tried to invade it. When this effort failed, it offered to buy Baja California – to no avail, however, as the area remained in Mexican hands.

A REGION LOOKING TOWARD THE UNITED STATES. In the late 19th century and throughout the 20th, the peninsula's evolution was largely determined by this new frontier and the relationship with the United States. When Prohibition was introduced after World War I, Americans would visit the northern cities of Tijuana and Ensenada to satisfy their thirst for alcohol (as well as for gambling, horse-racing and prostitution). This economy, established with the financial support of American mobsters, brought a new-found prosperity. Despite the closure of the casinos by Cárdenas in 1935, the leisure industry continued to thrive right through World War II, taking advantage of both the soldiers posted in the military base in San Diego and the smuggling of rationed products to the United States. Sustained migration across the border also prompted a substantial increase in the population; the flow started in 1880 and became massive in the 1940s, when the Mexican border towns served as staging posts. The demographic boom in Tijuana – from a small ranch town in 1889 to a city of 1.5 million today – is the archetypal example of this growth along the frontier. These days, the peninsula's economy mainly looks outward, on the basis of its dynamic trading relationship with the United States (it was a free trade zone for the entire 20th century) and its export industry, headed by the famous *maquiladoras* ▲ *379*, which are mainly concentrated by the frontier. Tourism provides another source of income.

A DRUG CORRIDOR
Large-scale drug smuggling – much of which now passes through Tijuana – is the logical consequence of the demand of the enormous American market, particularly California.

HERE'S WHAT I FELL INTO IN TIJUANA MEXICO

THE FRONTIER WALL
(*From the city center, head toward the airport. At the top of the hill, the road runs between the runways, to the right, and the wall, on the left.*) Ever since the construction of a second wall, illegal immigrants have ceased to cross the border from Tijuana but instead go further east, to steep canyons in desert areas, where the crossing is highly dangerous, or even fatal. A monument recalls this harsh reality: large crosses represent the victims of the frontier wall.

Tijuana ◆ A A1

In the north, this sprawling city hugs the frontier, marked by a corrugated-iron wall (*opposite*) taken from the fuselage of American warplanes used in the first Gulf War in 1991. In 1993 this was reinforced by a second wall of concrete slabs. In Playas, on the sea shore, the concrete wall divides the beach and plunges into the Pacific for a hundred yards, thereby extending the demarcation line into the sea.

THE OLD CENTER. Close to the main border post, the old center revolves around the AVENIDA REVOLUCIÓN, with its bars, nightclubs, souvenir stores selling craft goods of dubious authenticity and countless pharmacies aimed at American customers (medicines are easier to obtain and less expensive). The neo-Mozarabic JAI ALAI dates from 1925 and is a rare relic of that era (the famous casino burned down). Heading toward CALLE CONSTITUCIÓN, you will enter the city center, a hive of commercial activity (where few Americans venture) and the hub of the collective transport system, packed in the rush hour and crisscrossed by taxis and buses spewing black smoke. Tijuana is one of the few Mexican cities without a *zócalo*, as its cathedral stands in a simple street (*Calle Niños Héroes, between 1st and 2nd streets*), but the square of the PARQUE GUERRERO (*between 3rd Street and Calle F. Mártinez*), with its small garden, is imbued with all the provincial charm of a Mexican town.

THE MODERN CENTER. The Zona del Río, dominated by banks and shopping malls, is worth visiting for the CECUT. This cultural center, which opened in 1982, is an enormous

'TIJUANA LA HORRIBLE'
A visit to the Zona Norte (best seen at night, because of the atmosphere) represents a walk on the wild side of Tijuana. Right next to the frontier, small, recently renovated houses rub shoulders with exotically named nightclubs such as the Sans-Souci and the Manhattan. The city's bad reputation is derived from these streets teeming with prostitutes, transvestites, musicians and striptease bars. This is 'Tijuana la horrible'.

sphere containing a movie theater with a giant, 180°
panoramic screen. It also houses the MUSEO DE LAS
CALIFORNIAS, an excellent introduction to the history of the
peninsula through its missions and cave paintings.
VINICOLA L.Á. CETTO. Baja California is also a land of
wines. This company was founded by Don Angelo Cetto, an
Italian who emigrated to the United States in 1926, and it is
now run by his grandson. Its vineyards are in the nearby Valle
de Guadalupe. There are guided tours and wine tastings.

South of Tijuana

(*Take the Mex 1D turnpike.*) The panoramic freeway follows
the rocky coastline. A stop is called for at the MIRADOR, a
superb vantage point with a dizzying view down the cliffs,
before you make the descent to Ensenada Bay: in fine
weather, dolphins can be seen, and whales may appear
in the winter months.
FOX STUDIOS ◆ AA1. (*Just after passing Rosarito, take the
Popotla/La Paloma exit.*) These movie studios on the shores
of the ocean are currently the biggest in the world. They were
specially built to shoot *Titanic* (1997) and have since been
used for several other aquatic super-productions (*Pearl
Harbor, Master and Commander*, as well as some scenes from
the James Bond movie *Tomorrow Never Dies*). Alongside the
studio, the FOXPLORATION theme park delights children
with its Titanic Museum and interactive games revealing
the secrets of special effects and makeup. This beacon of
the movie industry has allowed Tijuana to recover some
of the glory of the 1920s and 1930s, when Hollywood stars
such as Rita Hayworth held court in the bars on Avenida
Revolución. After leaving the studio complex, stop off in
PUERTO NUEVO (follow the exit signposted on the highway)
to eat lobster.
ENSENADA ◆ AA1. Once the road reaches Ensenada, it
sweeps along the port, where an array of cheap restaurants
serve the famous *tacos de pescado* in front of the market.
Opposite the port, the cultural and civic center RIVIERA DEL
PACÍFICO – formerly a casino – occupies a large white
building typical of the neocolonial Californian style. The city
center, drawn up according to a grid plan inspired by the
neighboring American cities, is far more laid-back than that
of Tijuana and its tourist facilities cater to all the family,

**VALLE DE
GUADALUPE ◆ A** A1
(*Before entering
Ensenada, turn off in
the direction of
Tecate.*) Heading
inland, the Valle de
Guadalupe is the
biggest wine-making
region in Mexico.
Although the vines
and olive trees lining
the roads recall the
Mediterranean,
the vineyards are
designed on an
American scale:
the entire valley is
covered with acres
of vines, stretching
right up to the
mountains to the east.
The wine industry
has encouraged
an interest in
gastronomy, as
evidenced by the
recent opening of
several sophisticated
restaurants and stores
selling local produce.

▲ The Mexican deserts

CHAPARRAL BIRD
This earthbound cuckoo rarely flies and is
an indefatigable runner – hence its Spanish
name *correcaminos* (roadrunner).

The Mexican deserts, known locally as the *matorral*, account for
around 40% of the country's territory. These vast areas are
extremely diverse, but their common denominator is always
aridity. Generally, the vegetation does not grow above 3 feet
(1 m), although some isolated species can surpass 20 feet (6 m).
Plants tend to grow far apart from each other, leaving large, bare
spaces in between. Most of the species in these deserts are native
to Mexico and the southern United States.

**REDHEADED
URUBU**
It is not unusual to
see dozens of these
vultures circling
overhead, on the
lookout for carrion or
human refuse.

MOUNTAIN DESERT
(*Above*: Wirikuta Desert, State of San Luis Potosí)
In central Mexico, the cold areas deprived of rainfall in the
shadow of the Sierra Madre Oriental display typical desert
vegetation. Plants do not grow high and there are many species of
round, thorny cacti.

PEYOTE
The uninitiated will
have great problems
in finding this
legendary
hallucinogenic cactus
▲ 377. Its globular
shape, dull coloring
and small size make it
look like a pebble,
except when a flower
betrays its presence.

AGAVE
After living for
several years, this
plant produces a
spectacular bloom
and then dies ▲ 324.

'NOPAL'
It is possible to eat
the young prickly
leaves (*nopales*) and
fruit (*tunas*) of this
well-known cactus
● 67.

**ECHINOCACTUS
(OR MOTHER-IN-
LAW'S CUSHION)**
This fleshy, globular
cactus can grow to
heights of 10 feet
(3 m) in the mountain
deserts in central
Mexico. Its long, stiff
thorns protect it from
herbivores.

TARANTULA
Several thousand species of these spiders can
be found in the Tropics. They often live in a
burrow, where they lie in wait for their prey.
Their powerful fangs inject a poison that is
painful but not deadly to humans.

THE NORTHWEST (*Above*: landscape in Baja California)
This desert is endowed with a highly distinctive physiognomy, studded with trees over 33 feet (10 m) high but generally lacking in shrubs and grasses. The saguaro (candelabra cactus), yucca and fouquieria, with only a few, irregular branches, give these landscapes a curiously disjointed appearance. These species grow very slowly: a saguaro, for example, only reaches full maturity after 150 to 200 years.

THE VALLEYS OF TEHUACÁN AND CUICATLÁN
These valleys in the region of Puebla-Oaxaca ▲ *293* (*above*) contain Mexico's southernmost deserts. Here, the scattered cereus cacti and candelabras thrust their stems, gorged with water, straight up to the sky and dominate a shrubby layer of thorny, microphyllous plants. This region is the setting for several archeological studies investigating the origins of corn.

COYOTE
This animal is capable of changing its behavior, diet and social relationships to survive in a wide range of habitats, which are sometimes very hostile.

RATTLESNAKE
When a rattlesnake senses danger, it shakes its tail. The rattle is a signal to run fast!

FOUQUIERIA
This spiny, crassulaceous tree is only found in the deserts of northern Mexico. Its leaves drop off quickly in dry spells, but reappear just as quickly after rain (in a mere 72 hours).

VALLE DE LOS CIRIOS ★
In order to fully appreciate this fascinating lunar landscape, it is advisable to make a stopover in Cataviña.

Toward the Desierto Central

(*Via the 'Mex 1' or 'Transpeninsular', which extends to La Paz*)
Up to San Quintín, the road is largely governed by trucks carrying fruit and vegetables (especially tomatoes) from the huge San Quintín Valley to California. The towns on the way, with their dusty streets of beaten earth, are unremarkable.
SAN QUINTÍN ◆ A A2. (*100 miles/160 km from Ensenada. The road is signposted shortly after Lázaro Cárdenas.*) The Muelle Viejo (Old Port) of San Quintín is tucked into a quiet, isolated bay protected by an extinct volcano. After San Quintín, the road follows the coast before heading inland up to the central plateau.
VALLE DE LOS CIRIOS ◆ A B3. Some 100 miles (160 km) after San Quintín there begins the astonishing landscape of the Desierto Central, which lies between San Agustín and Punta Prieta. The Transpeninsular stretches out of view through a forest of cacti. The emblematic *cardón* (candelabra cactus) – often surpassing 15 feet (5 m) in height – and a colorful array of other species share the stage with the real star of the scene: the *Idria columnaris*, popularly known as *cirio* (cereus) ▲ *388*. Belonging to the north of the peninsula, this cactus (*above*) resembles a tapered yellowing tree trunk, sometimes supplemented by branches pointing skyward. Its shaft is covered with thorny protuberances and its summit sprouts flowers in summer, resembling a canopy of russet leaves. The best way to enjoy this startling landscape is by making a stopover in CATAVIÑA.

Excursions on the Mar de Cortés

SAN LUIS GONZAGA ◆ A B2-3. (*40 miles/59 km from the Transpeninsular, via a serviceable dirt road, signposted just opposite a tire repair store*) The road cuts through a wild, arid landscape before reaching the sea, where the blue-green water contrasts with the red of the stone. The small bay, protected by the rocky islands of the Gulf of California, plays

THE MISSIONS
(*Four-wheel-drive vehicles can reach Santa Borja by taking the track leading from Km 44 of the Bahía de los Ángeles road.*)
The outskirts of Bahía de los Ángeles boast the only two missions to be preserved in the State of Baja California Norte: San Francisco de Borja (1762) and Santa Gertrudis. All the others, built in adobe, are in ruins. The latter was first constructed in adobe by the Jesuits in 1752, but was subsequently rebuilt in stone by the Dominicans in 1796. It was finally abandoned in 1822.

SEAFOOD
The San Quintín region is a major supplier of oysters. The seaside restaurants
offer numerous specialties made with shellfish or crab's pincers and legs
(*head in the direction of the Muelle Viejo [Old Port] and the Molino Viejo
[Old Windmill] to the restaurants* Cielito Lindo *or* La Pinta).

host to San Luis Gonzaga, a village with a touch of the Wild West, where Americans have built houses around their old trailers.
BAHÍA DE LOS ÁNGELES ◆ A B3. *(45 miles/67 km from the Transpeninsular, via an asphalt road)* The descent to the bay offers hints of the blue sea, glimpsed between the red and ocher hills bristling with cacti, before throwing open views of countless

islets enclosed by rocky cliffs. Like San Luis Gonzaga, this old fishing village has taken in American settlers: some have opened a handful of hotels, while others live a more hand-to-mouth existence in improvised housing.

Guerrero Negro ◆ A B4

The 28th parallel marks the separation between the states of Baja California Norte and Baja California Sur. Amid the stark, flat expanse of the Desierto de Vizcaíno stands Guerrero Negro, an industrial town lashed by winds, with dark volcanic mountains on its horizons. The town's life revolves around the salt beds, which account for 70% of the local economy. The only reason to stop here is the nearby lagoon known as 'Ojo de Liebre' ('Hare's Eye'), which offers visitors a chance to observe whales at close quarters.
LAGUNA OJO DE LIEBRE ◆ A B4. *(Signposted on the right on the road heading south)* Gray whales come to breed in this lagoon – the biggest on the peninsula – between December and April, although they arc most abundant in February and March. Boat trips *(departure from Guerrero Negro, or directly from the shores of the lagoon)* take you to the middle of the lagoon, where it is not unusual for a female to approach the boat followed by her newly born cub; some lucky visitors may even be able to touch one.

THE GRAY WHALE
This animal (*above*) undertakes an extremely long migration, from the lagoons of Baja California, where it breeds in winter, to the Bering Sea, where it feeds in summer. The Laguna Ojo de Liebre was discovered in the mid-19th century by whale hunters, who threw themselves into their work with such gusto that the species came to the verge of extinction. In 1947, the gray whale came under the protection of the International Whaling Commission, and the Mexican government went on to classify the lagoon as a national park.

Bahía de Los Ángeles

PERMITS
A permit from the
National Institute of
Anthropology and
History is required
to visit the cave
paintings dotted
across the state.
This can be issued
in any village, which
will also furnish you
with a guide and
provisions.

SAN IGNACIO ★
Travelers from the
arid Transpeninsular
will be relieved to
encounter here all
the exuberance and
charm of a pueblo
with an atmosphere
that is distinctively
Mexican.

The San Ignacio de
Kadakaamán mission.

San Ignacio ◆ A C4

(*95 miles/142 km south of Guerrero Negro, via the
Transpeninsular*) On the approach to this fertile valley, the
aridity of the desert gradually gives way to an oasis, washed
by the waters of the San Ignacio River (*above*). Bordered by
high, dense palm groves, fruit trees and reeds, it has acquired
the indigenous name Kada Kaaman, or 'river of clumps of
reeds'. Arriving in the pueblo, you come to a square shaded
by large fig trees and, as in all Mexican villages, furnished
with a small central kiosk, which serves as the destination for
the inhabitants' nighttime promenade.

MISIÓN SAN IGNACIO DE KADAKAAMÁN. This was
founded by the Jesuits in 1728 and finally finished in 1786.
Unlike most of the missions on the peninsula, its magnificent
façade sculpted out of volcanic stone has survived the
centuries intact, complete with its four statues in niches and
its bell. Inside, visitors can admire a 17th-century altarpiece
made of gilded wood and embellished with oil paintings and,
in the center, the meticulously executed multicolored statue
of the village's patron, Saint Ignatius of Loyola. The mission
now houses the small MUSEUM OF CAVE PAINTINGS, which
contains displays of photographs, as well as archeological
remains and samples of the region's prehistoric art.

EIFFEL IN MEXICO
The Iglesia Santa Bárbara de Santa Rosalía (*below*) is a movable metal church designed by
Gustave Eiffel for the Paris Universal Exhibition in 1889 and later sent in pieces to Santa
Rosalía in 1895, for reasons that remain obscure. Whatever the explanation, this symbol of
modernity is of architectural interest for its body made of riveted metal sheets, its small clock
tower and its vault in the form of an upturned ship's hull.

The area around San Ignacio

LAGUNA SAN IGNACIO ◆ **A** B5. (*Around 40 miles/60 km to
the southwest of the town, via a dirt road in poor condition*)
This lagoon provides another natural refuge for the gray
whale ▲ *391*, which comes here to frolic with its young from
January to March, attracted by the warm waters.

**◪ CAVE PAINTINGS IN THE SIERRA DE SAN
FRANCISCO** ◆ **A** C4. (*Accessible in a 4-wheel-drive vehicle,
via a winding dirt road leading from the main road, 30 miles/
44 km north of San Ignacio to San Francisco; from there it is a
climb of about 25 miles/40 km by foot or by mule, which will
take around 4 hours.*) The climb from San Francisco down to
the CAÑON SAN PABLO is through impressive wild scenery
that alternates rock faces with dizzying gorges. The area is
dotted with cacti and lined with streams bordered by thick
palm groves. At the bottom lies the site of the CUEVA
PINTADA ('Painted Cavern'), with its impressive wall
490 feet (150 m) long and 30 feet (27 ft) high, adorned
with hundreds of human figures with raised arms, wearing
strange headdresses and grouped in hunting scenes. These
are complemented by animals, such as deer, rams and birds,
painted in red, black, yellow and white. Nearby, you can
also see the paintings in the CUEVA DEL RATÓN (the most
accessible), as well as those in the caves of EL PALMARITO I
and II and LA SERPIENTE ▲ *394*.

Santa Rosalía ◆ **A** C4

(*24 miles/35 km to the south, on the Transpeninsular*) On the
way here you'll get a good view of the Gulf of California.
Santa Rosalía, tucked between two mountains, looks nothing
like any other town on the peninsula or even in Mexico.
It has been marked by the presence of the French, who were
involved in its foundation in
1885, when El Boleo began to
mine copper here. Its unusual
but homogenous architecture
comprises colorful planked
houses with sloping roofs and
long verandahs. These come in
modest versions in the town
center and as opulent mansions
for the bosses on the Mesa
Francia ('French Plateau'). This
is also the site of the MUSEO, set
in the former offices of the
mining company. Also worth
noting are the Hotel Central,
Hotel Francés, the Palacio
Municipal, the Mahatma Gandhi
library, the House of Culture,
the El Boleo *panadería* (bakery)
and the Iglesia Santa Bárbara.
The old premises of the mines
and foundry can be seen on the
sea front.

EL BOLEO
In 1885, Porfirio
Díaz ● 28 signed a
contract with a
French company
exonerating it from
all taxes and all
customs duties on the
imported materials
required to set up its
business on this
plateau, where copper
deposits in the form
of balls (*boleos*) had
been found. In
exchange, the French
firm committed itself
to building a town,
supplying it with
water and attracting
settlers to this
parched land. El
Boleo was a thriving
concern in the early
years of the 20th
century, when it
provided 80% of all
the copper consumed
in Mexico. After the
Revolution, however,
the company slumped
into a long decline
that was only ended
by its sale. The mines
closed for good in
1985.

Below: Iglesia Santa
Bárbara
Bottom: house in
Santa Rosalía

From the southern tip of the peninsula right up to the American border, Baja California boasts one of the most exceptional legacies of cave paintings in the world. There are literally hundreds of sites with paintings or even engravings on the walls. The vast wealth of this heritage, hidden in the heart of an arid, inhospitable landscape, began to be explored in the 18th century. The most characteristic features of these sites are their inaccessibility, the large dimensions of certain figures (the Cueva Pintada, El Brinco and San Gregorio) and the precision of the compositions (El Batequi, Palmarito, El Serpiente). UNESCO has listed some of the caves in the Sierra de San Francisco, in the heart of the Reserva del Vizcaíno.

AN ARRAY OF SITES

Central Baja California – the sierras of San Francisco, San Borja, San Juan and Guadalupe – are particularly rich in monumental paintings, but countless examples of cave paintings can be found in the rest of the peninsula: paintings and engravings in the Sierra de la Rumorosa, to the north, and paintings on Cape San Lucas, particularly in Rancho Buena Vista and Punta Alamo.

Above: painted wall in Cataviña
Below: the Sierra de San Francisco

THE ICONOGRAPHIC REPERTORY

Apart from the simple geometric forms (lines and dots), most of the paintings display complex compositions featuring both human and animal figures (birds, quadrupeds, marine animals, snakes, and so forth). The most frequent subject is hunting scenes, which maybe served a propitiatory role in the attainment of food (game), but war scenes are not uncommon, as in San Borjitas (Sierra de Guadalupe). It is also possible that some artworks evoke the 'movements' of the sun.

OF BEASTS AND MEN

The deer drawn in thin, elegant lines in the Cueva de la Trinidad (Sierra de Guadalupe) suggest a herd led by a dominant male, while a sense of depth is created by the positioning of the females. At Palmarito (Sierra de San Francisco), the animals recall the bas-reliefs on the Gate of the Lionesses in Mycenae. The Cueva de la Serpiente (*above*) in Sierra de San Francisco, one of the most elaborate conceptually, is adorned with two huge reptiles with deer heads, around which are dozens of anthropomorphic figures with horned headdresses, evoking a brotherhood worshipping a mythological being.

DATING

Carbon 14 tests have established the date of a painting in San Borjitas as 5,500 BC. This finding means that the monumental paintings of Baja California are among the oldest examples of the genre found anywhere in the world. Not all the sites on the peninsula have been subjected to such dating tests, however, and it could be that some paintings are even older.

Right: Cueva de las Flechas (arrows) and Cueva Pintada

THE ANIMAL MASTER OF EL BATEQUI

El Batequi (Sierra de San Francisco) has given rise to a hypothesis of a belief in an 'animal master'. The crazy parade of various types of quadrupeds does indeed seem to be controlled by a human figure. The same wall depicts a female figure, recognizable by her breasts, and another male character with a corned headdress.

PIGMENTS

Manganese was used for black, hematite for red and ocher, and limestone for white.

BODY PAINTING AND COLOR SCHEMES

Body painting was a deeply rooted custom on the peninsula. The anthropomorphic figures reflect this tradition. Red and black were most widely used, often in combination, in either a vertical or horizontal arrangement. Although the symbolism of these colors remains uncertain, it seems to correspond to the principle of the *coincidentia oppositorum* (conciliation of opposites). Red and black may have been chosen to represent heat and cold in the body.

The oasis of Mulegé

Mulegé ◆ **A** C5

(*42 miles/63 km south of Santa Rosalía*) This is one of the oldest settlements in the region. Its name means 'river between two rocks' in the local language, and, in effect, Mulegé is an oasis between two arid massifs, separated by the meandering Santa Rosalía de Mulegé River, which flows past reeds and high palm trees into the transparent waters of the Mar de Cortés. Mulegé has adapted to the demands of tourism. In its restaurant, be sure to try the traditional *almejas* (clams), steamed with butter and garlic and garnished with coriander.

MISIÓN DE SANTA ROSALÍA. This mission, bounded by cacti, was founded by the Jesuits in 1705 and finally completed in 1766. Set just above a coastal river, it seems an integral part of the dry, mineral landscape all around it. Its rough, blind, dark stone walls require constant maintenance on account of the humidity.

The area around Mulegé

MULEGÉ'S OLD PRISON
The building erected in 1907 on the top of the hill, opposite the mission, served as a jail until the 1960s. It was known as 'the prison without gates', as its inmates could leave in the morning to work in the village and return at the end of the day.

CUEVAS DE SAN BORJITAS. (*Head 20 miles/30 km northward, then follow a winding track for a further 23 miles/ 35 km; a four-wheel-drive vehicle is highly recommended.*) Climb on foot, through the rocks, cacti and giant thistles, up to a cave 65 feet (20 m) deep, 13 feet (4 m) high and 146 feet (45 m) wide, with a total of 95 paintings, including the oldest known figurative representation in the Americas: a male figure with outstretched arms and a torso pierced with arrows and spears. It measures over 6½ feet (2 m) high and is painted in two vertical sections of red and black. Animals – quadrupeds and fish – are also depicted. Visitors to the site require an authorization from the INAH office in Mulegé, as well as the services of a good guide.

Bahía Concepción ◆ **A** C5

(*About 50 miles/80 km south of Mulegé*) The Transpeninsular provides a stunning panoramic view of this magnificent bay, closed off by a tongue of land, while the crystalline water laps against the thin strips of pale sand at the foot of the dry, red rocks. A few islets, dotted here and there close to the shore, add a delightful counterpoint to the landscape. The calm, warm water proves irresistible to swimmers, but it is also good for diving or snorkeling to observe the schools of multicolored fish. Most of the beaches offer basic camping facilities, in the form of rented *palapas* (huts with a palm roof). From north to south, the outstanding beaches include SANTISPAC (with a view taking in the entire bay),

The Transpeninsular,
running alongside
Bahía Concepción

ESCONDIDA, EL BURRO, EL COYOTE, BUENAVENTURA and
PLAYA REQUESÓN, with its photogenic bank of pale sand.

Loreto and its bay ◆ A C5

(*84 miles/135 km south of Mulegé*) The landscape begins to
acquire the characteristics of a desert, with vast plains dotted
with enormous cacti stretching for miles. This area, centered
on Loreto, sets up striking contrasts between the imposing
Sierra de la Giganta, the desert and the blue waters of the
Mar de Cortés, studded with the four islands of Coronado,
Carmel, Montserrat and Danzante. Once in Loreto, the
partially pedestrianized Avenida Salvatierra will lead you
into the tourist area. To the north, the *zócalo*, with its fig
trees and central kiosk, is bounded by the Palacio Municipal,
built in traditional Mexican style.
MISIÓN DE NUESTRA SEÑORA DE LORETO. This
magnificent building seems to be resisting the harsh climatic
conditions with stoicism. It has preserved its gilded wooden
altarpiece adorned with five oil paintings, along with its bell,
its crucifix, its Way of the Cross and its six other paintings; all
these date from the 17th century. The rooms lining the
cloister now house the MUSEO DE LAS MISIONES.

The Transpeninsular,
running alongside
Bahía Concepción

Near Loreto

The Misión San Javier

PEARLS FROM THE MAR DE CORTÉS
The explorers who discovered the islands in the Gulf of California in the first half of the 16th century soon realized that the waters contained huge banks of pearl oysters. The Isla del Espíritu Santo became known as the 'Island of Pearls' because of its extraordinary abundance of oysters, which also yielded the highly coveted black pearl. Californian pearls were in such demand that the banks were over-exploited and the trade ceased to be viable. In the late 1930s, the banks of pearl oysters were decimated by a mysterious disease.

THE BAY. Continue on foot to the *malecón* (seafront), with its small marinas and superb views of the Mar de Cortés. The bay's biodiversity has led it to be classified as a protected national marine park, spread over 775 sq. miles (2,007 sq. km). You can take a boat trip to the ISLA CORONADO to observe its colonies of sealions and birds, as well as visiting the abandoned saltworks of the ISLA DEL CARMEL, once a haven for pearl divers. The transparent bays offer divers the chance to see thousands of multicolored fish.

MISIÓN SAN JAVIER ◆ A C5. (*40 miles/65 km southwest of Loreto, via a dirt track open to vehicles*) The delightful road ascending the red-ocher Sierra Giganta, dotted with *cardones* and shrubs, runs alongside a small river lined with palm trees, gradually climbing to the mission and village of San Javier that nestles in the shadows of high mountains. The first settlers called the spot Viggé Biaundó ('high land above the gorges'), and it constitutes a small oasis amid arid mountain slopes. Its entrance is still guarded by a large stone colonial cross. The impressive mission, built by the Jesuits with black stone (1744–59), stands at the end of the village's

only street, flanked by white adobe houses with palm roofs. This dry, rugged setting has allowed the mission to survive better than most both the passing of time and the fierce sun of the desert. It has preserved a gilded altarpiece adorned with five oil paintings, a crucifix and two sculptures: one of Saint Xavier, the patron of the village, and another of the Virgin of Guadalupe. All the decor, along with its three bells (still in place), dates from the 17th century.

Statue of Christ in front of Saint Ignatius in the San Javier mission

La Paz ◆ A D6

For a long time, the capital of the State of Baja California Sur depended on the pearl industry. It now boasts a university and enjoys thriving shipping and commercial links with the nearby mainland; as a result, it does not revolve around tourism alone and has retained an authentic Mexican atmosphere. In the main square, the benches are always occupied, vendors of lottery tickets proclaim their presence and street traders hawk their *tacos*. The spectacular sunsets over the Mar de Cortés invite passersby to linger in wonderment on the recently restored *malecón*.

DISCOVERING THE OLD CITY. In the main square, the CATHEDRAL, built in 1861, displays 18th-century paintings brought here from other Jesuit missions. The square is lined by various colonial-style buildings, notably the PALACIO DEL GOBIERNO (1881), which contains the library of the history of the Californias. The MUSEO REGIONAL DE ANTROPOLOGÍA E HISTORIA DE BAJA CALIFORNIA SUR *corner of Calles Altamirano and 5 de Mayo)* is a mine of information on, among other things, 19th-century buccaneers and relations with the United States.

THE BEACHES. *(To the north of the city, via an asphalt road)* The bay of La Paz is closed off by a small peninsula, which is studded with beautiful beaches. The clean sea and white sand attract Mexican families at weekends and during school vacations; at these times, the *palapas* and refreshment stalls do a roaring trade. The first beach after the city, COROMUEL, is complemented by a small dolphinarium, making it particularly popular. On the way to Pichilingue (the departure point for ferries to the continent), the prettiest beach of all, TESORO, is tucked into the end of a tiny creek. After that come BALANDRA and TECOLOTE: the former is free of all infrastructure, while the second is a center for nautical activities. Beware! The other side of the peninsula, beyond Tecolote, is swept by dangerous tides.

The *malecón* in La Paz

ISLANDS IN THE BAY
(Rent a boat on Playa Tecolote) The ISLA DEL ESPÍRITU SANTO, 18 miles (29 km) offshore from La Paz, hides creeks with white sand that provide sanctuary for the red-tailed falcon and the gray heron, as well as sealions and numerous reptiles and rodents. Close by, to the northwest, the small island of PARTIDA is also home to colonies of sealions. Out in the open sea, shipwrecks have created artificial reefs that attract thousands of vividly colored fish, to the delight of divers and snorkelers.

▲ Baja California

Below: Hotel Western Regina, Los Cabos
Bottom: El Arco

TODOS SANTOS
◆ **A** A6
(*To the northwest of Cabo San Lucas*)
Several Americans have chosen Todos Santos as their home or getaway, attracted by the peaceful, leisurely lifestyle. Turning their back on the hubbub of 'Cabo', they have restored the colonial houses on this former missionary site and given birth to a luxurious hideout. A series of beautiful beaches extend to the south, but they can be dangerous for swimmers.

Los Cabos ◆ **A** AB6

The far south of the peninsula has been taken over by one of Mexico's most important tourist complexes, Los Cabos, which is made up of San José del Cabo, to the east, Cabo San Lucas, to the west, with the tourist corridor running between them.

SAN JOSÉ DEL CABO ◆ **A** A6. This official center of the municipality is a quiet community on the edge of the Mar de Cortés, at the mouth of the San José River; its clusters of reeds and soaring palms make it an oasis of greenery. The town has retained much of its colonial charm, thanks to its central square and streets lined with old, Spanish-style houses. The seafront, in contrast, has been endowed with touristy shops and restaurants and the usual modern beach facilities.

THE CORRIDOR TURÍSTICO. Large hotels, campsites for trailers and magnificent golf courses are spread over 18 miles (29 km) of sandy beaches washed by the warm waters of the Gulf of California, with the outlines of enormous cacti scattered over the desert to the rear.

CABO SAN LUCAS ◆ **A** A6. The nucleus of this resort complex is undoubtedly the most Americanized town on the peninsula, complete with shopping malls, luxury hotels, marinas, golf courses and intense, uninhibited revelry until dawn – all within the context of apparently unbridled property development. Apart from the frenetic nightlife, most of the activities on offer to visitors are linked to the sea. A boat can be rented in the port to visit EL ARCO, a rocky arch known as the 'Window on the Pacific'. Nearby, the PLAYA DEL AMOR is bathed on one side by the calm water of the Mar de Cortés, on the other by the livelier waves of the Pacific.

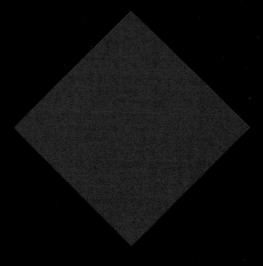

Practical information

◆ BEFORE YOU GO

The symbol ◆ refers to the practical information pages.

USEFUL ADDRESSES

→ IN THE US

■ **EMBASSY OF MEXICO**
1911 Pennsylvania Ave, NW
Washington, D.C. 20006
Tel. (202) 728-1600
www.embassyof
mexico.org

■ **MEXICAN CONSULATES**
– 2827 16th St, NW
Washington, D.C. 20009
Tel. (202) 736-1000
http://portal.sre.gob.
mx/washington
– 204 S. Ashland Ave
Chicago, IL 60607
Tel. (312) 855-1380
www.consulmexchicago
.com
– 27 East 39th St
New York, NY 10016
Tel. (212) 217-6400
www.consulmexny.org
– 2401 West 6th St,
Los Angeles,
CA 90057
Tel. (213) 351-6800
www.sre.gob.mx/
losangeles

■ **MEXICAN MINISTRY OF TOURISM**
Av. Presidente
Masaryk No. 172,
Col. Chapultepec
Morales,
C.P. 11587, México,
Distrito Federal
Tel. (55) 3002-6300
www.visitmexico.com
Tel. from USA or
Canada: 1-800-44-
MEXICO
(1-800-4463942)
contact@visitmexico
.com
Extensive and very
helpful information
both on the phone
(in Spanish or
English), and via its
Web site.

→ IN THE UK

■ **MEXICAN EMBASSY**
16 St George St,
Mayfair, London W1
Tel. 020 7499 8586
Fax 020 7495 4035
www.embamex.co.uk
To obtain a visa,
please contact the
Mexican Consulate

■ **MEXICAN CONSULATE**
8 Halkin St,
London SW1
Tel. 020 7235 6393
Tel. 020 7201 0962/
63 (Visa)
Mon–Fri 9am–1pm
www.mexican
consulate.org.uk

■ **MEXICAN TOURIST BOARD**
Wakefield House
41 Trinity Square
London EC3
Tel. 020 7488 9392
Fax 020 7265 0704
www.visitmexico.com

FLYING TO MEXICO

→ FROM THE US

Flight times to Mexico
vary depending on
the point of origin. A
direct flight from New
York City to Mexico
City is typically about
5½ hrs long; from
Los Angeles it is
about 3½ hrs.

■ **DELTA**
Tel. 800-241-4141
www.delta.com

■ **CONTINENTAL**
Tel. 1-800-523-3273
www.continental.com

■ **USEFUL WEB SITES**
www.cheapflights.com
www.hotwire.com
www.orbitz.com
www.priceline.com
www.sidestep.com
www.travelocity.com

→ FROM THE UK

There are no direct
flights to Mexico.
Planes connect in the
US (Atlanta, Chicago
or Houston) or you
can fly via Paris.

AIR FRANCE
Tel. 0870 142 4343
www.airfrance.co.uk

■ **DELTA**
Tel. 0845 600 0950
www.delta.com/uk

■ **CONTINENTAL**
Tel. 0845 607 6760
www.continental.com

■ **UNITED**
Tel. 0845 8444 777
www.unitedairlines
.co.uk

MONEY

→ CURRENCY

The national currency
is the Mexican peso
($), which is divided
into 100 centavos.
Note Do not confuse
the peso ($) with the
US dollar (US $).
$100 = US $9.50 or
£5.50
£1 = $18.20
US $1 = $10.50

■ **US DOLLARS**
Many places accept
dollars. It is worth
stocking up with
them, as the
conversion rates are
often advantageous
in hotels.

→ CHANGING MONEY

■ **IN BANKS**
The most common
banks exchange US
dollars for cash
(efectivo) or travelers'
checks (cheques de
viajero).

■ Euros are slightly
less easy to convert,
especially in less
touristy or very
Americanized areas.
Some banks accept
only travelers'
checks, others only
cash.

■ **IN FOREIGN EXCHANGE OFFICES ('CASAS DE CAMBIO')**
– Longer opening
hours and quicker
service than in banks.
– Exchange rates
generally less
favorable.

→ CREDIT CARDS

They are accepted in
up- and mid-market
restaurants and
hotels, and in stores
(except markets and
small grocer's shops).
Note Commission of
2.5% of the purchase
value (maximum of
US $9.20) is
deducted.
– They are refused in
gas stations.

■ **WITHDRAWING CASH**
Cash dispensers
accept international
cards: Eurocard-
Mastercard, Visa,
AmEx, etc.
Note: bank's
commission
deducted: US $3.60
+ 2% of the sum
withdrawn (maximum
of US $9.20). Avoid
multiple withdrawals.

■ **LOST OR STOLEN CARDS**
Should your credit
card be lost or stolen
while you're in
Mexico, call the
following numbers for
assistance.
Visa
001-800-847-2911
**Eurocard-
MasterCard**
001-800-307-7309
American Express
Call collect at 1-336-
393-1111.

→ TRAVELERS' CHECKS

Take travelers'
checks in dollars or
euros (less widely
accepted).
Note Keep travelers'
checks in a separate
place from their
receipts and the data
required in case of
loss.

INSURANCE

→ TRAVEL INSURANCE

It is highly advisable
to take out a travel
insurance policy
before leaving, to
cover ticket
cancellations, loss
or theft of baggage,
and to obtain a
repatriation service (in
case of accident or
sickness) and health
insurance.

→ CREDIT CARDS

Bleue, Visa, Premier,
Gold and MasterCard
offer medical
insurance and
repatriation.

TIME DIFFERENCE

Mexico extends over
three time zones.

■ **GMT – 6**
Most of Mexico,
including Mexico City
and the states of
Colima, Jalisco, and
Oaxaca, is in the
Central Time Zone,
6 hrs behind GMT, or
1 hr behind Eastern
Standard Time.
Mexico uses daylight
savings time in the

summer (*horario de verano*) from the first Sun in April to the last Sun in Oct.
■ **GMT – 7**
In the States of Baja California Sur, Nayarit, Sinaloa and Chihuahua.
■ **GMT – 8**
In Baja California Norte and Sonora.
Note: Mountain Time is often referred to as 'Pacific Time' since most of the states on 'Mountain Time' border the Pacific.

FORMALITIES

→ **VISA/PASSPORT**
For travelers from the United States, no visa is necessary for a tourist trip of up to 90 days. As of December 2006, a valid passport will be necessary to enter the country.
Travelers from the UK need a passport valid for at least 6 months from the intended date of entry.
www.consulmexny.org

→ **TOURIST CARD**
On arrival at the airport, or in the plane, or at border crossing points if you are traveling by road, you will be required to fill in a tourist card (FMT, *folleto de migración turística*). The FMT is stamped by customs and indicates the authorized length of your stay. Keep this card (and a photocopy in case of loss), as it will be requested when you leave.

→ **FRONTIERS**
TOWARD BELIZE AND GUATEMALA
There are no customs formalities; you just have to pay the necessary tax.
■ **TOWARD THE UNITED STATES**
Travelers from Europe will be asked to show a valid passport.

INTERNET

■ www.visitmexico.com
Tourist information (English and Spanish).
■ www.mexonline.com
General information (English).
■ www.mexperience.com
■ www.mexico.net/
■ www.arts-history.mx
In-depth survey of Mexican culture (in English and Spanish).
■ www.tiempolibre.com.mx
Program of leisure activities (in Spanish).
■ www.webdemexico.com.mx
Serious site from Guadalajara University (Spanish).
■ www.lanic.utexas.edu/la/mexico
Very complete portal on Mexico (English).
■ www.planeta.com/ecotravel/mexico/mexparks.html
On parks and protected areas
■ www.inah.gob.mx
On Mexican historic monuments (Spanish).

WHEN TO GO

→ **CLIMATE**
Two seasons: dry (Nov–Apr) and wet (May–Oct); rainfall varies from region to region ● 22.
■ **DESERTS AND STEPPES OF THE NORTH**
(Baja California, desert in Sonora in the northwest and the State of Coahuila in the northeast).
– The climate is hot and arid, the summers scorching.
– The highest temperatures are recorded here.
■ **HIGH PLATEAUS OF THE NORTH AND THE SIERRAS**
– Low rainfall, cold winters.
– Temperatures can drop to 26° F (-3° C) in Chihuahua, and lower in the mountain regions (sierras), where there is snow at high altitudes.

■ **MEXICO CITY AND THE CENTRAL REGION**
– Temperate climate: mean of 66–70° F (19–21° C).
– Wide gap between max. and min. daily temperature in winter (it can drop to 14° F/ –10° C) in Mexico City).
– Heavy rain from May to Oct.
■ **THE SOUTH AND THE COASTS**
– Tropical climate, hot all year round: mean of 77–82° F (25–28° C), with hottest peaks in summer.
– Annual rainfall above 80 inches (2,000 mm), with a very pronounced rainy season.
– The Caribbean coast is subject to hurricanes in Sep and Oct.

→ **TOURIST SEASON**
Traveling in the low season will greatly reduce your budget. The high season falls over the New Year celebrations and in Easter Week (reserve accommodation in advance).
■ **LOCAL EVENTS**
These attract crowds and push up the prices: whale-watching in Baja California (Jan–Mar), Festival of the Dead on Lake Pátzcuaro ◆ 411.
■ **INTERMEDIATE SEASON**
Summer constitutes an intermediary season, with mid-range prices – except in the Sierra Tarahumara, where it is the most welcoming season, and thus more expensive.

HEALTH

→ **THE RISKS**
■ **MALARIA**
Low risk, except in some more rural areas (Campeche, Chiapas, Guerrero, Michoacán, Nayarit,

Quintana Roo, Sinaloa and Tabasco), especially in the rainy season.
■ **VACCINATIONS**
No vaccinations are compulsory. A yellow fever vaccination (with certificate) is required, however, when entering from a country where the disease is endemic. Vaccination against typhoid fever is advisable, and check that your diphtheria/ tetanus and polio vaccinations are up to date.

TELEPHONE

■ **CALLING MEXICO**
From the US and Canada dial 01 + 52 (Mexico) + the city code + the number you require.
From the UK and Europe dial 00 + 52 (Mexico) + number.
See ◆ 409 for a list of city codes.

WHAT TO PACK

■ **CLOTHES**
– Light clothes plus a warm sweater or polar jacket.
– A hat, scarf and gloves are needed in winter for the Sierra Tarahumara and for the nights in San Cristóbal.
– Take rainwear and filled-in walking shoes in the wet season. See *Climate*.
■ **ELECTRICITY ◆ 406**
– You may need an adapter.
■ **PHOTOGRAPHY**
– Films for slides or those with an unusual sensitivity (ASA) may be hard to find (unlike accessories for a digital camera).
■ **PHARMACY ◆ 407**
– Personal hygiene accessories and common medicines can be bought.
– Take a good anti-mosquito spray and the appropriate treatment for insect bites.

◆ GETTING AROUND MEXICO

The symbol ▲ refers to the Itineraries section and ◆ refers to the practical information pages.

BY PLANE

→ INTERNAL FLIGHTS
Mexico has over fifty airports. The big cities are served by Aeroméxico and Mexicana; the smaller ones, by regional companies. Given the size of the country, this means of transportation is obviously useful for traveling from the center to the north (Chihuahua), Baja California (La Paz, Tijuana) and the Caribbean coast (Cancún) – but it is quite expensive.
Note Mexicana offers a system of combined tickets, the Mexipass (valid in Mexico, the United States, Central and South America and the Caribbean). A ticket to Mexico is sold with at least two coupons for internal flights. You'll find a list of fares from city to city on the student travel website STA:
www.statravel.com

→ AIRLINES
■ **AEROMÉXICO**
From Mexico City:
Tel. (55) 5133-4010
From the USA:
Tel. (800) 237-6639
From the UK:
Tel: 0052 55 5133-4000
www.aeromexico.com/mex/english/index.html
■ **MEXICANA**
From Mexico City:
Tel. (55) 5448-1050
From the rest of the Mexican Republic:
Tel. 01-800-509-8960
From the USA:
Tel. 1 (800) 531-7921
From the UK:
Tel: 020 8492 0000
www.mexicana.com

→ MAIN AIRPORTS
■ **MEXICO CITY**
(Benito Juarez International Airport)
Mexico City ▲ 127.
Airport code: MEX
www.aeropuertos
mexico.com/Ingles

– 5 miles (8 km) from the historic center.
To the city center:
by taxi
– 20 to 45 mins to the city center.
– Prepaid taxis to the left of the main exit (E4): Pro Taxi and Taxi Sitio 300 (less expensive).
by subway
The Terminal Aerea station (*línea 5*) is about 450 yards (410 m) to the left on leaving the airport.
with a rented car
The big international agencies are all represented. Go to the ground floor of the airport.
See By Car ◆ 405.

■ **CANCÚN**
(Cancún International Airport)
In Yucatán ▲ 202.
Airport code: CUN
www.cancun-airport.com
– 18 miles (30 km) from Cancún.
– Minibus and taxi links to the city center (45 mins).

■ **MÉRIDA**
In Yucatán ▲ 199.
– 6 miles (10 km) southwest of the city center (20 mins in minibus or taxi).

■ **JALISCO**
(Miguel Hidalgo y Costilla International Airport)
Airport code: GDL
www.aeropuertos
mexico.com

■ **MONTERREY**
(General Mariano Escobedo International Airport)
Airport code: MTY
www.aeropuertos
mexico.com

BY BOAT

Ferries and launches serve Isla de Mujeres (from Cancún), Cozumel (45 mins from Playa del Carmen) and Baja California (from Los Mochis).

BY BUS

This is the most popular and cheapest means of transportation in Mexico. A highly efficient private network provides regular links between cities and towns.

→ BUS STATIONS
(*central* or *terminal de autobuses*).
– There are often two bus stations in cities: one for first class and one for second. Sometimes a company may also have its own station.
– For long-distance trips, it is worth buying tickets in advance, especially in the tourist season.
– In some cities, you will find efficient, computerized Ticket-Bus offices centralize bookings for various companies.

→ FROM MEXICO CITY AIRPORT
There is a bus service from the first floor of the airport (Hall F – cross the bridge).
Departures 6.30am–12.30am to Cuernavaca (16 buses daily), Puebla (42 buses), Toluca (19 buses), Querétaro (14 buses) and Pachuca.

→ CLASSES
■ **SECOND CLASS**
(*segunda clase*)
– Cheap, but long trips (frequent stops).
– More suited to short journeys. Tiring for long distances or night trips.
Companies
Flecha Amarilla, Herradura de Plata, AU, Estrella Roja.

■ **FIRST CLASS**
(*primera clase*)
Quicker and more comfortable: reclining seats (more or less!), toilets, air-conditioning.

Companies
Cristóbal Colón, ADO, Pulman de Morelos, Estrella de Oro.

■ **DELUXE**
– More expensive.
– Worth considering for long journeys as they generally offer a high level of comfort: truly reclining seats, onboard drinks and sandwiches.
Companies
ETN, ADO-GI, UNO, Cristóbal Colón-Plus.
Note Luggage is safer in first-class and deluxe buses, as it is placed in the hold in exchange for a ticket; this is not the case with segunda.

→ MINIBUS
In areas with limited transportation, you can take:
– a minibus (*combi*, 10–12 passengers). Cheaper than a taxi, it will leave when full.
– a pickup (*camioneta*). Very cheap and extremely convivial.

BY 'COLECTIVOS' AND 'PESEROS'

Half-taxi, half-bus, the *colectivos* (known as *peseros* in Mexico City) travel along the main roads of the big cities. The route is indicated on the windshield. Hail the driver to get on and off – they will stop at any *cuadra* (street corner). In Mexico City, the *peseros* are ideal for getting to know the city.

BY TAXI

Taxis are readily available in cities. The average price of a trip is easily affordable.
Note When a taxi is not equipped with a meter, negotiate the price in advance or pay the standard fare.

For national calls: 01 followed by the city code, then the number.
For local calls: number with 7 (or 8) digits, without the code.

on journeys where this has been pre-established for all taxis.

→ TAXIS IN MEXICO CITY

There are two types of taxis.

■ 'TAXIS DE SITIO'

These are very safe taxis, controlled by a neighborhood HQ. They are distinguished by the 'S' on their license plate. They can be found on taxi ranks or called by taxi phone.

■ 'TAXIS LIBRES'

These bear an 'L' on their license plate. They can be hailed in the street. They are very cheap, but do not guarantee the same degree of safety as the *taxis de sitio*.
Beware!
Men pretending to be taxi drivers and incidents of theft and kidnapping are a reality in the capital.
Note:
– Ask the driver to switch on the meter (taximetro).
– If you are traveling at night, only use taxis de sitio.
– Never hesitate to ask to see the driver's identification document (carta de identificación).

■ COMPANIES

Radio Elite
Tel. (55) 56 60 11 22
Sitio 137 Durango (Roma)
Tel. (55) 55 14 27 00
Servi-Radio
Tel. (55) 57 63 54
51/00 29 93
Ciudad de México
Tel. (55) 57 71 76 66
Sitio Parque México
Tel. (55) 52 86 71
29/64
Note Always be clear where you want to be picked up when you telephone. See Getting Around for tips on Mexican addresses ◆ 407

BY TRAIN

Apart from the *Chihuahua al Pacífico* line, which still operates because it is a tourist attraction ▲ 370, (and because there is no other feasible route), Mexico's railroad network is largely out of service and of little use to travelers.

BY CAR

→ RENTAL

You must be at least twenty-one years old and have a credit card and a drivers' license. Worth considering, especially in regions like the Yucatán where many sights are far from towns and Baja California where there are few buses. Elsewhere, take a bus (or fly) to reach the cities and hire a car to visit the surrounding area once you're there.

■ FOUR-WHEEL-DRIVE VEHICLES

Generally of little use, unless you want to visit very isolated places (for example, some of the Mayan ruins in Yucatán). In contrast, they are highly recommended in Baja California, where a four-wheel-drive vehicle makes it possible for you to leave the region's only asphalt road and discover some of the hidden aspects of the peninsula.

■ AGENCIES
IN MEXICO CITY
Budget
Tel. (55) 57 84 30 11
Open 9am–11pm
Avis
Tel. (55) 57 62 11 66
Open 7am–11pm
Royal Rent a Car
Tel. (55) 57 26 01 10
Open 7am–10pm
Hertz
Tel. (55) 57 62 89 77
Open 7am–10.30pm

Note
– Book your car before leaving home.
– Avoid returning it to an agency other than the one at the point of departure because this works out far more expensive.

■ INSURANCE
– Consider taking out a complete civil insurance policy; this will cost about 10% of the value of the vehicle.
– Check that third-party damage (daño a tercero) is included; this is absolutely essential.

→ ROAD NETWORK

Most roads are asphalt, although some archeological sites can only be reached via dirt tracks. Wherever possible, it is advisable to take toll roads or turnpikes, as they are better maintained and are safer.
Beware!
The topes (speed bumps) on the outskirts of towns are not always visible or well signposted.

→ DRIVING
■ REGULATIONS
– Traffic drives on the right.
– The speed limit is 110 km/hr on freeways, 80 km/hr on roads and 60 km/hr in urban areas.
– Wearing a seatbelt is compulsory.

■ LOCAL DRIVING HABITS
– The left-hand indicator is particularly used to tell the car behind that it can pass.
– At *cuatro altos* (intersections where vehicles can come from all four sides and must stop), priority goes to the first to arrive, then the second, and so on.

– A red traffic light does not stop a car from turning right if the road is clear.
Note: To reduce pollution in Mexico City, every car must stay out of circulation at least once a week. This regulation does not apply to recent, non-polluting vehicles (these include rented cars).

→ GASOLINE

Gasoline is a state monopoly. Gas stations all belong to the PEMEX, which charges fixed prices throughout the country. Cars use two types of unleaded gas (*sin plomo*): Magna (green pump) or Premium (red pump, more expensive).
Note
When renting a car, ask about the type of gasoline required.

→ MAPS

The best map for getting around by car is the road atlas published by Guía Roji (which also produces maps of cities and states). This can be found in stores in the Sanborns chain (in all the big cities).

SIGNPOSTS
Alto: stop
Ceda el paso: give way
Despacio: slow down
E (estacionamiento): parking
E crossed: no parking
No girar: no turning
Peligro: danger
Tope: speed bump, humpback
Vado: ford
Via cuota: turnpike
Via libre: normal road

◆ THE A–Z OF STAYING IN MEXICO

The symbol ▲ refers to page numbers in the Itineraries section,
◆ to Practical Information and ● to the Encyclopedia section.

Peso ($)
$10 = US$0.95 / £0.55

USEFUL ADDRESSES

→ EMBASSIES
■ BRITISH EMBASSY
British Embassy
Río Lerma 71
Col Cuauhtémoc
06500 México
Tel. (55) 5242 8500
www.britishembassy
.gov.uk
Consular Section
Río Usumacinta 26
Col Cuauhtémoc
06500 México
Tel. (55) 5242 8500
Fax (55) 5242 8523
consular.mexico@
fco.gov.uk
Mon–Fri
8.30–11.30am
■ US EMBASSY
Embajada de Estados
Unidos
Paseo de la
Reforma 305,
Col. Cuauhtemoc
06500 México
Tel. (55) 5080-2000
Fax (55) 5511-9980
http://mexico
.usembassy.gov
Citizens Consular Services
Same address and
telephone number.
Room 101, ext. 4780.
Mon–Fri 9am–2pm,
3–5pm.
Passport, Citizenship & Notarials Unit
Room 106, ext. 4326.
Mon–Fri
8.30–10.30am.
ccs@usembassy
.net.mx

→ TOURIST OFFICES
The *oficinas de turismo* display varying degrees of efficiency. In the state capitals, the Secretariat of Tourism (Sectur or Sedetur) sometimes provides services.

ELECTRICITY

Electrical power at 110 V, with wall sockets following the American model. Equipment with other specifications will work only if it is fitted with an internal transformer (like most laptops).

ACCOMMODATION

→ CAMPING
Campsites are scarce. They are mainly found in Baja California (although they are mostly fitted out as trailer parks) and, to a lesser extent, on the Caribbean coast of Yucatán and in the region of Puerto Escondido, on the Pacific coast.
***Note** Avoid camping in the wild.*

→ HAMMOCKS AND 'CABAÑAS'
■ HAMMOCKS
In the beach resorts of Yucatán and on the Pacific coast (Puerto Escondido region), small hotels rent out a hammock and a place to hang it: generally a canopy of palms open on the sides (*palapa*).
You will sleep much better if you lie sideways across the hammock.
***Note** Don't forget to apply anti-mosquito spray and check that the hotel has lockers in which you can store your belongings.*

■ 'CABAÑAS'
These can be found by the beaches in the south (Caribbean coast, Oaxaca coast). The comfort afforded – and the price – will vary, from a rustic hut surrounded by sand to a luxury bungalow, with a bathroom, air-conditioning and kitchenette.

→ BOARDING HOUSES
(*Pensiones* or *casas de huespedes*) Generally situated in the historic center of cities. Despite their somewhat basic comfort, they are often very charming. Bathrooms can be private or communal (*baño compartido*).

→ HOTELS
A wide range is available, from a *hacienda*, or a converted house, to a modern hotel chain.

■ STANDOUTS
The *haciendas* of Yucatán are some of the most enchanting hotels in the country.
Beware!
The hotel tax (ISH, Impuesto Sobre Hospedaje) is not always included in the price of the room (it's about 2%, depending on the State). If in doubt, ask: ¿Está incluido el impuesto?

→ YOUTH HOSTELS
– They're usually well kept and conveniently situated. You can also stay in dormitories for a reasonable price. Communal areas (kitchen and bathrooms).
– Internet connection often available. Sheets and towels are normally provided and breakfast is included. Youth hostels also offer a few private rooms, with the same prices as a small hotel.

– Hostels can be independent or affiliated to Hostelling International. A Hostelling International or ISIC card is not compulsory, but does entitle the holder to discounts.
http://dyred.sureste
.com/hostelsnuevo
Note
In Mexico the International Student Identity Card (ISIC) is useful only for youth hostels and some small private museums.
www.isic.org

OPENING TIMES

■ OFFICES AND ADMINISTRATIVE BUILDINGS
Mon–Fri 9am–2pm and 4–7pm.

■ POST OFFICES
Mon–Fri 8am–3pm (o 5pm) and sometimes Sat 9am–1pm.
See under 'Mail'.

■ BANKS
Mon–Fri 9am–4pm (or 5pm).
Note In some banks, foreign currency is changed only in the morning; you'll be out of luck later.

■ STORES
Generally open Mon–Sat 9am–7pm, with a possible lunch break between 2 and 4pm.
Note Some stores open on Sundays and at night; hours can vary.

■ MARKETS
Usually in place 7am–6pm (or 7pm).

■ MUSEUMS AND SITES
Museums generally open Tue–Sun 9am (or 10am) – 5pm (or 6pm). Archeological sites are open daily 8am (or 9am) to 5pm

■ CHURCHES
Apart from the big cathedrals, which

THE A–Z OF STAYING IN MEXICO ◆

For national calls: dial 01 followed by the city code, then the number.
For local calls: dial the 7- (or 8-) digit number, without the code.
For a list of city codes ◆ 409.

have established opening times, churches tend to open according to their particular use – although, having said that, it is unusual to find a church closed in Mexico.

INTERNET

Internet cafés are everywhere. They are usually well equipped and open from morning to night. The average price is $5–15 per hr, but you can pay up to $30 or even $50 in Baja California.

MEDIA

→ NEWSPAPERS
La Jornada
This independent daily newspaper, popular with the middle class and intelligentsia, has served as a reference since 1983. Its articles are written by leading intellectuals from home and abroad. Excellent supplements.
El Universal
In existence since 1916. Close to the PRI, the party that has dominated Mexican politics for 75 years.
Reforma
Particularly read by the business class. It has a liberal standpoint and has earned a solid reputation for quality. Similar in style to an American newspaper.

→ TELEVISION
Televisa and TV Azteca dominate the audiovisual landscape. The schedules mainly feature light entertainment, football and telenovelas ▲ 140. Up-market hotels provide access to Spanish and American channels such as CNN).

GETTING AROUND

→ FINDING YOUR WAY
The Mexicans use blocks (*cuadras*, *manzanas*) as their reference, counted from the main thoroughfares.
Beware!
*A street can be very long and lacking in numbers. Take care to note the streets between which your destination is situated. The colonial urban model features a central square (*zócalo*) that serves as a convenient landmark. Some streets are known by a number, often qualified by one of the four cardinal points (1a Norte, 2a Sur Poniente).*

→ READING AN ADDRESS
– From left to right: name, then street number; with or without the specification *Calle* or *Avenida*.
– In the case of an apartment building (*edificio*), the no. of the apartment (*departamento*).
– Indication of the *Colonia* (equivalent of the neighborhood, abbreviated as *Col*), the town and the zip code.
– Name of the state, sometimes abbreviated (Gto for Guanajuato, Oax. for Oaxaca, DF for Distrito Federal)

PEOPLE WITH DISABILITIES

Few facilities for people with reduced mobility (*minus-válidos*). The website www.accessable.com (in English) lists hotels offering provisions for access and stays, specialized transportation organizations and

diving and leisure clubs.

MAIL

Post office is *correo* in Spanish.
– Letter (*carta*) of under 20 g or postcard (*tarjeta postal*): $10.50 for Europe and $8.50 for Canada. For airmail, write '*via aerea*' on the envelope.
– To ensure safe arrival, ask for a *registrado* ($16 more).
– For a 500 g parcel: $45 to Canada, $76 to Europe. Recorded mail (*encomienda*): $173 and $239.

→ DELIVERY TIME
Between 10 and 20 days to Europe; between 4 and 15 days to the United States and Canada. An express service called 'Mexpost' is available in some post offices.

TIPPING

– Tax (IVA) normally included in the prices
– Tip (*propina*) usually given in restaurants (10–15%) and appreciated for services rendered (gas stations, guides).

HEALTH

→ FOOD HYGIENE
– Drink only bottled water (*agua purificada*), either still (*natural*) or fizzy (*mineral*). If you're hiking miles from anywhere, purify your drinking water with disinfectants such as Micropur and Hydroclonazone.
– Avoid eating raw vegetables, fruit or seafood in stalls that may not guarantee good hygiene (food washed with bottled water).
– Wash fruit and vegetables bought in the market (apples, strawberries and so

on) with bottled water.
– Remember to wash your hands regularly, especially before meals.

→ SICKNESS
■ ALTITUDE SICKNESS
Mexico City and several other cities are at a high altitude. Be prepared for an adjustment period, with a risk of breathlessness, headaches and insomnia.
Note
– *Avoid copious meals and alcohol in the first few days.*
– *Rest at first and drink plenty of water.*
– *If the symptoms are acute or persistent, consult a doctor.*

■ DISORDERS ASSOCIATED WITH POLLUTION
Mexico City's peaks of pollution are generally recorded in winter, and in the morning. Travelers with cardiac or respiratory sickness should consult their doctor before going to Mexico City, take the recommended precautions and adjust their schedules accordingly.

■ INTESTINAL DISORDERS
Be aware of how uncooked food is cleaned, only drink bottled water and bring anti-diarrhea medicine with you.

→ PHARMACIES
A wide range of medicines and personal hygiene products is sold.
*Note You should be able to find pharmacies that specialize in generic drugs (*genéricos*).*

SAFETY

→ RISK AREAS
Mexico City; the cities on the

◆ THE A–Z TO STAYING IN MEXICO

The symbol ▲ refers to page numbers in the Itineraries section,
◆ to Practical Information and ● to the Encyclopedia section.

Peso ($
$10 = US$0.95 / £0.5!

American border; the State of Guerrero (away from the beach resorts). The political situation in Chiapas is relatively calm, but there is certain tension.
Note *Information about safety for travelers is available on the websites of the Foreign and Commonwealth Office (UK)* www.fco.gov.uk *and the US State Department* http://travel.state.gov

→ THEFT AND ATTACKS
■ SOME RECOMMENDATIONS
Avoid isolated areas: deserted beaches, bars open late, abandoned city neighborhoods, remote villages, little-used tracks.

■ IN A CAR
Never sleep in your car and never drive at night (greater risk of accidents and attacks). Do not pick up hitchhikers.

■ WOMEN ON THEIR OWN
Mexican women do not travel alone. A foreign woman therefore lays herself open to unwanted stares or propositions. Avert your gaze and gently but firmly reject any advances; avoid any overly flimsy or provocative clothes.

→ DRUGS
Drug smuggling (*narcotráfico*) is becoming more intense, and this goes to explain most of the military roadblocks on certain roads (Baja California and the South).
Note *Never accept the loan of a vehicle from someone you do not know – or even do not know very well. All drivers*

are held responsible for the contents of the vehicle they are driving. It is also a good idea to keep the original packaging and prescriptions for your medicines, along with a doctor's certificate justifying the possible use of syringes, to quell any suspicions.

→ NATURAL DANGERS
■ SWIMMING IN THE SEA
Except on the Caribbean coasts of Quintana Roo, swimming can be dangerous, particularly in the Pacific, where the waves can overwhelm even the strongest swimmers. Beaches very rarely have lifeguards. Opt for sheltered creeks and observe warning flags on the beaches.

■ CYCLONES
Especially in the rainy season (June 1 to late October). In the event of an alert, the utmost caution is recommended, on both the Atlantic and Pacific coasts and in the neighboring regions. Closely follow the instructions of the relevant authorities. Website of the Mexican weather bureau: http://smn.cna.gob.mx

■ EARTHQUAKES
This land of volcanoes and earthquakes has not experienced a disaster since the earthquake in Mexico City in 1986. The danger is ever-present, however. Website of the seismological service: www.ssn.unam.mx

SHOPPING

■ LEATHER
Specialty of the livestock regions in

northern Mexico. You can put together an entire *ranchero* outfit in Chihuahua ▲ 370: cowboy boots, belt and buckles, spurs, saddle, etc. Leather craft goods (bags, belts, etc.) are also available in the colonial towns of the north.

■ SILVER
The widest choice and lowest prices are found in Taxco ▲ 177, the silver capital. The colonial cities around Mexico City also sell silver jewelry and objects.

■ CRAFT GOODS
● 62 Standards have dropped and some markets hawk a wide range of imported products. The beautiful craft goods of Mexico are still available, however, in specialist markets.
Note *For a list of recommended craft workshops and state stores, see ◆ 410.*

■ POTTERY
Local production in many villages in Michoacán (black pottery from Pátzcuaro ▲ 314) and the Oaxaca region ▲ 294. Crockery made from *talavera* (*azulejos*) in Puebla ▲ 288.

■ TREES OF LIFE
These extraordinary multicolored terra-cotta sculptures are made in Metepec, near Toluca (State of Mexico).

■ ALEBRIJES
Small creatures sculpted out of wood in the Oaxaca region ● 65.

■ LACQUERED OBJECTS
Hand-painted and lacquered wooden boxes and chests are a particular specialty of Chiapa de Corzo ▲ 281.

■ TEXTILES
Embroidered *huipil* (traditional indigenous blouses) from Chiapas, wooler ponchos from Pátzcuaro, long lengths of fabric, colorful scarves, and many more.

■ OTHERS
Huichol craft goods (Guadalajara region) ▲ 328, guitars from Michoacán ▲ 319, Panamas from Mérida, papier-mâché objects from the Festival of the Dead ● 48, *guayabera* (typical shirts, Veracruz.)

SPORT AND LEISURE

→ HIKING AND MOUNTAIN-BIKING
Mexico is ideal for these activities, although there is no network of official footpaths and information centers are few and far between. Take your own camping and climbing equipment and find a guide in situ.

■ THE MAIN AREAS
La Barranca del Cobre
(Chihuahua, the North ▲ 368)
Hikes to the canyons or the waterfalls, leaving from Creel or Cerocahui. From May to Sept, and particularly during the hotter summer months when the waterfalls display their full splendor.
Baja California
▲ 383
A guide is essential and the rates are high. To be avoided in summer because of the suffocating heat.
Paricutín Volcano
Extraordinary walk leading to the village of San Juan, buried i lava, with only the belltower of the

THE A–Z TO STAYING IN MEXICO ◆

For national calls: dial 01 followed by the city code, then the number.
For local calls: dial the 7- (or 8-) digit number, without the code.
For a list of city codes ◆ 409.

old church visible
▲ 319.
Around San Cristóbal
(Chiapas ▲ 253)
Hills on the high
plateaus. A favorite
of hikers and
mountain bikers.
Sierra de Juárez
(north of Oaxaca)
Puebla–Oaxaca–
Pacific ▲ 306

→ **MOUNTAIN
CLIMBING**
The volcanoes
of Mexico offer
excellent climbs.
– The highest
mountains accessible
to climbers are
Ixtaccíhuatl ▲ 161,
between Mexico City
and Puebla, and the
spectacular Pico de
Orizaba, in Veracruz
▲ 190. Reckon on
two or three days to
reach the summits.
Take all your own
equipment. No
exceptional technical
expertise is required.
– Less high: El
Nevado de Toluca
(State of Mexico) and
the Cofre de Perote
(Veracruz).
– Rock climbers will
be in their element on
the outskirts of
Monterrey (Sierra
Madre Oriental).

→ **WATER SPORTS**
■ **DIVING AND
SNORKELING**
The Caribbean coast
(Yucatán peninsula)
includes some of the
world's most
beautiful seabeds
under its clear blue
waters (Cozumel
Island ▲ 204).
Another prime spot is
Loreto Bay ▲ 397, in
Baja California,
where kayaking is
also popular.

■ **SURFING AND
WINDSURFING**
The Pacific coast
attracts seasoned
surfers and
windsurfers
from all over the
world. It is not
recommended for
beginners, however.

Puerto Escondido
(Oaxaca ▲ 307) is
the hub, but most
of the Pacific
beaches are suitable.
Barra de Navidad
is particularly popular
with windsurfers
▲ 332.

→ **GOLF**
Mexico has around
forty public golf
courses and about
eighty private ones.
Most of these are
located close to the
big beach resorts, in
the area of Los
Cabos in Baja
California, near
Acapulco, Manzanillo
and Puerto Vallarta
on the Pacific coast
and near Cancún in
Yucatán. There are
also some to be
found in the central
regions.
www.golfinmexico.net
Note *Keen golfers
should not miss the
golf courses of Los
Cabos (Baja
California), by the
sea.*

SOCIAL
ETIQUETTE

→ **CLOTHING**
Women should avoid
shorts, except at the
seaside. Daring
swimsuits and
topless sunbathing is
forbidden on
beaches, although
the big international
resorts on the
Caribbean do have
nudist beaches.

→ **GOOD MANNERS**
Take the trouble to
learn and use some
polite formulas, as
Mexicans are very
courteous. Men
greet each other
by shaking hands,
women by kissing.
More informally,
the *abrazo* consists
of a handshake and
hug and a greeting,
accompanied by
pats on the back.
Beware!
*When asked for
directions, Mexicans*

*always indicate
a route, rather than
risk disappointing
by admitting that
they do not know
the way…*
See *Useful phrases*
◆ 412.

→ **AN IDEA OF TIME**
Punctuality is not
considered an
essential part of good
manners in Mexico.
Watch out for this
characteristic gesture
of the hand; the
forefinger touching
the thumb, with the
other fingers closed,
accompanied by a
'*momentito*'. This
'short moment' can
last … an eternity!
Any signs of
impatience on your
part may cause
surprise or even
irritation.

→ **PHOTOGRAPHS**
Never take photos
of Indians or their
places of worship,
as it will be perceived
as showing
disrespect for their
beliefs.

TELEPHONE

EMERGENCIES
Tel. 080

COLLECT CALLS
(*llamada por cobrar*).
From a booth, dial
090 to speak to an
operator.

**DIRECTORY
ENQUIRIES**
Tel. 040

→ **WHERE TO
CALL FROM**
■ **PHONE BOOTHS**
These work with
cards (*tarjetas
telefónicas*), which
are on sale in all
stores displaying the
sign '*Ladatel de venta
aquí*'. Phone booths
unfortunately cannot
receive incoming
calls.

■ **CALL CENTERS**
The charges in these
casetas telefónicas

are sometimes
slightly lower. The
cost is calculated
after the call.

■ **TELEPHONE
VIA THE INTERNET**
Some Internet cafés
and hotels offer a
telephone connection
via the Internet, and
this is a far cheaper
way to call home than
using a phone both
or call center.

→ **LOCAL CALLS**
Dial the 7-digit
number (8 in Mexico
City and Guadalajara)
without the city code.

→ **NATIONAL CALLS**
Dial 01 plus the city
code, then the
number.

→ **MEXICO TO
THE UK AND US**
For the UK, dial 00
44, then the number
(without the initial 0);
for the US, dial 00 1,
then the number.

→ **CALLING A
CELLPHONE**
Dial 044, then the city
code (even for a local
call) before the 7-digit
number.

→ **CITY CODES**

Mexico City	55
Acapulco	744
Cabo San Lucas	624
Cancún	998
Chihuahua	614
Ciudad Juarez	656
Cuernavaca	777
Durango	618
Ensenada	646
Guadalajara	33
Jalapa	932
Matamoros	871
Mazatlán	669
Mexicali	686
Mexico City	55
Monterrey	81
Nogales	631
Nuevo Laredo	867
Oaxaca de Juarez	951
Playa del Carmen	984
Puerto Vallarta	322
Tampico	833
Tijuana	664
Veracruz	229
Villahermosa	993

◆ CRAFT STORES AND WORKSHOPS

Abbreviations used below: b/w = between; Priv. = Privada (private); Calz. = Calzada (avenue); Col. = Colonia (neighborhood); Fracc. = Fraccionamento (neighborhood)

CRAFTSMEN

The following artists have been selected from Mexico's finest to participate in the program 'Great Masters of Popular Art from Mexico', promoted since 1986 by the foundation Fomento Cultural Banamex. It is possible to visit their workshops and watch them applying traditional techniques to create objects of an exceptionally high quality.

→ CAMPECHE ▲ 222
Horn goods
MIGUEL NADAL BURGOS
Calle 18 no. 419 int. b/w Prolongación Montecristo and Av. Colosio Col. Vicente Guerrero

→ CHIAPA DE CORZO ▲ 282
Masks
ANTONIO LÓPEZ HERNÁNDEZ
Av. Capitán Vicente López 321

→ GUADALUPE ▲ 345
Silver
CRAFTSMEN OF THE FORMER BERNÁRDEZ HACIENDA
Fracc. Lomas de Bernárdez

→ GUANAJUATO ▲ 349
Majolica
GORKY GONZÁLEZ QUIÑONES
Pastita Ex-Huerta de Montenegro s/n

Papier-mâché
MAURICIO HERNÁNDEZ COLMENERO
San Isidro no. 19 Calz. de Guadalupe

→ IZAMAL ▲ 242
Jewelry with cocoyol seeds
ESTEBAN ABAN
Calle 26 no. 344, b/w Calles 45 & 47

Carved wood
GABRIEL PÉREZ RAJÓN
Calle 21 no. 282 b/w Calles 22 & 24, Barrio el Zorro

→ IZÚCAR DE MATAMOROS (PUEBLA)
Terracotta
ALFONS CASTILLO ORTA
Callejón del Partidor 3

→ MÉRIDA ▲ 226
Gold and silver filigree
LEONARDO RAMOS COBOS & CARLOS RAMOS
Calle 36 no. 498, b/w 59 and 61

→ METEPEC (STATE OF MEXICO)
Trees of life
OSCAR SOTENO ELÍAS
Vialidad Metepec Carretera Ixtapan

→ MEXICO CITY ▲ 127
Alebrijes
LINARES FAMILY
Oriente 30 no. 251 Col. Merced Balbuena

Screens
PEDRO ORTEGA LOZANO
Av. Tláhuac 8041-B Barrio de la Asunción

Silver
ODILÓN MARMOLEJO SÁNCHEZ
Calle 11 no. 201, Col. Porvenir

→ OAXACA ▲ 294
Woolen tapestries
ARNULFO MENDOZA RUÍZ
Galería La Mano Mágica, Calle M. Alcala 203, Col. Centro

→ OCOTLÁN DE MORELOS ▲ 305
Terracotta statuettes
GUILLERMINA AGUILAR ALCANTARA
Prolongación de Morelos 430

→ OCUMICHO (MICHOACÁN) ▲ 319
Terracotta
ESPERANZA FELIPE MURATO *(ask for directions when you're at the site)*

→ OLINALÁ (GUERRERO)
Lacquered wood
FRANCISCO CORONEL NAVARRO
Juan Aldama 7 Barrio San Diego

Lacquered, engraved wood
DÁMASO AYALA JIMÉNEZ
Ramón Ibarra 27

→ PARACHO ▲ 319 (MICHOACÁN)
Shawls *(rebozos)*
CECILIA BAUTISTA CABALLERO
Matamoros 120 Ahuirán

→ PATAMBAN ▲ 319 (MICHOACÁN)
Terracotta
NEFTALÍ AYUNGUA SUÁREZ
Madero 17

→ PÁTZCUARO ▲ 314
Lacquered wood
MARIO AUGUSTÍN GASPAR RODRÍGUEZ
Priv. de Codallos 47

→ PUEBLA ▲ 288
Majolica
CÉSAR TORRES RAMÍREZ
Lirios 6117 Col. Bugambilias

→ SALAMANCA ▲ 352
Wax crêche
AURELIO AUGUSTÍN ARREDONDO RANGEL
Cuitláhuac 212, Fracc. Aztlán

→ SAN BARTOLO COYOTEPEC ▲ 305
Black terracotta
CARLOMAGNO PEDRO MARTÍNEZ
Guerrero 1

→ SAN CRISTÓBAL DE LAS CASAS ▲ 252
Weaving
SNA JOLOBIL (coop)
Calz. Lázaro Cárdenas 42 Barrio de Mexicanos

→ SANTA CLARA DEL COBRE ▲ 317
Beaten copper
IGNACIO PUNZO ÁNGEL
E. Huerta 105

→ SANTA MARÍA ATZOMPA
Terracotta dolls
IRMA GARCÍA BLANCO
Av. Juárez 302

→ TIXKKOKOB (YUCATÁN)
Embroidery, jewelry in gold and silver filigree, plus hammocks
ATELIER DE SAN ANTONIO MILLET
(ask at the site)

→ TLAQUEPAQUE ▲ 323
Terracotta
ZENÓN MARTÍNEZ GARCÍA
16 de Septiembre 406 (before 384)

→ TONALÁ ▲ 323
Terracotta miniatures
ÁNGEL SANTOS JUÁREZ
Ávila Camacho 123 Col. el Zapote

Terracotta
SALVADOR VÁZQUEZ CARMONA
López Cotilla 328 Col. El Zapote

JOSÉ BARNABE CAMPECHANO
Hidalgo 83 Col. Centro

→ URUAPAN ▲ 318
Lacquered plates
JOAQUÍN MENDOZA GÓMEZ
Priv. Emilio Carranza 7, Barrio Santiago

FONART STORES

This state-run chain of stores offers high-quality craft goods throughout the country.

Cuernavaca ▲ 175
Av. Morelos 271 Col. Centro
Mexico City (Center) ▲ 127
Av. Juárez 89
Mexico City (Col. Juárez)
Av. Paseo de la Reforma 116
Mexico City (Col. Michoacán)
Av. Patriotismo 691
Monterrey ▲ 378
Diego de Montemayo 510 Sur; Barrio Antiguo; Centro Cultural Santa Lucía
Querétaro ▲ 335
Av. 16 de Septiembre 44-C Poniente Centro Histórico
San Luis Potosí ▲ 33
Jardín Guerrero 5 Centro

FESTIVALS AND EVENTS ◆

A selection of the best. The symbols ● and ▲ refer to the pages on which these events are described.

FAIRS/FESTIVALS

APRIL 25–MAY 5	AGUASCALIENTES	**Feria de San Marcos**	▲ 348
JUNE 29	GUADALAJARA	**Festival de Tlaquepaque** *Mariachis, dancing, processions of floats*	
SEP–OCT	GUANAJUATO	**Festival Cervantino** *Theater, dance, music*	▲ 349
OCT	GUADALAJARA	**October festival** *Races, artistic and sporting events*	
LATE NOV– EARLY DEC	GUADALAJARA	**Book fair** *The most important in Latin America*	

NATIONAL HOLIDAYS ('FIESTAS PATRIAS')

FEB 5	Particularly COZUMEL, VERACRUZ, MAZÁTLAN	**Day of the Constitution** *Commemoration of the Constitution of 1917*	● 51
MARCH 21	OAXACA	**Celebration of the birthday of Juárez**	● 51
MAY 5	PUEBLA	**Anniversary of the Battle of Puebla** *Commemoration of the Mexicans' victory over the French in 1862; military parades*	▲ 287
SEP 15–16	MEXICO CITY	**Día de Independencia** *Reenactment of the 'grito de Dolores', the signal for rebellion issued by Father Hidalgo to his compatriots in 1810*	● 51
OCT 12	ALL OVER THE COUNTRY	**Día de la Raza** *Ceremony commemorating the discovery of America by Christopher Columbus in 1492*	
NOV 20	MEXICO CITY	**Día de la Revolución** *Parades for the anniversary of the Revolution*	● 51

RELIGIOUS AND FOLKLORIC FESTIVALS

JAN 6	Particularly TZINTZUNTZAN, PARRAL (CHIHUAHUA)	**Los Santos Reyes (Epiphany)** *As in Spain, the Three Kings bring children their Christmas presents.*	
JAN 18	TAXCO	**Santa Prisca (festival of the patron saint)**	
FEB 2	Particularly TLACOTALPAN, SAN JUAN DE LOS LAGOS, CHOLULA and METEPEC	**La Candelaría (Candlemas)** *Traditional dances, processions and bull runs*	
FEB–MARCH	Esp. VERACRUZ, ACAPULCO, CAMPECHE, MAZATLÁN	**Carnival**	
MARCH 21	CHICHÉN ITZÁ, TEOTIHUACÁN	**Festival of the Equinox**	▲ 165
MARCH–APRIL	Particularly MEXICO CITY, IXTAPALAPA, SAN LUIS POTOSÍ, SAN MIGUEL DE ALLENDE, TAXCO	**Easter Week** *Representation of the Passion, processions*	● 47
MAY 3	Particularly PÁTZCUARO and VALLE DE BRAVO	**Santa Cruz** *Houses are decorated with floral crosses*	
MAY 10	CUAUTLA (Morelos)	**Festival of the Charro** *Rodeos in honor of Emiliano Zapata*	
2nd THURSDAY AFTER PENTECOST	ALL OVER THE COUNTRY, particularly in PAPANTLA	**Corpus Christi** *Dance of the Palo Volador in Papantla*	▲ 193
JULY 18–31 (last 2 Mondays)	OAXACA	**Fiesta de la Guelaguetza**	▲ 295
AUG 27–31	ZACATECAS	**Morismas** *Traditional dances*	
SEP 1–8	ALL OVER THE COUNTRY	**Virgen de Natividad (Nativity)**	
	TEPOZTLÁN	**Festival of Tepoztecatl**	
	CHOLULA	**Celebration of the Virgen de los Remedios**	
SEP 21	CHICHÉN ITZÁ, TEOTIHUACÁN	**Festival of the Equinox**	▲ 165
SEP 27– 29	SAN MIGUEL DE ALLENDE	**Festival of the patron saint**	
SEP 27 – OCT 14	MÉRIDA	**Cristo de Amapolas (Christ of the Poppies)**	
NOV 1–2	Particularly JANITZIO (Lago de Pátzcuaro), MIXQUIC (Mexico City)	**All Saints and the Festival of the Dead (Día de Muertos)**	● 48
DEC 12	MEXICO (Basilica of La Guadalupe)	**Festival of the Virgin of Guadalupe**	▲ 146
DEC 16–24	Especially in the villages	**Posadas de Navidad**	● 51
DEC 23	OAXACA	**Festival of the Radish (Fiesta del Rabano)**	▲ 294

SPORTS EVENTS

NOVEMBER	PUERTO ESCONDIDO	**International surfing championship**	▲ 307
	BAJA CALIFORNIA	**Baja 1000** *Motorbike race*	

◆ USEFUL EXPRESSIONS

EVERYDAY WORDS AND PHRASES

Yes: sí
No: no
Good morning: buenos días
Good afternoon: buenas tardes
Good night: buenas noches
How are you? ¿Cómo esta? or ¿Qué tal?
Please: por favor
Thank you: gracias
You're welcome: de nada or no hay de que
Excuse me: perdón or con permiso
I'm British/American: Soy británico/ norteamericano (fem: británica/ norteamericana)
I can't speak Spanish: No hablo español
I don't understand: No entiendo
What is that in Spanish ¿Cómo se dice en español?
My name is: me llamo
What is your name? ¿Cómo se llama (Usted)?
Goodbye: Adiós
See you soon: Hasta luego
Safe journey: Buen viaje
Take care: Que le vaya bien

PEOPLE, FAMILY

Woman: mujer
Man: hombre
Surname: apellido
First name: nombre
Mother: madre
Father: padre
Daughter: hija
Son: hijo
Sister: hermana
Brother: hermano
My wife: mi esposa
My husband: mi marido or mi esposo
Mr: Señor
Mrs: Señora
Miss: Señorita

NUMBERS

◆ CARDINAL

One:	uno
Two:	dos
Three:	tres
Four:	cuatro
Five:	cinco
Six:	seis
Seven:	siete
Eight:	ocho
Nine:	nueve
Ten:	diez
Twenty:	veinte
Thirty:	treinta
Hundred:	cien(to)
Thousand:	mil
Million:	millón

◆ ORDINAL
(Useful for street names)
1st: primero(a)
2nd: segundo(a)
3rd: tercero(a)
4th: cuarto(a)
5th: quinto(a)
6th: sexto(a)
7th: séptimo(a)
8th: octavo(a)
9th: noven(a)
10th: decimo(a)

GETTING AROUND

◆ READING A MAP
Arcade: portal
Avenue: avenida, calzada, paseo
Bay: bahía
Beach: playa
Belvedere: mirador
Block: cuadra
Bullring: plaza de toros
Cave: cueva
City: ciudad
Forest: selva
Grotto: gruta
Hill: loma, cerro
Island: isla
Lake: lago
Main square: zócalo
Neighborhood: barrio, colonia, fraccionamiento
Parish: parroquia
Park, landscaped promenade: alameda
Passageway: andador
Port: muelle
River: río
Seafront: malecón
Square: plaza, plazuela (small)
Stream: arroyo
Street: calle, callejón (small)
Street corner: esquina (abbr. esq.)
Tower: torre
Town: pueblo
Valley: valle

◆ IN TOWN
Bank: banco
Bookstore: librería
Bus station: terminal de autobus, central camionera
Church: iglesia
City hall: palacio municipal, ayuntamiento
Grocery store: abarrotes
Hotel: hotel
Laundromat: lavandería
Market: mercado
Museum: museo
Parking lot: estacionamiento
Police: policía
Post office: correo
Restaurant: restaurante
Supermarket: supermercado
Taxi-bus: colectivo, pesero, microbus
Taxi rank: sitio de taxis
Tourist office: oficina de turismo

◆ ON THE ROAD
Bicycle: bicicleta
Car: carro, coche
Freeway: autopista
Gasoline: gasolina
Gas station: gasolinera
Road: carretera
Toll: cuota
Traffic circle: glorieta
Turnpike: autopista de cuota

◆ AT THE BUS STATION
Bus: bus/autobus, camión
Seat: asiento
Checkroom: guarda equipaje
Ticket: boleto
Platform: andén
When does the next bus for ... leave? ¿A qué hora sale el próximo bus para...?
I would like a ticket for... Quisiera un boleto para....
Return: ida y vuelta
What time does the bus arrive? ¿A qué hora llega el bus?

◆ ASKING FOR DIRECTIONS
Is there a...? ¿Hay...?
Where is the nearest pharmacy? ¿Donde está la farmacia más cercana?
Where is the road to...? ¿Donde está la carretera a...?
Is it far? ¿Está lejos?
How many kilometers? ¿A cuántos kilómetros?
Take the second street on the right: Tome la segunda calle a la derecha
I'm lost: Estoy perdido(a)
I'm looking for...: Busco or estoy buscando...
North: norte
South: sur
East: este
West: oeste
On the left: a la izquierda
On the right: a la derecha
Straight ahead: todo recto or derecho
Above: arriba
Below: abajo
Ground floor: piso bajo, planta baja
First floor: primer piso (or segundo piso, as the ground floor is sometimes considered the first level)

CALENDAR

◆ MONTHS
January: enero
February: febrero
March: marzo
April: abril
May: mayo
June: junio
July: julio
August: agosto
September: septiembre
October: octubre
November: noviembre
December: diciembre

◆ DAYS
Monday: lunes
Tuesday: martes
Wednesday: miércoles
Thursday: jueves
Friday: viernes
Saturday: sábado
Sunday: domingo

◆ TIME
Today: hoy
Yesterday: ayer
Day before yesterday: anteayer
Tomorrow: mañana
Day after tomorrow: pasado mañana
Next Tuesday: el próximo martes
This morning: esta mañana
Tonight: esta noche
Early: temprano
Late: tarde
Later: más tarde
See you later: Nos vemos más tarde
One moment, please: Espere un rato (ratito/momento/ momentito), por favor
What time is it? ¿Qué hora son?
It's 8.30 (am): Son las ocho y media (de la mañana)
It's 3 o'clock (pm): Son las tres (de la tarde

ACCOMMODATION

Campsite: camping
Tent: tienda
Bungalow: cabaña
Hammock: hamaca
Bed: cama
Single room: habitació simple (in most cases, bedrooms are double)
Double room: habitación doble
With private bathroom con baño privado
With shared bathroom con baño compartido
Shower: ducha
Toilets: baños
Breakfast included: desayuno incluido
Tax included: impuestos incluidos
Air-conditioned: aire acondicionado
Fan: ventilador
Key: llave
Swimming pool: alberca
Do you have a room? ¿Tiene una habitación?
I would like to reserve a room: Quisiera reservar una habitació

How much does the room cost? ¿Cuánto cuesta la habitación?
Does the room have a view of the sea? ¿Tiene vista al mar la habitación?
Can you show me the room? ¿Puede enseñarme la habitación?
Can you prepare the check? ¿Me puede hacer la cuenta?
Can you wake me up at 7am? ¿Me puede despertar a las siete?

SHOPPING

Closed: cerrado
Open: abierto
Expensive: caro(a)
Cheap: barato(a)
Free: gratuito(a), libre
Traveler's check: cheque de viajero
Credit card: tarjeta de crédito
Cash: efectivo
Banknote: billete
Stamp: estampilla
Envelope: sobre
Postcard: postal
What time does the store open? ¿A qué hora abre la tienda?
Do you have…? ¿Tiene…?
What is the price of…? ¿Cuánto cuesta…?
Do you accept credit cards? ¿Acepta tarjetas de crédito?

HEALTH AND HYGIENE

Hospital: hospital
Emergency service: urgencias, emergencias
Pharmacy: farmacia
Sun cream: bronceador
Mosquito repellent: repelente
Condom: preservativo
Tampon, sanitary towel: tampón, toalla higiénica, kotex
I need to see a doctor: Necesito ver a un médico

AT THE RESTAURANT

The menu: el menú
Menu of the day: menú del día, comida corrida
Breakfast: desayuno
Lunch: comida
Dinner: cenar
Dish: plato, platillo
Table: mesa
Chair: silla
Napkin: servilleta
Fork: tenedor
Knife: cuchillo
Spoon: cuchara

Plate: plato
Glass: vaso
Carafe: jarra
Bottle: botella
Tip: propina
Service included: servicio incluido
The check, please: la cuenta, por favor

FOOD

◆ FISH AND SEAFOOD
(Pescados y mariscos)

Almeja: clam
Atún: tuna
Bacalao: cod
Calamares: squid
Camarón: shrimp
Cangrejo: crab
Caracol: sea snail
Cazón: shark
Huachinango: sea bream
Langosta: lobster
Lenguado: sole
Mero: grouper
Ostión: oyster
Pezsierra: sawfish
Pez espada: swordfish
Pulpo: octopus
Trucha: trout

◆ DESSERTS AND SWEETS
(Postres y dulces)

Arroz con leche: rice pudding
Cajeta: fudge
Flan: crème caramel
Helado: ice cream
Mermelada, jalea: jam
Nieve: sorbet

◆ VEGETABLES AND CEREALS
(Verduras y cereales)

Aguacate: avocado
Ajo: garlic
Apio: celery
Arroz: rice
Berenjena: eggplant
Calabaza: marrow, zucchini
Cebolla: onion
Chayote: vegetable pear
Chícharos: peas
Chile: chili
Elote: corn on the cob
Ensalada: salad
Frijoles: black beans
Habas: broad beans
Judías: beans
Lechuga: lettuce
Maíz: corn
Nopal: nopal (cactus leaf)
Pan tostado: toast
Patata, papa: potato
Pepino: cucumber
Perejil: parsley
Pimiento/Morrón: red pepper
Jitomate: tomato
Tortilla: pancake made with corn or wheat (trigo or harina)
Zanahoria: carrot

◆ FRUITS
(Fruta)

Fresa: strawberry
Guayaba: guava
Lima: small, sweet lime
Limón: lemon
Manzana: apple
Naranja: orange
Piña: pineapple
Plátano: banana
Toronja: grapefruit
Tuna: nopal fruit

◆ MEAT, EGGS, DAIRY PRODUCE
(Carne, huevos, producto lácteo)

Albóndiga: meatball
Cerdo: pork
Chicharrón: pork cracklings
Chuletas: ribs
Conejo: rabbit
Cordero: lamb
Filete: steak
Huevos a la mexicana: scrambled eggs with tomato, onion and chili
Huevos revueltos: scrambled eggs
Jamón: ham
Mantequilla: butter
Pato: duck
Pavo: turkey
Pollo: chicken
Pechuga de pollo: chicken breast
Queso: cheese
Res: beef
Ternera: veal

◆ MEXICAN SPECIALTIES

Antojitos: any dish based on tortilla or tamal
Asado: grilled
Barbacoa: barbecue
Botana: small side dishes, served with a drink in a cantina
Burrito: stuffed wheat tortilla
Caldo: broth
Ceviche: fish or seafood salad (on the coasts)
Chilaquil: leftover tortilla, which is fried and served with a garnish or sauce
Chile relleno: stuffed chile serrano
Chiles en nogada: chilies stuffed with meat, fruit and spices, covered in fresh walnut sauce and garnished with pomegranate seeds
Empanada: stuffed turnover made with corn flour
Enchilada: stuffed corn tortilla
Menudo: tripe stew
Mixiote: lamb stew
Mole: thick sauce

based on chili, nuts (almonds, peanuts) and cacao
Mole poblano: the most famous mole, from Puebla
Panucho: corn tortilla stuffed with black beans (Yucatán)
Pibil: hot dish (Yucatán) based on chicken or pork)
Pipián: sauce based on marrow seeds
Poc chuc: grilled pork marinated in bitter orange juice and served with a sauce of tomato and onion (Yucatán)
Pozole: stew with pork (or chicken), vegetables and corn
Quesadilla: tortilla garnished with cheese
Relleno negro: chicken or turkey accompanied by a thick, black, very hot sauce (Yucatán)
Salsa: sauce
Sincronizada: corn or wheat tortilla garnished with ham and cheese
Sopa de lima: poultry soup with sweet lime (Yucatán)
Sopa: soup
Sopa de arroz: pilau rice
Taco: stuffed tortilla
Tamal: corn dough mixed with vegetables or meat, wrapped in a banana leaf and steamed
Torta: sandwich
Tostada: crispy, fried tortilla
Totopo: fried tortilla, cut in triangles

◆ DRINKS
(Bebidas)

Agua fresca: drink made from a mixture of fruit juice, sugar and water
Agua mineral: fizzy water
Agua natural or purificada: mineral or spring water
Atole: flavored drink based on corn flour
Café americano: white coffee
Café negro: black coffee
Cerveza: beer
Chocolate: hot chocolate
Jugo: fruit juice
Leche: milk
Licuado: fruit juice mixed with milk
Liquor: spirits
Naranjada: orangeade
Té negro: tea
Té de hierbas: herbal infusion
Vino blanco: white wine
Vino tinto: red wine

The best way to discover Mexico is to adapt to the 'Mexican rhythm'. Breakfast here is fairly copious and dinner very light. If Mexicans eat out, they tend to do so for lunch (*comida*), when many restaurants are full to bursting; at night, in contrast, many eateries in small towns are closed! Another unmissable opportunity to soak up the local atmosphere, get to meet people and sample typical fare is provided by the popular *comedores* in the markets.

THE MEXICAN RHYTHM

→ DESAYUNO
Desayuno (breakfast) ranges from the 'continental' formula (coffee, bread rolls or pastries) to a copious spread of eggs accompanied by black beans and *tortillas*, as well as hearty soups – for example, the *menudo* (made with beef tripe).

→ ALMUERZO
If you find the morning too long, an *almuerzo* (light snack) will help you last out until the most important meal of the day, the *comida*.

→ COMIDA
Served between 2 and 4pm. *Comida* generally consists of two courses: soup, followed by a meat or fish dish with rice and vegetables.

→ NIGHT-TIME SNACK
Mexicans have a light supper, at around 9pm, comprising hot chocolate and sweet bread rolls, or a few *tacos*.

WHERE TO EAT?

→ IN THE STREET
Street vendors offer various typical specialties: the *chicharrón*, a grilled piece of pig's skin; small bags of sliced fruit, garnished with lemon juice and pepper, like corncobs; or *gelatinas*, fragrant, multicolored jellies with somewhat artificial flavoring, which are served in small beakers.

→ IN MARKETS
From 7am to 6 or 7pm
You can take a table in the eating area (*comedor*) in a market, in front of stands serving an array of typical dishes: *tacos*, *tostadas*, grilled *tortillas* with a choice of fillings (avocado, *ceviche*, sliced chicken, mushrooms, cheese), corn soup, *chiles rellenos*, and so forth. Wash the food down with a soda or *agua fresca*. The markets in the following cities cannot be beaten for charm: Taxco, Oaxaca, Coyoacán (in Mexico City), Guanajuato, Puebla, Pátzcuaro and Tepoztlán.

→ IN TAQUERÍAS, LONCHERÍAS OR TORTERÍAS
These Mexican-style fast-food joints are found on every street corner. They serve all types of *tacos* and sandwiches, eaten standing or seated, often to a soundtrack of *rancheras*. The delicious *tacos* are less expensive than those found in restaurants. The atmosphere tends to be lively at night.

→ IN RESTAURANTS
At lunchtime, the *comida corrida* is the equivalent of the menu of the day (or *menú del día*). At between $30 and $40, this will generally be the cheapest choice.
Note
If you have failed in your attempts to adapt to the 'Mexican rhythm', you risk having problems finding a restaurant after 9pm, especially in small towns and places with few tourists. That said, however, cenadurías, restaurants open only at night, serve tacos and other antojitos (snacks), in some cities.

→ ICE CREAM PARLORS
Ice-cream parlors (*heladería, nevería*) also sell delicious yogurts in a variety of flavors. The Michoacana chain in particular offers exquisite homemade ice creams (*helados*), as well as sorbets (*nieves*) in cones or on sticks (*paletas*). Do not buy sorbets from street vendors, as you can never be sure of the quality of the water they have used to make them.

WHERE TO HAVE A DRINK

→ CANTINAS
These were once exclusively the domain of men, but now Mexican saloons are gradually opening their doors to women as well. Immerse yourself in a totally Mexican atmosphere at the peak times (during the afternoons and at weekends), and indulge in the *botana*: with every beer that is drunk, a light snack is offered (such as a small salad or a dish of guacamole).

→ CAFÉS AND BARS
No shots of black coffee here! Mexicans sip tall glasses of white coffee, cappuccino and mocha in the afternoon and evening. In some cities (Oaxaca, Veracruz, Guadalajara, the colonial cities of northern Mexico), there are a few up-market neighbor-hoods (Coyoacán and Condesa in Mexico City) that boast European-style cafés with pretty terraces.

TIPPING

In principle, tax (IVA) is included in the prices. A tip (*propina*) is customary and expected in restaurants (approx. 15%).

For more information about the ingredients and specialties of Mexican cooking, refer to ● 66–70. For some useful food terms, see ◆ 413.

HOTELS AND RESTAURANTS ◆

Towns and cities are listed in alphabetical order.
A A1: coordinates in the map section at the end of this guide.
Each telephone number is preceded by the city code in brackets. For information about
making phone calls, refer to ◆ *403* and *409*.

Key

☑	The editors' favorites
Ⅲ	Air conditioning
☐	Credit cards accepted
☐	Credit cards not accepted
Ｐ	Parking
☒	Tennis courts
☒	Swimming pool

HOTELS

Price for one person for one night in a double room, based on two sharing:

⊡	< \$350
⊡	\$350–500
⊞	\$500–1 500
⊞	> \$1 500

RESTAURANTS

Price for a three-course meal, excluding drinks and service:

◼	< \$70
◼	\$70–120
◼	\$120–450
⊞	> \$450

ACAPULCO

▲ *181*   **D** A5

HOTELS

☑ **Hotel
Los Flamingos**
López Mateos s/n,
Fracc. Las Playas
Tel. (744) 482 06 90
*One of the few places
in Acapulco that
preserves the legend
of this magnificent
bay – first Johnny
Weissmuller (Tarzan)
then John Wayne
ruled the roost here.
Perched on the top of
the peninsula that
closes off the Bahía
de Santa Lucia, the
hotel has small, dark
pink rooms spread
along the edge of the
cliff. The swimming
pool, distinguished by
its curved forms,
reflects a cluster of
palm trees, seemingly
suspended from the
rocks. The restaurant
is passable, and
breakfast is a delight*

---

when taken from this
vantage point.
☒ Ⅲ ☒ Ｐ ☐

☑ **Villa
Bahía Ancha**
Carretera Barra de
Coyuca, Av. Ejército
Nacional, Km 17
Tel. (744) 488 90 65
*An original hotel,
full of personality,
with seven spacious
rooms (under large,
bright red vaults) and
a swimming pool.
A charming cross
between a hacienda
and a Roman villa,
between a
contemporary
creation and a
converted colonial
residence.*
☒ ☒ ☐

RESTAURANTS

☑ **100% Natural**
Costera Miguel
Alemán 3126
Tel. (744) 484 84 40
www.100natural.com.
mx
Daily 7am–11pm
*This large landmark
on the seafront
explores some
innovative ideas
under its gigantic
palm roof. The menu
uses natural produce
to offer large plates of
fresh vegetable
dishes, guaranteed to
satisfy even the most
devoted carnivore, as
well as soups –
reinterpretations of
Mexican classics –
and, above all, a
wonderful range of
fruit and vegetable
cocktails.*
◼

Pipo
– Almirante Breton 3
Tel. (744) 482 22 37
Daily noon–8pm
– Costera Miguel
Alemán 105
Tel. (744) 484 01 65
Daily 1–9.30pm
*Under ceiling fans
and chandeliers
adorned with
seashells, waiters
dressed in yellow and
white serve dishes of
supreme freshness,
such as tasty fried*

---

fish or the Pipo
Cocktail Combo, a
copious ceviche.
◼

Baïkal
Carretera Escénica
16, 22
Playas Guitarrón
Tel. (744) 446 68 45
Daily 7pm–1am (2am
Fri–Sat)
*Modern decoration,
with large windows
overlooking the bay.
The menu mixes
French, Asian and
Mediterranean
flavors. Apart from
the Lake Baïkal fruit
salad, the house
specialties include
snails, lobsters and
abalones (abulones).
Good wine list,
complete with
informed advice.*
⊞

ÁLAMOS

▲ *375*   **A** E5

HOTELS

☑ **Casa de María
Félix**
Calle Galeana 41
Tel. (647) 428 09 29
www.casademaria
felix.com
*Lynda, the Canadian
owner, discovered
that the legendary
actress María Félix
was born in this
house, so she
unearthed the plans
and tried to restore it
to its original state.
Lynda has also
created a small
museum, containing
all the documents
and photos she
has managed to
assemble. She
offers three
comfortable,
personalized
bedrooms, two of
them with a kitchen
and jacuzzi. There's a
small swimming pool
in the garden.*
☒ ☒ ☐

☑ **Hacienda de los
Santos**
Calle Molina 8
Tel. (647) 428 02 22
www.haciendadelos
santos.com

One of the most
beautiful hotels in the
entire country, it was
built as a residence
by a Spanish baron in
the 17th century. The
chain of patios has
now been fitted with
four swimming pools.
Everything is cared
for down to the last
detail, and the huge
bedrooms have
princely bathrooms,
with mosaics, pieces
of religious art and
antique furniture.
The hotel also has
a beauty parlor/
wellness center
and a large garden
containing the
restaurant
(reservations only).
☒ ☒ Ｐ ☐

AREPONÁPUCHI

▲ *374*   **A** F4

HOTEL

**Posada Barrancas
Mirador**
Tel. (635) 578 30 20
or (668) 818 70 46
*The most prestigious
hotel in the Sierra
Tarahumara is built on
the side of a canyon,
with an unbeatable
panoramic view. You
can visit for a meal or
a drink, but the prices
match the location.
As for the rooms,
they are very
comfortable but
somewhat
impersonal.*
⊞ ☐

BACALAR

▲ *213*   **F** D5

RESTAURANT

☑ **Cenote Azul**
Access via Av.
Costera, 3 miles
(5 km) from the
center, or the federal
road (from Cancún,
2nd exit on the left
to Bacalar)
Daily 8am–6pm
(cenote 8am–8pm)
*A genuine institution,
alongside a natural
well (cenote), popular
with Mexican families,
who flock here at
weekends to eat and
swim in the turquoise*

See ◆ 415 for a complete list of symbols.

waters bordered by the tropical forest – with a depth of 300 ft (90 m), this cenote is one of the most impressive on the peninsula. Excellent food (ceviche, seafood cocktails and shrimp dishes).
◘

BARRA DE NAVIDAD
▲ *332*   **C** A4

HOTEL

Hotel Buenos Aires
Veracruz 209
Tel. (315) 355 69 67
hotelbuenosairesmx@
yahoo.com.mx
A comfortable hotel with a friendly Argentinian-American owner. The rooms are small but immaculate, with a strongbox, mosquito net, abundant hot water, air-conditioning and a fan. The highlight, however, is the bar-terrace on the roof, where you can enjoy a tequila while contemplating the stunning sunset.
◘ ▥ P

RESTAURANT

Veleros
Veracruz 64
Tel. (315) 355 59 07
The best fish restaurant in Barra de Navidad, with a delightful terrace on the banks of the lagoon. The fish on your plate will have been caught that very morning!
◘

CAMPECHE
▲ *222*   **F** B3-4

HOTELS

Hotel America
Calle 10, between calles 59 and 61
Tel. (981) 816 45 88
Large, impressive, two-story colonial house with patterned tile floors; the rooms are off an open patio. Though comfortable, they are not in the best of taste.
◘ ▭

⌂ Hacienda Uayamón
On the Edzná road, after China, on the right
Tel. (981) 829 75 27
www.haciendasmexico
.com
Of all the converted haciendas, this is one of the most luxurious. All the extremely inviting rooms have their own terrace, and some even boast a small private swimming pool. The large swimming pool is in the old engine room, with only its stone arches still intact. The gardens are full of splendid trees.
▦ ▥ ▩ ▭

RESTAURANTS

⌂ La Parroquia
Calle 55, between calles 10 and 12
Tel. (981) 816 25 30
Daily 24/7
Not to be missed in Campeche. This large eatery, which is decorated with frescos inspired by the Mayan and Spanish cultures, is never empty but is particularly busy for lunch (comida) ◆ 414. Superb traditional food, served in generous portions. À la carte, soups, antojitos, meat and fish. Be sure to try the chiles rellenos: a real treat! Set breakfast menu.

⌂ Los Portales
Av. Miguel Alemán
Tel. (981) 811 14 92
Daily 6pm–midnight
Don't leave town without dining in this Spanish-style cenaduria, in the Barrio de San Francisco, behind the church of the same name and under the arcade of an enchanting little square. Local families gather here to enjoy a sopa de lima or panuchos ◆ 413.

As for drinks, the house specialties include horchata de coco and agua de chaya.
◘

CANCÚN
▲ *202*   **F** F1

HOTELS

El Rey del Caribe
Uxmal 24, SM2-A
Tel. (998) 884 20 28
www.reycaribe.com
Large, quiet, comfortable rooms, set in a beautiful tropical garden, with a small swimming pool and a spa area. This hotel, a refuge in the bustling center of Cancún, is ecologically sound: rainwater is stored, solar panels have been installed to heat water and the garbage is recycled.
◘ ▥ ▩ ▭

Maroma Resort and Spa
Carretera 307, Km 51
Solidaridad,
Quintana Roo
(20 miles/32 km south of Cancun Airport)
Tel. (998) 872 82 00
www.maromahotel.com
This luxurious hideway has 65 rooms and suites in houses scattered among the lush gardens; there are several pools and tennis courts and three restaurants. The Kinan spa has a rooftop yoga pavilion with a 360-degree view of the jungle and the sea. The spectacular wide, white sand beach with no seaweed is one of the best on the coast.
◘ ▥ ▩ ▨ P ▭

Paraiso de la Bonita
Bahia Petempich
Puerto Morelos
(a 20-min drive from Cancún Airport)
Tel. (998) 872 8301
www.paraisodelabonita
resort.com

Secluded on 14 acres (5.6 ha) with a private beach, this exotic hotel with its thatched roof entry and dark wood Asian furniture has 90 generously sized and stylish suites; vast bathrooms include a large sunken tub for two, double sinks, a big glass shower. Ground floor suites have a small private pool, upstairs ones a generous terrace with beach views. A French chef is in charge of the several dining rooms. Barragán-like red walls give way to a 24,000 sq. ft (2,230 sq. m) Thalasso spa with a salt-water pool. A 50-foot (15-m) catamaran is available for picnics; there is an infinity pool and one tennis court.
◘ ▥ ▩ ▨ P ▭

RESTAURANTS

La Joya
Bd Kukulcán, Km 9,5
Beside the Coral Beach Hotel
Tel. (998) 881 32 00/ 88
Daily 6–11pm
Nouvelle Mexican cuisine is served at one of the most appealing restaurants in Cancún, which has won various international awards. Live music.
◘

La Dolce Vita
Bd Kukulcán,
Km14.6; Hotel area
Tel. (998) 885 01 61
Daily noon–11.30pm
Enjoy the large bay windows and pretty terrace overlooking the lagoon while eating a delicious meal: green tagliolini, medallions of lobster and shrimps in white wine, threadfin (boquinete) Dolce Vita and fillet of red snapper in pastry, with shrimps,

mushrooms and lobster bisque.
⊞

CATAVIÑA
▲ 390   A B3

HOTEL

☑ **Hotel La Pinta**
On the right, as you approach from the north
Tel. (555) 151 46 04 or (619) 275 45 00
www.lapintahotels.com
An oasis in the desert. The large, comfortable rooms are arranged around a big, leafy patio in various shades of ocher, with a swimming pool that proves irresistible in such a dry setting. Rooms 111 and 118 have the best view of the desert, while those with the lowest numbers give on to the road.
⊡ ⊞ ≋ ⊟

CELESTÚN
▲ 239   F B2

HOTELS

Ecohotel Flamingo Playa
At the northern end of the beach
Tel. (988) 916 21 33
The most attractive hotel in Celestún offers modern comforts and a pretty swimming pool overlooking the sea.
⊡ ⊞ ≋ ⊡ 🖪

☑ **Hacienda Santa Rosa**
Approx. 34 miles (55 km) from Celestún and 6 miles (10 km) from Maxcanu on the Chunchucmil road
Tel. (999) 910 48 52
www.starwoodhotels.com/luxury
Once a hacienda, this charming hotel now belongs to the Luxury Collection, although its facilities are more modest than others in this chain: it is smaller (eleven) and less ostentatious, albeit with the same high prices. The

rooms are set in the old engine room, while a swimming pool has been installed in the reservoir used for irrigation.
⊞ ⊞ ≋ ⊡ ⊟

CEROCAHUI
▲ 374   A E4-5

HOTEL

Paraíso del Oso Lodge
3 miles (5 km) from Cerocahui, on the station road
At the foot of a cliff, some distance from the town, the Paraíso lives up to its name. Raised up above a river bank, it is totally delightful. The rooms – some lit by oil lamps – are arranged around a lush patio. There's a magnificent dining room decorated with animal skins, guns and superb saddles.
⊡ 🖪

CHICHÉN-ITZÁ
(see Pisté)

CHIHUAHUA
▲ 370   B A1

HOTEL

Palacio del sol
Independencia 116
Tel. (614) 416 60 00
www.hotelpalaciodelsol.com
The most luxurious hotel in town, although efficiency takes precedence over style – with the exception of the presidential suite; it has a view over the city and a sitting room with a fireplace under the rafters.
⊡ ⊞ ⊟

BAR

☑ **Casa de los Milagros**
Victoria 812, close to the corner of Ocampo
A haven of tranquility in an old house with a pleasant patio. Legend has it that, in olden days, many a frustrated love affair

came to fruition in the 'house of miracles'! It now attracts the city's gilded youth, and is an ideal setting for reading over an afternoon coffee or sipping a night-time cocktail. Food is also served. There is a concert of romantic Latin music at 9pm, Thur–Sun.

CHOLULA
▲ 291   D BC3

BAR

☑ **Anónimo**
6 Norte 601
Tel. (222) 247 08 49
www.anonimodelared.com
Movie screenings: Tue–Sat 2–8pm
It is amazing to find such a high-tech establishment in the humble streets of Cholula, but the success of Anónimo could well spark off a revival of this neglected area. The small red armchairs invite guests to linger and relax. A movie theater offers themed screenings, while the large covered terrace is sometimes used for concerts.

COMITÁN DE DOMINGUEZ
▲ 271   E E4

HOTEL

Virrey
Av. Central Norte Between 1ª and 2ª Norte Poniente
Tel. (963) 632 18 11
This bright pink and white hotel with an inner courtyard has very comfortable rooms and attentive service. Friendly and good value.
⊡ ⊡ 🖪

COZUMEL
▲ 204   F F2

RESTAURANT

Alfredo di Roma
Hotel Presidente Intercontinental Resort & Spa, Chankanaab, Km 6.5

Tel. (987) 872 95 00/64 32
Daily 6–11.30pm
The Roman branch is famous for having invented fettucine Alfredo! The menu includes meat ravioli with tomato sauce and tagliolini with sliced vegetables and shrimps (all the pasta is homemade). Try the tiramisu for dessert. One of the best wine cellars in Cozumel.
🔣

CREEL
▲ 372   A F4

HOTEL

Margarita's Plaza Mexicana
Calle Elfido Batista Perpendicular to López Mateos
Tel. (635) 456 02 45
The large rooms surround a courtyard dotted with tables and chairs. International food is served in a European-style dining room, complete with white tablecloths.
⊡ 🖪

CUERNAVACA
▲ 175   D B3

HOTELS

☑ **Hotel Colonial**
Aragón y León 19
Tel. (777) 318 64 14
This cozy hotel has fourteen rooms around a little, peach-colored patio with plants. Note that comfortable rooms with a small terrace and smaller ones with no terrace cost the same. Hot water and fans.
⊡ 🖪

Hacienda de Cortés
Plaza Kennedy 90
Col. Atlacomulco
(2.5 miles/4 km southeast of the center)
Tel. (777) 316 08 67
www.hotelhaciendadecortes.com
Mexico from another time: a huge estate with buildings set

HOTELS
⊡ < $350
▣ $350–500
▦ $500–1 500
▦ > $1 500

around a garden filled with birds. Built by the Cortés family, it played host to all the aristocracy of New Spain in the 16th century. Enormous rooms, beds with a canopy or on a platform, decorative azulejos, secret gardens, stone vaults, open-air lounges… The tables for the buffet breakfast occupy an entire courtyard, while the swimming pool with a waterfall recalls Roman baths.
▦ �III ✕ P ⊟

RESTAURANTS

☐ Pozolería El Barco
Rayón 5
Tel. (777) 314 10 20
Daily 11am–midnight
Emiliano Zapata 618, Col. Buenavista
Tel. (777) 313 21 31
There are two branches of El Barco in Cuernavaca – modest restaurants with fast service and low prices. Good antojitos and seafood dishes. The house specialty is pozole, a spicy pork stew accompanied by corn, which comes in no less than forty varieties, depending on the size and the way it is prepared. It is a simple dish, but hearty and very tasty.
▣

La India Bonita
Dwight Morrow 15
Tel. (777) 312 50 21
Open Tue–Thu 8am–10pm; Sat 9am–11pm; Sun 9am–6pm
One of the oldest restaurants in Cuernavaca. Its name refers to the Indian mistress of the Emperor Maximilian of Hapsburg – as does the costume worn by the waitresses. Specialties include fajitas de pollo en salsa de tamarindo and traditional dishes:

enchiladas verde de pollo and homemade mole. The delightful, shady inner courtyard is a perfect place to linger over a drink, or enjoy the folk dancing organized on Sat (9pm).
▣

☐ Las Mañanitas
Ricardo Linares 107
Between Av. Morelos and Álvaro Obregón
Tel. (777) 314 14 66
Daily 8am–11pm
This is one of the best restaurants in Mexico, situated in the elegant hotel of the same name. Its tables offer views of the pretty gardens, the habitat of an array of exotic birds. It specializes in shrimp curry (camarones curry) and pescado cappy.
▦

BAR

☐ Los Arcos
Jardín de los Niños 4
Tel. (777) 318 27 57
Daily 8am–midnight
At weekends, salsa groups liven up the terrace of this bar, which looks onto the zócalo. From their very first note, the customers are on their feet and swinging their hips. Arrive early in the evening and order a Mexican snack washed down with a beer (Mexican, of course). Los Arcos also has a fish restaurant next door if you're still hungry (ceviches, oysters).

EL FUERTE
▲ 175   A E5

HOTEL

Hotel Villa del Pescador
Robles, between 5 de Mayo and García
Tel. (698) 893 01 60
Eight extremely comfortable, air-conditioned rooms set around a large courtyard with an

attractive swimming pool. It is advisable to make a reservation, especially during the New Year and Easter Week holidays.
⊡ III ✕ P ⊟

ENSENADA
▲ 387   A A1

RESTAURANTS

El Rey Sol
Av. López Mateos 1000 between Alvarado and Blancarte
Tel. (646) 178 17 33
Daily 7am–10pm
This classic of French cuisine, founded in 1947, has earned an international reputation as the oldest French restaurant in Mexico, and one of the best. Try the freshly caught fish and seafood, accompanied by a local wine.
▦

☐ Manzanilla
Riverol 122, between López Mateos and Calle 2
Tel. (646) 175 70 73
Open Tue–Sun 6pm–midnight
One of the best fish and seafood restaurants in the country. The chef has a personal approach, based on quality produce, resulting in dishes like mussels with six chilies (mejillones a los seis chiles), abalones (abulón) and red tuna (atún aleta azul). This is one of Mexico's main winemaking regions, and accordingly the wines are excellent – try one from a small vineyard.
▦

GUADALAJARA
▲ 320   C C3

HOTELS

☐ Posada San Pablo
Madero 429
Tel. (33) 36 14 28 11
posadasanpablo@prodigy.net.mx
Huge, colonial-style

rooms painted a spotless white, in a 19th-century house with a patio. The rooms upstairs get more light; the bathrooms are immaculate. Excellent value for money in a very pleasant neighborhood 5 minutes from the center. Worth reserving in advance.
⊡ ⊟

☐ Posada San Rafael
López Cotilla 619
Tel./fax (33) 36 14 91 46
http://sanrafael1.tripod.com
A stone's throw from the Posada San Pablo, eleven comfortable, recently refurbished rooms in an old Jesuit monastery with a large covered patio. Reservations advisable.
⊡ ⊟

Hotel de Mendoza
Venustiano Carranza 16
Tel. (33) 36 13 46 46
www.demendoza.com.mx
Of the 110 rooms of the old convent of the Church of Santa María de Gracia, the most appealing are on the third floor, with a view over the rooftops towards the church. Some are endowed with a private balcony. Beware! Some rooms are less attractive, as they are small and have no view.
▦ ✕ P ⊟

Hotel Francés
Maestranza 35
Tel. (33) 36 13 11 90/09 36
reserva@hotelfrances.com
The oldest hotel in town, set in an inn dating from 1610, close to the cathedral. Its two stories frame a patio with arcades (once

RESTAURANTS

■ < $70
■ $70–120
■ $120–450
⊞ > $450

used as stables).
Elegant comfort in
the sixty rooms. Good
value for money.
🅱 🅺 🅿 🖃

RESTAURANTS

**🍴 Birrería
Las Nueve Esquinas**
Colón 384
Corner of Galeana
Tel. (33) 36 13 62 60
Daily 9am–10pm
A welcoming dining
room, covered with
tiles and proverbs.
The restaurant made
its name with
specialties from
Jalisco: birria de
chivo, a goat stew left
to simmer for hours,
and barbacoa de
borrego en pencas
de maguey,
a tasty lamb stew.
Slightly outside the
historic center, it
gives onto the
pedestrianized Plaza
de las Nueve
Esquinas.
■

La Chata
Corona 126
Tel. (33) 36 13 13 15
Daily 8am–11.30pm
A classic that has
been packing them in
since 1942, on
account of its fine
dishes from Jalisco.
Try the house
specialty, the platillo
jaliscience (chicken
accompanied by
potatoes, a flauta and
an enchilada).
Excellent value for
money.
■

Tinto & Blanco
Francisco Javier
Gamboa 245, corner
of Guadalupe Zuno
Tel. (33) 36 15 95 35
Open Mon–Sat
1pm–1am
The international
dishes served here
are carefully
coordinated with the
wines. After dinner,
you can stay on to
listen to jazz or house
music. A space is
also reserved for
exhibitions.
■

BAR

🍷 La Maestranza
Maestranza 179
Tel. (33) 36 13 58 78/
20 65
www.lamaestranzacant
ina.com
A picturesque bar
with walls covered
with bullfighting
posters and stuffed
heads of toros
bravos. Nibble snacks
(botanos) while
sipping a mojito,
mescal or tequila.

GUANAJUATO
▲ 349   C E3

HOTELS

**🍷 Hotel Hostería
del Frayle**
Sopeña 3
Tel. (473) 732 11 79
Rooms of varying
quality (but all at the
same price) in a
colonial building:
those overlooking the
street are sumptuous,
those further back
less so. Nicely
appointed linens and
imposing high
ceilings.
🅱 🖃

**Posada Molino
del Rey**
Corner of
Belaunzaran
and Campanero
Tel. (473) 732 22 23
A two-story, colonial-
style building, with a
covered patio. The
deluxe rooms vary
greatly; those on the
first and second
floors have splendid
vaulted brick ceilings;
the best rooms are
the ones that
overlook the street.
🅱 🅵

ISLA HOLBOX
▲ 250   F F1

HOTEL

**Hotelito
Las Tortugas**
Approx. 330 yards
(300 m) to the right of
the main entrance to
the beach
Tel. (984) 875 21 29
www.holboxcasalastor
tugas.com

You can opt for a
room under a high
palapa (an open-
roofed canopy)
complete with a
belvedere, or a more
luxurious, tastefully
decorated cabaña
fitted with its own
kitchenette and an
attractive bathroom.
Either way, you'll be
right on the beach.
🅱 🖃

ISLA MUJERES
▲ 202   F F1

HOTEL

Na Balam
Calle Zazil-Há 118
Tel. (998) 877 02 79
www.nabalam.com
The best situated and
most elegant luxury
hotel on the island.
Rooms on the Playa
Norte with a view of
the sea, or wooden
cabañas in a garden
with a swimming pool
on the other side of
the street. Some
rooms have a private
jacuzzi on a terrace.
Austere but
sophisticated
decoration. Try to
avoid the rooms
facing east, as they
overlook an
unattractive resort.
⊞ 🗆🅺🅿🖃

RESTAURANT

Casa Rolandi
Hotel Villa Rolandi
Fracc. Laguna Mar
SM 7, Mza 75
Lotes 15 and 16
Carretera Sac-Bajo
Tel. (998) 877 05 00
www.rolandi.com
Daily 8am–10pm
This Italian restaurant
is one of the best
known on the
Mexican Caribbean
coast and attracts
celebrities from all
over the world. Some
of the dishes owe
their special appeal to
to the fact that they
are cooked in a log-
fired oven – the fish
prepared in this way
is superb. Delicious,
homemade fresh
pasta.
■

IZAMAL
▲ 242   F C2

HOTEL

Macanche
Calle 22, between
calles 33 and 35
Tel. (988) 954 02 87
www.macanche.com
A haven of tranquility
amidst an array of
tropical plants. Before
diving into the pool,
make your choice
from one of the
bungalows scattered
in the big garden.
They vary with
respect to the price
and degree of
comfort, but all are
attractively decorated
and spotlessly clean.
🅱 🗆🅺🅿🅵

JALPAN
▲ 359   B E6

HOTEL

Hotel Misión Jalpan
Fray Junípero
Tel. (441) 296 02 55
www.hoteles
mision.com.mx
A beautiful hotel set
in an old colonial
residence, situated
on the main square.
This is the most
comfortable option in
town.
🅱 🗆🅺🖃

LA PAZ
▲ 399   A A5

HOTEL

El Ángel Azul
Independencia 518
Corner of Prieto
Tel. (612) 125 51 30
www.elangelazul.com
An expertly restored
19th-century building
provides the setting
for this delightful
hotel, imbued with
unassuming luxury.
The well-kept garden
and the large patio
are an oasis of
tranquility. Tucked
under the arcades,
the rooms – with their
tiled floors, stark
décor and pale colors
– create a Zen-like
atmosphere.
Although the larger
ones are particularly
appealing, the

◆ HOTELS AND RESTAURANTS

See ◆ 415 for a complete list of symbols.

smaller, less striking rooms are cheaper.
🖼 ▦ ▭

LORETO
▲ 397   A C5

HOTEL

Hotel Plaza Loreto
Hidalgo 2, three blocks from the malecón, on the left
Tel. (613) 135 02 80
hotelplazaloreto@prodigy.net.mx
This large building brings to mind a kasbah, with its courtyard surrounded by high walls in roughcast ocher. On the second floor, the landing opens onto a small terrace looking onto the street, with a view of the church's bell-tower. Laundry service available.
🖼 ▦ P ▭

MAZUNTE
▲ 308   D D6

HOTEL

☑ El Copal
Calle de Panteón Playa Mermejita
www.elcopal.com
On a promontory above a deserted beach, a handful of thatched cabins have a stunning view of the Pacific. El Copal is undoubtedly the most beautiful spot on this part of the coast. Each cabin has four beds and is complemented by a terrace and a wonderful open-air bathroom area. The cabins are tucked into the forest. The one nearest the beach is easily the most attractive.
🖼 🖼

MÉRIDA
▲ 226   F C2

HOTELS

☑ Luz en Yucatán
Calle 55, between calles 58 and 60
Tel. (999) 924 00 35
www.luzenyucatan.com

This big house full of plants and birds makes an enticing hotel. An ideal base for a few days – even the small swimming pool has a romantic charm – and the rooms with tiled bathrooms are very pretty. It's possible to use a private kitchenette or the communal kitchen.
🖼 ▦ ▧ 🖼

☑ Casa Mexilio
Calle 68, between calles 59 and 57
Tel. (999) 928 25 05 or 01 800 538 68 02
The interior of this colonial residence is so authentic you expect to meet a Spanish dignitary at any moment. The salons with their bourgeois furnishings lead to a maze of small terraces and outdoor staircases up to the rooms, each with its own name and history. Below, the swimming pool is tucked away amid an array of tropical plants. This intimate hotel is both charming and sophisticated.
🖼 ▦ ▧ P ▭

Hacienda Temozón
Route 261, approx. 22 miles (36 km) from Umán; 2 miles (3 km) after Yaxcopoil, follow the signs to the Hacienda
Tel. (999) 923 80 89
www.haciendasmexico.com
Of all the lavish haciendas, Temozón is the most famous. Its 28 rooms are decorated in the 'hacienda style'. Luxury (private pool, terrace), tranquility and sensuality guaranteed. Behind this majestic, bright red mansion house, a long pool converted into a swimming pool leads to the old engine rooms.
🖼 ▦ ▧ P ▭

RESTAURANTS

La Flor de Santiago
Calle 70, between calles 59 and 57
Tel. (999) 928 55 91
Daily 6am–11pm
This large, airy European-style café, founded in 1926, is soaked in atmosphere, heightened by its décor of wood and wrought iron adorned with old photos. It opens onto the quiet Barrio de Santiago, and in the evening the locals come here to have a coffee and a sandwich. Also on offer: huevos al gusto and other breakfast dishes.
▣

Los Almendros
Hotel Fiesta Americana, Paseo de Montejo 451, corner Av. Colón and Cupules
Tel. (999) 942 11 11
Daily 12.30–10.30pm
This unmissable institution provides the perfect introduction to Yucatec cuisine, one of the finest to have emerged from Mexico's cultural melting pot: venison (venado) and wild boar with annatto (jabalí al achiote). This restaurant was responsible for inventing poc-chuc, a pork fillet grilled over charcoal, served with tomato, grilled onions, purée of fried beans (frijoles colados) and fresh tortillas.
▣

MEXICO CITY
▲ 128   D B2

CENTRO HISTÓRICO

HOTEL

Hotel Majestic Best Western
Madero 73
Tel. (55) 55 21 86 00/09
www.majestic.com.mx
The 85 rooms are pleasant and

spacious, with a mini-bar, TV and bathtubs; you can have a view of the street, the Zócalo or the inner courtyard. The restaurant is on the terrace, overlooking the Cathedral.
🖼 ▦ P ▭

RESTAURANTS

☑ Café de Tacuba
Tacuba 28
Tel. (55) 55 18 49 50
Daily 8am–11.30pm
A magnificent restaurant run by successive generations of the same family since 1912. Its very comprehensive menu offers an excellent overview of Mexican food: tamales, pollo al mole poblano and other enchiladas. The large, attractive dining room has a vaulted ceiling and tiled walls, and is enlivened by musicians at night. Friendly, efficient service.
▣

☑ Casa de los Azulejos
Madero 4
Tel. (55) 55 12 13 31
Daily 7am–1am
Set in an old 16th-century palace, it is immediately recognizable by its Churrigueresque façade covered with earthenware tiles. A fresco by José Clemente Orozco (1925) adorns the stairwell. The magnificent interior contains two good Sanborn's restaurants, a bar, a tea room and a few stores.
▣

☑ Sobia
Palma 40
Tel. (55) 55 18 68 34
Daily 1–6pm
Two large and attractive dining rooms, with meticulously designed classical

☑ *The editors' favorites*

decoration, set in a well-ventilated basement. The house specialties are lamb and kid – from the brain to the feet, via the loin and the leg.
◘

Hostería de Santo Domingo
Belisario Domínguez 72, between República de Chile and República de Brasil
Tel. (55) 55 10 14 34
Daily 9am–10.30pm (9pm Sun)
The city's oldest restaurant (founded in 1860) occupies the site of a former monastery. It is the temple of chiles en nogada, *which are available throughout the year. Also recommended are the* quesadillas *and* pechuga ranchera en nata *(breast of free-range poultry with cream and chilies).*
◘

CAFÉS

Balcón del Zócalo
5 de Mayo
Tel. (55) 55 21 21 22
Daily 7am–11pm
You can have breakfast or a drink here at any time during the day, a salad at lunchtime or a full meal at night – all the while savoring the view of the Zócalo.

☑ Café La Pagoda
5 de Mayo 10F
Tel. (55) 55 10 11 22/91 76
Daily 24/7
A large, comfortable cafeteria, with excellent white coffee, as strong as you could possibly wish for.

ZONA ROSA

Hotel María Cristina
Río Lerma 31
Tel. (55) 57 03 12 12
A delightful colonial house with a patio and garden. The communal spaces are

relaxing and the 150 rooms offer good value for money.
🅰 Ⅲ Ⓟ ▭

POLANCO

HOTELS

Hotel Camino Real
Mariano Escobedo 700. Col. Anzures
Tel. (55) 52 63 88 88
www.caminoreal.com/mexico
This hotel is easy to spot, thanks to its bright yellow façade and fuchsia-colored doorway. Inside, the large communal spaces are stark but sophisticated, and the 724 rooms (from doubles to a presidential suite) exude an elegant charm typical of the 1970s. The Blue Bar, with its armchairs looking down onto water, is simply stunning.
🆓 Ⅲ 🎿 Ⓟ ▭

Hotel Habita
Presidente Masaryk 201, corner of La Martine
Tel. (55) 52 82 31 00
www.hotelhabita.com
The glass façade of this hotel, opened in 2001, hides 36 extremely refined rooms, with gray carpets, glass tables, extra-large beds, TV areas, Japanese music and a Zen atmosphere: hip and beautiful.
🆓 Ⅲ 🎿 Ⓟ ▭

RESTAURANTS

Águila y Sol
Molière 42, between Dickens and Presidente Masaryk
Tel. (55) 52 81 83 54
Open Mon–Sat 1.30–11.30pm;
Sun 1.30– 6pm
The mecca of creative Mexican cooking. Be sure not to miss the quesadillas rojas de machaca norteña *or the chenopeds (indigenous*

vegetables) with goat's cheese (huazontle con queso de cabra). *There's a gallery in the entrance that displays Mexican craftwork.*
⊞

Pujol
Francisco Petrarca 254, between Horacio and Homero
Tel. (55) 55 45 41 11
Open Mon–Sat 1– 11pm
One of the best restaurants in the city, it serves original, inventive dishes that draw on a wide range of ingredients. Opt for the menú de degustación *(a selection of sample dishes), imaginatively linked to the extensive wine list.*
⊞

ROMA AND CONDESA

RESTAURANTS

La Flor de Lis
Huichapan 21
Tel. (55) 52 11 30 40
Founded in the 1930s by a local Francophile, the Fleur-de-lis is renowned for its excellent tamales. *While here, you should also try the* atole, *a filling drink based on corn and cinnamon.*
◘

Contramar
Durango 200
Tel. (55) 55 14 92 17
Daily 1.30–6.30pm
This restaurant, reputedly the best fish restaurant in the city, attracts both families and fashion victims. Everything is excellent here, including the desserts, but the tuna *tostadas are particularly outstanding. A table at Contramar is highly coveted, but reservations are only accepted up to 2.30pm.*
◘

COYOACÁN

RESTAURANT

El Tajín
Miguel Ángel de Quevedo 687, between Carrillo Puerto and the bridge of San Francisco Centro Cultural Veracruzano
Tel. (55) 56 59 57 59
Daily 1–6pm
In this restaurant devoted to the cooking of Veracruz, some recipes have not changed for almost twenty years, such as the shrimps in tamarind sauce with jalapeño or chipotle (camarones en salsa de tamarindo al chipotle). Other delights include crabs in an earthenware casserole (chilpachole de jaiba), tidbits grilled on a traditional clay or iron disk (antojitos al comal), and an assortment of fish with annatto, grilled with salt and accompanied by a sauce of citrus fruit and chilies (pescado tatemado con achiote). The terrace is recommended, but its tables are highly prized!
◘

AZCAPOTZALCO

RESTAURANT

☑ El Bajío
Av. Cuitláhuac 2709, between Biólogo Maximino and Poniente 54
Tel. (55) 52 34 37 63/65
Open Mon–Fri 8am–7pm; Sat–Sun 9am–6.30pm
Although it's not ostentatious, El Bajío has earned an enviable reputation among gourmets for its rendition of old Mexican classics like mole de olla *(stew), chiles en nogada *and the more elaborate duck in* mole *(mole de pato) sauce.*
◘

◆ HOTELS AND RESTAURANTS

HOTELS

⬚ < $350
⬚ $350–500
⬚ $500–1 500
⬚ > $1 500

MONTEBELLO (LAGUNAS DE)

▲ 280   E E5

HOTEL

❏ Parador-museo Santa María
Montebello lakes road, around 11 miles (18 km) before the entrance to the park, on the right
www.paradorsantamaria.com.mx
Tel. (963) 632 51 16
This small, remote hacienda, on the Comitán plain, has eight rooms, all different, decorated with 18th- and 19th-century furniture. The restaurant overlooks the garden. The chapel contains a small museum of sacred art (16th–19th century). Reservations are advisable.
⬚ Ⅲ ⬚

MONTERREY

▲ 378   B D3

HOTEL

Best Western Centro
Av. Juárez 359 Norte
Col. Centro
Tel. (818) 125 47 00
This hotel in the city center has no special charm but it is well-kept and provides a good base for a stay in Monterrey.
⬚ Ⅲ P ⬚

MORELIA

▲ 311   C E4

HOTELS

Posada Don Vasco
Vasco de Quiroga 232
Tel. (443) 312 14 84
posada–don–vasco
@hotmail.com
This old two-story monastery with a pretty patio is set in one of the busiest streets in the city center. The rooms are all different, and some are far more appealing than others so ask to have a look at those available.
⬚ ⬚

Hotel Virrey de Mendoza
Poniente 310
Tel. (443) 312 49 40
www.hotelvirrey.com
One of the most luxurious hotels in Morelia, set in the former palace of Antonio de Mendoza, the first viceroy of Mexico. The 55 rooms are all different, with period furniture and glass chandeliers.
⬚ Ⅲ P ⬚

RESTAURANTS

❏ Café del Conservatorio
Tapia 363
Tel. (443) 312 86 01
Open Mon–Fri 9am–9pm; Sat-Sun 1–9pm
This is the most charming terrace in town, situated in a leafy square opposite the Templo de la Rosa. Ideal for breakfast or a snack with a drink.
⬚

Los Comensales
Zaragoza 148
Tel. (443) 312 93 61
Daily 8am–9pm
Delicious food typical of Michoacán, served in both the large colonial dining room and on the superb patio.
⬚

OAXACA

▲ 294   D D5

HOTELS

❏ Hotel Cuilapan
Trujano 305
Tel. (951) 514 83 42
A long courtyard that serves as a parking lot with comfortable and well-kept rooms surrounding it, at ground level or upstairs with a balcony (these are preferable, as they receive more light). Very central location but, consequently, fairly noisy in the morning.
⬚ P ⬚

Posada del Centro
Independencia 403
Tel. (951) 516 18 74
Two small ocher-colored patios, with large flower pots overflowing with bougainvillea, glass tables and metal chairs, a gangway with dark tiles and attractive lamps; inside, austerely furnished rooms with comfortable beds. This distinctive hotel makes its guests feel at ease.
⬚ P ⬚

Hotel Trebol
Flores Magón 201
Corner of las Casas, opposite the Benito Juárez market
Tel. (951) 516 12 56
This colorful new hotel offers good value for money. Beautiful bathrooms tiled with azulejos.
⬚ P ⬚

La Casa de Mis Recuerdos
Pino Suárez 508
Tel. (951) 515 56 45
www.misrecuerdos.net
This charming boarding house is made up of two buildings separated by a flower garden. The silence in the small bedrooms, tucked away on courtyards and terraces, is only broken by the songbirds hidden in shady cages. A pretty lounge-dining room is available for breakfast. It has won a reputation for its fine food, and the hostess runs classes in traditional Oaxaca cooking.
⬚ Ⅲ ⬚

RESTAURANTS

Flor de Oaxaca
Lopez 311
Corner of Armenta
Tel. (951) 516 55 22
Daily 8am–10pm
The food here is so delicious that it is easy to forget that the dining room lacks style and tends to be noisy. Be sure to try the local specialty, the succulent mole negro con pollo. Other good options are the enchiladas oaxaqueñas con tasajo and the filete de res a la veracruzana. Finish off by treating yourself to chocolate, Oaxaca or Spanish style.
⬚

Casa Oaxaca
García Vigil 407
Tel. (951) 514 41 73
www.casa-oaxaca.com
It is worth booking in advance one of the tables with wicker armchairs in the pretty courtyard. The octopus ceviche is renowned, and the fish of the day varies according to the catch in the morning. Order a good wine from Spain, Argentina or Mexico (the local Cabernet Sauvignon is particularly full-bodied), and a memorable dinner is guaranteed.

La Casa de la Abuela
Av. Hidalgo 616, between the Alameda de León and the zócalo
Tel. (951) 516 35 44/ 76 56
Daily 1–10pm
Set in a colonial house in the center, 'Grandmother's House' offers home cooking at its best. Particularly recommended are the tamales (turnovers wrapped in a banana or corn leaf and steamed) with dried meat (tasajo) and the seven varieties of mole, particularly the black one. Adventurous souls should try the grilled grasshoppers (chapulines).
⬚

HOTELS AND RESTAURANTS ◆

RESTAURANTS

▣ < $70
▣ $70–120
▣ $120–450
⊞ > $450

Los Danzantes
Macedonio Alcalá
403-4, between
Nicolás Bravo and
Ignacio Allende
Tel. (951) 501 11 84/
87
Daily 1.30–11.30pm
*Los Danzantes serves
contemporary
Mexican food in an
old 16th-century
church, restored with
modern accents. The
specialties include
grilled leaves of
balsam herb, stuffed
with cream cheese
and goat's cheese
(hierba santa asada
rellena de quesillo
y queso de cabra),
and duck enchiladas
with marrow seeds
(enchiladas de pato
en pipián verde).
Make sure you try the
house mescal as well.*
▣

BAR

La Casa del Mezcal
Flores Magón 209
Open Mon–Sat
10am–1am
*The customers here
knock back their
mescal standing by
the impressively
carved wooden
counter. It seems a
pity to order anything
else in a bar with this
name, but beer, rum
and vodka are also
available.*

PALENQUE
▲ 266   E E3

HOTELS

La Cañada
On the way out of the
city, going toward
Villahermosa (on the
right, after the traffic
circle)
Tel. (916) 345 20 94
*La Cañada is a
residential
neighborhood on the
edge of Palenque.
Travelers who prefer
natural scenery but
want to explore the
city center will find
the cabañas here a
good compromise.
Air-conditioned
and extremely
comfortable, they*

are dotted around a
large garden, which is
also the setting for
the restaurant.*
◫ ▥ ❄ P ⎙

☙ Maya Bell
The road to the ruins,
Km 6, on the left
Tel. (916) 345 14 64
*An excellent stopover,
on account of the
comfort and simple
charm of its rooms,
its large tropical
garden and, above
all, its huge
swimming pool in the
midst of the forest
(illuminated at night).
The restaurant is
attractive but the
food unexceptional.
A meeting-place for
travelers of all types,
with a relaxed
atmosphere and live
music on Saturday
nights.*
◫ ▥ ❄ P ⎙

Chan-Kah
The road to the ruins,
Km 3, on the left
(fake Mayan arch in
the entrance)
Tel. (916) 345 11 00/
34
www.chankah.com.mx
*The most luxurious
hotel in Palenque
offers beautiful rooms
in small pavilions,
with big bay windows
overlooking the jungle
and the enormous
swimming pool,
designed to resemble
a lagoon. The large
number of rooms
reflects the hotel's
popularity with
groups – so, the
degree of intimacy
partly depends on the
season.*
◫ ▥ ❄ P ⎕

RESTAURANT

☙ Tinajas
20 de Noviembre,
corner of Abasolo
Daily 7am–10.30pm
*The best in town,
with friendly and
professional service,
and a menu that
includes excellent
meat, fish, seafood,
fresh vegetables and
a wide range of soups*

– all served in
generous portions.*
▣

PÁTZCUARO
▲ 374   C E4

HOTELS

☙ Posada Mandala
Lerin 14
Tel. (434) 342 41 76
engapo@hotmail.com
*A small gem of a
hotel, with just five
rooms, two with a
shared bathroom on
the ground floor and
three on the terrace
with a private
bathroom and an
unbeatable view of
the city's rooftops
and the Sagrano
Church. The large,
red floor tiles, the
Indian tapestries, the
wooden furniture and
the soft beds all
create a cozy
atmosphere.*
◫ ⎙

☙ Mesón
de San Antonio
Serrato 33
Tel. (434) 342 25 01/
63 76
*One of the most
charming hotels in
Pátzcuaro, set in a
huge late-17th-
century residence in
the upper part of the
city. The large rooms
with high ceilings and
red floor tiles are
furnished with double
beds and a wooden
table. On one side
they overlook an
orchard, on the other
a patio covered with
lush plants. There's a
magnificent lounge,
and tranquility and a
family atmosphere
are guaranteed.*
◫ ⎙

☙ Posada
de la Basílica
Arciga 6
Plaza de la Basílica
Tel. (434) 342 11 08
www.posadalabasilica
.com
*A genuine find,
opposite the basilica,
on the premises of a
private hotel from the
early 18th century.*

The twelve
sumptuous rooms are
gradually being
refurbished, so that
you can now expect
waxed parquet,
fireplaces, painted
wooden beds and
mirrors with gilded
frames, not to
mention antique
chests of drawers.
The dining room
boasts a dizzying
view of the city, the
mountains and the
lake.*
▣ P ⎕

RESTAURANT

Gran Hotel
Plaza Bocanegra 6
Tel. (434) 342 04 98
*A first-rate hotel
restaurant that is not
overly expensive,
despite its delightful
terrace under the
arches of the Plaza
Gertrudis Bocanegra.
Try the sopa tarasca
– one of the best in
town – with chicken
enchiladas and tacos
de res. Everything
here is fresh and
tasty.*
▣

PISTÉ (CHICHÉN ITZÁ)
▲ 244   F D2

HOTEL

Hacienda Chichén
Tel. (999) 924 21 50
www.haciendachichen.
com
*The most elegant
hotel imaginable,
right next to the
archeological site.
The reception and
restaurant are located
in the former house of
a hacienda owner,
with a pretty arched
verandah overlooking
the garden.*
◫ ▥ ❄ P ⎕

PLAYA DEL CARMEN
▲ 204   F F2

HOTELS

☙ Posada Sian
Ka'an
Calle 2, between
Av. 5ª and the sea
Tel. (984) 873 02 02
*The large undulating
garden near the*

See ◆ 415 for a complete list of symbols.

beach is a dazzling sight – it even has its own little cenote. The cheapest rooms are at ground level, looking out on the lawn. Upstairs there is more comfort and views of the sea.
🔲 Ⅲ ▣

Hotel Deseo
Av. 5ª, on the corner of Calle 12
Tel. (984) 879 36 20
www.hoteldeseo.com
The height of luxury combined with state-of-the-art design: frosted-glass screens, white set off by ice blue, sails suspended to serve as partitions, a minimalist pool area with a teak floor and four-poster beds. The hotel's only drawback is that it is not on the sea front.
🔲 Ⅲ ▨ ▣

BAR

Captain Tutix
At the end of Calle 4, on the beach
Tel. (984) 803 15 95
Daily until 4am
Inside, a bar resembling a pirate ship; outside, tables and round lamps on the beach, with clients sipping cocktails to a soundtrack of R&B. The joint starts to jump at 11pm, when a rock band takes over.

PUEBLA
▲ *288*   **D** C3

HOTELS

♥ Hotel Puebla Plaza
5 Poniente 111
Tel. (222) 246 31 75
www.hotelpueblaplaza.com
The monumental entrance to this hotel leads to a series of small patios with orange walls and a staircase going up to the bedrooms. A friendly welcome is guaranteed and value is very good.

Furthermore, the hotel is ideally situated, right by the Cathedral.
🔲 ▣

Hotel San Ángel
4 Poniente 504
Tel. (222) 232 27 66
Restaurant open 7.30am–9.30pm
This bright, spotless hotel, in a patio sheltered from the street, offers rooms giving on to a walkway. The restaurant serves salads, soups, fish, meat and local specialties.
🔲 ▣ ▣

Hotel Posada San Pedro
2 Oriente 202
Tel. (222) 246 50 77
The bar has a fireplace and the swimming pool is set in a lush patio, one story above street level. The rooms are unpretentious, and those with a pool view come with small balconies and are preferable to the ones overlooking the street.
🔲 ▨ ▣ ▣

RESTAURANTS

♥ Cantina de Los Remedios
Corner of Juárez and 25 Sur
Tel. (222) 249 08 43
Open Mon–Sat 1pm–1am
The immense dining room stretches alongside the boulevard, with large photos displayed on the walls and an amazing ceiling sporting an array of objects, from birdcages to oars…This restaurant is extremely noisy, smoky and colorful – in short, buzzing with life, and a perfect place to mingle unnoticed with a very mixed Mexican clientele. Grilled dishes, chicken enchiladas and an

extensive drinks menu (there are hundreds of bottles lined up above the bar).
▨

Fonda de Santa Clara
– 3 Poniente 307
Tel. (222) 242 26 59
– 3 Poniente 920
Tel. (222) 246 19 19
www.fondadesanta clara.com
The music may be somewhat overwhelming, but the food is very good, particularly the local specialties such as tinga poblana (pork cooked with tomatoes and accompanied by slices of avocado), the unusual starter of fresh fruit and cheese salad and the authentic, homemade guacamole.
▨

Mi Ciudad
Av. Juárez 2507, between Calle 25 and Hermanos Serdán
Tel. (222) 231 53 26/ 02 77
Open Mon–Sat 1.30pm–12.30am; Sun 1.30–5pm
Earthenware tiles, antiques and frescos in typical Puebla style decorate this restaurant, whose food is staunchly traditional. They do an outstanding mole served with fresh tortillas and several seasonal specialties such as chiles en nogada.
▨

PUERTO ÁNGEL
▲ *308*   **D** D6

HOTELS

Gundi y Tomas
Entrance via the road by the main beach
Tel. (958) 584 30 68
www.puertoangel-hotel.com
A very welcoming casa de huespedes (boarding house)

perched on a hill overlooking the sea. The colorful bedrooms, with attractive frescos of pre-Hispanic inspiration, have fitted wooden furniture and open onto the terrace. Some food is available, as well as a safe, laundry and money-changing facilities.
🔲 ▣

♥ Hotel Buena Vista
On the right hand side (going toward Zipolite) on the road behind the main beach
Tel. (958) 584 31 04
www.labuenavista.com
Coconut trees brush against the tiled roofs of the bedrooms, which have four-poster beds shrouded in a mosquito nets; each has a balcony and an attractively tiled bathroom. The terrace offers a stunning view of the sunrise over the port, with the vast expanse of the Pacific beyond.
🔲 ▨ ▣

RESTAURANTS

♥ Rincón del Mar
Playa Principal
Daily 4–11pm
At the top of a few steps, at the beginning of the ring road leading to the Playa del Panteón, the pretty little terrace of the Rincón de Mar is perched above the bay. You can hear the waves below crashing against the shore, and watch the fisherman in the harbor, in the shadows of the big boats. The sea is the source of the menu: fish of the day (à la veracruzana), shrimp soup, octopus and, occasionally, lobster. You can also come here just to have a drink.
▨

❑ The editors' favorites

Restaurant Maca
Playa Principal, on the beach, to the left, opposite the tourist office
The best restaurant in the port. For thirty years, Macaria Cruz Cabrera has been serving her specialties at the entrance to Puerto Ángel: octopus with a spicy sauce, shrimps with olives and a hot sauce, Hawaiian fish fillet (with pineapple). Customers averse to seafood can opt for salads or spaghetti. Breakfast is also available here.
🦞

PUERTO ESCONDIDO
▲ 307   D D6

HOTELS

Hotel Flor de María
1ª Entrada, Playa Marinero, on the right after the bridge, going toward Puerto Angel
Tel. (954) 582 05 36
www.mexonline.com/flordemaria.htm
Restaurant open daily 6–9pm
The spacious rooms, with naive pictures painted directly on the walls, surround a lush patio. Guests receive a warm welcome and attentive service. The restaurant is considered the best in town. The swimming pool on the roof terrace offers a spectacular panoramic view. Be warned, however, that the Flor de María is a favorite haunt of mosquitoes in the rainy season.
🏊📶🅿️🍴

❑ Hotel Hacienda Revolución
Andador Revolución 21, on the right of Pérez Gasga, coming from Carretera Costera
Tel. (954) 582 18 18
Impeccable cleanliness and

abundant charm are the order of the day in this hotel, an oasis of calm right in the town center. The beds are made of carved wood, while the extremely elegant bathrooms are covered with mosaics. Excellent value for money. The classy restaurant next door belongs to the hotel.*
📶🍴

PUERTO VALLARTA
▲ 332   C A3

HOTELS

Hotel Posada Roger
Badillo 237
Tel. (322) 222 08 36/06 39
An attractive two-story hotel, arranged around a cool, leafy patio. The spacious, tastefully decorated rooms are all equipped with cable TV, and some have a balcony. There's also a small swimming pool, restaurant, communal kitchen and free strongbox service. Be assured of a charming welcome.
📶📺🏊🅿️

Casa Kimberley
Zaragoza 445
Tel. (322) 222 13 36
casakimberley@yahoo.com
For travelers who are keen to sleep in the bed used by Elizabeth Taylor and Richard Burton. The couple's splendid old villa has been turned into a hotel, complete with their furniture and a museum chronicling their exploits.
📶📺🏊🍴

Hotel Posada Río Cuale
Serdan 242, corner of Vallarta
Tel. (322) 222 04 50
riocuale@pvnet.com.mx
A pleasant little hotel with a swimming pool, on the south

bank of the Río Cuale. The rooms are unusually big, with extra-wide beds, a lounge area and cable TV. Good value for money in summer, less so in winter.*
📶📶🏊🍴

RESTAURANTS

Archie's Wok
Rodríguez 130
Tel. (322) 222 04 11
Open Mon–Sat 2–11pm
An institution, created by John Huston's former personal chef. The setting is elegant and the menu entirely Asian: chicken kebabs with satay sauce, shrimps with green curry sauce and coconut milk.
🦞

Café des Artistes
Guadalupe Sánchez 740
Tel. (322) 222 32 28
Restaurant open Mon–Sat 6–11pm (closed Sep). Dress code; reservations advisable. Bar open daily 6–11.30pm
One of the best chefs in Mexico, Thierry Blouet, holds court here. Several different spaces, including one entirely devoted to the highly recommended menú de degustación (sample dishes), a bistro and a drinks lounge.
🍴

QUERÉTARO
▲ 335   C F3

HOTELS

Hotel Mesón Obispado
Andador 16 de Septiembre 13
Tel. (442) 224 24 64/65
mesondelobispado@att.net.mx
A superb old monastery built in an eclectic neoclassical style, with ironwork imported from Italy. The spacious rooms have high ceilings

and beautiful painted wooden beds dating from the 19th century. Be sure to book one of the quieter, interior rooms.*
📶🍴

❑ La Casa de la Marquesa
Madero 41
Tel. (442) 212 00 92
marquesa@albec.net.mx
Once upon a time, an extremely rich man fell in love with a beautiful nun. She gave two conditions for her favors: that he solved the city's water supply problems and that he built the most beautiful house in the world. The results were the Querétaro aqueduct, the pride of the city, and this ornate residence, in a baroque style mixed with Mudejar. La Casa is now a magnificent hotel with ten royal and three imperial suites. In the restaurant, be brave and try fricassee of gusanos de maguey (cactus worms) and succulent ants' eggs with tomato sauce…
📶📺🅿️🍴

RESTAURANT

San Miguelito
Andador 5 de Mayo 39
Tel. (442) 224 27 60
lacasona5@yahoo.com
Open Tue–Sun 1pm–midnight
The splendor of this baroque casona (mansion house) bears witness to the vast fortune accumulated by Romero de Terreros, the founder of the state-owned pawnshops and owner of the silver mines in Pachuca. It is best appreciated at lunchtime, as the artificial lighting dulls its impact at night. The menu offers a choice of well-prepared Mexican

HOTELS
▫ < $350
▪ $350–500
▦ $500–1 500
▦ > $1 500

and international dishes.
▦

CAFÉS

☑ Via Espresso
Plaza San Antonio, corner of Corregidora and Peralta
Daily 10am–11pm
A charming café on a delightful little square, ideal for reading a newspaper with a coffee and panino.

☑ El Arcángel
Guerrero Norte 1
Tel. (442) 212 65 42
A cozy, old-fashioned café, where waitresses in black-and-white aprons scurry between the tables with huge coffeepots and delicious homemade muffins. Lunch is also available.

SAN BLAS
▲ 327   C A2

HOTEL

Casa Roxanna
Callejón el Rey 1, behind the Posada del Rey
Tel. (323) 285 05 73
www.casaroxanna.com
Fully fledged apartments, spacious and comfortable, with a living room and fitted kitchen, set in bungalows surrounded by a cool, well-kept garden. Two sizes, with two or three double beds.
▫ Ⅲ ⌇ P ⌿

SAN CRISTÓBAL DE LAS CASAS
▲ 252   E D4

HOTELS

☑ Posada Jovel
Paniagua, between C. Colón and D. Dugelay
Tel. (967) 678 17 34
www.mundochiapas.com/hotelposadajovel
The outdoor staircases leading up to the two stories of this impeccable and colorful hotel are interrupted by small landing-terraces with

wrought-iron furniture, perfect for sitting in the sun. The management is extremely professional, and this is reflected in the comfort and cleanliness of the rooms. Those in the annex (more expensive) are bedecked with arum lilies. It is a shame that no heating is available for the cold winter nights.
▫ P ⌿

Diego de Mazariegos
5 de Febrero
Fracc. Utrilla
Tel. (967) 678 08 33
reserva@diegodemazariegos.com.mx
The prettiest patio in town – huge and perfectly proportioned – has a fountain and wooden arcades with a thatched roof. On the other side of the street, a second patio has been closed and converted into a dining room. Unfortunately the decoration was not up to the overall standard of this magnificent colonial building. The seventy rooms are standardized but have all the comforts (including heating) that you would expect of a luxury hotel.
▪ P ▭

☑ Na Bolom
Museo Na Bolom
Tel. (967) 678 14 18
www.nabolom.org
The rooms offered by the Na Bolom Museum are easily the most beautiful to be found in San Cristóbal, as well as being steeped in history and memories. It has all the charm of a real house, with its original furniture and fifteen rooms (all different) overlooking

a large garden. Be sure to have dinner here: around the large dining table, you will find gathered foreign researchers, students and Lacandon Indians.
▪ P ▭

Plaza Santo Domingo
Utrilla, Corner of Escuadrón 201
Tel. (967) 678 19 27
www.hotelplazasantodomingo.com
This pretty 19th-century patio in the Santo Domingo neighborhood is adorned with a sturdy palm tree in the center and provides a view of the top of the Iglesia de la Caridad. Some rooms are set in a more modern building, around the patio and behind it. The oldest ones are distinguished by the exposed beams on their ceiling, while a few boast bathrooms decorated with azulejos. The best: nos. 5 and 6, 101 to 107. Breakfast and snacks are served in the elegant dining room and on the patio.
▪ ▭

RESTAURANTS

La Casa del Pan
Dr Navarro, corner of B. Domínguez
Tel. (967) 678 58 95
Open Tue–Sun 8am–10pm
On an enchanting little square near Santo Domingo, the Casa del Pan follows a trend pioneered by the chic neighborhood of Tlalpán in Mexico City, bringing together organic food, fair trade and a Zen attitude – in perfect harmony with the type of tourism popular in San Cristóbal. It is an agreeable place, with friendly service and cosmopolitan food

(such as tofu fajitas). There's also a good range of soups, salads and vegetarian dishes. At breakfast, a range of teas and juices, as well as enticing homemade cakes.
▫

Pierre
Real de Guadalupe, between Santiago and La Almolonga
Open daily
Pierre, who settled here ten years ago, makes his own butter, pâtés and pasta, as well as curing his own ham. He chooses his meat meticulously and cooks with virgin olive oil; he has even managed to find a Mexican chocolate with 70% cacao to concoct an authentic French mousse! Other delights include ravioli, eggplant confit with Parmesan, beef au poivre or à la bordelaise, chicken chasseur with olives and Normandy-style tripe – all washed down with an excellent wine.
▦

SAN IGNACIO
▲ 392   A C4

HOTEL

Ignacio Springs B&B
On the road leading to the center, on the left
Tel. (615) 154 03 33
www.ignaciosprings.com
Imagine sleeping in a Canadian tent in the middle of a palm grove? The four round yurts pitched on the river bank and owned by a Canadian couple contain real rooms and an unexpected degree of comfort: parquet, solid furniture and a microwave. There is access to the river for kayaking or swimming.
▫ Ⅲ P ▭

RESTAURANTS
- ☒ < $70
- ☒ $70–120
- ☒ $120–450
- ⊞ > $450

▲ *400* A A6

RESTAURANT

☑ El Mesón del Ahorcado
Calle Pescadores, corner of Marinos
Open Tue–Sun 6pm–midnight
This irresistible, authentic Mexican taquería, some way from the town center, is worth a detour for its vibrant atmosphere and delicious food. On the menu, there is a wide array of tacos and quesadillas, some with ingredients rarely found in Baja California, such as flor de calabaza, nopal and huitlacoche. Try all the small portions of spicy sauces on the table. No alcohol, but an exquisite café de olla, prepared with chocolate and cinnamon.
☒

▲ *338* B D6

HOTEL

Hotel Filher
Universidad 375, corner of Zaragoza 3 cuadras, south of la Plaza de Armas
Tel. (444) 812 15 62
hotelfilher@hotmail com
A beautiful building from 1890 with a large patio and a monumental staircase leading to pretty rooms decorated with wooden furniture and reproductions of works by Frida Kahlo and Diego Rivera. The ones looking out on the street have high stone windows. Very central.
☒ P ☐

RESTAURANT

El Callejón de San Francisco
Callejón de Lozada 1
Tel. (444) 812 45 08
Daily 2pm–midnight
Situated in an alley running alongside the Church of San Francisco, in the square of the same name. The delightful terrace on the roof has a view of the church's towers and its dome covered with azulejos. They serve fish and meat specialties.
☒

▲ *352* C E3

HOTEL

☑ Hotel Sautto
Hernández Macías 59
Tel. (415) 152 00 52
An excellent hotel in every respect. Guests enter through the porch of an old colonial house to find themselves in a huge garden dotted with orange trees and lined with paths bordered by fragrant flowers, leading to the rooms, or rather small studios. They are cool and shady, and some are spread over two floors, or even boast a little terrace. Their bathrooms and kitchen areas are charmingly decorated with yellow tiles. The restaurant is excellent, albeit a little expensive.
☒ P ☐

Posada de Las Monjas
Canal 37
Tel. (415) 152 01 71
www.posadalasmonjas .com
A beautiful hotel, set in the annex of the neighboring Convento de la Concepción – many of the rooms still have large painted crosses on the walls. They are all spacious, with a sitting area and a bathroom covered with earthenware tiles. The interior decoration is austere but sophisticated. There's a panoramic view of the nearby hills from the dining room and a large parking lot.
☒ P ☐

☑ Hotel Posada Carmina
Cuna de Allende 7
Tel. (415) 152 88 88/ 04 58
www.posadacarmina .com
A splendid 18th-century colonial building, a stone's throw from the main square. The patio, replete with orange trees and bougainvilleas, is surrounded by sumptuous rooms, with impressively high ceilings and elegant decor. There's a delightful restaurant serving breakfast and lunch. The finest hotel in its category in the town.
☒ Ⅲ ☒ P ☐

RESTAURANTS

☑ Olé Olé
Loreto 66
Tel. (415) 152 08 96
Daily 1–9pm
The dining room here bears witness to the owner's passion for bullfighting, with its posters of corridas and stuffed heads of toros bravos. The fajitas mixtas are mouthwatering, as are the beef and chicken kebabs. Excellent Chilean red wine.
☒

La Capilla
Cuna de Allende 10
Tel. (415) 152 06 98
www.la-capilla.com
Open Wed–Mon noon–midnight
The most prestigious restaurant in San Miguel benefits from an exceptional setting, under the high walls of the cathedral. There are two separate areas: a cheaper eatery on the first floor, which serves light snacks, and a fully-fledged restaurant upstairs, with a superb terrace that presents live music (piano or guitar) at night.
☒

▲ *234* F B3

HOTEL

☑ Hotel Sacbe
Route 261, Km 127 from Uxmal, on the right after the second exit (to Santa Elena)
Tel. (985) 858 12 81
www.sacbebungalows .com.mx
The small but charming private rooms, impeccable and tastefully decorated, are set in bungalows in the middle of a large garden, which is alive with birdsong in the morning. The hotel is run by a Franco-Mexican couple, who also serve delicious meals and can provide a mine of information on the region.
☒ P

▲ *393* A C4

HOTEL

☑ Hotel Francés
On the esplanade of the Mesa Francia
Tel. (615) 152 20 52
This evocative hotel was founded in 1886, during the glory days of El Boleo. The large colonial building with a verandah dominates the Mesa Francia. Breakfast is served downstairs, in a cozy dining room that has retained its wood trim and wall hangings. This style is continued in the shady, paneled bedrooms, enhanced by a rocking chair on the verandah. No. 112 has a view of the sea. Small swimming pool.
☒ Ⅲ ☒ P ☐

See ◆ 415 for a complete list of symbols.

TAXCO
▲ *176*   **D** A3

HOTELS

Hotel Posada de la Misión
Cerro de la Misión 32
Tel. (762) 622 00 63
www.posadamision.com
Terracotta tiles on the floors, a balcony set in the tiled roof, hidden patios, lush vegetation, galleries and bold, cool colors. This old mission, imbued with a delightful smell of wood, invites its guests to lose themselves in its charms. The swimming pool is bounded by a splendid mural, painted by Juan O'Gorman ● 96. There's a superb view of the city from the terrace of the restaurant, which offers both a tourist menu and service à la carte (grilled meat, fish).
🞉 ≋ P ▭

🞉 Posada San Javier
Estacadas 32
Tel. (762) 622 31 77
A small oasis of greenery, set below ground level. It is located in the heart of the city, but its guests reading by the pool, amidst a wealth of flowers, can enjoy total tranquility. The rooms are comfortable, well kept and prettily decorated. Some have a small sitting area, while others are large apartments with their own kitchen.
🞉 ≋ ⇄

RESTAURANTS

Restaurant Bar Paco
On the *zócalo*, corner of Cuauhtémoc
Tel. (762) 622 00 64
Restaurant: open daily 1–11pm
Piano bar: daily (except Thu) from 8pm
This fine restaurant

takes trouble over the quality of both its food and service. It boasts one of the best situated terraces in Taxco: on an upper level, above the zócalo and opposite the stunning Church of Santa Prisca. The Mar y Tierra kebabs (fish and meat) are accompanied by a delicious purée and crispy vegetables. Also recommended are the tasty spinach salad, the chicken curry, the shrimps and the enchilada de mole. Musicians and singers perform at night.
🞉

Restaurant El Campanario
Carlos J. Nibbi 4
Tel. (762) 622 69 66
Daily 8am–11pm
The delightful terrace dominates the Plaza San Juan. The aim here is to serve meat 'in the purest Argentinian style'. So, the chicken kebabs and all the other meats are grilled over charcoal. Alternatives for non-carnivores include the superb paella la valenciana and the traditional chiles en nogada.
🞉

TEOTIHUACÁN
▲ *162*   **D** B2

RESTAURANT

La Gruta
Opposite Puerta 5
Tel. (594) 956 01 27
Daily 11am–7pm
As its name suggests, this restaurant is set in a natural grotto. Nearly eighty years of loyal service have made it an unmissable stopover for the tourists who come to visit the archeological site. Try the plato mexicano, with rice, fried beans, chicken taco, guacamole, tamal ◆ 413, chicken

enchilada ◆ 413 with red mole and grilled beef with cheese (carne tampiqueña). You can watch folk dancing at the weekend.
🞉

TEPOZTLÁN
▲ *172*   **D** B3

HOTEL

Posada del Tepozteco
Paraíso 3,
Barrio de San Miguel
Tel. (739) 395 00 10
www.tepozteco.com
Terraces, gardens, and lush plants set off the pretty swimming pools. This is a peaceful and comfortable refuge with a splendid view of the Tepoztlán plain. Some rooms occupy small private pavilions, thereby providing an enticing sense of independence.
🞉 ≋ ▭

RESTAURANT

🞉 El Ciruelo
Zaragoza 17,
between Revolución and Matamoros
La Santísima neighborhood
Tel. (739) 395 12 03/ 25 59
Open daily 1–6pm (11pm Fri–Sat)
This picturesque spot in an idyllic village boasts a garden with adobe walls and a terrace with views of the mountain and the pre-Columbian site. The outstanding dishes include the shrimp tacos with jalapeño chili sauce (tacos de camarón en salsa de chipotle), fillet steak with four chilies (filete de res a los quatro chiles) and chicken breast stuffed with mushrooms and corn and bathed in goat's cheese (pechuga de pollo rellena de cuitlacoche y bañada con queso de cabra).
🞉

TIJUANA
▲ *386*   **A** A1

HOTEL

Hotel Lucerna
Paseo de los Heroes 10902
Tel. (664) 633 39 00
www.hotel-lucerna. com.mx
Family hotels are few and far between in Tijuana, so the Lucerna stands apart. It has the virtue of being well kept and friendly, as well as being central (albeit removed from the touristy districts); it has 168 bedrooms and suites.
⊞ Ⅲ ≋ P ▭

RESTAURANT

Café La Especial
Revolución 718,
between 3ª and 4ª
Tel. (664) 685 66 54
Open daily
One of the best restaurants in town, and a meeting-place for toreros after the corridas. Its reputation has reached the ears of tourists, who can be seen rubbing shoulders with Mexican families in this vaulted brick cellar, decorated in bright colors. Top-class food and impeccable service.
🞉

TLAXCALA
▲ *284*   **D** C2-3

HOTEL

Hotel Posada Francisco
Plaza de la Constitución 17
Tel. (246) 462 60 22
www.posadasanfrancis co.com
A beautiful hotel in classic Mexican colors: dark blue, ocher, lemon yellow. It is has spacious communal areas: a large swimming pool, several dining rooms, a small lounge by a fountain. The bar is decorated with bullfighting posters

and mementoes. The superb bullrings of Tlaxcala are justly famous (*corridas* are mainly on Sundays).
⊞ �Ⅲ ≋ P P

RESTAURANT

❑ Gran Café del Zócalo
Portal Hidalgo 7A
Tel. (246) 462 18 54
Daily 7am–11pm
One of the restaurants under the weathered arcade of the Portal Hidalgo, running alongside the zócalo. The set menu includes a soup and two main courses (enchiladas, rice, grilled meat). At the weekend, the Gran Café offers a generous buffet for breakfast, lunch and dinner. The service is both attentive and friendly.
⊞

TODOS SANTOS
▲ *400*   A A6

HOTEL

B&B Las Casitas
Rangel, between Obregón and Hidalgo
Tel. (612) 145 02 55
www.lascasitasbandb.com
This hotel, set within a small tropical garden, is distinguished by its well-kept rooms and cheerful service. Brunch is served on Sunday in season.
⊞ ▭

TULUM
▲ *208*   F F3

HOTELS

❑ El Paraíso
Km 1
Tel. (984) 871 20 07
www.elparaisotulum.com
Try to book one of the four enchanting cabañas raised on piles, in an idyllic location by the sea. The hotel also has ten very comfortable bedrooms (though set back from the water and overlooking the

parking lot). The Paraíso's beach is ideal, with unobtrusive and tasteful facilities that include several yellow-and-white cotton hammocks, and a small bar with seats on swings. Parasols and chaises longues can also be reserved.
⊞ P P

❑ Los Arrecifes
Km 7
Tel. (cellphone) (044) 984 879 73 07
Perfect for sleeping by the sea, with a real sense of isolation: the hotel is off the beaten track, and it is complemented by a cluster of cabañas, set directly on the sand, furnished with only a bed (with mosquito net) and a wooden board for storing a suitcase. Given the high levels of humidity, however, it is unfortunate that the showers are set at the far end of the hotel. If you are put off by the sand and mugginess, the hotel itself offers well-ventilated rooms, slightly set back from the beach.
⊞ P

❑ Zamas
Km 5
Tel. (984) 877 85 23
www.zamas.com
The best hotel in Tulum, in a different league from the other cabañas. It combines an idyllic setting – on the edge of a cove – with highly original interior decoration and carefully calculated color schemes that steer well clear of Caribbean kitsch. Its rooms are all different and very comfortable, featuring details such as floors partially covered with glass bricks and bathroom windows with stunning views of the

jungle. Not all the cabañas are on the beach, but the suites on the other side of the road are equally attractive, with expansive terraces in clearings in the forest.
⊞ P P

RESTAURANT

¡Que fresco! Restaurante
Open daily until 10pm
The restaurant attached to Hotel Zamas enjoys a spectacular location above the beach, on a small outcrop that affords not only dazzling views but also a breeze – highly appreciated in summer. Attentive service, delicious pasta, enchiladas and pizzas, as well as fish and meat dishes (pollo en mole).
⊞

TUXTLA GUTIÉRREZ
▲ *281*   E D4

HOTEL

Maria Eugenia
Corner of Av. Central Oriente and 6ª Calle Oriente Norte
Tel. (961) 613 37 67
www.mariaeugenia.com.mx
This large, centrally located hotel with 83 rooms manages to combine comfort of an international standard with décor reminiscent of a hacienda. There is also a good restaurant.
⊞ Ⅲ ≋ P ▭

UXMAL
(See Santa Elena)

VALLADOLID
▲ *248*   F E2

HOTELS

❑ Hotel San Clemente
Calle 42
Tel. (985) 856 22 08/ 31 61
www.hotelsanclemente.com.mx

This hotel could not be more central. The building is modern, but appealingly decorated with azulejos and wrought iron, and its large, comfortable rooms overlook a courtyard with a swimming pool, orange trees and hibiscus plants. The view of the cathedral towers from the first floor is simply magical.
⊞ Ⅲ ≋ P ▭

❑ Hotel El Mesón del Marqués
Zócalo, Calle 39
Tel. (985) 856 20 73/ 30 42/35 71
www.mesondelmarques.com
The prettiest hotel in town occupies an old colonial house. The large patio with a fountain is lined with arcades, complete with impressive chandeliers and naive murals. Ask for a room on this side; the best (nos. 222, 224 and 226) have the bonus of views of the Cathedral. A second, more modern patio with a pool has been built to the rear. Note that almost all the bathrooms are equipped with tubs – highly unusual in Mexico!
⊞ Ⅲ ≋ P ▭

RESTAURANT

❑ Hosteria del Marqués
Zócalo, Calle 39
Daily 7am–10.30pm
A delicious treat is guaranteed in this restaurant, set in the patio of the hotel of the same name. It offers a highly varied menu, combining Mexican and international food with excellent regional specialties (pollo en relleno negro), a wide range of soups, meat and seafood dishes, as well as low-calorie specialties for guests

◆ HOTELS AND RESTAURANTS

See ◆ 415 for a complete list of symbols.

anxious for a break from tacos! Also open for breakfast and drinks. Very thoughtful service.
⬛

VERACRUZ
▲ 185   D E3

HOTELS

Hotel Colonial
Miguel Lerdo 117
Tel. (229) 932 01 93
You will need time to find your way around the maze of corridors of this hotel with its old, pink façade. The terrace on the fifth floor offers stunning views of the zócalo below, while the second story boasts a swimming pool. The restaurant of the same name (under the arcade) is first rate.
🔲 🎚 ⬛ P ⬜

Mesón del Mar
Calle Esteban Morales 543
Tel. (229) 932 50 43
reservaciones@meson delmar.com.mx
Set in a beautiful 18th-century colonial building with large, cool arcades. Efficient and friendly service. Charming, quiet rooms with their own Internet connection.
🔲 🎚 ⬜

RESTAURANTS

Gran Café de la Parroquia
Gómez Farias 34
Tel. (229) 932 25 84
Daily 6am–1am
One of the outstanding restaurants in Veracruz (despite the ferocious air conditioning!). The menu includes fine local dishes (frijoles a la veracruzana, enchilada special Parroquia), as well as an array of drinks: from beer with milk chocolate to refrescos naturales con agua mineral. These consist of

pieces of fresh fruit in a large glass of fizzy water: eat the fruit, then drink the flavored water. Delicious and refreshing.
⬛

Gran Café del Portal
Corner of Zamora and Independencia
Tel. (229) 312 71 59
Daily 7am–midnight
This is another institution, set on the premises of an old confectioner's store dating from 1824. This famous café has served as a meeting place for countless politicians and intellectuals, and its central location still makes it a convenient rendezvous today. You can come here to eat an excellent meal or merely enjoy a drink or coffee, but head for the terrace on the street rather than the dining room, with its glacial air-conditioning.
⬛

Mesón del Mar
Same details as the hotel (*left*)
The hotel runs a restaurant that serves fresh fish – the owners are a family of fishermen – as well as meat dishes and local specialties.
⬛

VILLAHERMOSA
▲ 198   E D3

HOTEL

Best Western Hotel Madan
Madero 408
Between Lerdo de Tejada and Reforma
Tel. (993) 314 05 24/ 18
The accommodation in Villahermosa is undistinguished on the whole, and the Madan stands out as a reliable, comfortable and spotlessly clean option. The charming restaurant-cafeteria

on the first floor is usually packed, often with local businessmen relaxing between meetings.
🔲 ⬛ P ⬜

XILITLA
▲ 362   B E6

HOTEL

♥ El Castillo Guest House
Ocampo 105
Tel. (489) 365 00 38
info@junglegossip.com
This guest house was once the home of Dalí's famous English patron, Edward James. The architecture is a surprising mixture of Mexican, English and Moorish elements. Las Pozas, the Surrealist garden designed by James, is close by.
🔲 🎚 P 🔳

ZACATECAS
▲ 341   B C5

HOTELS

Hostal Reyna Soledad
Tacuba 170
Tel. (492) 925 20 49
www.hostalreynasole dad.com.mx
A haven of tranquility, right in the city center. Patios bedecked with flowers, comfortable rooms decorated in rustic style (wooden furniture and colored fabrics) and a very warm welcome.
🔲 P ⬜

♥ Mesón de Jobito
Jardín Juárez 143
Tel. (492) 924 17 22
www.mesondejobito. com
An old vecindad (residential building divided into apartments arranged around a patio) has been transformed into a hotel, its picturesque alleys – painted yellow and red – now serving as corridors. This unusual conversion has been proved

successful, but the rooms are overloaded with an ostentatious display of luxury.
🔲 ⬛ P ⬜

RESTAURANTS

La Cantera Musical
Under the Mercado González Ortega
Entrance via Tacuba
Daily 1–11pm
One of the best restaurants in town, popular with both locals and passing celebrities. On the menu: regional dishes like the mole rojo de Zacatecas (whose recipe is a closely guarded secret), traditional specialties and soups. Attentive service.
⬛

El Pueblito
Av. Hidalgo 403-D
Tel. (492) 924 38 18
Open daily
noon–10pm
This restaurant in a reconstruction of a typical Mexican village is set in a colonial-style house. Be sure to try the delicia zacatecana, a popular local dish served at festivals in the region: it consists of pork in sauce (a type of mole), accompanied by noodles, beans and rice. Craft goods on sale at reasonable prices.
⬛

PLACES TO VISIT ◆

The symbol ★ indicates sites not to be missed.
The symbol ▲ refers to the description within the itineraries.
D A5 provides, when applicable, a grid reference for the maps at the end of this guide.

GENERAL INFORMATION

CHURCHES	*Only the most important churches have fixed opening times; others are opened according to demand; they are, however, rarely closed.*
ROCK PAINTINGS FROM BAJA CALIFORNIA	*The INAH (National Institute of Anthropology and History) has branches in cities close to archeological sites, and will issue the necessary permit for all visits. These offices can provide guides and snacks are also available.*
MARKETS	*Most are open daily from 7am to 6 or 7pm.*
MUSEUMS	*Usually closed on Mondays.*
ARCHEOLOGICAL SITES	*Usually open daily from 8 or 9am to 5pm. Bring some drinking water and an anti-mosquito spray if you're traveling to a tropical forest in summer. There's a fee of $30 for the use of a camcorder.*
MISSIONARY SITES	*Opening times vary a lot. It's best to visit between 9am and 1pm.*

ACAPULCO   D A5 ▲ 181

Fuerte de San Diego
Av. Costera Miguel Alemán
Open Tue–Sun 9.30am–6.30pm.

ACATZINGO   D C3 ▲ 293

FRANCISCAN MONASTERY
Tel. (249) 424 00 08
Open daily 7am–8pm.

ACOLMAN   D B2 ▲ 166

EX-CONVENTO
A colonial museum: open Tue–Sun 10am–5pm.

ACTOPAN   D B1 ▲ 366

SAN NICOLÁS DE TOLENTINO ★
Open Tue–Sun 10am–2pm and 4–7pm.

AGUASCALIENTES   B C6 ▲ 345

MUSEO DE AGUASCALIENTES
Calle Zaragoza 507
Tel. (449) 915 90 43
Open Tue–Sun 9am–6pm.

AMATITÁN   C B3 ▲ 323

HACIENDA SAN JOSÉ DEL REFUGIO
Tequila Herradura
Tel. (374) 745 04 15
Open Mon–Fri 9am–3pm, Sat 9–11am.
Guided tours every hour; call beforehand.

ANGANGUEO   C F4 ▲ 311

SANTUARIO SIERRA EL CAMPANARIO ★
Tel. (7) 156 00 44/01 800 450 23 00
Guided tours (3½ hrs) from Feb 10 to April 1: daily 9am–3pm.

ATOTONILCO EL GRANDE   D B1 ▲ 365

EX-CONVENTO DE SAN AGUSTÍN
Open daily 8am–7pm.

BALAMKU   F B5 ▲ 221

ARCHEOLOGICAL SITE
50 miles from Escárcega on road 186.
Open daily 8am–5pm.

BECÁN   F C5 ▲ 220

ARCHEOLOGICAL SITE ★
1¾ miles from Xpuhi on road 186.
Open daily 8am–5pm.

BONAMPAK   E F4 ▲ 271

ARCHEOLOGICAL SITE ★
93 miles (148 km) from Palenque on the frontier road.
Open daily 8am–5pm.
Bring food, water and a flashlight.

CACAXTLA   D B3 ▲ 286

ARCHEOLOGICAL SITE ★
Freeway 150, exit San Rafael Atoyatenco
Tel. (246) 416 00 00
Open Tue–Sun 10am–5pm.

CALAKMUL   F C6 ▲ 221

ARCHEOLOGICAL SITE
Close to Xpuhil.
Open daily 8am–5pm.

◆ PLACES TO VISIT

Towns and sites are listed alphabetically.

CAMPECHE
F B3-4 and map **M** ▲ *222*

CASA DE ARTESANIAS TULKUNA Calle 10 Tel. (981) 816 21 88	*Open Mon–Sat 9am–8pm.*
FUERTE SAN MIGUEL – MUSEO ARQUEOLÓGICO ★ Av. Escénica (road to Champotón)	*Open Tue–Sun 8am–8pm.*
JARDÍN BOTÁNICO XMUCH HALTÚN Corner of Av. 16 de Septiembre and Calle 49	*Open Mon–Fri 8am–3pm and 6.20–8.30pm, Sat 9am–1pm and 5–8pm, Sun 9am–1pm.*
MUSEO DE LA CIUDAD Baluarte de San Carlos Between *calles* 63 and 65	*Open Tue–Sat 8am–7.30pm, Sun 8am–6pm.*
MUSEO DE LAS ESTELAS Baluarte de la Soledad Corner of *calles* 8 and 57	*Open Tue–Sun 8am–7.30pm.*

CANCÚN
F F1 and map **L** ▲ *202*

ARCHEOLOGICAL SITE OF EL REY *11 miles (17.6 km) from the city center.* *Coach 'Hoteles-Downtown' to 'Ruinas'.*	*Open daily 8am–5pm.*

CELESTÚN
F B2 ▲ *239*

BIOSPHERE RESERVE ★ Cultur Organization Tel. (988) 916 21 75	*Excursions in small boats.*

CHAPINGO
D B2 ▲ *166*

ESCUELA DE AGRICULTURA Universidad Autónoma Carr. Mexico-Veracruz, Km 38,50 Tel. (595) 952 17 01	*Open Mon–Fri 10am–3pm, Sat–Sun 10am–5pm.* *Proof of identity compulsory for any visit.*

CHETUMAL
F E5 ▲ *213*

MUSEO DE LA CULTURA MAYA Corner of Héroes and M. Gandhi Tel. (983) 832 68 38	*Open Tue–Thu 9am–7pm, Fri-Sat 9am–8pm.*

CHIAPA DE CORZO
E D4 ▲ *281*

EX-CONVENT OF SANTO DOMINGO *8¾ miles (14 km) from Tuxtla Gutiérrez.*	*Open Tue–Sun 9am–4pm.*

CHICANNÁ
F C5 ▲ *220*

ARCHEOLOGICAL SITE ★ *7½ miles (12 km) from Xpuhil.*	*Open daily 8am–5pm.*

CHICHÉN ITZÁ
F D2 ▲ *244*

ARCHEOLOGICAL SITE ★ *76 miles (121 km) from Mérida and 1½ miles (2.4 km) from Pisté.* Tel. (985) 851 01 37	*Open daily 8am–6pm (ticket office closes at 4.30pm). Entrance to the Castillo interior pyramid 11am–3pm and 4–5pm. Son-and-lumière daily 7pm (winter) and 8pm (summer).*

CHIHUAHUA
A F4 ▲ *370*

CALABOZO DE HIDALGO Av. Juárez Tel. (614) 410 10 77	*Open Tue–Sat 9am–1pm and 3–7pm, Sun 10am–4pm.*
CASA REDONDA Corner of Colón and Escudero Tel. (614) 414 90 31	*Open Tue–Sun 10am–8pm.* *Guided tours.*
CATEDRAL Corner of Calle Libertad and Calle 2	*Contains a Museo de Arte Sacro, open Mon–Fri 10am–2pm and 4pm-6pm.*
MUSEO DE LA REVOLUCIÓN ★ Calle 10ª 3010 Tel. (614) 416 29 58	*Open Tue–Sat 9am–7pm, Sun-Mon 10am–4pm.*
PALACIO DE GOBIERNO Calle Aldama, corner of Carranza Tel. (614) 429 33 00	*Open daily 8am–7pm.*
QUINTA GAMEROS Corner of Paseo Bolivar 401 and Calle 4ª Tel. (614) 416 66 84/54 74	*Open Tue–Sun 11am–2pm and 4–7pm.*

For national calls: dial 01 followed by the city code, then the number.
For local calls: dial the 7- (or 8-) digit number, without the code. For a list of city codes ◆ 409.

CHINKULTIC		**E** E5 ▲ 277
ARCHEOLOGICAL SITE ★ *Track situated 4½ miles (7.5 km) before the Montebello lakes.*	*Open Tue–Sun 10am–7pm.*	

CHOLULA		**D** BC3 ▲ 291
AFRICAM *10 miles (16 km) from Cholula.* www.africamsafari.com.mx	*Open daily 10am–5pm.*	
SANTUARIO DE LOS REMEDIOS ★	*Open daily 9am–6pm.* *Entrance fee to visit the pyramid's galleries.*	

CIUDAD VALLES		**B** E6 ▲ 362
MUSEO REGIONAL HUASTECO Corner of Artes and Rosario Tel. (481) 381 14 48	*Open Tue–Sun 10am–5pm.*	
MUSEO TAMUAZAN Corner of Bd México Larendo and Libramiento Sur Tel. (481) 381 26 75	*Open Tue–Sun 10am–5pm.* *Guided tours.*	

COBÁ		**F** E2 ▲ 211
ARCHEOLOGICAL SITE ★ *27 miles (43 km) west of Tulum.*	*Open daily 8am–5pm.*	

COIXTLAHUACA		**D** D4 ▲ 293
CONVENT	*Open daily 7am–8.30pm.*	

COLIMA		**C** B4 ▲ 330
CASA DE LA CULTURA Calle Ejército Nacional	*Houses the Museo de las Culturas del Occidente.* *Open Tue–Sun 9am–7pm.*	
MUSEO ALEJANDRO RANGEL *In the former Nogueras hacienda.*	*Open Tue–Fri 10am–2pm and 5–7.30pm,* *Sat–Sun 8am–8.30pm.*	

COMITÁN DE DOMÍNGUEZ		**E** E4 ▲ 276
MUSEO BELISARIO DOMÍNGUEZ Calle Belisario Domínguez Sur 35 Tel. (963) 632 13 00	*Open Mon–Sat 10am–6.45pm, Sun* *9am–12.45pm.*	

CONCÁ		**B** E6 ▲ 360
SAN MIGUEL DE CONCÁ ★	*Open daily 9am–5pm.*	

CREEL		**A** F4 ▲ 372
MUSEO TARAHUMARA *Close to the railway station.* Tel. (635) 456 00 80	*Open Mon–Sat 9am–6pm, Sun 9am–1pm.*	

CUERNAVACA		**D** B3 ▲ 175
PALACIO DE CORTÉS Calle Leyva 100 Tel. (777) 312 81 71	*Houses the Museo Cuauhnáhuac.* *Open Tue–Sun 10am–5pm.*	

CUETZALAN		**D** C2 ▲ 190
ARCHEOLOGICAL SITE: YOHUALICHAN *5½ miles (8.8 km) from Cuetzalan.*	*Open daily 10am–5pm.*	

CUILAPÁN		▲ 305
MUSEUM	*Open daily 10am–5pm.*	

CUITZEO		**C** E4 ▲ 313
CONVENTO DE STA MARÍA MAGDALENA Tel. (455) 357 01 75	*Open daily 10am–6pm.*	

CUYUTLÁN		**C** B5 ▲ 331
MUSEO COMUNITARIO DE LA SAL Calle Juárez, corner of Progreso Tel. (313) 33 22 01 01	*Open Wed–Sun 9am–7pm.*	

DAINZÚ		**D** D5 ▲ 303
ARCHEOLOGICAL SITE *12½ miles (20 km) from Oaxaca.*	*Open daily 10am–5pm.*	

◆ PLACES TO VISIT

DZIBILCHALTÚN	F C2 ▲ 239
ARCHEOLOGICAL SITE *7½ miles (12 km) north of Mérida on Progreso. Turn right at Km 13.*	*Open Tue–Sun 8am–5pm.*

DZIBILNOCAC	F C4 ▲ 225
ARCHEOLOGICAL SITE	*Open daily 8am–5pm.*

EDZNÁ	F B4 ▲ 224
ARCHEOLOGICAL SITE ★ *30 miles (48 km) from Campeche on the China road (toward the airport).*	*Open daily 8am–5pm.*

EK'BALAM	F E2 ▲ 249
ARCHEOLOGICAL SITE *15½ miles (24.8 km) from Valladolid, toward Tizimín.*	*Open daily 9am–5pm.*

EL TAJÍN	D C1 ▲ 191
ARCHEOLOGICAL SITE ★ *10 miles (16 km) southeast of Papantla.*	*Open daily 9am–6pm.*

EPAZOYUCAN	D B2 ▲ 366
CONVENTO DE SAN ANDRÉS	*Open daily 9am–6pm.*

FILOBOBOS	D D2 ▲ 187
NATURE RESERVE *77 miles (123 km) from Xalapa, toward Perote, then Rancho Nuevo.*	*Open daily 8am–5pm.*

GUADALAJARA	C C3 and map T ▲ 320
INSTITUTO CULTURAL CABAÑAS ★ Calle Cabañas 8 Tel. (33) 36 68 16 40	*Open Tue–Sat 10am–6pm, Sun 10am–3pm.*
MUSEO REGIONAL Calle Liceo 60 Tel. (33) 36 13 99 57/52 57	*Open Tue–Sat 9am–5.30pm, Sun 9am–4.30pm.*
PALACIO DE GOBIERNO Plaza de Armas Tel. (33) 36 68 18 04	*Open daily 9.30am–8.20pm.*
TEMPLO DE SAN FRANCISCO 16 de Septiembre 295, between Prisciliano Sánchez and Miguel Blanco	*Open daily 7am–1pm and 4–8.30pm.*

GUADALUPE	B C5 ▲ 345
CONVENTO AND MUSEO VIRREINAL ★ Jardín Juárez	*Open daily 10am–4.30pm.*

GUANAJUATO	C E2-3 and map V ▲ 349
CASA DE LOS MARQUESES DE SAN JUAN DE RAYAS Calle Pócitos 7 Tel. (473) 732 29 90	*Houses the Museo del Pueblo de Guanajuato. Open Tue–Sat 10am–6.30pm, Sun 10am–2.30pm.*
FORMER HACIENDA OF SAN GABRIEL DE BARRERA 1½ miles (2.4 km) from Guanajuato. Tel. (473) 732 06 19	*Houses a museum open daily 9am–6pm.*
MUSEO CASA DIEGO RIVERA Calle Pócitos 47 Tel. (473) 732 11 97	*Open Tue–Sat 10am–6.30pm, Sun 10am–2.30pm*
MUSEO DE ALHÓNDIGA DE GRANADITAS Calle de Mendizábal 6 Tel. (473) 732 11 12	*Open Tue–Sun 10am–1.30pm and 4–5.30pm.*
MUSEO DE LAS MOMIAS Esplanada del Panteón Tel. (473) 732 12 45	*Open daily 9am–6pm (8pm during holidays).*

HIERVE EL AGUA	D E5 ▲ 304
SPRINGS *4⅓ miles (7 km) from Mitla.*	*Open daily 10am–5pm. Small entrance fee payable to two Indian communities.*

The symbol ★ indicates sites not to be missed.
The symbol ▲ refers to the description within the itineraries.
D A5 provides, when applicable, a grid reference for the maps at the end of this guide.

HOCHOB		F C4 ▲ 225
ARCHEOLOGICAL SITE	*Open daily 8am–5pm.*	

HORMIGUERO		F C6 ▲ 219
ARCHEOLOGICAL SITE *13½ miles (22 km) from Xpuhil.*	*Open daily 8am–5pm.* *Take a taxi from Xpuhil.*	

HUAZALINGO		D B1 ▲ 364
MISIÓN SAN JOSÉ	*Open daily 8am–4pm.*	

HUEJOTZINGO		D B3 ▲ 287
FRANCISCAN MONASTERY OF SAN MIGUEL ★ Plazuela Fray Juan de Alameda Tel. (227) 276 02 28	*Houses the Museo de la Evangelización* *Franciscana. Open Tue–Sun 9am–6pm.*	

HUEJUTLA DE REYES		D B1 ▲ 364
MISIÓN *Can be reached from Ciudad Valles* *or Xilitla on road 105.*	*Open daily 8am–2pm and 4–8pm.*	

ISLA COZUMEL		F F2 ▲ 204
MUSEO Corner of Av. Rafael Melgar and Calle 6	*Open daily 9am–5pm.*	
ARCHEOLOGICAL SITE SAN GERVASIO	*Open daily 7am–4pm.*	

ISLA MUJERES		F F1 ▲ 203
HACIENDA MUNDACA Playa Lancheros	*Open daily 9am–5pm.*	
ANCIENT TEMPLE OF IXCHEL	*Open daily 9am–5pm.*	

IXMIQUILPAN		D B1 ▲ 366
TEMPLO AND EX-CONVENTO DE SAN MIGUEL ARCÁNGEL Tel. (759) 728 70 15 (town hall)	*Church open daily 9am–2pm and 4–7pm.* *Convent open daily 9am–6pm.*	

IZAMAL		F C2 ▲ 242
EX-CONVENTO DE SAN ANTONIO DE PADUA ★	*Open daily 8am–noon and 3–8pm. Son-and-* *lumière.*	

KABAH		F C3 ▲ 236
ARCHEOLOGICAL SITE ★ *15½ miles (25 km) from Uxmal.*	*See 'Ruta Puuc'.* *Open daily 8am–5pm.*	

KOHUNLICH		F D6 ▲ 218
ARCHEOLOGICAL SITE ★ *5½ miles (9 km) from the village.*	*Open daily 8am–5pm.*	

LABNÁ		F C3 ▲ 237
ARCHEOLOGICAL SITE ★ *24 miles (39 km) from Uxmal.*	*See 'Ruta Puuc'.* *Open daily 8am–5pm.*	

LAGUNA DE BACALAR		F DE5 ▲ 213
CENOTE AZUL *Take the Av. Costera, approx. 3 miles* *from the center on the federal road.*	*Open daily 8am–8pm.*	
FUERTE DE SAN FELIPE *Below the zócalo.*	*Houses the regional Museo de Historia:* *open Tue–Sun 9am–5pm.*	

LANDA		B E6 ▲ 360
NUESTRA SEÑORA DEL AGUA ★ Corner of Av. Juárez and 5 de Mayo	*Open daily 7am–6pm.*	

LA PAZ		A A5 ▲ 399
MUSEO DE ANTROPOLOGÍA E HISTORIA Corner of Altamirano and 5 de Mayo Tel. (612) 122 01 62	*Open Mon–Fri 8am–6pm, Sat 9am–2pm.*	

LA QUEMADA		B C6 ▲ 345
ARCHEOLOGICAL SITE *35 miles (56 km) from Zacatecas.*	*Open Tue–Sun 10am–5pm.*	

◆ PLACES TO VISIT

Towns and sites are listed alphabetically.

LOLTÚN	**F** C3	▲ 230
GROTTOES *68 miles (110 km) south of Mérida on federal road 180.*	*Open daily.* *Guided tours at 9am, 1pm and 4pm.*	
LORETO	**A** C5	▲ 397
MISIÓN DE NUESTRA SEÑORA DE LORETO Calle Salvatierra 6	*Houses the Museo de las Misiones.* *Open daily 9am–7pm.*	
LOS TORILES	**B** B6	▲ 327
ARCHEOLOGICAL SITE *5½ miles (9 km) from Ixtlán del Río.*	*Open daily 9am–5pm.*	
MALINALCO	**D** A3	▲ 174
ARCHEOLOGICAL SITE	*Open Tue–Sun 10am–5pm.*	
MAYAPÁN	**F** C3	▲ 229
ARCHEOLOGICAL SITE *1½ miles (2 km) from Telchalquillo.*	*Open Tue–Sun 10am–5pm.*	
MÉRIDA	**F** C2 and map **N**	▲ 226
CATEDRAL DE SAN ILDEFONSO	*Open daily 6am–noon and 4–8pm.*	
CONVENTO DE LA MEJORADA	*Currently being restored.*	
EX-CONVENTO DE LAS MONJAS	*Open 8am–8pm, Sun 8am–2pm.*	
MACAY Pasaje de la Revolución 1907 Tel. (999) 928 32 36	*Open Mon and Wed–Sat 9am–8pm,* *Sun 9am–2pm.*	
MUSEO DE ANTROPOLOGÍA ★ Corner of Calle 43 and Paseo de Montejo Tel. (999) 923 05 57	*Open Tue–Sat 8am–8pm, Sun 8am–2pm.*	
PALACIO DE GOBIERNO	*Open daily 8am–8pm.*	
METZTITLÁN	**D** B1	▲ 365
CONVENTO DE LOS SANTOS REYES	*Open daily 8am–6pm.*	
MEXICO CITY	**D** B2 and maps **G** to **K**	▲ 127
ANAHUACALLI Calle del Museo 150 Tel. (55) 56 17 37 94	*Open Tue–Sun 10am–6pm.*	▲ 154
BASÍLICA DE GUADALUPE Plaza de las Americas 1 Tel. (55) 57 48 20 85	*Open daily 6am–8pm.*	▲ 144
CASA ESTUDIO DIEGO RIVERA ★ Corner of Diego Rivera 2 and Altavista Tel. (55) 55 50 11 89	*Open Tue–Sun 10am–6pm.*	▲ 154
CASA MUSEO LUIS BARRAGÁN ★ General Francisco Ramírez 14 Tel. (55) 55 15 49 08	*Open Mon–Fri 10am–2pm and 4–6pm,* *Sat 10am–1pm. By appointment only.*	▲ 151
CASTILLO DE CHAPULTEPEC Chapultepec Wood, 1ª Sección Tel. (55) 52 41 31 00	*Houses the Museo Nacional de Historia.* *Open Tue–Sun 9am–5pm.*	▲ 148
CATEDRAL METROPOLITANA ★ **AND SAGRARIO METROPOLITANO** Tel. (55) 55 18 10 03	*Open daily 7.30am–8pm. Guided tours of the* *cathedral: Sat 10.30am–1pm;* *clocktower: Mon–Fri 10.30am–2.20pm and* *4–6pm; sacristy: Mon–Fri 11am–2pm.*	▲ 130
CONVENTO DEL CARMEN Corner of Revolución and Monasterio Tel. (55) 55 50 48 96 www.museodeelcarmen.org	*Open Tue–Sun 10am–5pm.*	▲ 154
MUSEO DE ARTE MODERNO Corner of Paseo de la Reforma and Gandhi. Tel. (55) 52 11 83 31	*Open Tue–Sun 10am–5pm 30.* *Guided tours for groups.*	▲ 148
MUSEO DEL CHOPO Dr Enrique González Martínez 10 Tel. (55) 55 46 84 90 www.chopo.unam.mx	*Open Tue–Sun 10am–2pm and 3pm-7pm.* *Closed July and Dec.*	▲ 148
MUSEO DE LA CIUDAD DE MÉXICO Calle Pino Suárez 30 Tel. (55) 55 22 99 36	*Open Tue–Sun 10am–6pm.*	▲ 138

For national calls: dial 01 followed by the city code, then the number.
For local calls: dial the 7- (or 8-) digit number, without the code. For a list of city codes ◆ 409.

MUSEO DOLORES OLMEDO ★ Av. México 5843 Tel. (55) 55 55 12 21	*Open Tue–Sun 10am–6pm.*	▲ 158
MUSEO FRANZ MAYER ★ Av. Hidalgo 45 Tel. (55) 55 18 22 66 www.franzmayer.org.mx	*Open Tue–Sun 10am–5pm, Wed 10am–7pm.*	▲ 142
MUSEO FRIDA KAHLO ★ Calle Londres 247 Tel. (55) 55 54 59 99	*Open Tue–Sun 10am–6pm.*	▲ 154
MUSEO JOSÉ LUIS CUEVAS Calle Academia 13 Tel. (55) 55 22 01 56	*Open Tue–Sun 10am–5pm.*	▲ 136
MUSEO MURAL DIEGO RIVERA At the western point of the Alameda. Tel. (55) 55 12 07 54	*Open Tue–Sun 10am–6pm.*	▲ 143
MUSEO NACIONAL DE ANTROPOLOGÍA ★ Corner of Paseo de la Reforma and Gandhi Tel. (55) 52 86 38 50 www.mna.inah.gob.mx	*Open Tue–Sun 9am–7pm.* *Free guided tours.*	▲ 149
MUSEO NACIONAL DE ARTE Calle Tacuba 8 Tel. (55) 51 30 34 00	*Open Tue–Sun 10.30am–5.30pm.*	▲ 139
MUSEO NACIONAL DE LA ESTAMPA Av. Hidalgo 39 Tel. (55) 55 21 22 44	*Open Tue–Sun 9am–6pm.*	▲ 142
MUSEO RUFINO TAMAYO Corner of Paseo de la Reforma and Gandhi Tel. (55) 52 86 65 19	*Open Tue–Sun 10am–6pm.*	▲ 148
MUSEO SAN ILDEFONSO Calle Justo Sierra 16 Tel. (55) 57 89 68 45	*Open Tue–Sun 10am–5.30pm.*	▲ 137
MUSEO SOUMAYA Corner of Av. Revolución and Río Magdalena Tel. (55) 56 16 37 61 www.soumaya.com.mx	*Open Mon, Thu and Sun 10.30am–6.30pm,* *Wed, Fri–Sat 10.30am–8.30pm.* *Guided tours Fri–Sat noon, 2pm, 4pm and 6pm,* *Sun noon and 4pm.*	▲ 154
MUSEO DE TROTSKI Río Churubusco 410 Tel. (55) 55 54 06 87	*Open Tue–Sun 10am–5pm.*	▲ 154
PALACIO DE BELLAS ARTES ★ Corner of Juárez 1 and Lázaro Cárdenas Tel. (55) 55 18 27 99	*Open Tue–Sun 10am–5.45pm.*	▲ 142
PALACIO DE CORREOS Corner of Tacuba 1 and Lázaro Cárdenas Tel. (55) 55 10 29 99	*Visite Tue–Sun 10am–6pm.* *Proof of identity needed.*	▲ 142
PALACIO DE MINERÍA Calle Tacuba 5 Tel. (55) 56 23 29 81	*Open Mon–Fri 9am–3pm and 4–7pm*	▲ 139
PALACIO NACIONAL ★ Zócalo Tel. (55) 91 58 12 61	*Museum open Tue–Sun 9am–5pm. Access to* *Diego Rivera's mural paintings daily 9am–5pm.* *Proof of identity needed.*	▲ 130
PIRÁMIDE, MUSEO DE CUICUILCO Av. Insurgentes, Km 16, at crossroads with Anillo Periférico	*Open daily 9am–5pm.*	▲ 158
SECRETARÍA DE EDUCACIÓN PÚBLICA ★ República Argentina 28	*Open Mon–Fri 9am–6pm.*	▲ 137
TEMPLO MAYOR AND MUSEO ★ Seminario 8 Tel. (55) 55 22 18 49	*Open Tue–Sun 9am–5pm.*	▲ 132
TORRE LATINOAMERICANA Corner of Madero and Lázaro Cárdenas Tel. (55) 51 30 28 32	*Open daily 9am–10pm.*	▲ 139

MITLA   **D**E5

ARCHEOLOGICAL SITE 26½ miles (43 km) from Oaxaca.	*Open daily 8am–5pm.*	▲ 304

◆ PLACES TO VISIT

MOLANGO — **D** B1 ▲ 364
| MISIÓN SANTA MARÍA MOLANGO | Open daily 7am–4pm. |

MONTE ALBÁN — **D** D5 ▲ 299
| ARCHEOLOGICAL SITE ★
6¼ miles (10 km) southeast of Oaxaca
Tel. (951) 516 12 15 | Open daily 8am–5pm. |

MONTERREY — **B** D3 ▲ 378
| MUSEO DE ARTE CONTEMPORÁNEO ★
Macroplaza
Tel. (81) 82 62 45 00 | Open Tue–Sun 10am–6pm, Wed 10am–8pm. |

MORELIA — **C** E4 and map **R** ▲ 311
BIBLIOTECA PÚBLICA Corner of Calle Nigromante and Av. Madero	Open Mon–Sat 9am–7pm.
CONVENTO DEL CARMEN Av. Morelo Norte Tel. (443) 313 13 20	Houses the Casa de la Cultura. Open Mon–Fri 9am–9pm, Sat–Sun 9am–6pm.
CONVENTO DE SAN FRANCISCO Plaza San Francisco Tel. (443) 312 08 48	Houses the Casa de las Artesanías. Open Mon–Sat 10am–8pm, Sun 10am–2pm.
MUSEO DE ARTE COLONIAL Calle Juárez 240	Open Tue–Sun 9am–8pm.
MUSEO DEL ESTADO Calle Prieto 176 Tel. (443) 313 06 29	Open Mon–Fri 9am–8pm, Sat–Sun 10am–6pm.
MUSEO REGIONAL MICHOACANO Calle Allende 305 Tel. (443) 312 04 17	Open Tue–Sat 9am–7pm, Sun 9am–4pm.
MERCADO DE ARTESANÍA Plaza Valladolid	Open daily 9am–6pm.
MERCADO DE DULCE Calle Valentín Gómez Farias	Open daily 9am–7pm.
PALACIO DE GOBIERNO Av. Madero	Open daily 8am–9pm.

MUYIL (CHUNYAXCHÉ) — **F** E3 ▲ 212
| ARCHEOLOGICAL SITE
10½ miles from Tulum on the 307. | Open daily 8am–5pm. |

NANCIYAGA — **D** F3 ▲ 195
| NATURE RESERVE
Exit the 'Isla de los Tuxtlas' freeway,
direction of Catemaco.
Tel. (294) 943 01 99
www.nanciyaga.com | Special guided tour to discover pre-hispanic traditions such as the tezmacal (Mayan steam baths). |

OAXACA — **D** D5 and map **Q** ▲ 294
EX-CONVENTO DE SANTO DOMINGO ★ Corner of Macedonio Alcalá and Adolfo Gurrión Tel. (951) 516 29 91	Houses the Museo de las Culturas de Oaxaca. Open Tue–Sun 10am–8pm.
MUSEO DE ARTE CONTEMPORÁNEO Calle Macedonio Alcalá 202	Open Wed–Mon 10.30am–8pm.
MUSEO RUFINO TAMAYO Calle Morelos 503 Tel. (951) 516 47 50	Open Mon and Wed–Fri 10am–2pm and 4–7pm, Sat–Sun 10am–3pm.
TEMPLO DE SANTO DOMINGO ★ Corner of Macedonio Alcalá and Adolfo Gurrión	Open daily 1–4pm.

OCUITUCO — **D** B3 ▲ 173
| TEMPLO DE SANTIAGO APOSTOL | Open daily 7am–8pm. |

PALENQUE — **E** E3 ▲ 266
| ARCHEOLOGICAL SITE ★
5 miles (8 km) from town. | Open daily 8am–5pm (last entry 4.30pm). |

The symbol ★ indicates sites not to be missed.
The symbol ▲ refers to the description within the itineraries.
D A5 provides, when applicable, a grid reference for the maps at the end of this guide.

MUSEO DEL SITIO	*Open Tue–Sun 9am–4.30pm.*

PAQUIMÉ		**A** E2 ▲ 371
ARCHEOLOGICAL SITE *In the surroundings of Casas Grandes.*	*Open daily 8am–5pm.*	

PARICUTÍN		**C** D4 ▲ 319
VOLCÁN PARICUTÍN ★ *Follow directions from Uruapan;* *Parque Nacional, then Paricutín.*	*The ascent is possible if you start from* *Angahuán (six- or seven-hour hike, return).*	

PÁTZCUARO		**C** E4 ▲ 314
EX-CONVENTO DE SAN AGUSTÍN Plaza Gertrudis Bocanegra	*Open Mon–Fri 9am–6pm.*	

PUEBLA		**D** C3 and map **O** ▲ 288
BIBLIOTECA PALAFOXIANA Calle 5 Oriente Tel. (222) 246 80 74	*Houses a museum.* *Open Tue–Fri 10am–5pm, Sat 10am–4pm.*	
CASA DEL ALFEÑIQUE Corner of 4 Oriente and 6 Norte Tel. (222) 234 04 58	*Open Tue–Sun 10am–4.30pm.*	
CATEDRAL	*Open Mon–Sat 6.30am–12.30pm and 4–7.30pm.*	
IGLESIA DE LA COMPAÑÍA Corner of Av. Camacho and Calle 4 Sur	*Open Mon–Thu 9am–5.30pm, Fri 9am–1pm.* *Small museum open daily 8am–1pm, 4–8pm.*	
IGLESIA SANTO DOMINGO ★ Calle 5 de Mayo	*Open daily 8am–1pm and 4–9pm.*	
MUSEO AMPARO ★ Calle 2 Sur 708 Tel. (222) 229 38 50	*Open Tue–Sun 10am–6pm.* *Guided tours.*	
MUSEO JOSÉ LUIS BELLO Calle 3 Poniente 302	*Open Tue–Sun 10am–5pm.*	

QUERÉTARO		**C** F3 and map **S** ▲ 335
CONVENTO DE SAN FRANCISCO Corner of Corregidora Sur and Madero Tel. (442) 212 20 31	*Houses the Querétaro Museo Regional.* *Open Tue–Sun 10am–7pm.*	
IGLESIA SAN AGUSTÍN Calle Allende Sur 14 Tel. (442) 212 23 57/35 23	*Houses the Museo de Arte de Querétaro.* *Open Tue–Sun 10am–6pm.*	
TEMPLO DE SANTA CLARA ★ Corner of Madero and Allende	*Open daily 9am–7pm.*	
TEMPLO DE SANTA ROSA DE VITERBO ★ Corner of Arteaga and Ezequiel Montes Tel. (442) 214 16 91	*Open daily 8am–1pm and 4–8pm.*	

RÍO LAGARTOS		**F** DE1 ▲ 250
RÉSERVE DE BIOSPHÈRE *From the village, follow the sea front* *toward the west, then 'Isla Contoy'.* www.riolagartos.com	*The tourist guides from the Isla Contoy travel* *agency, tel. (986) 862 00 02, are knowledgeable* *about the area's fauna and flora; discovery of the* *Las Coloradas' natural salt marshes; night* *excursions to see crocodiles.*	

RUTA PUUC		**F** BC3 ▲ 236
75-mile (120-km) loop (departs from *Muna). 'Ruta Puuc' coach (coach* *terminal): corner of calles 68 and 69.* Tel. (999) 923 22 87	*Day excursion aboard a coach that drives around* *the loop and stops at each remarkable site.* *Departure from Mérida daily 8am.* *Bring anti-mosquito lotion and water.*	

SALTILLO		**B** D4 ▲ 381
BIRD MUSEUM Corner of Hidalgo and Bolivar 151 Tel. (844) 414 01 67/68/69	*Open Tue–Sat 10am–6pm, Sun 11am–7pm.* *Independent guides.*	
DESERT MUSEUM In the Parque las Maravillas. Tel. (844) 410 66 23/33/36	*Open Tue–Sun 10am–5pm. Screening of* *documentaries Sat–Sun 1pm and 3pm.*	

SAN CRISTÓBAL DE LAS CASAS		**E** D4 and map **P** ▲ 252
CASA NA BOLOM ★ Calle Guerrero (northermost point) Tel. (967) 678 14 18	*Open daily 9am–2pm. Guided tours in Spanish* *and in English 11.30 and 2pm.*	

Towns and sites are listed alphabetically.

CATEDRAL	*Open Tue–Sun 10am–2pm and 4–7pm.*
MUSEO DEL ÁMBAR DE CHIAPAS Calle Diego de Mazariegos Tel. (967) 67 89716	
MUSEO SERGIO CASTRO Calle Guadalupe Victoria Tel. (967) 678 42 89	*Visit by appointments only.*
PALACIO MUNICIPAL	*Open daily 8am–10pm.*
TEMPLO AND EX-CONVENTO **DE SANTO DOMINGO ★** Gardens of the Alameda Tel. (967) 978 16 09/28 06	*Houses the Centro Cultural de los Altos:* *open Tue–Sat 9am–6pm and the Sna Jolobil* *('Weaving House'): open Tue–Sat 9am–2pm and* *4–7pm.*

SAN IGNACIO   A C4 ▲ 392

MISIÓN SAN IGNACIO DE KADAKAAMÁN Tel. (615) 154 02 22	*Houses a small museum dedicated to rock painting.* *Open Mon–Sat 8am–5pm.*
INAH OFFICE *Next to the museum* Tel. (615) 154 02 22	*Come here to obtain the necessary authorization* *to visit the painted grottoes of the Sierra de San* *Francisco.*

SAN JOSÉ MOGOTE   D D5 ▲ 306

ARCHEOLOGICAL SITE *7½ miles (11 km) southwest of Oaxaca*	*Open daily 8am–6pm.*

SAN JUAN CHAMULA   E D4 ▲ 261

CHURCH *6¼ miles (10 km) from San Cristóbal.*	*Open daily 11am–2pm and 5–8pm. Organized tours* *from San Cristóbal (see under 'Zinacantán').*

SAN LUIS POTOSÍ   C E1 ▲ 338

CASA DE LA CULTURA Av. Venustiano Carranza	*Open Tue-Sun 10am–2pm and 4–6pm.*
CONVENTO DE SAN FRANCISCO Calle Galeana 450 Tel. (444) 814 35 72	*Houses the Museo Regional Potosino :* *open Tue–Sat 10am–7pm, Sun 10am–3pm.*
MUSEO NACIONAL DE LA MÁSCARA Calle Villerías 2 Tel. (444) 812 30 25	*Open Tue–Fri 10am–2pm and 5–7pm,* *Sat–Sun 10am–2pm.*

SAN MIGUEL DE ALLENDE   C E3 and map W ▲ 352

JARDÍN BOTÁNICO *On the Querétaro road, then turn* *left after the statue of Allende.* Tel. (415) 154 47 15 www.laneta.apc.org/charco	*Open daily 8am–5pm (greenhouses 9am–4pm).*
ORATORIO DE SAN FELIPE NERI Plaza Cívica	*Open daily 9am–9pm.*

SANTA MARÍA XOXOTECO   D B1 ▲ 365

MISIÓN	*Open daily 7am–7pm.*

SANTA ROSALÍA   A C4 ▲ 393

MUSEO DE HISTORIA DE LA MINERÍA Esplanade Mesa Francia Tel. (615) 152 29 99	*Open Mon–Fri 8am–3pm, Sat 9am–1pm.*

SANTIAGO TUXTLA   D F3 ▲ 194

MUSEO TUXTECO Circuito Lic. Angel Carvajal Tel. (249) 70 196	*Open Mon–Sat 9am–6pm, Sun 9am–3pm.*
ARCHEOLOGICAL SITE TRES ZAPOTE *8 miles (13 km) from Santiago Tuxtla.*	*Open Tue–Sun 9am–5pm.*

SAYIL   F C3 ▲ 236

ARCHEOLOGICAL SITE ★ *18 miles (29 km) from Uxmal.*	*See 'Ruta Puuc'.* *Open daily 8am–5pm.*

SIHUAPAN   D F3 ▲ 195

CIGAR FACTORY Corner of Av. Tabamex and Carr. Costera del Golfo Tel. (294) 942 42 62/fax 03 13	*Visits by appointment. Send a fax with your name* *and fax number.*

PLACES TO VISIT ◆

For national calls: dial 01 followed by the city code, then the number.
For local calls: dial the 7- (or 8-) digit number, without the code. For a list of city codes ◆ 409.

TEHUACÁN		D C3 ▲ 293
MUSEO DEL VALLE DE TEHUACÁN Reforma Norte 210	*Open Tue–Sun 10am–5pm.*	

TENAM PUENTE		E E5 ▲ 277
ARCHEOLOGICAL SITE ★ 9⅓ miles (15 km) south from Comitán.	*Open daily 9am–4pm.*	

TEOTIHUACÁN		D B2 ▲ 162
ARCHEOLOGICAL SITE ★	*Open daily 7am–6pm.*	

TEPIC		C A2 ▲ 327
MUSEO DE ANTROPOLOGÍA E HISTORIA Corner of Av. Mexico and Morelos	*Open Mon–Fri 9am–7pm, Sat 9am–3pm.*	

TEPOSCOLULA		D C4 ▲ 293
IGLESIA DE SAN PEDRO Y SAN PABLO ★	*Open daily 8am–5pm.*	

TEPOTZOTLÁN		D A2 ▲ 167
MUSEO NATIONAL DEL VIRREINATO ★ Plaza Hidalgo 99 Tel. (55) 58 76 27 71	*Houses the Museo de Sitio (church): open Tue–Sun 9am–6pm and the Museo Histórico (art collections): open Wed–Sun 9am–6pm.*	

TEPOZTLÁN		D B3 ▲ 172
TEMPLO DE TEPOZTÉCATL	*Reached after a 1½ -hour walk; bring water and wear sensible shoes. Open daily 10am–5pm.*	
DOMINICAN MONASTERY ★	*Houses a museum containing pre-Hispanic objects: open Tue–Sun 10am–6pm.*	

TEQUILA		C B3 ▲ 323
MUSEO SAUZA Tel. (374) 742 24 10	*Open Tue–Sun 10am–4pm.*	

TIJUANA		A A1 ▲ 386
FOXPLORATION 20½ miles (33 km) from Tijuana, on the Ensenada road. Tel. (661) 614 94 44	*Amusement park adjacent to the Fox Studios. Open Wed–Fri 9am–5.30pm, Sat–Sun 10am–6.30pm.*	
MUSEO DE LAS CALIFORNIAS Centro Cultural, Paseo de los Héroes Tel. (664) 687 96 50	*Open Tue–Sun 10am–6pm.*	
VINICOLA L. A. CETTO Av. Cañon Johnson 2 108 Tel. (664) 155 24 64/22 69	*Open Mon–Fri 10am–6.30pm, Sat 10am–5pm.*	

TILACO		B E6 ▲ 361
SAN FRANCISCO DE TILACO	*Open daily 7am–6pm.*	

TIRIPITIO		C E4 ▲ 318
AUGUSTINIAN MONASTERY	*House a museum, open daily 9am–6pm.*	

TLACOCHAHUAYA		D D5 ▲ 303
DOMINICAN MONASTERY OF SAN JERÓNIMO Tel. (951) 516 39 56 (Instituto de Organo)	*Open daily 9am–6pm. Organ playing every November during a festival.*	

TLANCHINOL		D B1 ▲ 365
TEMPLO SAN AGUSTÍN	*Open daily 9am–7pm.*	

TLAQUEPAQUE		C C3 ▲ 323
MUSEO REGIONAL DE LA CERÁMICA Corner of Independencia 237 and Alfareros Tel. (33) 36 35 54 04	*Open Tue–Sat 10am–6pm, Sun 10am–3pm.*	

TLAXCALA		D C2-3 ▲ 284
EX-CONVENTO DE SAN FRANCISCO Calzada de San Francisco	*Houses the Museo Regional de Tlaxcala. Open Mon–Fri 10am–9pm, Sat 10am–3pm.*	
SANTUARIO DE OCOTLÁN ★ *About 1 mile/1.5 km from town.*	*Open daily 7am–9pm.*	

◆ PLACES TO VISIT

TLAYACAPAN		D B3 ▲ 173
CONVENTO DE SAN JUAN	*Open Tue–Sun 10am–5pm.*	

TONANTZINTLA		D B3 ▲ 292
TEMPLO DE SANTA MARÍA ★ *2 miles (3 km) southwest of Cholula.*	*Open Mon–Fri 7am–2pm and 4–8pm,* *Sat–Sun 7am–8pm.*	

TONINÁ		E E4 ▲ 263
ARCHEOLOGICAL SITE AND MUSEUM ★ *7½ miles (12 km) to the east of* *Ocosingo.*	*Site: open daily 9am–4pm.* *Museum: open Tue–Sun 8am–5pm.*	

TOTOLAPAN		D B3 ▲ 173
MISSIONARY SITE OF SAN GUILLERMO	*Open Thu–Tue 9am–8pm.*	

TULA		D A2 ▲ 171
ARCHEOLOGICAL SITE *40 miles from Mexico on road 57.*	*Open Tue–Sun 10am–6pm.*	

TULUM		F F3 ▲ 208
ARCHEOLOGICAL SITE ★ *81 miles (131 km) from Cancún.* *Follow the direction 'ZA'.*	*Open daily 8am–5pm.*	

TUPATARO		C E4 ▲ 317
TEMPLO SANTIAGO CABALLERO	*Open daily 9am–2pm.*	

TUXTLA GUTIÉRREZ		E D4 ▲ 281
MUSEO REGIONAL DE CHIAPAS Calzada de los Hombres Ilustres Tel. (961) 613 44 79	*Open Tue–Sun 9am–6pm.* *Guided tours by appointment.*	
PARQUE MARIMBA Av. Central Poniente	*Concerts: Mon–Sat 7–9pm, Sun 7–10pm.*	
ZOOMAT Tel. (961) 614 47 00 *Bus (line 70) from Plaza Mariachis.*	*Open Tue 8am–4pm, Wed–Sun 8.30am–4.30pm.*	

TZINTZUNTZAN		C E4 ▲ 316
CONVENTO DE SAN FRANCISCO ★	*Open daily 9am–8pm.*	
ARCHEOLOGICAL SITE	*Open daily 9am–6pm.*	

URUAPAN		C D4 ▲ 318
MUSEO HUATÁPERA Tel. (452) 524 71 99/34 34	*Open Tue–Sun 10am–6pm.*	
PARQUE NACIONAL EDUARDO RUIZ Calzada Juan de San Miguel	*Open daily 8am–6pm.*	

UXMAL		F B3 ▲ 284
ARCHEOLOGICAL SITE ★ *50 miles from Mérida on road 261.*	*Open daily 8am–5pm.* *Son-and-lumière 7pm (winter) and 8pm (summer).*	

VALENCIANA		C E2-3 ▲ 352
MINAS DE VALENCIANA Tel. (473) 732 05 07	*Open daily 9am–6pm.*	

VALLADOLID		F E2 ▲ 248
CENOTE DE ZACI Calle 36	*Open daily 8.30am–6.30pm.*	
CENOTE DE DZITNUP *13⅗ miles (22 km) from Valladolid.*	*Open daily 7am–6pm.*	

VERACRUZ		D E3 ▲ 185
ACUARIO DE VERACRUZ Bd M. Ávila Camacho, Playa de Hornos Tel. (229) 931 10 20	*Open daily 10am–7pm.*	
FUERTE DE SAN JUAN DE ULÚA	*Open Tue–Sun 9.30am–4.30pm.*	

VILLAHERMOSA		E D3 ▲ 198
PARQUE-MUSEO LA VENTA ★ Ruiz Cortines Tel. (993) 314 16 52	*Open daily 8am–4pm.*	

The symbol ★ indicates sites not to be missed.
The symbol ▲ refers to the description within the itineraries.
D A5 provides, when applicable, a grid reference for the maps at the end of this guide.

XALAPA		**D** D2 ▲ 188
HACIENDA DEL LANCERO 7 ½ miles from Xalapa toward Veracruz.	*Open Tue–Sun 10am–5pm.*	
MUSEO DE ANTROPOLOGÍA ★ Corner of Xalapa and 1 de Mayo Tel. (228) 815 49 52	*Open Tue–Sun 9am–5pm.* *Free guided tours at 11.30am.*	

XEL-HA		**F** F2 ▲ 208
PARC DE LOISIRS Tel. (984) 875 60 00	*Open daily 9am–6pm.*	

XILITLA		**B** E6 ▲ 362
LAS POZAS ★ Tel. (489) 365 00 12	*The Surrealist botanical garden of Edward James.* *Open daily 9am–5pm.*	

XOCHICALCO		**D** A3 ▲ 176
ARCHEOLOGICAL SITE ★ 23½ miles (38 km) from Cuernavaca.	*Open daily 10am–5pm.*	

XOCHITÉCATL		**D** B2-3 ▲ 286
ARCHEOLOGICAL SITE On foot from Cacaxtla, or by car outside San Miguel del Milagro.	*Open Tue–Sun 9am–5pm.*	

XPUHIL		**F** C5 ▲ 219
ARCHEOLOGICAL SITE ★ 6¼ miles (10 km) before Xpuhil on the 186.	*Open daily 8am–5pm.*	

YAGUL		**D** D5 ▲ 304
ARCHEOLOGICAL SITE	*Open daily 8am–5pm.*	

YANHUITLÁN		**D** C4 ▲ 306
IGLESIA DE SANTO DOMINGO	*Closed during restoration.*	

YAXCHILÁN		**E** F4 ▲ 274
ARCHEOLOGICAL SITE ★ On the Palenque-Frontera Corozal road, then by boat.	*Open Mon–Sun 10am–5pm.*	

YAXCOPOIL		**D** C2 ▲ 231
HACIENDA Tel. (999) 910 44 69	*Now a museum, open Tue–Sat 8am–5pm,* *Sun 9am–1pm.*	

YURIRIA		**C** E3 ▲ 313
CONVENTO DE SAN PABLO YURIRIA ★ Explanada Juárez	*Open Tue–Sun 9.30am–2pm and 3–5pm.*	

ZAACHILA		**D** D5 ▲ 305
ARCHEOLOGICAL SITE	*Open daily 8am–6pm.*	

ZACATECAS		**B** C5 and map **U** ▲ 341
CATEDRAL ★ Plaza de Armas	*Open daily 7am–1pm and 5–8pm.*	
MUSEO PEDRO CORONEL ★ Plaza de Santo Domingo Tel. (492) 922 80 21	*Open Fri–Wed 10am–5pm.*	
MUSEO RAFAEL CORONEL ★ Calle Abasolo Tel. (492) 922 81 16	*Open Wed–Mon 10am–5pm.*	
MINA EL EDÉN	*Open daily 10am–6pm.*	
MUSEO MANUEL FELGUÉREZ Corner of Calle Colón and Seminario Tel. (492) 924 37 05	*Open Wed–Mon 10am–5pm.*	
MUSEO ZACATECANO Dr Hierro 301, 2nd floor Tel. (492) 922 65 80	*In the former Casa de la Moneda.* *Open Wed–Mon 10am–5pm.*	

ZINACANTÁN		**E** D4 ▲ 261
6¼ miles (10 km) from San Cristóbal.	*Guided tour of Zinacantán and Chamula organized* *by the Na Bolom Museum in San Cristóbal*	

◆ BIBLIOGRAPHY, FILMOGRAPHY, DISCOGRAPHY

GENERAL

◆ *The Route of the Mayas*, Knopf Guides, Alfred A. Knopf, 2004
◆ BRUMFIELD (JAMES MCNAY): *A Tourist in the Yucatán*, Tres Picos Press, 2004
◆ DAY (NANCY RAINES): *Your Travel Guide to the Ancient Mayan Civilization*, Runestone Press, 2000
◆ HUMPHREY (CHRIS): *Mexico City*, Moon Handbook, 2005
◆ KEROUAC (JACK): *Mexico City Blues*, Grove Press/Atlantic Monthly Press, 1990
◆ STEPHENS (JOHN LLOYD): *Incidents of Travel in the Yucatán*, National Geographic, 2006

HISTORY

◆ BAUDEZ (CLAUDE-FRANÇOIS), PICASSO (SYDNEY): *Lost Cities of the Maya*, Thames & Hudson, 1992
◆ BULMER-THOMAS (VICTOR), COATSWORTH (JOHN) and CORTES-CONDE (ROBERTO), eds: *The Cambridge Economic History of Latin America*, Cambridge University Press, 2006
◆ CASTELOT (ANDRÉ): *Maximilien et Charlotte du Mexique*, Perrin, 2002
◆ CHARTRAND (RENE) and HOOK (RICHARD): *The Mexican Adventure, 1861–7*, Osprey, 1994
◆ COLLIS (MAURICE): *Cortés and Montezuma*, New Directions Publishing, 1999
◆ CONRAD (GEOFFREY W.) and DEMAREST (ARTHUR A.): *Religion and Empire: the Dynamics of Aztec and Inca Expansionism*, Cambridge University Press, 1988
◆ DALTON (WILLIAM): *Stories of the Conquest of Mexico and Peru, with a Sketch of the Early Adventures of the Spaniards in the New World*, Elibron Classics, 2001

◆ EISENHOWER (JOHN D.): *So Far from God, the US War with Mexico 1846–8*, University of Chicago Press, 2000
◆ EVANS (SUSAN TOBY) and WEBSTER (DAVID L.), eds: *Archaeology of Ancient Mexico and Central America, an Encyclopedia*, Garland Science, 2001
◆ GRUZINSKI (SERGE): *Images at War: Mexico from Columbus to Blade Runner (1492–2019)*, Duke University Press, 2001
◆ GRUZINSKI (SERGE): *The Aztecs: Rise and Fall of an Empire*, Thames & Hudson, 1992
◆ GRUZINSKI (SERGE): *Painting the Conquest: Mexican Indians and the European Renaissance*, Flammarion, 1992
◆ GRUZINSKI (SERGE): *The Mestizo Mind: The Intellectual Dynamics of Colonization and Globalization*, Routledge, 2002
◆ JOWLETT (PHILIP) ET AL: *The Mexican Revolution 1910–1920*, Osprey, 2006
◆ MEED, DOUGLAS V.: *The Mexican War 1846–8*, Osprey, 2002
◆ MCLYNN (FRANK): *Villa and Zapata: A Biography of the Mexican Revolution*, Pimlico, 2001
◆ PRESCOTT (WILLIAM HICKLING): *History of the Conquest of Mexico*, Weidenfeld & Nicholson, 2002
◆ SMITH (MICHAEL E.) and MASSON (MARILYN A.), eds: *The Ancient Civilizations of MesoAmerica: A Reader*, Blackwell Publishers, 2000
◆ SMITH (MICHAEL E.): *Aztecs (Peoples of America series)*, Blackwell Publishing, 2002
◆ WOMACK (JOHN): *Zapata and the Mexican Revolution*, Vintage Books, 1970

ARCHITECTURE

◆ BERNAL (IGNACIO), SIMONI-ABBAT (MIREILLE): *Le Mexique, des origines aux Aztèques*, collection 'L'Univers des formes', Gallimard, 1986
◆ DUVERGER (CHRISTIAN): *La Méso-Amérique*, Flammarion, 1999
◆ DUVERGER (CHRISTIAN): *Pierres métisses. L'Art sacré des Indiens du Mexique au xvie siècle*, Éd. du Seuil, 2003
◆ GENDROP (PAUL), HEYDEN (DORIS): *Architecture méso-américaine*, collection 'Histoire de l'architecture', Gallimard, 1993
◆ HERZOG (LAWRENCE A.): *From Aztec to High Tech: Architecture and Landscape across the Mexico-United States Border*, John Hopkins University Press, 2001
◆ HYAMS (GINA) and LEVICK (MELBA): *In a Mexican Garden*, Chronicle Books, 2005
◆ LEVICK (MELBA): *Mexicana: The Spirit and Design of Mexican Inns and Haciendas*, Chronicle Books 2002
◆ MIROW (GREGORY): *Ancient Mexican Designs*, Dover Publications, 1999
◆ PORTER (ELIOT) and AUERBACH (ELLEN): *Mexican Churches*, Chronicle Books, 1999

ART

◆ BURRI (RENÉ): *Barragán*, Phaidon Press, 2000
◆ FUENTES (CARLOS): *Juan Rulfo's Mexico*, Smithsonian Books, 2002
◆ HERRARA (HAYDEN): *Frida: The Biography of Frida Kahlo*, Bloomsbury, 2003
◆ HERRARA (HAYDEN): *Frida Kahlo: The Paintings*, HarperPerennial, 1993

◆ HOOKS (MARGARET): *Tina Modotti*, Phaidon, 2006
◆ HOOKS (MARGARET): *Tina Modotti: Photographer and Revolutionary*, Da Capo Press, 2000
◆ JULBEZ (PALOMAR) and JULBEZ (EGUIARTE): *The Life and Work of Luis Barragan*, Rizzoli International Editions, 1997
◆ KAHLO (FRIDA): *The Diary of Frida Kahlo*, introduction by Carlos Fuentes, Harry N. Abrams, 2006
◆ KAHLO (FRIDA) and PRIGNITZ-PODA (HELGA): *Frida Kahlo, the Painter and her Work*, Schimer/Mosel, 2004
◆ LOWE (SARAH M.): *Tina Modotti: Photographs*, Harry N. Abrams, 1995
◆ PORTUGAL (ARMANDO SALAS): *Luis Barragan, The Architecture of Light, Colour and Form*, Rizzoli International Editions, 1992
◆ ROGUE (ALFREDO VILCHIS) and SCHWARTZ (PIERRE): *Infinitas Gracias, Contemporary Mexican Painting*, Chronicle Books, 2004
◆ VIDELA (KHRISTAAN): *Contemporary Mexican Design*, Gibbs M. Smith Inc, 2003

SPANISH CHRONICLES OF THE CONQUEST

◆ CHAMPLAIN (SAMUEL DE): *Narrative of a Voyage to the West Indies and Mexico in the Years 1599–1602*, Elibron Classics, 2001
◆ CORTÉS (HERNAN): *Letters from Mexico*, Yale University Press, 2001
◆ CORTÉS (HERNAN): *Letters of Cortés – The Five Letters of Relation from Fernando Cortés to the Emperor Charles V*, G.P. Putnams' Sons, 1908

◆ DÍAZ DEL CASTILLO (BERNAL): *The Conquest of New Spain*, J.M. Cohen (ed), Penguin Books, 1969

◆ DIAZ DEL CASTILLO (BERNAL): *The Discovery and Conquest of Mexico*, Da Capo Press, 1996

◆ GOETZ (DELIA) and MORLEY (SYLVANUS G.), eds: *Popol Vuh – the Sacred Book of the Ancient Quiche Maya*, William Hodge & Co., 1951

◆ SALAZAR (FRANCISCO CERVANTES DE): *Life in the Imperial and Loyal City of Mexico in New Spain*, University of Texas Press, 1953

LITERATURE

◆ ARTAUD (ANTONIN): *Les Tarahumaras*, Gallimard, 1987

◆ BEDORD (SYBIL): *A Visit to Don Otavio*, William Collins, 1960

◆ BRENNER (ANITA): *Idols behind Altars*, Chapman & Hall, 1939

◆ CALDERON DE LA BARCA (FRANCES): *Life in Mexico*, Chapman & Hall, 1843

◆ GAGE (THOMAS): *Thomas Gage's Travels in the New World*, University of Oklahoma Press, 1969

◆ GREENE (GRAHAM): *The Power and the Glory*, William Heinemann Ltd, 1940

◆ HUXLEY (ALDOUS): *Beyond the Mexique Bay*, Chatto and Windus, 1934

◆ KEROUAC (JACK): *Mexico City Blues*, Christian Bourgois, 1995

◆ LAWRENCE (DAVID HERBERT): *Mornings in Mexico*, Martin Secker, 1930

◆ LOWRY (MALCOLM): *Under the Volcano*, Jonathan Cape, 1947

◆ McCARTHY (CORMAC): *Border Trilogy*, Pan Books, 1993

◆ PORTER (KATHERINE ANNE): *Flowering Judas and Other Stories*, Harrison, 1934

◆ STEINBECK (JOHN): *The Log from the Sea of Cortez*, Penguin, 2001

◆ STEINBECK (JOHN): *Zapata*, Penguin, 1993

◆ STEINBECK (JOHN): *A Life in Letters*, Heinemann, 1975

◆ THEROUX (PAUL): *The Old Patagonian Express*, Mariner Books, 1979

◆ WAUGH (EVELYN): *Robbery Under Law: The Mexican Object Lesson*, Chapman & Hall, 1939

◆ WEST (REBECCA): *Survivors in Mexico*, Yale University Press, 2003

MEXICAN LITERATURE

◆ CASTANEDA (CARLOS): *The Power of Silence*, Black Swan, 1988

◆ CASTANEDA (CARLOS): *Magical Passes*, HarperCollins, 1998

◆ CASTANEDA (CARLOS): *The Fire from Within*, Black Swan, 1984

◆ DEL PASO (FERNANDO): *Obras I*, Fondo de Cultura Economica USA, 2001

◆ ESQUIVEL (LAURA): *Like Water for Chocolate*, Black Swan, 1993

◆ ESQUIVEL (LAURA): *Malinche*, Simon & Schuster, 2006

◆ FUENTES (CARLOS): *Terra Nostra*, Dalkey Archive Press, 2003

◆ FUENTES (CARLOS): *La Región más transparente*, collection 'Folio', Gallimard, 1982

◆ FUENTES (CARLOS): *La Muerte de Artemio Cruz*, collection 'Folio', Gallimard, 1995

◆ FUENTES (CARLOS): *El Naranjo, collection "Folio"*, Gallimard, 1995

◆ FUENTES (CARLOS): *Los Años con Laura Díaz*, collection 'Folio', Gallimard, 2003

◆ GARRO (ELENA): *Los Recuerdos del porvenir*, Joaquin Mortiz Editorial, 2003

◆ PACHECO (JOSÉ EMILIO): *An Ark for the Next Millennium: Poems*, University of Texas Press, 1993

◆ PAZ (OCTAVIO): *The Labyrinth of Solitude; The Other Mexico; Return to the Labyrinth of Solitude; Mexico and the United States; The Philanthropic Ogre*, Avalon Travel Publishing, 1985

◆ PAZ (OCTAVIO): *Alternating Current*, Little Brown & Co, 2006

◆ PAZ (OCTAVIO): *The Collected Poems 1957–87*, Carcanet Press, 2001

◆ PAZ (OCTAVIO): *El Fuego de cada día*, collection 'Du monde entier', Gallimard, 1986

◆ PAZ (OCTAVIO): *Libertad bajo palabra*, collection 'Du monde entier', Gallimard, 1990

◆ REYES (ALFONSO): *An Anthology of Mexican Poetry*, Thames & Hudson, 1959

◆ RULFO (JUAN): *El Llano en llamas)*, collection 'Folio', Gallimard, 2003

◆ RULFO (JUAN): *Pedro Páramo*, collection 'L'Imaginaire', Gallimard, 1979

FILMS

◆ AKERMAN (CHANTAL): *From the Other Side*, 2002

◆ ARAU (ALFONSO): *Like Water for Chocolate*, 1992

◆ BUÑUEL (LUIS): *Los Olvidados (The Young and the Damned)*, 1950

◆ BUÑUEL (LUIS): *Ensayo de un Crimen (Rehearsal for a Crime; The Criminal Life of Archibaldo de la Cruz)*, 1955

◆ CARRERA (CARLOS): *El Crimen del padre Amaro (The Crime of Father Amaro)*, 2002

◆ CUARÓN (ALFONSO): *Y tu mama también (And Your Mother Too)*, 2001

◆ EISENSTEIN (SERGEÏ M.): *¡Que viva México!*, 1930

◆ HUSTON (JOHN): *The Treasure of the Sierra Madre*, 1948

◆ HUSTON (JOHN): *The Night of the Iguana*,1964

◆ IÑÁRRITU (ALEJANDRO GONZÁLEZ): *Amores Perros*, 2000

◆ IÑÁRRITU (ALEJANDRO GONZÁLEZ): *Babel*, 2006

◆ KAZAN (ELIA): *Viva Zapata!*, 1952

◆ MALLE (LOUIS): *Viva María!*, 1965

◆ REYGADAS (CARLOS): *Batalla en el Cielo (Battle in Heaven)*, 2005

◆ RIPSTEIN (ARTURO): *El Castillo de la pureza (Castle of Purity)*, 1973

◆ RIPSTEIN (ARTURO): *Profundo carmesí (Deep Crimson)*, 1996

◆ RODRÍGUEZ (HUGO): *Nicotina*, 2003

◆ SERRANO (ANTONIO): *La Hija del Canibal (Lucia, Lucia)*, 2003

◆ SODERBERGH (STEPHEN): *Traffic*, 2000

◆ TAYMOR (JULIE): *Frida*, 2002

MUSIC

◆ CAFÉ TACUBA: *Cuatro Caminos*, 2003

◆ DOWNS (LILA): *La Linea (Border)*, 2001

◆ DOWNS (LILA): *Una Sangre – One Blood*, 2004

◆ *Frida*, original film soundtrack, 2003

◆ K-PAZ DE LA SIERRA: *Pensando en ti*, 2004

◆ MANÁ: *Revolución de amor*, 2003

◆ MIGUEL (LUIS): *Mis boleros favoritos*, 2003

◆ NORTEC: *Tijuana Sessions*, 2002

◆ RIVERA (LUPILLO): *Amorcito corazón*, 2002

◆ THALÍA: *Arrasando*, (2000)

◆ VARGAS (CHAVELA): *La Llorona*, 1993; *Volver volver*, 1995

◆ LIST OF ILLUSTRATIONS

447

◆ LIST OF ILLUSTRATIONS

LIST OF ILLUSTRATIONS ◆

We have been unable to locate the heirs or publishers of some pictures and documents; an account has been opened for them.

Grateful acknowledgment is made to the following for permission to reprint previously published material.

Harcourt, Inc. and **Barbara Thompson Davis**:
Excerpt from 'Hacienda' from Flowering Judas and Other Stories. Copyright 1935 and renewed 1963 by Katherine Anne Portor. Reprinted by permission of Harcourt, Inc. and Barbara Thompson Davis.

Indiana University Press:
Excerpt from 'Tarahumara Herbs' by Reyes from Anthology of Mexican Poetry edited by Octavio Paz and translated by Samuel Beckett. Reprinted by permission of Indiana University Press.

University of Oklahoma Press:
Excerpt from Popul Vuh: The Sacred Book of the Ancient Quiche Maya by Adrian Recinos. Reprinted by permission of University of Oklahoma Press.

Yale University Press:
Excerpt from Survivors in Mexico by Rebecca West, ed. by Bernard Schweizer. Copyright © 2003 by Literary Estate of Rebecca West. Editing and Introduction copyright © 2003 by Bernard Schweizer. Reprinted by permission of Yale University Press.

The Random House Group Ltd:
Excerpt from Under the Volcano by Malcolm Lowry (Jonathan Cape). Reprinted by permission of The Random House Group Ltd.

◆ INDEX

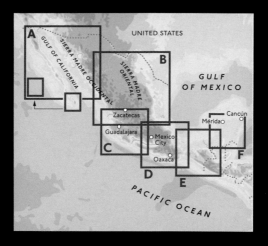

Map section

SAN DIEGO

A B C

Tijuana
Tecate
Rosarito
Yuma
SIERRA DE JUAREZ
LAGUNA SALADA
RÍO COLORADO
San Luis Río Colorado
UNITED STATE

Ensenada
La Bufadora
DESIERTO DE ALTAR
Sonoyta
Lukeville

San Vicente
PARQUE NACIONAL SAN PEDRO MÁRTIR
SIERRA DE SAN PEDRO MÁRTIR
La Trinidad (El Chinero)
RÍO SONOYTA
Puerto Peñasco
BAHÍA DE SAN JORGE

Camalú
▲ PICO DEL DIABLO 3 078 M
San Felipe
GULF OF CALIFORNIA
RÍO ASUNCIÓN

San Quintín
BAHÍA SAN QUINTÍN
BAJA CALIFORNIA NORTE
Caborca
EL BAMURI

El Rosario de Arriba

San Agustín
Cataviña
BAHÍA SAN LUIS GONZAGA
San Luis Gonzaga
PARQUE NATURAL DEL DESIERTO CENTRAL DE BAJA CALIFORNIA
ISLA ÁNGEL DE LA GUARDA

Chapala
BAHÍA DE LOS ÁNGELES
ISLA TIBURÓN
Mi Ale

Punta Prieta
Bahía de los Angeles
ISLA SAN LORENZO
Bahía Kino

PACIFIC OCEAN
ISLA CEDROS
SIERRA SAN BORJA
MisiónSan Fco de Borja
ISLA SAN ESTEBAN

BAHÍA SEBASTIÁN VIZCAÍNO
BOCA CARDONAL
BOCA TASTIOTA

PUNTA FALSA
Santo Domingo
Guerrero Negro
SIERRA DE SAN FRANCISCO
San Francisco de la Sierra

LAGUNA DE OJO DE LIEBRE
RESERVA DE LA BIOSFERA EL VIZCAÍNO
Santa Rosalía
ISLA SAN MARCOS

SIERRA DE VIZCAÍNO
DESIERTO DE VIZCAÍNO
San Ignacio
Mulegé
PUNTA CONCEPCIÓ

Laguna San Ignacio
San José de Gracia
BAHÍA CONCEPCIÓN

BAHÍA DE BALLENAS
Rosarito

BAJA CALIFORNIA SUR
SIERRA DE LA GIGANTA

Puerto San Andrecito
San Javier

El Cajete
BAHÍA LA PAZ
Pichilingue
La Paz
ISLA CERRALVO

San Pedro

Ciudad Insurgentes
BOCA SANTO DOMINGO

Todos Santos
SIERRA LA LAGUNA
SIERRA DE SAN LÁZARO
Puerto Adolfo López Mateos
ISLA MAGDALENA
San Carlos
Ciudad Constitución

San José del Cabo
Cabo San Lucas
CABO SAN LUCAS
BAHÍA MAGDALENA
ISLA SANTA MARGARITA

0   30   60 miles
1/4 600 000 - 1/2 in : 30 miles

A B C

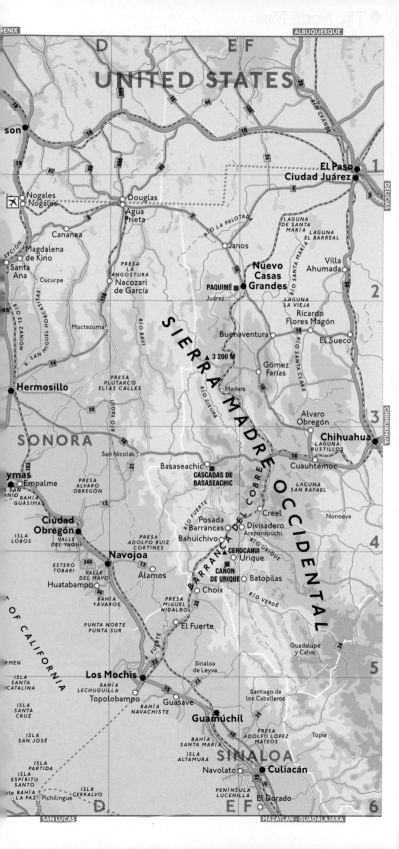

B

A B C

SIERRA EL FIERRO

Presidio

Ojinaga

RÍO CONCHOS

RÍO GRANDE
RÍO BRAVO

Boquillas
Boquillas
del Carmen

SIERRA
DEL CARME

Tres Marías

Aldama

Alvaro
Obregón

LAGUNA
BUSTILLOS

Chihuahua

Cuauhtémoc

CHIHUAHUA

PARQUE
INT. DEL
RÍO BRAVO

1

HERMOSILLO

Meoqui
Delicias

Rosales

RÍO SANTA CRUZ

Nonoava

Ciudad
Camargo

PRESA
LA BOQUILLA

**MESETA
DEL NORTE
BOLSÓN
DE MAPIMÍ**

LAGUNA
LA LECHE

**Hidalgo
del Parral**

Jiménez

LAGUNA
DEL REY

COAHUIL

San Francisco
del Oro

2

Santa
Bárbara

Emiliano
Zapata

LAGUNA
PALOMAS

SIERR

RÍO VERDE

Villa
Ocampo

Charcos
de Risa

DESIERTO
DE MAYRAN

Guanaceví

PRESA
LÁZARO
CÁRDENAS

El Zape

El Palmito

San Pedro
de las Colonias

Topia

RÍO PIAXTLA

SIERRA

DURANGO

Vizcaíno

RÍO NAZAS

**Gómez
Palacio
Torreón**

Matamoros

Parras d
la Fuen

BAJÍO
LOS
LLANOS

3

Santiago
Papasquiaro

LAGUNA
SANTIAGUILLO

Cuencamé

BAJÍO
LA VACA

R. AGUENAVA

Estación
Simón

Canatlán

MADRE

Juan
Adalma

4

LOS MOCHIS

RÍO PRESIDIO

OCCIDENTAL

Durango

Vicente
Guerrero

Río
Grande

El
Salto

Mezquital

Sombrerete

ZACATECA

Mazatlán

Rosario

La
Rastra

Mineral
de Cucharas

Fresnillo

Escuinapa de Hidalgo

LAGUNA
EL CAIMANERO

Calera de
Víctor Rosales

Acaponeta

Valparaíso

Jerez de
García Salinas

Zacatec

5

Tecuala

El Novillero

Santa
Teresa

Santa Lucía
de la Sierra

La Quemada

GUADALUPE

Ojc
Cal

RÍO SAN PEDRO MEZQUITAL

RÍO ATENGO

Mezquitic

Víboras

LA QUEMADA

Loreto

LAGUNA DE
AGUA BRAVA

Mesa
del Nayar

Monte
Escobedo

Villanueva

AGUASCALIEN

Santa Cruz
Mexcaltitán

San Pedro
Ixcatán

Villa Guerrero

Aguascalie

Santiago Ixcuintla

NAYARIT

Túxpan

Tlatenango de
Sánchez Román

Joaquín
Amaro

Calvillo

Encarnac
de Díaz

ISLA
ISABELA

ISLAS MARÍAS

San
Blas

La Tovara

RÍO BOTANOS

Jalpa

2 792 M

70

6

Santa
Cruz

Tepic

Benito
Juárez

Nochistlán
de Mejía

71

43

Compostela

Las Varas

Ixtlán
del Río

Moyahua
de Estrada

San Juan
de los Lagos

ENSENADA CHACALÁ

200

LOS TORILES

A B C

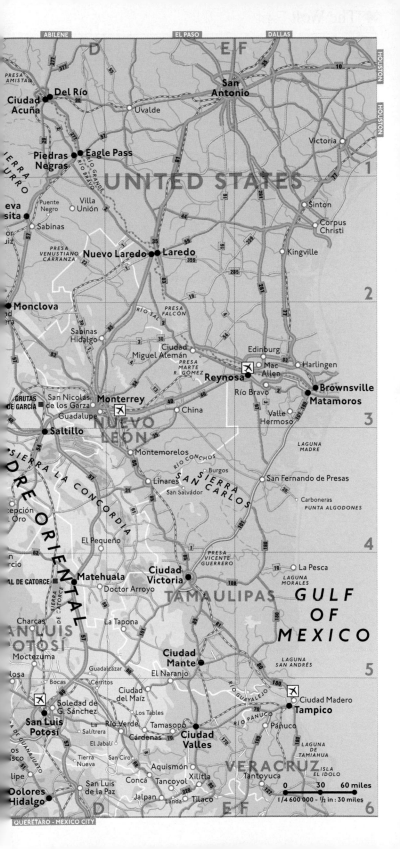

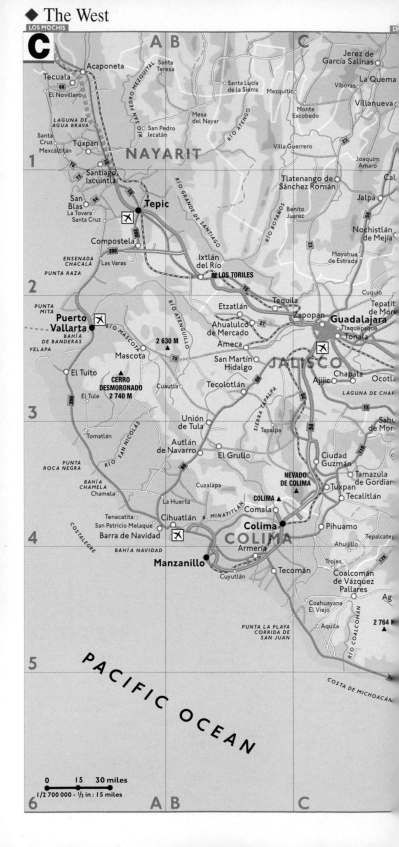

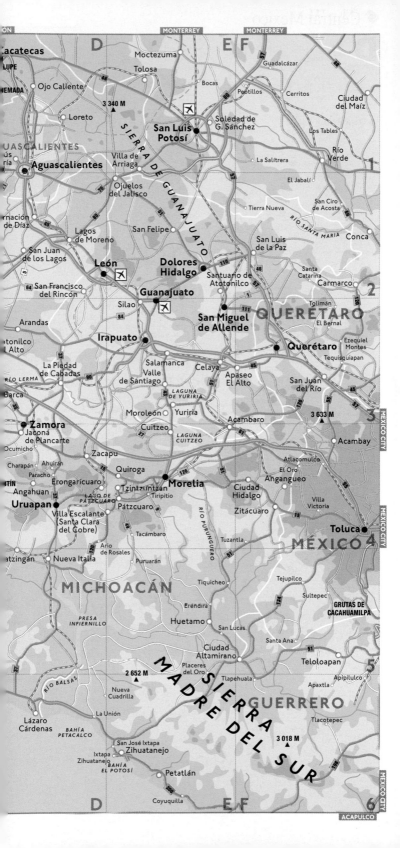

◆ Central Mexico

D

SAN LUIS POTOSÍ
AGUASCALIENTES
GUADALAJARA
MANZANILLO

A   B   C

Santa   Carmarco   Tlanchinol   Huejutla
Catarina   de Reyes   Tuxpa.
Tolimán   Alamo
QUERÉTARO   Molango   Tianguistenco   190
El Bernal   Eloxochitlán   Huazalingo   Po
Ezequiel   Orizabita   Ixhuatlán   Metlaltoyuca   R
Montes   Metztitlán
● Querétaro   Tecozautla   Ixmiquilpan   Metzquititlán   EL
Tequisquiapan   Xoxoteco   Coyutla
HIDALGO   Mineral   Atotonilco   Metlatoyuca   Xicotepec
San Juan   120   del Chico   el Grande   130
del Río   45   Huichapan   Huauchinango
Mixquiahuala   Actopan   Pachuca   130
Tula   Tezontepec   Mineral   Cuetza
57   TULA ■   del Monte   Tulancingo   Zacatlán   Tezi
3 633 M ▲   17   Epazoyucan   Chignahuapan   130
Acambay   10   Tetela
Tepotzotlán   Zumpango   Ciudad   Apan   de Ocampo
Atlacomulco   Villa   Sahagún   Tlaxco
El Oro   Nicolás Romero   Coacalco   TEOTIHUACÁN   TLAXCALA
Angangueo   Jiquipilco   126   ACOLMAN   136   Apizaco   Ori
Villa   Mexico City   136   Zac
Victoria   134   Chapingo   Texmelucan   VOLCAN   135
Toluca   DISTRITO   150   Tlaxcala   LA MALINCHE   San Sal
MEXICO   LAGOS   FEDERAL   IXTACCÍHUATL   CACAXTLA   4 461 M ▲   El Se
DE ZEMPOALA   5 286 M ▲   Huejotzingo   Tepetlaxco
55   106   Amecameca   113   Cholula   ● Puebla   Acatzin
MALINALCO   Cuernavaca   POPOCATÉPETL   Tetela   150
XOCHICALCO   166   5 452 M ▲   del Volcan   Tecamachalco
GRUTAS DE   Tepoztlán   PUEBLA
CACAHUAMILPA   115   Cuautla
Taxco   Puente   MORELOS   Atlixco
de Ixtla   Zacatepec   Izúcar de
Santa Ana   Huitzuco   Axochiapan   Matamoros
51   Iguala   Chiautla   160   San Juan   Tehuac
Teloloapan   Apipilulco   Ixcaquixtla
Apaxtla   Atenango   Acatlán   Zapotitlán
del Río   Salinas
GUERRERO   95   Ixcamilpa   Chila   125
Mezcala   Olinalá   Huajuapan   Santa
Tlacotepec   Milpillas   Huamuxtitlán   de León   Camo
▲ 3 018 M   Zilala   Santo Domingo   Tepe
Zumpango   Tonalá   Villa de   de N
del Río   Tlapa de   Tamazulapan
Chilpancingo   Comonfort   Yan
Quechultenango   Santiago   Tepos
Juxtlahuaca
SIERRA   Tlacuapa   San Juan Mixtepec   Santa M
Tlaxia
MADRE   DEL   SUR   Laguna   S
El Carrizal   Ayutla de   San Luis   Santa
RÍO OMITLÁN   los Libres   Acatlán   Yoson
Pie de la Cuesta   La Palma   Azoyu   Zimatlán
Acapulco   San Marcos   Cruz   Xochistlahuaca   Llano
BAHÍA ACAPULCO   200   Grande   Ometepec   Grande
LAGUNA   Copala   RÍO QUETZALA   San Juan Cacahuatepec
TRES
PALOS   LAGUNA   Cuajinicuilapa   Pinotepa de
TECOMATE   Don Luis   Chayuco
LAGUNA   PUNTA MALDONADO   Llano   Santiago   Santiago
CHANTENGO   Grande   Pinotepa   Jamiltepec
Nacional   P.N.
LAGU
DE CHAC

PACIFIC   OCEAN

6   A   B   C

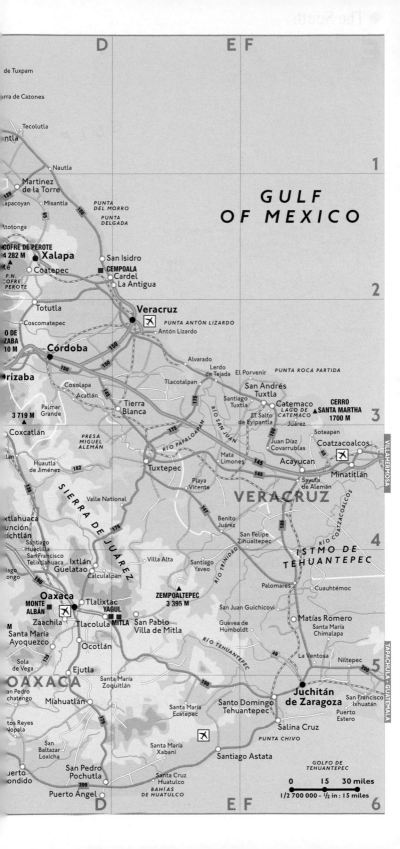

E

GULF OF

GOLFO
DE CAMPECHE

1

VERACRUZ

CÓRDOBA · MÉXICO

PUNTA ANTÓN LIZARDO
Antón Lizardo

Alvarado
Lerdo
de Tejada   El Porvenir   PUNTA ROCA PARTIDA
Tlacotalpan

San Andrés
Tuxtla
Santiago
Tuxtla   Catemaco   CERRO
LAGO DE   SANTA MARTHA
CATEMACO   1700 M
El Salto
de Eyipantla   Juárez
Soteapan
Juan Díaz
Covarrublas

El Alacrán   Par

Sánchez   LAGUNA   Comal
Magallanes   DEL CARMEN
Lázaro
Cárdenas
La Venta   Hero
Cárde

RÍO SAN JUAN

RÍO PAPALOAPAN

2

Tuxtepec
Playa
Vicente

Mata
Limones   Acayucan
Sayula
de Alemán

Coatzacoalcos

Minatitlán

Las Choapas   180
LAGUNA
EL ROSARIO
Francisco
Rueda   Chontalpa
Yucatecal
El Chichón   Ós

VERACRUZ

Benito
Juárez
San Felipe
Zihualtepec

RÍO COATZACOALCOS

ISTMO DE
TEHUANTEPEC

RÍO UXPANAPA   181

3

Santiago
Yaveo

ZEMPOALTEPEC
3 395 M

RÍO TRINIDAD

Palomares

Cuauhtémoc

REGIÓN DE
LOS CHIMALAPAS

Raudales   Tec
PRESA
NEZAHUALCÓYOTL
Apic-Pac

San Juan Guichicovi

Guevea de
Humboldt   Matías Romero
Santa María
Chimalapa

Ocozocoautla
Cintalapa

RÍO TEHUANTEPEC

49   La Ventosa   Niltepec   200

San Pedro
Tapanatepec   180

4

OAXACA

190

Santa María
Ecatepec   Santo Domingo
Tehuantepec

**Juchitán
de Zaragoza**

Salina Cruz

San Francisco
Ixhuatán

Puerto
Estero

Emiliano
Zapata   Arriaga   SIER

Tonalá

Santa María
Xabani

Santiago Astata   PUNTA CHIVO

Puerto
Arista

Santa Cruz
Huatulco   El Manguito
BAHÍAS
DE HUATULCO

GOLFO DE
TEHUANTEPEC

5

PACIFIC OCEAN

0   15   30 miles
1/2 700 000 · 1/2 in : 15 miles

6

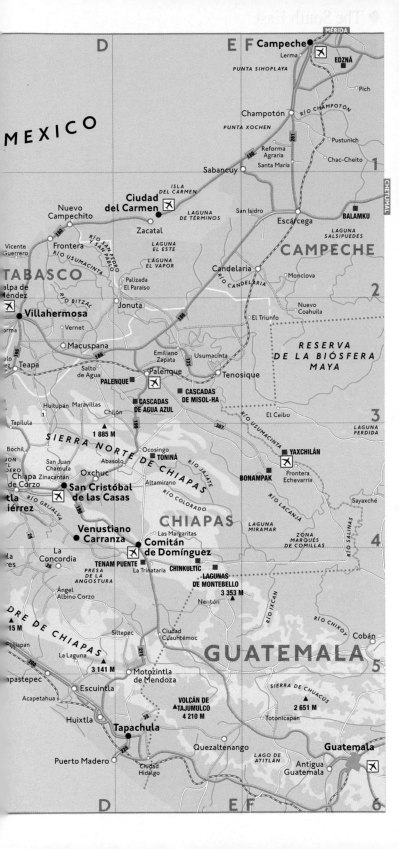

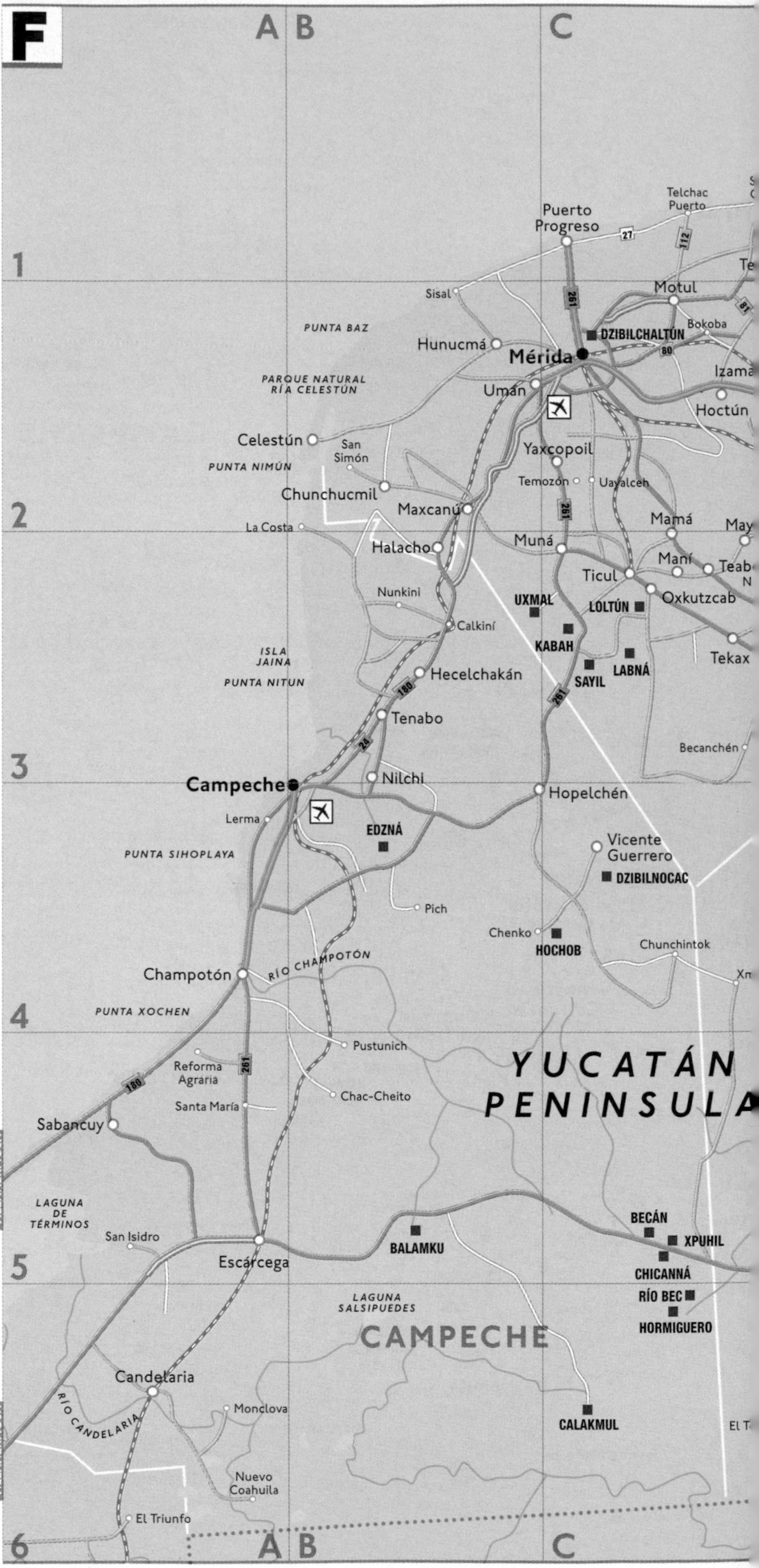

F

A B C

1

Puerto
Progreso

Telchac
Puerto

Motul

Sisal

Bokoba

DZIBILCHALTÚN

PUNTA BAZ

Hunucmá

Mérida

Izama

PARQUE NATURAL
RÍA CELESTÚN

Umán

Hoctún

Celestún

San
Simón

Yaxcopoil

PUNTA NIMÚN

Temozón

Uayalceh

Chunchucmil

Maxcanú

Muná

Mamá

May

2

La Costa

Halacho

Ticul

Maní

Teab

Nunkini

UXMAL

LÓLTÚN

Oxkutzcab

Calkiní

KABAH

Tekax

ISLA
JAINA

SAYIL

LABNÁ

PUNTA NITUN

Hecelchakán

Becanchén

Tenabo

3

Campeche

Nilchi

Hopelchén

Lerma

Vicente
Guerrero

PUNTA SIHOPLAYA

EDZNÁ

DZIBILNOCAC

Pich

Chenko

HOCHOB

Chunchintok

Champotón

RÍO CHAMPOTÓN

Xn

4

PUNTA XOCHEN

Pustunich

YUCATÁN
PENINSULA

Reforma
Agraria

Chac-Cheito

Santa María

Sabancuy

LAGUNA
DE
TÉRMINOS

San Isidro

BECÁN

XPUHIL

5

Escárcega

BALAMKU

CHICANNÁ

RÍO BEC

LAGUNA
SALSIPUEDES

HORMIGUERO

CAMPECHE

Candelaria

Monclova

RÍO CANDELARIA

CALAKMUL

El T

Nuevo
Coahuila

6

El Triunfo

A B C

VILLAHERMOSA

VILLAHERMOSA

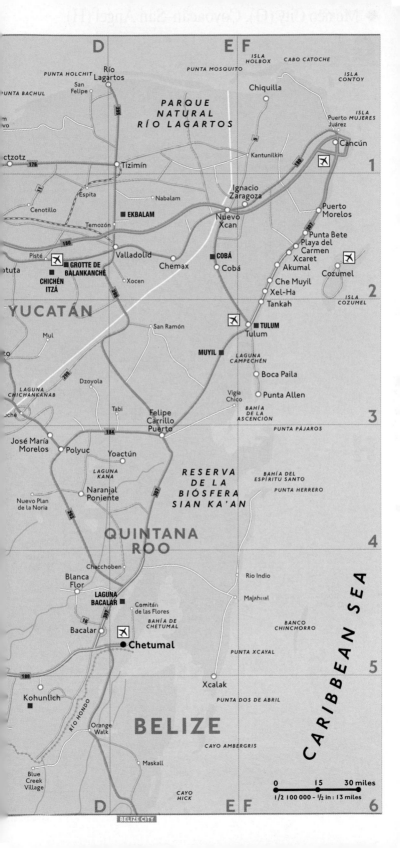

◆ Mexico City (G), Coyoacán–San Ángel (H)

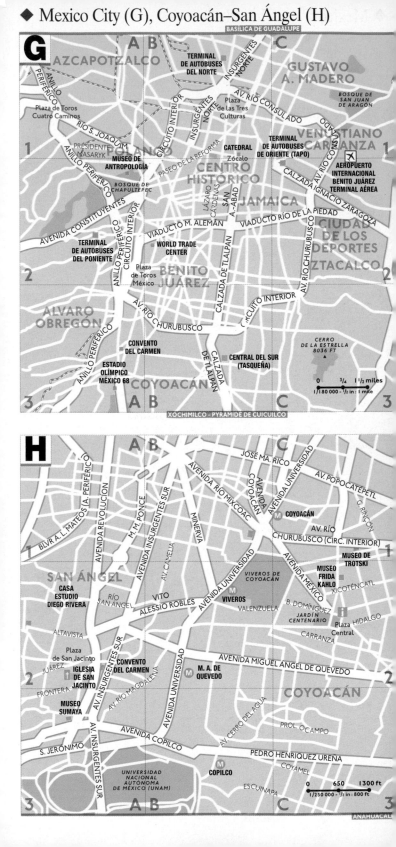

G

AZCAPOTZALCO

TERMINAL DE AUTOBUSES DEL NORTE

INSURGENTES NORTE

GUSTAVO A. MADERO

BOSQUE DE SAN JUAN DE ARAGÓN

ANILLO PERIFÉRICO

Plaza de Toros Cuatro Caminos

RÍO S. JOAQUIN

PRESIDENTE MASARYK

ANILLO PERIFÉRICO

CIRCUITO INTERIOR

INSURGENTES NORTE

AV. RÍO CONSULADO

OCEANIA

VENUSTIANO CARRANZA

Plaza de las Tres Culturas

CATEDRAL

Zócalo

TERMINAL DE AUTOBUSES DE ORIENTE (TAPO)

AV. RÍO CONSULADO

AEROPUERTO INTERNACIONAL BENITO JUÁREZ TERMINAL AÉREA

MUSEO DE ANTROPOLOGÍA

PASEO DE LA REFORMA

CENTRO HISTÓRICO

CALZADA IGNACIO ZARAGOZA

BOSQUE DE CHAPULTEPEC

LÁZARO CÁRDENAS

SAN A.-ABAD

JAMAICA

AV. RÍO CHURUBUSCO

AVENIDA CONSTITUYENTES

ANILLO PERIFÉRICO CIRCUITO INTERIOR

VIADUCTO M. ALEMÁN

CALZADA DE TLALPAN

VIADUCTO RÍO DE LA PIEDAD

CIUDAD DE LOS DEPORTES

IZTACALCO

TERMINAL DE AUTOBUSES DEL PONIENTE

WORLD TRADE CENTER

BENITO JUÁREZ

Plaza de Toros México

ÁLVARO OBREGÓN

ANILLO PERIFÉRICO

AV. RÍO CHURUBUSCO

CIRCUITO INTERIOR

AV. RÍO CHURUBUSCO

CONVENTO DEL CARMEN

CALZADA DE TLALPAN

CENTRAL DEL SUR (TASQUEÑA)

CERRO DE LA ESTRELLA 8036 FT ▲

ESTADIO OLÍMPICO MÉXICO 68

COYOACÁN

0   ³⁄₄   1 ½ miles
1/180 000 - ½ in : 1 mile

H

JOSÉ MA. RICO

AV. POPOCATÉPETL

AVENIDA RÍO MIXCOAC

AVENIDA COYOACÁN

AVENIDA UNIVERSIDAD

COYOACÁN

G. RINCÓN

BLVR A. L. MATEOS (A. PERIFÉRICO)

AVENIDA REVOLUCIÓN

M. M. PONCE

AVENIDA INSURGENTES SUR

MINERVA

AV. RÍO CHURUBUSCO (CIRC. INTERIOR)

AVENIDA MÉXICO

MUSEO DE TROTSKI

SAN ÁNGEL

AV. CAMELIA

VIVEROS DE COYOACÁN

MUSEO FRIDA KAHLO

XICOTÉNCATL

CASA ESTUDIO DIEGO RIVERA

RÍO SAN ÁNGEL

VITO

ALESSIO ROBLES

AVENIDA UNIVERSIDAD

VIVEROS

VALENZUELA

B. DOMÍNGUEZ

JARDÍN CENTENARIO

ALTAVISTA

CARRANZA

Plaza Central

Plaza HIDALGO

Plaza de San Jacinto

JUÁREZ

IGLESIA DE SAN JACINTO

CONVENTO DEL CARMEN

M. A. DE QUEVEDO

AVENIDA MIGUEL ÁNGEL DE QUEVEDO

FRONTERA

MUSEO SUMAYA

AV. INSURGENTES SUR

AV. RÍO MAGDALENA

AVENIDA UNIVERSIDAD

COYOACÁN

S. JERÓNIMO

AVENIDA COPILCO

AV. CERRO DEL AGUA

PROL. OCAMPO

PEDRO HENRIQUEZ UREÑA

COYAMEL

AV. INSURGENTES SUR

UNIVERSIDAD NACIONAL AUTÓNOMA DE MÉXICO (UNAM)

COPILCO

ESCUINAPA

0   650   1300 ft
1/250 000 - ½ in : 800 ft

I

A B C

ARCOS DE BELEN

AV DE LA REPUBLICA

BALDERAS

R0SALES GUERRERO

DR. RIO DE LA LOZA

DR. VERTIZ

NIÑOS HEROES

PTE DE ALVARADO

Plaza de la República

CHRISTOPHER COLOMBUS MONUMENT

BUCARELI

AVENIDA CUAUHTEMOC

1

EL CHOPO

RIBERA DE SAN COSME

AV SAN COSME

INSURGENTES NORTE

MONUMENT TO THE REVOLUTION

AVENIDA INSURGENTES NORTE

PASEO DE LA REFORMA

CUAUHTEMOC

MORELIA

ALVARO OBREGON

GUANAJUATO

CORDOBA

1

SAN RAFAEL

MAESTRO

AV. ANTONIO CASO

AV. PARQUE VIA SULLIVAN

CUAUHTEMOC Monument

DINAMARCA

C HAVRE

CASA DE FRANCIA

AV. CHAPULTEPEC

PUEBLA

Plaza Rio de Janeiro

MARSELLA

INSURGENTES

OAXACA

ROMA NORTE

MONTERREY

YUCATAN

MEDELLIN

2

AV. MARINA NACIONAL

BAHIA ASCENCION

(CIRCUITO INTERIOR)

RIO TIBER

RIO LERMA

COLUMN OF INDEPENDENCE ('EL ÁNGEL')

FLORENCIA

CALZ. MELCHOR OCAMPO

AV. INSURGENTES SUR

AMSTERDAM

CASA LAMM

2

VERONICA ANZURES

AVENIDA EJERCITO NACIONAL

GUTENBERG

THIERS

RIO MISISIPI

RIO TIBER

DIANA CAZADORA

PASEO DE LA REFORMA

SEVILLA

HAMBURGO

AV. CHAPULTEPEC

DURANGO

SALAMANCA

HUICHAPAN

PARQUE ESPAÑA

JARDIN CATEREPEC

PARQUE MEXICO

3

THIERS

CALZ. MARIANO ESCOBEDO

NUEVA ANZURES

LIEJA

SEVILLA

CHAPULTEPEC

VERACRUZ

JUAN ESCUTIA

AMATLAN

MAZATLAN

AV. YODESM

JOSE VASCONCELOS

3

POLANCO

HORACIO

AVENIDA PRESIDENTE MASARYK

MUSEO DE ARTE MODERNO

MUSEO RUFINO TAMAYO

MUSEO DE ANTROPOLOGIA

PASEO DE LA REFORMA

CASTILLO DE CHAPULTEPEC

AVENIDA CONSTITUYENTES

4

AV. RIO SAN JOAQUIN

JARDIN ZOOLÓGICO

BOSQUE DE CHAPULTEPEC

AUDITORIO

CALZ. CHIVATITO

C. GENERAL F. RAMIREZ

CONSTITUYENTES

4

HORACIO

AVENIDA EJERCITO NACIONAL

AVENIDA PRESIDENTE MASARYK

PASEO DE LA REFORMA

BLVR PDTE ADOLFO LOPEZ MATEOS (ANILLO PERIFÉRICO)

CASA ESTUDIO LUIS BARRAGAN

5

PRESA FALCON

AV. C. DE GUERNAVACA

HORACIO

PASEO DE LAS PALMAS

PASEO DE LA REFORMA

5

AVENIDA EJÉRCITO NACIONAL

0   1000   2000 ft

1/333 000 – 1/2 in : 1090 ft

6

A B C

6

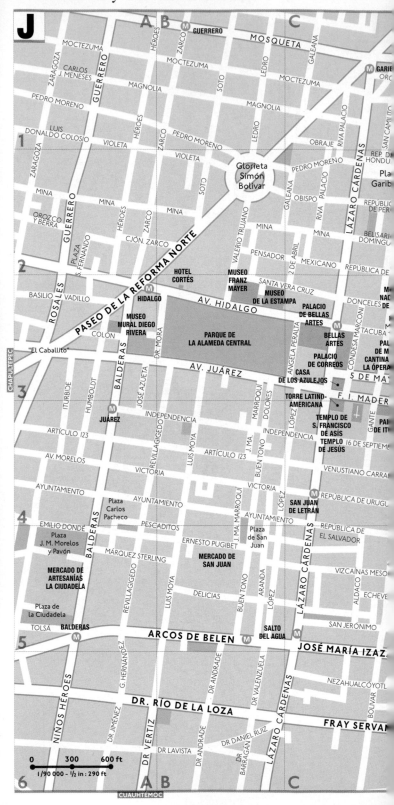

J

MOCTEZUMA
MOCTEZUMA
MOSQUETA
GUERRERO
MAGNOLIA
MOCTEZUMA
MAGNOLIA
PEDRO MORENO
LUIS DONALDO COLOSIO
VIOLETA
PEDRO MORENO
OBRAJE
ZARAGOZA
CARLOS J. MENESES
ZARAGOZA
VIOLETA
PEDRO MORENO
Glorieta Simón Bolívar
Pla Garib
MINA
MINA
OROZCO Y BERRA
MINA
CJÓN. ZARCO
PENSADOR
MINA
MINA
2 DE ABRIL
MEXICANO
REPÚBLICA DE
REP D HONDU
SAN CAMILO
RIVA PALACIO
LÁZARO CÁRDENAS
PLAZA S. FERNANDO
GUERRERO
HÉROES
ZARCO
SOTO
VALERIO TRUJANO
PASEO DE LA REFORMA NORTE
GALEANA
OBISPO
PALACIO
RIVA
BELISARI DOMÍNGU
BASILIO
ROSALES
VADILLO
SANTA VERA CRUZ
HOTEL CORTÉS
MUSEO FRANZ MAYER
MUSEO DE LA ESTAMPA
PALACIO DE BELLAS ARTES
M NAC DE
DONCELES
HIDALGO
MUSEO MURAL DIEGO RIVERA
AV. HIDALGO
BELLAS ARTES
TACUBA
"El Caballito"
COLÓN
DR. MORA
PARQUE DE LA ALAMEDA CENTRAL
ANGELA PERALTA
CONDESA MARCONI
PALACIO DE CORREOS
PAL DE M
CANTINA LA ÓPERA
BALDERAS
AV. JUÁREZ
CASA DE LOS AZULEJOS
5 DE MA
ITURBIDE
HUMBOLDT
JOSÉ AZUETA
INDEPENDENCIA
MARROQUI
DOLORES
TORRE LATINO-AMERICANA
F. I. MADER
JUÁREZ
LÓPEZ
GANTE
PAI DE IT
ARTÍCULO 123
REVILLAGIGEDO
LUIS MOYA
ARTÍCULO 123
J. MA.
BUEN TONO
INDEPENDENCIA
TEMPLO DE S. FRANCISCO DE ASÍS
16 DE SEPTIEM
AV. MORELOS
VICTORIA
TEMPLO DE JESÚS
VICTORIA
VENUSTIANO CARRA
AYUNTAMIENTO
AYUNTAMIENTO
LÓPEZ
SAN JUAN DE LETRÁN
REPÚBLICA DE URUGU
Plaza Carlos Pacheco
AYUNTAMIENTO
J. MA. MARROQUI
AYUNTAMIENTO
Plaza de San Juan
REPÚBLICA DE EL SALVADOR
EMILIO DONDÉ
PESCADITOS
Plaza J. M. Morelos y Pavón
BALDERAS
MÁRQUEZ STERLING
ERNESTO PUGIBET
MERCADO DE SAN JUAN
ARANDA
LÓPEZ
VIZCAÍNAS MESO
MERCADO DE ARTESANÍAS LA CIUDADELA
REVILLAGIGEDO
LUIS MOYA
DELICIAS
BUEN TONO
LÁZARO CÁRDENAS
ALDACO
ECHEVE
Plaza de la Ciudadela
TOLSÁ
BALDERAS
ARCOS DE BELEN
SALTO DEL AGUA
SAN JERÓNIMO
JOSÉ MARÍA IZAZ.
NIÑOS HÉROES
G. HERNÁNDEZ
DR VERTIZ
DR. RÍO DE LA LOZA
DR ANDRADE
DR VALENZUELA
LÁZARO CÁRDENAS
NEZAHUALCÓYOTL
BOLÍVAR
FRAY SERVA
DR JIMÉNEZ
DR LAVISTA
DR DANIEL RUIZ
DR BARRAGÁN RUIZ

0   300   600 ft
1/90 000 - ½ in : 290 ft

CHAPULTEPEC
CUAUHTÉMOC

A   B   C

GUERRERO
GARI
ORC

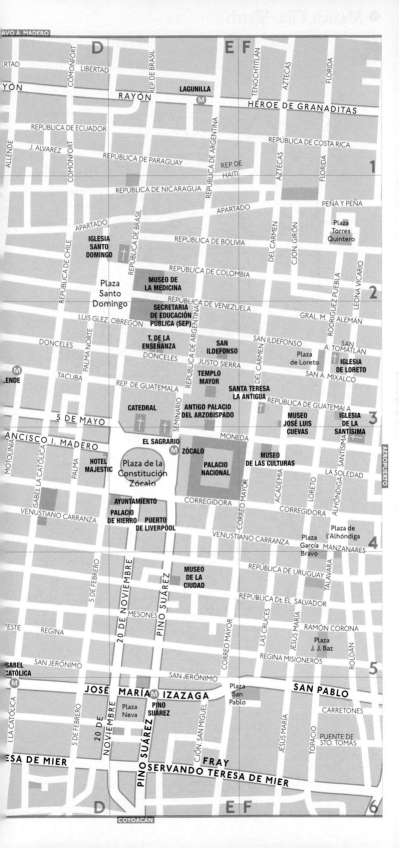

◆ Mexico City: Metro

K

A B C

El Rosario 7 6
Tezozómoco
Azcapotzalco
Ferrería
Norte 45
Vallejo
Aquiles Serdán
Camarones
Refinería
Politécnico 5
Instituto del Petróleo
Lindavista
Indios Verdes
Deportivo 18 de Marzo
La Villa Basílica
Ciudad Azteca B
Plaza Aragón
Olímpica
Tecnológico
M. Muzquiz
Martín Carrera 6 4
Talismán
Río de los Remedios
Impulsora
Continentes
Villa Aragón
Bosque de Aragón
Deportivo Oceanía
Oceanía
Romero Rubio
Terminal Aérea

Autobuses del Norte
Potrero
La Raza
Misterios
Valle Gómez
Bondojito
Aragón
E. Molina
Consulado

2 Panteones
Tacuba
Cuitláhuac
Popotla
Cuatro Caminos
Colegio Milit.
Normal
San Cosme
Revolución
Hidalgo
San Joaquín
Tlatelolco
Buenavista B
Guerrero
Garibaldi
Lagunilla
Bellas Artes
Allende
S. Juan de Letrán
Zócalo
Tepito
C. D. Norte
Morelos
Candelaria
R. Flores Magón
S. Lázaro
Moctezuma

Polanco
Juárez
Cuauhtémoc
Insurgentes
Sevilla
Balderas
Salto del Agua
Isabel la Católica
Pino Suárez
Merced
Balbuena
Bd. Puerto Aéreo
Gómez Farías
Hangares
Pantitlán 5 1 9 A

Auditorio
Constituyent.
Chapultepec
Niños Héroes
Hospital Gen.
Centro Médico
Doctores
S. Antonio Abad
Chabacano
Fray Servando
Jamaica
Mixihuca
Zaragoza
Agrícola Oriental

Tacubaya 1 9
Observatorio
Patriotismo
Chilpancingo
Lázaro Cárdenas
Viaducto
La Viga
Velódromo
Cd. Deportiva
Puebla
Canal San Juan
Tepalcates
Guelatao

San Pedro de los Pinos
San Antonio
Etiopía
Eugenia
División del Norte
Xola
Coyuya
Iztacalco
Apatlaco
Aculco
Peñón Viejo
Acatitla

Mixcoac
Zapata
Villa de Cortés
Portales
Natividad
Ermita
Santa Anita 4
Escuadrón 201
Santa Martha
Los Reyes
La Paz A

Coyoacán
Gen. Anaya
2
Tasqueña
Iztapalapa
Atlalilco
Cerro de la Estrella
Uam-I
8
Constitución de 1917

M. A. de Quevedo
Copilco
Viveros
Las Torres
Cd. Jardín
La Virgen
Xotepingo
Barranca del Muerto 7

Universidad 3
Nezahualpilli
Reg. Federal
Textitlán
El Vergel
Estadio Azteca
Huipulco
Xomali
Periférico
Tepepan
La Noria
Huichapan
Xochimilco

Embarcadero

○ Station | *La Paz* Terminus
◎ Interchange station | ▬ Tren ligero

1 2 3 4 5 6

Cancún (L), Campeche (M) ◆

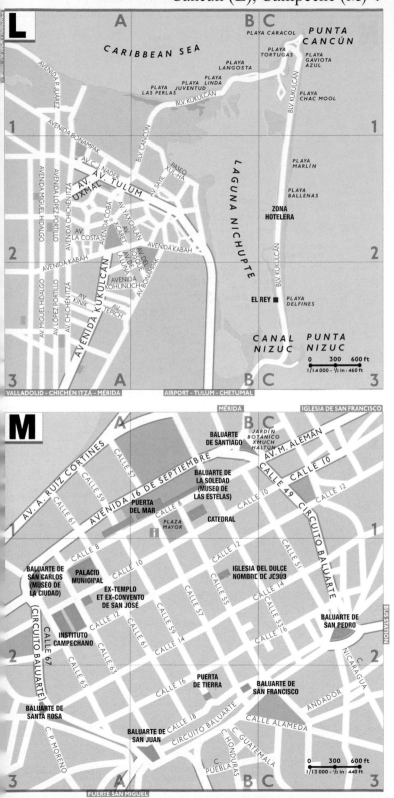

L

CARIBBEAN SEA

A | B | C

PLAYA CARACOL

PUNTA CANCÚN

PLAYA TORTUGAS

PLAYA GAVIOTA AZUL

AVENIDA P. JUÁREZ

PLAYA LANGOSTA

PLAYA LINDA

PLAYA JUVENTUD

PLAYA LAS PERLAS

BLV. KUKULCÁN

PLAYA CHAC MOOL

AVENIDA BONAMPAK

BLV. CANCÚN

PASEO XUL-HA

AV. SAYIL

LAGUNA NICHUPTE

PLAYA MARLÍN

AV. CLJ NADER

AV. TULUM

UXMAL

AVENIDA LÓPEZ PORTILLO

AVENIDA MIGUEL HIDALGO

AVENIDA CHICHÉN ITZÁ

AV. YAXCHILÁN

AV. COBÁ

AV. LA COSTA

AV. ACARET

AV. DEL BOSQUE

AVENIDA KABAH

PLAYA BALLENAS

ZONA HOTELERA

AVENIDA KABAH

AV. LÓPEZ PORTILLO

AV. MIGUEL HIDALGO

AV. CHICHÉN ITZÁ

AV. KINIK

AVENIDA KUKULCÁN

AV. DE LA LUNA

AVENIDA BONAMPAK

AVENIDA KOHUNLICH

AV. TEPICH

EL REY ■

PLAYA DELFINES

BLV. KUKULCÁN

CANAL NIZUC

PUNTA NIZUC

0   300   600 ft

1/14 000 - ½ in : 460 ft

VALLADOLID - CHICHÉN ITZÁ - MÉRIDA

AIRPORT - TULUM - CHETUMAL

M

MÉRIDA

IGLESIA DE SAN FRANCISCO

A | B | C

BALUARTE DE SANTIAGO

JARDÍN BOTÁNICO XMUCH HALTÚN

AV. M. ALEMÁN

AV. A. RUIZ CORTINES

CALLE 57

AVENIDA 16 DE SEPTIEMBRE

CALLE 59

CALLE 61

BALUARTE DE LA SOLEDAD (MUSEO DE LAS ESTELAS)

PUERTA DEL MAR

PLAZA MAYOR

CATEDRAL

CALLE 8

CALLE 49

CALLE 10

CALLE 12

CIRCUITO BALUARTE

CALLE 8

CALLE 10

CALLE 12

CALLE 51

BALUARTE DE SAN CARLOS (MUSEO DE LA CIUDAD)

PALACIO MUNICIPAL

EX-TEMPLO ET EX-CONVENTO DE SAN JOSÉ

IGLESIA DEL DULCE NOMBRE DE JESÚS

CALLE 55

CALLE 53-6

CALLE 14

BALUARTE DE SAN PEDRO

INSTITUTO CAMPECHANO

CALLE 10

CALLE 12

CALLE 57

CALLE 59

CALLE 61

CALLE 63

CALLE 65

CALLE 67 (CIRCUITO BALUARTE)

BUS STATION

C. NICARAGUA

PUERTA DE TIERRA

BALUARTE DE SAN FRANCISCO

ANDADOR

CALLE 16

CALLE 18

BALUARTE DE SANTA ROSA

BALUARTE DE SAN JUAN

CIRCUITO BALUARTE

CALLE ALAMEDA

C. GUATEMALA

C. HONDURAS

C. P. MORENO

C. PUEBLAS

0   300   600 ft

1/13 000 - ½ in : 440 ft

FUERTE SAN MIGUEL

◆ Mérida (N), San Cristóbal de las Casas (P)

N

CAUCEL – CELESTÚN

PALACIO CANTÓN

CALLE 74-A, CALLE 74, CALLE 72, CALLE 70, CALLE 68, CALLE 66, CALLE 64, CALLE 62, CALLE 60, CALLE 58, P. DE MONTEJO, CALLE 56, CALLE 41, CALLE 50, CALLE 43, CALLE 45, CALLE 54, CALLE 47, CALLE 52, CALLE 49, CALLE 50, CALLE 51, CALLE 48, CALLE 53, CALLE 46

CALLE 43
CALLE 45
IGLESIA SANTA ANA
CALLE 47
CALLE 49
CALLE 53
CALLE 55

Plaza de Santiago

CALLE 57

UNIVERSIDAD AUTÓNOMA DE YUCATÁN

TEATRO JOSÉ PEÓN CONTRERAS

IGLESIA SANTA LUCÍA

CALLE 59

CALLE 55
CALLE 57

IGLESIA DEL TERCER ORDEN

CONVENTO DE LA MEJORADA

PALACIO DEL GOBIERNO

Plaza Hidalgo

EX-CONVENTO DE LAS MONJAS

CALLE 61
CALLE 63

PALACIO MUNICIPAL

Plaza Mayor

CATEDRAL

MACAY

CASA DE MONTEJO

MERCADO CENTRAL

CALLE 59
CALLE 61
CALLE 63
CALLE 65
CALLE 67
CALLE 69
CALLE 71

CALLE 70, CALLE 68, CALLE 66, CALLE 64, CALLE 62, CALLE 60, CALLE 58, CALLE 56-A, CALLE 56, CALLE 54, CALLE 50, CALLE 48, CALLE 46, CALLE 44, CALLE 52

0   650   1300 ft
1/27 000 - 1/2 in : 890 ft

P

CHAMULA – TUXTLA G.

BARRIO DE MEXICANOS

CALLE ECUADOR

REAL DE MEXICANOS

CALZADA LÁZARO CÁRDENAS

MERCADO MUNICIPAL

BERMUDAS
D. ARRIAGA

CENTRO CULTURAL DE LOS ALTOS

IGLESIA DE SANTO DOMINGO

CHIAPA DE CORZO

CASA NA BOLOM

VENEZUELA

IGLESIA DE LA CARIDAD

COMITÁN

COMITÁN

TAPACHULA

BARRIO LA MERCED

ESCUADRÓN 201

DR NAVARRO

CINTALAPA

AV. 16 DE SEPTIEMBRE

28 DE AGOSTO

EJÉRCITO NACIONAL

DE OCTUBRE

20 DE NOVIEMBRE

1° DE MARZO

AV. GENERAL UTRILLA

AV. BELISARIO DOMÍNGUEZ

AV. CRISTÓBAL COLÓN

FLAVIO A. PANIAGUA

AV. DIEGO DUGELAY

12 DE SEPTIEMBRE

12

5 DE FEBRERO

MARÍA ADELINA

AV. DIEGO FLORES

MUSEO SERGIO CASTRO

AVENIDA 5 DE MAYO

CATEDRAL

IGLESIA DE SAN NICOLÁS

GUADALUPE VICTORIA

REAL DE GUADALUPE

AV. VICENTE GUERRERO

IGLESIA DE LA MERCED

MATAMOROS

DIEGO DE MAZARIEGOS

FRANCISCO MADERO

BARRIO DE GUADALUPE

MUSEO DEL ÁMBAR DE CHIAPAS

LA PALMA

CUAUHTÉMOC

DR JOSÉ FELIPE FLORES

SANTIAGO

AV. I. ALLENDE

NIÑOS HÉROES

AV. MIGUEL HIDALGO

FRANCISCO LEÓN

IGLESIA DEL CERRITO SAN CRISTÓBAL

H. DOMÍNGUEZ

AV. INSURGENTES

PEDRO MORENO

IGLESIA ET ARCO DEL CARMEN

JULIO M. CORZO

IGLESIA DE SAN FRANCISCO

BARRIO DE SAN ANTONIO

0   300   600 ft
1/11 000 - 1/2 in : 360 ft

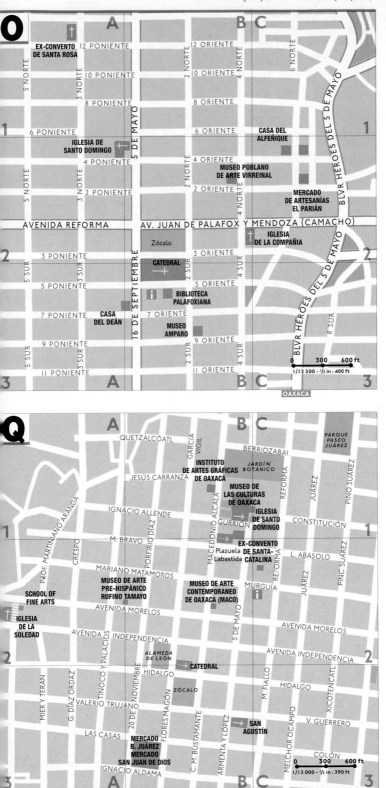

O

A · **B** · **C**

EX-CONVENTO
DE SANTA ROSA

12 PONIENTE — 12 ORIENTE

10 PONIENTE — 10 ORIENTE

8 PONIENTE — 8 ORIENTE

1 6 PONIENTE — 6 ORIENTE — CASA DEL ALFEÑIQUE **1**

IGLESIA DE SANTO DOMINGO

4 PONIENTE — 4 ORIENTE — MUSEO POBLANO DE ARTE VIRREINAL

2 PONIENTE — 2 ORIENTE — MERCADO DE ARTESANÍAS EL PARIÁN

AVENIDA REFORMA — AV. JUAN DE PALAFOX Y MENDOZA (CAMACHO)

Zócalo — IGLESIA DE LA COMPAÑÍA

2 3 PONIENTE — 3 ORIENTE **2**

CATEDRAL

5 PONIENTE — 5 ORIENTE

BIBLIOTECA PALAFOXIANA

7 PONIENTE — CASA DEL DEÁN — 7 ORIENTE

MUSEO AMPARO

9 PONIENTE — 9 ORIENTE

3 11 PONIENTE — 11 ORIENTE **3**

5 NORTE · 3 NORTE · 5 DE MAYO · 2 NORTE · 4 NORTE · 6 NORTE · BLVR HÉROES DEL 5 DE MAYO

5 SUR · 3 SUR · 16 DE SEPTIEMBRE · 2 SUR · 4 SUR · 8 SUR

0   300   600 ft
1/12 500 - ½ in = 400 ft

OAXACA

Q

A · **B** · **C**

QUETZALCÓATL — GARCÍA VIGIL — PARQUE PASEO JUÁREZ

BERRIOZABAI

INSTITUTO DE ARTES GRÁFICAS DE OAXACA — JARDÍN BOTÁNICO

JESÚS CARRANZA — MUSEO DE LAS CULTURAS DE OAXACA

IGNACIO ALLENDE — IGLESIA DE SANTO DOMINGO

GURRIÓN

1 M. BRAVO — EX-CONVENTO DE SANTA CATALINA **1**

Plazuela de Santa-Labastida

MARIANO MATAMOROS — MUSEO DE ARTE PRE-HISPÁNICO RUFINO TAMAYO — MUSEO DE ARTE CONTEMPORÁNEO DE OAXACA (MACO)

SCHOOL OF FINE ARTS — AVENIDA MORELOS — MURGUÍA

IGLESIA DE LA SOLEDAD

AVENIDA INDEPENDENCIA — AVENIDA MORELOS

2 ALAMEDA DE LEÓN — AVENIDA INDEPENDENCIA **2**

HIDALGO — CATEDRAL — HIDALGO

Zócalo

LAS CASAS — SAN AGUSTÍN

MERCADO B. JUÁREZ — MERCADO SAN JUAN DE DIOS — COLÓN

3 IGNACIO ALDAMA **3**

PROF. MARTINIANO ARANDA · CRESPO · PORFIRIO DÍAZ · MACEDONIO ALCALÁ · REFORMA · JUÁREZ · PINO SUÁREZ · CONSTITUCIÓN · L. ABASOLO · JUÁREZ · PINC SUÁREZ

MIER Y TERÁN · G. DÍAZ ORDAZ · TINOCO Y PALACIOS · 20 DE NOVIEMBRE · VALERIO TRUJANO · FLORES MAGÓN · C. M. BUSTAMANTE · ARMENTA Y LÓPEZ · M. FIALLO · MELCHOR OCAMPO · XICOTÉNCATL · V. GUERRERO

5 DE MAYO

0   300   600 ft
1/12 000 - ½ in = 390 ft

◆ Morelia (R), Guadalajara (T)

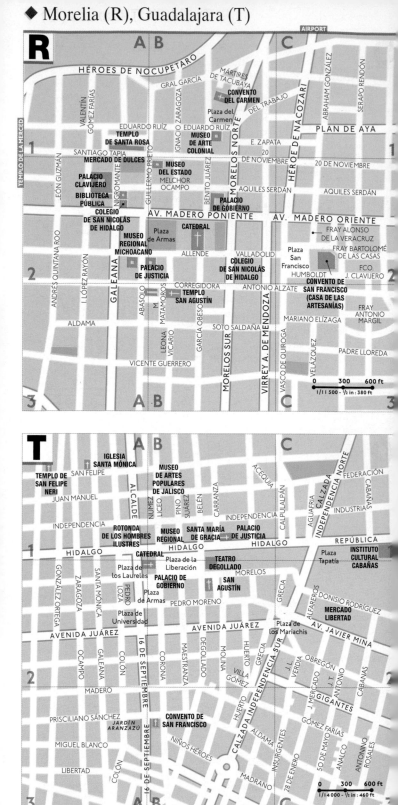

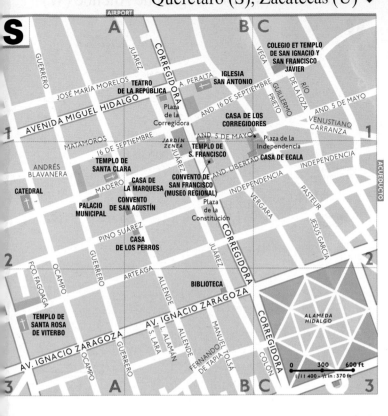

MEXICO IN FIGURES

AREA
756,061 sq miles (1,958,200 sq km), about a fifth of the size of the US; the Islas Revillagigedo are a Pacific archipelago.

POPULATION
(in 2000) 104 million.

The State of Mexico is the most populous (13,096,686 inhabitants), while Baja California Sur has the fewest inhabitants (424,041). Population density: 130 inhabitants per sq mile (50/sq km).

Birth rate: 19.3 per thousand (2003). Mortality rate: 4.5 per thousand (2003).

POLITICAL STRUCTURE
A federal republic with a presidential regime; 31 states and 1 federal district (DF): Mexico.

Main political parties (at the legislative elections of July 2003): the PRI (center right) took 38% of the seats in the Chamber of Deputies; the PAN (conservative), 32%; the PRD (left wing), 18%.